Managing & Using Information Systems: A Strategic Approach

Authors

Carol S. Saunders • Dennis F. Galletta • Keri E. Pearlson

University of Massachusetts Amherst

ISBN 9781119346760

Printed in the United States of America 10 9 8 7 6 5 4 3 2 1

List of Titles

Managing and Using Information Systems: A Strategic Approach, Binder Ready Version, 6th edition

by Keri E. Pearlson, Carol S. Saunders, and Dennis F. Galletta

Copyright © 2016, ISBN: 978-1-119-24428-8

Table of Contents

Managing and Using Information Systems

A STRATEGIC APPROACH

Sixth Edition

Keri E. Pearlson
KP Partners

Carol S. Saunders
W.A. Franke College of Business
Northern Arizona University
Dr. Theo and Friedl Schoeller Research Center for Business and Society

Dennis F. Galletta
Katz Graduate School of Business
University of Pittsburgh, Pittsburgh, PA

VICE PRESIDENT & DIRECTOR	George Hoffman
EXECUTIVE EDITOR	Lise Johnson
DEVELOPMENT EDITOR	Jennifer Manias
ASSOCIATE DEVELOPMENT EDITOR	Kyla Buckingham
SENIOR PRODUCT DESIGNER	Allison Morris
MARKET SOLUTIONS ASSISTANT	Amanda Dallas
SENIOR DIRECTOR	Don Fowley
PROJECT MANAGER	Gladys Soto
PROJECT SPECIALIST	Nichole Urban
PROJECT ASSISTANT	Anna Melhorn
EXECUTIVE MARKETING MANAGER	Christopher DeJohn
ASSISTANT MARKETING MANAGER	Puja Katariwala
ASSOCIATE DIRECTOR	Kevin Holm
SENIOR CONTENT SPECIALIST	Nicole Repasky
PRODUCTION EDITOR	Loganathan Kandan

This book was set in 10/12 Times Roman by SPi Global and printed and bound by Courier Kendallville.

This book is printed on acid free paper.

Founded in 1807, John Wiley & Sons, Inc. has been a valued source of knowledge and understanding for more than 200 years, helping people around the world meet their needs and fulfill their aspirations. Our company is built on a foundation of principles that include responsibility to the communities we serve and where we live and work. In 2008, we launched a Corporate Citizenship Initiative, a global effort to address the environmental, social, economic, and ethical challenges we face in our business. Among the issues we are addressing are carbon impact, paper specifications and procurement, ethical conduct within our business and among our vendors, and community and charitable support. For more information, please visit our website: www.wiley.com/go/citizenship.

ISBN: 978-1-119-24428-8 (BRV)
ISBN: 978-1-119-24807-1 (EVALC)

Library of Congress Cataloging-in-Publication Data

Names: Pearlson, Keri E. | Saunders, Carol S. | Galletta, Dennis F.
Title: Managing and using information systems: a strategic approach / Keri E. Pearlson, Carol S. Saunders, Dennis F. Galletta.
Description: 6th edition. | Hoboken, NJ : John Wiley & Sons, Inc., [2015] | Includes index.
Identifiers: LCCN 2015041210 (print) | LCCN 2015041579 (ebook) | ISBN 9781119244288 (loose-leaf : alk. paper) | ISBN 9781119255208 (pdf) | ISBN 9781119255246 (epub)
Subjects: LCSH: Knowledge management. | Information technology—Management. | Management information systems. | Electronic commerce.
Classification: LCC HD30.2 .P4 2015 (print) | LCC HD30.2 (ebook) | DDC 658.4/038011—dc23
LC record available at http://lccn.loc.gov/2015041210

Printing identification and country of origin will either be included on this page and/or the end of the book. In addition, if the ISBN on this page and the back cover do not match, the ISBN on the back cover should be considered the correct ISBN.

Printed in the United States of America

10 9 8 7 6 5 4 3 2 1

To Yale & Hana

To Rusty, Russell, Janel & Kristin

To Carole, Christy, Lauren, Matt, Gracie, and Jacob

Preface

Information technology and business are becoming inextricably interwoven. I don't think anybody can talk meaningfully about one without the talking about the other.

Bill Gates
Microsoft[1]

I'm not hiring MBA students for the technology you learn while in school, but for your ability to learn about, use and subsequently manage new technologies when you get out.

IT Executive
Federal Express[2]

Give me a fish and I eat for a day; teach me to fish and I eat for a lifetime.

Proverb

Managers do not have the luxury of abdicating participation in decisions regarding information systems (IS). Managers who choose to do so risk limiting their future business options. IS are at the heart of virtually every business interaction, process, and decision, especially when the vast penetration of the Web over the last 20 years is considered. Mobile and social technologies have brought IS to an entirely new level within firms and between individuals in their personal lives. Managers who let someone else make decisions about their IS are letting someone else make decisions about the very foundation of their business. This is a textbook about managing and using information written for current and future managers as a way to introduce the broader implications of the impact of IS.

The goal of this book is to assist managers in becoming knowledgeable participants in IS decisions. Becoming a knowledgeable participant means learning the basics and feeling comfortable enough to ask questions. It does not mean having all the answers or having a deep understanding of all the technologies out in the world today. No text will provide managers everything they need to know to make important IS decisions. Some texts instruct on the basic technical background of IS. Others discuss applications and their life cycles. Some take a comprehensive view of the management information systems (MIS) field and offer readers snapshots of current systems along with chapters describing how those technologies are designed, used, and integrated into business life.

This book takes a different approach. It is intended to provide the reader a foundation of basic concepts relevant to using and managing information. This text is not intended to provide a comprehensive treatment on any one aspect of MIS, for certainly each aspect is itself a topic of many books. This text is not intended to provide readers enough technological knowledge to make them MIS experts. It is not intended to be a source of discussion of any particular technology. This text is written to help managers begin to form a point of view of how IS will help or hinder their organizations and create opportunities for them.

The idea for this text grew out of discussions with colleagues in the MIS area. Many faculties use a series of case studies, trade and popular press readings, and Web sites to teach their MIS courses. Others simply rely on one of the classic texts, which include dozens of pages of diagrams, frameworks, and technologies. The initial idea for this text emerged from a core MIS course taught at the business school at the University of Texas at Austin. That course was considered an "appetizer" course—a brief introduction into the world of MIS for MBA students. The course had two main topics: using information and managing information. At the time, there was no text like this

[1] Bill Gates, *Business @ the Speed of Thought*. New York: Warner Books, Inc. 1999.
[2] Source: Private conversation with one of the authors.

one; hence, students had to purchase thick reading packets made up of articles and case studies to provide them the basic concepts. The course was structured to provide general MBA students enough knowledge of the MIS field so that they could recognize opportunities to use the rapidly changing technologies available to them. The course was an appetizer to the menu of specialty courses, each of which went much more deeply into the various topics. But completion of the appetizer course meant that students were able to feel comfortable listening to, contributing to, and ultimately participating in IS decisions.

Today, many students are digital natives—people who have grown up using information technologies (IT) all of their lives. That means that students come to their courses with significantly more knowledge about things such as tablets, apps, personal computers, smartphones, texting, the Web, social networking, file downloading, online purchasing, and social media than their counterparts in school just a few years ago. This is a significant trend that is projected to continue; students will be increasingly knowledgeable the personal use of technologies. That knowledge has begun to change the corporate environment. Today's digital natives expect to find in corporations IS that provide at least the functionality they have at home. At the same time, these users expect to be able to work in ways that take advantage of the technologies they have grown to depend on for social interaction, collaboration, and innovation. We believe that the basic foundation is still needed for managing and using IS, but we understand that the assumptions and knowledge base of today's students is significantly different.

Also different today is the vast amount of information amassed by firms, sometimes called the "big data" problem. Organizations have figured out that there is an enormous amount of data around their processes, their interactions with customers, their products, and their suppliers. These organizations also recognize that with the increase in communities and social interactions on the Web, there is additional pressure to collect and analyze vast amounts of unstructured information contained in these conversations to identify trends, needs, and projections. We believe that today's managers face an increasing amount of pressure to understand what is being said by those inside and outside their corporations and to join those conversations reasonably and responsibly. That is significantly different from just a few years ago.

This book includes an introduction, 13 chapters of text and mini cases, and a set of case studies, supplemental readings, and teaching support on a community hub at http://pearlsonandsaunders.com. The Hub provides faculty members who adopt the text additional resources organized by chapter, including recent news items with teaching suggestions, videos with usage suggestions, blog posts and discussions from the community, class activities, additional cases, cartoons, and more. Supplemental materials, including longer cases from all over the globe, can be found on the Web. Please visit http://www.wiley.com/college/pearlson or the Hub for more information.

The introduction to this text defends the argument presented in this preface that managers must be knowledgeable participants in making IS decisions. The first few chapters build a basic framework of relationships among business strategy, IS strategy, and organizational strategy and explore the links among them. The strategy chapters are followed by ones on work design and business processes that discuss the use of IS. General managers also need some foundation on how IT is managed if they are to successfully discuss their next business needs with IT professionals who can help them. Therefore, the remaining chapters describe the basics of information architecture and infrastructure, IT security, the business of IT, the governance of the IS organization, IS sourcing, project management, business analytics, and relevant ethical issues.

Given the acceleration of security breaches, readers will find a new chapter on IS security in this sixth edition of the text. Also, the material on analytics and "big data" has been extensively updated to reflect the growing importance of the topic. Further, the chapter on work design has been reorganized and extensively revised. Each of the other chapters has been revised with newer concepts added, discussions of more current topics fleshed out, and old, outdated topics removed or at least their discussion shortened.

Similar to the fifth edition, every chapter begins with a navigation "box" to help the reader understand the flow and key topics of the chapter. Further, most chapters continue to have a Social Business Lens or a Geographic Lens feature. The Social Business Lens feature reflects on an issue related to the chapter's main topic but is enabled by or fundamental to using social technologies in the enterprise. The Geographic Lens feature offers a single idea about a global issue related to the chapter's main topic.

No text in the field of MIS is completely current. The process of writing the text coupled with the publication process makes a book somewhat out-of-date prior to delivery to its audience. With that in mind, this text is written to summarize the "timeless" elements of using and managing information. Although this text is complete in and of itself, learning is enhanced by combining the chapters with the most current readings and cases. Faculty are encouraged to read the news items on the faculty Hub before each class in case one might be relevant to the topic of the day. Students are encouraged to search the Web for examples related to topics and current events and bring them into the discussions of the issues at hand. The format of each chapter begins with a navigational guide, a short case study, and the basic language for a set of important management issues. These are followed by a set of managerial concerns related to the topic. The chapter concludes with a summary, key terms, a set of discussion questions, and case studies.

Who should read this book? General managers interested in participating in IS decisions will find this a good reference resource for the language and concepts of IS. Managers in the IS field will find the book a good resource for beginning to understand the general manager's view of how IS affect business decisions. And IS students will be able to use the book's readings and concepts as the beginning in their journey to become informed and successful businesspeople.

The information revolution is here. Where do you fit in?

Keri E. Pearlson, Carol S. Saunders, and Dennis F. Galletta

Acknowledgments

Books of this nature are written only with the support of many individuals. We would like to personally thank several individuals who helped with this text. Although we've made every attempt to include everyone who helped make this book a reality, there is always the possibility of unintentionally leaving some out. We apologize in advance if that is the case here.

Thank you goes to Dr. William Turner of LeftFour, in Austin, Texas, for help with the infrastructure and architecture concepts and to Alan Shimel, Editor-in-Chief at DevOps.com for initial ideas for the new security chapter.

We also want to acknowledge and thank pbwiki.com. Without its incredible and free wiki, we would have been relegated to e-mailing drafts of chapters back and forth, or saving countless files in an external drop box without any opportunity to include explanations or status messages. For this edition, as with earlier editions, we wanted to use Web 2.0 tools as we wrote about them. We found that having used the wiki for our previous editions, we were able to get up and running much faster than if we had to start over without the platform.

We have been blessed with the help of our colleagues in this and in previous editions of the book. They helped us by writing cases and reviewing the text. Our thanks continue to go out to Jonathan Trower, Espen Andersen, Janis Gogan, Ashok Rho, Yvonne Lederer Antonucci, E. Jose Proenca, Bruce Rollier, Dave Oliver, Celia Romm, Ed Watson, D. Guiter, S. Vaught, Kala Saravanamuthu, Ron Murch, John Greenwod, Tom Rohleder, Sam Lubbe, Thomas Kern, Mark Dekker, Anne Rutkowski, Kathy Hurtt, Kay Nelson, Janice Sipior, Craig Tidwell, and John Butler. Although we cannot thank them by name, we also greatly appreciate the comments of the anonymous reviewers who have made a mark on this edition.

The book would not have been started were it not for the initial suggestion of a wonderful editor in 1999 at John Wiley & Sons, Beth Lang Golub. Her persistence and patience helped shepherd this book through many previous editions. We also appreciate the help of our current editor, Lise Johnson. Special thanks go to Jane Miller, Gladys Soto, Loganathan Kandan, and the conscientious JaNoel Lowe who very patiently helped us through the revision process. We also appreciate the help of all the staff at Wiley who have made this edition a reality.

We would be remiss if we did not also thank Lars Linden for the work he has done on the Pearlson and Saunders Faculty Hub for this book. Our vision included a Web-based community for discussing teaching ideas and posting current articles that supplement this text. Lars made that vision into a reality starting with the last edition and continuing through the present. Thank you, Lars!

From Keri: Thank you to my husband, Yale, and my daughter, Hana, a business and computer science student at Tulane University. Writing a book like this happens in the white space of our lives—the time in between everything else going on. This edition came due at a particularly frenetic time, but they listened to ideas, made suggestions, and celebrated the book's completion with us. I know how lucky I am to have this family. I love you guys!

From Carol: I would like to thank the Dr. Theo and Friedl Schoeller Research Center of Business and Society for their generous support of my research. Rusty, thank you for being my compass and my release valve. I couldn't do it without you. Paraphrasing the words of an Alan Jackson song ("Work in Progress"): I may not be what you want me to be, but I'm trying really hard. Just be patient because I'm a work in progress. I love you, Kristin, Russell, and Janel very much!

From Dennis: Thanks to my terrific family: my wife Carole, my daughters Christy and Lauren, and my granddaughter Gracie. Also thanks to Matt and Jacob, two lovable guys who take wonderful care of my daughters. Finally, thanks to our parents and sisters' families. We are also blessed with a large number of great, caring neighbors whom we see quite often. I love you all, and you make it all worthwhile!

About the Authors

Dr. Keri E. Pearlson is President of KP Partners, an advisory services firm working with business leaders on issues related to the strategic use of information systems (IS) and organizational design. She is an entrepreneur, teacher, researcher, consultant, and thought leader. Dr. Pearlson has held various positions in academia and industry. She has been a member of the faculty at the Graduate School of Business at the University of Texas at Austin where she taught management IS courses to MBAs and executives and at Babson College where she helped design the popular IS course for the Fast Track MBA program. Dr. Pearlson has held positions at the Harvard Business School, CSC, nGenera (formerly the Concours Group), AT&T, and Hughes Aircraft Company. While writing this edition, she was the Research Director for the Analytics Leadership Consortium at the International Institute of Analytics and was named the Leader of the Year by the national Society of Information Management (SIM) 2014.

Dr. Pearlson is coauthor of *Zero Time: Providing Instant Customer Value—Every Time, All the Time* (John Wiley, 2000). Her work has been published in numerous places including *Sloan Management Review, Academy of Management Executive, and Information Resources Management Journal.* Many of her case studies have been published by Harvard Business Publishing and are used all over the world. She currently writes a blog on issues at the intersection of IT and business strategy. It's available at www.kppartners.com.

Dr. Pearlson holds a Doctorate in Business Administration (DBA) in Management Information Systems from the Harvard Business School and both a Master's Degree in Industrial Engineering Management and a Bachelor's Degree in Applied Mathematics from Stanford University.

Dr. Carol S. Saunders is Research Professor at the W. A. Franke College of Business, Northern Arizona University in Flagstaff, Arizona, and is a Schoeller Senior Fellow at the Friedrich-Alexander University of Erlangen-Nuremberg, Germany. She served as General Conference Chair of the International Conference on Information Systems (ICIS) in 1999 and as Program Co-Chair of the Americas Conference of Information Systems (AMCIS) in 2015. Dr. Saunders was the Chair of the ICIS Executive Committee in 2000. For three years, she served as Editor-in-Chief of *MIS Quarterly*. She is currently on the editorial boards of *Journal of Strategic Information Systems* and *Organization Science* and serves on the advisory board of *Business & Information Systems Engineering*. Dr. Saunders has been recognized for her lifetime achievements by the Association of Information Systems (AIS) with a LEO award and by the Organizational Communication and Information Systems Division of the Academy of Management. She is a Fellow of the AIS.

Dr. Saunders' current research interests include the impact of IS on power and communication, overload, virtual teams, time, sourcing, and interorganizational linkages. Her research is published in a number of journals including *MIS Quarterly, Information Systems Research, Journal of MIS, Communications of the ACM, Journal of Strategic Information Systems, Journal of the AIS, Academy of Management Journal, Academy of Management Review, Communications Research*, and *Organization Science*.

Dr. Dennis F. Galletta is Professor of Business Administration at the Katz Graduate School of Business, University of Pittsburgh in Pennsylvania. He is also the Director of the Katz School's doctoral program and has taught IS Management graduate courses in Harvard's summer program each year since 2009. He obtained his doctorate from the University of Minnesota in 1985 and is a Certified Public Accountant. Dr. Galletta served as President of the Association of Information Systems (AIS) in 2007. Like Dr. Saunders, he is both a Fellow of the AIS and has won a LEO lifetime achievement award. He was a member of the AIS Council for five years. He also served in leadership roles for the International Conference on Information Systems (ICIS): Program Co-Chair in 2005 (Las Vegas) and Conference Co-Chair in 2011 (Shanghai); as Program Co-Chair for the

Americas Conference on Information Systems (AMCIS) in 2003 (Tampa, Florida) and Inaugural Conference Chair in 1995 (Pittsburgh). The Pittsburgh conference had several "firsts" for an IS conference, including the first on-line submissions, reviews, conference registration and payment, placement service, and storage of all papers in advance on a website. Dr. Galletta served as ICIS Treasurer from 1994 to 1998 and Chair of the ICIS Executive Committee in 2012. He taught IS courses on the Fall 1999 Semester at Sea voyage (Institute for Shipboard Education) and established the concept of Special Interest Groups in AIS in 2000. In 2014, he won an Emerald Citation of Excellence for a co-authored article that reached the top 50 in citations and ratings from the fields of management, business, and economics.

Dr. Galletta's current research addresses online and mobile usability and behavioral security issues such as phishing, protection motivation, and antecedents of security-related decision making. He has published his research in journals such as *Management Science; MIS Quarterly; Information Systems Research; Journal of MIS; European Journal of Information Systems; Journal of the AIS; Communications of the ACM; Accounting, Management, and Information Technologies; Data Base;* and *Decision Sciences* and in proceedings of conferences such as ICIS, AMCIS, and the Hawaii International Conference on Systems Sciences. Dr. Galletta's editorship includes working as current and founding Coeditor in Chief for *AIS Transactions on Human-Computer Interaction* and on editorial boards at journals such as *MIS Quarterly, Information Systems Research, Journal of MIS,* and *Journal of the AIS.* He is currently on the Pre-eminent Scholars Board of *Data Base.* He won a Developmental Associate Editor Award at the *MIS Quarterly* in 2006. And during the off-hours, Dr. Galletta's fervent hobby and obsession is digital photography, often squinting through his eyepiece to make portrait, macro, Milky Way, and lightning photos when he should be writing.

Introduction

Why do managers need to understand and participate in the information systems decisions of their organizations? After all, most corporations maintain entire departments dedicated to the management of information systems (IS). These departments are staffed with highly skilled professionals devoted to the field of technology. Shouldn't managers rely on experts to analyze all the aspects of IS and to make the best decisions for the organization? The answer to that question is an emphatic "no."

Managing information is a critical skill for success in today's business environment. All decisions made by companies involve, at some level, the management and use of IS and the interpretation of data from the business and its environment. Managers today need to know about their organization's capabilities and uses of information as much as they need to understand how to obtain and budget financial resources. The ubiquity of personal devices such as smart phones, laptops, and tablets and of access to apps within corporations and externally over the Internet, highlights this fact. Today's technologies form the backbone for virtually all business models. This backbone easily crosses oceans, adding the need for a global competency to the manager's skill set. Further, the proliferation of supply chain partnerships and the vast amount of technology available to individuals outside of the corporation have extended the urgent need for business managers to be involved in information systems decisions. In addition, the availability of seemingly free (or at least very inexpensive) applications, collaboration tools, and innovation engines in the consumer arena has put powerful tools in everyone's hands, increasing the difficulty of ensuring that corporate systems are robust, secure, and protected. A manager who doesn't understand the basics of managing and using information can't be successful in this business environment.

The majority of U.S. adults own a smart phone and access online apps. According to the Pew Research Center, in 2014, 90% of U.S. adults had a cell phone of some kind, and 87% of American adults used the Internet.[1] Essentially the use of these types of devices implies that individuals now manage a "personal IS" and make decisions about usage, data, and applications. Doesn't that give them insight into managing information systems in corporations? Students often think they are experts in corporate IS because of their personal experience with technology. Although there is some truth in that perspective, it's a very dangerous perspective for managers to take. Certainly knowing about interesting apps, being able to use a variety of technologies for different personal purposes, and being familiar with the ups and downs of networking for their personal information systems provide some experience that is useful in the corporate setting. But in a corporate setting, information systems must be enterprise-ready. They must be scalable for a large number of employees; they must be delivered in an appropriate manner for the enterprise; they must be managed with corporate guidelines and appropriate governmental regulations in mind. Issues like security, privacy, risk, support, and architecture take on a new meaning within an enterprise, and someone has to manage them. Enterprise-level management and use of information systems require a unique perspective and a different skill set.

[1] Internet Use and Cell Phone Demographics, http://www.pewinternet.org/data-trend/internet-use/internet-use-over-time (accessed August 18, 2015).

1

Consider the now-historic rise of companies such as Amazon.com, Google, and Zappos. Amazon.com began as an online bookseller and rapidly outpaced traditional brick-and-mortar businesses like Barnes and Noble, Borders, and Waterstones. Management at the traditional companies responded by having their IS support personnel build Web sites to compete. But upstart Amazon.com moved ahead, keeping its leadership position on the Web by leveraging its business model into other marketplaces, such as music, electronics, health and beauty products, lawn and garden products, auctions, tools and hardware, and more. It cleared the profitability hurdle by achieving a good mix of IS and business basics: capitalizing on operational efficiencies derived from inventory software and smarter storage, cost cutting, and effectively partnering with such companies as Toys "R" Us Inc. and Target Corporation.[2] More recently, Amazon.com changed the basis of competition in another market, but this time it was the Web services business. Amazon.com Web services offers clients the extensive technology platform used for Amazon.com but in an on-demand fashion for developing and running the client's own applications. Shoe retailer Zappos.com challenged Amazon's business model, in part by coupling a social business strategy with exemplary service and sales. It was so successful that Amazon.com bought Zappos.

Likewise, Google built a business that is revolutionizing the way information is found. Google began in 1999 as a basic search company but its managers quickly learned that its unique business model could be leveraged for future success in seemingly unrelated areas. The company changed the way people think about Web content by making it available in a searchable format with an incredibly fast response time and in a host of languages. Further, Google's keyword-targeted advertising program revolutionized the way companies advertise. Then Google expanded, offering a suite of Web-based applications, such as calendaring, office tools, e-mail, collaboration, shopping, and maps and then enhanced the applications further by combining them with social tools to increase collaboration. Google Drive is one of the most popular file-sharing tools and Gmail one of the most popular email apps. In 2015, Google's mission was to "organize the world's information and make it universally accessible and useful." It is offering its customers very inexpensive fiber connections. In so doing, Google further expanded into infrastructure and on-demand services.[3]

These and other online businesses are able to succeed where traditional companies have not, in part because their management understood the power of information, IS, and the Web. These exemplary online businesses aren't succeeding because their managers could build Web pages or assemble an IS network. Rather, the executives in these new businesses understand the fundamentals of managing and using information and can marry that knowledge with a sound, unique business vision to dominate their intended market spaces.

The goal of this book is to provide the foundation to help the general business manager become a knowledgeable participant in IS decisions because any IS decision in which the manager doesn't participate can greatly affect the organization's ability to succeed in the future. This introduction outlines the fundamental reasons for taking the initiative to participate in IS decisions. Moreover, because effective participation requires a unique set of managerial skills, this introduction identifies the most important ones. These skills are helpful for making both IS decisions and all business decisions. We describe how managers should participate in the decision-making process. Finally, this introduction presents relevant models for understanding the nature of business and information systems. These models provide a framework for the discussions that follow in subsequent chapters.

The Case for Participating in Decisions about Information Systems

In today's business environment, maintaining a back-office view of technology is certain to cost market share and could ultimately lead to the failure of the organization. Managers who claim ignorance of IS can damage their reputation. Technology has become entwined with all the classic functions of business—operations, marketing, accounting, finance—to such an extent that understanding its role is necessary for making intelligent and effective decisions about any of them. Furthermore, a general understanding of key IS concepts is possible without the extensive technological knowledge required just a few years ago. Most managers today have personal technology

[2] Robert Hof, "How Amazon Cleared the Profitability Hurdle" (February 4, 2002), http://www.bloomberg.com/bw/stories/2002-02-03/how-amazon-cleared-the-profitability-hurdle (accessed on October 29, 2015).

[3] For more information on the latest services by these two companies, see http://aws.amazon.com/ec2 and http://www.google.com/enterprise/cloud/.

Reasons
IS must be managed as a critical resource since it permeates almost every aspect of business.
IS enable change in the way people work both inside and outside of the enterprise.
IS are at the heart of integrated Internet-based solutions that are replacing standard business processes.
IS enable or inhibit business opportunities and new strategies.
IS can be used to combat business challenges from competitors.
IS enable customers to have greater pull on businesses and communities by giving them new options for voicing their concerns and opinions using social media.
IS can support data-driven decision making.
IS can help ensure the security of key assets.

FIGURE I-1 Reasons why business managers should participate in information systems decisions.

such as a smart phone or tablet that is more functional than many corporate-supported personal computers provided by enterprises just a few years ago. In fact, the proliferation of personal technologies makes everyone a "pseudo-expert." Each individual must manage applications on smart phones, make decisions about applications to purchase, and procure technical support when the systems fail. Finally, with the robust number of consumer applications available on the Web, many decisions historically made by the IS group are increasingly being made by individuals outside that group, sometimes to the detriment of corporate objectives.

Therefore, understanding basic fundamentals about using and managing information is worth the investment of time. The reasons for this investment are summarized in Figure I-1 and are discussed next.

A Business View of Critical Resources

Information technology (IT) is a critical resource for today's businesses. It both supports and consumes a significant amount of an organization's resources. Just like the other three major types of business resources—people, money, and machines—it needs to be managed wisely.

IT spending represents a significant portion of corporate budgets. Worldwide IT spending topped $3.7 trillion in 2014. It is projected to continue to increase.[4] A Gartner study of where this money goes groups spending into five categories including devices (e.g., PCs, tablets, and mobile phones), data center systems (e.g., network equipment, servers, and storage equipment), enterprise software and apps (e.g., companywide software applications), IT services (e.g., support and consulting services), and telecommunications (e.g., the expenses paid to vendors for voice and data services).

Resources must return value, or they will be invested elsewhere. The business manager, not the IS specialist, decides which activities receive funding, estimates the risk associated with the investment, and develops metrics for evaluating the investment's performance. Therefore, the business manager needs a basic grounding in managing and using information. On the flip side, IS managers need a business view to be able to explain how technology impacts the business and what its trade-offs are.

People and Technology Work Together

In addition to financial issues, managers must know how to mesh technology and people to create effective work processes. Collaboration is increasingly common, especially with the rise of social networking. Companies are reaching out to individual customers using social technologies such as Facebook, Twitter, Reddit, Renren, YouTube, and numerous other tools. In fact, **Web 2.0** describes the use of the World Wide Web applications that incorporate information sharing, user-centered design, interoperability, and collaboration among users. Technology facilitates

[4] http://www.gartner.com/newsroom/id/2959717/ (accessed March 5, 2015).

the work that people do and the way they interact with each other. Appropriately incorporating IS into the design of a business model enables managers to focus their time and resources on issues that bear directly on customer satisfaction and other revenue- and profit-generating activities.

Adding a new IS to an existing organization, however, requires the ability to manage change. Skilled business managers must balance the benefits of introducing new technology with the costs associated with changing the existing behaviors of people in the workplace. There are many choices of technology solutions, each with a different impact. Managers' decisions must incorporate a clear understanding of the consequences. Making this assessment doesn't require detailed technical knowledge. It does require an understanding of short-term and long-term consequences risk mitigation, and why adopting new technology may be more appropriate in some instances than in others. Understanding these issues also helps managers know when it may prove effective to replace people with technology at certain steps in a process.

Integrating Business with Information Systems

IS are integrated with almost every aspect of business and have been for quite some time. For example, the CTO of @WalmartLabs, Jeremy King, wrote in a blog,

> There used to be a big distinction between tech companies: those that develop enterprise technology for businesses, and the global companies that depend on those products. But that distinction is now diminishing for this simple reason: every global company is becoming a tech company. . . . we're seeing technology as a critical component for business success.[5]

Walmart built platforms to support all of its ecommerce and digital shopping experiences around the world. Walmart's teams created a new search engine to enable engaging and efficient ways for on-line customers to find items in inventory. IS placed information in the hands of Walmart associates so that decisions could be made closer to the customer. IS simplified organizational activities and processes such as moving goods, stocking shelves, and communicating with suppliers. For example, handheld scanners provide floor associates with immediate and real-time access to inventory in their store and the ability to locate items in surrounding stores, if necessary.

Opportunities and New Strategies Derived from Rapid Changes in Technology

The proliferation of new technologies creates a business environment filled with opportunities. The rate of adoption of these new technologies has increased due in part to the changing demographics of the workforce and the integration of "**digital natives**," individuals whose entire lives have been lived in an era with Internet availability. Therefore digital natives are completely fluent in the use of personal technologies and the Web. Even today, innovative uses of the Internet produce new types of online businesses that keep every manager and executive on alert. New business opportunities spring up with little advance warning. The manager's role is to frame these opportunities so that others can understand them, evaluate them against existing business needs and choices, and then pursue those that fit with an articulated business strategy. The quality of the information at hand affects the quality of both decisions and their implementation. Managers must develop an understanding of what information is crucial to the decisions, how to get it, and how to use it. They must lead the changes driven by IS.

Competitive Challenges

Competitors come from both expected and unexpected places. General managers are in the best position to see the emerging threats and utilize IS effectively to combat ever-changing competitive challenges. Further, general managers are often called on to demonstrate a clear understanding of how their own technology programs and products

---

[5] Jeremy King, "Why Every Company Is a Tech Company" (November 21, 2013), http://www.walmartlabs.com/2013/11/21/why-every-company-is-a-tech-company-by-jeremy-king-cto-of-walmartlabs (accessed August 18, 2015).

compare with those of their competitors. A deep understanding of the capabilities of the organization coupled with existing IS can create competitive advantages and change the competitive landscape for the entire industry.

Customer Pull

With the emergence of social networks like Facebook, microblogs like Twitter, and other Web applications like Yelp, businesses have had to redesign their existing business models to account for the change in power now wielded by customers and others in their communities. Social media and other web apps have given powerful voices to customers and communities, and businesses must listen. Redesigning the customer experience when interacting with a company is paramount for many managers and the key driver is IS. Social IT enables new and often deeper relationships with a large number of customers, and companies are learning how to integrate and leverage this capability into existing and new business models.

Data-Driven Decision Making

Managers are increasingly using evidence-based management to make decisions based on data gathered from experiments, internal files, and other relevant sources. Data-driven decision making, based on new techniques for analytics, data management, and business intelligence, has taken on increased importance. Social media have created a rich stream of real-time data that gives managers increased insights to the impact of decisions much faster than traditional systems. Mid-course corrections are much easier to make. Predictive and prescriptive analytics give suggestions that are eerily close to what happens. Big data stores can be mined for insights that were unavailable with traditional IS, creating competitive advantage for companies with the right tools and techniques.

Securing Key Assets

As the use of the Internet grows, so does the opportunity for new and unforeseen threats to company assets. Taking measures to ensure the security of these assets is increasingly important. But decisions about security measures also impact the way IS can be used. It's possible to put so much security around IT assets that they are locked down in a manner that gets in the way of business. At the same time, too little security opens up the possibility of theft, hacking, phishing, and other Web-based mischief that can disrupt business. Managers must be involved in decisions about risk and security to ensure that business operations are in sync with the resulting security measures.

What If a Manager Doesn't Participate?

Decisions about IS directly affect the profits of a business. The basic formula Profit = Revenue − Expenses can be used to evaluate the impact of these decisions. Adopting the wrong technologies can cause a company to miss business opportunities and any revenues those opportunities would generate. For example, inadequate IS can cause a breakdown in servicing customers, which hurts sales. Poorly deployed social IT resources can badly damage the reputation of a strong brand. On the expense side, a miscalculated investment in technology can lead to overspending and excess capacity or underspending and restricted opportunity. Inefficient business processes sustained by ill-fitting IS also increase expenses. Lags in implementation or poor process adaptation reduces profits and therefore growth. IS decisions can dramatically affect the bottom line.

Failure to consider IS strategy when planning business strategy and organizational strategy leads to one of three business consequences: (1) IS that fail to support business goals, (2) IS that fail to support organizational systems, and (3) a misalignment between business goals and organizational capabilities. These consequences are discussed briefly in the following section and in more detail in later chapters. The driving questions to consider are the potential effects on an organization's ability to achieve its business goals. How will the consequences impact the way people work? Will the organization still be able to implement its business strategy?

Information Systems Must Support Business Goals

IS represent a major investment for any firm in today's business environment. Yet poorly chosen IS can actually become an obstacle to achieving business goals. The results can be disastrous if the systems do not allow the organization to realize its goals. When IS lack the capacity needed to collect, store, and transfer critical information for the business, decisions can be impacted and options limited. Customers will be dissatisfied or even lost. Production costs may be excessive. Worst of all, management may not be able to pursue desired business directions that are blocked by inappropriate IS. Victoria's Secret experienced this problem when a Superbowl ad promoting an online fashion show generated so many inquiries to its Web site that the Web site crashed. Spending large amounts of money on the advertisement was wasted when potential customers could not access the site. Likewise, Toys "R" Us experienced a similar calamity when its well-publicized Web site was unable to process and fulfill orders fast enough one holiday season. It not only lost those customers, but it also had a major customer-relations issue to manage as a result.

Information Systems Must Support Organizational Systems

Organizational systems represent the fundamental elements of a business—its people, work processes, tasks, structure, and control systems—and the plan that enables them to work efficiently to achieve business goals. If the company's IS fail to support its organizational systems, the result is a misalignment of the resources needed to achieve its goals. For example, it seems odd to think that a manager might add functionality to a corporate Web site without providing the training the employees need to use the tool effectively. Yet, this mistake—and many more costly ones—occurs in businesses every day. Managers make major IS decisions without informing all the staff of resulting changes in their daily work. For example, an enterprise resource planning (ERP) system often dictates how many business processes are executed and the organizational systems must change to reflect the new processes. Deploying technology without thinking through how it actually will be used in the organization—who will use it, how they will use it, and how to make sure the applications chosen will actually accomplish what is intended—results in significant expense. In another example, a company may decide to block access to the Internet, thinking that it is prohibiting employees from accessing offensive or unsecure sites. But that decision also means that employees can't access social networking sites that may be useful for collaboration or other Web-based applications that may offer functionality to make the business more efficient.

The general manager, who, after all, is charged with ensuring that company resources are used effectively, must guarantee that the company's IS support its organizational systems and that changes made in one system are reflected in the other. For example, a company that plans to allow employees to work remotely needs an information system strategy compatible with its organizational strategy. Desktop PCs located within the corporate office aren't the right solution for a telecommuting organization. Instead, laptop computers or tablets with applications that are accessible online anywhere and anytime and networks that facilitate information sharing are needed. Employees may want to use tablets or smart phones remotely, too, and those entail a different set of IS processes. If the organization allows the purchase of only desktop PCs and builds systems accessible from desks within the office, the telecommuting program is doomed to failure.

Skills Needed to Participate Effectively in Information Technology Decisions

Participating in IT decisions means bringing a clear set of skills to the table. All managers are asked to take on tasks that require different skills at different times. Those tasks can be divided into three types: visionary tasks, or those that provide leadership and direction for the group; informational/interpersonal tasks, or those that provide information and knowledge the group needs to be successful; and structural tasks, those that organize the group. Figure I-2 lists basic skills required of managers who wish to participate successfully in key IT decisions. Not only does this list emphasize understanding, organizing, planning, and solving the business needs of the organization, but also it is an excellent checklist for all managers' professional growth.

Managerial Role	Skills
Visionary	Creativity Curiosity Confidence Focus on business solutions Flexibility
Informational and Interpersonal	Communication Listening Information gathering Interpersonal skills
Structural	Project management Analytical Organizational Planning Leading Controlling

FIGURE I-2 Skills for successful IT use by managerial role.

These skills may not look much different from those required of any successful manager, which is the main point of this book: General managers can be successful participants in IS decisions without an extensive technical background. General managers who understand a basic set of IS concepts and who have outstanding managerial skills, such as those listed in Figure I-2, are ready for the digital economy.

How to Participate in Information Systems Decisions

Technical wizardry isn't required to become a knowledgeable participant in the IS decisions of a business. Managers need curiosity, creativity, and the confidence to ask questions in order to learn and understand. A solid framework that identifies key management issues and relates them to aspects of IS provides the background needed to participate in business IS decisions.

The goal of this book is to provide that framework. The way in which managers use and manage information is directly linked to business goals and the business strategy driving both organizational and IS decisions. Aligning business and IS decisions is critical. Business, organizational, and information strategies are fundamentally linked in what is called the *Information Systems Strategy Triangle,* discussed in the next chapter. Failing to understand this relationship is detrimental to a business. Failing to plan for the consequences in all three areas can cost a manager his or her job. This book provides a foundation for understanding business issues related to IS from a managerial perspective.

Organization of the Book

To be knowledgeable participants, managers must know about both using and managing information. The first five chapters offer basic frameworks to make this understanding easier. Chapter 1 uses the Information Systems Strategy Triangle framework to discuss alignment of IS and the business. This chapter also provides a brief overview of relevant frameworks for business strategy and organizational strategy. It is provided as background for those who have not formally studied organization theory or business strategy. For those who have studied these areas, this chapter is a brief refresher of major concepts used throughout the remaining chapters of the book.

Subsequent chapters provide frameworks and sets of examples for understanding the links between IS and business strategy (Chapter 2), links between IS and organizational strategy (Chapter 3), collaboration and individual work (Chapter 4), and business processes (Chapter 5).

The rest of the text covers issues related to the business manager's role in managing IS itself. These chapters are the building blocks of an IS strategy. Chapter 6 provides a framework for understanding the four components of IS architecture: hardware, software, networks, and data. Chapter 7 discusses how managers might participate in decisions about IS security. Chapter 8 focuses on the business of IT with a look at IS organization, funding models, portfolios, and monitoring options. Chapter 9 describes the governance of IS resources. Chapter 10 explores sourcing and how companies provision IS resources. Chapter 11 focuses on project and change management. Chapter 12 concerns business intelligence, knowledge management, and analytics and provides an overview of how companies manage knowledge and create a competitive advantage using business analytics. And finally, Chapter 13 discusses the ethical use of information and privacy.

Basic Assumptions

Every book is based on certain assumptions, and understanding those assumptions makes a difference in interpreting the text. The first assumption made by this text is that managers must be knowledgeable participants in the IS decisions made within and affecting their organizations. That means that the general manager must develop a basic understanding of the business and technology issues related to IS. Because technology changes rapidly, this text also assumes that today's technology is different from yesterday's technology. In fact, the technology available to readers of this text today might even differ significantly from that available when the text was being written. Therefore, this text focuses on generic concepts that are, to the extent possible, technology independent. It provides frameworks on which to hang more up-to-the-minute technological evolutions and revolutions, such as new uses of the Web, new social tools, or new cloud-based services. We assume that the reader will supplement the discussions of this text with current case studies and up-to-date information about the latest technology.

A second, perhaps controversial, assumption is that the roles of a general manager and of an IS manager require different skill sets and levels of technical competency. General managers must have a basic understanding of IS in order to be a knowledgeable participant in business decisions. Without that level of understanding, their decisions may have serious negative implications for the business. On the other hand, IS managers must have more in-depth knowledge of technology so they can partner with general managers who will use the IS. As digital natives take on increasingly more managerial roles in corporations, this second assumption may change—all managers may need deeper technical understanding. But for this text, we assume a different, more technical skill set for the IS manager and we do not attempt to provide that here.

Assumptions about Management

Although many books have been written describing the activities of managers, organizational theorist Henry Mintzberg offers a view that works especially well with a perspective relevant to IS management. Mintzberg's model describes management in behavioral terms by categorizing the three major roles a manager fills: interpersonal, informational, and decisional (see Figure I-3). This model is useful because it considers the chaotic nature of the environment in which managers actually work. Managers rarely have time to be reflective in their approaches to problems. They work at an unrelenting pace, and their activities are brief and often interrupted. Thus, quality information becomes even more crucial to effective decision making. The classic view is often seen as a tactical approach to management, whereas some describe Mintzberg's view as more strategic.

Assumptions about Business

Everyone has an internal understanding of what constitutes a business, which is based on readings and experiences with different firms. This understanding forms a model that provides the basis for comprehending actions, interpreting decisions, and communicating ideas. Managers use their internal model to make sense of otherwise

Type of Roles	Manager's Roles	IS Examples
Interpersonal	Figurehead	CIO greets touring dignitaries.
	Leader	IS manager puts in long hours to help motivate project team to complete project on schedule in an environment of heavy budget cuts.
	Liaison	CIO works with the marketing and human resource vice presidents to make sure that the reward and compensation system is changed to encourage use of the new IS supporting sales.
Informational	Monitor	Division manager compares progress on IS project for the division with milestones developed during the project's initiation and feasibility phase.
	Disseminator	CIO conveys organization's business strategy to IS department and demonstrates how IS strategy supports the business strategy.
	Spokesperson	IS manager represents IS department at organization's recruiting fair.
Decisional	Entrepreneur	IS division manager suggests an application of a new technology that improves the division's operational efficiency.
	Disturbance handler	IS division manager, as project team leader, helps resolve design disagreements between division personnel who will be using the system and systems analysts who are designing it.
	Resource allocator	CIO allocates additional personnel positions to various departments based upon the business strategy.
	Negotiator	IS manager negotiates for additional personnel needed to respond to recent user requests for enhanced functionality in a system that is being implemented.

FIGURE I-3 Managers' roles.
Source: Adapted from H. Mintzberg, *The Nature of Managerial Work* (New York: Harper & Row, 1973).

chaotic and random activities. This book uses several conceptual models of business. Some take a functional view and others take a process view.

Functional View

The classical view of a business is based on the functions that people perform, such as accounting, finance, marketing, operations, and human resources. The business organizes around these functions to coordinate them and to gain economies of scale within specialized sets of tasks. Information first flows vertically up and down between line positions and management; after analysis, it may be transmitted across other functions for use elsewhere in the company (see Figure I-4).

Process View

Michael Porter of Harvard Business School describes a business in terms of the primary and support activities that are performed to create, deliver, and support a product or service. The primary activities are not limited to specific functions, but rather are cross-functional processes (see Figure I-5). For example, an accounts payable process

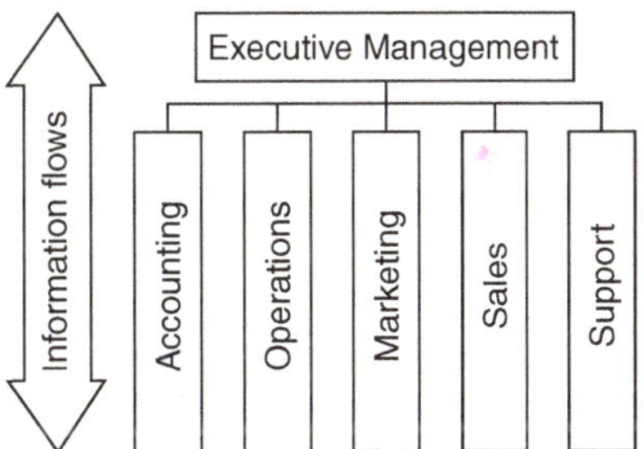

FIGURE I-4 Hierarchical view of the firm.

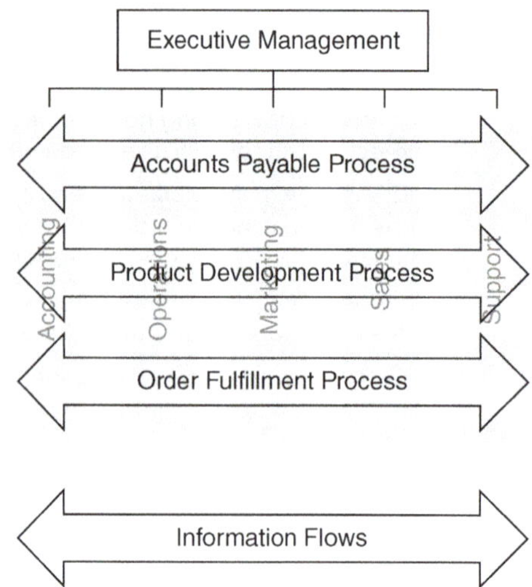

FIGURE I-5 **Process view of the firm: Cross-functional processes.**

might involve steps taken by other departments that generate obligations, which the accounting department pays. Likewise, the product creation process might begin with an idea from R&D, which is transferred to an operations organization that builds the actual product and involves marketing to get the word out, sales to sell and deliver the product, and support to provide customer assistance as needed. This view takes into account the activities in each functional area that are needed to complete a process, and any organization can be described by the processes it performs. Improving coordination among activities increases business profit. Organizations that effectively manage core processes across functional boundaries are often the industry leaders because they have made efficiencies that are not visible from the functional viewpoint. IS are often the key to process improvement and cross-functional coordination.

Both the process and functional views are important to understanding IS. The functional view is useful when similar activities must be explained, coordinated, executed, or communicated. For example, understanding a marketing information system means understanding the functional approach to business in general and the marketing function in particular. The process view, on the other hand, is useful when examining the flow of information throughout a business. For example, understanding the information associated with order fulfillment, product development, or customer service means taking a process view of the business. This text assumes that both views are important for participating in IS decisions.

Assumptions about Information Systems

Consider the components of an information system from the manager's viewpoint rather than from the technologist's viewpoint. Both the nature of information (hierarchy and economics) and the context of an information system must be examined to understand the basic assumptions of this text.

Information Hierarchy

The terms *data, information*, and *knowledge* are often used interchangeably, but have significant and discrete meanings within the knowledge management domain (and are more fully explored in Chapter 12). Tom Davenport, in his book *Information Ecology*, pointed out that getting everyone in any given organization to agree on common definitions is difficult. However, his work (summarized in Figure I-6) provides a nice starting point for understanding the subtle but important differences.

The information hierarchy begins with data, or simple observations; **data** are sets of specific, objective facts or observations, such as "inventory contains 45 units." Standing alone, such facts have no intrinsic meaning but can be easily captured, transmitted, and stored electronically.

	Data	Information	Knowledge
Definition	Simple observations of the state of the world	Data endowed with relevance and purpose	Information from the human mind (includes reflection, synthesis, context)
Characteristics	• Easily structured • Easily captured on machines • Often quantified • Easily transferred • Mere facts	• Requires unit of analysis • Data that have been processed • Human mediation necessary	• Hard to structure • Difficult to capture on machines • Often tacit • Hard to transfer
Example	Daily inventory report of all inventory items sent to the CEO of a large manufacturing company	Daily inventory report of items that are below economic order quantity levels sent to inventory manager	Inventory manager's knowledge of which items need to be reordered in light of daily inventory report, anticipated labor strikes, and a flood in Brazil that affects the supply of a major component

FIGURE I-6 Comparison of data, information, and knowledge.
Source: Adapted from Thomas Davenport, *Information Ecology* (New York: Oxford University Press, 1997).

Information is data endowed with relevance and purpose.[6] People turn data into information by organizing data into some unit of analysis (e.g., dollars, dates, or customers). For example, a mashup of location data and housing prices adds something beyond what the data provide individually, and that makes it information. A **mashup** is the term used for applications that combine data from different sources to create a new application on the Web.

To be relevant and have a purpose, information must be considered within the context in which it is received and used. Because of differences in context, information needs vary across functions and hierarchical levels. For example, when considering functional differences related to a sales transaction, a marketing department manager may be interested in the demographic characteristics of buyers, such as their age, gender, and home address. A manager in the accounting department probably won't be interested in any of these details, but instead wants to know details about the transaction itself, such as method of payment and date of payment.

Similarly, information needs may vary across hierarchical levels. These needs are summarized in Figure I-7 and reflect the different activities performed at each level. At the supervisory level, activities are narrow in scope and focused on the production or the execution of the business's basic transactions. At this level, information is focused on day-to-day activities that are internally oriented and accurately defined in a detailed manner. The activities of senior management are much broader in scope. Senior management performs long-term planning and needs

	Top Management	Middle Management	Supervisory and Lower-Level Management
Time Horizon	Long: years	Medium: weeks, months, years	Short: day to day
Level of Detail	Highly aggregated Less accurate More predictive	Summarized Integrated Often financial	Very detailed Very accurate Often nonfinancial
Source	Primarily external	Primarily internal with limited external	Internal
Decision	Extremely judgmental Uses creativity and analytical skills	Relatively judgmental	Heavily reliant on rules

FIGURE I-7 Information characteristics across hierarchical levels.
Source: G. Adapted from Anthony Gorry and Michael S. Scott Morton, "A Framework for Management Information Systems," *Sloan Management Review* 13, no. 1, 55–70.

[6] Peter F. Drucker, "The Coming of the New Organization," *Harvard Business Review* (January–February 1988), 45–53.

information that is aggregated, externally oriented, and more subjective than supervisors require. The information needs of middle managers in terms of these characteristics fall between the needs of supervisors and of senior management. Because information needs vary across levels, a daily inventory report of a large manufacturing firm may serve as information for a low-level inventory manager whereas the CEO would consider such a report to be merely data. The context in which the report is used must be considered in determining whether it is information.

Knowledge is information that is synthesized and contextualized to provide value. It is information with the most value. Knowledge consists of a mix of contextual information, values, experiences, and rules. For example, the mashup of locations and housing prices means one thing to a real estate agent, another thing to a potential buyer, and yet something else to an economist. It is richer and deeper than information and more valuable because someone thought deeply about that information and added his or her own unique experience and judgment. Knowledge also involves the synthesis of multiple sources of information over time.[7] The amount of human contribution increases along the continuum from data to information to knowledge. Computers work well for managing data but are less efficient at managing information and knowledge.

Some people think there is a fourth level in the information hierarchy: wisdom. **Wisdom** is knowledge fused with intuition and judgment that facilitates the ability to make decisions. Wisdom is that level of the information hierarchy used by subject matter experts, gurus, and individuals with a high degree of experience who seem to "just know" what to do and how to apply the knowledge they gain. This is consistent with Aristotle's view of wisdom as the ability to balance different and conflicting elements together in ways that are only learned through experience.

Economics of Information versus Economics of Things

In their groundbreaking book, *Blown to Bits*, Evans and Wurster argued that every business is in the information business.[8] Even those businesses not typically considered information businesses have business strategies in which information plays a critical role. The physical world of manufacturing is shaped by information that dominates products as well as processes. For example, an automobile contains as much computing power as a personal computer. Information-intensive processes in the manufacturing and marketing of the automobile include design, market research, logistics, advertising, and inventory management. The automobile itself, with its millions of lines of code, has become a computer on wheels with specialized computers and sensors alerting the driver of its health and road conditions. When taken in for service, maintenance crews simply plug an electronic monitor into the automobile to analyze and identify worn parts or other areas in need of upgrades and repair.

As our world is reshaped by information-intensive industries, it becomes even more important for business strategies to differentiate the timeworn economics of things from the evolving economics of information. Things wear out; things can be replicated at the expense of the manufacturer; things exist in a tangible location. When sold, the seller no longer owns the thing. The price of a thing is typically based on production costs. In contrast, information never wears out, although it can become obsolete or untrue. Information can be replicated at virtually no cost without limit; information exists in the ether. When sold, the seller still retains the information, but this ownership provides little value if the ability of others to copy it is not limited. Finally, information is often costly to produce but cheap to reproduce. Rather than pricing it to recover the sunk cost of its initial production, its price is typically based on its value to the consumer. Figure I-8 summarizes the major differences between the economics of goods and the economics of information.

Evans and Wurster suggest that traditionally the economics of information has been bundled with the economics of things. However, in this Information Age, firms are vulnerable if they do not separate the two. The Encyclopedia Britannica story serves as an example. Bundling the economics of things with the economics of information made it difficult for Encyclopedia Britannica to gauge two serious threats. The first threat was posed by Encarta, an entire encyclopedia on a CD-ROM that was given away to promote the sale of computers and peripherals. The second was Wikipedia, which is freely available to all and updated on a nearly real-time basis continuously by thousands of

[7] Thomas H. Davenport, *Information Ecology* (New York: Oxford University Press, 1997), 9–10.
[8] Philip Evans and Thomas Wurster, *Blown to Bits* (Boston: Harvard Business School Press, 2000).

Things	Information
Wear out	Doesn't wear out but can become obsolete or untrue
Are replicated at the expense of the manufacturer	Is replicated at almost zero cost without limit
Exist in a tangible location	Does not physically exist
When sold, possession changes hands	When sold, seller may still possess and sell again
Price based on production costs	Price based on value to consumer

FIGURE I-8 Comparison of the economics of things with the economics of information.

volunteers; currently Wikipedia reports that it holds over 4.9 million articles, receives 10 edits per second globally, and boasts 750 new pages added each day.[9] In contrast, Encyclopedia Britannica published volumes every several years and the price was between $1,500 and $2,200, covering printing and binding ($250) and sales commissions ($500 to $600).[10]

Britannica focused on its centuries-old tradition of providing information in richly bound tomes sold to the public through a well-trained sales force. Only when it was threatened with its very survival did Encyclopedia Britannica grasp the need to separate the economics of information from economics of things and sell bits of information online. Clearly, Encyclopedia Britannica's business strategy, like that of many other companies, needed to reflect the difference between the economics of things from the economics of information.

Internet of Things

More recently, a new concept has emerged to describe the explosive growth in the data generated by sensors traveling over the Web. The **Internet of things** (IoT) is the term used to refer to machines and sensors talking to each other over the network, taking Evans and Wurster's concepts even further. Although the term IoT was coined in1999,[11] it was not widely discussed until the current decade. The earliest example of its functions was reported before the Internet even existed—in a Coke machine at Carnegie Mellon University in the mid-1970s. Staff members and students in the Computer Science Department were able to use a network connecting a minicomputer and sensors in the machine to monitor not only the machine's inventory but even which button to push for the coldest bottles.[12]

A more broadly used early application of IoT was provided by Otis Elevator in the late 1980s and later copied by most other elevator companies.[13] Sensors in elevators send alerts over a network to a service center's computer when parts need replacing, and service technicians arrive without the builder owner knowing about the potential problem. Extending IoT even further, today's elevator systems alert handheld devices of nearby repair technicians who then visit the elevator to make the repair. Devices may connect to the Internet over a wireless connection or through a hard-wired connection.

Many say that we are on the brink of a new revolution that will be as impactful as the popularization of the World-Wide Web. The IoT has already been applied to large number of "things"—extending to home appliances, automobiles, thermostats, lighting, pets, and even people.[14] Many people can already perform futuristic functions using smartphone apps. They can remotely check the status of their heart monitor, tire pressure, or subway train's location. They can locate a lost pet or valuable object. They can reset their thermostat, turn off lights, and record a program on their DVR even after having left for vacation.

[9] Wikipedia Statistics, http://en.wikipedia.org/wiki/Wikipedia:Statistics (accessed August 18, 2015).
[10] Evans and Wurster, *Blown to Bits*.
[11] K. Ashton, "That 'Internet of Things' Thing," *RFID Journal* (June 22, 2009), http://www.rfidjournal.com/articles/view?4986 (accessed May 26, 2015).
[12] Attributed to The Carnegie Mellon University Computer Science Department Coke Machine, "The 'Only' Coke Machine on the Internet," https://www.cs.cmu.edu/~coke/history_long.txt (accessed May 26, 2015).
[13] D. Freedman, "The Myth of Strategic IS," *CIO Magazine* (July 1991), 42–48.
[14] Internet of Things, Whatis.com, http://whatis.techtarget.com/definition/Internet-of-Things (accessed May 26, 2015).

Social Business Lens

The explosion of consumer-based technologies, coupled with applications such as Facebook, Renren, Sina Weibo, Twitter, LinkedIn, YouTube, Foursquare, Skype, Pinterest, and more have brought into focus the concept of a social business. Some call this trend the *consumerization of technology*. *Consumerization* means that technologies such as social tools, mobile phones, and Web applications targeted at individual, personal users are creating pressures for companies in new and unexpected ways. At the same time, technologies initially intended for the corporation, like cloud computing, are being retooled and "consumerized" to appeal to individuals outside the corporation.

In this text, we use the term **social business** to refer to an enterprise using social IT for business applications, activities and processes. We sometimes say that a social business has infused social capabilities into business processes.

Social business is permeating every facet of business. There are new business models based on a social IT platform that offer new ways of connecting with stakeholders in functions such as governing, collaborating, doing work, and measuring results. In this book, we are particular about the terminology we use. *Social IT* is the term we use for all technologies in this space. We define **social IT** as the technologies used for people to collaborate, network, and interact over the Web. These include social networks and other applications that provide for interaction between people.

Many use the term **social media** as an overarching term for this space, but increasingly, *social media* refers to the marketing and sales applications of social IT, and we use it that way. Social networks are a specific type of tool, like Facebook, Ning, and similar tools. **Social networking** is the use of these types of social IT tools in a community. As of the writing of this text, the social space is still like the Wild West; there are no widely accepted conventions about the terms and their meanings or the uses and their impacts. But we have enough experience with social IT that we know it's a major force bursting on to the enterprise scene and it must be addressed in discussions of managing and using information systems.

Look in chapters for the feature "Social Business Lens" where we explore one topic related to that chapter from a social business perspective.

The reader might already be using the IoT with one or more of these apps. However, vendors tell us we "ain't seen nothing yet." The potential impact of IoT is limited by the number of objects connected and apps available to monitor and control them. As the number of devices directly connected to the Internet increases, researchers and IT

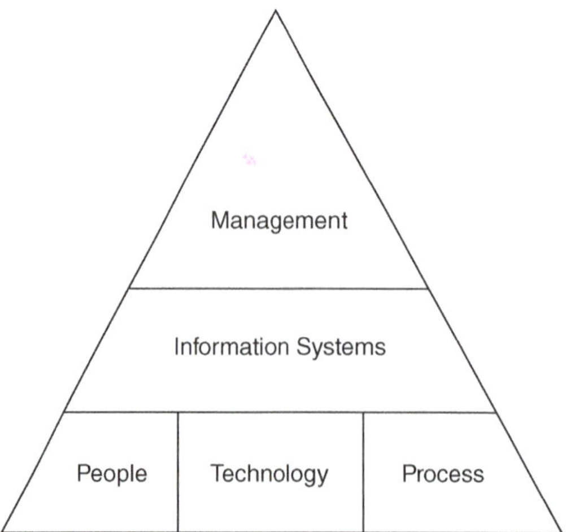

FIGURE I-9 System hierarchy.

professionals expect an exponential increase in IoT functionality and usage.[15] In the coming years, Internet traffic will dramatically increase along with an explosion in the amount of information generated by these devices.

System Hierarchy

Information systems are composed of three main elements: technology, people, and process (see Figure I-9). When most people use the term *information system*, they actually refer only to the technology element as defined by the organization's infrastructure. In this text, the term **infrastructure** refers to everything that supports the flow and processing of information in an organization, including hardware, software, data, and network components whereas **architecture** refers to the blueprint that reflects strategy implicit in combining these components. **Information systems (IS)** are defined more broadly as the *combination* of technology (the "what"), people (the "who"), and process (the "how") that an organization uses to produce and manage information. In contrast, information technology (IT) focuses only on the technical devices and tools used in the system. We define **information technology** as all forms of technology used to create, store, exchange, and use information. Many people use the terms IS and IT interchangeably. In recent years, "IT" has been more fashionable, but that changes as fashions change.

SUMMARY

Aligning information systems and business decisions is no longer an option; it's an imperative for business. Every business operates as an information-based enterprise. In addition, the explosive growth of smart phones, tablets, social tools, and Web-based businesses provides all managers with some experience in information systems and some idea of the complexity involved in providing enterprise-level systems. This highlights the need for all managers to be skilled in managing and using IS.

It is no longer acceptable to delegate IS decisions to the management information systems (MIS) department alone. The general manager must be involved to both execute business plans and protect options for future business vision. IS and business maturity must be aligned to provide the right level of information resources to the business.

This chapter makes the case for general managers' full participation in strategic business decisions concerning IS. It outlines the skills required for such participation, and it makes explicit certain key assumptions about the nature of business, management, and IS that will underlie the remaining discussions. Subsequent chapters are designed to build on these concepts by addressing the following questions.

Frameworks and Foundations

- How should information strategy be aligned with business and organizational strategies? (Chapter 1)
- How can a business achieve competitive advantages using its IS? (Chapter 2)
- How do organizational decisions impact IS decisions? (Chapter 3)
- How is the work of the individual in an organization affected by decisions concerning IS? (Chapter 4)
- How are information systems integrated with business processes? (Chapter 5)

IS Management Issues

- What are the components of an IS architecture? (Chapter 6)
- How are IS kept secure? (Chapter 7)
- How is the IT organization managed and funded? (Chapter 8)
- How are IS decisions made? (Chapter 9)
- What source should provide IS services and how and where should they be provided? (Chapter 10)

[15] Jared Newman, "Right Now, the Internet of Things Is Like the Internet of the 1990s," *Fast Company* (March 27, 2015I, http://www.fastcompany.com/3044375/sector-forecasting/the-future-of-the-internet-of-things-is-like-the-internet-of-the-1990s (last accessed May 26, 2015).

- How are IS projects managed and risks from change management mitigated? (Chapter 11)
- How is business intelligence managed within an organization? (Chapter 12)
- What ethical and moral considerations bind the uses of information in business? (Chapter 13)

KEY TERMS

architecture (p. 14)
data (p. 10)
digital natives (p. 4)
information (p. 11)
information system (p. 14)
information technology (p. 14)
infrastructure (p. 14)
internet of things (p. 13)
knowledge (p. 12)
mashup (p. 11)
social business (p. 15)
social IT (p. 15)
social media (p. 15)
social networking (p. 15)
Web 2.0 (p. 3)
wisdom (p. 12)

The Information Systems Strategy Triangle

chapter

1

The Information Systems Strategy Triangle highlights the alignment necessary between decisions regarding business strategy, information systems, and organizational design. This chapter reviews models of business strategy, organizational strategy and design, and information systems strategy. It concludes with a simple framework for creating a social business strategy.

In February 2015,[1] health care giant Kaiser Permanente named Dick Daniels to the CIO position and the leadership team for the next stage of the company's business strategy: to provide better health care at lower costs. To achieve those goals, Kaiser Permanente, one of the nation's largest not-for-profit health care systems with over 9.5 million members and 2014 operating revenue of $56.4 billion, invested in numerous information systems projects aimed at streamlining operations, offering new services, and meeting government obligations. For example, in 2014, 13% of all the medical appointments were fulfilled digitally—through e-mail—to the delight of patients who did not have to make a trip to the doctor's office and to the delight of doctors who were able to check in on their patients, particularly those with chronic conditions, more frequently. Doctors particularly liked this because their annual bonuses were based, in part, on improvements in patient health metrics such as lower blood pressure, reduced blood sugar levels if at risk for diabetes, and improvement in cholesterol scores rather than on the number of tests they ordered or the total billing they brought in. The organization invested heavily in video conferencing technology, mobile apps, and analytics as they finished implementing a $4 billion electronic health records system, KP HealthConnect.

KP HealthConnect began in 2003, but by 2008, all members had online access to their health records; by 2010, all system services were available at all medical offices and hospitals in the system; and by 2012, all members had access to their health records on mobile devices. Kaiser Permanente has been a regular innovator in the use of technologies, being one of the first health care organizations to experiment with chat rooms, secure messaging, and private e-mail correspondence between patients, physicians, and care providers. The new system connects each member to all caregivers and services available at Kaiser Permanente. Further, it enabled patients to participate in the health care they received at a new level and access information directly from the system.

The organizational design supported the business strategy of better health care at lower costs.[2] At the core of this strategy was a shift from a "fix-me system" with which patients seek health care when something is broken and needs repair to a system that was truly proactive and focused on promoting health. Under the "fix-me system," health care was expensive and often sought too late to

[1] http://blogs.wsj.com/cio/2015/02/09/kaiser-permanente-names-richard-dick-daniels-cio/; http://fortune.com/2015/04/29/kaiser-ceo-on-healthcare/; http://fortune.com/2014/07/24/a-health-care-model-thats-working/; Paul Gray, Omar Sawy, Guillermo Asper, and Magnus Thordarson, "Realizing Strategic Value Through Center-Edge Digital Transformation in Consumer-Centric Industries," *MIS Quarterly Executive* 12, no. 1 (March 2013).

[2] Note that the organizational design puts the organizational strategy into practice. For instance, rewarding billings, sharing little information, and late involvement with patients are organizational design elements of a "fix-me" organizational strategy.

fix the problem. Instead, the Kaiser Permanente strategy focused on promoting health, enabling identification of problems before they became serious issues. For example, those in need of more exercise may receive a prescription to take a walk and an e-mail reminder from health care providers to reinforce the new behavior. Staff incentive systems were aligned with this behavior, too. Physicians were all paid a flat salary and end-of-year bonuses if their patients achieved better health. All caregivers were rewarded for guiding people into making behavioral choices that were likely to keep them well.

The success at Kaiser Permanente was achieved in part because of the alignment between its business strategy, its information systems strategy, and its organization design. Physicians were part of the decision-making processes. Managers were involved in the design and implementation of the information systems. The decision to move from a "fix-me system" to a "proactive health system" was not made in isolation from the organization or the information systems.

The information systems (IS) department is not an island within a firm. Rather, IS manages an infrastructure that is essential to the firm's functioning. Further, the Kaiser Permanente case illustrates that a firm's IS must be aligned with the way it manages its employees and processes. For Kaiser Permanente, it was clear that not only did the physicians need a fast, inexpensive, and useful way to communicate with patients outside of regular in-person appointments but also incentive systems and patient service processes had to be updated. Information systems provided a solution in conjunction with new operational and control processes.

This chapter introduces a simple framework for describing the alignment necessary with business systems and for understanding the impact of IS on organizations. This framework is called the **Information Systems Strategy Triangle** because it relates business strategy with IS strategy and organizational strategy. This chapter also presents key frameworks from organization theory that describe the context in which IS operates as well as the business imperatives that IS support. The Information Systems Strategy Triangle presented in Figure 1.1 suggests three key points about strategy.

1. **Successful firms have an overriding business strategy that drives both organizational strategy and IS strategy.** The decisions made regarding the structure, hiring practices, vendor policies, and other components of the organizational design, as well as decisions regarding applications, hardware, and other IS components, are all driven by the firm's business objectives, strategies, and tactics. Successful firms carefully balance these three strategies—they purposely design their organization and their IS strategies to complement their business strategy.

2. **IS strategy can itself affect and is affected by changes in a firm's business and organizational design.** To perpetuate the balance needed for successful operation, changes in the IS strategy must be accompanied by changes in the organizational strategy and must accommodate the overall business strategy. If a firm designs its business strategy to use IS to gain strategic advantage, the leadership position in IS can be sustained only by constant innovation. The business, IS, and organizational strategies must constantly be adjusted.

3. **IS strategy always involves consequences—intended or not—within business and organizational strategies.** Avoiding harmful unintended consequences means remembering to consider business and organizational strategies when designing IS implementation. For example, deploying tablets to employees without an accompanying set of changes to job expectations, process design, compensation plans, and business tactics will fail to achieve expected productivity improvements. Success can be achieved only by specifically designing all three components of the strategy triangle so they properly complement each other.

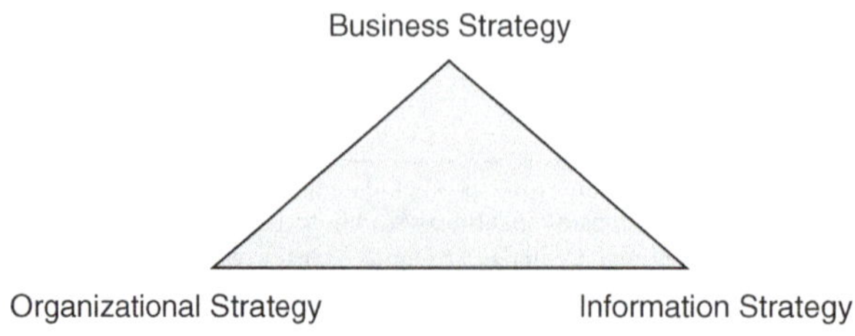

FIGURE 1.1 The Information Systems Strategy Triangle.

Before the changes at Kaiser Permanente, incentives for doctors were misaligned with the goals of better health care. Its IS Strategy Triangle was out of alignment at that time. Its organizational strategy (e.g., a "fix-me" system) was not supported by the IS strategy (e.g., tracking and reporting billable procedures). Neither the organizational strategy nor the IS strategy adequately supported their purported business strategy (helping patients at lower cost). For Kaiser Permanente, success could be achieved only by specifically designing all three components of the strategy triangle to work together.

Of course, once a firm is out of alignment, it does not mean that it has to stay that way. To correct the misalignment described earlier, Kaiser Permanente used on-line services to enable quick communications between patients, physicians, and care providers. Further, it changed its bonus structure to focus on health rather than billing amounts. The new systems realign people, process, and technology to provide better service, save time, and save money.

What does *alignment* mean? The book *Winning the 3-Legged Race* defines *alignment* as the situation in which a company's current and emerging business strategy is enabled and supported yet unconstrained by technology. The authors suggest that although alignment is good, there are higher states, namely synchronization and convergence, toward which companies should strive. With synchronization, technology not only enables current business strategy but also anticipates and shapes future business strategy. Convergence goes one step further by exhibiting a state in which business strategy and technology strategy are intertwined and the leadership team members operate almost interchangeably. Although we appreciate the distinction and agree that firms should strive for synchronization and convergence, *alignment* in this text means any of these states, and it pertains to the balance between organizational strategy, IS strategy, and business strategy.[3]

A word of explanation is needed here. Studying IS alone does not provide general managers with the appropriate perspective. This chapter and subsequent chapters address questions of IS strategy squarely within the context of business strategy. Although this is not a textbook of business strategy, a foundation for IS discussions is built on some basic business strategy frameworks and organizational theories presented in this and the next chapter. To be effective, managers need a solid sense of how IS are used and managed within the organization. Studying details of technologies is also outside the scope of this text. Details of the technologies are relevant, of course, and it is important that any organization maintain a sufficient knowledge base to plan for and adequately align with business priorities. However, because technologies change so rapidly, keeping a textbook current is impossible. Instead, this text takes the perspective that understanding what questions to ask and having a framework for interpreting the answers are skills more fundamental to the general manager than understanding any particular technology. That understanding must be constantly refreshed using the most current articles and information from experts. This text provides readers with an appreciation of the need to ask questions, a framework from which to derive the questions to ask, and a foundation sufficient to understand the answers received. The remaining chapters build on the foundation provided in the Information Systems Strategy Triangle.

Brief Overview of Business Strategy Frameworks

A **strategy** is a coordinated set of actions to fulfill objectives, purposes, and goals. The essence of a strategy is setting limits on what the business will seek to accomplish. Strategy starts with a mission. A **mission** is a clear and compelling statement that unifies an organization's effort and describes what the firm is all about (i.e., its purpose). Mark Zuckerberg's reflection on the mission of Facebook provides an interesting example. Originally conceived as a product rather than a service, the CEO of Facebook commented, "after we started hiring more people and building out the team, I began to get an appreciation that a company is a great way to get a lot of people involved in a mission you're trying to push forward. Our mission is getting people to connect."[4]

In a few words, the mission statement sums up what is unique about the firm. The information in Figure 1.2 indicates that even though Zappos, Amazon, and L.L. Bean are all in the retail industry, they view their missions quite differently. For example, Zappos' focus is on customer service, Amazon is about customer sets, and L.L. Bean is

[3] F. Hogue, V. Sambamurthy, R. Zmud, T. Trainer, and C. Wilson, *Winning the 3-Legged Race* (Upper Saddle River, NJ: Prentice Hall, 2005).

[4] Shayndi Raice, "Is Facebook Ready for the Big Time?" *The Wall Street Journal* (January 14–15, 2012), B1.

Company	Mission Statement
Zappos	To provide the best customer service possible. Internally we call this our WOW philosophy.[a]
Amazon	We seek to be Earth's most customer-centric company for three primary customer sets: consumer customers, seller customers and developer customers.[b]
L.L. Bean	Sell good merchandise at a reasonable profit, treat your customers like human beings and they will always come back for more.[c]

[a] http://about.zappos.com (accessed March 19, 2015).
[b] http://www.amazon.com Mission Statement on Amazon Investor Relations page (accessed March 19, 2015).
[c] http://www.llbean.com/customerService/aboutLLBean/company_values.html (accessed March 19, 2015).

FIGURE 1.2 Mission statements of three retail businesses.

about the merchandise and treating people the right way. It's interesting to note that although Amazon purchased Zappos in 2009, the acquisition agreement specified that Zappos would continue to run independently of its new parent. Today, Zappos continues to remain both culturally and physically separate from Amazon. Zappos is located near Las Vegas, Nevada, and Amazon is in Seattle, Washington.

A **business strategy** is a plan articulating where a business seeks to go and how it expects to get there. It is the means by which a business communicates its goals. Management constructs this plan in response to market forces, customer demands, and organizational capabilities. Market forces create the competitive context for the business. Some markets, such as those faced by package delivery firms, laptop computer manufacturers, and credit card issuers, face many competitors and a high level of competition, such that product differentiation becomes increasingly difficult. Other markets, such as those for airlines and automobiles, are similarly characterized by high competition, but product differentiation is better established. Customer demands comprise the wants and needs of the individuals and companies who purchase the products and services available in the marketplace. Organizational capabilities include the skills and experience that give the corporation a currency that can add value in the marketplace.

Consider Dell, originally a personal computer company. Initially Dell's business strategy was to sell personal computers directly to the customer without going through an intermediary. Reaching customers in this way was less expensive and more responsive than selling the computers in retail stores. The Internet, combined with Dell's well-designed IS infrastructure, allowed customers to electronically contact Dell, which then designed a PC for a customer's specific needs. Dell's ordering system was integrated with its production system and shared information automatically with each supplier of PC components. This IS enabled the assembly of the most current computers without the expense of storing large inventories, and inventory uncertainties were pushed back to the vendors. Cost savings were passed on to the customer, and the direct-to-customer model allowed Dell to focus its production capacity on building only the most current products. With small profit margins and new products quickly able to replace existing products, IS aligned with Dell's business strategy to provide low-cost PCs. The cost savings from the IS was reflected in the price of systems. In addition, Dell executives achieved a strategic advantage in reducing response time, building custom computers that had one of the industry's lowest costs, and eliminating inventories that could become obsolete before they are sold. Thus, this business strategy was consistent with Dell's mission of delivering the best customer experience in the markets it serves.

But things aren't always as they seem. If the direct-to-customer strategy was so effective, why is Dell now also selling its computers at major retail outlets such as Walmart, Staples, and Best Buy? It is likely that the sales figures and profit margins were not measuring up to Dell's stated objectives and performance targets. And Dell has branched out to other hardware, such as printers and servers, and more recently, providing IT services. Consequently, Dell adjusted its business strategy, and we can expect to see changes in its organizational design and information systems to reflect its altered direction.

Now consider your favorite dot-com company. Every dot-com company has a business strategy of delivering its products or services over the Internet. To do so, the dot-coms need organizations filled with individuals and processes that support this business strategy. Their employees must be Internet savvy; that is, they must have

Business Models versus Business Strategy

Some new managers confuse the concept of a business model with the concept of a business strategy. The **business strategy**, as discussed in this chapter, is the coordinated set of actions used to meet the business goals and objectives. It's the path a company takes to achieve its goals. One of the components of the business strategy is the business model, the design of how the business will make money and how customers will get value from its products and services. Some might argue that a business model is the outcome of strategy.*

Some examples of business models commonly seen in the digital world include†:

- *Subscription:* Customers pay a recurring fee for the product or service.
- *Advertising:* Customers access the product or service for "free," and sponsors or vendors pay fees for advertising that goes with the product or service.
- *Cost plus:* Somewhat like a traditional retailer, customers purchase the product or service for a specific price that is usually the cost plus some markup for profit.
- *Renting/Licensing:* Customers pay a fee to use the product or service for a specified period of time.
- *All-you-can-Eat:* Customers pay one fee for access to as much of the product or service as they want to consume, usually over a specific period of time.
- *Freemium:* Customers get something for "free," and the company makes money from selling customers something after they get the giveaway. This is similar to a business model used in brick-and-mortar businesses that give away something or sell something for a very low price, but the customer has to pay for refills or upgrades such as giving razors away but making money from selling razor blades.

*For a more detailed treatment of the concepts of business models, strategy, and tactics, see Ramon Casadesus-Masanell and Joan Ricart, "From Strategy to Business Models and to Tactics," Harvard Business School working paper 10-036, http://www.hbs.edu/faculty/Publication%20Files/10-036.pdf (accessed August 21, 2015).

†For a list of 15 different business models, see http://www.digitalbusinessmodelguru.com/2012/12/15-business-models-complete-list.html (accessed August 21, 2015).

skills and knowledge that are relevant to the dot-com business. Their processes must support the dot-com strategy. Imagine what would happen if the order process for their services was not Internet based. It seems silly to even consider a dot-com that would insist that orders be placed in person or even by telephone. The dot-com processes are aligned with companies' on-line-based business strategy. Further, their IS strategy must also be aligned with their processes. It would be equally silly to expect information to be based on paper files rather than electronic files.

A classic, widely used model developed by Michael Porter still frames most discussions of business strategy. In the next section, we review Porter's generic strategies framework as well as dynamic environment strategies.[5] We then share questions that a general manager must answer to understand the business' strategy.

The Generic Strategies Framework

Companies sell their products and services in a marketplace populated with competitors. Michael Porter's framework helps managers understand the strategies they may choose to build a competitive advantage. In his book *Competitive Advantage*, Porter claims that the "fundamental basis of above-average performance in the long run is sustainable competitive advantage."[6] Porter identified three primary strategies for achieving competitive advantage: (1) cost leadership, (2) differentiation, and (3) focus. These advantages derive from the company's relative position

[5] Another popular model by Michael Porter, the value chain, provides a useful model for discussing internal operations of an organization. Some find it a useful model for understanding how to link two firms. This framework is used in Chapter 5 to examine business process design. For further information, see M. Porter, *Competitive Advantage,* 1st ed. (New York: The Free Press, 1985).

[6] M. Porter, *Competitive Advantage: Creating and Sustaining Superior Performance,* 2nd ed. (New York: The Free Press, 1998).

	Strategic Advantage		
Strategic Target		Uniqueness perceived by customer	Low-cost position
	Industrywide	Differentiation	Cost leadership
	Particular segment only	Focus	

FIGURE 1.3 Three strategies for achieving competitive advantage.
Source: Adapted from M. Porter, *Competitive Advantage*, 1st ed. (New York: The Free Press, 1985) and *Competitive Advantage: Creating and Sustaining Superior Performance*, 2nd ed. (New York: The Free Press, 1998).

in the marketplace, and they depend on the strategies and tactics used by competitors. See Figure 1.3 for a summary of these three strategies for achieving competitive advantage.

Cost leadership results when the organization aims to be the lowest-cost producer in the marketplace. The organization enjoys above-average performance by minimizing costs. The product or service offered must be comparable in quality to those offered by others in the industry so that customers perceive its relative value. Typically, only one cost leader exists within an industry. If more than one organization seeks an advantage with this strategy, a price war ensues, which eventually may drive the organization with the higher cost structure out of the marketplace. Through mass distribution, economies of scale, and IS to generate operating efficiencies, Walmart epitomizes the cost-leadership strategy.

Through **differentiation**, the organization offers its product or service in a way that appears unique in the marketplace. The organization identifies which qualitative dimensions are most important to its customers and then finds ways to add value along one or more of those dimensions. For this strategy to work, the price charged customers for the differentiator must seem fair relative to the price charged by competitors. Typically, multiple firms in any given market employ this strategy. Progressive Insurance is able to differentiate itself from other automobile insurance companies.

In its earlier days, Progressive Insurance's service was unique. Representatives responded to accident claims 24-7, arriving at the scene of the accident with powerful laptops and software that enabled them to settle claims and cut a check on the spot. More recently, Progressive was the first to offer a usage-based insurance product, called Snapshot, that bases insurance rates on the miles driven by customers. These innovations enabled a strategy that spurred Progressive's growth and widened its profit margins. Apple Inc. is another example of a company that competes in its markets on its ability to differentiate its products. Apple's various innovations in its operating system, laptop design, iPads, iPhones, iPods, iTunes and iWatches have created a strategy based on the uniqueness of its products and services.

Focus allows an organization to limit its scope to a narrower segment of the market and tailor its offerings to that group of customers. This strategy has two variants: (1) *cost focus*, in which the organization seeks a cost advantage within its segment and (2) *differentiation focus*, in which it seeks to distinguish its products or services within the segment. This strategy allows the organization to achieve a local competitive advantage even if it does not achieve competitive advantage in the marketplace overall. Porter explains how the focuser can achieve competitive advantage by focusing exclusively on certain market segments:

> Breadth of target is clearly a matter of degree, but the essence of focus is the exploitation of a narrow target's differences from the balance of the industry. Narrow focus in and of itself is not sufficient for above-average performance.[7]

Marriott International demonstrates both types of focus with two of its hotel chains: Marriott has a cost focus, and Ritz-Carlton has a differentiation focus. To better serve its business travelers and cut operational expenses, Marriott properties have check-in kiosks that interface with their Marriott Rewards loyalty program. A guest can swipe a credit card or Marriott Rewards card at the kiosk in the lobby and receive a room assignment and keycard

[7] Porter, *Competitive Advantage: Creating and Sustaining*.

from the machine. She can also print airline boarding passes at the kiosks. Further, the kiosks help the Marriott chain implement its cost focus by cutting down on the personnel needed in at the front desk. The kiosk system is integrated with other systems such as billing and customer relationship management (CRM) to generate operating efficiencies and enhanced corporate standardization.

In contrast, stand-alone kiosks in the lobby would destroy the feeling that the Ritz-Carlton chain, acquired by Marriott in 1995, creates. To the Ritz-Carlton chain, CRM means capturing and using information about guests, such as their preference for wines, a hometown newspaper, or a sunny room. Each Ritz-Carlton employee is expected to promote personalized service by identifying and recording individual guest preferences. To demonstrate how this rule could be implemented, a waiter, after hearing a guest exclaim that she loves tulips, could log the guest's comments into the Ritz-Carlton CRM system called "Class." On her next visit to a Ritz-Carlton hotel, tulips could be placed in the guest's room after querying Class to learn more about her as her visit approaches. The CRM is instrumental in implementing the differentiation-focus strategy of the Ritz-Carlton chain.[8] Its strategy allows the Ritz-Carlton chain to live up to its unique motto which emphasizes that its staff members are distinguished people with distinguished customers.

Airline JetBlue adopted a differentiation strategy based on low costs coupled with unique customer experience. It might be called a "value-based strategy." It is not the lowest cost carrier in the airline industry; at 12.3 cents per passenger seat mile, JetBlue has one of the lowest costs, but Virgin America, Spirit, and Allegiant had even lower per seat mile costs in 2013. But JetBlue manages its operational costs carefully, making decisions that keep its per passenger costs among the lowest in the business, such as a limited number of airplane models in its fleet, gates at less congested airports, paperless cockpit and many other operations, and snacks instead of meals on flights. JetBlue has one of the longest stage length averages (the length of the average flight) in the industry, and the longer the flight, the lower the unit costs. Competing network carriers, who are more well known and established, may have different pay scales because they've been in the business longer and have a different composition of staff. These carriers also have higher maintenance costs for their older, more diverse fleets. If it could realize its plans for growth while maintaining its low cost structure, JetBlue could move from its cost focus based on serving a limited, but growing, number of market segments to a cost leadership strategy.[9]

While sustaining a cost focus, JetBlue's chairman believes that JetBlue can compete on more than price, which is part of its unique differentiation strategy. It is why the airline continually strives to keep customers satisfied with frills such as extra leg room, leather seats, prompt baggage delivery, DirectTV, and movies. It has been recognized with many awards for customer satisfaction in the North American airline industry.

Dynamic Environment Strategies

Porter's generic strategies model is useful for diagnostics, for understanding how a business seeks to profit in its chosen marketplace, and for prescriptions, or building new opportunities for advantage. It reflects a careful balancing of countervailing competitive forces posed by buyers, suppliers, competitors, new entrants, and substitute products and services within an industry. As is the case with many models, dynamic environment strategies offer managers useful tools for thinking about strategy.

However, the Porter model was developed at a time when competitive advantage was sustainable because the rate of change in any given industry was relatively slow and manageable. Since the late 1980s, when this framework was at the height of its popularity, newer models have been developed to take into account the increasing turbulence and velocity of the marketplace. Organizations need to be able to respond instantly and change rapidly, which requires dynamic structures and processes. One example of this type of approach is the hypercompetition framework. Discussions of hypercompetition take a perspective different from that of the previous framework. Porter's framework focuses on creating competitive advantage in relatively stable markets, whereas **hypercompetition** frameworks suggest that the speed and aggressiveness of the moves and countermoves in a highly competitive and

[8] Scott Berinato, "Room for Two," *CIO.com* (May 15, 2002), http://www.cio.com/archive/051502/two_content.html.

[9] http://www.oliverwyman.com/content/dam/oliver-wyman/global/en/2014/nov/Airline_Economic_Analysis_Screen_OW_Nov_2014.pdf (accessed March 23, 2015).

turbulent market create an environment in which advantages are rapidly created and eroded. In a hypercompetitive market, trying to sustain a specific competitive advantage can be a deadly distraction because the environment and the marketplace change rapidly. To manage the rapid speed of change, firms value agility and focus on quickly adjusting their organizational resources to gain competitive advantage. Successful concepts in hypercompetitive markets include dynamic capabilities, creative destruction, and blue ocean strategy.[10]

Dynamic capabilities are means of orchestrating a firm's resources in the face of turbulent environments. In particular, the dynamic capabilities framework focuses on the ways a firm can integrate, build, and reconfigure internal and external capabilities, or abilities, to address rapidly changing environments. These capabilities are built rather than bought. They are embedded in firm-specific routines, processes, and asset positions. Thus, they are difficult for rivals to imitate. In sum, they help determine the speed and degree to which the firm can marshal and align its resources and competences to match the opportunities and requirements of the business environment.[11]

Since the 1990s, a competitive practice, called **creative destruction**, has emerged. First predicted over 60 years ago by the economist Joseph Schumpeter, it was made popular more recently by Harvard Professor Clay Christensen. Coincidentally (or maybe not), the accelerated competition has occurred concomitantly with sharp increases in the quality and quantity of information technology (IT) investment. The changes in competitive dynamics are particularly striking in sectors that spend the most on IT.[12]

One example of using dynamic models was implemented by leadership guru Jack Welch at General Electric (GE). Often nicknamed "Neutron Jack" because of the way businesses were radically changed, Welch's approach to creative destruction was termed *destroy your business* (DYB). Welch recognized that GE could sustain its competitive advantage only for a limited time as competitors attempted to outmaneuver the company. He knew that if GE did not identify its weaknesses, its competitors would relish doing so. DYB is an approach that places GE employees in the shoes of their competitors.[13] Through the DYB lenses, GE employees develop strategies to destroy the company's competitive advantage. Then, in light of their revelations, they apply the grow your business (GYB) strategy to find fresh ways to reach new customers and better serve existing ones. This allows GE to protect its business from its competitors and sustain its position in the marketplace over the long run.

A similar strategy of cannibalizing its own products was used by Apple. Steve Jobs, Apple's founder and former CEO, felt strongly that if a company was not willing to cannibalize its own products, someone else would come along and do it for them. That was evident in the way Apple introduced the iPhone while iPod sales were brisk and the iPad while its Macintosh sales were strong.[14] Apple continues to exhibit this strategy with subsequent releases of new models of all of its products.

Most discussions of strategy focus on gaining competitive advantage in currently existing industries and marketplaces, which are referred to by Kim and Mauborgne as **red ocean strategy**. Using a red ocean strategy, firms fiercely compete to earn a larger share of existing demand. Kim and Mauborgne recommend a better approach: Firms adopt a **blue ocean strategy** in which they create new demand in untapped marketspaces where they have the "water" to themselves. When applying the blue ocean strategy, the goal is not to beat the competition but to make it irrelevant. This is what Dell did when it challenged current industry logic by changing the computer purchasing and delivery experiences of its customers. "With its direct sales to customers, Dell was able to sell its PCs for 40 percent less than IBM dealers while still making money."[15] Dell also introduced into unchartered seas an unprecedented delivery process that allowed buyers to receive their new computers within four days of ordering them as compared to the red ocean process, which typically required 10 weeks.

---

[10] For more information, please see Don Goeltz, "Hypercompetition," vol. 1 of *The Encyclopedia of Management Theory,* ed. Eric Kessler (Los Angeles: Sage, 2013), 359–60.

[11] D. J. Teece, G. Pisano, and A. Shuen, "Dynamic Capabilities and Strategic Management," *Strategic Management Journal* 18 (1997), 509–33; David Teece, "Dynamic Capabilities," vol. 1 of *The Encyclopedia of Management Theory,* ed. Eric Kessler (Los Angeles: Sage, 2013), 221–24.

[12] Andrew McAfee and Erik Brynjolfsson, "Investing in the IT That Makes a Competitive Difference," *Harvard Business Review* (July–August 2008), 98–107.

[13] M. Levinson, "GE Uses the Internet to Grow Business," *CIO* (October 15, 2001), http://www.cio.com/article/30624/HOT_TOPIC_E_BUSINESS_GE_Uses_the_Internet_to_Grow_Business_ (accessed May 5, 2012).

[14] Walter Isaacson, *Steve Jobs* (New York: Simon and Shuster, 2011).

[15] W. Chan Kim and Renee Mauborgne, *Blue Ocean Strategy* (Cambridge, MA: Harvard Business School, 2005), 202.

Strategic Approach	Key Idea	Application to Information Systems
Porter's generic strategies	Firms achieve competitive advantage through cost leadership, differentiation, or focus.	Understanding which strategy is chosen by a firm is critical to choosing IS to complement the strategy.
Dynamic environment strategies	Speed, agility, and aggressive moves and countermoves by a firm create competitive advantage.	The speed of change is too fast for manual response, making IS critical to achieving business goals.

FIGURE 1.4 Summary of strategic approaches and IT applications.

Why Are Strategic Advantage Models Essential to Planning for Information Systems?

A general manager who relies solely on IS personnel to make IS decisions may not only give up any authority over IS strategy but also hamper crucial future business decisions. In fact, business strategy should drive IS decision making, and changes in business strategy should entail reassessments of IS. Moreover, changes in IS potential should trigger reassessments of business strategy—as in the case of the Internet when companies that understood or even considered its implications for the marketplace quickly outpaced their competitors who failed to do so. For the purposes of our model, the Information Systems Strategy Triangle, understanding business strategy means answering the following questions:

1. What is the business goal or objective?
2. What is the plan for achieving it? What is the role of IS in this plan?
3. Who are the crucial competitors and partners, and what is required of a successful player in this marketplace?
4. What are the industry forces in this marketplace?

Porter's generic strategies framework and the dynamic frameworks (summarized in Figure 1.4) are revisited in the next few chapters. They are especially helpful in discussing the role of IS in building and sustaining competitive advantages (Chapter 2) and for incorporating IS into business strategy. The next section of this chapter establishes a foundation for understanding organizational strategies.

Brief Overview of Organizational Strategies

Organizational strategy includes the organization's design as well as the choices it makes to define, set up, coordinate, and control its work processes. How a manager designs the organization impacts every aspect of operations from dealing with innovation to relationships with customers, suppliers, and employees. The organizational strategy is a plan that answers the question: "How will the company organize to achieve its goals and implement its business strategy?"

A useful framework for organizational design can be found in the book *Building the Information Age Organization* by Cash, Eccles, Nohria, and Nolan.[16] This framework (Figure 1.5) suggests that the successful execution of a company's organizational strategy comprises the best combination of organizational, control, and cultural variables. Organizational variables include decision rights, business processes, formal reporting relationships, and informal networks. Control variables include the availability of data, nature and quality of planning, effectiveness of performance measurement and evaluation systems, and incentives to do good work. Cultural variables comprise the values of the organization. These organizational, control, and cultural variables are **managerial levers** used by decision makers to effect changes in their organizations. These managerial levers are discussed in detail in Chapter 3.

[16] James I. Cash, Robert G. Eccles, Nitin Nohria, and Richard L. Nolan, *Building the Information Age Organization* (Homewood, IL: Richard D. Irwin, 1994).

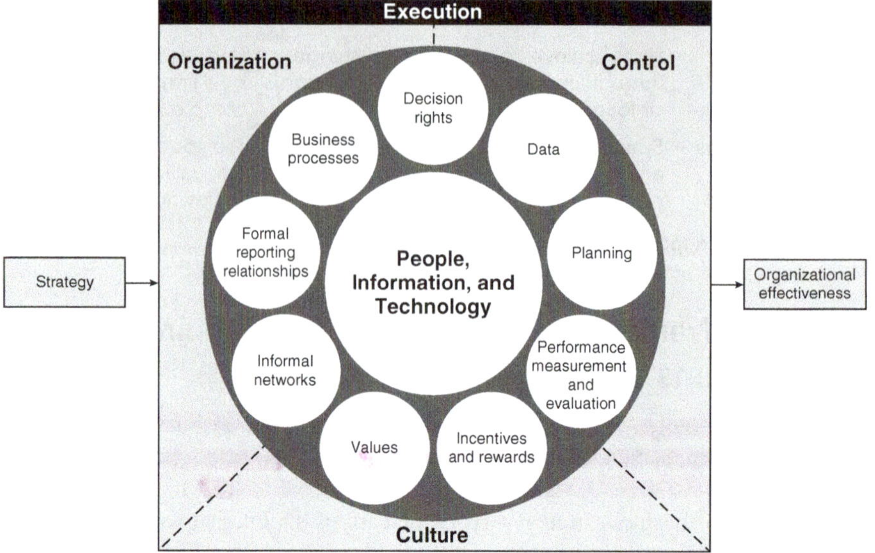

FIGURE 1.5 Managerial Levers model.
Source: J. Cash, R. G. Eccles, N. Nohria, and R. L. Nolan, *Building the Information Age Organization* (Homewood, IL: Richard D. Irwin, 1994).

Our objective is to give the manager a framework to use in evaluating various aspects of organizational design. In this way, the manager can review the current organization and assess which components may be missing and what future options are available. Understanding organizational design means answering the following questions:

1. What are the important structures and reporting relationships within the organization?
2. Who holds the decision rights to critical decisions?
3. What are the important people-based networks (social and informational), and how can we use them to get work done better?
4. What are the characteristics, experiences, and skill levels of the people within the organization?
5. What are the key business processes?
6. What control systems (management and measurement systems) are in place?
7. What are the culture, values, and beliefs of the organization?

The answers to these questions inform the assessment of the organization's use of IS. Chapters 3, 4, and 5 use the Managerial Levers model to assess the impact of information systems (IS) on the firm. Chapters 8 and 9 use this same list to understand the business and governance of the IS organization.

Brief Overview of Information Systems Strategy

IS strategy is the plan an organization uses to provide information services. IS allow a company to implement its business strategy. JetBlue's former Vice President for People explains it nicely: "We define what the business needs and then go find the technology to support that."[17]

Business strategy is a function of competition (What does the customer want and what does the competition do?), positioning (In what way does the firm want to compete?), and capabilities (What can the firm do?). IS help

[17] Hogue et al., *Winning the 3-Legged Race*, 111.

	What	Who	Where
Hardware	The physical devices of the system	System users and managers	Physical location of devices (cloud, data center, etc.)
Software	The programs, applications, and utilities	System users and managers	The hardware it resides on and physical location of that hardware
Networking	The way hardware is connected to other hardware, to the Internet, and to other outside networks	System users and managers; company that provides the service	Where the nodes, the wires, and other transport media are located
Data	Bits of information stored in the system	Owners of data; data administrators	Where the information resides

FIGURE 1.6 IS strategy matrix.

determine the company's capabilities. An entire chapter is devoted to understanding key issues facing general managers concerning IT architecture, but for now a more basic framework is used to understand the decisions related to IS that an organization must make.

The purpose of the matrix in Figure 1.6 is to give the manager a high-level view of the relation between the four IS infrastructure components and the other resource considerations that are keys to IS strategy. Infrastructure

Social Business Lens: Building a Social Business Strategy

Some companies use social IT as point solutions for business opportunities, but others build a social business strategy that considers the application of social IT tools and capabilities to solve business opportunities holistically. A **social business strategy** is a plan of how the firm will use social IT that is aligned with its organizational strategy and IS strategy. Social business strategy includes a vision of how the business would operate if it seamlessly and thoroughly incorporated social and collaborative capabilities throughout the business model. It answers the same type of questions of what, how, and who, as do many other business strategies.

Social businesses infuse social capabilities into their business processes. Most of the social business opportunities fall into one of three categories:

Collaboration—using social IT to extend the reach of stakeholders, both employees and those outside the enterprise walls. Social IT such as social networks enable individuals to find and connect with each other to share ideas, information, and expertise.

Engagement—using social IT to involve stakeholders in the traditional business of the enterprise. Social IT such as communities and blogs provide a platform for individuals to join in conversations, create new conversations, and offer support to each other and other activities that create a deeper feeling of connection to the company, brand, or enterprise.

Innovation—using social IT to identify, describe, prioritize, and create new ideas for the enterprise. Social IT offers community members a "super idea box" where individuals suggest new ideas, comment on other ideas, and vote for their favorite idea, giving managers a new way to generate and decide on products and services.

National Instruments (ni.com) is an example of a company that has embraced social IT and created a social business strategy. Managers developed a branded community consisting of a number of social IT tools like Facebook, Twitter, blogs, forums, and more. By thinking holistically about all the ways that customers and employees might interact with one another, the branded community has become the hub of collaboration, engagement, and idea generation.

Source: Adapted from Keri Pearlson, "Killer Apps for a Social Business" (February 17, 2011), http://instantlyresponsive.wordpress.com/2011/02/27/killer-apps-for-a-social-business/ (accessed March 19, 2015). For more information on National Instruments, see Harvard Business school case study 813001, "National Instruments" by Lynda Applegate, Keri Pearlson, and Natalie Kindred.

includes hardware, such as desktop units and servers. It also includes software, such as the programs used to do business, to manage the computer itself and to communicate between systems. The third component of IS infrastructure is the network, which is the physical means by which information is exchanged among hardware components. Examples include fiber networks such as Google Fiber, cable networks such as those provided by Time Warner, AT&T, and Comcast, WiFi provided by many local services, and 3G/4G/WiMax technologies (which are actually Internet communication standards, but some phone companies adopt those terms as the name of networks they offer). Some communications are conducted through a private digital network, managed by an internal unit). Finally, the fourth part of the infrastructure is the data. The data include the bits and bytes stored in the system. In current systems, data are not necessarily stored alongside the programs that use them; hence, it is important to understand what data are in the system and where they are stored. Many more detailed models of IS infrastructure exist, and interested readers may refer to any of the dozens of books that describe them. For the purposes of this text, the IS strategy matrix provides sufficient information to allow the general manager to assess the critical issues in information management.

Because of the advanced state of technology, many managers are more familiar with the use of platforms and applications, or apps. Platforms are technically any set of technologies upon which other technologies or applications run. Often they are a combination of hardware and operating system software. Microsoft Windows and Apple's Macintosh with its latest operating system are two examples of platforms. Also common are mobile platforms such as the iPhone and Samsung/Android phone. Applications or **apps**, on the other hand, are self-contained software programs that fulfill a specific purpose and run on a platform. The term "apps" became popular from the smart phone industry, beginning when Apple offered an online marketplace for customers to download small programs to run on their devices. But more recently, because all platforms have applications that run on them, the term *apps* has taken on a broader meaning.

SUMMARY

The Information Systems Strategy Triangle represents a simple framework for understanding the impact of IS on businesses. It relates business strategy with IS strategy and organizational strategy and implies the balance that must be maintained in business planning. The Information Systems Strategy Triangle suggests the following management principles.

Business Strategy

Business strategy drives organizational strategy and IS strategy. The organization and its IS should clearly support defined business goals and objectives.

- Definition: A well-articulated vision of where a business seeks to go and how it expects to get there
- Example Models: Porter's generic strategies model; dynamic environment models

Organizational Strategy

Organizational strategy must complement business strategy. The way a business is organized either supports the implementation of its business strategy or it gets in the way.

- Definition: The organization's design, as well as the choices it makes to define, set up, coordinate, and control its work processes
- Example Model: managerial levers

IS Strategy

IS strategy must complement business strategy. When IS support business goals, the business appears to be working well. IS strategy can itself affect and is affected by changes in a firm's business and organizational strategies. Moreover, IS strategy always has consequences—intended or not—on business and organizational strategies.

- Definition: The plan the organization uses in providing information systems and services
- Models: A basic framework for understanding IS decisions for platform, applications, network and data-relating architecture (the "what"), and the other resource considerations ("who" and "where") that represent important planning constraints

Strategic Relationships

Organizational strategy and information strategy must complement each other. They must be designed so that they support, rather than hinder, each other. If a decision is made to change one corner of the triangle, it is necessary to evaluate the other two corners to ensure that balance is preserved. Changing business strategy without thinking through the effects on the organization and IS strategies will cause the business to struggle until balance is restored. Likewise, changing IS or the organization alone will cause an imbalance.

KEY TERMS

apps (p. 27)
blue ocean strategy (p. 24)
business model (p. 20)
business strategy (p. 21)
collaboration (p. 28)
cost leadership (p. 22)
creative destruction (p. 24)
differentiation (p. 22)
dynamic capabilities (p. 24)
engagement (p. 28)
focus (p. 22)
hypercompetition (p. 23)
Information Systems Strategy Triangle (p. 18)
innovation (p. 28)
IS strategy (p. 26)
managerial levers (p. 25)
mission (p. 19)
organizational strategy (p. 25)
red ocean strategy (p. 24)
social business strategy (p. 27)
strategy (p. 19)

DISCUSSION QUESTIONS

1. Why is it important for business strategy to drive organizational strategy and IS strategy? What might happen if the business strategy was not the driver?
2. In 2015, the NFL decided to hand out Microsoft Surface tablets to all coaches for use during games, and there are reports that in the future, they will add HoloLens devices to provide augmented reality.[18] A HoloLens device is a high-definition, head-mounted display that allows coaches to see the plays with text and animation superimposed right on the live images. If the NFL simply handed them out without making any other formal changes in organizational strategy or business strategy, what might be the outcome? What unintended consequences might occur?
3. Consider a traditional manufacturing company that wants to build a social business strategy. What might be a reasonable business strategy, and how would organization and IS strategy need to change? How would this differ for a restaurant chain? A consumer products company? A nonprofit?
4. This chapter describes key components of an IS strategy. Describe the IS strategy of a consulting firm using the matrix framework.
5. What does this tip from *Fast Company* mean: "The job of the CIO is to provide organizational and strategic flexibility"?[19]

---

[18] Sean Michael, "NFL Teams Will Use Surface Pro 3s in 2015 and May Use HoloLens in the Future," WinBeta (August 7, 2015), http://www.winbeta.org/news/nfl-teams-will-use-surface-pro-3s-2015-and-may-use-hololens-future (accessed August 21, 2015).

[19] "Technology: How much? How fast? How revolutionary? How expensive?" *Fast Company* (March 2002), http://www.fastcompany.com/44651/technology-how-much-how-fast-how-revolutionary-how-expensive (accessed August 21, 2015).

CASE STUDY 1-1 Lego

Lego has long been an industry leader in children's toys with its simple yet unique building block-style products. A Danish carpenter whose family still owns Lego today founded the privately held company in 1932. But by 2004, the company found itself close to extinction, losing $1 million a day. A new CEO was brought in, and within five years sales were strong, profits were up, and naysayers who felt the new strategy was going to fail were proved wrong. In fact, sales, revenues and profits continued to be strong. Revenues grew from 16 billion Danish krone (DKK) in 2010 to over 28 billion DKK in 2014, and in the same period, profit almost doubled from 3.7 billion DKK to 7 billion DKK.

With the advent of high-tech forms of entertainment, such as the iPod and PlayStation, Lego found itself more antique than cutting edge in the toy world. When new CEO Jorgen Vig Knudstorp, a father and former McKinsey consultant, took over, the company was struggling with poor performance, missed deadlines, long development times, and a poor delivery record. The most popular toys frequently would be out of stock, and the company was unable to ship enough products or manage the production of its more complicated sets. Retail stores were frustrated, and that translated into reduced shelf space and ultimately to business losses.

Knudstorp changed all of that. He reached out to top retailers, cut costs, and added missing links to the supply chain. For example, prior to the new strategy, 90% of the components were used in just one design. Designers were encouraged to reuse components in their new products, which resulted in a reduction from about 13,000 different Lego components to 7,000. Because each component's mold could cost up to 50,000 euros on average to create, this reduction saved significant expense.

Lego was known for its traditional blocks and components that would allow children to build just about anything their imagination could create. The new strategy broadened the products, targeting new customer segments. Lego managers created products based on themes of popular movies, such as *Star Wars* and the Indiana Jones series. The company moved into video games, which featured animated Lego characters sometimes based on movies. The company created a product strategy for adults and engaged the communities who had already set up thousands of Web sites and blogs featuring Lego creations. It embraced the community who thought of Lego as a way to create art rather than simply as a building toy. And the company designed a line of Legos aimed at girls because the majority of its products had primarily targeted boys.

The culture of Lego changed to one that refused to accept nonperformance. The company's past showed a tendency to focus on innovation and creativity, often at the expense of profits. But that changed. "Knudstorp . . . made it clear that results, not simply feeling good about making the best toys, would be essential if Lego was to succeed. . . . Its business may still be fun and games, but working here isn't,"[20] describes the current culture at Lego.

Some of the most drastic changes came from within the Lego organization structure. After its massive losses in 2004, Lego switched its employee pay structure, offering incentives for appropriate product innovation and sales. Key performance indicators encourage product innovation that catalyzes sales while decreasing costs. Development time dropped by 50%, and some manufacturing and distribution functions were moved to less expensive locations, but the focus on quality remained. The creation of reusable parts alleviated some of the strain on Lego's supply chain, which in turn helped its bottom line.

Lego also expanded into the virtual world, extending into video gaming and virtual-interaction games on the Internet. Thinking outside the company's previous product concepts cut costs while encouraging real-time feedback from customers across a global market. Additionally, Lego created brand ambassadors who organized conventions across the world to discuss product innovation and to build communities of fellow customers. With increased revenue, Lego managers considered entering the movie-making business—a risky proposition for a toy company. However, Lego's success with Hollywood-type action figures fueled its interest in a movie-making endeavor.

The growth put strains on the IS supporting the business. Order management and fulfillment were particularly affected, resulting in the inability to meet customer demand. Employee management systems were stretched as new employees were added to support the growth and additional locations. Product design and development, especially the virtual and video games, required new technology, too.

To solve some of these problems, Lego managers used the same approach they used for their blocks. They created a modularized and standardized architecture for their IS, making it possible to expand more quickly and add capacity and functionality as it was needed. They implemented an integrated enterprise system that gave them new applications for human capital management, operations support, product life cycle management, and data management. The new systems and services, purchased from vendors such as SAP and IBM, simplified the IT architecture and the management processes needed to oversee the IS.

[20] Nelson D. Schwartz, "Turning to Tie-Ins, Lego Thinks Beyond the Brick," *The New York Times*, September 5, 2009, http://www.nytimes.com/2009/09/06/business/global/06lego.html?pagewanted=all&_r=0 (accessed August 21, 2015).

One manager at Lego summed it up nicely, "The toy world moves onwards constantly, and Lego needs to re-invent itself continuously. Significant corporate re-shaping introduced new energy to the company." [21] He went on to say that simplifying Lego's IT systems and implementing an efficient product development process that was able to maintain quality and cost favorably positioned Lego to respond to the fast changing pace of the toy industry.

Discussion Questions

1. How did the information systems and the organization design changes implemented by Knudstorp align with the changes in business strategy?
2. Which of the generic strategies does Lego appear to be using based on this case? Provide support for your choice.
3. Are the changes implemented by Knudstorp an indication of hypercompetition? Defend your position.
4. What advice would you give Knudstorp to keep Lego competitive, growing, and relevant?

Sources: Adapted from http://www.nytimes.com/2009/09/06/business/global/06lego.html (accessed August 21, 2015); Brad Wieners, "Lego Is for Girls" (December 19, 2011), 68–73; information from Lego's 2012 annual report, http://www.lego.com/en-us/aboutus/news-room/2013/february/annual-result-2012 (accessed March 29, 2015); and "Lego Case Study," http://thelegocasestudy.com (accessed March 29, 2015).

CASE STUDY 1-2 Google

Started in the late 1990s, Google grew rapidly to become one of the leading companies in the world. Its mission is "to organize the world's information and make it universally accessible and useful." It is operating on a simple but innovative business model of attracting Internet users to its free search services and earning revenue from targeted advertising. In the winner-takes-all business of Internet search, Google has captured considerably more market share than its next highest rival, Yahoo. This has turned Google's Web pages into the Web's most valuable real (virtual) estate. Through its two flagship programs, AdWords and AdSense, Google has capitalized on this leadership position in searching to capture the lion's share in advertisement spending. AdWords enables businesses to place ads on Google and its network of publishing partners using an auction-engine algorithm to decide which ad will appear on a given page. On the other hand, Google uses AdSense to push advertisements on publishing partners' Web sites targeting a specific audience and share ad revenue with the publishing partner. This creates a win–win situation for both advertisers and publishers; Google makes more than 90% of its revenue from ads.

Even as a large company, Google continues to take risks and expand into new markets. Innovation is at the core of their enterprise. Sergey Brin and Larry Page, the founders, declared in Google's IPO prospectus, "We would fund projects that have a 10% chance of earning a billion dollars over the long term. . . We place smaller bets in areas that seem very speculative or even strange. As the ratio of reward to risk increases, we will accept projects further outside our normal areas." They add that they are especially likely to fund new types of projects when the initial investment is small.

Google promotes a culture of creativity and innovation in a number of ways. It encourages innovation in all employees by allowing them to spend 20% of their time on a project of their own choosing. In addition, the company offers benefits such as free meals, on-site gym, on-site dentist, and even washing machines at the company for busy employees.

Despite an open and free work culture, a rigid and procedure-filled structure is imposed for making timely decisions and executing plans. For example, when designing new features, the team and senior managers meet in a large conference room. They use the right side of the conference room walls to digitally project new features and the left side to project any transcribed critique with a timer clock giving everyone 10 minutes to lay out ideas and finalize features. Thus, Google utilizes rigorous, data-driven procedures for evaluating new ideas in the midst of a chaotic innovation process.

Nine notions of innovations are embedded in the organizational culture, processes, and structure of Google:[22]

1. "Innovation Comes from Anywhere": All Google employees can innovate.
2. "Focus on the User": When focus is on the user, the money and all else will follow.

[21] https://www.vmware.com/files/pdf/partners/sap/sap-vmware-lego-cs-en.pdf (accessed September 11, 2015).

[22] Kathy Chin Long, "Google Reveals its Nine Principles of Innovations," *Fast Company*, http://www.fastcompany.com/3021956/how-to-be-a-success-at-everything/googles-nine-principles-of-innovation (accessed March 30, 2015).

3. "Aim to be Ten Times Better": To get radical and revolutionary innovation, think 10 times improvement to force out-of-the-box thinking.
4. "Bet on Technical Insights": Trust your organization's unique insights and bet on them for major innovation.
5. "Ship and Iterate": Do not wait for perfection; let users help you to "iterate."
6. "Give Employees 20 Percent Time": Employees will delight you with their creative thinking. Give them 20 percent of their work time to pursue projects they are passionate about.
7. "Default to Open Processes": Make processes open to all to tap into the collective energy of the user base to find great ideas.
8. "Fail Well": Do not attach stigma to failure. If you do not fail often, you are not trying hard enough. Let people and projects fail with pride.
9. "Have a Mission That Matters": Google believes that its work has a positive impact on millions of people and that this is motivating its people every day.

Keeping up with the organizational strategy of Google, its IT department provides free and open access to IT for all employees. Rather than keeping tight control, Google allows employees to choose from several options for computer and operating systems, download software themselves, and maintain official and unofficial blog sites. Google's intranet provides employees information about every piece of work at any part of the company. In this way, employees can find and join hands with others working on similar technologies or features.

In building the necessary IT infrastructure, Google's IT department balances buying and making its own software depending on its needs and off-the-shelf availability. Google thinks of every IT decision "at Web Scale" to make sure its technology works well for its customers. Given the nature of business, security of information resources is critical for Google. For instance, its master search algorithm is considered a more valuable secret formula than Coca-Cola's. However, rather than improving IT security by stifling freedom through preventive policy controls, Google puts security in the infrastructure and focuses more on detective and corrective controls. Its network management software tools combined with a team of security engineers constantly look for viruses and spyware as well as strange network traffic patterns associated with intrusion.

Discussion Questions

1. How is Google's mission statement related to its business strategy?
2. How does Google's information systems strategy support its business strategy?
3. How does Google's organizational strategy support its business strategy?
4. Which of Porter's three generic strategies does Google appear to be using based on this case? Provide a rationale for your response.
5. Analyze Google's strategy and the type of market disruption it has created using a dynamic environment perspective.

Sources: Adapted from Michelle Colin, "Champions of Innovation," *Businessweek* 3989 (June 18, 2006), 18–26, http://www.bloomberg.com/bw/stories/2006-06-18/champions-of-innovation; Vauhini Vara, "Pleasing Google's Tech-Savvy Staff" (March 18, 2008), B6; Jason Bloomberg, "Google's Three-Pronged Enterprise Strategy," Forbes Online (December 12, 2014); and Connor Forrest, "Four Ways Google Makes Money," *TechRepublic* (January 16, 2015), http://www.techrepublic.com/article/four-ways-google-makes-money-outside-of-advertising/ (accessed August 21, 2015).

Strategic Use of Information Resources

chapter

2

This chapter introduces the concept of building competitive advantage using information systems-based applications. It begins with a discussion of a set of eras that describe the use of information resources historically. It then presents information resources as strategic tools, discussing information technology (*IT*) assets and IT capabilities. Michael Porter's Five Competitive Forces model then provides a framework for discussing strategic advantage, and his Value Chain model addresses tactical ways organizations link their business processes to create strategic partnerships. We then introduce the Piccoli and Ive's model to show how strategic advantage may be sustained in light of competitive barriers while the Resource-Based View focuses on gaining and maintaining strategic advantage through information and other resources of the firm. The chapter concludes with a brief discussion of strategic alliances, co-opetition, risks of strategic use of IT, and cocreating IT and business strategy. Just as a note: this chapter uses the terms *competitive advantage* and *strategic advantage* interchangeably.

Zara, a global retail and apparel manufacturer based in Arteixo, Spain, needed a dynamic business model to keep up with the ever-changing demands of its customers and industry. At the heart of its model was a set of business processes and an information system that linked demand to manufacturing and manufacturing to distribution. The strategy at Zara stores was simply to have a continuous flow of new products that were typically in limited supply. As a result, regular customers visited their stores often—an average of 17 times a year whereas many retail stores averaged only four times a year. When customers saw something they liked, they bought it on the spot because they knew it would probably be gone the next time they visited the store. The result was a very loyal and satisfied customer base and a wildly profitable business model.

How did Zara do it? It was possible in part because the company aligned its information system strategy with its business strategy. Its corporate Web site gave some insight:

> Zara's approach to design is closely linked to our customers. A non-stop flow of information from stores conveys shoppers' desires and demands, inspiring our 200-person strong creative team.[1]

The entire process from factory to shop floor is coordinated from Zara's headquarters by using information systems. The point-of-sale (POS) system on the shop floor records the information from each sale, and the information is transmitted to headquarters at the end of each business day. Using a handheld device, the Zara shop managers also report daily to the designers at headquarters to let them know what has sold and what the customers wanted but couldn't find. The information is used to determine which product lines and colors should be kept and which should be altered or dropped.

[1] Inditex Web site, http://www.inditex.com/en/who_we_are/concepts/zara (accessed February 20, 2012); http://www.marinabaysands.com/shopping/zara.html (accessed May 2, 2015).

The designers communicate directly with the production staff to plan for the incredible number of designs—more than 30,000—that will be manufactured every year.[2]

The shop managers have the option to order new designs twice a week using handheld computers. Before ordering, they can use these devices to check out the new designs. Once an order is received at the manufacturing plant at headquarters, a large computer-controlled piece of equipment calculates how to position patterns to minimize scrap and cut up to 100 layers of fabric at a time. The cut fabric is then sent from Zara factories to external workshops for sewing. The completed products are sent to distribution centers where miles of automated conveyor belts are used to sort the garments and recombine them into shipments for each store. Zara's Information Systems (IS) department wrote the applications controlling the conveyors, often in collaboration with vendors of the conveyor equipment.

As the Zara example illustrates, innovative use of a firm's information resources can provide it substantial and sustainable advantages over competitors. Every business depends on IS, making its use a necessary resource every manager must consider. IS also can create a strategic advantage for firms who bring creativity, vision, and innovation to their IS use. The Zara case is an example. This chapter uses the business strategy foundation from Chapter 1 to help general managers visualize how to use information resources for competitive advantage. This chapter highlights the difference between simply using IS and using IS strategically. It also explores the use of information resources to support the strategic goals of an organization.

The material in this chapter can enable a general manager to understand the linkages between business strategy and information strategy on the Information Systems Strategy Triangle. General managers want to find answers to questions such as: Does using information resources provide a sustainable and defendable competitive advantage? What tools are available to help shape strategic use of information? What are the risks of using information resources to gain strategic advantage?

Evolution of Information Resources

The Eras model (Figure 2.1) summarizes the evolution of information resources over the past six decades. To think strategically about how to use information resources now and in the future within the firm, a manager must understand how the company arrived at where it is today. This model provides a good overview of trends and uses that have gotten the company from simple automation of tasks to extending relationships and managing their business ecosystems to where it is today.

IS strategy from the 1960s to the 1990s was driven by internal organizational needs. First came the need to lower existing transaction costs. Next was the need to provide support for managers by collecting and distributing information followed by the need to redesign business processes. As competitors built similar systems, organizations lost any advantages they had derived from their IS, and competition within a given industry once again was driven by forces that existed prior to the new technology. Most recently, enterprises have found that social IT platforms and capabilities drive a new evolution of applications, processes, and strategic opportunities that often involve an ecosystems of partners rather than a list of suppliers. **Business ecosystems** are collections of interacting participants, including vendors, customers, and other related parties, acting in concert to do business.[3]

In Eras I through III, the value of information was tied to physical delivery mechanisms. In these eras, value was derived from scarcity reflected in the cost to produce the information. Information, like diamonds, gold, and MBA degrees, was more valuable because it was found in limited quantities. However, the networked economy beginning in Era IV drove a new model of value—value from plenitude. **Network effects** offered a reason for value derived from plenitude; the value of a network node to a person or organization in the network increased when others joined the network. For example, an e-mail account has no value without at least one other e-mail account with which to communicate. As e-mail accounts become relatively ubiquitous, the value of having an e-mail account increases as its potential for use increases. Further, copying additional people on an e-mail is done at a very low cost (virtually zero), and the information does not wear out (although it can become obsolete). As the cost of producing an

[2] Shenay Kentish, Zara (October 18, 2011), http://unilifemagazine.com.au/special-interest/zara/ (accessed April 10, 2012).

[3] For further discussion of business ecosystems, please refer to Nicholas Vitalari and Hayden Shaughnessy, *The Elastic Enterprise* (Longboat Key, FL: Telemachus Press, 2012).

	Era I 1960s	Era II 1970s	Era III 1980s	Era IV 1990s	Era V 2000s	Era VI 2010+	
Primary Role of IT	Efficiency	Effectiveness	Strategy	Strategy	Value creation	Value extension	
	Automate existing paper-based processes	Solve problems and create opportunities	Increase individual and group effectiveness	Transform industry/ organization	Create collaborative partnerships	Create community and social business	Connecting intelligent devices
Justify IT Expenditures	Return on investment	Increase in productivity and better decision quality	Competitive position	Competitive position	Added value	Creation of relationships	Automated information exchange
Target of Systems	Organization	Organization/ Group	Individual manager/ Group	Business processes	Customer/ Supplier relationships	Customer/ Employee/ supplier ecosystem	Intelligent devices
Information Models	Application specific	Data driven	User driven	Business driven	Knowledge driven	People driven (or relationship driven)	Data exchange driven
Dominant Technology	Mainframe, "centralized intelligence"	Minicomputer, mostly "centralized intelligence"	Microcomputer, "decentralized intelligence"	Client server, "distributed intelligence"	Internet, global "ubiquitous intelligence"	Social platforms, social networks, mobile, cloud	Intelligent devices, sensors, electronics
Basis of Value	Scarcity	Scarcity	Scarcity	Plenitude	Plenitude	Hyperplenitude	
Underlying Economics	Economics of information bundled with economics of things	Economics of information bundled with economics of things	Economics of information bundled with economics of things	Economics of information separated from economics of things	Economics of information separated from economics of things	Economics of relationships bundled with economics of information	Economics of information bundled with economics of things

FIGURE 2.1 Eras of information usage in organizations.

additional copy of an information product within a network becomes trivial, the value of that network increases. Therefore, rather than using production *costs* to guide the determination of price, information products might be priced to reflect their *value* to the buyer.[4]

As each era begins, organizations adopt a strategic role for IS to address not only the firm's internal circumstances but also its external circumstances. Thus, in the value-creation era (Era V), companies seek those applications that again provide them an advantage over their competition and keep them from being outgunned by start-ups with innovative business models or traditional companies entering new markets. For example, companies like Microsoft, Google, Apple, and Facebook have created and maintained a competitive advantage by building technical platforms and organizational competencies that allow them to bring in partners as necessary to create new products and services for their customers. Their business ecosystems give them agility as well as access to talent and knowledge, extending the capabilities of their internal staff. Other firms simply try to solve all customer requests themselves.

Era VI has brought another paradigm shift in the use of information with an era of hyperplenitude: seemingly unlimited availability of information resources such as the Internet and processing and storage through

[4] Adapted from M. Broadbent, P. Weill, and D. Clair. "The Implications of Information Technology Infrastructure for Business Process Redesign," *MIS Quarterly* 23, no. 2 (1999), 163.

cloud computing sparked new value sources such as community and social business and the Internet of Things (connecting intelligent devices, sensors, and other electronics).

The Information System Strategy Triangle introduced in Chapter 1 reflects the linkages between a firm's IS strategy, organizational strategy, and business strategy. A link between IS strategy and business strategy focuses on the firm's external requirements whereas a link between IS strategy and organizational strategy fulfills and enhances internal requirements of the firm. Maximizing the effectiveness of the firm's business strategy requires that the general manager be able both to identify and use information resources. This chapter describes how information resources can be used strategically by general managers.

Information Resources as Strategic Tools

Crafting a strategic advantage requires the general manager to cleverly combine all the firm's resources, including financial, production, human, and information, and to consider external resources such as the Internet and opportunities in the global arena. Information resources are more than just the infrastructure. This generic term, **information resources**, is defined as the available data, technology, people, and processes within an organization to be used by the manager to perform business processes and tasks. Information resources can either be assets or capabilities. An **IT asset** is any thing, tangible or intangible, that can be used by a firm to create, produce, and/or offer its products (goods or services). Examples of IT assets include a firm's Web site, data files, or computer equipment. An **IT capability** is something that is learned or developed over time for the firm to create, produce, or offer its products. An IT capability makes it possible for a firm to use its IT assets effectively.[5] The ability and knowledge to create a Web site, work with data files, and take advantage of IT equipment are examples of capabilities.

An *IS infrastructure* (a concept that is discussed in detail in Chapter 6) is an IT asset. It includes each of an information resource's constituent components (i.e., data, technology, people, and processes). The infrastructure provides the foundation for the delivery of a firm's products or services. Another IT asset is an *information repository*, which is logically related data captured, organized, and retrieved by the firm. Some information repositories are filled with internally oriented information designed to improve the firm's efficiency. Other repositories tap the external environment and contain significant knowledge about the industry, the competitors, and the customers. Although most firms have these types of information repositories, not all firms use them effectively.

In the continually expanding Web space, the view of IT assets is broadening to include potential resources that are available to the firm but that are not necessarily owned by it. These additional information resources are often available as a service rather than as a system to be procured and implemented internally. For example, Internet-based software (also called *software as a service, or SAAS*), such as SalesForce.com, offers managers the opportunity to find new ways to manage their customer information with an externally based IT resource. Social networking systems such as Facebook and LinkedIn offer managers the opportunity to find expertise or an entire network of individuals ready to participate in the corporate innovation processes using relatively little capital or expense.

The three major categories of IT capabilities are technical skills, IT management skills, and relationship skills. *Technical skills* are applied to designing, developing, and implementing information systems. *IT management skills* are critical for managing the IS department and IS projects. They include an understanding of business processes, the ability to oversee the development and maintenance of systems to support these processes effectively, and the ability to plan and work with the business units in undertaking change. *Relationship skills* can be focused either externally or internally. An externally focused relationship skill includes the ability to respond to the firm's market and to work with customers and suppliers. The internal relationship between a firm's IS managers and its business managers is a spanning relationship skill and includes the ability of IS to manage partnerships with the business units. Even though it focuses on relationships in the firm, it requires spanning beyond the IS department. Relationship skills develop over time and require mutual respect and trust. They, like the other information resources, can create a unique advantage for a firm. Figure 2.2 summarizes the different types of information resources and provides examples of each.

---

[5] G. Piccoli and B. Ives, "IT-Dependent Strategic Initiatives and Sustained Competitive Advantage: A Review and Synthesis of the Literature," *MIS Quarterly* 29, no. 4 (2003), 747–76.

IT Assets	IT Capabilities
IT Infrastructure • Hardware • Software and company apps • Network • Data • Web site Information Repository • Customer information • Employee information • Marketplace information • Vendor information	Technical Skills • Proficiency in systems analysis • Programming and Web design skills • Data analysis/data scientist skills • Network design and implementation skills IT Management Skills • Business process knowledge • Ability to evaluate technology options • Project management skills • Envisioning innovative IT solutions Relationship Skills • Spanning skills such as business-IT relationship management • External skills such as vendor management

FIGURE 2.2 Information resources.
Source: Adapted from G. Piccoli and B. Ives, "IT-Dependent Strategic Initiatives and Sustained Competitive Advantage: A Review and Synthesis of the Literature," *MIS Quarterly* 29, no. 4 (2005), 755.

Information resources exist in a company alongside other resources. The general manager is responsible for organizing all resources so that business goals are met. Understanding the nature of the resources at hand is a prerequisite to using them effectively. By aligning IS strategy with business strategy, the general manager maximizes the company's profit potential. To ensure that information resources being deployed for strategic advantage are used wisely, the general manager must identify what makes the information resource valuable (and the Eras model may provide some direction) and sustainable. Meanwhile, the firm's competitors are working to do the same. In this competitive environment, how should the information resources be organized and applied to enable the organization to compete most effectively?

How Can Information Resources Be Used Strategically?

The general manager confronts many elements that influence the competitive environment of his or her enterprise. Overlooking a single element can bring about disastrous results for the firm. This slim tolerance for error requires the manager to take multiple views of the strategic landscape. Three such views can help a general manager align IS strategy with business strategy. The first view uses the *five competitive forces model* by Michael Porter to look at the major influences on a firm's competitive environment. Information resources should be directed strategically to alter the competitive forces to benefit the firm's position in the industry. The second view uses Porter's *value chain model* to assess the internal operations of the organization and partners in its supply chain. Information resources should be directed at altering the value-creating or value-supporting activities of the firm. We extend this view further to consider the value chain of an entire industry to identify opportunities for the organization to gain competitive advantage. The third view specifically focuses on the types of *IS resources* needed to gain and sustain competitive advantage. These three views provide a general manager with varied perspectives from which to identify strategic opportunities to apply the firm's information resources.

Using Information Resources to Influence Competitive Forces

Porter provides the general manager a classic view of the major forces that shape the competitive environment of an industry, which affects firms within the industry. These five competitive forces are shown in Figure 2.3 along with some examples of how information resources can be applied to influence each force. This view reminds the general

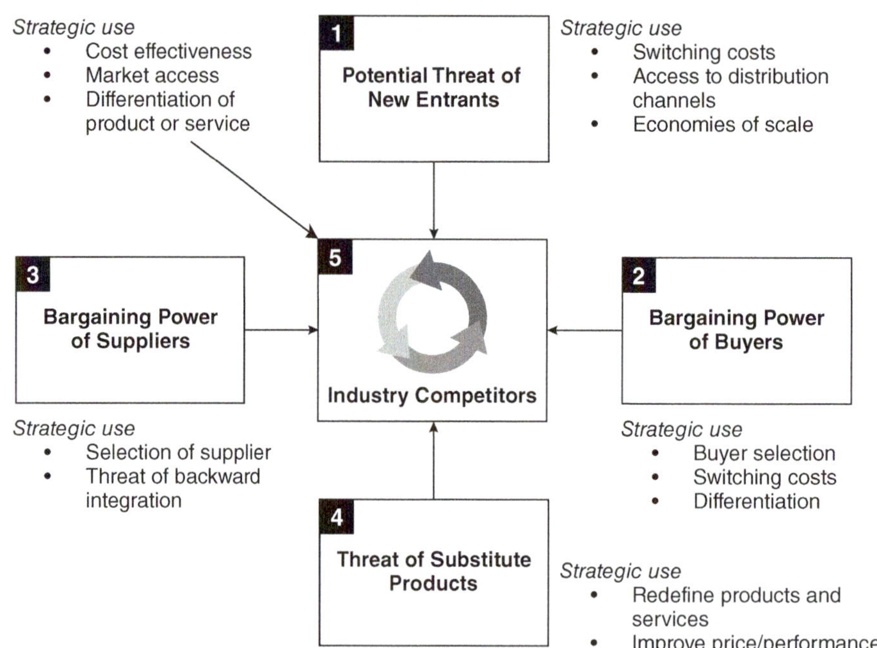

FIGURE 2.3 Five competitive forces with potential strategic use of information resources.
Sources: Adapted from M. Porter, *Competitive Strategy* (New York: The Free Press, 1998); and Lynda M. Applegate, F. Warren McFarlan, and James L. McKenney, *Corporate Information Systems Management : The Issues Facing Senior Executives*, 4th ed. (Homewood, IL: Irwin, 1996).

manager that competitive forces result from more than just the actions of direct competitors. We explore each force in detail from an IS perspective.

Potential Threat of New Entrants

Existing firms within an industry often try to reduce the threat of new entrants to the marketplace by erecting barriers to entry. New entrants seem to come out of nowhere; established firms can diversify their business models and begin to compete in the space occupied by existing firms, or an enterprising entrepreneur can create a new business that changes the game for existing firms. Barriers to entry— including a firm's controlled access to limited distribution channels, public image of a firm, unique relationships with customers, and an understanding of their industry's government regulations—help the firm create a stronghold by offering products or services that are difficult to displace in the eyes of customers based on apparently unique features. Information resources also can be used to build barriers that discourage competitors from entering an industry. For example, Google's search algorithm is a source of competitive advantage for the search company, and it's a barrier of entry for new entrants that would have to create something better to compete against Google. New entrants have failed to erode Google's market share, which holds fast at 65% in the United States and at over 90% in Europe.[6] Walmart, another example, effectively blocks competition with its inventory control system, which helps it drive down expenses and ultimately offer lower costs to customers. Any company entering Walmart's marketplace would have to spend millions of dollars to build the inventory control system and IS required to provide its operations with the same capabilities. Therefore, the system at Walmart may be a barrier to entry for new companies.

Search engine optimization (actions that a firm can take to improve its prominence in search results) has served as a barrier to entry for some businesses. Consider the Web site that has the number one position in a user's search. There is only one number one position, making it an advantage for the company enjoying that position and a barrier for all other Web sites seeking that position.

[6] "Viewed as a Monopoly in Europe, Google Takes on Role as a Wireless Trust-Buster in U.S.," *New York Times* (May 8, 2015), B1, B6.

Bargaining Power of Buyers

Customers often have substantial power to affect the competitive environment. This power can take the form of easy consumer access to several retail outlets to purchase the same product or the opportunity to purchase in large volumes at superstores like Walmart. Information resources can be used to build switching costs that make it less attractive for customers to purchase from competitors. Switching costs can be any aspect of a buyer's purchasing decision that decreases the likelihood of "switching" his or her purchase to a competitor. Such an approach requires a deep understanding of how a customer obtains the product or service. For example, Amazon.com's patented One Click option encourages return purchases by making buying easier. Amazon.com stores buyer information, including a default credit card number, shipping method, and "ship-to" address so that purchases can be made with one click, saving consumers the effort of data reentry and further repetitive choices. Similarly, Apple's iTunes simple-to-use interface and proprietary software for downloading and listening to music makes it difficult for customers to use other formats and technologies, effectively reducing the power of the buyers, the customers.

Bargaining Power of Suppliers

Suppliers' bargaining power can reduce a firm's options and ultimately its profitability. Suppliers often strive to "lock in" customers through the use of systems (and other mechanisms). For example, there are many options for individuals to back up their laptop data, including many "cloud" options. The power of any one supplier is low because there are a number of options. But Apple's operating system enables easy creation of backups and increases Apple's bargaining power. Millions of customers find it easy to use the iCloud, and they do.

The force of bargaining power is strongest when a firm has few suppliers from which to choose, the quality of supplier inputs is crucial to the finished product, or the volume of purchases is insignificant to the supplier. For example, steel firms lost some of their bargaining power over the automobile industry because car manufacturers developed technologically advanced quality control systems for evaluating the steel they purchase. Manufacturers can now reject steel from suppliers when it does not meet the required quality levels.

Through the Internet, firms continue to provide information for free as they attempt to increase their share of visitors to their Web sites and gather information about them. This decision reduces the power of information suppliers and necessitates finding new ways for content providers to develop and distribute information. Many Internet firms are integrating backward or sideways within the industry, that is, creating their own information supply and reselling it to other Internet sites. Well-funded firms simply acquire these content providers, which is often quicker than building the capability from scratch. One example of this was Amazon.com's purchase of Zappos, the shoe retailer. More recently, in 2015 LinkedIn acquired online learning company Lynda.com to add a capability to offer professional development to the company's business of networking, recruitment, and advertising.

Threat of Substitute Products

The potential of a substitute product in the marketplace depends on the buyers' willingness to substitute, the relative price-to-performance ratio of the substitute, and the level of switching costs a buyer faces. Information resources can create advantages by reducing the threat of substitution. Substitutes that cause a threat come from many sources. Internal innovations can cannibalize existing revenue streams for a firm. For example, new iPhones motivate current customers to upgrade, essentially cannibalizing the older product line revenue. Of course, this is also a preemptive move to keep customers in the iPhone product family rather than to switch to another competitor's product. The threat might come from potentially new innovations that make the previous product obsolete. Tablets have reduced the market for laptops and personal computers. GPS systems have become substitutes for paper maps, digital cameras have made film and film cameras obsolete, and MP3 music has sharply reduced the market for vinyl records, record players, CDs, and CD players. Free Web-based applications are a threat to software vendors who charge for their products and who do not have Web-based delivery. Revolutions of many kinds and levels of maturity seem to be lurking everywhere. Cloud services are a substitute for data centers. Uber offers a substitute for taxicabs. Managers must watch for potential substitutes from many different sources to fully manage this competitive threat.

5 ## Industry Competitors

Rivalry among the firms competing within an industry is high when it is expensive for a firm to leave the industry, the growth rate of the industry is declining, or products have lost differentiation. Under these circumstances, the firm must focus on the competitive actions of rivals to protect its own market share. Intense rivalry in an industry ensures that competitors respond quickly to any strategic actions. Facebook enjoys a competitive advantage in the social networking industry. Other sites have tried to compete with Facebook by offering a different focus, either a different type of interface or additional ways to network. Competition is fierce and many start-ups hope to "be the next Facebook." However, Facebook continues to lead the industry, in part by continued innovation and in part by its huge customer base, which continues to raise the bar for competitors.

The processes that firms use to manage their operations and to lower costs or increase efficiencies can provide an advantage for cost-focus firms. However, as firms within an industry begin to implement standard business processes and technologies—often using enterprisewide systems such as those of SAP and Oracle—the industry becomes more attractive to consolidation through acquisition. Standardizing IS lowers the coordination costs of merging two enterprises and can result in a less competitive environment in the industry.

One way competitors differentiate themselves with an otherwise undifferentiated product is through creative use of IS. Information provides advantages in such competition when added to an existing product. For example, the iPod, iPhone, iPad, and iWatch are differentiated in part because of the iTunes store and the applications available only to users of these devices. Competitors offer some of the same information services, but Apple was able to take an early lead by using information systems to differentiate their products. Credit card companies normally compete on financial services such as interest rate, fees, and payment period. But Capital One differentiated its credit cards by adding information to its services; it provided customers their credit scores.

Each of the competitive forces identified by Porter's model is acting on firms at all times, but perhaps to a greater or lesser degree. There are forces from potential new entrants, buyers, sellers, substitutes, and competitors at all times, but their threat varies. Consider Zara, the case discussed in at the beginning of this chapter. See Figure 2.4 for a summary of these five forces working simultaneously at the retailer and manufacturer.

General managers can use the five competitive forces model to identify the key forces currently affecting competition, to recognize uses of information resources to influence forces, and to consider likely changes in these forces

Competitive Force	IT Influence on Competitive Force
Threat of New Entrant	Zara's IT supports its tightly knit group of designers, market specialists, production managers, and production planners. New entrants are unlikely to be able to provide IT to support such relationships that have been built over time at Zara. Further, it has a rich information repository about customers that would be hard to replicate.
Bargaining Power of Buyers	Recently, Zara has employed laser technology to measure 10,000 women volunteers so that it can add the measurements of "real" customers into its information repositories. This means that the new products will be more likely to fit Zara customers.
Bargaining Power of Suppliers	Its computer-controlled cutting machine cuts up to 1,000 layers at a time. A large number of sellers are available for the simple task of sewing the pieces together. Zara has great flexibility in choosing the sewing companies.
Industry Competitors	Zara tracks breaking trends and focuses on meeting customer preferences for trendy, low-cost fashion. The result is the highest sales per square foot in its industry, virtually no advertising, only 10% of stock remaining unsold, very low inventory levels, new products offered in 15 days from idea to shelves, and extremely efficient manufacturing and distribution operations.
Threat of Substitute Products	IT helps Zara offer extremely fashionable lines that are expected to last for approximately 10 wears. IT enables Zara to offer trendy, appealing apparel at hard-to-beat prices, making substitutes difficult.

FIGURE 2.4 Application of five competitive forces model for Zara.

over time. The changing forces drive both the business strategy and IS strategy, and this model provides a way to think about how information resources can create competitive advantage for a business unit and, even more broadly, for the firm. The forces also can reshape an entire industry—compelling general managers to take actions to help their firm gain or sustain competitive advantage.

Using Information Resources to Alter the Value Chain

A second lens for describing the strategic use of information systems is Porter's value chain. The value chain model addresses the activities that create, deliver, and support a company's product or service. Porter divided these activities into two broad categories (Figure 2.5): support and primary activities. Primary activities relate directly to the value created in a product or service whereas support activities make it possible for the primary activities to exist and remain coordinated. Each activity may affect how other activities are performed, suggesting that information resources should not be applied in isolation. For example, more efficient IS for repairing a product may increase the possible number of repairs per week, but the customer does not receive any value unless his or her product is repaired, which requires that the spare parts be available. Changing the rate of repair also affects the rate of spare parts ordering. If information resources are focused too narrowly on a specific activity, then the expected value may not be realized because other parts of the chain have not adjusted.

The value chain framework suggests that competition stems from two sources: lowering the cost to perform activities and adding value to a product or service so that buyers will pay more. To achieve true competitive advantage, a firm requires accurate information on elements outside itself. Lowering activity costs achieves an advantage only if the firm possesses information about its competitors' cost structures. Even though reducing isolated costs can improve profits temporarily, it does not provide a clear competitive advantage unless the firm can lower its costs below a competitor's. Doing so enables the firm to lower its prices as a way to grow its market share.

For example, many Web sites sell memory to upgrade laptops. But some sites, such as crucial.com, have an option that automates the process prior to the sales process. These sites have the "Crucial System Scanner Tool," which scans the customer's laptop, identifies the current configuration and the capacity, and then suggests compatible memory upgrade kits. The customer uses the scanner, which identifies the configuration of the laptop, and automatically opens a Web page with the appropriate memory upgrades. The customer does not have to figure out the configuration or requirements; it's done automatically. By combining a software program like its configurator with the sales process, crucial.com has added value to the customer's experience by automating a key process.

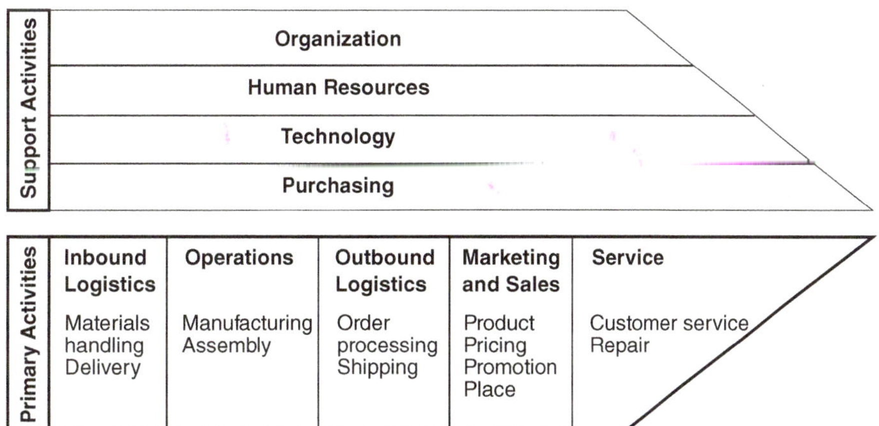

FIGURE 2.5 Value chain of the firm.
Source: Adapted from Michael Porter and Victor Millar, "How Information Gives You Competitive Advantage," *Harvard Business Review* (July–August 1985), reprint no. 85415.

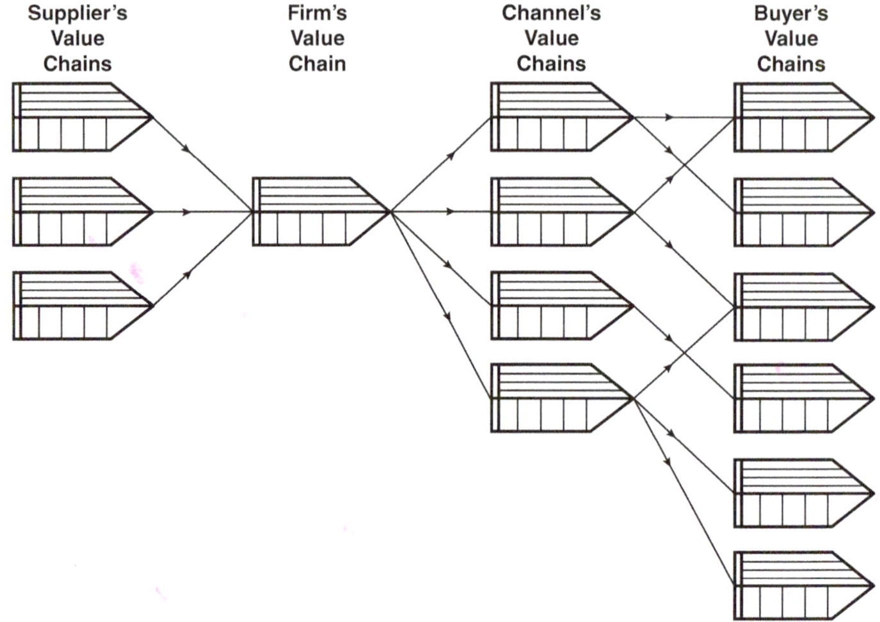

FIGURE 2.6 The value system: Interconnecting relationships between organizations.

Although the value chain framework emphasizes the activities of the individual firm, it can be extended, as in Figure 2.6, to include the firm in a larger value system. This value system is a collection of firm value chains connected through a business relationship and through technology. From this perspective, a variety of strategic opportunities exist to use information resources to gain a competitive advantage. Understanding how information is used within each value chain of the system can lead to new opportunities to change the information component of value-added activities. It can also lead to shakeouts within the industry as firms that fail to provide value are forced out and as surviving firms adopt new business models.

Opportunity also exists in the transfer of information across value chains. For example, sales forecasts generated by a manufacturer, such as a computer or automotive company, and linked to supplier systems create orders for the manufacture of the necessary components for the computer or vehicle. Often this coupling is repeated from manufacturing company to vendor/supplier for several layers, linking the value chains of multiple organizations. In this way, each member of the supply chain adds value by directly linking the elements of its value chains to others.

Optimizing a company's internal processes, such as its supply chain, operations, and customer relationship processes, can be another source of competitive advantage. Tools are routinely used to automate the internal operations of a firm's value chain, such as **supply chain management (SCM)** to source materials for operations, **enterprise resource planning (ERP)** systems to automate functions of the operations activities of the value chain, and **customer relationship management (CRM)** systems to optimize the processing of customer information. These systems are discussed in more detail in Chapter 5.

In an application of the value chain model to the Zara example discussed earlier, Figure 2.7 describes the value added to Zara's primary and support activities provided by information systems. The focus in Figure 2.7 is on value added to Zara's processes, but suppliers and customers in its supply chain also realize the value added by information systems. Most notably, the customer is better served as a result of the systems. For example, the stores place orders twice a week over personal digital assistants (PDAs). Each night, managers use their PDAs to learn about newly available garments. The orders are received and promptly processed and delivered. In this way, Zara can be very timely in responding to customer preferences.

Unlike the five competitive forces model, which focuses on industry dynamics, the focus of the value chain is on the firm's activities. Yet, using the value chain as a lens for understanding strategic use of information resources affects competitive forces because technology innovations add value to suppliers, customers, or even competitors and potential new entrants.

Activity	Zara's Value Chain
Primary Activities	
Inbound Logistics	IT-enabled just-in-time (JIT) strategy results in inventory being received when needed. Most dyes are purchased from its own subsidiaries to better support JIT strategy and reduce costs. Many suppliers are located near its production facilities.
Operations	Information systems support decisions about the fabric, cut, and price points. Cloth is ironed and products are packed on hangers so they don't need ironing when they arrive at stores. Price tags are already on the products. Zara produces 60% of its merchandise in house. Fabric is cut and dyed by robots in 23 highly automated Spanish factories.
Outbound Logistics	Clothes move on miles of automated conveyor belts at distribution centers and reach stores within 48 hours of the order.
Marketing and Sales	Limited inventory allows low percentage of unsold inventory (10%); POS at stores linked to headquarters track how items are selling; customers ask for what they want, and this information is transmitted daily from stores to designers over handheld computers.
Service	No focus on service on products.
Support Activities	
Organization	IT supports tightly knit collaboration among designers, store managers, market specialists, production managers, and production planners.
Human Resources	Managers are trained to understand what's selling and report data to designers every day. The manager is key to making customers feel listened to and to communicating with headquarters to keep each store and the entire Zara clothing line at the cutting edge of fashion.
Technology	Technology is integrated to support all primary activities. Zara's IT staff works with vendors to develop automated conveyors to support distribution activities.
Purchasing	Vertical integration reduces amount of purchasing needed.

FIGURE 2.7 Application of value chain model to Zara.

Sustaining Competitive Advantage

It might seem obvious that a firm would try to sustain its competitive advantage. After all, the firm might have worked very hard to create advantages, such as those previously discussed. However, there is some controversy about trying to sustain a competitive advantage.

On one side are those who warn of hypercompetition as discussed in Chapter 1.[7] In an industry facing hypercompetition, recall that trying to sustain an advantage can be a deadly distraction. Consider the banking industry as a good example that has undergone much change over the past five decades. In the 1960s, people needed to visit a physical bank for all transactions, including withdrawing from or depositing to their accounts and transferring among accounts. In the 1970s, some banks took a chance and invested in automated teller machines (ATMs) and were among the innovators in the industry. In the 1980s, some banks pioneered "bank-by-phone" services that enabled customers to pay bills by phone, attempting to establish competitive advantage with technology. In the late 1990s, Web sites served to augment banking services, and "bank-by-web" was the new, exciting way to compete. Most recently, many banks are providing mobile banking, enabling customers to make deposits by using their smartphone camera to take photos of checks that previously needed to be turned in physically. Then the checks can be destroyed.

The obvious picture to paint here is that competitors caught up with the leaders very quickly, and competitive advantage was brief. When ATMs were introduced, it did not take long for others to adopt the same technology. Even small banks found that they could band together with competitors and invest in the same technologies. The same imitation game took place with "bank by phone," "bank by Web," and mobile banking.

More interestingly, what sounds like an exciting way to show off the power of technology can also be interpreted as a way to increase the cost of doing business. Although some investments, such as using ATMs to replace tellers, lowered costs, other investments raised costs (such as needing to offer phone, Web, *and* mobile banking options to customers).

[7] Don Goeltz, "Hypercompetition," vol. 1 of *The Encyclopedia of Management Theory*, ed. Eric Kessler (Los Angeles: Sage, 2013), 359–60.

Barrier	Definition	Examples
IT project barrier	It would be a large undertaking for a competitor to build the system to copy the capability.	• Requires a large investment • Requires a long time to build • Complicated to build
IT assets and capabilities barrier	Competitors might lack the IT resources to copy the capability.	• Database of customers that cannot be copied • Expert developers or project managers
Complementary resources barrier	The firm has other resources that create a synergy with the IT that provides competitive advantage.	• Respected brand • Partnership agreements • Exclusivity arrangements • Good location
Preemption barrier	The firm "got there first."	• Loyal customer base built at the beginning • Firm known as "the" source

FIGURE 2.8 Barriers to competition and building sustainability.

Rather than arguing that sustaining a competitive advantage is a deadly distraction, Piccoli and Ives[8] provide a framework that outlines the ways in which a firm can provide barriers to competitors, which would build sustainability. The framework outlines four types of barriers: IT project barrier, IT resources and capabilities barrier, complementary resources barrier, and preemption barrier. See Figure 2.8 for a brief definition and a few examples of each.

So, should a firm focus attention on building barriers to the competition, or should it just give up on the established competitive advantage and focus on seeking the next revolution? Given that some technologies can be copied quickly, or even just purchased from the same well-known vendor who supplied it to the leader, it seems prudent to spend some time to explore each technological option in the Piccoli and Ives' framework and determine where the firm can increase sustainability. If the project is rather small, then the firm should focus on the other three barriers. If the firm can build loyalty with customers who appreciate innovation, a two-month competitive advantage might turn into a two-year or longer advantage (thus building a preemption barrier). If a firm can capture valuable data right at the beginning, a copycat firm may fall further behind. Also, building partnerships or securing exclusive rights to some of the technologies can further slow down a competitor.

It would not be wise to stop there, however. The firm should continue to seek ways in which IT can improve offerings or service to customers. And the firm should go beyond those steps, focusing on how it might change its entire industry. One example is the way in which Netflix continued to speed its DVD delivery service while focusing on movie streaming, a technology that will someday make the delivery service obsolete. Netflix was more than aware that its revenue was falling every quarter, but it expected and embraced the shortfall with its strategic move into streaming.[9] Given that other services such as Amazon and many cable companies had begun streaming, Netflix has created original series offerings such as *House of Cards* and *Orange Is the New Black.*

Therefore, a firm might (1) seek ways to build sustainability by looking into each of the four potential barriers to identify promising ways to block the competition and at the same time (2) continue to innovate and change the industry. Netflix has done both by building a dependable and efficient mailing business and creating new business models such as streaming and series production. Focusing only on building sustainability has the potential effect of fighting a losing battle, and focusing only on new business models might be too risky as the sole source of growth. The last strategic framework, resource-based view, is more general and emphasizes ways in which to exploit its many potential resources. The framework, described next, can be helpful for sustaining and creating competitive advantage.

[8] Piccoli and Ives, "IT-Dependent Strategic Initiatives and Sustained Competitive Advantage," 755.
[9] Greg Sandoval, "Netflix CEO, DVD Subscribers to Decline Now and Forever," *CNET*, http://www.cnet.com/news/netflix-ceo-dvd-subscribers-to-decline-now-and-forever (accessed August 19, 2015).

Using the Resource-Based View (RBV)

A fourth framework, the **resource-based view (RBV)**,[10] is useful for determining whether a firm's strategy has created value by using IT. Like the value chain model, the RBV concentrates on areas that add value to the firm. Whereas the value chain model focuses on a firm's activities, the resource-based view focuses on the resources that it can manage strategically in a rapidly changing competitive environment. Like the Piccoli and Ives framework, the RBV focuses on sustaining competitive advantage but through use of resources rather than by raising competitive barriers.

The RBV has been applied in the area of IS to help identify two types of information resources: those that enable a firm to *attain* competitive advantage and those that enable a firm to *sustain* the advantage over the long term. From the IS perspective,[11] some types of resources are better than others for creating attributes that enable a firm to attain competitive advantage (i.e., value, rarity) whereas other resources are better for creating attributes to sustain competitive value (e.g., low substitutability, low mobility, low imitability).

Resources to Attain Competitive Advantage

Valuable and rare resources that firms must leverage to establish a superior resource position help companies attain competitive advantage. A resource is considered valuable when it enables the firm to become more efficient, effective, or innovative. It is a rare resource when other firms do not possess it. For example, many banks today would not think of doing business without a mobile banking app. Mobile banking apps are very valuable to the banks in terms of their operations. A bank's customers expect it to provide a mobile banking app that can be used on any mobile device. However, because many other banks also have mobile banking apps, they are not a rare resource, and they do not offer a strategic advantage. Some call them *table stakes* or resources required just to be in the business. Many systems in Eras I and II, and especially Era III, were justified on their ability to provide a rare and valuable resource. In some cases these very systems have become table stakes.

Resources to Sustain Competitive Advantage

Many firms that invested in systems learned that gaining a competitive advantage does not automatically mean that they could sustain it over the long term. The only way to do that is to continue to innovate and to protect against resource imitation, substitution, or transfer. For example, Walmart's complex logistics management is deeply embedded in both its own and its suppliers' operations so that imitations by other firms is unlikely. The Oakland Athletics' use of information systems propelled it to victory, as depicted in the movie *Moneyball,* but as soon as other teams learned about the secret behind the success Oakland was having with analytics and information systems, they, too began to use similar techniques, reducing the advantage Oakland initially enjoyed. Finally, to sustain competitive advantage, resources must be difficult to transfer or replicate, or relatively immobile. Some information resources can be easily bought. However, technical knowledge—especially that which relates to a firm's operation—an aggressive and opportunistic company culture, deep relationships with customers, and managerial experience in the firm's environment is less easy to obtain and, hence, considered harder to transfer to other firms.

Some IT management skills are general enough in nature to make them easier to transfer and imitate. Although it clearly is important for IS executives to manage internally oriented resources such as IS infrastructure, systems development, and running cost-effective IS operations, these skills can be acquired in many different forms. They are basic IT management skills possessed by virtually all good IS managers. Other skills, however, are unique to a firm and require considerable time and resources to develop. For example, it takes time to learn how the firm operates and to understand its critical processes and socially complex working relationships. However, the message suggested by the RBV is that IS executives must look beyond their own IS shop and concentrate on cultivating resources

[10] The resource-based view was originally proposed by management researchers, most prominently Jay Barney, "Firm Resources and Sustained Competitive Advantage," *Journal of Management* 17, no. 1 (1991), 99–120 and "Is the Resource-Based 'View' a Useful Perspective for Strategic Management Research? Yes," *Academy of Management Review* 26, no. 1 (2001), 41–56; M. Wade and J. Hulland, "Review: The Resource-Based View and Information Systems Research: Review, Extension and Suggestions for Future Research," *MIS Quarterly* 28, no. 1 (2004), 107–42. This article reviewed the resource-based view's application in the MIS literature and derived a framework to better understand its application to IS resources.

[11] http://www.minonline.com/best_of_web/Best-of-the-Web-CommunitySocial-Networking_10185.html (accessed January 1, 2012).

that help the firm understand changing business environments and allow it to work well with all its external stakeholders. Even when considering internally oriented information resources, there are differences in the extent to which these resources add value. Many argue that IS personnel are willing to move, especially when offered higher salaries by firms needing these skills. Yet, some technical skills, such as knowledge of a firm's use of technology to support business processes, and technology integration skills are not easily exported to, or imported from, another firm. Further, hardware and many software applications can be purchased or outsourced, making them highly imitable and transferrable. Because it is unlikely that two firms have exactly the same strategic alternatives, resources at one firm might have only moderate substitutability in the other firm.

Zara and RBV

Figure 2.9 indicates the extent to which the attributes of each information resource may add value to Zara, the company discussed earlier in the chapter. Zara's advantage did not come from the specific hardware or software technologies it employed. Its management spent five to ten times less on technology than its rivals. In contrast,

	Value Creation		**Value Sustainability**		
Resource/Attribute	**Value**	**Rarity**	**Imitation**	**Substitution**	**Transfer**
IT ASSET					
IT Infrastructure	**Moderate** because of its skillful use of the POS equipment, handheld computers, automated conveyors, and computer-controlled equipment to cut patterns, but similar technology could be purchased and used by competitors		**Easy** to imitate and transfer its infrastructure **Moderate** for substitution of infrastructure (automated conveyers)		
Information Repository	**High** value and rarity because of its information about customers' preferences and body types, which Zara leverages strategically; well integrated with Zara's operations and personnel; retail information analyzed by designers to identify future products		**Difficult** to imitate and transfer **Extremely difficult** to substitute because of the volume and nature of the data		
IT CAPABILITY					
Technical Skills	**Low** value/rarity because IS professionals could be hired relatively easily to perform the technical work		**Moderately difficult** to imitate, substitute, or transfer; some sustainability results because the skills are used to integrate across a range of systems		
IT Management Skills	**High** value/rarity because they were acquired over time		**Difficult** to imitate, substitute, or transfer; resources leveraged well		
Relationship Skills—*Externally Focused*	**High** value from relationships with European manufacturers **Moderate** rarity because other companies also have relationships with manufacturers although required time to develop the relationship		**Difficult** to imitate, substitute, or transfer; turnaround time of under 5 weeks from conception to distribution		
Relationship Skills—*Spanning*	**High** rarity of spanning		**Difficult** to imitate, substitute, or transfer spanning; unusual tight-knit teams at headquarters not easy to imitate or purchase in the marketplace, allowing the ability to correctly interpret and quickly respond to customer needs		

FIGURE 2.9 Information resources at Zara, by attribute.
Source: Based on M. Wade and J. Hulland, "The Resource-Based View and Information Systems Research: Review, Extension and Suggestions for Future Research," *MIS Quarterly* 28, no. 1 (2004), 107–42.

Social Business Lens: Social Capital

A management theory that is gaining in popularity as a tool in understanding a social business is the social capital theory. **Social capital** is the sum of the actual and potential resources embedded within, available through, and derived from the network of relationships possessed by an individual or social unit. Relationships associated with networks have the potential of being a valuable resource for businesses. The theory's focus is not on managing individuals but on managing relationships.

The value from networks may be derived in one of three interrelated ways: structural, relational, and cognitive. The *structural* dimension is concerned with the pattern of relationships in the network—who is connected to whom. The *relational* dimension looks at the nature of relationships among members in the network (i.e., respect, friendship)—how the connected people interact. The third *cognitive* dimension looks at the way people think about things in the network, in particular whether they have a shared language, system of meanings or interpretations—how the connected people think. The unusual thing about social capital is that no one person owns it. Rather, the people in the relationship own it jointly. Thus, it can't be traded easily, but it can be used to do certain things more easily. In particular, in social business applications, social capital may make it easier to get the information needed to perform a task or connect with certain key people. In IS development teams, social capital may improve the willingness and ability of team members to coordinate their tasks in completing a project.

Source: J. Nahapiet and S. Ghosal, "Social Capital, Intellectual Capital and the Organizational Value, "*Academy of Management Review*, 23, no. 2 (1998), 242–66.

Zara has created considerable value from the other information asset—its valuable information repository with customers' preferences and body types.

In terms of information capability, much of Zara's value creation is from its valuable and rare IT management skills. Zara's relationship skills also serve as a tool for value creation and sustainability. Overall, Zara is able to create high value from its IT management and relationship skills. It would be moderately to extremely difficult to substitute, imitate, or transfer them.

The resource-based theory, although highly cited, has received its share of criticism.[12] The major criticism is that it doesn't clearly distinguish between value and strategic competitive advantage. Another criticism of the original theory is that it doesn't consider different types of resources. However, IS researchers addressed this concern when they categorized resources into assets and capabilities and then provided examples of each. In applying the theory, it is important to recognize that it is focused on internal sources of a firm's competitive advantage and, thus, does not thoroughly take into account the environment in which the firm is embedded, especially when the environment is quite dynamic.

Most firms don't really have a choice of creating competitive advantage by manipulating industry forces either through their use of information resources or IT-enhanced activities. Yet, like Zara, they can leverage the IT resources they do have to create and sustain strategic value for their firms.

Strategic Alliances

The value chain helps a firm focus on adding value to the areas of most value to its partners. The resource-based view suggests adding value using externally oriented relationship skills. The Eras framework emphasizes the importance of collaborative partnerships and relationships. The increasing number of Web applications focused on collaboration and social networking only foreshadow even more emphasis on alliances. These relationships can take many forms, including joint ventures, joint projects, trade associations, buyer–supplier partnerships, or cartels. Often such partnerships use information technologies to support strategic alliances and integrate data across

[12] For an excellent discussion of criticisms of the resource-based view, see J. Kraaijenbrink, J-C Spender, and A. J. Groen "The Resource-Based View: A Review and Assessment of Its Critiques," *Journal of Management*, 36, no. 1, (2010), 349–72.

partners' information systems. A **strategic alliance** is an interorganizational relationship that affords one or more companies in the relationship a strategic advantage. An example is the strategic alliance between game maker Zynga and Facebook. As documented in Facebook's IPO filing in January 2012, the relationship is a mutually beneficial one. Zynga developed some of the most popular games found on Facebook, including Mafia Wars, Farmville, and WordsWithFriends. Facebook has exclusive rights to Zynga's games, many of which have generated thousands of new members for Facebook. It also gained access to Zynga's customer database. The alliance generates significant revenue for both parties because players of these games purchase virtual goods with real money and Zynga purchases significant advertising space from Facebook to promote its games. Zynga benefits from the revenue resulting from its gamers on Facebook community.[13]

Business ecosystems are often groups of strategic alliances in which a number of partners provide important services to each other and jointly create value for customers. The Facebook ecosystem could be said to include many of the companies that use that platform to deliver their apps, that allow customers to post directly on their Facebook page from the app, or that allow customers to log on to their site using their Facebook account. This adds value for customers by providing greater convenience, and by offering the ability to automatically update their activity stream with information from the app, and both Facebook and the app provider benefit from their alliance.

IS often provides the platform upon which a strategic alliance functions. Technology can help produce the product developed by the alliance, share information resources across the partners' existing value systems, or facilitate communication and coordination among the partners. Because many services are information based today, an IS platform is used to deliver these services to customers. The Facebook– Zynga alliance is an example of this type of IS platform. Further, linking value chains through supply chain management (SCM) is another way that firms build an IT-facilitated strategic alliance.

Co-opetition

Clearly, not all strategic alliances are formed with suppliers or customers as partners. Rather, co-opetition is an increasingly popular alternative model. As defined by Brandenburg and Nalebuff in their book of the same name, **co-opetition** is a strategy whereby companies cooperate and compete at the same time with companies in their value net.[14] The value net includes a company and its competitors and complementors as well as its customers and suppliers and the interactions among all of them. A *complementor* is a company whose product or service is used in conjunction with a particular product or service to make a more useful set for the customer. For example, Goodyear is a complementor to Ford and GM because tires are a complementary product to vehicles. Likewise, Amazon is a complementor to Apple in part because the Amazon reading application, the Kindle, the reading tablet that Amazon sells, is one of the most popular apps for the iPad. Finally, a cellular service is a complementor to Google's search engine because the service allows more consumers to use Google's search function.

Co-opetition, then, is the strategy for creating the best possible outcome for a business by optimally combining competition and cooperation. It can also be used as a strategy for sourcing as discussed in Chapter 10. It frequently creates competitive advantage by giving power in the form of information to other organizations or groups. For example, Covisint.com hosts the auto industry's e-marketplace, which grew out of a consortium of competitors, including General Motors, Ford, DaimlerChrysler, Nissan, and Renault. By addressing multiple automotive functional needs across the entire product life cycle, Covisint offers support for collaboration, supply chain management, procurement, and quality management. Covisint.com has extended this business-to-partner platform to other industries including health care, manufacturing, life sciences, food and beverage, and oil and gas. Thus, co-opetition as demonstrated by Covisint not only streamlines the internal operations of its backers but also has the potential to transform an industry.

[13] Adapted from N. Wingfield, "Virtual Products, Real Profits" *The Wall Street Journal* (September 9, 2011), A1, 16; L. B. Baker, "Zynga's Sales Soar on Facebook Connection," *Reuters News* (February 2, 2012), http://www.reuters.com/article/2012/02/02/us-zynga-shares-idUSTRE8111PO20120202 (accessed September 14, 2015); Jackie Cohen, "So Much for the Facebook Effect: Zynga Sees $978.6 Million Loss In 2011," *Yahoo News* (February 14, 2012), http://www.allfacebook.com/facebook-zynga-eps-2012-02 (accessed February 20, 2012).

[14] A. Brandenburg and B. Nalebuff, *Co-opetition* (New York: Doubleday, 1996).

Risks

As demonstrated throughout this chapter, information resources may be used to gain strategic advantage even if that advantage is fleeting. When information systems are chosen as the tool to outpace a firm's competitors, executives should be aware of the many risks that may surface. Some of these risks include the following:

- *Awakening a sleeping giant:* A firm can implement IS to gain competitive advantage only to find that it nudged a larger competitor with deeper pockets into implementing an IS with even better features. FedEx offered its customers the ability to trace the transit and delivery of their packages online. FedEx's much larger competitor, UPS, rose to the challenge. UPS not only implemented the same services but also added a new set of features eroding some of the advantages FedEx enjoyed, causing FedEx to update its offerings. Both the UPS and FedEx sites passed through multiple Web site iterations as the dueling delivery companies continue to struggle for competitive advantage.
- *Demonstrating bad timing:* Sometimes customers are not ready to use the technology designed to gain strategic advantage. For example, Grid Systems created the GRiDPAD in 1989. It was a tablet computer designed for businesses to use in the field and was well reviewed at that time. But it didn't get traction. Three decades later, in 2010, Apple introduced the iPad, and tablet computing took off.
- *Implementing IS poorly:* Stories abound of information systems that fail because they are poorly implemented. Typically, these systems are complex and often global in their reach. An implementation fiasco took place at Hershey Foods when it attempted to implement its supply and inventory system. Hershey developers brought the complex system up too quickly and then failed to test it adequately. Related systems problems crippled shipments during the critical Halloween shopping season, resulting in large declines in sales and net income. More recently, in 2012, more than 100,000 Austin Energy customers received incorrect utility bills due to problems with the company's vendor-supplied bill collection system. Some customers went months without a bill, and others were incorrectly billed. Some businesses that owed $3,000 were billed $300,000. Still others tried to pay their bill online only to be told that the payment had not recorded when it had been. The utility calculated that the problems cost it more than $8 million.[15]
- *Failing to deliver what users want:* Systems that do not meet the needs of the firm's target market are likely to fail. For example, in 2011, Netflix leadership divided the company into two, calling the DVD-rental business Qwikster and keeping the streaming business under Netflix. But customers complained, and worse, closed their accounts, and less than a month later, Qwikster was gone. Netflix reunited both businesses under the Netflix name.[16]
- *Running afoul of the law:* Using IS strategically may promote litigation if the IS results in the violation of laws or regulations. Years ago, American Airlines' reservation system, Sabre, was challenged by the airline's competitors on the grounds that it violated antitrust laws. More recently, in 2010, Google said it was no longer willing to adhere to Chinese censorship. The Chinese government responded by banning searching via all Google search sites (not only google.cn but all language versions, e.g., google.co.jp, google.com.au), including Google Mobile. Google then created an automatic redirect to Google Hong Kong, which stopped June 30, 2010, so that Google would not lose its license to operate in China. Today, Google, Inc. is acting in compliance with the Chinese government's censorship laws and Chinese users of Google.cn see filtered results as before. More recently, European antitrust officials claimed that Google's search engine unfairly generates results that favor its shopping sites over those of its competitors and that its Android mobile phone operating system unfairly features Google as the default search engine.[17]

---

[15] Marty Toohey, "More Than 100,000 Austin Energy Customers Hit by Billing Errors from $55 Million IBM System," *Statesman* (February 18, 2012), http://www.statesman.com/news/local/more-than-100-000-austin-energy-customers-hit-2185031.html (accessed February 20, 2012).

[16] Qwikster = Gonester (October 10, 2011), http://www.breakingcopy.com/netflix-kills-qwikster (accessed February 20, 2012).

[17] "Viewed as a Monopoly in Europe, Google Takes on Role as a Wireless Trust-Buster in U.S.," *The New York Times* (May 8, 2015), B1, B6.

Geographic Box: Mobile-Only Internet Users Dominate Emerging Countries

More than 25% of mobile Web users in emerging markets connect to the Internet solely through mobile devices. This is the case for 70% of mobile Web users in Egypt, 59% in India, and 50% in Nigeria but only for 25% of U.S. and 22% of U.K. mobile Web users. Malaysia is emerging as a test case for a mobile-only Internet. It has rolled out a next-generation, high-speed broadband network that covers most of its population. This infrastructure makes it possible to make video calls with Apple's FaceTime application in locations throughout the country using a tiny pocket router that accesses a WiMAX wireless-broadband network set up by a local conglomerate, YTL Corp. Bhd. To further encourage the spread of Internet, Malaysia's leaders have pledged not to censor the Internet.

Sources: G. Dunaway, "Mobile-Only Internet Users Dominate Emerging Markets" Adotas.com (October 24, 2011), http://www.adotas.com/201w1/10/mobile-only-internet-users-dominate-emerging-markets/ (accessed August 19, 2015); J. Hookway, "Broadband in the Tropics," *The Wall Street Journal* (September 21, 2011), B6.

Every business decision has risks associated with it. However, with the large expenditure of IT resources needed to create sustainable, strategic advantages, the manager should carefully identify and then design a mitigation strategy to manage the associated risks.

Co-Creating IT and Business Strategy

This chapter has discussed the alignment of IT strategy with business strategy. Certainly, the two strategies must be carefully choreographed to ensure receiving maximum value from IT investments and obtaining the maximum opportunity to achieve the business strategy. However, in the fast-paced business environment where information is increasingly a core component of the product or service offered by the firm, managers must co-create IT and business strategy. That is to say that IT strategy *is* business strategy; one cannot be created independently of the other. In many cases, they are now one in the same.

For companies whose main product is information, such as financial services companies, it's clear that information management is the core of the business strategy itself. How an investment firm manages the clients' accounts, how its clients interact with the company, and how investments are made are all done through the management of information. A financial services company must co-create business and IT strategy.

But consider a company like FedEx, most well known as the package delivery company. Are customers paying to have a package delivered or to have information about that package's delivery route and timetable? One could argue that they are one in the same and that increasingly the company's business strategy *is* its IS strategy. Certainly, there are components of the operation that are more than just information. There are actual packages to be loaded on actual trucks and planes, which are then actually delivered to their destinations. However, to make it all work, the company must rely on IS. Should the IS stop working or have a serious failure, FedEx would be unable to do business. A company like this must co-create IT strategy and business strategy.

This was not true a few years ago. Companies could often separate IS strategy from business strategy in part because their products or services did not have a large information component. For example, a few years ago, should the IS of a trucking company stop working, the trucks would still be able to take their shipments to their destination and pick up new ones. It might be slower or a bit more chaotic, but the business wouldn't stop. Today, that's not the case. Complicated logistics are the norm, and IS are the foundation of the business as seen at FedEx.

With the increasing number of IS applications on the Web and on mobile devices, firms increasingly need to co-create business and IT strategy. Managers who think they can build a business model without considering the opportunities and impact of information systems, using both the resources owned by the firm and those available on the Web, will find they have significant difficulties creating business opportunities as well as sustainable advantage in their marketplace.

SUMMARY

- Information resources include data, technology, people, and processes within an organization. Information resources can be either assets or capabilities.
- IT infrastructure and information repositories are IT assets. Three major categories of IT capabilities are technical skills, IT management skills, and relationship skills.
- Using IS for strategic advantage requires an awareness of the many relationships that affect both competitive business and information strategies.
- The five competitive forces model implies that more than just the local competitors influence the reality of the business situation. Analyzing the five competitive forces—threat of new entrants, buyers' bargaining power, suppliers' bargaining power, industry competitors, and threat of substitute products—from both a business view and an information systems view helps general managers use information resources to minimize the effect of these forces on the organization.
- The value chain highlights how information systems add value to the primary and support activities of a firm's internal operations as well as to the activities of its customers and of other components of its supply chain.
- The resource-based view (RBV) helps a firm understand the value created by its strategy. RBV maintains that competitive advantage comes from a firm's information resources. Resources enable a firm to attain and sustain competitive advantage.
- IT can facilitate strategic alliances. *Ecosystems* are groups of strategic alliances working together to deliver goods and services. Supply chain management (SCM) is a mechanism that may be used for creating strategic alliances.
- *Co-opetition* is the complex arrangement through which companies cooperate and compete at the same time with other companies in their value net.
- Numerous risks are associated with using information systems to gain strategic advantage: awaking a sleeping giant, demonstrating bad timing, implementing poorly, failing to deliver what customers want, avoiding mobile-based alternatives, and running afoul of the law.

KEY TERMS

business ecosystem (p. 34)
co-opetition (p. 48)
customer relationship management (CRM) (p. 42)
enterprise resource planning (ERP) (p. 42)
information resources (p. 36)
IT asset (p. 36)
IT capability (p. 36)
network effects (p. 34)
resource-based view (RBV) (p. 45)
strategic alliance (p. 48)
social capital (p. 47)
supply chain management (SCM) (p. 42)

DISCUSSION QUESTIONS

1. How can information itself provide a competitive advantage to an organization? Give two or three examples. For each example, describe its associated risks.
2. Use the five competitive forces model as described in this chapter to describe how information technology might be used to provide a winning position for each of these businesses:
   a. A global advertising agency
   b. A local restaurant
   c. A mobile applications provider
   d. An insurance company
   e. A Web-based audio book service

3. Using the value chain model, describe how information technology might be used to provide a winning position for each of these businesses:
   a. A global advertising agency
   b. A local restaurant
   c. A mobile applications provider
   d. An insurance company
   e. A Web-based audio book service
4. Use the resource-based view as described in this chapter to describe how information technology might be used to provide and sustain a winning position for each of these businesses:
   a. A global advertising agency
   b. A local restaurant
   c. A mobile applications provider
   d. An insurance company
   e. A Web-based audio book service
5. Some claim that the only sustainable competitive advantage for an organization is its relationships with its customers. All other advantages eventually erode. Do you agree or disagree? How can information systems play a role in maintaining the organization's relationship with its customers? Defend your position.
6. Cisco Systems has a network of component suppliers, distributors, and contract manufacturers that are linked through Cisco's extranet. When a customer orders a Cisco product at its Web site, the order triggers contracts to manufacturers of printed circuit board assemblies when appropriate and alerts distributors and component suppliers. Cisco's contract manufacturers are aware of the order because they can log on to its extranet and link with Cisco's own manufacturing execution systems. What are the advantages of Cisco's strategic alliances? What are the risks to Cisco? To the suppliers?

CASE STUDY 2-1 Groupon

Groupon, Inc. raised $700 million at its IPO in the fall of 2011, instantly providing a valuation of almost $13 billion for a company that was only three years old at the time. Some question the value, claiming Groupon has no sustainable competitive advantage. Others see Groupon as an innovative company with high potential.

Groupon sells Internet coupons for events, services, and other popular items that customers might want to buy. Customers sign up for daily e-mails targeted to their local market. The daily deal, offered for one-day only and only if a predetermined minimum number of customers buy it, gives customers 50% off the "retail" price. For example, a $100 three-month health club membership would sell for $50 on Groupon. The customer pays $50 to Groupon and prints a certificate to redeem at the health club. Groupon keeps 50% of the revenue, or $25 in this case, and gives the rest to the health club. Effectively, retailers are offering 75% off with the customer saving 50% and Groupon taking the rest.

Groupon pays the retailer when the coupon is redeemed, making money both on the float between the time revenue is collected and the time the retailer is paid and on the certificates that are never redeemed at all, which the industry calls *breakage*. Retailers make money in the long run by introducing customers to their products, selling them additional products and services when they come in to redeem their coupons, and turning them into repeat customers. And retailers benefit from the buzz created when their business is on Groupon.

In August 2010, Groupon launched its first national deal, a coupon worth $50 of Gap apparel and accessories for $25. It sold over 440,000 coupons, netting Groupon and the Gap close to $11 million. But not all vendors are the size of the Gap, and smaller vendors have been overwhelmed with too many coupons. One local business owner said the company lost $8,000 on its Groupon promotion when too many coupons were issued. In fact, a study of 150 retailers showed that only 66% found their deals profitable.

Around the time of the IPO, analysts and observers alike claimed that Groupon's business model was not sustainable. In addition to the large number of retailers who found their deals unprofitable, observers noted that Groupon does not produce anything of value, and it isn't adding value to the retailers. Further, there are no barriers to entry to stop competitors. In May 2011, more than 450 competitors offering discounts and deals included LivingSocial, another daily deal site; restaurant.com, a site for restaurant gift certificates at a deep discount; and overstock.com and woot.com, sites offering discounted merchandise, not to mention deep-pocketed competitors like Amazon.com.

But Groupon added to its business strategy with mobile capability and new services. In February 2012, it purchased Kima Labs, a mobile payment specialist, and Hyperpublic, a company that builds databases of local information. In May 2011, in a few cities, the company launched Groupon Now, a time-based local application that gives customers instant deals at merchants nearby using location-based software. CEO Andrew Mason told Wall Street analysts in February 2012 that he saw significant growth potential, including working on new features that will help customers personalize offers and avoid deals they don't want.

Discussion Questions

1. How does information technology help Groupon compete?
2. Do you agree or disagree with the statement that "Groupon has no sustainable competitive advantage?" Please explain your point of view.
3. How does Groupon add value to the companies whose offers are sold on the site?
4. What impact, if any, will Groupon Now have on Groupon's competitive position? Explain.
5. What would you advise Groupon leaders to consider as their next application?
6. Analyze the business model of Groupon using Porter's five forces model.

Sources: Adapted from http://mashable.com/2010/08/19/gap-groupon/ (accessed February 21, 2012); http://www.forbes.com/sites/petercohan/2011/06/06/memo-to-sec-groupon-has-no-competitive-advantage-stop-its-ipo/ (accessed February 21, 2012); http://blogs.wsj.com/venturecapital/2010/09/29/rice-university-study-groupon-renewal-rate-not-so-hot/ (accessed February 21, 2012); http://articles.chicagotribune.com/2011-05-18/business/ct-biz-0519-groupon-now-20110518_1_groupon-chief-executive-andrew-mason-first-phase (accessed February 21, 2012); http://www.reuters.com/article/2012/02/09/us-groupon-idUSTRE81727 B20120209 (accessed February 21, 2012).

CASE STUDY 2-2 Zipcar

Zipcar is an answer for customers who want to rent a car for a few hours in their home city rather than for a few days from a traditional rental agency. Car reservations are for a specific pick-up time and location around the city, often in neighborhoods so the customers need only to walk to pick up their reserved car. Customers apply for a Zipcard, which enables them to reserve a car online and unlock their car when they arrive at its location.

The company operates with a very small staff compared to traditional rental agencies. Very little human interaction is required between the customer and Zipcar for a transaction. A customer reserves a car online, enters into the reserved car by waving the RFID-enabled Zipcard against the card reader mounted behind the driver's side windshield, returns the car to the same location, and is billed on the credit card already on file. The customer can check all rental records and print receipts from the online reservation system. The system also has a color-coded time chart showing the availability and location of all rental cars in the vicinity. This transparent information exchange allows a customer to pick the car he or she wants, if available, or delay the reservation until that car is returned by another customer. Zipcar also created and installed a GPS-enabled wireless device in each car, which allows members to find and reserve a vehicle nearby using a cell phone. Customers also can use an iPhone or Android app on their iPhone or Android mobile device to find and reserve a Zipcar on a 24/7 basis. Zipcar sends text alerts near the end of the rental period, and customers can text back if they want to extend their rental time.

All cars were outfitted with patented wireless technology. Zipcar's proprietary IT platform carries information flow between customers, vehicles, and the company. It is used to monitor car security, fulfill reservations, record hourly usage, and maintain mileage information. The platform also relays vital technical information such as battery voltage and fuel level. It even informs the central system if a customer forgot to turn off headlights, which can quickly drain battery power.

This business model provides unique advantages over traditional car rentals. Customers do not have to stand in line or fill out papers to rent a car. They know exactly which make and model they will be getting. Unlike most off-airport rental agency locations, which are open only during business hours, Zipcar locations are open 24 hours. The company's rates also include the cost of gas and insurance as well as reserved parking spots at some locations.

Additionally, the company uses social networking technologies to develop an online community of Zipcar members—Zipsters. It encourages Zipsters to talk about their Ziptrips (i.e., share their personal experiences with Zipcar).

Thus, information technology is not only the key enabler of this business model but also a facilitator in creating a buzz and encouraging community development around the concept. Zipcar changed the rules of the rental car industry by bringing the new Web 2.0 mind-set of focusing on automation, customer empowerment, transparency, and community. Zipcar is very successful; as of August 2015, its Website boasts over 900,000 paying members and renting over 10,000 vehicles in 30 major metro markets in the United States, Canada, and the United Kingdom, as well as 400 college campuses and 50 airports.

Discussion Questions

1. Apply the resource-based view to Zipcar's business model to show how information resources may be used to gain and sustain competitive advantage.
2. Discuss the synergy between the business strategy of Zipcar and information technology.
3. What *network effects* are part of Zipcar's strategy? How do they add value?
4. As the CEO of Zipcar, what is your most threatening competition? What would you do to sustain a competitive advantage?

Sources: Adapted from Paul Boutin, "A Self-Service Rental Car," *Businessweek* (May 3, 2006), http://www.bloomberg.com/bw/stories/2006-05-03/a-self-service-rental-car (accessed August 19, 2015); Mary K. Pratt, "RFID: A Ticket to Ride," *Computerworld* (December 18, 2006), http://www.computerworld.com/article/2554153/mobile-wireless/rfid—a-ticket-to-ride.html (accessed August 19, 2015); "Zipcar: Our Technology Downloaded," http://www.zipcar.com/how/technology; Zipcar: "Zipcar Overview," http://www.zipcar.com/press/overview (accessed August 19, 2015).

Organizational Strategy and Information Systems

chapter 3

In order for information systems (IS) to support an organization in achieving its goals, the organization must reflect the business strategy and be coordinated with the organizational strategy. This chapter focuses on linking and coordinating the IS strategy with the three components of organizational strategy:

- Organizational design (decision rights, formal reporting relationships and structure, informal networks)
- Management control systems (planning, data collection, performance measurement, evaluation, incentives, and rewards)
- Internal culture (values, locus of control)

After 20 years of fast growth, in 2014 Cognizant Technology Solutions was a company with $8.84 billion in revenues from providing IS outsourcing services. However, growing at such a breakneck speed, it had to reinvent its organizational structure many times to make sure that it facilitated the flow of information. Initially, its India-centric structure located managers of each group in India along with software engineers. Employees at customer locations worldwide reported to the managers. As the company grew and its focus shifted from simple, cost-based solutions to complex, relationship-based solutions, this structure had to be changed to be more customer oriented. Under the redesigned reporting structure, managers were moved to customer locations but software engineers remained in India. This change improved customer relations but brought about new headaches on the technical side. Under the new arrangement, managers had to spend their days with customers and unexpectedly ended up spending their nights with software engineers to clarify customer requirements and fix bugs. This created a tremendous strain on managers, who threatened to quit. It also hampered the company's business of systems development. Thus, neither of these organizational structures was working well. Neither structure was well aligned with the business strategy and the IS strategy

However, Cognizant found that despite these problems, some work teams were working and performing well. Upon an extensive analysis of those groups, the company decided to adopt a matrix structure of comanagement throughout the company. In this matrix structure, each project has two managers equally responsible for the project in a location. One manager is in India and the other is at the client site. They work out among themselves how and when to deal with issues. And both managers are equally responsible for customer satisfaction, project deadlines, and group revenue. The new structure (Figure 3.1) enables Cognizant to work more closely with its clients to focus on improving operations. That is, the new matrix structure makes it possible to build IS that the customers wanted.

During the same time period in 2008, the largest outsourcing company and software exporter in India, Tata Consultancy Services (TCS), also found that growth led to problems. "As we scale up over 100,000 employees, TCS needs a structure that allows us to build a nimble organization to

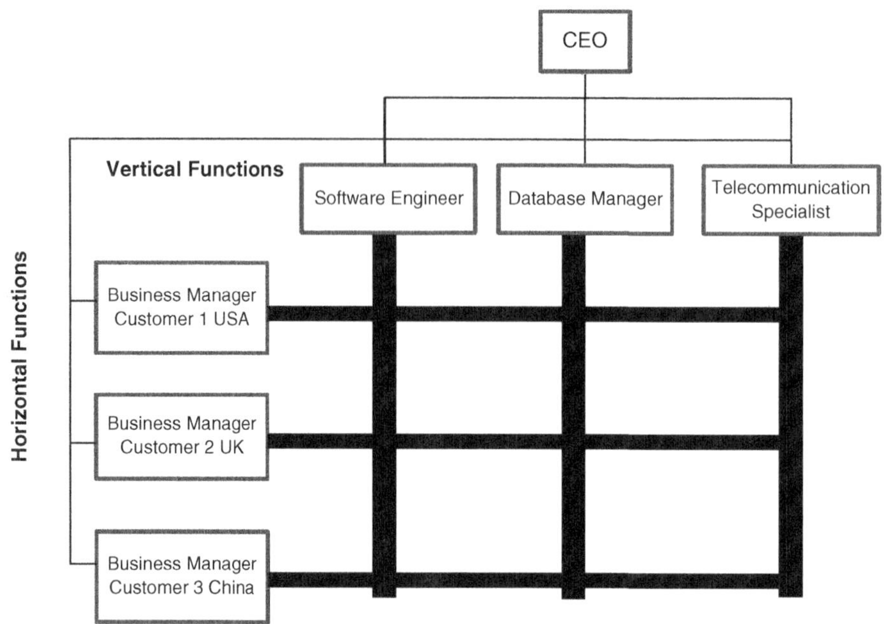

FIGURE 3.1 Example of possible cognizant matrix structure.
Source: Adapted from "The Issue: For Cognizant, Two's Company," *Businessweek* (January 17, 2008), http://www.bloomberg.com/bw/stories/2008-01-17/the-issue-for-cognizant-twos-companybusinessweek-business-news-stock-market-and-financial-advice (accessed August 20, 2015).

capture new growth opportunities," said then TCS CEO and Managing Director S. Ramadorai.[1] Growth led to a high volume of issues that needed the attention of the CEO and COO, and eventually it was difficult to keep up. At the same time, there was a need to spend significantly more time investigating new potential markets and new strategic initiatives than the CEO/COO could spare. In 2011, the new TCS CEO N. Chandrasekaran modified the structure and added a new layer of leaders to oversee the businesses and free up their time to work on strategy (see Figure 3.2). The new layer focuses on customers and aims to boost revenue growth.[2]

While both Cognizant and TCS are large Indian outsourcing companies that found they needed to reorganize to respond to problems resulting from growth, their problems were profoundly different. Cognizant's main problem was its lack of necessary information flows between the software engineers in India and the customer service managers on the client location. Its complex problems resulted in a correspondingly complex matrix structure. It focused on the delivery of information systems that reflect refined technical solutions to their problems to its customers. Its new organization structure both improves customer responsiveness and necessary information flows. It focuses on system development and delivery and seeks to address the information flow problem that Cognizant previously experienced in building systems.

In contrast, TCS's organization chart reflects a focus not only on current customers but also on future markets. That is why it added major units called "New Growth Markets" and "Strategic Initiative Unit." The Business Process Outsourcing and Small and Medium Enterprise solutions in this latter major unit indicate the strategic directions that TCS wants to take. The organizational structure is designed to emphasize these new growth areas and facilitate information flows along these lines in the organization. Its focus is on building an ever bigger market for its IS and the IS services that it provides.

[1] "Reinvented Blog by Prashanth Rai" (March 19, 2008), http://cio-reinvented.typepad.com/cioreinvented/2008/03/tcs—new-organ.html (accessed December 19, 2011).
[2] N. Shivapriya, "TCS CEO N Chandrasekaran Creates New Layer to Oversee Verticals" (May 25, 2011), http://articles.economictimes.indiatimes.com/2011-05-25/news/29581999_1_tcs-ceo-n-chandrasekaran-tcs-spokesperson-structure (accessed December 19, 2011).

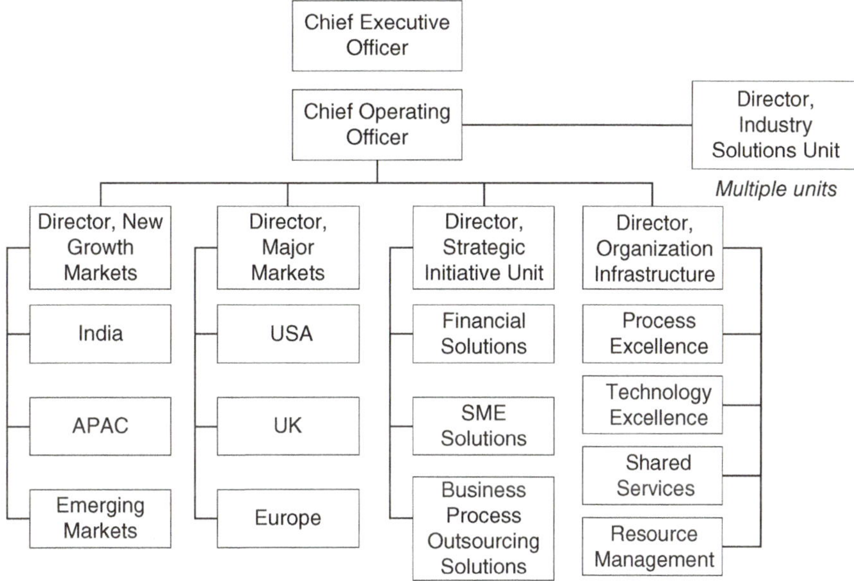

FIGURE 3.2 Tata Consultancy Services.
Source: "TCS Plans New Organizational Structure" (February 12, 2008), http://www.livemint.com/Companies/2ODg7L1mCcRlFowK1ktX5N/TCS-plans-new-organisational-structure.html (accessed August 20, 2015).

Cognizant and TCS are both in the same business but chose different organizational structures to carry out their objectives. The point is that different organizational structures reflect different organizational strategies that are used to implement business strategies and accomplish organizational goals. These organizational strategies need to be aligned with IS strategies. When used appropriately, IS leverage human resources, capital, and materials to create an organization that optimizes performance. Companies that design organizational strategy without considering IS strategies run into problems like those Cognizant experienced. A synergy results from designing organizations with IS strategy in mind—a synergy that cannot be achieved when IS strategy is just added on.

Chapter 1 introduced a simple framework for understanding the role of IS in organizations. The Information Systems Strategy Triangle relates business strategy with IS strategy and organizational strategy. In an organization that operates successfully, an overriding business strategy drives both organizational strategy and information strategy. The most effective businesses optimize the interrelationships between the organization and its IS, maximizing efficiency and productivity.

Organizational strategy includes the organization's design, as well as the managerial choices that define, set up, coordinate, and control its work processes. As discussed in Chapter 1, many models of organizational strategy are available. One is the managerial levers framework that includes the complementary design variables shown in Figure 3.3. Optimized organizational designs support optimal business processes, and they, in turn, reflect the firm's values and culture. Organizational strategy may be considered as the coordinated set of actions that leverages the use of organizational design, management control systems, and organizational culture to make the organization effective by achieving its objectives. The organizational strategy works best when it meshes well with the IS strategy.

This chapter builds on the managerial levers model. Of primary concern is how IS impact the three types of managerial levers: organizational, control, and cultural. This chapter looks at organizational designs that incorporate IS to define the flow of information throughout the organization, explores how IS can facilitate management control at the organizational and individual levels, and concludes with some ideas about how culture impacts IS and organizational performance. It focuses on organizational-level issues related to strategy. The next two chapters complement these concepts with a discussion of new approaches to work and organizational processes.

Variable	Description
Organizational variables	
Decision rights	The authority to initiate, approve, implement, and control various types of decisions necessary to plan and run the business
Business processes	The set of ordered tasks needed to complete key objectives of the business
Formal reporting relationships	The structure set up to ensure coordination among all units within the organization; reflects allocation of decision rights
Informal networks	Mechanisms, such as ad hoc groups, which work to coordinate and transfer information outside the formal reporting relationships
Control variables	
Data	The facts collected, stored, and used by the organization
Planning	The processes by which future direction is established, communicated, and implemented
Performance measurement and evaluation	The set of measures that are used to assess success in the execution of plans and the processes by which such measures are used to improve the quality of work
Incentives	The monetary and nonmonetary devices used to motivate behavior within an organization
Cultural variables	
Values	The set of implicit and explicit beliefs that underlies decisions made and actions taken; reflects aspirations about the way things should be done
Locus	The span of the culture, i.e., local, national, regional

FIGURE 3.3 Organizational design variables.
Source: Adapted from James I. Cash, Robert G. Eccles, Nitin Nohria, and Richard L. Nolan, *Building the Information Age Organization* (Homewood, IL: Richard D. Irwin, 1994).

Information Systems and Organizational Design

Organizations must be designed in a way that enables them to perform effectively. Different designs accomplish different goals. This section examines organizational variables. It focuses on how IS are designed in conjunction with an organization's structure. Ideally, an organizational structure is designed to facilitate the communication and work processes necessary for it to accomplish the organization's goals, and the use of IS is often the way coordination and workflow are done. The organizational structures of Cognizant and TCS, while very different, reflect and support the goals of each company. Perhaps intuitively, organizational designers at those companies used organizational variables described in Figure 3.3 to build their structures. Those variables include decision rights that underlie formal structures, formal reporting relationships, and informal networks. Organizational processes are another important design component discussed in more detail in Chapter 5.

Decision Rights

Decision rights indicate who in the organization has the responsibility to initiate, supply information for, approve, implement, and control various types of decisions. Ideally, the individual who has the most information about a decision and who is in the best position to understand all of the relevant issues should be the person who has its decision rights. But this may not happen, especially in organizations in which senior leaders make most of the important decisions. Much of the discussion of IT governance and accountability in Chapter 9 is based upon who has the decision rights for critical IS decisions. When talking about accountability, one has to start with the person who is responsible for the decision—that is, the person who has the decision rights. Organizational design is all about making sure that decision rights are properly assigned—and reflected in the structure of formal reporting relationships. IS support decision rights by getting the right information to the decision maker at the right time and then transmitting the decision to those who are affected. In some cases, IS enables a centralized decision maker to pass information that has been gathered from operations and stored centrally down through the organization. If information systems fail to deliver the right information, or worse, deliver the wrong information to the decision maker, poor decisions are bound to be made.

Consider the case of Zara from the last chapter. Each of its 1,000 stores orders clothes in the same way, using the same type of handheld devices, and follows a rigid weekly timetable for ordering, which provides the headquarters commercial team with the information needed to manage fulfillment. Many other large retailers make the decision centrally about what to send to their stores, using forecasting and inventory control models. However, at Zara, store managers have decision rights for ordering, enabling each store to reflect the tastes and preferences of customers in its localized area. But, the store managers do not have decision rights for order fulfillment because they have no way of knowing the consolidated demand of stores in their area. The decision rights for order fulfillment lie with the commercial team in headquarters because it is the team that knows about overall demand, overall supply, and store performance in their assigned areas. The information from the commercial team then flows directly to designers and production, allowing them to respond quickly to customer preferences.[3]

Formal Reporting Relationships and Organizational Structures

Organizational structure is the design element that ensures that decision rights are correctly allocated. The structure of reporting relationships typically reflects the flow of communication and decision making throughout the organization. Traditional organizational structures are hierarchical, flat, or matrix. The networked structure is a newer organizational form. A comparison of these four types of organizational structures may be found in Figure 3.4.

Hierarchical Organizational Structure

As business organizations entered the 20th century, their growth prompted a need for systems for processing and storing information. A new class of worker—the clerical worker—flourished. From 1870 to 1920 alone, the number of U.S. clerical workers mushroomed from 74,200 to more than a quarter of a million.[4]

	Hierarchical	**Flat**	**Matrix**	**Networked**
Description	Bureaucratic form with defined levels of management	Decision making pushed down to the lowest level in the organization	Workers assigned to multiple supervisors in an effort to promote integration	Formal and informal communication networks that connect all parts of the company
Characteristics	Division of labor, specialization, unity of command, formalization	Informal roles, planning, and control; often small and young organizations	Dual reporting relationships based on function and purpose	Known for flexibility and adaptability
Type of Environment Best Supported	Stable, certain	Dynamic uncertain	Dynamic uncertain	Dynamic uncertain
Basis of Structuring	Primarily function	Very loose	Function and purpose (i.e., location, product, customer)	Networks
Power Structure	Centralized	Decentralized	Distributed (matrix managers)	Distributed (network)

FIGURE 3.4 Comparison of organizational structures.

[3] Andrew McAfee and Erik Brynjolfsson, "Investing in the IT That Makes a Competitive Difference, https://cb.hbsp.harvard.edu/cbmp/product/R0807J-PDF-ENG (accessed August 20, 2015); James Surowiecki, *The Wisdom of Crowds* (New York: Anchor Books, 2005).

[4] Frances Cairncross, *The Company of the Future* (London: Profile Books, 2002).

Factories and offices structured themselves using the model that Max Weber observed when studying the Catholic Church and the German army. This model, called a **bureaucracy**, was based on a hierarchical organizational structure.

Hierarchical organizational structure is an organizational form based on the concepts of division of labor, specialization, span of control, and unity of command. Decision rights are highly specified and centralized. When work needs to be done, orders typically come from the top and work is subjected to the division of labor. That means it is segmented into smaller and smaller pieces until it reaches the level of the business in which it will be done. Middle managers do the primary information processing and communicating, telling their subordinates what to do and telling senior managers the outcome of what was done. Jobs within the enterprise are specialized and often organized around particular functions, such as marketing, accounting, manufacturing, and so on. **Span of control** indicates the number of direct reports. The new TCS CEO, N. Chandrasekaran, revised the organizational structure to lower his span of control by inserting a new layer with only a few leaders reporting directly to him. **Unity of command** means that each person has a single supervisor. Rules and policies are established to handle the routine work performed by employees of the organization. When in doubt about how to complete a task, employees turn to the rules. If a rule doesn't exist to handle the situation, employees turn to a supervisor in the hierarchy for the decision. Key decisions are made at the top and filter down through the organization in a centralized fashion. Hierarchical structures, which are sometimes called *vertical structures,* are most suited to relatively stable, certain environments in which the top-level executives are in command of the information needed to make critical decisions. This allows them to make decisions quickly.

IS are typically used to store and communicate information and to support the information needs of managers throughout the hierarchy. IS convey the decisions of top managers downward and data from operations are sent upward through the hierarchy using IS. Hierarchical structures are also very compatible with efforts to organize and manage data centrally. The data from operations that have been captured at lower levels and conveyed through IS increasingly need to be consolidated, managed, and made secure at a high level. The data are integrated into databases that are designed so that employees at all levels of the organization can see the information that they need when they need it. Often there is an information dashboard for executives, a system that provides a summary of key performance indicators (KPIs). Each level of KPI has additional detail behind it and executives can drill down into the details as necessary. For example, a KPI revealing lower profitability might have been caused by higher costs or lower sales, and managers would need to drill down through additional levels of information to understand why the KPI changed. Managers throughout the hierarchy often have similar dashboards with the KPIs for their organization so that up and down the hierarchy, managers are looking at the same information consolidated for their level of decision making.

2. Flat Organizational Structure

In contrast to the hierarchical structure, the **flat, or horizontal, organizational structure** has a less well-defined chain of command. You often don't see an actual organization chart for a flat organization because the relationships are fluid and the jobs are loosely defined. That is, drawing an organization chart for a flat organization is like trying to tie a ribbon around a puddle. In flat organizations, everyone does whatever needs to be done to conduct business. There are very few "middle managers." For this reason, flat organizations can respond quickly to dynamic, uncertain environments. Entrepreneurial organizations, as well as smaller organizations, often use this structure because they typically have fewer employees, and even when they grow, they initially build on the premise that everyone must do whatever is needed. Teamwork is important in flat organizations. To increase flexibility and innovation, decision rights may not be clearly defined. Hence, the decision making is often decentralized because it is spread across the organization to where the decisions are made. It is also time consuming. As the work grows, new individuals are added to the organization, and eventually a hierarchy is formed where divisions are responsible for segments of the work processes. Many companies strive to keep the "entrepreneurial spirit," but in reality, work is done in much the same way as with the hierarchy described previously. Flat organizations often use IS to off-load certain routine work in order to avoid hiring additional employees. As a hierarchy develops, the IS become the glue tying together parts of the organization that otherwise would not communicate. IS also enable flat organizations to respond quickly to their environment.

3. Matrix Organizational Structure

The third popular form, which Cognizant ultimately adopted, is the **matrix organizational structure**. It typically assigns employees to two or more supervisors in an effort to make sure multiple dimensions of the business are integrated. Each supervisor directs a different aspect of the employee's work. For example, a member of a matrix team from marketing would have a supervisor for marketing decisions and a different supervisor for a specific product line. The team member would report to both, and both would be responsible in some measure for that member's performance and development. That is, the marketing manager would oversee the employee's development of marketing skills and the product manager would make sure that the employee develops skills related to the product. Thus, decision rights are shared between the managers. The matrix structure allows organizations to concentrate on both functions and purpose. The matrix structure allows the flexible sharing of human resources and achieves the coordination necessary to meet dual sets of organizational demands. It is suited for complex decision making and dynamic and uncertain environments. IS reduce the operating complexity of matrix organizations by allowing information sharing among the different managerial functions. For example, a saleswoman's sales would be entered into the information system and appear in the results of all managers to whom she reports.

Cognizant might have moved to the matrix structure (see Figure 3.1) from a hierarchical structure because the complexity of its projects had increased. "As part of the structure of a Cognizant engagement, we always pair our technologists with people who have business context experience," says Raj Mamodia, who was then the Assistant Vice President of Cognizant's Consumer Goods business unit. The purpose of these formally structured relationships is to meet the customer's needs, and not just focus on "how beautiful the technology is in and of itself."[5]

The matrix organizational structure carries its own set of weaknesses. Although theoretically each boss has a well-defined area of authority, the employees often find the matrix organizational structure frustrating and confusing because they are frequently subjected to two authorities with conflicting opinions. Consequently, working in a matrix organizational structure can be time consuming because confusion must be dealt with through frequent meetings and conflict resolution sessions. Matrix organizations often make it difficult for managers to achieve their business strategies because they flood managers with more information than they can process.

4. Networked Organizational Structure

Made possible by advances in IT, a fourth type of organizational structure emerged: the **networked organizational structure**. Networked organizations characteristically feel flat and hierarchical at the same time. An article published in the *Harvard Business Review* describes this type of organization: "Rigid hierarchies are replaced by formal and informal communication networks that connect all parts of the company. . . . [This type of organizational structure] is well known for its flexibility and adaptiveness."[6] It is particularly suited to dynamic, unstable environments.

Networked organizational structures are those that rely on highly decentralized decision rights and utilize distributed information and communication systems to replace inflexible hierarchical controls with controls based in IS. Networked organizations are defined by their ability to promote creativity and flexibility while maintaining operational process control. Because networked structures are distributed, many employees throughout the organization can share their knowledge and experience and participate in making key organizational decisions. IS are fundamental to process design; they improve process efficiency, effectiveness, and flexibility. As part of the execution of these processes, data are gathered and stored in centralized data warehouses for use in analysis and decision making. In theory at least, decision making is more timely and accurate because data are collected and stored instantly. The extensive use of communication technologies and networks also renders it easier to coordinate across functional boundaries. In short, the networked organization is one in which IT ties together people, processes, and units.

The organization feels flat when IT is used primarily as a communication vehicle. Traditional hierarchical lines of authority are used for tasks other than communication when everyone can communicate with everyone else, at

[5] Cognizant Computer Goods Technology, "Creating a Culture of Innovation: 10 Steps to Transform the Consumer Goods Enterprise" (October 2009), 6, http://www.cognizant.com/InsightsWhitepapers/Cognizant_Innovation.pdf (accessed August 20, 2015).

[6] L. M. Applegate, J. I. Cash, and D. Q. Mills, "Information Technology and Tomorrow's Manager," *Harvard Business Review* (November–December 1988), 128–36.

least in theory. The term used is *technological leveling* because the technology enables individuals from all parts of the organization to reach all of its other parts.

Portions of Zara's organizational structure appear networked. Being networked enables the store managers to use technology to communicate directly with designers. Zara uses the technology-supported structure to coordinate the actions and decisions of tens of thousands of its employees so that they can focus their attention on the same goal of making and selling clothes that people want to buy.

Other Organizational Structures

An organization is seldom a pure form of one of the four structures described here. It is much more common to see a hybrid structure in which different parts of the organization use different structures depending on the information needs and desired work processes. For example, the IS department may use a hierarchical structure that allows more control over data warehouses and hardware, whereas the research and development (R&D) department may employ a networked structure to capitalize on knowledge sharing. In the hierarchical IS department, information flows from top to bottom, whereas in the networked R&D department, all researchers may be connected to one another.

Further, IS are enabling even more advanced organization forms such as the adaptive organization, the zero time organization,[7] and the elastic enterprise.[8] Common to these advanced forms is the idea of agile, responsive organizations that can configure resources and people quickly. These organizations are flexible enough to sense and respond to changing demands. Elastic enterprises, for example, have a core competency of adding partners as necessary to quickly respond to customer needs. They do this by creating a platform and common interfaces to reduce the effort and friction of partnering. Building in the capability to respond instantly means designing the organization so that each of the key structural elements is able to respond instantly.

Informal Networks

The organization chart reflects the authority derived from formal reporting relationships in the organization's formal structure. However, informal relationships also exist and can play an important role in an organization's functioning. Informal networks, in addition to formal structures, are important for alignment with the organization's business strategy.

Sometimes, management designs some of the informal relationships or networks. For example, when working on a special project, an employee might be asked to let the manager in another department know what is going on. This is considered an informal reporting relationship. Or a company may have a job rotation program that provides employees with broad-based training by allowing them to work a short time in a variety of areas. Long after they have moved on to another job, employees on job rotations may keep in touch informally with former colleagues, or call upon their past co-workers when a situation arises that their input may be helpful. Hewlett Packard's Decision Support and Analytics Services unit encouraged the development of work-related informal networks when it established focused interest group/forums known as Domain Excellence Platforms (DEPs). An IT-enabled DEP allows at least five people who hold a common interest related to the business to form a team to share their knowledge on a topic (e.g., cloud computing, Web analytics). For nonbusiness related topics, the employees can join conferences to talk about the topic and get to know one another better. The hope is that they will start thinking beyond their work silos.[9]

However, not all informal relationships are a consequence of a plan by management. Some networks unintended by management develop for a variety of other factors including work proximity, friendship, shared interests, family ties, and so on. The employees can make friends with employees in another department when they play together on

[7] For more information on zero time organizations, see R. Yeh, K. Pearlson, and G. Kozmetsky, *ZeroTime: Providing Instant Customer Value Every Time, All the Time* (Hoboken, NJ: John Wiley, 2000).

[8] For more information on elastic enterprises, see N. Vitalari and H. Shaughnessy, *The Elastic Enterprise* (Longboat Key, FL: Telemachus Press, 2012).

[9] T. S. H. Teo, R. Nishant, M. Goh, and S. Agarwal, "Leveraging Collaborative Technologies to Build a Knowledge Sharing Culture at HP Analytics," *MIS Quarterly Executive* 10, no. 1 (March 2011), 1–18.

Social Business Lens: Social Networks

Social networks are a form of informal networks. They even have begun to supplement and possibly replace organization charts in enterprises. A **social network** is an IT-enabled network that links individuals together in ways that enable them to find experts, get to know colleagues, and see who has relevant experience for projects across traditional organization lines. Much like the networked organization, a social network provides an IT backbone linking all individuals in the enterprise, regardless of their formal title or position. Some might regard a social network as a "super-directory" that provides not only the names of the individuals but also their role in the company, their title, their contact information, and their location. It might even list details such as their supervisor (and their direct reports and peers), the project(s) they are currently working on, and personal information specific to the enterprise.

What differentiates a social network from previous IT solutions to connect individuals is that it is integrated with the work processes themselves. Conversations can take place, work activities can be recorded, and information repositories can be linked or merely represented within the structure of the social network.

IBM has a good example of how a social network permeates an organization, changing its culture, structure, and collaboration processes. With over 400,000 employees, the company has a flurry of social activity embodied in more than 17,000 individual blogs, 1 million daily page views of internal wikis and Web sites, and 400,000 employee profiles on IBM Connections. Its social network allows employees to share status updates, collaborate on internal systems, and share files. There have been 15 million downloads of employee-generated videos and podcasts so far.

Source: http://www.forbes.com/sites/haydnshaughnessy/2011/12/09/is-social-business-the-same-as-social-media/ (accessed April 5, 2012).

the company softball team, share the same lunch period in the company cafeteria, or see one another at social gatherings. Informal networks can also arise for political reasons. Employees can cross over departmental, functional, or divisional lines in an effort to create political coalitions to further their goals. Some informal networks even cross organizational boundaries. As computer and information technologies facilitate collaboration across distances, social networks and virtual communities are formed. Many of these prove useful in getting a job done, even if not all of the members of the network belong to the same organization. LinkedIn is an example of a tool that enables large, global informal networks.

Information Systems and Management Control Systems

Controls are the second type of managerial lever. Not only does IS change the way organizations are structured, but also it profoundly affects the way managers control their organizations. Management control is concerned with how planning is performed in organizations and how people and processes are monitored, evaluated, and compensated or rewarded. Ultimately, it means that senior leaders make sure the things that are supposed to happen actually happen.

Management control systems are similar to room thermostats. Thermostats register the desired temperature. A sensing device within the thermostat determines whether the temperature in the room is within a specified range of the one desired. If the temperature is beyond the desired range, a mechanism is activated to adjust the temperature. For instance, if the thermostat is set at 70 degrees and the temperature in the room is 69, then the heater can be activated (if it is winter) or the air conditioning can be turned off (if it is summer). Similarly, management control systems must respond to the goals established through planning. Measurements are taken periodically and if the variance is too great, adjustments are made to organizational processes or practices. For example, operating processes might need to be changed to achieve the desired goals.

IS offer new opportunities for collecting and organizing data for three management control processes:

1. *Data collection:* IS enable the collection of information that helps managers determine whether they are satisfactorily progressing toward realizing the organization's mission as reflected in its stated goals.

2. *Evaluation:* IS facilitate the comparison of actual performance with the desired performance that is established as a result of planning.

3. *Communication:* IS speed the flow of information from where it is generated to where it is needed. This allows an analysis of the situation and a determination about what can be done to correct for problematic situations.

When managers need to control work, IS can play a crucial role. IS provide decision models for scenario planning and evaluation. For example, the airlines routinely use decision models to study the effects of changing routes or schedules. IS collect and analyze information from automated processes, and they can make automatic adjustments to the processes. For example, a paper mill uses IS to monitor the mixing of ingredients in a batch of paper and to add more ingredients or change the temperature of the boiler as necessary. IS collect, evaluate, and communicate information, leaving managers with time to make more strategic decisions.

Planning and Information Systems

In the first chapter, the importance of aligning organizational strategy with the business strategy was discussed. An output of the strategizing process is a plan to guide in achieving the strategic objectives. IS can play a role in planning in four ways:

- IS can provide the necessary data to develop the strategic plan. They can be especially useful in collecting data from organizational units and integrating the data to transform those data into information for the strategic decision makers.
- IS can provide scenario and sensitivity analysis through simulation and data analysis.
- IS can be a major component of the planning process.
- In some instances, an information system is a major component of a strategic plan. That is, as discussed in Chapters 1 and 2, information systems can be used to gain strategic advantage.

Data and Information Systems

In addition to focusing on organizational-level planning and control, managers use information systems to build controls for individuals. An important part of management control lies in making sure that individuals perform appropriately. At the individual level, IS can streamline the process of data collection (usually through monitoring and analytical processes that use the collected data, as Chapter 4 discusses) and support performance measurement and evaluation as well as compensation through salaries, incentives, and rewards.

Monitoring work can take on a completely new meaning with the use of information technologies. IS make it possible to collect such data as the number of keystrokes, the precise time spent on a task, exactly who was contacted, and the specific data that passed through the process. The data collected from operations creates large data stores that can be analyzed for trends. For example, a call center that handles customer service telephone calls is typically monitored by an information system that collects data on the number of calls each representative received and the length of time each representative took to answer each call and then to respond to the question or request for service. Managers at call centers can easily and nonintrusively collect data on virtually any part of the process. The organizational design challenge in data collection is twofold: (1) to embed monitoring tasks within everyday work and (2) to reduce the negative impacts to employees being monitored. Workers perceive their regular tasks as value adding but have difficulty in seeing how value is added by tasks designed to provide information for management control. Research has found that monitoring does not always increase stress of the employee, especially when it fits the task and is automatic and nonintrusive.[10] But employees often avoid activities aimed at monitoring their work

[10] D. Galletta and R. Grant, "Silicon Supervisors and Stress: Merging New Evidence from the Field," *Accounting, Management and Information Technology* 5, no. 3 (1995), 163–83.

or worse, find ways to ensure that data recorded are inaccurate, falsified, or untimely. Collecting monitoring data directly from work tasks—or embedding the creation and storage of performance information into software used to perform work—renders the data more reliable.

A large number of software products are available for companies to monitor employees. Software monitoring products are installed by companies to get specific data about what employees are doing. This information can help ensure that work is being performed correctly. It can also be used to avoid barriers to employee productivity from "cyberslacking" and "cyberslouching."[11] The intention may seem both ethical and in the best interest of business, but in practice, the reverse may actually be true. In many cases, employees are not informed that they are being monitored or that the information gleaned is being used to measure their productivity. In these cases, monitoring violates both privacy and personal freedoms. Managers need to take into account employee privacy rights and try to balance their right to privacy against the needs of the business to have surveillance mechanisms in place.

Performance Measurement, Evaluation, and Information Systems

IS make it possible to evaluate actual performance data against reams of standard and historical data, often by using models and simulations. Analytics and big data tools have changed the way many companies use data to make decisions. Managers can more easily and completely understand work progress and performance. In fact, the ready availability of so much information catches some managers in "analysis paralysis": analyzing too much or too long. In our example of the call center, a manager can compare an employee's output to that of colleagues, to earlier output, and to historical outputs reflecting similar work conditions at other times. Even though evaluation constitutes an important use of IS, how the information is used has significant organizational consequences. Information collected for evaluation may be used to provide feedback so that the employee can improve personal performance; it also can be used to determine rewards and compensation. The former use—for improvement in performance—is nonthreatening and generally welcomed.

Using the same information for determining compensation or rewards, however, can be threatening. Suppose a call center manager is evaluating the number and duration of calls that service representatives answer on a given day. The manager's goal is to make sure all calls are answered quickly, and he communicates that goal to his staff. Now think about how the evaluation information is used.

If the manager simply provides the employees with information, then the evaluation is not threatening. If handled this way, employees might respond by improving their call numbers and duration. A discussion may even occur in which the service representative highlights other important considerations, such as customer satisfaction and quality. Perhaps the representative takes longer than average on each call because she believes that the attention devoted to the customer would result in higher customer satisfaction.

On the other hand, some managers use the same information to rank employees so that top-ranked employees are rewarded and those lower ranked are, in some way, punished or reprimanded. This may cause employees to feel threatened and respond accordingly. The representative who is not on the top of the list might shorten calls or deliver less quality, consequently decreasing customer satisfaction, while increasing the values of the metrics that are measured. The lesson for managers is to pay attention to what is monitored and how the information is used. Metrics for performance must be meaningful in terms of the organization's broader goals, and measured, managed, and communicated appropriately.

How feedback is communicated in the organization plays a role in affecting behavior. Some feedback can be communicated via IS themselves. A simple example is the feedback built into an electronic form that will not allow it to be submitted until it is properly filled out. For more complex feedback, IS may not be the appropriate vehicle. For example, no one would want to be told she or he was doing a poor job via e-mail or voice mail. Negative feedback of significant consequence often is best delivered in person.

IS can allow for feedback from a variety of participants who otherwise could not be involved. Many companies provide "360-degree" feedback in which the individual's supervisors, subordinates, and co-workers all provide

[11] Bernd Carsten Stahl, "The Impact of the UK Human Rights Act 1998 on Privacy Protection in the Workplace," *Computer Security, Privacy and Politics: Current Issues, Challenges and Solutions* (Hershey, PA: Idea Group Publishing, 2008), 55–68.

formal input. Social tools are making inroads in evaluation, too. For example, a "thumbs up" or "1–5 stars" evaluation system makes it easy and fast to provide informal feedback and evaluate activities. Because that feedback is received more quickly, improvements can be made faster.

Incentives and Rewards and Information Systems

Incentives and rewards are the ways organizations encourage good performance. A clever reward system can make employees feel good without paying them more money. IS can affect these processes, too. Some organizations use their Web sites to recognize high performers, giving them electronic badges that are displayed on the social network to identify them as award recipients. Others reward them with new technology. At one organization, top performers get new computers every year, while lower performers get the "hand-me-downs."

IS make it easier to design complex incentive systems, such as shared or team-based incentives. IS make it easier to keep track of contributions of team members and, in conjunction with qualitative inputs, allocate rewards according to complex formulas. For example, in a call center, agents can be motivated to perform better by providing rewards based on tracking metrics, such as average time per call, number of calls answered, and customer satisfaction. Information systems can provide measures of all of these on a real-time basis—even customer satisfaction through automated audio or Web site questionnaires after a customer interaction.

When specifying reward metrics, managers must be careful because they tend to drive the behavior they specify. For example, call center agents who know they will be evaluated only by the volume of calls they process may rush callers and provide poorer service in order to maximize their performance according to the narrow metric. Those measured only by customer satisfaction might spend more time than necessary on each call and perhaps try endlessly to solve problems that should be routed to more technical personnel.

Information Systems and Culture

The third managerial lever of organizational strategy is culture. Culture plays an increasingly important role in information system management and use. Because information systems management and use are complicated by human factors, it is important to consider culture's impact. **Culture** is defined as the set of "shared values and beliefs" that a group holds and that determines how the group perceives, thinks about, and appropriately reacts to its various environments.[12]

A "collective programming of the mind" distinguishes not only societies (or nations) but also industries, professions, and organizations.[13] **Beliefs** are the perceptions that people hold about how things are done in their community whereas **values** reflect the community's aspirations about the way things should be done. Culture is something of a moving target because it evolves over time as the group solves problems adapting to the environment and internal operations.

Culture has been compared to an iceberg because, like an iceberg, only part of the culture is visible from the surface. In fact, it is necessary to look below the surface to understand the deep-rooted aspects of culture that are not visible. That is, culture may be thought of in terms of layers: observable artifacts, values, and assumptions. **Observable artifacts** are the most visible level. They include such physical manifestations as type of dress, symbols in art, acronyms, awards, myths and stories told about the group, rituals, and ceremonies. **Espoused values** are the explicitly stated preferred organizational values. Ideally, they should be consistent with the **enacted values**, which are the values and norms that are actually exhibited or displayed in employee behavior. For example, if an organization says that it believes in a good work–life balance for its employees but actually requires them to work 12-hour days and on weekends, the enacted values don't match with the espoused ones. The deepest layer of culture is the underlying assumption layer, or the fundamental part of every culture that helps discern what is real

[12] A. Kinicki, *Organizational Behavior: Core Concepts* (Boston, MA: McGraw-Hill Irwin, 2008), 183.

[13] G. J. Hofstede, *Culture's Consequences: Comparing Values, Behaviors, Institutions, and Organizations Across Nations*, 2nd ed. (Thousand Oaks, CA: Sage Publications, 2001).

and important to the group. **Assumptions** are unobservable because they reflect organizational values that have become taken for granted to such an extent that they guide organizational behavior without any group members thinking about them.[14]

Levels of Culture and IT

Culture can vary depending upon which group you are studying. Countries, organizations, and subgroups in organizations all have a culture. IS management and use can be impacted by culture at all these levels. IS can even play a role in promoting it. For instance, Cognizant used IT to implement "10/10/10," a program designed to keep its associates focused on innovation. On the tenth workday of each month at 10 A.M., everyone's computer screen is frozen, allowing the entire Cognizant workforce to spend 10 minutes thinking about and sharing innovative ideas.[15]

With the growth of analytics and the availability of large stores of data, many organizations are adopting a data-driven culture in which virtually all decisions are made with the support of analytics. In a data-driven culture, managers are typically expected to provide data to support their recommendations and to back up decisions. Information is often freely shared in this culture, and IS take on the important role of collecting, storing, analyzing, and delivering data and information to all levels of the organization. Dell, Procter and Gamble, GE, Google, and Facebook are examples of companies that are known to have a data-driven culture. Sometimes the employees in these companies are said to "speak the language of data" as part of their culture.

When IS developers have values that differ from the clients in the same organization for whom they are developing systems, cultures can clash. For example, clients may favor computer-based development practices that encourage reusability of components to enable flexibility and fast turnaround. Developers, on the other hand, may prefer a development approach that favors stability and control but tends to be slower. Both national and organizational cultures can affect IT management and usage and vice versa. National culture may affect IT in a variety of ways, impacting information systems development, technology adoption and diffusion, system use and outcomes, and management and strategy. These relationships are shown in Figure 3.5 and described next. The model and the discussion of the impact of culture on IT issues draws heavily from the work of Leidner and Kayworth.[16]

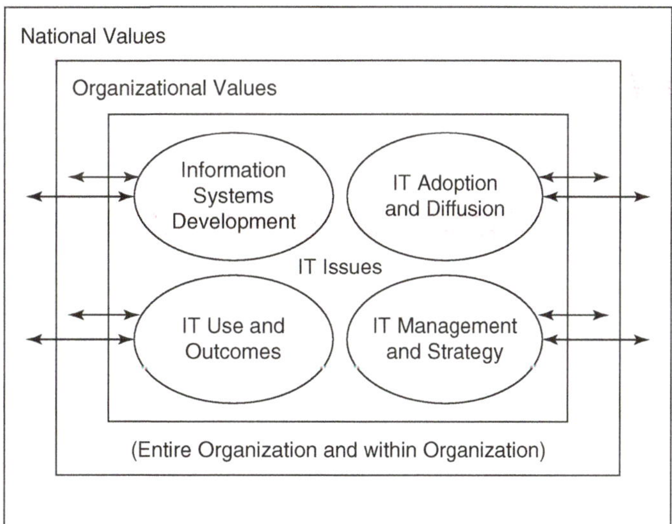

FIGURE 3.5 Levels of culture.
Source: Adapted from D. Leidner and T. Kayworth, "A Review of Culture in Information Systems Research: Toward a Theory of Information Technology Culture Conflict," *MIS Quarterly* 30, no. 2 (2006), 372, Figure 1.

[14] E. Schein, *Organizational Change and Leadership*, 4th ed. (San Francisco, CA: Jossey-Bass, 2010).
[15] Cognizant Computer Goods Technology, "Creating a Culture of Innovation," 1–6.
[16] D. Leidner and T. Kayworth, "A Review of Culture in Information Systems Research: Toward a Theory of Information Technology Culture Conflict," *MIS Quarterly* 30, no. 2 (2006), 357–99.

Culture and Information Systems Development

Variation across national cultures may lead to differing perceptions and approaches to IS development. In particular, systems designers may have different perceptions of the end users and how the systems would be used. For example, Danish designers who had more socialist values were more concerned about people-related issues when compared to Canadian designers with more capitalist values. The Canadian designers were more interested in technical issues. National culture may also affect the perceptions of project risk and risk management behaviors. At the organizational level, cultural values can affect the features of new software and the way it is implemented.

Culture and Information Technology Adoption and Diffusion

National cultures that are more willing to accept risk appear to be more likely to adopt new technologies. Those cultures that are less concerned about power differences among people (i.e., have low power distance) are more likely to adopt technologies that help promote equality. People are more likely to adopt a new technology if they think that the technology's embedded values match those of their national culture. Further, if a technology is to be successfully implemented into an organization, either the technology must fit with the organization's culture or the culture must be shaped to fit the behavioral requirements of the technology. For example, a dashboard that shares analytics and key performance indicators to all employees would reduce the "power" of leaders in a hierarchical organization in which only the senior managers have access to the data. In such organizations, implementation of such an information system would likely be very slow or rejected altogether because the culture would not support broad information sharing.

Culture and Information Technology Use and Outcomes

Research has shown that differences in culture result in differences in the use and outcomes of IT. At the organizational level, cultural values are often related to satisfied users, successful IS implementations or knowledge management successes. At the national level, e-mail adoption was much slower in Japan than in the United States. Japanese prefer richer forms of communication such as meeting face-to-face. The lean e-mail can't accommodate the symbols in their language as easily as a fax. Further, in countries that are more likely to avoid uncertainty like Japan and Brazil, IT is used often for planning and forecasting, whereas in countries that are less concerned about risk and uncertainty, IT is more often used for maintaining flexibility. Furthermore, some things are acceptable in one country but not another. For example, DitchWitch could not use its logo globally because a witch is offensive in some countries.

Culture and Information Technology Management and Strategy

National and organizational culture affects planning, governance, and perceptions of service quality. For example, having planning cultures at the top levels of an organization typically signal that strategic systems investment is important. At Adidas, a multinational sports apparel company headquartered in Germany, national culture played a role in its multisourcing strategy. Adidas' managers selected an Eastern European vendor because they were looking for a provider whose culture was similar to their own. They thought that vendor's employees were more likely to question system requirements and to make creative, innovative contributions than the Indian vendors they had hired.[17]

National Cultural Dimensions and Their Application

One of the best-known (and prolific) researchers in the area of differences in the values across national cultures is Geert Hofstede. Most studies about the impact of national cultures on IS have used Hofstede's dimensions of national culture. Hofstede[18] originally identified four major dimensions of national culture: power distance,

[17] Martin Wiener and Carol Saunders, "Forced Coopetition in IT Multi-Sourcing," *Journal of Strategic Information Systems* 23, no. 3 (2014), 210–25.
[18] G. Hofstede, *Culture's Consequences: International Differences in Work-Related Values* (London: Sage, 1980).

uncertainty avoidance, individualism-collectivism, and masculinity-femininity.[19] To correct for a possible bias toward Western values, a new dimension, Confucian work dynamism, also referred to "short-term vs. long-term orientation," was added.[20] Many others have used, built upon, or tried to correct problems related to Hofstede's four dimensions. One notable project is the Global Leadership and Organizational Behavior Effectiveness (GLOBE) research program, which is a team of 150 researchers who have collected data on cultural values and practices and leadership attributes from over 18,000 managers in 62 countries. The GLOBE project has uncovered nine cultural dimensions, six of which have their origins in Hofstede's pioneering work. The Hofstede dimensions and their relationship to the GLOBE dimensions are summarized in Figure 3.6.

Hofstede Dimensions (*Related GLOBE Dimensions*)	**Description**[a]	**Examples of Effect on IT**[b]
Uncertainty Avoidance (*Uncertainty Avoidance*)	Extent to which a society tolerates uncertainty and ambiguity; extent to which members of an organization or society strive to avoid uncertainty by reliance on social norms, rituals, and bureaucratic practices to alleviate the unpredictability of future events.	Countries with high uncertainty avoidance are less likely to adopt new IT and have higher perceptions of project risk than countries with low uncertainty avoidance.
Power Distance (*Power Distance*)	Degree to which members of an organization or society expect and agree that power should be equally shared.	Individuals from high power distance countries are found to be less innovative and less trusting of technology than individuals from low power distance countries.
Individualism/Collectivism (*Societal and In-Group Collectivism*)	Degree to which individuals are integrated into groups; extent to which organizational and societal institutional practices encourage and reward collective distribution of resources and collective action.	Individualistic cultures are more predisposed than collectivistic cultures to report bad news about troubled IT projects; companies in collectivist societies are more likely than individualistic societies to fill an IS position from within the company.
Masculinity/Femininity (*General Egalitarianism and Assertiveness*)	Degree to which emotional roles are distributed between the genders; extent to which an organization or society minimizes gender role differences and gender discrimination; often focuses on caring and assertive behaviors.	Australian groups (high masculinity) generated more conflict and relied less on conflict resolution strategies than Singaporean groups (low masculinity).
Confucian Work Dynamism (*Future Orientation*)	Extent to which society rewards behaviors related to long- or short-term orientations; degree to which individuals in organizations or societies engage in future-oriented behaviors such as planning, investing in the future, and delaying gratification.	When considering future orientation, studies found differences in the use of Executive Information Systems and the evaluation of service quality across countries.

[a] Adapted from R. House, M. Javidan, P. Hanges, and P. Dorfman, "Understanding Cultures and Implicit Leadership Theories across the Globe: An Introduction to Project GLOBE," *Journal of World Business* 37, no. 1 (2002), 3–10; and G. Hofstede and G. J. Hofstede, Dimensions of National Culture, http://www.geerthofstede.nl/dimensions-of-national-cultures.aspx (accessed August 20, 2015).
[b] Examples were provided in D. Leidner and T. Kayworth, "A Review of Culture in Information Systems Research: Toward a Theory of Information Technology Culture Conflict," *MIS Quarterly* 30, no. 2 (2006), 357–99.

FIGURE 3.6 National cultural dimensions.

[19] Ibid.
[20] G. Hofstede and M. H. Bond, "The Confucius Connection: From Cultural Roots to Economic Growth," *Organizational Dynamics* 16 (1988), 4021.

Geographic Lens: Does National Culture Affect Firm Investment in IS Training?

In a massive study of 6,000 firms in 21 countries, Hilla Peretz and Zehava Rosenblatt found that differences along Hofstede's cultural dimensions do affect employee training. In particular, firms in countries that embrace low power distance (i.e., Germanic countries, Anglo-American countries, the Netherlands, and Israel) tend to invest more in training than firms in countries with high power distance (i.e., some Asian, Latin America, and Middle Eastern countries).

Why might this be the case? Perhaps firms in high power distance societies view investment in training as less favorable because it might narrow the power gaps by making a higher level of skills available across all levels of the organization. Those in power might not want to see a leveling of power throughout the organization.

Peretz and Rosenblatt also discovered that firms in countries that had a strong orientation toward the future (i.e., some Asian countries) were more likely to invest in training than firms in countries with a shorter-term orientation (i.e., some Anglo-American countries). The researchers think this might be so because training is all about helping employees develop so that they can perform better in the future. Better-trained employees help the firm's competitive prospects down the line.

Finally, the researchers found that firms in countries with high uncertainty avoidance (i.e., some Hispanic cultures, Japan, South Korea, Israel, and Russia) spend more on training than countries with low uncertainty avoidance (i.e., the United Kingdom, Ireland, Hong Kong, and Singapore)—maybe because employee training may be seen as a way to reduce uncertainty.

Although the study was about training in general, the findings are even more likely to hold for IS training. Because IS change so quickly, IS professionals need considerable training to stay current and do their jobs well.

Source: H. Peretz and Z. Rosenblatt, "The Role of Societal Cultural Practices in Organizational Investment in Training: A Comparative Study in 21 Countries," *Journal of Cross-Cultural Psychology* 42, no. 5 (2011), 817–31.

Even though the world may be becoming "flatter," cultural differences have not totally disappeared. But some leadership traits, such as being trustworthy, just, and honest; having foresight and planning ahead; being positive, dynamic, encouraging, and motivational; and being communicative and informed are seen as universally acceptable across cultures.[21]

The generally accepted view is that the national culture predisposes citizens of a nation to act in a certain way along a Hofstede or GLOBE dimension, such as in an individualistic way in England or in a collectivist way in China. Yet, the extent of the influence of a national culture may vary among individuals, and culturally based idiosyncrasies may surface based upon the experiences that shape each person's ultimate orientation on a dimension. Having an understanding and appreciation for cultural values, practices, and subtleties can help in smoothing the challenges that occur in dealing with these idiosyncrasies. An awareness of the Hofstede or GLOBE dimensions may help to improve communications and reduce conflict.

Effective communication means listening, framing the message in a way that is understandable to the receiver, and responding to feedback. Effective cross-cultural communication involves each of these plus searching for an integrated solution that can be accepted and implemented by members of diverse cultures. This may not be as simple as it sounds. For instance, typical American managers, noted for their high-performance orientation, prefer direct and explicit language full of facts and figures. However, managers in lower performance-oriented countries like Russia or Greece tend to prefer indirect and vague language that encourages the exploration of ideas.[22] Communication differences surfaced when one of this book's authors was designing a database in Malaysia. She asked questions that required a "yes" or "no" response. In trying to reconcile the strange set of responses she received, the author learned that Malaysians are hesitant to ever say "no." Communication in meetings is also subject to cultural differences. In countries with high levels of uncertainty avoidance such as Switzerland and

[21] Mansour Javidan and R. J. House, "Cultural Acumen for the Global Manager," *Organizational Dynamics* 29, no. 4 (2001), 289–305.
[22] Ibid.

Austria, meetings should be planned in advance with a clear agenda. The managers in Greece or Russia who come from a low uncertainty avoidance culture often shy away from agendas or planned meetings.

Knowing that a society tends to score high or low on certain dimensions helps a manager anticipate how a person from that society might react. However, this provides only a starting point because each person is different. Importantly, without being aware of cultural differences, a company is unlikely to develop IS or to use it effectively.

SUMMARY

- Organizational strategy reflects the use of the managerial levers of an organization's design, organizational culture, and management control systems that coordinate and control work processes.
- Organizational designers today must have a working knowledge of what information systems can do and how the choice of information system will affect the organization itself.
- Organizational structures can facilitate or inhibit information flows.
- Organizational design should take into account decision rights, organizational structure, and informal networks.
- Structures such as flat, hierarchical, matrix and, networked organizations are being enhanced by information technology. Increasingly information technology enables and supports networked organizations that can better respond to dynamic, uncertain organizational environments.
- Information technology affects managerial control mechanisms: planning, data, performance measurement and evaluation, incentives and rewards.
- Management control at the individual level is concerned with monitoring (i.e., data collection), evaluating, providing feedback, compensating, and rewarding. It is the job of the manager to ensure that the proper control mechanisms are in place and the interactions between the organization and the information systems do not undermine the managerial objectives.
- Organizational and national culture should be taken into account when designing, managing, and using IS.

KEY TERMS

assumptions (p. 67)
beliefs (p. 66)
bureaucracy (p. 60)
culture (p. 66)
decision rights (p. 58)
enacted values (p. 66)
espoused values (p. 66)
flat organizational structure (p. 60)
hierarchical organizational structure (p. 60)
matrix organizational structure (p. 61)
networked organizational structure (p. 61)
observable artifacts (p. 66)
organizational strategy (p. 57)
social network (p. 63)
span of control (p. 60)
unity of command (p. 60)
values (p. 66)

DISCUSSION QUESTIONS

1. How might IS change a manager's job?
2. Is monitoring an employee's work on a computer a desirable or undesirable activity from a manager's perspective? From the employee's perspective? How does the organization's culture impact your position? Defend your position.
3. Consider the brief description of the elastic enterprise. What is an example of a control system that would be critical to manage for success in elastic enterprise? Why?
4. Mary Kay, Inc. sells facial skin care products and cosmetics around the globe. The business model is to provide one-on-one, highly personalized service. More than 500,000 Independent Beauty Consultants (IBCs) sell in 43 markets worldwide. Each IBC runs his or her own business by developing a client base and then providing services and products for sale to those clients. The IBCs were offered support through an e-commerce system with two major components: mymk.com and Mary

Kay InTouch. Mymk.com allows IBCs to create instant online sites where customers can shop anytime directly with their personal IBC. Mary Kay InTouch streamlines the ordering process by automatically calculating discounts, detecting promotion eligibility, allowing the IBCs to access up-to-date product catalogs, and providing a faster way to transact business with the company.[23]

a. How would the organizational strategy need to change to respond to Mary Kay's new business strategy and information system?

b. What changes would you suggest Mary Kay, Inc. managers make in their management systems in order to realize the intended benefits of the new systems? Specifically, what types of changes would you expect to make in the evaluation systems, the reward systems, and feedback systems?

CASE STUDY 3-1 The Merger of Airtran by Southwest Airlines: Will the Organizational Cultures Merge?[24]

Southwest Airlines' merger with AirTran Airlines, valued at over US$3 billion, made Southwest the largest domestic carrier based on number of passengers flown.[25] The merger increases Southwest's presence in a number of major cities, most notably New York (LaGuardia) and Washington D.C. (Ronald Reagan National Airport). Thanks to AirTran, Southwest now flies into the coveted Atlanta's Hartsfield-Jackson Atlanta International, the world's busiest airport, along with a number of international vacation destinations such as Aruba, Puerto Rico, and the Bahamas. In all, 21 new cities were added, 7 of which were in the international market, positioning Southwest to expand in Central and South America. The result was a significant increase in profitability for Southwest, growing from $178 million in 2011 to $1.1 billion in 2014.[26]

Southwest has grown organically, acquiring only two other smaller carriers—Morris Air and Muse Air—in the 1980s. This has made it easier to maintain its quirky identity. On the other hand, AirTran was created from several airlines, including the former ValuJet, about 15 years ago. It is known mostly as a low-cost, on-time carrier. The Company Culture page on AirTran's Web site prior to the merger claimed that "loyal crew members keep AirTran airways customers soaring" and who have a "timely and accommodating demeanor." AirTran's values included a total commitment to safety, technical excellence, continuous learning, fun, and profit.[27]

Southwest, headquartered at Love Field in Dallas, uses the ticker symbol LUV and uses all kinds of ways to show that "Luv" to their customers. Southwest has cultivated a corporate culture that focuses on employees and customers having a good time while flying. The company carefully selects its employees using interviews that involve creative activities and even asking the recruits to wear tutus. Southwest's training program with karaoke and amusing challenges is designed to socialize the new recruits into the airline's fun-loving culture. According to its Web site, its cultural values include "A Warrior Spirit, A Servant's Heart, A Fun-Luving Attitude."[28]

Wharton management professor Peter Cappelli commented just after the merger was announced in 2010 that "Southwest's whole business model is built on a particular approach to managing employees. It's a big bet they are making that they can swallow AirTran . . . . This is a very different approach, taking thousands of AirTran employees, dumping them into the system and hoping it works. It's a pretty risky move." Cappelli adds that airline mergers are always difficult because integration has to take place while a carrier continues to carry out complex operations. Thousands of employees can't easily be put through an orientation program in the merger's short time frame, and the information systems supporting the complex operations of two airlines can't be easily changed.[29]

---

[23] Adapted from "Mary Kay, Inc.," *Fortune* (Microsoft supplement, November 8, 1999).

[24] An earlier version of this case was written by Parul Acharya.

[25] "What Has AirTran Done for Southwest Airlines," *Forbes* (December 11, 2014), http://www.forbes.com/sites/greatspeculations/2014/12/11/what-has-airtran-done-for-southwest-airlines/ (accessed April 27, 2015).

[26] Charisse Jones, "Southwest Scores Record Profit—Again" *USA Today* (January 22, 2015), http://www.usatoday.com/story/money/2015/01/22/southwest-sees-record-profits-in-2014/22166225/ (accessed August 20, 2015).

[27] www.airtran.com (accessed April 2011).

[28] Southwest Airlines, http://www.southwest.com/html/about-southwest/careers/culture.html (accessed January 27, 2012).

[29] "By Acquiring AirTran, Will Southwest Continue to Spread the LUV?" Knowledge@Wharton (October 13, 2010), http://knowledge.wharton.upenn.edu/article.cfm?articleid=2614 (accessed August 20, 2015); and B. Snyder, "How the Southwest-AirTran Merger Creates a Labor Problem," *CBS Money* (October 5, 2010), http://www.cbsnews.com/8301-505123_162-43642550/how-the-southwest-airtran-merger-creates-a-labor-problem/ (accessed April 12, 2012).

In November 2011, Southwest Airlines' more than 6,000 pilots and AirTran Airways' 1,700 pilots overwhelmingly approved a plan to combine the seniority lists of the two carriers with five of six pilots voting in favor.[30] The personnel systems had to be modified to reflect the new seniority and pay systems.

The disparate cultures of Southwest and AirTran also posed problems for the merger of their online reservation systems and their frequent-flyer programs. Southwest switched from Sabre to Amadeus system to better accommodate merchandising and international flights. AirTran's reservations system vendor was Navitaire.[31] AirTran and Southwest had diametrically opposed views on distribution through online travel agencies. Southwest usually sold its tickets via telephone or through its Web site whereas AirTran preferred online reservation systems such as Orbitz and Expedia.[32] It took several years after to figure out how to blend the two different reservations systems. The Southwest frequent-flyer program was the last system to be updated to include the top customers of AirTran. In December 2014, the new merged airline was just finishing up the integration. Will the cultures of Southwest and AirTran come together? People are optimistic, but the real answer lies in the future.

Discussion Questions

1. Discuss the layers of culture that are evident in this case. Why do you think Southwest has preferred to grow organically over its history?
2. What are the similarities and dissimilarities between the cultures, values, and beliefs of Southwest and AirTran airlines? Where would you expect the differences to be most difficult to manage? Why?
3. What problems could arise due to the different perspectives of both airlines toward online reservation systems? What do you recommend the managers do to solve these problems?
4. What would you recommend managers to do ensure a smooth integration of the information systems given the culture differences?

■ CASE STUDY 3-2 The FBI

The Federal Bureau of Investigation of the U.S. government, the FBI, was forced to scrap its $170 million virtual case file (VCF) management system. Official reports blamed numerous delays, cost overruns, and incompatible software. But a deeper examination of the cause of this failure uncovered issues of control, culture, and incompatible organizational systems.

Among its many duties, the FBI is charged with the responsibility to fight crime and terrorism. To do so requires a large number of agents located within the United States and around the world. That means agents must be able to share information among themselves within the bureau and with other federal, state, and local law enforcement agencies. But sharing information has never been standard operating procedure for this agency. According to one source, "agents are accustomed to holding information close to their bulletproof vests and scorn the idea of sharing information." This turned out to be a real problem in an investigation of DarkMarket, an Internet forum that connected buyers and sellers so that they could exchange stolen information such as bank details and credit card numbers. When both the FBI and Secret Service agents were investigating each other as criminals, it took their British colleagues, who knew the secrets of both agencies, to avert a crisis.

Enter the FBI's efforts to modernize its infrastructure, codenamed "Trilogy." The efforts included providing agents with 30,000 desktop PCs, high-bandwidth networks to connect FBI locations around the world, and the VCF project to facilitate sharing of case information worldwide. The FBI Director explained to Congress that VCF would provide "an electronic means for agents to globally send field notes, documents, pieces of intelligence and other evidence so they could hopefully act faster on leads." It was designed to replace a paper-intensive process with an electronic, Web-based process. With such a reasonable goal, why didn't it work?

[30] T. Maxon, "Southwest Airlines, AirTran Pilots Overwhelming Approve Plan to Combine Seniority Lists," Aviationblog, *Dallas News* (November 7, 2011), http://aviationblog.dallasnews.com/archives/mergers-consolidation/ (accessed November 7, 2011); Snyder, "How the Southwest-AirTran Merger Creates a Labor Problem."

[31] D. Schall, "Distribution Questions Loom Following US Approval of Southwest-AirTran Merger," tnooz.com (April, 27, 2011), http://www.tnooz.com/2011/04/27/news/distribution-questions-loom-following-us-approval-of-southwest-airtran-merger/ (accessed April 12, 2012).

[32] J. Brancatelli, "The Fight Stuff: Why the Airlines Are Fighting Travel Sites," Portfolio.com (January 5, 2011), http://www.portfolio.com/business-travel/2011/01/05/why-legacy-airlines-are-warring-with-expedia-and-orbitz/ (accessed November 7, 2011).

The CIO of the FBI offered one explanation. He claimed that the FBI needed to change its culture. "If the Bureau is ever going to get the high-tech analysis and surveillance tools it needs to. . . fight terrorism, we must move from a decentralized amalgam of 56 field offices. . . to a seamlessly integrated global intelligence operation capable of sharing information and preventing crimes in real-time." He added that the Bureau personnel were also very distrustful of the technology, as well as others not only in other organizations but also within the FBI.

A former project manager at the FBI further explained, "They work under the idea that everything needs to be kept secret. But everything doesn't have to be kept secret. To do this right, you have to share information."

The VCF system has been shut down, but the CIO is working on a new approach. He is busy trying to win buy-in from agents in the field so that the next case management system will work. In addition, he is working to establish a portfolio management plan that will cover all of the FBI's IT projects, even those begun in decentralized offices. His team has been designing an enterprise architecture that will lay out standards for a bureauwide information system. The Director of the FBI has helped too. He reorganized the governance of IT, taking its budget control away from the districts and giving total IT budget authority to the CIO.

The FBI is building a new case management system called Sentinel in four phases. The first two phases have been deployed and, according to the Federal IT dashboard, the project is on schedule and on budget. The new system, according to the CIO, will include workflow, document management, record management, audit trails, access control, and single sign-on. It will provide enhanced information sharing, search, and analysis capabilities to FBI agents and facilitate information sharing with members of the law enforcement and intelligence communities. To manage the expectations of the agents, the CIO plans to communicate often and significantly increase the training program for the new system. The CIO commented, "We want to automate those things that are the most manually cumbersome for the agents so they can see that technology can actually enhance their productivity. That is how to change their attitudes."

The FBI also has a billion-dollar Next Generation Identification (NGI) system with 52 million searchable facial images and 100 million individual fingerprint records as well as millions of palm prints, DNA samples, and iris scans. NGI can scan mug shots for a match and pick out suspects from a crowd scanned by a security camera or in a photograph on the Internet. The information can be exchanged with 18,000 law enforcement agencies 24 hours a day, 365 days a year.[33] When combined with Sentinel, NGI will further enhance the effectiveness of the FBI's antiterror efforts.

Discussion Questions

1. What do you think were the real reasons why the VCF system failed?
2. What were the points of alignment and misalignment between the information systems strategy and the FBI organization?
3. What do you think of the CIO's final comment about how to change attitudes? Do you think it will work? Why or why not?
4. If you were the CIO, what would you do to help the FBI modernize and make better use of information technology?

Sources: Adapted from Allan Holmes, "Why the G-Men Aren't IT Men" *CIO* (June 15, 2005), 42–45; IT Dashboard, "FBI Sentinel," http://www.itdashboard.gov/investment?buscid=441; Marc Goodman, *Future Crimes* (Toronto, Canada: Random House, 2015).

[33] Federal Bureau of Investigation, "FBI Announces Full Operational Capability of the Next Generation Identification System" (September 15, 2014), https://www.fbi.gov/news/pressrel/press-releases/fbi-announces-full-operational-capability-of-the-next-generation-identification-system (accessed August 20, 2015).

Digital Systems and the Design of Work

chapter

4

New approaches to work such as workplace flexibility and remote work combined with newer collaboration and social technologies, mobile technologies, and cloud computing have drastically changed the way we work. This chapter explores the impact technology has on the nature and design of work. A Work Design Framework is used to explore how digital technology can be used effectively to support these changes and help make employees more effective. In particular, this chapter discusses technologies to support communication and collaboration, new types of work, new ways of doing traditional work, new challenges in managing employees, and issues in working remotely and on virtual teams. It concludes with a section on change management.

Consumer financial services powerhouse American Express viewed workplace flexibility as a strategic lever. Its award-winning BlueWork program was a good example of turning strategic intent into action. In addition to receiving the Chairman's Award for Innovation—Top Innovators Prize, the BlueWork program enabled increased employee productivity and more than $10 million in annual savings from reduced cost of office space.[1] BlueWork was Amex's term for arrangements for flexibility in workspace. Integrated into the company's human resource policies, the flexibility included staggered working hours, off-site work areas such as home/virtual office arrangements, shared office space, touch-down (laptop-focused, temporary) space, and telecommuting. The corporate focus is on results rather than on hours clocked in the office and face-to-face time. But BlueWork also supported the sustainability and corporate social responsibility objectives. According to the Amex Web site,

> Our sustainable facilities story is also woven into the fabric of our employees' daily routine. BlueWork, our flexible workplace program, allows American Express employees to better utilize company work space and work remotely. The installation of 63 telepresence studios in 46 office locations encourages virtual meetings, reduces the need for travel, and contributes positively to our carbon reduction target.[2]

Employees are assigned to a type of work arrangement based on their role. Hub employees require a fixed desk because they work in the office every day. Club employees can share time between the office and other locations because their roles involve both face-to-face and virtual meetings. Home employees work from home at least three days a week. Roam employees are on the road or at customer sites. Susan Chapman, SVP at American Express commented on the importance of

---

[1] Christopher Palafax, "American Express's New Design Team," *American Builders Quarterly* (April/May/June 2014), http://americanbuildersquarterly.com/2014/american-express/ (accessed August 25, 2015); http://www.employeralliance.sg/toolkit/toolkit/tk1_13_2a.html (accessed August 25, 2015); Monak Mitra, "Best Companies to Work for 2012," *The Economic Times*, http://articles.economictimes.indiatimes.com/2012-07-16/news/32698433_1_employee-benefits-jyoti-rai-american-express-india (accessed August 25, 2015); Jeanne Meister, "Flexible Workspaces: Employee Perk or Business Tool to Recruit Top Talent?" *Forbes* (April 1, 2013), http://www.forbes.com/sites/jeannemeister/2013/04/01/flexible-workspaces-another-workplace-perk-or-a-must-have-to-attract-top-talent/ (accessed August 25, 2015).

[2] American Express Corporate Social Responsibility Report, Quarter 3 2014 Update, http://about.americanexpress.com/csr/crr-2014-q3.aspx (accessed August 25, 2015).

technology's role in alternative work arrangements, "Technology drives workplace flexibility. . . . Technology has become a strategic competency that drives revenue growth. It's not just about enabling productivity."[3]

How has BlueWork impacted the staff? In addition to the productivity improvements and savings in office expense, overall employee satisfaction is up. American Express managers are happy with these arrangements too. They have found employees to be more engaged while working, more committed to the company, and better able to drive needed results.[4] American Express has clearly adopted one of the most accommodating approaches to work hours, but many employers allow their employees some flexibility in their work schedule. A third or more of IBM, Aetna, and AT&T employees have no official desks at the company. Communications giant Cisco, which has over 75,000 employees on six continents, uses technology-enabled flexible work practices such as telecommuting, remote work, and flex time.[5] Sun Microsystems Inc. calculates that it has saved over $400 million in real estate costs by allowing nearly half of its employees to work anywhere they want.[6] Even the U.S. Government has a flexible work program, Flexiwork, that enables eligible employees to do their job under alternative work arrangements such as work from home.[7]

The American Express example illustrates how the nature of work has changed—and information technology is supporting, if not propelling, the changes. In preindustrial societies, work was seamlessly interwoven into everyday life. Activities all revolved around nature's cyclical rhythms (i.e., the season, day, and night; the pangs of hunger) and the necessities of living. The Industrial Revolution changed this. With the practice of dividing time into measurable, homogeneous units for which they could be paid, people started to separate work from other spheres of life. Their workday was distinguished from family, community, and leisure time by punching a time clock or responding to the blast of a factory whistle. Work was also separated into space as well as time as people went to a particular place to work.[8]

Technology and new work arrangements have once again enabled an integration of work activities into everyday life. Technologies have made it possible for employees to do their work in their own homes, on the road, or at an alternative work space at times that accommodate home life and leisure activities.[9] Paradoxically, however, employees often want to create a sense of belonging within the space where they work. That is, they wish to create a sense of "place," which is a bounded domain in space that structures their experiences and interactions with objects that they use and other people that they meet in their work "place." People learn to identify with these "places," or locations in space, based on a personal sharing of experiences with others within the space. Over time, visitors to the place associate it with a set of appropriate behaviors.[10] Increasingly "places" are being constructed in space with Web tools that encourage collaboration, allowing people to easily communicate on an ongoing basis, once again changing the nature of where work is done.

The Information Systems Strategy Triangle, discussed in Chapter 1, suggests that changing information systems (IS) results in altered organizational characteristics. Significant changes in IS and the work environments in which they function are bound to coincide with significant changes in the way that companies are structured and how people experience work in their daily lives. Chapter 3 explores how information technology (IT) influences organizational design. This chapter moves the focus to the way IT is changing the nature of work, the rise of new work environments, and IT's impact on different types of employees, where and when they do their work, and how they collaborate. This chapter looks at how IT enables and facilitates a shift toward collaborative and virtual work. The terms *IS* and *IT* are used interchangeably in this chapter, and only basic details are provided on technologies used. The point of this chapter is to look at the impact of IT on the way work is done by individuals and teams. This chapter should help managers understand the challenges in designing technology-intensive work and develop a sense of how to address these challenges and overcome resistance to IT in our rapidly changing world.

---

[3] Gensler, Dialog 22, http://www.gensler.com/uploads/documents/Dialogue-22.pdf (accessed August 25, 2015).

[4] http://www.forbes.com/sites/jeannemeister/2013/04/01/flexible-workspaces-another-workplace-perk-or-a-must-have-to-attract-top-talent/.

[5] http://csr.cisco.com/casestudy/flexible-work (accessed May 30, 2015).

[6] "Smashing the Clock," *Bloomberg News* (December 10, 2006), http://www.bloomberg.com/bw/stories/2006-12-10/smashing-the-clock (accessed May 29, 2015).

[7] The IRS is one example of these U.S. government programs. For more information, see http://www.irs.gov/irm/part6/irm_06-800-002.html (accessed May 29, 2015).

[8] S. Barley and G. Kunda, "Bringing Work Back In," *Organizational Science* 12, no. 1 (2001), 76–95.

[9] S. Harrison and P. Dourish, "Re-Place-ing Space: The Roles of Place and Space in Collaborative Systems," Proceedings of the 1996 ACM Conference on Computer Supported Cooperative Work (1996), 67–76.

[10] C. Saunders, A. F. Rutkowski, M. Genuchten, D. Vogel, and J. M. Orrega, "Virtual Space and Place: Theory and Test," *MIS Quarterly* 35, no. 4 (2011), 1079–98.

Work Design Framework

As the place and time of work becomes less distinguishable from other aspects of people's lives, the concept of "jobs" is changing and being replaced by the concept of work. Prior to the Industrial Revolution, a job meant a discrete task of a short duration with a clear beginning and end.[11] By the mid-20th century, the concept of job had evolved into an ongoing, often unending stream of meaningful activities that allowed the worker to fulfill a distinct role. More recently, organizations are moving away from organization structures built around particular jobs to a setting in which a person's work is defined in terms of what needs to be done.[12] In many organizations, it is no longer appropriate for people to establish their turfs and narrowly define their jobs to address only specific functions. Yet, as jobs "disappear," IT can enable employees to better perform their roles in tomorrow's workplace; that is, IT can help employees function and collaborate in accomplishing work that more broadly encompasses all the tasks that need to be done.

In this chapter, a simple framework is used to assess how emerging technologies may affect work. As is suggested by the Information Systems Strategy Triangle (in Chapter 1), this framework links the organizational strategy with IS decisions. This framework is useful in designing characteristics of work by asking key questions and helping identify where IS can affect how the work is done.

Consider the following questions:

- *What work will be performed?* Understanding what tasks are needed to complete the process being done by the employee requires an assessment of specific desired outcomes, inputs, and transformation needed to turn inputs into outcomes. Many types of work are based upon recurring operations such as those found in manufacturing plants or service industries. The value chain helps in understanding the workflow for key tasks that are performed (i.e., purchasing, materials handling, manufacturing, customer service, repair). Increasingly, much work is done at a keyboard and involves managing knowledge, information, or data. Each type of work has a unique set of characteristics and tasks that needs to be supported by information technology.
- *Who is going to do the work?* Sometimes the work can be automated. However, if a person is going to do the work, who should that person be? What skills are needed? From what part of the organization should that person come? If a team is going to do the work, many of these same questions need to be asked. However, they are asked within the context of the team: Who should be on the team? What skills do the team members need? What parts of the organization need to be represented by the team? Will the team members be dispersed?
- *Where will the work be performed?* With the increasing availability of networks, Web tools, apps, mobile devices, cloud-based computing, and the Internet in general, managers can now design work for employees who come to the office or who work remotely. Does the work need to be performed locally at a company office? Can it be done remotely at home? On the road?
- *When will the work be performed?* Traditionally, work was done during "normal business hours," which meant 9 A.M. to 5 P.M. In many parts of the world, a job between the hours of 9 and 5 is an anomaly. Technologies also make it easier to work whenever necessary. The reality of modern technologies is that they often tether employees to a schedule of 24 hours a day, seven days a week (24/7) when they are always accessible to calls or other communications through their mobile devices.
- *How can the acceptance of IT-induced change be increased?* In this text, the overarching questions are how to leverage IT to help improve work and how to keep IT from inhibiting work. Sometimes this means automating certain tasks. For example, computers are much better at keeping track of inventory, calculating compensation, and many other repetitious tasks that are opportunities for human error. On the other hand, technologies provide increasing support for tasks at which humans excel, such as decision making, communication, and collaboration tasks among employees. Using a structured change management approach to manage IT-induced change will increase the probability of success.

[11] William Bridges, *JobShift: How to Prosper in a Workplace without Jobs* (New York: Addison-Wesley, 1995).

[12] Ibid.

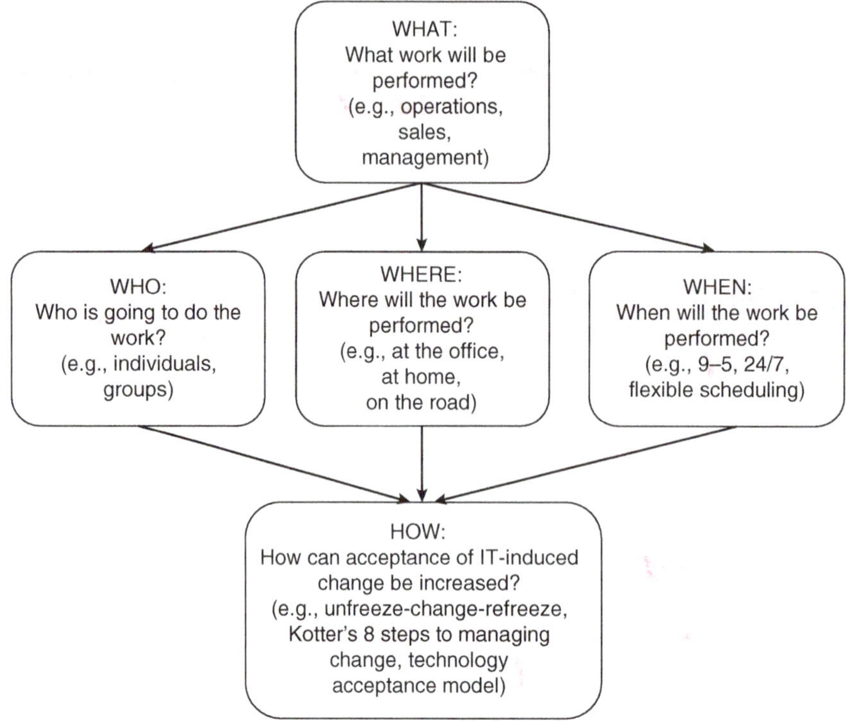

FIGURE 4.1 Framework for work design.

Figure 4.1 shows how these questions can be used in a framework to incorporate technologies into the design of work. Although it is outside the scope of this chapter to discuss the current research on either work or job design, you are encouraged to read these rich literatures.

How Information Technology Changes the Nature of Work

Advances in IT provide an expanding set of tools that make individual employees more productive and broaden their capabilities. They transform the way work is performed—and the nature of the work itself. This section examines three ways in which new IT alters employee life: by creating new types of work, by enabling new ways to do traditional work, and by supporting new ways to manage people.

Creating New Types of Work

IT often leads to the creation of new jobs or redefines existing ones. The high-tech field has emerged in its entirety over the past 60 years and has created a wide range of positions in the IT sector, such as programmers, analysts, managers, hardware assemblers, Web site designers, software sales personnel, social media specialists, and consultants. A study based on the Bureau of Labor statistics places the number of IT employees in the United States at an all-time high of 4.9 million.[13] Even within traditional non-IT organizations, the growing reliance on IS creates new types of jobs, such as data scientists who mine for insights in the company's data, community managers who manage the firm's online communities, and communications managers who manage the use of communication technologies for the business. IS departments also employ individuals who help create and manage the technologies, such

[13] TechServe Alliance, "IT Employment Grows Modestly in April," http://www.techservealliance.org/pressroom/documents/Press_Release_May2015_MBR.pdf (accessed May 30, 2015).

as systems analysts, database administrators, network administrators, and network security advisors. The Internet has given rise to many other types of jobs, such as Web masters and site designers. Virtually every department in every business has someone who "knows the information systems" as part of her or his job.

New Ways to Do Traditional Work

Changing the Way Work Is Done

IT has changed the way work is done. Many traditional jobs are now done by computers. For example, computers can check spelling in documents, whereas traditionally that was the job of an editor or writer. Jobs once done by art and skill are often greatly changed by the introduction of IT. Workers at one time needed an understanding of not only what to do but also how to do it; now their main task often is to make sure the computer is working because the computer does the task for them. Sadly, many cashiers no longer seem to be able to add, subtract, or take discounts because they have grown up letting the computer in their point-of-sale (POS) terminal do the calculations for them. Workers once were familiar with others in their organization because they passed work to them; now they may never know those co-employees because the IT routes the work. In sum, the introduction of IT into an organization can greatly change the day-to-day tasks performed by its employees.

In her landmark research, Shoshana Zuboff describes a paper mill in which papermakers' jobs were radically changed with the introduction of computers.[14] The papermakers mixed big vats of paper and knew when the paper was ready by the smell, consistency, and other subjective attributes of the mixture. For example, one employee could judge the amount of chlorine in the mixture by sniffing and squeezing the pulp. They were masters at their craft, but they were not able to explicitly describe to anyone else exactly what was done to make paper. An apprenticeship was needed to train new generations of masters, and the process of learning how to smell and squeeze the paper pulp was arduous. The company, in an effort to increase productivity in the papermaking process, installed an information and control system. Instead of the employees looking at and personally testing the vats of paper, the system continuously tested parameters and displayed the results on a panel located in the control room. The papermakers sat in the control room, reading the numbers, and making decisions on how to make the paper. Many found it much more difficult, if not impossible, to make the same quality paper when watching the control panel instead of personally testing, smelling, and looking at the vats. The introduction of the information system resulted in the need for different skills to make paper. Abstracting the entire process and displaying the results on electronic readouts required skills to interpret the measurements, conditions, and data generated by the new computer system.

In another example, sales and delivery people at a snack company have portable devices that not only keep track of inventory but also help them in the selling function. Prior to the information system, the salespeople used manual processes to keep track of inventory in their trucks. When visiting customers, it was possible only to tell them what was missing from their shelves and to replenish any stock they wanted. With IT, the salespeople have become more like marketing and sales consultants, helping the customers with models and data of previous sales, floor layouts, and replenishment as well as forecasting demand based on analysis of the data histories stored in the IS. The salespeople need to do more than be persuasive. They now must also do data analysis and floor plan design in addition to using the computer. Thus, the skills needed by the salespeople as well as the workflow, have greatly changed with the introduction of IT.

One of the biggest changes in workflow has been in the area of data entry. In the past, the workflow included capturing the data, keying it into the system, rekeying it to check its accuracy, and then processing it. The workflow has now changed to capture the data directly when it is entered by the user in a variety of ways such as from the Web, with a GPS signal, or by reading the RFID code. A program may check its accuracy when it is captured and then process it. Companies are moving way from entering sales data at all; customers enter it for them when they place an order. As data entry tasks are eliminated, the steps in the workflow are drastically reduced, and the process is much faster.

---

[14] Shoshana Zuboff, *In the Age of the Smart Machine: The Future of Work and Power* (New York: Basic Books, 1988), 211.

A study by Frey and Osborn examined 702 occupations and noted that 47% of total U.S. employment is at high risk of being automated in the next few years. Least likely to be automated are those jobs with nonroutine tasks involving complex perception and manipulation as well as creative and social intelligence.[15] Even knowledge employees, who once felt safe in their jobs because of the high degree of analysis and diagnosis they performed, are at risk of automation as analytics and cognitive intelligence systems become increasingly more accurate in their predictions and diagnoses.

The Internet enables changes in many types of work. For example, within minutes, financial analysts can download an annual report from a corporate Web site to their smartphones and check what others have said about the company's growth prospects on social networks. Librarians can check the holdings of other libraries online and request that particular volumes be routed to their own clients or download the articles from a growing number of databases. Marketing professionals can pretest the reactions of consumers to potential products in virtual worlds. Technical support agents diagnose and resolve problems on remote client computers using the Internet. The cost and time required to access information has plummeted, increasing personal productivity and giving employees new tools. It is hard to imagine a job today that doesn't have a significant information systems component.

For those tasks that must be done by people, companies can use information technology to find willing employees at what may seem like bargain rates. Amazon's Mechanical Turk has created a marketplace site on which an organization can post tasks at specified rates. Willing employees can use this site to find those tasks. For example, a company posted that it wanted employees to enter data from photos of cash register receipts. Another company posted a task offer of transcribing a 25-second audiotape. Many of these task offers involve very small amounts, often $.05 to $.25. Some tasks take a significant portion of an hour and pay up to $5 or more. Some of the employees do very brief tasks at low pay so they can gain higher status and qualify for higher-paying tasks. Although this isn't automating a task inside an organization, from the manager's perspective, it's another way to use IT to change the work done by the employees of the organization.

Changing Communication Patterns

All one has to do is observe people walking down a busy downtown street or a college campus to note changes in communication patterns over a period as short as the last decade. Some people are talking on their cell phones, but even more are texting or using apps for all kinds of reasons, such as checking out game scores, specials at nearby restaurants, or movie times. Or observe what happens when a plane lands. It seems that over half the people on the plane whip out their portable devices or cell phones as soon as the plane touches down. They are busy making arrangements to meet the people who are picking them up at the airport or checking to see the calls or e-mails they missed while in flight. Finally, consider meeting a friend at a busy subway station in Hong Kong. It is virtually impossible without the aid of a cell phone to locate each other. Some may say that we are addicted to our mobile technologies, unable to put them away even when driving or walking, unfortunately sometimes leading to dangerous behaviors.

Applications (Apps) such as iMessage, Skype, Twitter, and Sina Weibo (Chinese Twitter) have changed how people communicate. Traditionally, people found each other in person to have a conversation in the moment. With the telephone, people called each other and both parties had to participate at the same time to have a conversation. Along came e-mail, which rapidly became the communication technology of choice because it eliminated the need for those involved in the conversation to participate at the same time. Today, people have an array of communications technologies, and, once again, IT is changing communication patterns. Some rely on texting, others on video conferences, such as Facetime or Skype, and still others on social networks such as Facebook or Renren, for their primary communications channel. The challenge created by the large number of choices is that individuals now must have a presence on numerous platforms to ensure that they can be contacted. Further, one must know how not only to contact someone but also to recognize that the person's preferred medium might change during the day, week, or month. For example, during normal business hours, an employee might prefer to receive e-mail or a phone call. But after hours, he or she might prefer a text, and late at night, while surfing the Web, may prefer a message on

[15] C. B. Frey and M. Osborn, "The Future of Employment: How Susceptible Are Jobs to Computerisation?" (September 17, 2013), http://www.oxfordmartin.ox.ac.uk/downloads/academic/The_Future_of_Employment.pdf (accessed August 25, 2015).

Facebook Messenger or Skype. Without knowledge of the recipients' preferences for how to receive the message, the sender is likely to be unsuccessful in communicating with the recipients over the proper channel. A sender who doesn't know which medium the recipient prefers might use one medium (e.g., e-mail) to see whether the recipient is open to using another medium (e.g., phone).

Similarly, IT is changing the communication patterns of employees. There are still some employees who do not need to communicate with others for the bulk of their workday. For example, many truck drivers do not interact with others in their organization while driving to their destination. But there are other ways communication technologies have changed the work done by truck drivers. Consider the example of a Walmart driver who picks up goods dropped off by manufacturers at the Walmart distribution center and then delivers them in small batches to one or more Walmart stores. Walmart has provided its drivers with radios and satellite systems so that, on short notice, on their way back to the distribution center to load up for the next delivery, they can opportunistically pick up goods from manufacturers and take them to the distribution center. In this way, the company saves the delivery charges from that manufacturer and conserves energy in the process. Walmart office staff and drivers therefore use IT to save money by enhancing their communications with suppliers.[16]

Many changes in communication have been supported, if not propelled, by IT. Some communication technologies, such as social networking and microblogs, are rather new and unfamiliar, motivating managers in many organizations to understand how to apply them to work-related applications in a way that adds value to their business. These and other communication tools help make large companies feel smaller by bringing together employees from geographic disparate locations and from a variety of divisions and levels in the organization. Large companies can feel smaller because communications technology enables individuals to find each other despite the organization's size. These tools also help small companies feel like large companies because, to some degree, they level the playing field in the ways companies communicate and collaborate. Thomas Friedman, the author of the popular *The World Is Flat* and other books, argues that collaboration is the way that small companies can "act big" and flourish in today's flat world. The key to success is for such companies "to take advantage of all the new tools for collaboration to reach farther, faster, wider and deeper."[17] For example, any company can have a Facebook page or a Twitter feed, making it difficult to distinguish between small and large organizations simply by interacting over these technologies.

Changing Organizational Decision Making and Information Processing

IT changes not only organizational decision-making processes but also the information used in making those decisions. Data processed to create more accurate and timely information are being captured earlier in a process. Analytics (see Chapter 12) have made it possible to mine data stores and identify insights, make predictions, and even suggest decisions. Through information technologies, information that employees need to do their job can be pushed to them in real time or saved and made available when they need it.

IT can change the amount and type of information available to employees. For example, salespeople can use technology to get quick answers to customer questions. Further, IT-based tools allow salespeople to search for best practices on a marketing topic over a social network and to benefit from blogs and wikis written by informed employees in their company. Organizations now maintain large comprehensive business databases, called *data warehouses,* that can be mined by using tools to analyze patterns, trends, and relationships. We discuss data management in Chapter 12.

Modern devices with voice interfaces have assistants that further change decision-making processes. Apps such as Siri, Cortana, and Google-Now allow users to talk to their devices, often mobile ones, to access information from either their devices or the Internet. These types of interfaces are increasingly being built into enterprise systems to supplement ways employees gather information, increasing employee efficiency.

In their classic 1958 *Harvard Business Review* article, Leavitt and Whisler boldly predicted that IT would shrink the ranks of middle management by the 1980s.[18] Because of IT, top-level executives would have access

[16] Thomas L. Friedman, *The World is Flat* (New York: Farrar, Straus and Giroux, 2005), 145.

[17] Ibid.

[18] Harold Leavitt and Thomas Whisler, "Management in the 1980s," *Harvard Business Review* (November–December 1958), 41–48.

to information and decision-making tools and models that would allow them to easily assume tasks previously performed by middle managers. Other tasks clearly in the typical job description of middle managers at the time would become so routinized and programmed because of IT that lower-level managers could perform them. As Leavitt and Whisler predicted, the 1980s saw a shrinking in the ranks of middle managers. This trend was partly attributable to widespread corporate downsizing, which forced many organizations to find alternatives to getting the work done and IT solutions to proliferate to fill the gap. However, it was also attributable to changes in decision making induced by IT. Since the 1980s, IT has become an even more commonly employed tool of executive decision makers. IT has increased the flow of information to them and provided tools for filtering and analyzing the information.

Changing Collaboration

IT helps make work more team oriented and collaborative. Technologies such as texting (SMS), instant messaging (IM), Web logs (blogs), virtual worlds, groupware, wikis, social networking, and video teleconferencing are at the heart of collaboration today. Groups can form and share documents with less effort using these platforms. Group members can seek or provide information from or to each other much more easily than ever before. And groups can connect by voice or with voice and video using these platforms.

Collaboration takes place in one of four ways. Teams are collocated and work together at the same time, they are collocated but work at different times, they are not located in the same place but work at the same time, or they work from different places at different times. Figure 4.2 summarizes these options and lists representative technologies that facilitate collaboration for each type of team.

Consider the New York-based marketing firm CoActive Digital whose president decided to implement a wiki to have a common place where 25 to 30 people could go to share a variety of documents ranging from large files to meeting notes and PowerPoint presentations.[19] An added benefit was that the wiki was encrypted, protected, and could be used only with a virtual private network (VPN). The president recognized that the challenge for implementing the wiki would be to change a culture in which e-mail had long been the staple for communication. Consequently, he decided to work closely with the leader of the business development group. This group handles inquiries from customers and coordinates the work (i.e., marketing campaigns) internally. The group needed to hold many meetings and share much work. He populated the wiki site with the documents that had formerly been traded over e-mail and asked the leader to encourage her group members to use the wikis. It took some effort, but eventually the group learned to appreciate the benefits of the wiki for collaboration and to reduce members' dependence on e-mail.

Verifone's company culture is one that encourages information sharing. A story is told of a new salesperson who was trying to close a particularly big deal. He was about to get a customer signature on the contract when he was asked about the competition's system. Being new to the company, he did not have an answer, but he knew he could

	Team Works at the Same Time	**Team Works at Different Time**
Team Works in the Same Place	Face-to-face meetings	Electronic bulletin boards
	Meeting room technologies	Document sharing systems (wikis)
	Document sharing systems (wikis)	
Team Works in Different Places	Video conferencing	E-mail
	Chat rooms	Microblogs (e.g., Twitter)
	Texting (SMS) and instant messaging (IM)	Texting (SMS) and instant messaging (IM)
	Document sharing systems (wikis)	Document sharing systems (wikis)

FIGURE 4.2 Collaboration technologies matrix: Examples of key enabling technologies.
Source: Adapted from Geraldine DeSanctis and R. Brent Gallupe, "A Foundation for the Study of Group Decision Support Systems," *Management Science* 33, no. 5 (May 1987), 589–609.

[19] C. G. Lynch, "How a Marketing Firm Implemented an Enterprise Wiki," http://www.cio.com/article/print/413063 (accessed July 9, 2008).

count on the company's information network for help. He asked his customer for 24 hours to research the answer. He then sent an e-mail to everyone in the company asking the questions posed by the customer. The next morning, he had several responses from others around the company. He went to his client with the answers and closed the deal. What is interesting about this example is that others around the world treated the "new guy" as a colleague even though they did not know him personally. He was also able to collaborate with them instantaneously. It was standard procedure, not panic time, because of the culture of collaboration in this company. With increased use of social networks and other social tools, instantaneous collaboration is commonplace.[20]

The Internet has greatly enhanced collaboration. Beyond sharing and conversing, teams can also use the Web to create something together. An example of this is Wikipedia on which individuals who do not know each other contribute to the information on a topic. At computer company Dell, a Web-based site named IdeaStorm has been used since 2008 for idea generation, discussion, and prioritization between and among individuals in the Dell community, including staff, executives, customers, and potential customers. Recent statistics show that over 23,000 ideas have been submitted, over 747,000 votes for ideas have been recorded, and over 100,000 comments have been posted about the ideas suggested. Dell's management has implemented over 500 of the ideas. Ideas can range from small incremental improvements such as adding a port to an existing product to large sweeping changes such as creating a new product line. Some ideas, such as how to change the retail experience or support activities, are process oriented. Some ideas are about education, the environment, and other topics related to Dell's business. The company has since implemented an internal version of this system, Employee Storm, only open to internal staff. Employee Storm invites ideas on company benefits, innovations, ways to work better, and other company-focused issues. Many other companies have implemented similar platforms, including IBM's Think-Place, BestBuy's BlueShirt Nation, and ESPN's SportsNation.

Changing the Ways to Connect

Probably one of the biggest changes that people are experiencing as a result of new technologies is that they are always connected. In fact, many feel tethered to their mobile phones, tablets, or laptops to such a large extent that they must be available at all times so that they can respond to requests from their supervisors, colleagues, or customers. As a result, the boundaries between work and play have become blurred, now causing people to struggle even more with work–life balance.

Businesses are still trying to understand the technological advances that have become commonplace. Many in the workforce find that their technology at home differs from that at work and prefer those at home. For example, while although many use social media tools on their tablets, laptops, or smartphones during the weekend at home, on Monday morning, they find themselves working on an older desktop system with slow access to the files and Web-based systems they want to use for their work.[21] They find this quite bothersome. In fact, a Cisco Systems survey of young professionals and college students found that one in three believes the Internet is as important as air, water, food, and shelter. Two people in five say they would accept a lower-paying job that had more flexibility with regard to device choice, social media access, and mobility over a higher-paying job with less flexibility.[22] In commenting on the survey findings, Marie Hattar, vice president, Enterprise Marketing, Cisco, stated:

> The results of the Cisco Connected World Technology Report should make businesses re-examine how they need to evolve in order to attract talent and shape their business models. Without a doubt, our world is changing to be much more Internet-focused, and becomes even more so with each new generation.
>
> CIOs need to plan and scale their networks now to address the security and mobility demands that the next generation workforce will put on their infrastructure, and they need to do this in conjunction with a proper assessment of corporate policies.[23]

---

[20] Hossam Galal, Donna Stoddard, Richard Nolan, and Jon Kao, "VeriFone: The Transaction Automation Company," Harvard Business School Case Study 195–088, July 1994.

[21] Cognizant, "The Future of Work Has Arrived: Time to Re-Focus IT" (February 2011), 1–15, http://www.cognizant.com/SiteDocuments/CBC_FoW_Time_to_Refocus_IT.pdf (accessed August 25, 2015).

[22] Cisco Connected World Technology Report, 2011 Findings, http://www.cisco.com/en/US/netsol/ns1120/index.html#~2011 (accessed August 25, 2015).

[23] "Air, Food, Water, Internet—Cisco Study Reveals Just How Important Internet and Networks Have Become as Fundamental Resources in Daily Life," http://newsroom.cisco.com/press-release-content?type=webcontent&articleId=474852 (accessed August 25, 2015).

Social Business Lens: Activity Streams

An *activity stream* is a list of activities on a Web site that briefly highlight what the individuals connected to that stream are doing. Activity streams can include posts by individuals who share what they are doing or thinking and posts directly by other programs, which deposit an update about what an individual is doing. By collecting all of these posts in a single feed, the activity stream gives a reader a good sense of what is happening in a community.

Examples of activity streams are Facebook's news feed and Salesforce.com's Chatter. Companies that incorporate activity streams in their social business platform report that teams using that technology had fewer face-to-face meetings, reduced e-mail, faster information flows, better collaboration, and increased responsiveness. An activity stream can keep staff updated on the happenings around an organization. For example, SAS, the international statistics and analytics software company, implemented an activity stream for its employees. Staff were able to keep track of what others were working on over an activity stream that mimicked the news feed that Facebook users see on their home page. Staff could share, comment on, or "like" pages and documents they found in their systems or on the Web and those entries would show up in the activity stream.

Source: David F. Carr, "SAS Creates Internal Facebook with Socialcast" (April 29, 2011), http://www.informationweek.com/thebrainyard/news/social_networking_private_platforms/229402527/sas-institute-creates-internal-facebook-with-socialcast (accessed on April 5, 2012).

Consider IBM's SmallBlue—an opt-in social network analysis tool that maps the knowledge and the connections of IBM employees. SmallBlue can be used to find employees with specific knowledge or skills, display employee networks on particular topics, validate a person's expertise based on her or his corporate profile, and display a visualization of an employees' personal social networks. IBM claims that SmallBlue has promoted innovation, effectiveness, and efficiency.[24]

The preceding examples show how technologies have become a key component in the design of work. IT has greatly changed day-to-day tasks, which in turn has changed the skills needed by employees. The examples show how adding IT to a work environment can change the way that work is done.

New Ways to Manage People

New working arrangements create new challenges in how employees are supervised, evaluated, compensated, and even hired. When most work was performed individually in a central location, supervision and evaluation were relatively easy. A manager could directly observe the employee who spent much of his or her day in an office. It was fairly simple to determine whether or not the employee was present and productive.

Modern organizations often face the challenge of managing a workforce that is spread across the world in isolation from direct supervision and working mostly in teams. Sales work is one area in which we see this. Rather than working in a central office, external salespeople work remotely, relying on laptop computers, smart phones, the Web and apps linking them to customers, office colleagues, sales support information, and other databases. The technical complexity of some products, such as enterprise software, necessitates a team-based sales approach combining the expertise of many individuals, and technologies connect the team together.

Modern organizations must also choose among three types of formal controls to ensure that work is done properly.[25] **Behavior controls** involve direct monitoring and supervision of employee actions while the work is being done. Vivid depictions of behavior controls are provided in road construction projects that have one employee digging and another watching, motionless with arms folded. On the other hand, **outcome controls** involve examining work outcomes rather than work actions. Finally, **personnel controls** represent a proper fit between the person and the job, often involving picking the right person for the task.

[24] For additional information on SmallBlue, see http://www.watson.ibm.com/cambridge/Projects/project8.shtml (accessed May 31, 2015).

[25] L. J. Kirsch, "Portfolios of Control Modes and IS Project Management," *Information Systems Research* 8, no. 3 (1997), 215–239; W. G. Ouchi, "The Transmission of Control through Organizational Hierarchy," *Academy of Management Journal* 21, no. 2 (1978), 173–92; K. A. Merchant, *Modern Management Control Systems, Text and Cases* (Upper Saddle River, NJ: Prentice-Hall, 1998).

It is important for a firm to choose the right type of control for each position being supervised. Behavior controls make the most sense for physical labor in which incorrect particular body movements might be inefficient or even dangerous. Programmers would consider it quite insulting to have a supervisor exercise action control and watch every keystroke whereas transcriptionists might understand the need to track each keystroke. Outcome controls make more sense not only for programmers but also for many other personnel, such as engineers, sales managers, and ad writers. However, personnel controls are more useful when it would take several years to evaluate the results of work, which is often the case when goals are indefinable, conflicting, or confusing and the stakes are high. For instance, when Apple was having difficulty defining a meaningful product line in the mid-1990s, the firm resorted to personnel controls when it determined that the right way to redefine its mission was to bring back Steve Jobs. After two decades, hindsight shows that Jobs was the right choice. Personnel controls are useful for situations in which it is difficult not only *when* to expect results but also to define *what* results should even be expected.

When the results of work are fairly well defined, technology can change dramatically how it is monitored. One technological solution, electronic employee monitoring (introduced in Chapter 3), can replace direct supervision and provide detailed behavior controls, automatically logging keystrokes, listing the Web sites visited, or even recording the contents of an employee's screen. Technology can also provide outcome controls by tracking the number of calls processed, e-mail messages sent, or time spent surfing the Web. When output is monitored digitally, pay-for-performance compensation strategies reward employees for deliverables produced or targets met as opposed to vague subjective factors such as "attitude" or "teamwork." Further, supervisors can spend time coaching, motivating, and planning rather than personally monitoring performance because they can utilize the information gathered from electronic monitoring systems for that task. The introduction of BlueWork at American Express illustrates the need to change from an approach in which managers watch employees and count the hours they spend at their desks to one that focuses instead on the work they actually do. These changes are summarized in Figure 4.3.

IT has also impacted the way employees are hired, becoming an essential part of that process for many firms. Open positions are posted on job Web sites, and applicants submit resumes over the Web, complete applications on line, and refer potential employers to their personal Web sites. When researching candidates, companies often look at their Facebook pages and do online searches of the candidates to see what pops up. Social networking provides a forum for informal introductions and casual conversations in cyberspace. Interviews can be arranged in virtual worlds or via teleconferencing to reduce travel costs. A face-to-face interview is usually eventually required, but recruiters can significantly and more effectively filter the applicant pool, reducing the number of expensive site visits.

In addition, companies increasingly realize that hiring is changing and that recruiting efforts should reflect the new approaches people are using to look for jobs. Tech-savvy job applicants are now using business-oriented social networks such as LinkedIn to seek contacts for jobs and online job search engines like Monster.com and CareerBuilder.com to find job listings. A Facebook app, BeKnown, provides a profile detailing an individual's work experience, a news feed for contact updates and actions, a search tool to locate people and connect with them, and

	Traditional Approach: Subjective Observation	**Digital Approach: Objective Assessment**
Supervision	It is personal and informal. Manager is usually present or relies on others to ensure that the employee is present and productive.	It is electronic or assessed by deliverables. As long as the employee is producing value, he or she does not need direct formal supervision.
Evaluation	Behavior controls are predominant. Focus is on process through direct observation. Manager sees how employee performs at work. Subjective (personal) factors are very important.	Outcome controls are predominant. Focus is on output by deliverable (e.g., produce a report by a certain date) or by target (e.g., meet a sales quota). Fewer subjective measures are used.
Compensation and Rewards	It is often individually based.	It is often team based or contractually spelled out.
Hiring	Hiring is done through meetings with HR personnel with little concern for computer skills.	It is often electronic with recruiting Web sites and electronic testing for more information-based work that requires a higher level of IT skills.

FIGURE 4.3 Changes to supervision, evaluations, compensation, and hiring.

a way to recommend other users or display badges earned for completing certain professional goals. The app also is integrated with Monster.com's job listings.[26]

Furthermore, the way an organization uses IT affects the array of technical and nontechnical skills needed in its employees. For example many basic clerical tasks can be performed expeditiously with IT, so fewer employees with those basic skills are required, making room for those with more targeted skills. Just to be sure employees are IT savvy, too, the actual hiring process may require applicants to complete an assessment or perform other activities online. In this way, hiring managers can raise the overall IT competency exhibited by employees in their businesses. Employees who cannot keep pace with IT are increasingly unemployable.

The design of the work needed by an organization is a function of the skill mix required for its work processes and of the flow of those processes themselves. Thus, a company that infuses technology effectively and employs a workforce with a high level of IT skills designs itself differently from a company that does not. The skill mix required by an IT-savvy firm reflects a high capacity for using the technology itself. For example, because many clerical skills are now embedded in the technologies staff use, fewer clerical staff are needed and those who are hired by the company often do specialized work that is not easily automated or subsumed by technology.

As workforce demographics shift, so do the IT needs and opportunities to change work. Digital natives—people who have grown up using computers, social networking sites, texting, and the Web as a normal, integrated part of their daily lives—are finding new and innovative ways to do their work. There are widely varying impacts from the skills these employees bring to their work, including how to do their work in a new, and often more efficient, manner.

IT has drastically changed the landscape of work today. As a result of IT, many new jobs have been created. In the next section, we examine how IT can change where work is done, when it is done, and who does it.

Where Work Is Done and Who Does It: Mobile and Virtual Work Arrangements

This section examines another important effect of IT on work: the ability of some employees to work anywhere at any time. With WiFi virtually ubiquitous, individual employees can connect to the Web from almost anywhere. And with powerful technologies available in the consumer space, employees often find the tools and apps they have at home function as well as, or even better than, their workplace technologies. Research also suggests that employees—especially those younger employees who have never known a world without ubiquitous access to personal smart devices and the Web—prefer to have the work–life flexibility that remote and mobile work arrangements provide. At the group level, virtual teams have become standard operating mechanisms to bring the best individuals available to work together on a task. We explore remote work from the perspective of both individuals and teams in the next section.

Remote Work and Virtual Teams

Flexible work arrangements, although not the norm for many organizations, have been gaining support as technologies enable employees to be "virtually present" for their employers. The terms *telecommuting*, *mobile worker,* and *remote worker* are often used to describe flexible work arrangements. **Telecommuting**, sometimes called *teleworking,* refers to employees working from home, at a customer site, or from other convenient locations instead of coming into the corporate office. The word *telecommute* is derived from combining "telecommunications" with "commuting," indicating that these employees use telecommunications instead of driving, or commuting, to the office. **Mobile workers** are those who work from wherever they are. They are outfitted with the technology necessary for access to co-workers, company computers, intranets, and other information sources. We use the term **remote workers** when we refer to both telecommuters and mobile workers.

[26] Kristin Burnham, "Monster.com Brings Professional Social Networking to Facebook," CIO.com (July 15, 2011), http://blogs.cio.com/print/16406 (accessed February 2, 2012).

Phase	Preparation	Launch	Performance Management	Team Development	Disbanding
Key Activities	Mission statement Personnel selection Task design Rewards system Technology selection and installment	Kick-off meetings Getting acquainted Goal clarification Norm development	Leadership Communication Conflict resolution Task accomplishment Motivation Knowledge management Norm enforcement and shaping	Assessment of needs/deficits Individual and/or team training Evaluation of training effects Trust building	Recognition of achievements Re-integration of team members

FIGURE 4.4 Key activities in the life cycle of teams.
Source: Adapted from Guido Hertel, Susanne Geister, and Udo Konradt, "Managing Virtual Teams: A Review of Current Empirical Research," *Human Resource Management Review* 15, no. 1 (2005), 69–95.

Such employees work not only on a remotely independent basis but also with remote members on virtual teams. **Virtual teams** are defined as two or more people who (1) work together interdependently with mutual accountability for achieving common goals, (2) do not work in either the same place and/or at the same time, and (3) must use electronic communication and other digital technologies to communicate, coordinate their activities, and complete their team's tasks. Initially, virtual teams were seen as an alternative to conventional teams that meet face-to-face. However, it is simplistic to view teams as either meeting totally face-to-face or totally virtually. Rather, teams may reflect varying degrees of virtuality. Virtual team members may be in different locations, organizations, time zones, or work shifts (day, evening, or overnight). Further, like most teams, virtual teams may have distinct, relatively permanent membership, or they may be relatively fluid as they evolve to respond to changing task requirements and as members leave and are replaced by new members.

Virtual teams are thought to have a life cycle like most teams.[27] Their lifecycle, shown in Figure 4.4, is noteworthy because it the important activities in team development: Teams are formed; their work is completed; and, the team is disbanded.

Factors Driving Use of Remote Work and Virtual Teams

Remote working has been around since the 1970s, but it has steadily been gaining popularity since the late 1990s. One poll of 11,300 employees in 22 countries found that one 1 of 6 telecommute worldwide.[28] And as managers move to build teams of the best talent available, they inevitably turn to virtual teams as the mechanism to bring people together for a task. Several factors that drive these trends are shown in Figure 4.5.

The first factor is that work is increasingly knowledge based. The United States and many other world economies continue to shift from manufacturing to service industries. Equipped with the right IT, employees can create, assimilate, and distribute knowledge as effectively from home as they can from an office. The shift to knowledge-based work thus tends to minimize the need for a particular locus of activity.

The second factor is that remote workers and virtual team members often shift the time of their work to accommodate their lifestyles. For instance, parents modify their work schedules to allow time to take their children to school and attend extracurricular activities. Telecommuting provides an attractive alternative for parents who might otherwise decide to take leaves of absence from work for child rearing. Telecommuting also enables people who are housebound by illness, disability, or the lack of access to transportation to join the workforce.

[27] G. Hertel, S. Geister, and U. Konradt, "Managing Virtual Teams: A Review of Current Empirical Research," *Human Resource Management Review* 15, no. 1 (2005), 69–95.
[28] The actual statistics for the number of telecommuters is hard to find. These figures were obtained from Smart Planet, http://www.smartplanet.com/blog/business-brains/one-sixth-of-the-worlds-employees-now-telecommute-survey/21616 (accessed June 19, 2015).

Geographic Lens: How Do People Around the World Feel About Working Remotely?

A recent survey by Cisco found marked national differences about how professionals viewed their ability to be productive when working remotely. On average, 39% of the 1,303 professionals in 13 countries surveyed answered "yes" when asked whether it was necessary for them to be in the office to make decisions more effectively and efficiently (i.e., nothing replaces daily in-person interaction), but only 7% answered "yes" in India whereas 56% and 57% answered "yes" in Japan and Germany, respectively. That is, a large percentage of people in Japan and Germany thought they had to come into the physical office to be productive. This wasn't the case at all in India. A very small percentage of Indians felt they had to be tethered to a desk in a physical office. They could do their work by staying connected to their workplaces through a variety of devices including their laptops, tablets, and smartphones.

Source: "The Cisco Connected World Report" (October 2010), http://newsroom.cisco.com/dlls/2010/ekits/ccwr_final.pdf (accessed February 4, 2012).

Driver	Effect
Shift to knowledge-based work	Eliminates requirement that certain work be performed in a specific place
Changing demographics and lifestyle preferences	Provides workers geographic and time-shifting flexibility
New technologies with enhanced bandwidth	Makes remotely performed work practical and cost effective
Reliance on Web	Provides employees the ability to stay connected to co-workers and customers and to access work-related apps, even on a 24/7 basis
Energy concerns	Reduces the cost of commuting (for telecommuters), energy costs associated with real estate (for companies) and travel costs (for companies and for people on virtual teams)

FIGURE 4.5 Driving factors of remote work and virtual teams.

Remote work also provides employees and virtual team members enormous geographic flexibility. The freedom to live where one wishes, even at a location remote from one's corporate office, can boost employee morale and job satisfaction. As a workplace policy, it may also lead to improved employee retention. For example, American Express employees use the BlueWork program as part of its recruiting pitch. Further, productivity and employee satisfaction for those on the BlueWork program are markedly higher, and voluntary turnover is down. Many employees can be more productive at home, and they actually work more hours than if they commuted to an office. Furthermore, such impediments to productivity as traffic delays, canceled flights, bad weather, and mild illnesses become less significant. Companies enjoy this benefit, too. Those who build in remote work as a standard work practice are able to hire employees from a much larger talent pool than those companies that require geographical presence.

The third driving factor is that the new technologies, which make work in remote locations viable, are becoming better, cheaper, and more widely available. Telecommunication and PC speeds are increasing exponentially at the same time that their costs are plummeting. The oft-cited time frame involved in this progression is a doubling of computer capabilities (such as speed) every 18 months.[29] The drastic increase in capabilities of portable technologies makes small devices more powerful than the computers of yesterday, enabling effective and productive mobile work. Applications also provide integration between applications. Virtual team members can use Skype, Webex, Zoom, or any number of video and audio conferencing technologies to work together. Cloud computing also has contributed to this trend because applications are moved from computers housed in company data centers to Web-based hosts such as Amazon Web Services (AWS), Rackspace, and other service providers.

[29] Gordon Moore, head of Intel, observed that the capacity of microprocessors doubled roughly every 12 to 18 months. Even though this observation was made in 1965, it still holds true. Eventually, it became known in the industry as Moore's law.

A fourth driving factor is the increasing reliance on Web-based technologies by all generations, especially younger generations, such as Generation Y and the Millennials. The younger generations are at ease with Web-based social relationships and are adept at using social networking tools to grow these relationships. Face-to-face work arrangements are not necessary for these employees to build productive connections. Web-based tools allow them to stay connected with their co-workers and customers. Further, as more and more organizations turn to flexible working hours in programs such as BlueWork implemented by American Express and as 24/7 becomes the norm in terms of service, the Web becomes the standard platform to allow employees to respond to work's increasing demands.

A fifth factor is the increasing emphasis on energy conservation. As concerns about greenhouse gasses, carbon footprints, and even potential future gasoline price increases, employees are looking for ways to be more responsible and frugal at the same time. Telecommuting is quite appealing in such a scenario, especially when public transportation is not readily available. Companies can also experience lower energy usage and costs from telecommuting. SAP reduced its global greenhouse footprint by encouraging employees to shift their commuting behavior. As a result of these ongoing efforts, emissions from employees' commutes dropped. In addition to telecommuting and encouraging the use of mass transit and carpooling, SAP also began providing employees information on their carbon footprint from commuting through a new internal dashboard aimed at ensuring greater transparency and accountability.[30]

Many employees no longer need to be tied to official desks. Thus, the real estate needs of their employers are shrinking, and companies are saving costs by reducing the office space they own or rent. This reduction lowers their energy needs by no longer needing to heat, cool, or maintain these spaces. Companies are realizing that they can comply with the Clean Air Act and be praised for their "green computing" practices at the same time they are reaping considerable cost savings.

Advantages and Disadvantages of Remote Work

There are clearly advantages to remote work. Employees have greater flexibility in where they work. They can work from home or from just about any location as long as they have a laptop and a WiFi connection. Employees often find that they are more productive because they can work in the environment of their choosing without the distractions of the office. Homebound individuals can work for a company that embraces remote work. Employees also seem to have higher morale and lower absenteeism in part because they can work from wherever they are, wearing whatever clothes they want. A remote employee who has a cold may not want to go into the office and risk spreading the germs to others but can work from home. Employers find advantages of enabling remote work compelling, too. They are able to hire employees who do not live in the geographic area of the office. They don't have to monitor the employees the same way, freeing up their time to focus on exceptions and issues that require a

Geographic Lens: Who Telecommutes? A Look at Global Telecommuting Habits

Flexible work arrangements have been around for decades, but as technologies enable new capabilities for work away from a traditional office, telework has been gaining popularity. In 2015, advisory services firm EY surveyed about 9,700 employees in the eight top economies across the globe—the United States, United Kingdom, India, Japan, China, Germany, Mexico, and Brazil. The firm found flexible work arrangements varied significantly by country. The report cited countries with the highest and lowest percentages of employees with flexible work schedules. Germany (70%), India (61%), and the United States (61%) had the highest percentage, and Japan (30%) and China (22%) had the lowest.

Source: "EY Global Generations: A Global Study on Work-Life Challenges Across Generations," EY.com, http://www.ey.com/Publication/vwLUAssets/EY-global-generations-a-global-study-on-work-life-challenges-across-generations/$FILE/EY-global-generations-a-global-study-on-work-life-challenges-across-generations.pdf (accessed August 26, 2015), 6.

[30] SAP Sustainability Report, Greenhouse Gas Footprint, http://www.sapsustainabilityreport.com/greenhouse-gas-footprint (accessed February 2, 2012).

supervisor. And employers often find that it is less expensive to provide a remote employee the tools needed than to pay for the office space to house the employee.

Remote employees sometimes report that work–life balance often suffers. Because work can be done anyplace and anytime, they sometimes find the option attractive because of the ability to work around the schedules of children or other family members. Paradoxically, it is often difficult for them to separate work from their home life. Consequently, they may work many more hours than the standard nine-to-five employee or experience the stress of trying to separate work from play.

Remote work challenges managers to address performance evaluation and compensation. Managers of remote workers must evaluate employee performance in terms of results or deliverables. Virtual offices make it more difficult for managers to appreciate the skills of the people reporting to them, which in turn makes it more difficult to evaluate their performance. Managers must rely heavily on the remote worker's self-discipline to ensure that work is done. As a result, managers may feel they are losing control over their employees, and some remote employees do, in fact, abuse their privileges. Managers accustomed to traditional work models in which they are able to exert control more easily may strongly resist remote working. In fact, managers are often the biggest impediment to implementing remote work programs.

Self-discipline is a key concern for many remote workers. Workers who go to an office or who must make appearances at customer locations have a structure that gets them up and out of their home. But remote workers find that working from home, in particular, is full of distractions such as personal phone calls, visitors, the television, Facebook and other social networking sites, and inconvenient family disruptions. A remote worker must carefully set up a home-work environment and develop strategies to enable quality time for the work task.

Remote work also requires managers to undertake special planning and communicating activities. In terms of planning, business and support tasks must be designed to support remote workers. Managers must also work to coordinate schedules, ensure adequate communication among all workers, establish policies to support communications, and build business processes to support remote workers.

Working remotely can disconnect employees from their company's culture and make them feel isolated. The casual, face-to-face encounters that take place in offices transmit extensive cultural, political, and other organizational information. These encounters are lost to an employee who seldom, if ever, works at the office. Consequently, telecommuters need to undertake special efforts to stay connected. They must engage in forms of conversation to replace "water cooler" talk. This could take the form of instant messaging or participating in telephone calls/conferences, e-mail, social networking, blogs, or even video conferencing. The most successful remote work arrangements do include regular visits to the office to solidify personal connections.

Not all jobs are suitable for remote work. Some jobs, such as server in a restaurant, a clerk in a grocery store, and a facilities manager in a high-rise building, require the employee to be at the work location. Further, new employees who need to be socialized into the organization's practices and culture are not good candidates for remote work. Finally, some organizations' culture does not support remote workers. Notably, when Marissa Meyer took over as President of Yahoo, one of her first decisions was to eliminate remote work and bring everyone back into the home office. She felt that the culture had taken a wrong turn and the only way to fix it was to have everyone in the same place.

Remote work also raises the specter of **offshoring**, or foreign outsourcing of jobs once performed internally in the organization. Once a company establishes an infrastructure for remote work, it often can be performed abroad as easily as domestically. U.S. immigration laws limit the number of foreigners who may work in the United States. However, no such limitations exist on work performed outside this country by employees who transmit their work to the United States electronically. Because such work is not subject to minimum wage controls, companies may have a strong economic incentive to outsource work abroad. They find it particularly easy to outsource clerical work related to electronic production, such as data processing and computer programming. Sourcing is further discussed in Chapter 9. Benefits and potential problems associated with telecommuting are summarized in Figure 4.6.

Security is another issue for remote workers who might bring to the office an infected computer and plug it into the network, posing a threat to other office computers. Further, as demonstrated by the Department of Veterans Affairs (VA) employee whose laptop carrying unencrypted, sensitive personal information on more that 2.2 million active-duty military personnel was stolen from the employee's home, remote workers can be the source of security

Advantages of Remote Working	Potential Problems
Reduced stress due to increased ability to meet schedules and to have fewer work-related distractions	Increased stress from inability to separate work life from home life
Higher morale; lower absenteeism	Harder for managers to evaluate and communicate about performance
Geographic flexibility for worker; capitalization on distant expertise for organization	Employee may become disconnected from company culture
Higher personal productivity	Lack of suitability for all jobs or employees
Inclusion of housebound individuals in the workforce	Telecommuters more easily replaced by offshore workers
Very informal dress is acceptable	Harder to achieve high security

FIGURE 4.6 Some advantages and disadvantages of remote work.

breaches.[31] Organizational security mechanisms are continually increasing in effectiveness; however, it is impossible for organizations to make remote workers totally secure. General managers need to get involved in assessing the areas and severity of risk and take appropriate steps, via policies, education, and technology, to reduce the risks and make remote workers as secure as possible. IS leaders are aware that even with the best policies and tools available, breaches occur. The IS organizations typically has many levels of security to sense and respond to threats. IT security is discussed more fully in Chapter 7.

Advantages and Disadvantages of Virtual Teams

Virtual teams clearly offer advantages in terms of expanding the knowledge base through team membership. Thanks to new and ever-emerging communication and information technologies, managers can draw team members with needed skills or expertise from around the globe without having to commit to huge travel expenses. Further, virtual teams can benefit from *following the sun*. One classic example of this can be found in software development. London members of a virtual team of software developers at Tandem Services Corporation initially code a project and transmit its code each evening to a U.S. team for testing. The U.S. team forwards the tested code to Tokyo for debugging. London team members start their next day with the code debugged by the Japanese team, and another cycle is initiated.[32] Increasingly, growing pressure for faster turn around time for systems has resulted in systems development by global virtual teams whose members are located around the world.

There are some clear disadvantages to virtual teams. For example, different time zones, although helpful when following the sun, can work against virtual team members when they are forced to stay up late or work in the middle of the night to communicate with team members in other time zones. There also are a considerable number of challenges that if not correctly managed could turn into disadvantages. A summary of these challenges in comparison with more traditional teams can be found in Figure 4.7.

Managing Remote Workers and Virtual Teams

Managers cannot manage remote workers or virtual teams in the same way that they manage in-office workers or traditional teams. The differences in management control activities are particularly pronounced because managers cannot observe the actual behavior of remote workers or virtual team members. Thus, monitoring behavior is likely to be more limited. As stated earlier, performance for both remote workers and virtual teams is more likely to be evaluated through outcomes controls rather than behavior controls. Because team members and remote workers are dispersed, providing feedback is especially important—not just at the end of a project, but throughout the workers' employment and the team's life.

[31] Robert Lemos, "VA Data Theft Affects Most Soldiers" (June 7, 2006), http://www.securityfocus.com/brief/224 (accessed May 7, 2012).
[32] Marie-Claude Boudreau, Karen Loch, Daniel Robey, and Detmar Straub, "Going Global: Using Information Technology to Advance the Competitiveness of the Virtual Transnational Organization," *Academy of Management Executive* 12, no. 4 (1998), 120–28.

Challenges	Virtual Teams (VT)	Traditional Teams
Communication	• Difficulties in terms of scheduling meetings and interactions • Increased inefficiencies when passing work between time zones • Altered communication dynamics such as facial expressions, vocal inflections, verbal cues, and gestures	• Collocated in same time zone. Scheduling is less difficult • Use of richer communication media, including face-to-face discussions
Technology	• Need for proficiency across wide range of technologies • Automatic creation of electronic repository to build organizational memory • Need for ability to align group structure and technology with the task environment	• Support for face-to-face interaction without replacing it • Electronic communication skills not needed by team members • Task technology fit less critical
Team Diversity	• Harder to establish a group identity • Require better communication skills • More difficult to build trust, norms, and shared meanings about roles because team members have fewer cues about their teammates' performance • More likely to have different perceptions about time and deadlines	• Group identity easier to create • Easier communication among members

FIGURE 4.7 Comparison of challenges facing virtual teams and traditional teams.

Compensation for virtual teams must be based heavily on the team's performance and ability to reach its goal rather than on individually measured performance. Compensating team members for individual performance may result in "hot-rodding" or lack of cooperation among team members. Organizational reward systems must be aligned with the accomplishment of desired team goals. This alignment is especially difficult when virtual team members belong to different organizations, each with her or his own unique reward and compensation system, each of which may affect individual performance in a different way. Managers need to be aware of differences and discover ways to provide motivating rewards to all team members. Further, policies about the selection, evaluation, and compensation of virtual team members may need to be enacted.

In addition to management control challenges, there are other challenges as included in Figure 4.7. The rest of this section is devoted to managing the challenges.

Managing Communication Challenges

Because virtual teams and remote workers communicate differently than workers in the office, managers must make sure the communications policies and practices support these work arrangements. For example, holding a team meeting in the office and expecting remote members to listen in requires the manager to prepare differently for the meeting. Any presentation slides to be used in the meeting must also be shared with the remote participants, either over a video conference with meeting software or beforehand. When most of the co-workers are in the office and only one or two are dialing in from other locations, the remote participants miss all the nonverbal communication that takes place in the meeting room. Soft-spoken individuals are often difficult to hear. Managers must make sure key messages are being conveyed to the remote participants or the results of the meeting are sub-optimal.

Team leaders may decide to initiate or supplement a team's virtual activity with a face-to-face meeting so that the seeds of trust can be planted and team members feel as if they know one another on a more personal basis. Face-to-face meetings indeed appear to contribute to successful global virtual teams. An in-depth study of three global virtual teams found that the two effective teams created a rhythm organized around regularly scheduled face-to-face meetings coupled with virtual meetings as needed. Before each face-to-face meeting, there was a flurry of communication and activity as team members prepared for the meeting. After the meeting, there were many follow-up messages and tasks. The ineffective team did not demonstrate a similar pattern.[33] Because not all teams can meet face-to-face, well-managed synchronous meetings using video teleconferencing or in a virtual world can activate the rhythm and accelerate the workflow.

[33] M. L. Maznevski and K. Chudoba, "Bridging Space Over Time: Global Virtual Team Dynamics and Effectiveness," *Organization Science* 11, no. 5 (2000), 373–92.

Because team leaders cannot always see what their team members are doing or whether they are experiencing any problems, frequent communications are important. If remote employee or team members are quiet, the team leader must reach out to them to identify their participation and ensure that they feel their contributions are appreciated. Further, team leaders can scrutinize the team's asynchronous communications and its repository to evaluate and give feedback about each team member's contributions. Even when a majority of team members are in one location, the team leader should rotate meeting times to alternate the convenience among team members. The rule of thumb is that "more communication is better than less" because it is very difficult to "overcommunicate." Managers and team leaders with remote participants must make sure to think about how their remote colleagues are receiving the information they need, not just how the managers are communicating it.

Managing Technology Challenges

Information and communication technologies are at the heart of the success of remote work and virtual team accomplishments. However, managers must ensure that their remote colleagues have access to the technologies and support they need. All team members must have the ability to connect to the information sources and communications pathways used by the group. Well-designed Web-based conferencing applications make this easier because any device connected to the Internet can access them. Managers must make sure meetings over video or audio conference tools are well coordinated and all attendees have the right access codes and meeting times. Time zone differences often confuse this issue, so it is critical to make sure everyone knows the right time for a meeting.

Support processes for technologies must also be designed with remote employees in mind. If the only support for them is in the office, they will find it difficult if not impossible to access the help they need. Bringing a laptop to the office during normal business hours may not be possible if the remote worker is hundreds or thousands of miles away. Processes must be designed to accommodate the remote employee or team member.

Managers must ensure that all employees and team members have the tools they need to do their jobs. That might mean providing seamless telephone transfers, desktop support, network connectivity, and security support to the remote workers. How and where information is stored must be considered because all workers must have access to the files and applications they need to do their work. And, of course, the importance of security for remote work cannot be overstated. A good rule of thumb is to design work processes so they work for remote workers, and consider the office as just another location. If the process works for the remote workers, it most likely will work for someone in the office, but the converse is not necessarily true. Unforeseen problems can develop for those remotely located.

Further, managers must also provide the framework for using the technology. Policies and norms or unwritten rules about how all employees should use the technology to work with one another must be established.[34] These include norms about telephone, e-mail, and videoconferencing etiquette (i.e., how often to check for messages, the maximum time to wait to return e-mails, and alerting team members about absences or national holidays), work to be performed, and so on. Such norms are especially important when team members are not in the same office and cannot see when team members are unavailable. For example, leaving a paper note on someone's desk works fine if that person is in the office, but that option does not exist for remote participants. Leaving an e-mail or sending texts may be a better alternative because both work for everyone.

Managing Diversity Challenges

Managers may also seek to provide technologies to support diverse team member characteristics. For example, team members from different parts of the globe may have different views of time. Team members from Anglo-American cultures (i.e., United States, United Kingdom, Canada, Australia, New Zealand) may view time as a continuum from past to present and future. For such team members, each unit of time is the same. These team members are likely to be concerned with deadlines and often prefer to complete one task before starting another (i.e., are monochronic). For team members who are conscious of deadlines, planning and scheduling software may

[34] C. Saunders, C. Slyke, and D. R. Vogel, "My Time or Yours? Managing Time Visions in Global Virtual Teams," *Academy of Management Executive* 18, no. 1 (2004), 19–31.

be especially useful. In contrast, team members from India often have a cyclical view of time. They do not get excited about deadlines and there is no hurry to make a decision because it is likely to cycle back—at which time the team member may be in a better position to make the decision. Many people from India tend to be polychronic, preferring to do several activities at one time. Team members who are polychronic may benefit from having instant messaging or instant video chats available to them so that they can communicate with their teammates and still work on other tasks.[35]

In addition to providing the appropriate technologies, managers with team members who have different views of time need to be aware of the differences and try to develop strategies to motivate those who are not concerned with deadlines to deliver their assigned tasks on time. Or the managers may wish to assign these team members to do tasks that are not sensitive to deadlines.

Of course, views of time are only one dimension of diversity. Although team diversity has been demonstrated to lead to more creative solutions, it can also make it harder for team members to learn to communicate, to trust one another, and to form a single group identity. Through open communications, managers may be able to uncover and deal with other areas of diversity, such as culture, training, gender, personality, position, and language, that positively or negatively affect the team.[36] Managers may establish an expertise directory at the start of the team's life or encourage other ways of getting team members to know more about one another. The rule of thumb here is to not assume a team will work just because it has been created by management. Specific thought must be giving to helping the team members function together and embrace, rather than reject, the differences diversity brings to the table.

Gaining Acceptance for IT-Induced Change

The changes described in this chapter no doubt alter the frames of reference of organizational employees and may be a major source of concern for them. Employees may resist the changes if they view the changes as negatively affecting them. In the case of a new information system that they do not fully understand or are not prepared to operate, they may resist in several ways:

- They may deny that the system is up and running.
- They may sabotage the system by distorting or otherwise altering inputs.
- They may try to convince themselves, and others, that the new system really will not change the status quo.
- They may refuse to use the new system when its usage is voluntary.

Managing Change

To help avoid these resistance behaviors, John Kotter[37] builds upon Kurt Lewin's[38] change model of unfreezing, changing, and refreezing. Kotter recommends eight specific steps to bring about change. Kotter's steps are related to Lewin's changes and listed in Figure 4.8.

Managers can keep these eight steps in mind as they introduce change into their workplaces. It is important for managers to make clear why the change is being made before it is implemented, and they must follow the change with reinforcement behaviors such as rewarding those employees who have successfully adopted new desired behaviors.

[35] Ibid.

[36] Terri R. Kurtzberg and Teresa M. Amabile, "From Guilford to Creative Synergy: Opening the Black Box of Team-Level Creativity," *Creativity Research Journal* 13, no. 3–4 (2001), 285–94.

[37] John Kotter, *Leading Change* (Boston, MA: Harvard Business School Press, 1996).

[38] Kurt Lewin, "Frontiers in Group Dynamics II. Channels of Group Life; Social Planning and Action Research," *Human Relations* 1, no. 22 (1947), 143–53.

Lewin's Stage	Unfreezing	Changing	Refreezing
Definition	Creating motivation to change	Providing stakeholders with new information, systems, products, or services	Reinforcing change by integrating stakeholders' changed behaviors and attitudes into new operations resulting from change
Kotter's Steps	1. Establish a sense of urgency: Create a compelling reason why change is needed. 2. Create the guiding coalition: Select a team with enough expertise and power to lead the change. 3. Develop a vision and strategy: Use the vision and strategic plan to guide the change process. 4. Communicate the change vision: Devise and implement a communication strategy to consistently convey the vision.	5. Empower broad-based action: Encourage risk-taking and creative problem solving to overcome barriers to change. 6. Generate short-term wins: Celebrate short-term improvements and reward contributions to change effort. 7. Consolidate gains and produce more change: Use credibility from short-term wins to promote more change so that change cascades throughout the organization.	8. Anchor new approaches in the culture: Reinforce change by highlighting areas in which new behaviors and processes are linked to success.

FIGURE 4.8 Stages and steps in change management.
Source: Adapted from John Kotter, Leading change (Boston, MA: Harvard Business School Press, 1996).

Technology Acceptance Model and Its Variants

To avoid the negative consequences of resistance to change, those implementing change must actively manage the change process and gain acceptance for new IS. To help explain how to gain acceptance for a new technology, Professor Fred Davis and his colleagues developed the Technology Acceptance Model (TAM). Many variations of TAM exist, but its most basic form is displayed on the right-hand side in Figure 4.9. TAM suggests that managers

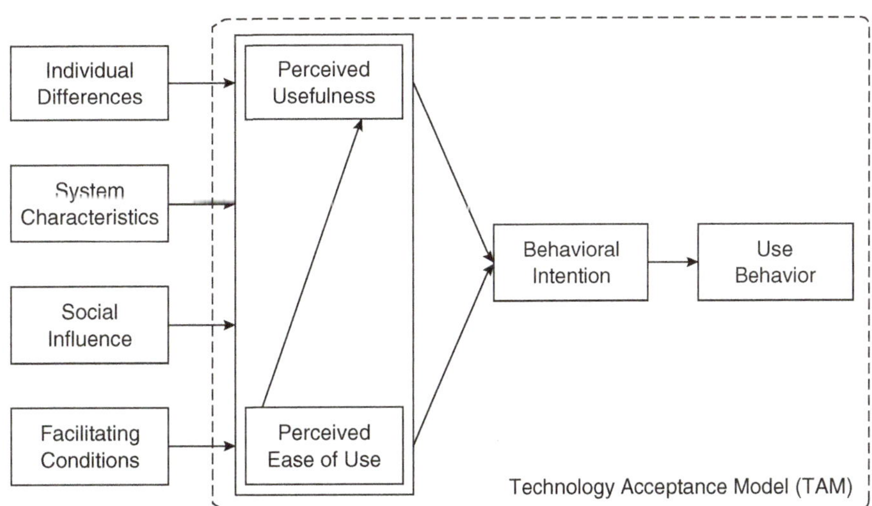

FIGURE 4.9 Simplified technology acceptance model (TAM3).
Source: Viswanath Venkatesh and Hillol Bala, "Technology Acceptance Model 3 and a Research Agenda on Interventions," *Decision Sciences* 39, no. 2 (2008), 276.

cannot get employees to use a system until they want to use it. To convince employees to want to use the system, managers may need to employ unfreezing tactics to change employee attitudes about the system. Attitudes may change if employees believe that the system will allow them to do more or better work for the same amount of effort (perceived usefulness), and that it is easy to use. Training, documentation, and user support consultants are external variables that may help explain the usefulness of the system and make it easier to use.

The left-hand side of Figure 4.9 provides four categories of determinants of perceived usefulness and perceived ease of use from the point of view of organizational users. Specifically, they are *individual differences* (e.g., gender, age), *system characteristics* (e.g., output quality and job relevance that help individuals develop favorable or unfavorable views about the system), *social influence* (e.g., subjective norms), and *facilitating conditions* (e.g., top management support). TAM assumes that system use is under the control of the individual users. When employees are mandated to use the system, they may use it in the short run, but over the long run, negative consequences of their resistance may surface. Thus, gaining acceptance of the system is important, even in those situations where it is mandated.

SUMMARY

- The nature of work is changing, and IT supports, if not propels, these changes.
- Communication and collaboration are vital for today's work. Technology to support communication includes e-mail, intranets, instant messaging (IM), video conferences, virtual private networks (VPN), and file transfer software. Technology to support collaboration includes social networking sites, Web logs (blogs), virtual worlds, wikis, teleconference systems, groupware, microblogs and Internet sharing sites.
- IT affects work by creating new work, creating new working arrangements, and presenting new managerial challenges in employee supervision, evaluation, compensation, and hiring.
- Newer approaches to management reflect increased use of computer and information technology in hiring and supervising employees, a more intense focus on output (compared to behavior), and an increased team orientation.
- The shift to knowledge-based work, changing demographics and lifestyle preferences, new technologies, growing reliance on the Web, and energy concerns contribute to the increase in remote work and virtual teams.
- Companies find that building telecommuting capabilities can be an important tool for attracting and retaining employees, increasing their productivity, providing flexibility to otherwise overworked individuals, reducing office space and associated costs, responding to environmental concerns about energy consumption, and complying with the Clean Air Act. Alternative work arrangements also promise employees potential benefits: schedule flexibility, higher personal productivity, less commuting time and fewer expenses, and increased geographic flexibility.
- Disadvantages of remote work include increased stress from trying to maintain work–life balance; difficulties in planning, communicating, and evaluating performance; feelings of isolation among employees; easier displacement of employees by offshoring; and limitations of jobs and employees in its application.
- Virtual teams can be defined as two or more people who (1) work together interdependently with mutual accountability for achieving common goals, (2) do not work in either the same place and/or at the same time, and (3) must use electronic communication technology to communicate, coordinate their activities, and complete their team's tasks. They are an increasingly common organizational phenomenon and must be managed differently than more traditional teams.
- Managers of remote workers and virtual teams must focus on overcoming the challenges of communication, technology, and diversity of team members.
- To gain acceptance of a new technology, potential users must exhibit a favorable attitude toward the technology. In the case of information systems, the users' beliefs about its perceived usefulness and perceived ease of use color their attitudes about the system. Kotter provides some suggested steps for change management that are related to Lewin's three stages of change: unfreezing, change, and refreezing.

KEY TERMS

behavior controls (p. 84)
mobile workers (p. 86)
offshoring (p. 90)
outcome controls (p. 84)
personnel controls (p. 84)
remote workers (p. 86)
telecommuting (p. 86)
virtual teams (p. 87)

DISCUSSION QUESTIONS

1. Why might an employee resist the implementation of a new technology? What are some of the possible consequences of asking an employee to use a computer or similar device in his or her job?
2. How can IT alter an individual's work? How can a manager ensure that the impact is positive rather than negative?
3. What current technologies do you predict will show the most impact on the way work is done? Why?
4. Given the growth in telecommuting and other mobile work arrangements, how might offices physically change in the coming years? Will offices as we think of them today exist by 2030? Why or why not?
5. How is working at an online retailer different from working at a brick-and-mortar retailer? What types of jobs are necessary at each? What skills are important?
6. Paul Saffo, former director of the Institute for the Future, noted, "Telecommuting is a reality for many today, and will continue to be more so in the future. But beware, this doesn't mean we will travel less. In fact, the more one uses electronics, the more they are likely to travel."[39] Do you agree with this statement? Why or why not?
7. The explosion of information-driven self-serve options in the consumer world is evident at the gas station where customers pay, pump gas, and purchase a car wash without ever seeing an employee; in the retail store such as Walmart, Home Depot, and the local grocery where self-service checkout stands mean that customers can purchase a basket of items without ever speaking to a sales agent; at the airport where customers make reservations and pay for and print tickets without the help of an agent; and at the bank, where ATMs have long replaced tellers for most transactions. But a backlash is coming, experts predict. Some say that people are more isolated than they used to be in the days of face-to-face service, and they question how much time people are really saving if they have to continually learn new processes, operate new machines, and overcome new glitches. Labor-saving technologies were supposed to liberate people from mundane tasks, but it appears that these technologies are actually shifting some tasks to the customer. On the other hand, many people like the convenience of using these self-service systems, especially because it means customers can visit a bank for cash or order books or gifts from an online retailer 24 hours a day. Does this mean the end of "doing business the old-fashioned way"? Will this put a burden on the elderly or the poor when corporations begin charging for face-to-face services?[40]

■ CASE STUDY 4-1 Trash and Waste Pickup Services, Inc.

Martin Andersen is responsible for 143 of Trash and Waste Pickup Services, Inc.'s (TWPS's) garbage trucks. TWPS is a commercial and household trash hauler. When a caller recently complained to Andersen that a brown and green Trash and Waste Pickup Services truck was speeding down Farm Route 2244, Andersen turned to the company's information system. He learned that the driver of a company front-loader had been on that very road at 7:22 A.M., doing 51 miles per hour (mph) in a 35 mph zone. The driver of that truck was in trouble!

The TWPS information system uses a global positioning system (GPS) not only to smooth its operations but also to keep closer track of its employees, who may not always be doing what they are supposed to be doing during work hours. Andersen pointed out, "If you're not out there babysitting them, you don't know how long it takes to do the route. The guy could be driving around the world, he could be at his girlfriend's house."

[39] "Online Forum: Companies of the Future," http://www.msnbc.com/news/738363.asp (accessed June 11, 2002).
[40] Stevenson Swanson, "Are Self-Serve Options a Disservice?" *Chicago Tribune* (May 8, 2005), Section H, 1d.

Before TWPS installed the GPS system, the drivers of his 37 front-loaders clocked in approximately 250 hours a week of overtime at one and a half times pay. Once TWPS started monitoring the time they spent in the yard before and after completing their routes and the time and location of stops that they made, the number of overtime hours plummeted to 70 per week. This translated to substantial savings for a company whose drivers earn about $20 an hour.

TWPS also installed GPS receivers in salesmen's cars. Andersen was not surprised to learn that some of the company's salespeople frequented The Zone, a local bar, around 4 P.M. when they were supposed to be calling on customers. Andersen decided to set digital boundaries around the bar.

Understandably, the drivers and salespeople aren't entirely happy with the new GPS-based system. Ron Simon, a TWPS driver, admits: "It's kind of like Big Brother is watching a little bit. But it's where we're heading in this society. . . . I get testy in the deli when I'm waiting in line for coffee, because it's like, hey, they're (managers) watching. I've got to go."

Andersen counters that employers have a right to know what their employees are up to: "If you come to work here, and I pay you and you're driving one of my vehicles, I should have the right to know what you're doing."

Discussion Questions

1. What are the positive and negative aspects of Andersen's use of the GPS-based system to monitor his drivers and salespeople?
2. What advice do you have for Andersen about the use of the system for supervising, evaluating, and compensating his drivers and salespeople?
3. As more and more companies turn to IS to help them monitor their employees, what do you anticipate the impact will be on employee privacy? Can anything be done to ensure employee privacy?

Source: This is a fictitious case. Any resemblance to an actual company is purely coincidental.

CASE STUDY 4-2 Social Networking: How Does IBM Do It?

IBM's award-winning developerWorks site was established in 2000 as a technical resource repository for the company's global development community. Designed to share knowledge and skills related to IBM products and other key technologies, it has been a solid success. The site attracts about 4 million unique visitors a month—including students, professionals, and developers from almost all the world's countries—who search its library of 30,000 articles, demos, podcasts, and tutorials. developerWorks is available in eight languages, including Russian, Chinese, and Spanish, and about 70% of its visitors come from outside IBM.

My developerWorks, a social networking function, was added to the repository platform in 2009 to allow developers to connect, communicate, and collaborate on projects. Soon the network had added more than 600,000 user profiles as well as numerous blogs and forums. In addition to allowing established business, start-ups, and partners to collaborate, it has also helped users find answers to support questions that would otherwise go to IBM's call centers and help desks, thus saving the company an estimated $100 million.

Alice Chou, Director of IBM developerWorks, carefully monitored the number of My developerWorks profiles and the volume of traffic to the site. She looked at unique visitors, developer demographics, time spent on the site, and patterns of page views. She created a reward and recognition framework so that when users contributed a highly regarded article or blogpost to the site, "they got the kudos they deserve."

Discussion Questions

1. How might My developerWorks leverage changes in the way people work?
2. Why do you think Alice Chou carefully monitors the My developerWorks site? What would be an example of an insight she would gain from the data she's collecting?
3. Why do you think Alice Chou thinks a rewards program is necessary for My developerWorks because so many profiles have already been developed. Do you agree that a reward would be necessary?

Sources: IBM, www.ibm.com/developerworks (accessed April 17, 2012); Ellen Traudt and Richard Vancil, "Becoming a Social Business: The IBM Story," IDC White Paper #226706 (January 2011), 1–14 (quote on p. 6, developerWorks at http://www.ibm.com/developerworks/).

Information Systems and Business Transformation

chapter

5

Transformation requires discontinuous thinking—recognizing and shedding outdated rules and fundamental assumptions that underlie operations. Business processes, the cross-functional sets of activities that turn inputs into outputs, are at the heart of how businesses operate and how transformation takes place. This chapter discusses business processes and the systems that support them. The chapter begins with a discussion of a functional (silo) versus a process perspective of a firm, including agile and dynamic business processes. The chapter then focuses on the way managers change business processes, including incremental and radical approaches. Information systems (*IS*) including workflow and business process management systems and enterprise systems that support and automate business processes follow. The chapter concludes by examining when IS drive business transformations and the complexities that arise when companies integrate systems.

Business strategy at Sloan Valve Company,[1] a family-owned global manufacturer of plumbing products, had executives launching a range of new products every year. The new product development (NPD) process was both core and strategic for Sloan, but it was also complex and slow; over 16 functional units were involved, and it often took 18–24 months to bring a new product to market. Sloan Valve's process of initiating and screening new product ideas was broken. More than 50% of the ideas that began the process didn't make it through, resulting in wasted resources. Further, no one was accountable for the process, making it difficult to get a handle on process management and improvement. Information flow was blocked in part because of the structure of the organization.

Management initially invested in an enterprise system to automate the company's internal processes, believing that IS would provide a common language, database, and platform. Despite successful implementation, the communication and coordination problems continued. Further, the new system did not provide an NPD process. Upon deeper analysis by a new CIO brought in to "fix things," management realized that the enterprise system was working fine, but the underlying process was broken. Top management decided to redesign the NPD process.

The NPD process redesign team was led by an IT manager with considerable process experience and involved members from manufacturing, engineering, IT, finance, marketing, operations, and quality assurance. The director of design engineering was made process owner to provide oversight for all changes. The team spent nine months assessing the current way of working and proposed a new end-to-end NPD process. The reengineered NPD process included six subprocesses: ideation, business case development, project portfolio management, product development, product and process validation, and launch. The underlying information system was the enterprise system upgraded to include newer modules, which supported product life cycle management.

[1] Adapted from S. Balaji, C. Ranganathan, and T. Coleman, "IT-Led Process Reengineering: How Sloan Valve Redesigned Its New Product Development Process," *MIS Quarterly Executive* 10, no. 2 (June 2011), 81–92.

The quality, timing, and output of NPD greatly improved. The new NPD process reduced time-to-market to less than 12 months. New product ideas that were unlikely to work were filtered out early, eliminating problems of wasting resources. Synthesis of product and process information improved. Customer feedback was easier to access. And accountability increased, smoothing out responsibilities and workflow.

Not all IS enterprise system implementations are as successful as that at Sloan Valve. There are hundreds of stories of companies that ran into significant problems when automating and transforming their business processes, especially when an information system is at the heart of the change. Overstock.com's order tracking system failed for a full week when it rolled out a new enterprise system. By rushing to implement the new system, a glitch put the enterprise system out of sync with the accounting system, causing the company to have to restate more than five years of earnings, which showed lower revenue and higher losses. Clothing manufacturer Levi Strauss had similar problems with its new enterprise system, causing shipping errors and issues with its financial control systems. The latter was blamed for the company's 98% decrease in net income for the second quarter in 2008. Avis Europe attempted to implement an enterprise system, but project delays and cost overruns caused the company to cancel the project and write off £28 million on its books. With so much at risk, general managers must be informed and involved in these types of complex information systems that change business processes.[2]

IS can enable or impede business change. The right design coupled with the right technology can result in changes such as those experienced by Sloan Valve. The wrong business process design or the wrong technology, however, can force a company into operational, and sometimes financial, crisis as the Overstock.com, Levi Strauss, and Avis Europe examples show.

To a manager in today's business environment, an understanding of how IS enable business change is essential. The terms *management* and *change management* are used almost synonymously in today's business vocabulary: To manage effectively means to manage change effectively. As IS become ever more prevalent and more powerful, the speed and magnitude of the changes that organizations must address to remain competitive continue to increase. To be a successful manager, one must understand how IS enable change in a business; one must gain a process perspective of business and must understand how to transform business processes effectively. This chapter provides managers a view of business process change. It provides tools for analyzing how a company currently does business and for thinking about how to effectively manage the inevitable changes that result from competition and the availability of IS. This chapter also describes an IT-based solution commonly known as *enterprise IS*.

A brief word to the reader is needed. The term *process* is used extensively in this chapter. In some instances, it is used to refer to the steps taken to change aspects of the business. At other times, it is used to refer to the part of the business to be changed: the business process. The reader should be sensitive to the potentially confusing use of the term *process*.

Silo Perspective versus Business Process Perspective

When effectively linked with improvements to business processes, advances in IS enable changes that make it possible to do business in a new way, one that is better and more competitive than before. On the other hand, IS can also inhibit change, which occurs when managers fail to adapt business processes because they rely on inflexible systems to support those processes. Finally, IS can also drive change for better or for worse. Examples abound of industries that were fundamentally changed by advances in IS and of companies whose success or failure depended on the ability of their managers to adapt. This chapter considers IS as an enabler of business transformation, a partner in transforming business processes to achieve competitive advantages. We begin by comparing a process view of the firm with a functional view.

Transformation requires discontinuous thinking—recognizing and shedding outdated rules and fundamental assumptions that underlie operations. "Unless we change these rules, we are merely rearranging the deck chairs on the *Titanic*. We cannot achieve breakthroughs in performance by cutting fat or automating existing processes.

[2] Adapted from http://www.baselinemag.com/c/a/ERP/Five-ERP-Disasters-Explained-878312/ (accessed February 24, 2012).

Rather, we must challenge old assumptions and shed the old rules that made the business under perform in the first place."[3]

Functional (Silo) Perspective

Many think of business by imagining a hierarchical structure (described in Chapter 3) organized around a set of functions. Looking at a traditional organization chart allows an understanding of what the business does to achieve its goals. A typical hierarchical structure, organized by function, results in disconnected silos that might look like the one in Figure 5.1.

When an organization has silos, departments are organized on the basis of their core competencies. Specialized silos allow them to focus on what they do best. For example, the operations department focuses on operations, the marketing department focuses on marketing, and so on. Each major function within the organization usually forms a separate department to ensure that work is done by groups of experts in that function. This functional structure is widespread in today's organizations and is reinforced by business education curricula, which generally follow functional structures, that is, students take courses in functions (i.e., marketing, management, accounting) and major in functions and then are predisposed to think in terms of these same functions.

Even when companies use the perspective of the value chain model (as discussed in Chapter 2), they still focus on functions that deliver their portion of the process and "throwing it over the wall" to the next group on the value chain. These silos become self-contained functional units, which can be useful for several reasons. First, they allow an organization to optimize expertise and training. For example, all the marketing people can belong to the same department, allowing them to informally network and learn from each other. Second, the silos allow the organization to avoid redundancy in expertise by hiring one person who can be assigned to projects across functions on an as-needed basis instead of hiring an expert in each function. Third, with a silo organization, it is easier to benchmark outside organizations, utilize bodies of knowledge created for each function, and easily understand the role of each silo.

On the other hand, silo organizations can experience significant suboptimization. First, individual departments often recreate information maintained by other departments. Second, communication gaps between departments are often wide. Third, handoffs between silos are often a source of problems, such as finger-pointing and lost information. Finally, silos tend to lose sight of the objective of the overall organization and operate in a way that maximizes their local goals. The last point is illustrated by a production department that pushes the concept of a small number of product sizes or options while the marketing department urges management to consider a larger variety or highly customized products. Such conflicts do arise in many organizations, and it can be difficult to negotiate to find a solution that is best, overall, for the firm.

A firm's work changes over time. In a functionally organized silo business, each group is primarily concerned with its own set of objectives. The executive officers jointly seek to ensure that these functions work together to create value, but the task of providing the "big picture" to so many functionally oriented personnel can prove extremely challenging. As time passes and business circumstances change, new work is created that relies on more than one of the old functional departments. Departments that took different directions must now work together. They negotiate the terms of any new work processes with their own functional interests in mind, and the "big

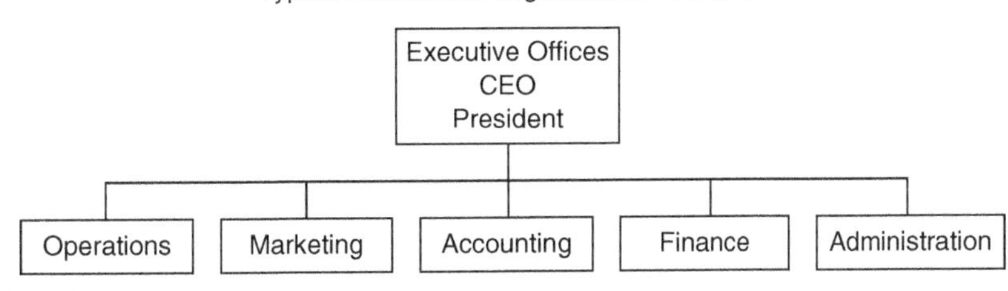

FIGURE 5.1 Hierarchical structure.

[3] Michael Hammer, "Reengineering Work: Don't Automate, Obliterate" *Harvard Business Review* 68, no. 4 (July–August 1990), 104–12.

picture" optimum gets scrapped in favor of suboptimal compromises among the silos. These compromises then become repeated processes; they become standard operating procedures.

Losing the big picture means losing business effectiveness. After all, a business's main objective is to create as much value as possible for its shareholders and other stakeholders by satisfying its customers to stimulate repeat sales and positive word of mouth. When functional groups duplicate work, fail to communicate with one another, or lose the big picture and establish suboptimal processes, the customers and stakeholders are not being well served.

Business Process Perspective

A manager can avoid such suboptimization—or begin to "fix" it—by managing from a business process perspective. A **business process perspective**, or more simply a **process perspective**, keeps the big picture in view and allows the manager to concentrate on the work that must be done to ensure the optimal creation of value. A process perspective helps the manager avoid or reduce duplicate work, facilitate cross-functional communication, optimize business processes, and ultimately, best serve the customers and stakeholders.

In business, a **process** is defined as an interrelated, sequential set of activities and tasks that turns inputs into outputs and includes the following:

- A beginning and an end
- Inputs and outputs
- A set of tasks (subprocesses or activities) that transform the inputs into outputs
- A set of metrics for measuring effectiveness

Metrics are important because they focus managers on the critical dimensions of the process. Metrics for a business process are things like **throughput**, which is how many outputs can be produced per unit time, or **cycle time**, which is how long it takes for an entire process to execute. Examples of process measures are the number of handoffs in the process or actual work versus total cycle time. Other metrics are based on the outputs themselves, such as customer satisfaction, revenue per output, profit per output, and quality of the output.

Examples of business processes include customer order fulfillment, manufacturing planning and execution, payroll, financial reporting, and procurement. A procurement process might look like the sample in Figure 5.2. The process has a beginning and an end, inputs (requirements for goods or services) and outputs (receipt of goods, vendor payment), and subprocesses (filling out a purchase order, verifying the invoice). Metrics of the success of the process might include turnaround time and the number of paperwork errors.

The procurement process in Figure 5.2 cuts across the functional lines of a traditionally structured business. For example, the requirements for goods might originate in the operations department based on guidelines from the finance department. Paperwork would likely flow through the administration department, and the accounting department would be responsible for paying the vendor.

Focusing on business processes ensures focusing on the business's goals (the "big picture") because each process has an "endpoint" that is usually a deliverable to a customer, supplier, or other stakeholder. A business process perspective recognizes that processes are often cross-functional. In the diagram in Figure 5.3, the vertical bars represent functional departments within a business. The horizontal bars represent processes that flow across those functional departments. A business process perspective requires an understanding that processes properly exist to serve the larger goals of the business and that functional departments must work together to optimize processes in regard to these goals.

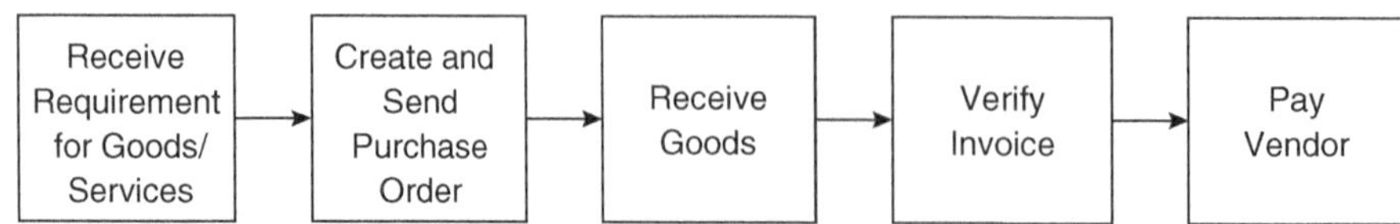

FIGURE 5.2 Sample procurement business process.

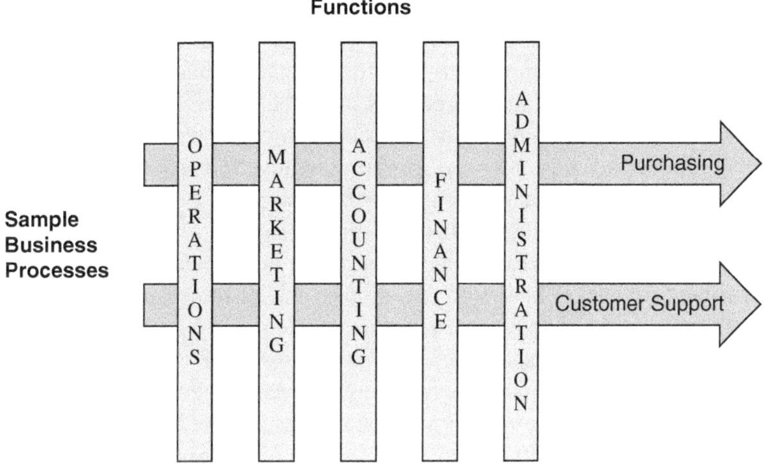

FIGURE 5.3 Cross-functional nature of business processes.

For example, an order-fulfillment process might include payment, order delivery, product implementation, and after-sales service tasks. This process would involve multiple functions, including operations, accounting, service, and sales, making it a cross-functional business process. The "sales order" would be the input for this process. A satisfied customer might be the output, and a number of metrics, such as a survey of the customer's satisfaction, time to complete the order fulfillment process, number of defects (or other quality measure), can be used to measure success.

When managers take a business process perspective, they are able to optimize the value that customers and stakeholders receive by managing the flow as well as the tasks. They begin to manage processes by:

- Identifying the customers of processes (who receives the output of the process?)
- Identifying these customers' requirements (what are the criteria for successful implementation of the process?)
- Clarifying the value that each process adds to the overall goals of the organization
- Sharing their perspective with other organizational members until the organization itself becomes more process focused

The differences between the silo and business process perspectives are summarized in Figure 5.4. A **silo perspective** refers to self-contained functional units such as marketing, operations, finance, and so on. Unlike a

	Silo Perspective	Business Process Perspective
Definition	Self-contained functional units such as marketing, operations, finance, and so on	Interrelated, sequential set of activities and tasks that turns inputs into outputs
Focus	Function	Cross-function
Goal Accomplishment	Goals optimized for the function, which may be suboptimal for the organization	Goals optimized for the organization, or the "big picture"
Benefits	Core competencies highlighted and developed; functional efficiencies	Avoidance of work duplication and cross-functional communication gaps; organizational effectiveness
Problems	Redundancy of information throughout the organization; cross-functional inefficiencies; communication difficulties	Difficulty in finding staff who can be knowledgeable generalists; need for sophisticated software

FIGURE 5.4 Comparison of silo perspective and business process perspective.

silo perspective, a business process perspective recognizes that businesses operate as a set of processes that flow across functional departments. The business process perspective enables a manger to analyze the processes of the business in regard to its larger goals in comparison to the functional orientation of the silo perspective. Finally, it provides a manager with insights into how those processes might better serve these goals.

An example illustrates the problem. Using a silo perspective, a customer with a warranty issue would need to explain a problem with a product to a customer service representative in the service department. If the problem is technical, the call would be transferred to a technical support person (in a different department), and the customer might need to explain the entire problem again. If the technical support representative determined that a part is needed, the customer would be transferred to the sales department and would need to explain the issue yet another time. Because the departments are not talking with one another, the customer might even need to provide proof of purchase several times to avoid having to pay for a warranty problem.

In contrast, with a business process perspective, either one representative would work with the customer on all problems or an **enterprise system** would enable the representative to transfer both the call and notes with the details to any specialists who are needed along the way. Having one representative handle all problems is not always possible because it is often difficult to find staff able to handle an entire process for the same reasons that support the functional hierarchical structure: People are normally trained in a function, such as marketing or accounting, not in a process that requires many different skill sets. For example, individuals who excel at marketing may not also possess the accounting skills needed to fix a billing problem.

Zara's Cross-Functional Business Processes

Consider Spanish clothing retailer Zara (introduced in Chapter 2). With over 1,600 stores in 78 countries around the world and a well-designed set of cross-functional business processes, Zara often is able to design, produce, and deliver a garment within 15 days. For this to happen, its managers must regularly create and rapidly replenish small batches of goods all over the world. Zara's organization, operational procedures, performance measures, and even its office layout are all designed to make information transfer easy.

Zara's designers are colocated with the production team, including marketing, procurement, and production planners. Prototypes are created nearby, facilitating easy discussion about the latest design. Large circular tables in the middle of the production process encourage impromptu meetings where ideas are readily exchanged among the designers, market specialists, and production planners. The speed and quality of the design process is greatly enhanced by the colocation of the entire team because the designers can quickly check their ideas with others on their cross-functional teams. For example, the market specialists can quickly respond to designs in terms of the style, color, and fabric whereas the procurement and production planners can update these specialists about manufacturing costs and available capacity.

Zara's information technology provides a platform but does not preclude informal face-to-face conversations. Retail store managers are linked to marketing specialists through customized handheld computers but sometimes use the telephone to share order data, sales trends, and customer reactions to a new style. Zara's cross-functional teams enable information sharing among everyone who "needs to know" and therefore creates the opportunity to change directions quickly to respond to new market trends.

Building Agile and Dynamic Business Processes

To stay competitive and consistently meet changing customer demands, organizations build **dynamic business processes** or **agile business processes**, processes that repeat through a constant renewal cycle of design, deliver, evaluate, redesign, and so on. Agile business processes are designed to simplify redesign and reconfiguration. They are designed to be flexible and easily adaptable to changes in the business environment and can be incrementally changed with little effort. Dynamic business processes, on the other hand, reconfigure themselves as they "learn" and the business utilizes them.

To be agile or dynamic, a process necessitates a high degree of IT use. The more of the process that can be done with software, the easier it is to change, and the more likely it can be designed to be agile or dynamic.

Examples of agile processes are often found in manufacturing operations, where production lines are reconfigured regularly to accommodate new products and technologies. For example, automobile production lines produce large numbers of vehicles, but very few are identical to the one made before or after it on the production line. Also, vehicles are often built with space and wiring for options (such as a remote starter) that can be added by a dealer quickly and with minimal labor. The design of the line is such that many changes in design, features, or options are just incorporated into the assembly of the vehicle at hand.

Another common example is in software development. Agile software development methodologies underlie an incremental and iterative development process that is often used to rapidly and collaboratively create working and relevant software.

More recently, with the use of the Internet and social technologies, building agility into business processes is increasingly common. Processes run entirely in the digital world. Some common examples are order management, service/product provisioning, human resource support, and bill payment. The pervasiveness of the digital world has necessitated rethinking many business processes; customers, employees, and other stakeholders expect to be able to access processes on the Web and perform self-service.

In fact, many processes have been designed as an app, as described in the Introduction. Consider smart phones or tablets. Each app loaded on these devices is, in reality, an automated business process. And because it's an app, it's relatively easy for the developer to upgrade, fix, and enhance. Apps are good examples of software that supports agile processes.

An example of a dynamic process is a network with a changing flow of data. The network could have sensors built in to monitor the flow, and when flow is greater than the current network configuration can handle, the network automatically redistributes or requisitions more capacity to handle the additional data and reconfigures itself to balance the flow over the new channels. Another example, with a more physical configuration, would be a call center. Call center systems are designed to monitor the flow of calls coming into a center and the time it takes for agents to respond to them. These systems can automatically redistribute calls to or from other centers as volume increases or decreases. The system might be sufficiently sophisticated so that it can add additional agents to the schedule or alert a supervisor of an increase and route calls to standby agents. Enabling the system to redistribute incoming calls to respond to changes in the center is an important capability.

Dynamic IT applications, a component of software defined architecture, described more fully in Chapter 6, are required for dynamic business processes. When the underlying IT is not designed with this goal in mind, the business process itself cannot adapt as necessary to changing requirements of the business environment. The benefits of agile and dynamic business processes are operational efficiency gained by the ease of incrementally improving the process as necessary and the ability to create game-changing innovative processes more quickly.

Sloan Valve's NPD process is another example of a more flexible approach. Previously steeped in the old way of doing things, and tied to legacy information systems, the redesigned NPD process was faster and enabled detection of and reaction to customer feedback, process problems, and team misalignments.

Changing Business Processes

Sloan Valve decided to do a complete redesign of its NPD process. After trying to incrementally change it with a new IS, and minor changes to the process, managers realized that a complete transformation was necessary.

Transforming a business today means redesigning business processes. Two techniques used to transform a static business process are: (1) radical process redesign, which is sometimes called **business process reengineering (BPR)** or simply reengineering and (2) incremental, continuous process improvement, which includes **total quality management (TQM)** and **Six Sigma**. Radical and incremental improvement concepts are important; they continue to be different tools a manager can use to effect change in the way his or her organization does business. The basis of both approaches is viewing the business as a set of business processes rather than using a silo perspective.

Incremental Change

At one end of the continuum, managers use incremental change approaches to improve business processes through small, incremental changes. This improvement process generally involves the following activities:

- Choosing a business process to improve
- Choosing a metric by which to measure the business process
- Enabling personnel to find ways to improve the business process based on the metric

Personnel often react favorably to incremental change because it gives them control and ownership of improvements and, therefore, renders change less threatening. The improvements grow from their grassroots efforts. TQM is one such approach that incorporates methods of continuous process improvement. At the core of the TQM method is W. Edwards Deming's "14 Points," or key principles to transform business processes. The principles outline a set of activities for increasing quality and improving productivity.[4] TQM has lost some of its luster in the United States, but it continues to be very popular in Europe and Asia.

Six Sigma is an incremental and data-driven quality management approach for eliminating defects from a process. The term *six sigma* comes from the idea that if the quality of all output from a process were to be mapped on a bell-shaped curve, the tail of the curve, six sigma (standard deviations) from the mean, would represent less than 3.4 defects per million. Such a low rate of defects would be close to perfect. The Six Sigma methodology is carried out by experts known as *Green Belts* and more experienced experts known as *Black Belts,* who have taken special Six Sigma training and worked on numerous Six Sigma projects. Motorola was one of the first companies in the United States to use Six Sigma, but GE made the method a part of its business culture driving significant and continuous improvement throughout the corporation. The GE Web site states "Six Sigma is a highly disciplined process that helps us focus on developing and delivering near-perfect products and services."[5]

Radical Change

Incremental change approaches work well for tweaking existing processes. However, they tend to be less effective for addressing cross-functional processes. Major changes usually associated with cross-functional processes require a different type of management tool. At the other end of the change continuum, radical change enables the organization to attain aggressive improvement goals (again, as defined by a set of metrics). The goal of radical change is to make a rapid, breakthrough impact on key metrics. Some businesses even have made radical process reconfiguration a core competency so that they can better serve customers whose demands are constantly changing.

Sloan Valve is an example of a company that set aggressive improvement goals and reached them with a radical change approach. The company set out to dramatically improve new products' time to market and was able to reduce it from 18–24 months to 12 months.

The difference in the incremental and radical approaches over time is illustrated by the graph in Figure 5.5. The vertical axis measures, in one sense, how well a business process meets its goals. Improvements are made either incrementally or radically. The horizontal axis measures time.

Not surprisingly, radical change typically faces greater internal resistance than does incremental change. Therefore, radical change processes should be carefully planned and used only when major change is needed in a short time. Some examples of situations requiring radical change are when the company is in trouble, when it imminently

[4] For more information about TQM and Deming's 14 Point approach to quality management, see the ASQ (Formerly known as the American Society for Quality), a global community of experts on quality and the administrators of the Malcolm Baldrige National Quality Award program, http://asq.org/learn-about-quality/total-quality-management/overview/overview.html (accessed August 26, 2015).

[5] http://www.ge.com/en/company/companyinfo/quality/whatis.htm (accessed August 27, 2015).

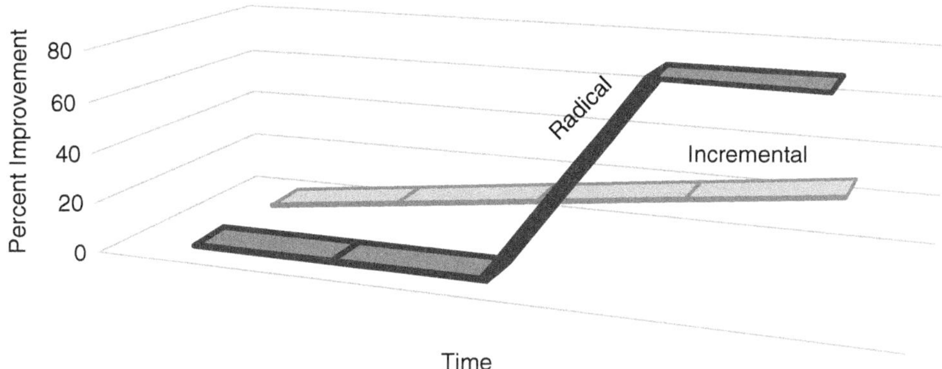

FIGURE 5.5 Comparison of radical and incremental improvement.

faces a major change in the operating environment, or when it must change significantly to outpace its competition. Key aspects of radical change approaches include the following:

- Need for major change in a short amount of time
- Thinking from a cross-functional process perspective
- Challenge to old assumptions
- Networked (cross-functional) organization
- Empowerment of individuals in the process
- Measurement of success via metrics tied directly to business goals and the effectiveness of new processes (e.g., production cost, cycle time, scrap and rework rates, customer satisfaction, revenues, and quality)

Workflow and Mapping Processes

Workflow in its most basic meaning is the series of connected tasks and activities performed by people and computers that together form a business process. Consideration of workflow is a way to assess a cross-functional process. But the term *workflow* has come also to mean software products that document and automate processes. Workflow software facilitates the design of business processes and creates a digital workflow diagram. workflow software lets the manager diagram answers to questions such as how a process will work, who will do what, what the information system will do, and what decisions will be made and by whom. When combined with business process management modules, processes can be managed, monitored, and modified.

The tool used to understand a business process is a **workflow diagram**, which shows a picture, or map, of the sequence and detail of each process step. More than 200 products are available for helping managers diagram the workflow. The objective of process mapping is to understand and communicate the dimensions of the current process. Typically, process engineers begin the process mapping procedure by defining the scope, mission, and boundaries of the business process. Next, engineers develop a high-level overview flowchart of the process and a detailed flow diagram of everything that happens in the process. The diagram uses active verbs to describe activities and identifies all process actors, inputs, and outputs. The engineers verify the detailed diagram for accuracy with the actors in the process and adjust it accordingly.

Business Process Management (BPM)

Thinking about the business as a set of processes has become more common, but managing the business as a set of processes is another story. Some claim that to have truly dynamic or agile business processes requires a well-defined and optimized set of IT processes, tools, and skills called **business process management (BPM)**. In the 1990s, a class of systems to help manage workflows in the business emerged. The systems primarily helped track document-based processes where people executed the steps of the workflow. BPM systems go way beyond document management capabilities and include features that manage person-to-person process steps, system-to-system steps, and those processes that include a combination of them. Systems include process modeling, simulation, code generation, process execution, monitoring, and integration capabilities for both company-based and Web-based systems. The tools allow an organization to actively manage and improve its processes from beginning to end.

Enterprise Rent-a-Car, one of the largest car rental companies in the world with 7,000 locations and more than 65,000 employees worldwide, used BPM to model, manage, and streamline its IT-based processes. It used BPM to build Request Online, the system through which employees requested laptops, software and applications, system access, reports, and other services available from the IS department. The prior system was mostly manual, not scalable as volume increased, and not automatable. Not surprisingly, it was difficult to make improvements to that system. Using a BPM system, the IT staff developed a model that copied the way service requests were already handled so the experience would be familiar and added features slowly to enhance the experience. The result was a BPM-based system that provided better management capabilities and created a common platform for rapid change and capacity for future growth. That proved critical when Enterprise acquired National Car Rental and Alamo Rent A Car, creating much more demand for Request Online. Enterprise was able to shift development to less costly IT staff who could make process modifications directly through the BPM. Finally, the usability of the system was increased as the BPM facilitated the creation of customized interfaces based on characteristics of the specific users.[6]

BPM systems provide a way to build, execute, and monitor automated processes that may go across organizational boundaries. Some of the functionality of a BPM may be found in enterprise applications such as enterprise resource planning (ERP), customer relationship management (CRM), and financial software because these systems also manage processes within a corporation. But BPM systems go outside a specific application to help companies manage across processes. Some BPM systems manage front office applications that are often person-to-person processes such as sales or ordering. These processes are people centric and incorporate social IT. Other BPM systems support back-office processes that often are more system-to-system oriented and possibly extend outside the corporation to include Web-based components. See Figure 5.6 for a representative illustration of the components of a BPM system.

Enterprise's Request Online used a BPM system by Appian, which includes components to help a company design, manage, and optimize core business processes. Appian offers sophisticated features that combine social

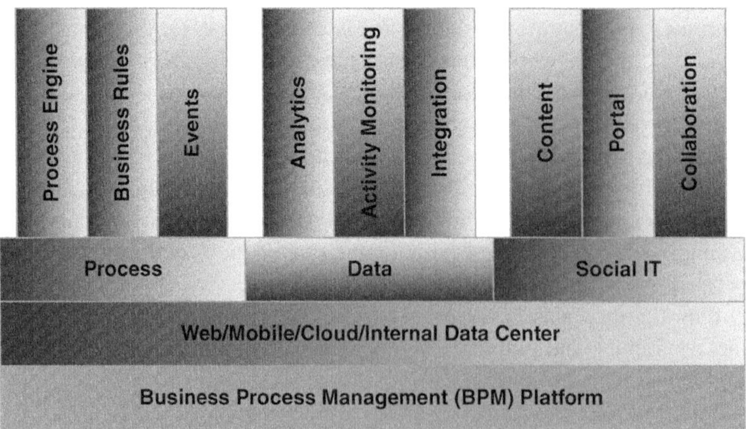

FIGURE 5.6 Sample BPM architecture.
Source: Adapted from www.appian.com (accessed May 1, 2012).

[6] Adapted from http://www.appian.com/about/news-item/enterprise-rent-car-goes-live-appian-enterprise/ (accessed August 27, 2015).

IT capabilities with process modeling, content management, data management, and integration with existing enterprise systems. Microsoft's SharePoint, one of the most popular collaboration environments, can be managed through Appian's suite, creating a one-stop-shop for managing business processes in an enterprise.

Two other common vendors for BPM are IBM and SoftwareAG's ARIS, which stands for architecture of integrated information systems. ARIS has also come to mean an entire modeling approach. ARIS structures four views of the enterprise, including an organizational view, a data view, a functional view, and a control view. Using ARIS, managers can model the business, including its processes, using a common language and set of procedures.

Integration versus Standardization

Processes are the ways organizations deliver goods and services to customers. Designing, building, and executing processes is one of the roles of management. Dr. Jeanne Ross, Principal Research Scientist at MIT's Center for Information Research, suggested that the level of integration and standardization of business processes, another management decision, determines the role of IS. Ross pointed out that "Companies make two important choices in the design of their operations: (1) how standardized their business processes should be across operational units (business units, region, function, market segment) and (2) how integrated their business processes should be across those units." The resulting model defines important IT and business capabilities (see the following figure). The level of process integration and standardization defines the necessary IS capabilities and ultimately the investment the firm will need to make in IS.

Process Integration versus Standardization

		Business Process Standardization	
		Low	High
Business Process Integration	High	The business is focused on process integration, usually creating a single face to customers and suppliers but does not usually impose process standards on operating units.	The business has a centralized design with high needs for reliability, predictability, and sharing data across business units, creating a single view of the process.
	Low	The business has a decentralized design with which business units make local decisions on processes to meet customer needs.	The business is focused on process standardization in which tasks are done the same way with the same systems across business units, but the business units have little need to interact.

CEMEX, the multinational cement company based in Monterrey, Mexico, built a business high in process standardization and low in process integration. CEMEX standardized on eight information systems-based business processes to cover logistics, manufacturing, accounting, planning, operations, procurement, finance, and HR. Each operating unit uses the same processes and creates similar data, but each runs autonomously, rarely sharing data. This approach provides a competitive advantage because it enables the company to grow quickly, easing the assimilation of acquired companies.

Merrill Lynch's Global Private Client business with high integration and low standardization provides a wide range of financial services to clients across multiple channels such as financial advisory services, online services, and help center support services. The key to the company's success is integration across processes to provide a single view of the customer, which can then be leveraged when new products and services are announced. At the same time, the company does not expect standardization across processes; each operating unit can create what it needs as long as it uses a standardized technology platform that supports the integrated design. That is, the separate systems need to coordinate the various information resources among themselves.

Source: J. Ross, "*Forget Strategy: Focus IT on Your Operating Model*," MIT Center for Information Research, Research Briefing (December 2005), V(3C), http://cisr.mit.edu/blog/documents/2005/12/09/2005_12_3c_operatingmodels.pdf/ (accessed May 23, 2015).

Enterprise Systems

Information technology is a critical component of almost every business process today because information flow is at its core. A class of IT applications called **enterprise systems** is a set of information systems tools that many organizations use to enable this information flow within and between processes across the organization. These tools help ensure integration and coordination across functions such as accounting, production, customer management, and supplier management. Some are designed to support a particular industry such as health care, retail, and manufacturing.

Computer systems in the 1960s and early 1970s were typically designed around a specific application. These early systems were often not connected with each other and often had their own version of data. One of the authors moved to another home in 1980 and visited the bank to change his address. He had to fill out a separate form for his checking and savings account. It was lucky that the post office forwarded mail for a year after the move; four months after moving, the bank sent a year-end auto loan summary document via his old address, requiring another update of the address, and nearly a year later, the bank sent his safe deposit box renewal form via his old address too, requiring yet another update. It was obvious that each system contained its own copy of redundant data and existed in its own silo.

Organizational computing groups faced the challenge of linking and maintaining the patchwork of loosely overlapping, redundant systems. In the 1980s and 1990s, software companies in a number of countries, including the United States, Germany, and the Netherlands, began developing integrated software packages that used a common database and cut across organizational systems. Some of these packages were developed from administrative systems (e.g., finance and human resources), and others evolved from materials resource planning (MRP) in manufacturing. These comprehensive software packages that incorporate all modules needed to run the operations of a business are called **enterprise information systems (EIS)** or simply *enterprise systems.* Enterprise systems include ERP, supply chain management (SCM), CRM, and product life cycle management (PLM) systems (see Figure 5.7). Some companies develop proprietary enterprise systems to support mission-critical processes when they believe these processes give them an advantage and using a vendor-supplied system would jeopardize that advantage. Other enterprise systems may be developed specifically to integrate organizational processes. Figure 5.8 describes some examples of the processes supported by an enterprise system.

Two of the largest vendors of enterprise systems are German-based SAP and California-based Oracle. Initially, SAP defined the ERP software space, and Oracle had the database system supporting it. But more recently, SAP has moved to its own database system, and Oracle has acquired many other smaller vendors, creating their own suite of enterprise software solutions.

Sloan Valve, the case introduced at the beginning of this chapter, used SAP. Initially, Sloan implemented the ERP module, but as the design emerged for the NPD process, the PLM module was key. It enabled the process owner to keep track of targets, look at efficiencies in the process, and understand process problems. It also helped track and allocate resources for each new product idea and enabled coordination between all the cross-functional team members.

Enterprise Resource Planning (ERP)

Enterprise resource planning (ERP) was designed to help large companies manage the fragmentation of information stored in hundreds of individual desktop, department, and business unit computers across the organization. These modules offered the IS department in many large organizations an option for switching from underperforming, obsolete mainframe systems to client-server environments designed to handle the changing business demands of their operational counterparts. Many firms moved from their troubled systems in the late 1990s to avoid the year 2000 (Y2K) problem[7] and to standardize processes across their businesses.

[7] The Y2K problem was of great concern in the 1990s because many old systems used two digits instead of four digits to represent the year, making it impossible to distinguish between years such as 2000 and 1900.

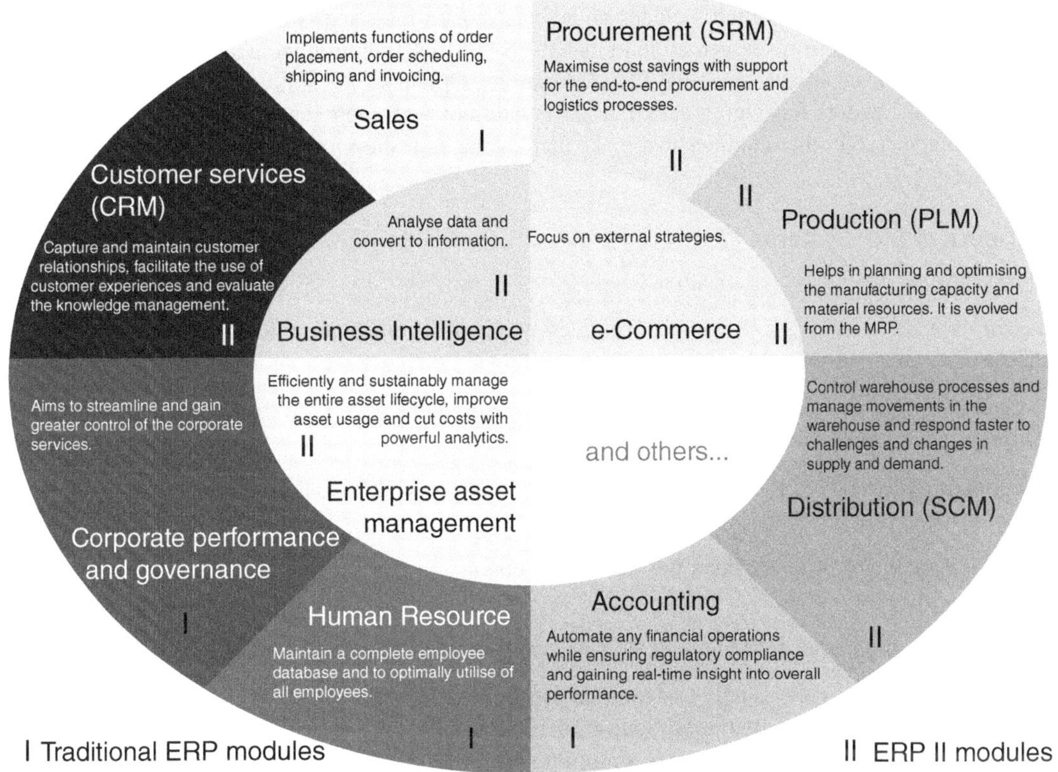

FIGURE 5.7 Enterprise systems and the processes they automate.
Source: Adapted from Shing Hin Yeung, http://commons.wikimedia.org/wiki/File:ERP_Modules.png (accessed August 27, 2015).

Enterprise System	**Sample Processes**
Enterprise resource planning (ERP)	Financial management (accounting, financial close, invoice to pay process, receivable management); human capital management (talent management, payrolls, succession planning); operations management (procurement, logistics, requisition invoice payment, parts inventory)
Customer relationship management (CRM)	Marketing (brand management, campaign management); lead management; loyalty program management; sales planning and forecasting; territory and account management; customer service and support (claims, returns, warranties)
Supply chain management (SCM)	Supply chain design; order fulfillment; warehouse management; demand planning, forecasting; sales and operations planning; service parts planning; source-to-pay/procurement process; supplier life cycle management; supply contract management
Product life cycle management (PLM)	Innovation management (strategy and planning, idea capture and management, program/project management); product development and management; product compliance management

FIGURE 5.8 Enterprise systems and examples of processes they support.

The next generation of enterprise system emerged: ERP II systems. Whereas an ERP makes company information immediately available to all departments throughout the company, ERP II also makes company information immediately available to *external stakeholders*, such as customers and partners. ERP II enables e-business by integrating business processes between an enterprise and its trading partners. More recently, a move to better manage information systems using the cloud has again called into question the design of some business processes.

Today, ERP systems include all of the ERP II functionality plus social and collaboration features. A good example is Chatter from Salesforce.com,[8] which includes an activity stream interface (similar to Facebook) for employees with easy connections to the firm's information in its ERP. SAP's ERP solution includes SAP ERP Financials, SAP ERP Human Capital Management, and SAP ERP Operations. Oracle's ERP solution, EnterpriseOne, offers these same functions. Both vendors have integrated their ERP solutions with their supply chain/logistics solutions, their CRM solutions, and several other modules that make them a one-stop shop for software that provides the backbone of an enterprise.

Characteristics of ERP Systems

ERP systems have several characteristics:[9]

- *Integration.* ERP systems are designed to seamlessly integrate information flows throughout the company. ERP systems are configured by installing various modules, such as:
  - Manufacturing (materials management, inventory, plant maintenance, production planning, routing, shipping, purchasing, etc.)
  - Accounting (general ledger, accounts payable, accounts receivable, cash management, forecasting, cost accounting, profitability analysis, etc.)
  - Human resources (employee data, position management, skills inventory, time accounting, payroll, travel expenses, etc.)
  - Sales (order entry, order management, delivery support, sales planning, pricing, etc.)
- *Packages.* ERP systems are usually commercial packages purchased from software vendors. Unlike many packages, ERP systems usually require long-term relationships with software vendors because the complex systems must typically be modified on a continuing basis to meet the organization's needs.
- *Best practices.* ERP systems reflect industry best (or at least "very good") practices for generic business processes. To implement them, businesses often have to change their processes in some way to accommodate the software.
- *Some assembly required.* The ERP system is software that needs to be integrated with the organization's hardware, operating systems, databases, and network. Further, ERP systems often need to be integrated with proprietary legacy systems. It often requires that **middleware** (software used to connect processes running in one or more computers across a network) or "bolt-on" systems be used to make all the components operational. Vendor-supplied ERP systems have a number of configurable components, too, which need to be set up to best fit with the organization. Rarely does an organization use an ERP system directly "out of the box" without configuration.
- *Evolving.* ERP systems were designed first for mainframe systems, then for client-server architectures, and now for Web-enabled or cloud-based delivery.

Integrating ERP packages with other software in a firm is often a major challenge. For example, integrating internal ERP applications with supply chain management software seems to create issues. Making sure the linkages between the systems happen seamlessly is a challenge. One important problem in meeting this challenge is to allow companies to be more flexible in sourcing from multiple (or alternative) suppliers while also increasing the transparency in tightly coupled supply chains. A second problem is to integrate ERP's transaction-driven focus into a firm's workflow.[10]

---

[8] See http://www.salesforce.com/chatter/overview/ (accessed August 27, 2015).

[9] M. Lynne Markus and Cornelis Tanis, "The Enterprise System Experience—From Adoption to Success," *Framing the Domains of IT Management: Projecting the Future Through the Past,* ed. R. Zmud (Cincinnati, OH: Pinaflex Educational Resources, 2000), 176–79.

[10] Amit Basu and Akhil Kumar, "Research Commentary: Workflow Management Issues in e-Business," *Information Systems Research* 13, no. 1 (March 2002), 1–14.

Managing Customer Relationships

A type of software package that is increasingly considered an enterprise system is customer relationship management systems. **Customer relationship management (CRM)** is a set of software programs that supports management activities performed to obtain, enhance relationships with, and retain customers. They include sales, support, and service processes. Today, CRM has come to mean the enterprise systems that support these processes, and the term is used interchangeably with the set of activities.

CRM processes create ways to learn more about customers' needs and behaviors with the objective of developing stronger relationships. CRM systems consist of technological components as well as many pieces of information about customers, sales, marketing effectiveness, responsiveness, and market trends. Optimized CRM processes and systems can lead to better customer service, more efficient call centers, product cross-selling, simplified sales and marketing efforts, more efficient sales transactions, and increased customer revenues. The goal of CRM is to provide more effective interaction with customers and bring together all information the company has on a customer.

The top-selling CRM systems are from Salesforce.com, SAP, Oracle, and Microsoft Dynamics.[11] Oracle and SAP have CRM systems that integrate with their other enterprise systems. Oracle's CRM system includes modules for pricing, sales force automation, sales order management, support activities, customer self-service, and

Geographic Lens: Global vs. Local ERPs

ERP systems are usually designed around best practices—but whose best practices? SAP and Oracle, the leading vendors of ERP systems, have a Western bias. More specifically, best practices at the heart of their systems are based upon business processes that are found in successful companies in Germany and North America. However, when these systems are transplanted into Asian companies, problematic "misfits" have been found to occur.

An example is the use of ERP systems designed for hospitals. Western health care models are decidedly different from those used in Singapore. In Western countries, insurance enables patients to pay a fraction of their medical expenses themselves, and the government or private insurance covers the rest. Singapore has a completely different model. In Singapore, health care expenses are covered primarily by the individual. Government subsidies and other community support is minimal.

How does this affect processes embedded in ERP systems in hospitals? When ERP systems are designed for Western hospitals, they include modules that help manage the complexity of billing and collections that result from claims submissions and insurance verification. When the primary payment is from individuals paying at the time of service or in installments, the collections process is significantly different. Further, "bed class" is important in Singapore where patients in public hospitals can choose from a variety of plans ranging from one bed to six or more per room. The Western model is simpler because single-bed rooms are more common.

Because of differences and "misfits," businesses in many non-Western companies are turning to local vendors that have developed systems reflecting local best practices. For example, local ERP vendors in Taiwan have developed ERP systems to support the majority of firms in the market space—small- to medium-sized Taiwanese companies with sophisticated, adaptive logistic networks. The local ERP vendors have adopted a strategy of customization and are more willing to modify their systems to satisfy local needs than are their large global competitors.

These examples suggest that another factor needs to be considered when designing and implementing and ERP: It should not be implemented if the system is based on a cultural model that conflicts with the local customs and that cannot easily be accommodated.

Sources: C. Soh, S. K. Sia, and J. Tay-Yap, "Cultural Fits and Misfits: Is ERP a Universal Solution," *Communications of the ACM* 43, no. 4 (2000), 47–51; E. T. G. Wang, G. Kleing, and J. J. Jiang, "ERP Misfit: Country of Origin and Organizational Factors," *Journal of Management Information Systems* 23, no. 1 (2006), 263–92.

[11] Louis Columbus, "Gartner CRM Market Share Update: 41% Of CRM Systems Are SaaS-based, Salesforce Dominating Market Growth," *Forbes*, May 6, 2014, http://www.forbes.com/sites/louiscolumbus/2014/05/06/gartners-crm-market-share-update-shows-41-of-crm-systems-are-saas-based-with-salesforce-dominating-market-growth/ (accessed August 27, 2015).

service management. SAP's CRM system has similar modules plus marketing support such as resource and brand management, campaign management, real-time offer management, loyalty management, and e-marketing. There is also an e-commerce module that facilitates personalized interface and self-service applications for customers. Salesforce.com is a different type of CRM. Whereas Oracle and SAP came from the enterprise systems space and then created a CRM module, Salesforce.com started with a CRM solution. In addition, the products by Oracle and SAP grew from on-premise enterprise systems, and each company eventually built Web-based versions of its products, but Salesforce.com started as a Web-based cloud system. Managers who seek a CRM system for their organizations should compare the features and delivery systems of these and other solutions provided by niche vendors who specialize in systems optimized for specific industry applications.

Social IT is increasingly integrated into CRM solutions. Providing software or Web applications that extend the brand, engage customers, allow customers to interact with each other and with employees, and provide service options generates additional "touches" with customers. CRM systems record these touches. The information becomes an additional channel of data useful for building customer relationships. Salesforce.com teamed with Dun & Bradstreet to use Data.com, a cloud-based storehouse of company and customer contact information for use in CRM systems. Data.com uses a crowd-sourcing model to collect up-to-date information with users of the server contributing data and helping to keep that data accurate.

In Chapter 1, we described the Ritz-Carlton's CRM, Class, which captures information about guest preferences and enables the chain to provide enhanced, customized service during future visits. Web sites collect information from customers who visit, make purchases, or request information. That information is stored in the company's CRM and used in many ways to better meet customer needs and enhance the customer experience. For example, movie site Netflix stores all the purchases and product reviews a customer makes in its CRM. Using that information, the site recommends additional films the customer might enjoy based on analysis of the data in the CRM.

Managing Supply Chains

Another type of enterprise system in common use is a **supply chain management (SCM)** system, which manages the integrated supply chain. Business processes are not just internal to a company. With the help of information technologies, many processes are linked across companies with a companion process at a customer or supplier, creating an integrated supply chain. Technology, especially Web-based technology, allows the supply chains of a company's customers and suppliers to be linked through a single network that optimizes costs and opportunities for all companies in the supply chain. By sharing information across the network, guesswork about order quantities for raw materials and products can be reduced, and suppliers can make sure they have enough on hand if demand for their products unexpectedly rises.

The supply chain of a business is the process that begins with raw materials and ends with a product or service ready to be delivered (or in some cases actually delivered) to a customer. It typically includes the procurement of materials or components, the activities to turn these materials into larger subsystems or final products, and the distribution of these final products to warehouses or customers. But with the increase in information systems use, the supply chain may also include product design, product planning, contract management, logistics, and sourcing. Globalization of business and ubiquity of communication networks and information technology have enabled businesses to use suppliers from almost anywhere in the world. At the same time, this has created an additional level of complexity for managing the supply chain. *Supply chain integration* is the approach of technically linking supply chains of vendors and customers to streamline the process and to increase efficiency and accuracy.

Without such linking, a temporary increase in demand from a retailer might become interpreted by its suppliers as permanent, and the changes can become magnified by each supplier up the chain when each supplier attempts to add another percent or two just to be "safe." Those erratic and wild changes are called the *bullwhip effect*. Linking synchronizes all suppliers to the same demand increase up and down the chain and prevents that effect.

Integrated supply chains have several challenges, primarily resulting from different degrees of integration and coordination among supply chain members.[12] At the most basic level, there is the issue of information integration. Partners must agree on the type of information to share, the format of that information, the technological standards they both use to share it, and the security they use to ensure that only authorized partners access it. Trust must be established so the partners can solve higher-level issues that may arise. At the next level is the issue of synchronized planning. At this level, the partners must agree on a joint system of planning, forecasting, and replenishment. The partners, having already agreed on what information to share, now have to agree on what to do with it. The third level can be described as workflow coordination—the coordination, integration, and automation of critical business processes between partners. For some supply chains, this might mean simply using a third party to link the procurement process to the preferred vendors or to communities of vendors who compete virtually for the business. For others, it might be a more complex process of integrating order processing and payment systems. Ultimately, supply chain integration leads to new business models as varied as the visionaries who think them up. These business models are based on new ideas of coordination and integration made possible by the Internet and information-based supply chains. In some cases, new services have been designed by the partnership between supplier and customer, such as new financial services offered when banks link up electronically with businesses to accept online payments for goods and services purchased by the businesses' customers. In other cases, a new business model for sourcing has resulted, such as one in which companies list their supply needs and vendors electronically bid to be the supplier for that business.

Demand-driven supply networks are the next step for companies with highly evolved supply chain capabilities. Kimberly Clark, the 135-year-old consumer products company, is one such example. Its vision is for a highly integrated suite of supply chain systems that provide end-to-end visibility of the supply processes in real time. Key processes in the company's demand-driven supply network are forecast to stock and order to cash. Using an integrated suite of systems allows the firm's users to share the same information as close to real time as possible and to use the data in their systems for continually updating their supply chain, category management, and consumer insight processes. IS have allowed managers to reduce the problems of handing off data from one system or process to another (because now everything is in one system), having employees work from different databases (because it's now one database), and working with old data (because it's as real time as possible). This has improved managers' ability to see what's going on in the marketplace and evaluate the impact of promotions, production, and inventory much more quickly.

Integrated supply chains are truly global in nature. Thomas Friedman, in his book *The World is Flat*, describes how the Dell computer that he had ordered for writing his book was developed from the contributions of an integrated supply chain that involved about four hundred companies in North America, Europe, and, primarily, Asia. However, the globalization of integrated supply chains faces a growing challenge from skyrocketing transportation costs. For example, Tesla Motors, a pioneer in electric-power cars, had originally planned the production of a luxury roadster for the U.S. market based on an integrated global supply chain. The 1,000-pound battery packs for the cars were to be manufactured in Thailand, shipped to Britain for installation, and then shipped to the United States where they would be assembled into cars. However, because of the extensive costs associated with shipping the batteries more than 5,000 miles, Tesla decided to make the batteries and assemble the cars near its headquarters in California. Darryl Siry, Tesla's Senior Vice President of Global Sales, Marketing, and Service explains: "It was kind of a no-brain decision for us. A major reason was to avoid the transportation costs, which are terrible." Economists warn managers to expect the "neighborhood effect" in which factories may be built closer to component suppliers and consumers to reduce transportation costs. This effect may apply not only to cars and steel but also to chickens and avocados and a wide range of other items.[13]

[12] Hau Lee and Seungjin Whang, "E-Business and Supply Chain Integration," Stanford University Global Supply Chain Management Forum (November 2001).

[13] Larry Rohter, "Shipping Costs Start to Crimp Globalization" *The New York Times,* 1, 10, http://www.nytimes.com/2008/08/03/business/worldbusiness/03global.html (accessed August 27, 2015).

Dell continues to be not only a great example of an integrated supply chain but also of the neighborhood effect. Its "build-to-order" strategy of building computers as they are ordered rather than to mass-produce them for inventory requires an integrated supply chain. One of the authors of this textbook visited a Dell plant in Malaysia with several dozen students. An official there described how the plant's zero inventory goal was accomplished by ordering components only when computers were ordered, to arrive on the day of assembly. Also, suppliers were strategically located in adjacent buildings surrounding the plant with an airport practically in walking distance. In this way, suppliers are closely linked with the actual production process.

Product Life Cycle Management (PLM)

A less well-known type of enterprise system is a **product life cycle management (PLM)** system. PLM systems automate the steps that take ideas for products and turn them into actual products. *PLM* refers to the process that starts with the idea for a product and ends with the "end of life" of a product. It includes the innovation activities, new product development, and management, design, and product compliance (if necessary). PLM systems contain all the information about a product such as design, production, maintenance, components, vendors, customer feedback, and marketing.

Advantages and Disadvantages of Enterprise Systems

One major benefit of enterprise systems is that they represent a set of industry best practices. One confidential story relayed to the authors described a large university that had suffered for years with inconsistent, incomplete, and immature processes. The university's leader announced in advance that rather than customize a new ERP to fit those processes, the directive was to replace completely those poor processes provided by the ERP. As a result, the ERP's best practices dramatically improved the university's ability to provide information services to faculty, staff, and students and also to track the entire "life cycle" of people from initial inquiry to graduation and beyond.

Another major benefit of an enterprise system is that all modules of the information system easily communicate with each other, offering enormous efficiencies over stand-alone systems. In business, information from one functional area is often needed by another area. For example, an inventory system stores information about vendors who supply specific parts. This same information is required by the accounts payable system, which pays vendors for their goods. It makes sense to integrate these two systems to have a single accurate record of vendors and to use an enterprise system to facilitate that integration.

Because of the focus on integration, enterprise systems are useful tools for an organization seeking to centralize operations and decision making. As described earlier in the Integration versus Standardization box about the Ross framework, high integration allows units to coordinate easily and unify their data for global access. Redundant data entry and duplicate data may be eliminated; standards for numbering, naming, and coding may be enforced; and data and records can be cleaned up through standardization. Further, the enterprise system can reinforce the use of standard procedures across different locations.

The obvious benefits notwithstanding, implementing an enterprise system represents an enormous amount of work. For example, if an organization has allowed both the manufacturing and the accounting departments to keep their own records of vendors, then most likely these records are kept in somewhat different forms (one department may enter the vendor name as IBM, the other as International Business Machines or even IBM Corp., all of which make it difficult to integrate the databases). Making matters worse, a simple data item's name itself might be stored differently in different systems. In one system, it might be named Phone_No, but in another, it might be simply Phone. Such inconsistencies in data items and values must be recognized and fixed so that the enterprise system can provide optimal advantage.

Moreover, even though enterprise systems are flexible and customizable to a point, most also require business processes to be redesigned to achieve optimal performance of the integrated modules. It is rare that an off-the-shelf system is perfectly harmonious with an existing business process; the software usually requires significant modification or customization to fit with the existing processes, or the processes must change to fit the software.

In most installations of enterprise systems, both take place. The system is usually customized when it is installed in a business by setting a number of parameters. Many ERP projects are massive undertakings, requiring formal, structured project management tools (as discussed in Chapter 11).

All systems make assumptions about how the business processes work, and at some level, customization is not possible. For example, one major Fortune 500 company refused to implement a vendor's enterprise system because the company manufactured products in lots of "one," and the vendor's system would not handle the volume this company generated. If the company had decided to use the ERP, a complete overhaul of its manufacturing process in a way that executives were unwilling to do would have been necessary.

Implementing enterprise systems requires organizations to make changes beyond just the processes, but also in their organization structure. Recall from Chapter 1 that the Information Systems Strategy Triangle suggests that implementing an information system must be accompanied with appropriate organizational changes to be effective. Implementing an enterprise system is no different; a 2014 Panorama report stated directly that only firms that allocate enough of the project budget to organizational change management will achieve the best results.[14] For example, who will now be responsible for entering the vendor information that was formerly kept in two locations? How will that information be entered into the enterprise system? The answer to such simple operational questions often requires managers minimally to modify business processes and more likely to redesign them completely to accommodate the information system.

Enterprise systems are also risky. The number of enterprise system horror stories demonstrates this risk. For example, Kmart wrote off its $130 million ERP investment. American LaFrance (ALF), the manufacturer of highly customized emergency vehicles, declared bankruptcy, blaming its IT vendor and its ERP implementation. The problems with the implementation kept ALF from being able to manufacture many preordered vehicles.[15] Two months after the installation of a new ERP system, the Fort Worth Police Officers Association complained that paychecks were not being received correctly or on a timely basis by officers. Some officers had not been paid since the installation, and others were shortchanged in their paychecks because the new system was not able to handle odd hours and shift work.

Furthermore, enterprise systems and the organizational changes they induce tend to come with a hefty price tag. In a study of the initial acquisition and implementation costs of ERP systems in primarily midsize companies (with $100 million to $1 billion in annual revenues), half of the responding 157 chief financial officers (CFOs) admitted spending *more than* $1 million for the license, service, and first year's maintenance on their current ERP systems. Nine of 10 respondents said they spent a minimum of $250,000. Unreported were additional hidden costs in the form of technical and business changes, likely to be necessary when implementing an enterprise system. These include project management, user training, and IT support costs.[16] Some surveys uncover negative impacts on performance. For instance, in 2014, overruns in costs were found to plague 54% of ERP projects, and 72% of the firms reporting encountered implementation delays. Perhaps more important were disruptions in service such as difficulties in shipping products, experienced by 51% of the firms surveyed.[17]

One of the reasons that ERP systems are so expensive is that they are sold as a suite, such as financials or manufacturing, and not as individual modules. Because buying modules separately is difficult, companies implementing ERP software often find the price of modules they won't use hidden in the cost of the suite.

Seventy percent of survey respondents report that they are satisfied with their ERP systems in spite of the large expense, overruns, delays, and disruptions experienced, largely due to the capabilities of ERP systems. However, only 63% considered the project a "success," perhaps due to overruns.[18] A set of advantages and disadvantages of enterprise systems is provided in Figure 5.9.

---

[14] Panorama Consulting, "Organizational Issues Number One Reason for Extended Durations," http://panorama-consulting.com/company/press-releases/panorama-consulting-solutions-releases-2014-erp-report/ (accessed February 26, 2015).

[15] For additional examples of IT failures in general and enterprise systems failures in particular, please visit the blog written by Michael Krigsman, http://blogs.zdnet.com/projectfailures/.

[16] T. Wailgum, "Why CEOs and CFOs Hate It: ERP" (April 8, 2009), http://advice.cio.com/thomas_wailgum/why_cfos_and_ceos_hate_it_erp (accessed February 14, 2012).

[17] Panorama Consulting 2014 Report.

[18] Ibid.

Advantages	Disadvantages
• Represent "best practices" • Allow modules throughout the organization to communicate with each other • Enable centralized decision making • Eliminate redundant data entry • Enable standardized procedures in different locations	• Require enormous amount of work • Require redesign of business practices for maximum benefit • Have very high cost • Are sold as a suite, not individual modules • Require organizational changes • Have high risk of failure

FIGURE 5.9 Advantages and disadvantages of enterprise systems.

When the System Drives the Transformation

When is it appropriate to use the enterprise system to drive transformation and business process redesign, and when is it appropriate to redesign the process first and then implement an enterprise system? Although it may seem like the process should be redesigned first and then the information system aligned to the new design, there are times when it is appropriate to let the enterprise system drive business process redesign. First, when an organization is just starting out and processes do not yet exist, it is appropriate to begin with an enterprise system as a way to structure operational business processes. After all, most processes embedded in the "plain vanilla" enterprise system from a top vendor are based on the best practices of corporations that have been in business for years. Second, when an organization does not rely on its operational business processes as a source of competitive advantage, then using an enterprise system to redesign these processes is appropriate. Third, it is reasonable when the current systems are in

Social Business Lens: Crowdsourcing Changes Innovation Processes

One business process that has been radically changed by the use of social IT is the way innovation is managed using crowdsourcing. Enterprises have found ways to use a social IT platform to solicit, discuss, and prioritize new ideas. Anyone in the community can add an idea, and then the entire community can discuss, comment on, and rate the idea. Managers then have a wealth of ideas along with community input to use as input into the innovation process.

One of the original examples of this is Dell's Ideastorm. Anyone in the community can access Ideastorm to view ideas posted by the community, post an idea for Dell products or services, vote on the ideas presented, and see what Dell managers have decided to do with the ideas presented. Ideas presented by the community range from suggestions for new features on existing systems to new products and services Dell might offer. By allowing the community to comment and vote on ideas, managers get a sense of the importance and viability of implementing the innovation.

Similar social platforms have been implemented by numerous other companies including Starbucks' mystarbucksidea.com and Best Buy's IdeaX. Companies have also taken this idea inside the corporation to solicit ideas and innovations about processes, products, and other enterprise issues. Dell's EmployeeStorm and the City of New York's Simplicity are two social IT examples of soliciting ideas to improve processes and efficiencies from employees.

Companies have also embraced the crowd for individual projects; Sam Adams, the beer company, used a Facebook application for crowdsourcing the next flavor of beer. The application let fans select the color, clarity, body, malt, hops, and yeast components of a recipe. For each component, the crowdsourcing application educated fans about the contribution each component made to the resulting beer. The company collected the crowd's preferences, sharing them along the way for comment and discussion. The results not only gave Sam Adams managers information about preferences of their fans but also prioritized ideas about the next product to create with a high probability that it will have a large fan base to get it started.

Sources: https://gigaom.com/2011/01/19/new-york-city-crowdsourcing/ (accessed August 27, 2015); http://www.facebook.com/SamuelAdams?sk=app_299970113373932 (accessed January 19, 2012); http://www.ideastorm.com (accessed on August 30, 2015).

crisis and there is not enough time, resources, or knowledge in the firm to fix them. Even though it is not an optimal situation, managers must make tough decisions about how to fix the problems. A business must have working operational processes; therefore, using an enterprise system as the basis for process design may be the only workable plan. It was precisely this situation that many companies faced with Y2K.

Likewise, it is sometimes inappropriate to let an enterprise system drive business process change. When an organization derives a strategic advantage through its operational business processes, it is usually not advisable for it to buy a vendor's enterprise system. Using a standard, publicly available information system that both the company and its competitors can buy from a vendor may mean that any system-related competitive advantage is lost. For example, consider a major computer manufacturer that relied on its ability to process orders faster than its competitors to gain strategic advantage. Adopting an enterprise system's approach would result in a loss of that advantage. Furthermore, the manufacturer might find that relying on a third party as the provider of such a strategic system would be a mistake in the long run because any problems with the system due to bugs or changed business needs would require negotiating with the ERP vendor for the needed changes. With a system designed in house, the manufacturer was able to ensure complete control over the IS that drives its critical processes.

Another situation in which it would be inappropriate to let an enterprise system drive business process change is when the features of available packages and the needs of the business do not fit. An organization may use specialized processes that cannot be accommodated by the available enterprise systems. For example, many ERPs were developed for discrete part manufacturing and do not support some processes in paper, food, or other process industries.[19]

A third situation would result from lack of top management support, company growth, a desire for strategic flexibility, or decentralized decision making that render the enterprise system inappropriate. For example, Dell stopped the full implementation of SAP R/3 after only the human resources module had been installed because the CIO did not think that the software would be able to keep pace with Dell's extraordinary growth. Enterprise systems were also viewed as culturally inappropriate at the highly decentralized Kraft Foods.

Challenges for Integrating Enterprise Systems Between Companies

With the widespread use of enterprise systems, the issue of linking supplier and customer systems to the business's systems brings many challenges. As with integrated supply chains, there are issues of deciding what to share, how to share it, and what to do with it when the sharing takes place. There are also issues of security and agreement on encryption or other measures to protect data integrity as well as to ensure that only authorized parties have access.

Some companies have tried to reduce the complexity of this integration by insisting on standards either at the industry level or at the system level. An example of an industry-level standard is the bar coding used by all who do business in the consumer products industry. An example of a system-level standard is the use of SAP or Oracle to provide the ERP system used by both supplier and customer. And the increasing use of cloud-based systems with standard interfaces makes the integration easier.

SUMMARY

- Most business processes today have a significant information systems component to them. Either the process is completely executed through software or an important information component complements the physical execution of the process. Transforming business, therefore, involves rethinking the information systems that support business processes.
- IS can enable or impede business process change. IS enables change by providing both the tools to implement the change and the tools on which the change is based. IS can impede change, particularly when the process flow is mismatched with the capabilities of the IS.
- To understand the role IS plays in business transformation, one must take a business process rather than a functional (silo) perspective. Business processes are well-defined, ordered sets of tasks characterized by a beginning and an end,

[19] Markus and Tanis, "The Enterprise System Experience," 176–79.

sets of associated metrics, and cross-functional boundaries. Most businesses operate business processes even if their organization charts are structured by functions rather than by processes.

- Agile business processes are processes that are designed to be easily reconfigurable. Dynamic processes are designed to automatically update themselves as conditions change. Both types of processes require a high degree of information systems, which makes the task of changing the process a software activity rather than a physical activity.
- Making changes in business processes typically involves either incremental or radical change. Incremental change with TQM and Six Sigma implies an evolutionary approach. Radical change with a BPR approach, on the other hand, is more sudden. Either approach can be disruptive to the normal flow of the business; hence, strong project management skills are needed.
- BPM systems are used to help managers design, control, and document business processes and ultimately the workflow in an organization.
- An enterprise system is a large information system that provides the core functionality needed to run a business. These systems are typically implemented to help organizations share data between divisions. However, in some cases, enterprise systems are used to effect organizational transformation by imposing a set of assumptions on the business processes they manage.
- An ERP system is a type of enterprise system used to manage resources including financial, human resources, and operations.
- A CRM system is a type of enterprise system used to manage the processes related to customers and the relationships developed with customers.
- An integrated supply chain is often managed using an SCM system, an enterprise system that crosses company boundaries and connects vendors and suppliers with organizations to synchronize and streamline planning and deliver products to all members of the supply chain.
- A PLM system is a type of enterprise system support product development from its first idea up through its end.
- Information systems are useful as tools to both enable and manage business transformation. The general manager must take care to ensure that consequences of the tools themselves are well understood and well managed.

KEY TERMS

agile business processes (p. 104)
business process management (BPM) (p. 107)
business process perspective (p. 102)
business process reengineering (BPR) (p. 105)
customer relationship management (CRM) (p. 113)
cycle time (p. 102)
dynamic business processes (p. 104)
Enterprise Information Systems (EIS) (p. 110)
enterprise resource planning (ERP) (p. 110)
enterprise systems (p. 110)
middleware (p. 112)
process (p. 102)
process perspective (p. 102)
product life cycle management (PLM) (p. 116)
silo perspective (p.103)
Six Sigma (p. 105)
supply chain management (SCM) (p. 114)
throughput (p. 102)
total quality management (TQM) (p. 105)
workflow (p. 107)
workflow diagram (p. 107)

DISCUSSION QUESTIONS

1. Why was radical design of business processes embraced so quickly and so deeply by senior managers of so many companies? In your opinion, and using hindsight, was its popularity a benefit for businesses? Why or why not?
2. Off-the-shelf enterprise IS often forces an organization to redesign its business processes. What are the critical success factors to make sure the implementation of an enterprise system is successful?
3. ERP systems are usually designed around best practices. But whose best practices are the right ones? A Western bias is common; practices found in North America or Europe are often the foundation. When transferred to Asia, however, the

resulting systems may be problematic. Why do you think this is the case? What might be different in the way different countries use processes (besides the standard "language" difference)?

4. Have you been involved with a company doing a redesign of its business processes? If so, what were the key things that went right? What went wrong? What could have been done better to minimize the risk of failure?

5. What do you think the former CIO of Dell, Jerry Gregoire, meant when he said, "Don't automate broken business processes"?[20]

6. What might an integrated supply chain look like for a financial services company such as an insurance provider or a bank? What are the components of the process? What would the customer relationship management process look like for this same firm?

7. Tesco, the U.K. retail grocery chain, used its CRM system to generate annual incremental sales of £100 million. Using a frequent shopper card, a customer got discounts at the time of purchase, and the company got information about the customer's purchases, creating a detailed database of customer preferences. Tesco then categorized customers and customized discounts and mailings, generating increased sales and identifying new products to expand the organization's offerings. At the individual stores, data showed which products must be priced below competitors, which products had fewer price-sensitive customers, and which products must have regular low prices to be successful. In some cases, prices were store specific, based on the customer information. The information system has enabled Tesco to expand beyond groceries to books, DVDs, consumer electronics, flowers, and wine. The chain also offers services such as loans, credit cards, savings accounts, and travel planning. What can Tesco management do now that the company has a CRM that it could not do prior to the CRM implementation? How does this system enable Tesco to increase the value provided to customers?

CASE STUDY 5-1 Santa Cruz Bicycles

Bicycle enthusiasts not only love the ride their bikes provide but also are often willing to pay for newer technology, especially when it will increase their speed or comfort. Innovating new technologies for bikes is only half the battle for bike manufacturers. Designing the process to manufacture the bikes is often the more daunting challenge.

Consider the case of Santa Cruz Bicycles. It digitally designs and builds mountain bikes and tests them under the most extreme conditions to bring the best possible product to its customers. A few years back, the company designed and patented the Virtual Pivot Point (VPP) suspension system, a means to absorb the shocks that mountain bikers encounter when on the rough terrain of the off-road ride. One feature of the new design allowed the rear wheel to bounce 10 inches without hitting the frame or seat, providing shock absorption without feeling like the rider was sitting on a coiled spring.

The first few prototypes did not work well; in one case, the VPP joint's upper link snapped after a quick jump. The experience was motivation for a complete overhaul of the design and engineering process to find a way to go from design to prototype faster. The 25-person company adopted a similar system used by large, global manufacturers: product life cycle management (PLM) software.

The research and development team had been using computer-aided-design (CAD) software, but it took seven months to develop a new design, and if the design failed, starting over would be the only solution. This design approach was a drain not only on the company's time but also on its finances. The design team found a PLM system that helped members analyze and model capabilities in a much more robust manner. The team used simulation capabilities to watch the impact of the new designs on rough mountain terrain. The software tracks all the variables the designers and engineers need so they can quickly and easily make adjustments to the design. The new system allows the team to run a simulation in a few minutes, representing a very large improvement over their previous design software, which took seven hours to run a simulation.

The software was just one component of the new process design. The company also hired a new master frame builder to build and test prototypes in house and invested in a van-size machine that can fabricate intricate parts for the prototypes, a process the company previously outsourced. The result was a significant decrease in its design-to-prototype process. What once averaged about 28 months from start of design to shipping of the new bike now takes 12 to 14 months.

[20] "Technology: How Much? How Fast? How Revolutionary? How Expensive?" *Fast Company* 56, no. 62, http://www.fastcompany.com/online/56/fasttalk.html (accessed May 30, 2002).

Discussion Questions

1. Would you consider this transformation to be incremental or radical? Why?
2. What, in your opinion, was the key factor in Santa Cruz Bicycles' successful process redesign? Why was that factor the key?
3. What outside factors had to come together for Santa Cruz Bicycles to be able to make the changes it did?
4. Why is this story more about change management than software implementation?

Source: Adapted from Mel Duvall, "Santa Cruz Bicycles," www.baselinemag.com (accessed February 24, 2008).

CASE STUDY 5-2 Boeing 787 Dreamliner

The first Boeing 787 Dreamliner was delivered to Japan's ANA in the third quarter of 2011, more than three years after the initial planned delivery date. Its complicated, unique design (including a one-piece fuselage that eliminated the need for 1,500 aluminum sheets and 50,000 fasteners and reduced the resulting weight of the plane proportionally) promised both a reduction in out-of-service maintenance time and a 20% increase in fuel economy, but problems with early testing of the new design contributed to the giant project's troubles. Even after those delays, the 787 was grounded in January 2013 because the main battery had problems of overheating and subsequently burning. The problems were finally reported solved in December 2014.

Delivery of Boeing's 787 Dreamliner project was delayed, in part, because of the company's global supply chain network, which was touted to reduce cost and development time. In reality, the network turned out to be a major cause for problems. Boeing decided to change the rules of the way large passenger aircraft were developed through its Dreamliner program; rather than simply relying on technological know-how, it decided to use collaboration as a competitive tool embedded in a new global supply chain process.

With the Dreamliner project, Boeing not only attempted to create a new aircraft through the innovative design and new material but also radically changed the production process. It built an incredibly complex supply chain involving over 50 partners scattered in 103 locations all over the world. The goal was to reduce both the financial risks involved in a $10 billion-plus project for designing and developing a new aircraft and the new product development cycle time. Boeing tapped the expertise of various firms in different areas such as composite materials, aerodynamics, and IT infrastructure to create a network in which partners' skills complement each other. This changed the basis of competition to skill set rather than the traditional basis of low cost. In addition, this was the first time Boeing had outsourced the production on the two most critical parts of the plane—the wings and the fuselage.

The first sign of problems showed up just six months into the trial production. Engineers discovered unexpected bubbles in the skin of the fuselage during baking of the composite material. This delayed the project a month. Boeing officials insisted that they could make up the time and all things were under control. But next to fail was the test version of the nose section. This time, a problem was found in the software programs, which were designed by various manufacturers. They failed to communicate with each other, leading to a breakdown in the integrated supply chain. Then problems popped up in the integration of electronics. The Dreamliner program entered the danger zone when Boeing declared that it was having trouble getting enough permanent titanium fasteners to hold together various parts of the aircraft. The global supply network did not integrate well for Boeing and left it highly dependent on a few suppliers.

The battery problems involved lithium-ion batteries that could not recover from a situation involving a rare but serious internal short circuit that would cause flames to spread from one cell to another. Lithium-ion batteries had not previously been used in an airplane and had not been tested under an assumption of a short circuit.

This case clearly underscores the hazards in relying on an extensive supply chain, failing to expect the worst case with critical new parts, and encountering information exchange problems that caused long delays and seriously compromised a company's ability to carry out business as planned. Creating a radically different process can mean encountering unexpected problems. In some cases, it would put a company so far behind its competition that it was doomed to fail. However, in this case, the major competitor to the Dreamliner, the Airbus 380 program, was also using a global supply chain model, and its program was delayed by a couple of years. The result for Boeing was a much-anticipated plane with fuel economy and outstanding design that made the wait worth it. However, because of compromises in design, the Dreamliner holds only up to 250 passengers, compared to the A380, which has a seating capacity between 525 and 853.

Discussion Questions

1. Why did Boeing adopt the radical change approach for designing and developing the 787 Dreamliner? What were the risks? In your opinion, was it a good move? Defend your choice.
2. Using the silo perspective versus business process perspective, analyze the Dreamliner program.
3. What are your conclusions about the design of the integrated supply chain? Give some specific ideas about what could have been done to integrate it better.
4. If you were the program manager, what would you have done differently to avoid the problems faced by the Dreamliner program?

Sources: Adapted from J. Lynn Lunsford, "Boeing Scrambles to Repair Problems with New Plane," *The Wall Street Journal* (December 7, 2007), A1, 13; Stanley Holmes, "The 787 Encounters Turbulence," *Businessweek* (June 19, 2006), 38–40; Zach Honig, "Boeing 787 Review: ANA's Dreamliner Flies Across Japan, We Join for the Ride" (December 16, 2011), http://www.engadget.com/2011/12/16/boeing-787-review-anas-dreamliner-flies-across-japan-we-join/ (accessed August 27, 2015); J. Mouawad, "Report on Boeing 787 Dreamliner Battery Flaws Finds Lapses at Multiple Points," *The New York Times* (December 1, 2014), http://www.nytimes.com/2014/12/02/business/report-on-boeing-787-dreamliner-batteries-assigns-some-blame-for-flaws.html?

chapter

6

Architecture and Infrastructure

This chapter provides managers with an overview of IT architecture and infrastructure issues and designs. It begins by translating a business into IT architecture and then from the architecture into infrastructure. The manager's role is then discussed, and an example of a fictitious company, GiantCo.com, is used to show how strategy leads to infrastructure. The framework used to describe the basic components of architecture and infrastructure, introduced in Chapter 1, is revisited here, providing a language and structure for describing hardware, software, network, and data considerations. Common architectures are then presented, including centralized, decentralized and Web-based service-oriented architecture (SOA). Architectural principles are covered, followed by a discussion of enterprise architecture. Virtualization and cloud computing, two current architectural considerations, are reviewed. The chapter concludes with a discussion of managerial considerations that apply to any architecture.

Mohawk,[1] a paper mill in upstate New York, was established in 1931. Contrary to a common assumption that information technology is not critical to old technology industry players facing a declining market, the firm has not only embraced cloud computing but also has been able to transform its business because of the cloud in three ways: (1) moving from manufacturing as its primary focus to providing service, (2) shifting from a self-sufficient model to one of collaboration with a network of partners, and (3) ensuring that the partner network is flexible and its capabilities are integrated with those of Mohawk. Mohawk accomplished this flexibility by using service-oriented architecture (SOA) tools, which enable a firm to scale technology services (and expenses) up and down instantaneously according to its needs.[2] Also, applications under SOA can be added or subtracted as needed.

Mohawk's new envelope manufacturing facility serves as a vivid example to illustrate the benefits of flexibility. Along the way, the company learned of the anticipated bankruptcy of the largest envelope manufacturing firm in the United States and developed a list of six outsourced firms to turn its premium papers into envelopes. After six months of using those suppliers and investing in building its own in-house envelope manufacturing capabilities, Mohawk was able to shift to an insourcing model for 90% of its volume. The cloud services approach avoided the information systems difficulties usually inherent in such a transformation.

There are also benefits to internal flexibility as well. As processing volumes increase and decrease, sometimes on a seasonal basis and sometimes due to new or discontinued lines of business, Mohawk experiences corresponding increases and decreases in its requirements for space, servers, and processing. Its cloud approach allows the company to set up or dismantle servers quickly.

[1] Adapted from Paul J. Stamas, Michelle L. Kaarst-Brown, and Scott A. Bernard, "The Business Transformation Payoffs of Cloud Services at Mohawk," *MIS Quarterly Executive* 13, no. 4 (2014).

[2] Christopher Hale: "Liaison Technologies to Deliver SOA-in-the-Cloud Services to Mohawk Papers," *Business Wire* (February 24, 2010), http://www.businesswire.com/news/home/20100224006065/en/Liaison-Technologies-Deliver-SOA-in-the-Cloud-Services-Mohawk-Papers#.VYFh_0ZZWjs (accessed June 17, 2015).

Mohawk's experience shows that cloud computing is not just a mechanism to avoid or reduce costs or to gain operational benefits. The cloud can enable transformation of the business itself. Mohawk's mission changed from "making paper" to "making connections," which involves being able to sell directly to consumers five times the number of products than in the pre-2011 period when it mainly sold a few lines of paper to 10–15 large distributors. Partners now offer many of those products, and the system provides the capabilities to sell from Mohawk's own inventory or from the partners in a seamless way directly to many thousands of small businesses and consumers via its Web site.

Mohawk was able to make the changes it believed were necessary by shifting from an electronic data interchange (EDI) approach to a simpler, more interchangeable format using XML and other tools. Liaison Technologies, its integration consulting firm, enabled these changes by first developing what it calls a cloud integration platform and building upon that platform in several stages to ultimately arrive at an enhanced Web services platform that enabled other organizations and customers to request information, inquire about freight charges and pricing, place orders, and pay for their orders through connections with banks. The platform enables designers to "mash up" (combine) applications as needed on Web sites that can be built rather quickly. Each feature "plugs in" using tools that make it easy to connect the Web sites to existing databases.

Payoffs to Mohawk included:

- Shaking the precloud annual earnings decreases of 2%–5% per year to tripling its earnings in two years
- Automating its transaction processes, saving $1 million to $2 million annually in staff costs
- Increasing its product variety fivefold
- Increasing its customer base from 10–15 distributors to 100 business partners and many thousands of direct customers

Not all firms can base their entire operations on a cloud platform that permits integration with other organizations. Mohawk's experiences can be considered to be "cutting edge," and integration consulting is a rather new phenomenon. Further, even if firms use a cloud approach, they will need to estimate the extent of services they will need to purchase up front. The Mohawk story illustrates how infrastructure can enable the strategic objectives of a firm. However, building such an infrastructure cannot come first. Firms must begin by determining a strategic vision, determining the IS architecture needed to fulfill that vision, and then making it all tangible by putting together an IS infrastructure.

This chapter examines the mechanisms by which business strategy is transformed into tangible IS architecture and infrastructure. The terms *architecture* and *infrastructure* are often used interchangeably in the context of IS. This chapter discusses how the two differ and the important role each plays in realizing a business strategy. Then this chapter examines some common architectural components for IS today.

From Vision to Implementation

As shown in Figure 6.1, architecture translates strategy into infrastructure. Building a house is similar: The owner has a vision of how the final product should look and function. The owner must decide on a strategy about where to live—in an apartment or in a house. The owner's strategy also includes deciding how to live in the house in terms of taking advantage of a beautiful view, having an open floor plan, or planning for special interests by designing such special areas as a game room, study, music room, or other amenities. The architect develops plans based on this vision. These plans, or blueprints, provide a guide—unchangeable in some areas but subject to interpretation in others—for the carpenters, plumbers, and electricians who actually construct the house. Guided by past experience and by industry standards, these builders select the materials and construction techniques best suited to the plan. The plan helps them determine where to put the plumbing and wiring, important parts of the home's infrastructure. When the process works, the completed house fulfills its owner's vision, even though he or she did not participate in the actual construction.

An IT **architecture** provides a blueprint for translating business strategy into a plan for IS. An IT **infrastructure** is everything that supports the flow and processing of information in an organization, including hardware, software, data, and network components. It consists of components, chosen and assembled in a manner that best suits the

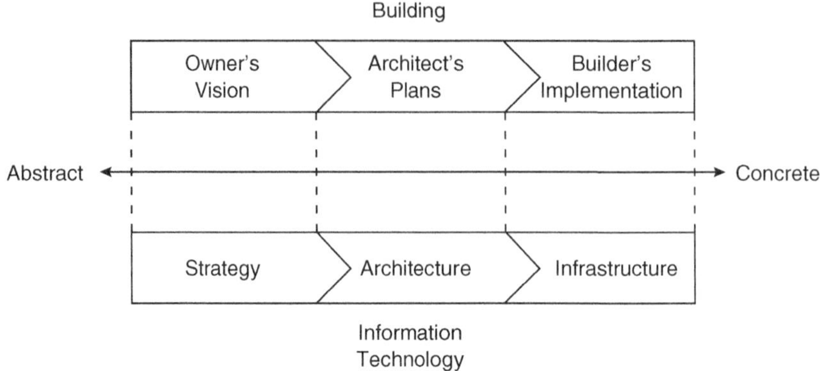

FIGURE 6.1 From the abstract to the concrete—building versus IT.

plan and therefore best enables the overarching business strategy.[3] Infrastructure in an organization is similar to the beams, plumbing, and wiring in a house; it's the actual hardware, software, network, and data used to create the information system.

The Manager's Role

Even though he or she is not drawing up plans or pounding nails, the homeowner in this example needs to know what to reasonably expect from the architect and builders. The homeowner must know enough about architecture, specifically about styling and layout, to work effectively with the architect who draws up the plans. Similarly, the homeowner must know enough about construction details such as the benefits of various types of siding, windows, and insulation to set reasonable expectations for the builders.

Like the homeowner, managers must understand what to expect from IT architecture and infrastructure to be able to make full and realistic use of them. The manager must effectively communicate his or her business vision to IT architects and implementers and, if necessary, modify the plans if IT cannot realistically create or support those plans. Without the involvement of the manager, IT architects could inadvertently make decisions that limit the manager's business options in the future.

For example, a sales manager for a large distribution company did not want to partake in discussions about providing sales force automation systems for his group. He felt that a standard package offered by a well-known vendor would work fine. After all, it worked for many other companies, he rationalized, so it would be fine for his company. No architecture was designed, and no long-range thought was given to how the application might support or inhibit the sales group. After implementation, it became clear that the application had limitations and did not support the type of sales process in use at this company. He approached the IT department for help, and in the discussions that ensued, he learned that earlier infrastructure decisions now made it prohibitively expensive to implement the capability he wanted. Involvement with earlier decisions and the ability to convey his vision of what the sales group wanted to do might have resulted in an IT infrastructure that provided a platform for the changes the manager now wanted to make. Instead, the infrastructure lacked an architecture that met the business objectives of the sales and marketing departments.

The Leap from Strategy to Architecture to Infrastructure

The huge number of IT choices available coupled with the incredible speed of technology advances makes the manager's task of designing an IT infrastructure seem nearly impossible. However, in this chapter, the task is broken down into two major steps: first, translating strategy into architecture and second, translating architecture into

[3] Gordon Hay and Rick Muñoz, "Establishing an IT Architecture Strategy," *Information Systems Management* 14, no. 3 (Summer 1997), 67–69.

infrastructure. This chapter describes a simple framework to help managers sort through IT issues. This framework stresses the need to consider business strategy when defining an organization's IT building blocks. Although this framework may not cover every possible architectural issue, it does highlight major issues associated with effectively defining IT architecture and infrastructure.

From Strategy to Architecture

The manager must start out with a strategy and then use the strategy to develop more specific goals as shown in Figure 6.2. Then detailed business requirements are derived from each goal. In the Mohawk case, the business strategy was to integrate its own product offerings with those from partners and to present the larger product line directly to a large number of customers as well as an expanded list of wholesalers. The business requirements were to integrate the disparate functionality into a modular, flexible system. By outlining the overarching business strategy and then fleshing out the business requirements associated with each goal, the manager can provide the architect with a clear picture of what IS must accomplish and the governance arrangements needed to ensure their smooth development, implementation, and use. The governance arrangements specify who in the company retains control of and responsibility for the IS. Preferably this is somebody in upper management.

Of course, the manager's job is not finished here. Continuing with Figure 6.2, the manager must work with the IT architect to translate these business requirements into a more detailed view of the systems requirements, standards, and processes that shape an IT architecture. This more detailed view, the architectural requirements, includes consideration of such things as data and process demands as well as security objectives. These are the architectural requirements. The IT architect takes the architectural requirements and designs the IT architecture.

From Architecture to Infrastructure

Mohawk's decision to use a service-oriented architecture led to the design of a number of services and composite applications. This illustrates the next step, translating the architecture into infrastructure. This task entails adding yet more detail to the architectural plan that emerged in the previous phase. Now the detail comprises actual hardware, data, networking, and software. Details extend to location of data and access procedures, location of firewalls, link specifications, interconnection design, and so on. This phase is also illustrated in Figure 6.2 where the architecture is translated into functional specifications. The functional specifications can be broken down into hardware specifications, software specifications, storage specifications, interface specifications, network specifications, and so on. Then decisions are made about how to implement these specifications: what hardware, software, storage, interface, network, and so forth to use in the infrastructure.

When we speak about infrastructure, we are referring to more than the components. Plumbing, electrical wiring, walls, and a roof do not make a house. Rather, these components must be assembled according to the blueprint to create a structure in which people can live. Similarly, hardware, software, data, and networks must be combined in a coherent pattern to have a viable infrastructure. This infrastructure can be considered at several levels. At the most global level, the term may be focused on the enterprise and refer to the infrastructure for the entire organization. The term may also focus on the interorganizational level by laying the foundation for communicating with customers, suppliers, or other stakeholders across organizational boundaries. Sometimes *infrastructure* refers to those components needed for an individual application. When considering the structure of a particular application, it is important to consider databases and program components, as well as the devices and operating environments on which they run.

Often when referring to an infrastructure, the underlying computer system is called the platform. The term has been used in a variety of ways: to identify the hardware and operating system of a computer, such as Microsoft Windows, Apple OSX, or Linux, or smartphone and tablet operating systems, such as Android and iOS. Vendors need to provide an entirely separate version of their software on each chosen platform, and they often have tools that allow their programs to produce, nearly automatically, versions that run on multiple platforms.

A platform can also refer to a firm's collection of cloud-based, modular tools as the example from Mohawk illustrated. Such platforms use open standards for easy "plugging-in" of components, enabling "mashing-up" of a

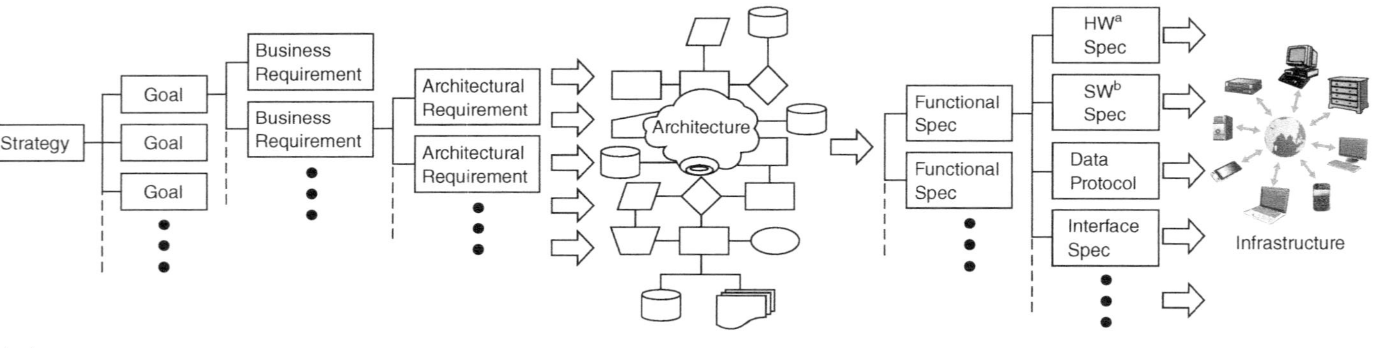

[a] Hardware.
[b] Software.

FIGURE 6.2 From strategy to architecture to infrastructure.

variety of resources at once. Google Maps is an excellent example of a standardized resource that can be accessed by any platform that provides the proper requests.

Framework for the Infrastructure and Architecture Analysis

When developing a framework for transforming business strategy into architecture and then into infrastructure, these basic components should be considered:

- *Hardware:* The physical components that handle computation, storage, or transmission of data (e.g., personal computers, servers, mainframes, hard drives, RAM, fiber-optic cabling, modems, and telephone lines).
- *Software:* The programs that run on the hardware to enable work to be performed (e.g., operating systems, databases, accounting packages, word processors, sales force automation, and enterprise resource planning systems). Software is usually divided into two groups: **system software**, such as Microsoft Windows, Apple OSX, and Linux, and **applications**, such as word processors, spreadsheets, and digital photo editors. System software is often referred to as a **platform** because application software runs upon it, sometimes only on a particular version.
- *Network:* Software and hardware components for local or long-distance networking. Local networking components include switches, hubs, and routers; long-distance networking components include cable, fiber, and microwave paths for communication and data sharing. All work according to a common protocol, most often Internet protocol (IP). Some networks are private, requiring credentials to connect. Others, like the Internet, are public.
- *Data:* The electronic representation of the numbers and text. Here, the main concern is the quantity and format of data and how often it must be transferred from one piece of hardware to another or translated from one format to another.

The framework that guides the analysis of these components was introduced in the first chapter in Figure 1.6 This framework is simplified to make the point that initially understanding an organization's infrastructure is not difficult. Understanding the technology behind each component of the infrastructure and the technical requirements of the architecture is a much more complex task. The main point is that the general manager must begin with an overview that is complete and that delivers a big picture.

This framework asks three types of questions that must be answered for each infrastructure component: what, who, and where. The "what" questions are those most commonly asked and that identify the specific type of technology. The "who" questions seek to understand what individuals, groups, and departments are involved. In most cases, the individual user is not the owner of the system or even the person who maintains it. In many cases, the systems are leased, not owned, by the company, making the owner a party completely outside the organization. In understanding the infrastructure, it is important to get a picture of the people involved. The third set of questions addresses "where" issues. With the proliferation of networks, many IS are designed and built with components in multiple locations, often even crossing oceans. Learning about infrastructure means understanding where everything is located.

We can expand the use of this framework to also understand architecture. To illustrate the connections between strategy and systems, the table in Figure 6.3 has been populated with questions that typify those asked in addressing architecture and infrastructure issues associated with each component.

The questions shown in Figure 6.3 are only representative of many that would need to be addressed; the specific questions depend on the business strategy the organizations are following. However, this framework can help IT staff ask managers to provide further information as they seek to translate business strategy into architecture and ultimately into infrastructure in their organizations. The answers derived with IT architects and implementers should provide a robust picture of the IT environment. That means that the IT architecture includes plans for the data and information, the technology (the standards to be followed and the infrastructure that provides the foundation), and the applications to be accessed via the company's IT system.

Component	What		Who		Where	
	Architecture	Infrastructure	Architecture	Infrastructure	Architecture	Infrastructure
Hardware	What type of personal device will our users use?	What size hard drives do we equip our laptops with?	Who knows the most about servers in our organization?	Who will operate the server?	Does our architecture require centralized or distributed servers?	What specific computers will we put in our Tokyo data center?
Software	Does fulfillment of our strategy require ERP software?	Shall we go with SAP or Oracle applications?	Who is affected by a move to SAP?	Who will need SAP training?	Does our geographical organization require multiple database instances?	Can we use a cloud instance of Oracle for our database?
Network	How should the network be structured to fulfill our strategy?	Will a particular Cisco switch be fast enough for what we need?	Who needs a connection to the network?	Who provides our wireless network?	Will we let each user's phone be a hotspot?	Shall we lease a cable or use satellite?
Data	What data do we need for our sales management system?	What format will we store our data in?	Who needs access to sensitive data?	How will authorized users identify themselves?	Will backups be stored on-site or off-site?	Will data be in the cloud or in our data center?

FIGURE 6.3 Infrastructure and architecture analysis framework with sample questions.

Traditionally, there are three common configurations of IT architecture as shown in Figure 6.4. Enterprises sometimes like the idea of a **centralized architecture** with everything purchased, supported, and managed centrally, usually in a **data center**, to eliminate the difficulties that come with managing a distributed infrastructure. In addition, almost every sizable enterprise has a large data center with servers and/or large **mainframe** computers that support many simultaneous users. Because of that history, there are a significant number of legacy mainframe environments still in operation today. However, one large computer at the center of the IT architecture is not used as regularly today as it was in the past. Instead, many smaller computers are linked together to form a centralized IT core that operates very much like the mainframe, providing the bulk of IT services necessary for the business.

A more common configuration is a **decentralized architecture**. The hardware, software, networking, and data are arranged in a way that distributes the processing and functionality between multiple small computers, servers, and devices, and they rely heavily on a network to connect them together. Typically, a decentralized architecture uses numerous servers, often located in different physical locations, at the backbone of the infrastructure, called a **server-based architecture**.

A third increasingly common configuration is **service-oriented architecture (SOA)**, the architecture that Mohawk, in this chapter's opening case, decided to use. An example of a service is an online employment form that, when completed, generates a file with the data for use in another service. Another example is a ticket-processing service that identifies available concert seats and allocates them. These relatively small chunks of functionality are available for many applications through **reuse**. The type of software used in an SOA architecture is often referred to as **software-as-a-service**, or SaaS. Another term for these applications when delivered over the Internet is **Web services**.

A cutting-edge type of configuration is one that can allocate or remove resources by itself, referred to as a **software-defined architecture**.[4] Two illustrations can provide an idea of this trend. The first is a true story of a

[4] See K. Pearlson, "Software Defined Future: Instant Provisioning of IT Services," *Connect-Converge* (Fall 2014), http://connect-converge.com/issues/2014_fall/A1767E8395A03D54262BE6F0B892F986/Converge%20C2-2014-Fall.pdf (accessed August 27, 2015).

Architecture	Description	Other Terms	When to Use?
Centralized Architecture	• A large central computer system runs all applications and stores all data. • Typically, the computer is housed in a data center and managed directly by the IT department. • Networking allows users to access remotely.	Mainframe architecture	• To make it easier to manage—all functionality is located in one place • When the business is highly centralized
Decentralized Architecture	• Computing power is spread out among a number of devices in different locations. • Servers in different locations, personal computers, laptops, smartphones, and tablets are also included. • The "client" devices can perform many of the services needed with only occasional requests to central servers for data and services.	Server-based architecture	• To modularize and address concerns about scalability • When the business is primarily decentralized
Service-Oriented Architecture (SOA)	• Software is broken down into services "orchestrated" and connected to each other. • Together those services form an application for an entire business process. • The services are often offered from multiple vendors on the Internet and are combined to form applications.	Cloud-based architecture	• To be agile—reusability and componentization can create new apps • When the business is new and rapid app design is important
Software-Defined Architecture	• Infrastructure reconfigures based on load or time of day. • Infrastructure can be reconfigured autonomously based on rules.	Software-defined network, network virtualization	• When resources need to be flexible and reconfigured often • When usage varies dramatically depending on time of day

FIGURE 6.4 Common architectures.

company selling 10 bird baths per month. It had a Web site for its small family business. For a while, the site was adequate for its needs. However, when Oprah Winfrey featured the company's high-quality designs on her show, the number of monthly orders jumped to 80,000. Fortunately, the firm's IT consultants were able to create a software-defined network that adapted to the increase in orders. It was able to sense a change in the volume of orders and allocate additional resources such as storage and processing power to keep the Web site working. A typical hosting provider would have treated a monthly 8,000-fold volume increase as an attack and would shut down the site to protect it. Also, a typical provider would not have enough storage allocated for the orders. The software-defined network saved thousands of sales (and hundreds of thousands of dollars) from being lost.

Sometimes software-defined networks can even change the architecture on the fly. For example, many fast-food restaurants and coffee shops offer free WiFi to customers. This capability requires more than one connection to the Internet in very busy locations, and the shop itself needs its own secure, dedicated connection to record sales transactions and inventory updates from individual restaurant and shop operations. If that operation connection fails, a software-defined network could automatically reconfigure to switch one of the customer connections to become a substitute operations connection. Customers might find their WiFi connections to be a little slower until the situation returns to normal, but the automatic reconfiguration prevents the restaurant or shop from having to close or revert to a very clumsy manual system. Even without a catastrophe, customer traffic on the WiFi system and the need for operations capacity can fluctuate as well. After closing, the WiFi system for customers is not needed, but during busy times, it might be saturated. When software updates are performed or large volumes of transactions are transmitted, the operations connection might be overwhelmed. Shifting resources automatically from one separate architectural component to another is a powerful way to reduce costs.

A manager must be aware of the trade-offs when considering architectural decisions. For example, decentralized architectures are more modular than centralized architectures, allowing other servers to be added with relative ease and provide increased flexibility for adding clients with specific functionality for specific users. Decentralized organizational governance, such as that associated with the networked organization structure (discussed in Chapter 3), is consistent with decentralized architectures. In contrast, a centralized architecture is easier to manage in some ways because all functionality is centralized in the main computer instead of distributed throughout all the devices and servers. A centralized architecture tends to be a better match in companies with highly centralized governance, for example, those with hierarchical organization structures. SOA is increasingly popular because the design enables large units of functionality to be built almost entirely from existing software service components. SOA is useful for building applications quickly because it offers managers a modular and componentized design and, therefore, a more easily modifiable approach to building applications. **Software-defined architectures** are even easier to manage because they self-manage many of their features. However, each self-managing feature must be imagined and defined; the systems are not autonomous beyond those features.

An example of an organization making these trade-offs is the Veterans Health Administration (VHA), a part of the Department of Veterans Affairs of the U.S. federal government.[5] The organization included 14 different business units that served various administrative and organizational needs. The primary objective of the organization was to provide health care for veterans and their families. In addition, the VHA was a major contributor to medical research, allowing medical students to train at VHA hospitals. The medical centers operated independently and sometimes competed against each other. When the U.S. Congress passed an act that enabled the VHA to restructure itself from a system of hospitals to a single health care system, the IT architecture was reconfigured from a very centralized design, which enabled the Office of Data Management and Telecommunications to retain control, to a decentralized hospital-based architecture that gave local physicians and administrators the opportunity to deploy applications addressing local needs while ensuring that standards were developed across the different locations. The VA then introduced the "One-VA" architecture to unify the decentralized systems and "to provide an accessible source of consistent, reliable, accurate, useful, and secure information and knowledge to veterans and their families. . . ."[6] Efforts were made to encrypt, secure, and account for every piece of computer hardware in the system, and a national and regional data warehouse initiative was launched to standardize business data storage and management.

Technological advances such as peer-to-peer architecture and wireless or mobile infrastructure make possible a wide variety of options. These designs can either augment a firm's existing way of operating or become its main focus. For example, a **peer-to-peer** architecture allows networked computers to share resources without needing a central server to play a dominant role. ThePirateBay.org, the Web site for sharing music, movies, games, and more, and Skype, a site for teleconferencing, texting, and telephoning, are examples of businesses that use a peer-to-peer architecture. **Wireless (mobile) infrastructures** allow communication from remote locations using a variety of wireless technologies (e.g., fixed microwave links; wireless LANs; data over cellular networks; wireless WANs; satellite links; digital dispatch networks; one-way and two-way paging networks; diffuse infrared, laser-based communications; keyless car entry; and global positioning systems).

Web-based and **cloud architectures** locate significant hardware, software, and possibly even data elements on the Internet. Web-based architectures offers greater flexibility when used as a source for **capacity-on-demand**, or the availability of additional processing capability for a fee. IT managers like the concept of capacity on demand to help manage peak processing periods when additional capacity is needed. It allows them to use the Web-available capacity as needed, rather than purchasing additional computers to handle the larger loads.

---

[5] Adapted from V. Venkatesh, H. Bala, S. Venkatraman, and J. Bates, "Enterprise Architecture Maturity: The Story of the Veterans Health Administration," *MIS Quarterly Executive* 6, no. 2 (June 2007),79–90; and J. Walters, "IBM Transformation Series, 2009," http://www.businessofgovernment.org/report/transforming-information-technology-department-veterans-affairs (accessed August 27, 2015).

[6] Venkatesh, Venkatraman, and Bates, "Enterprise Architecture Maturity," p. 86.

With the proliferation of smartphones and tablets, enterprises increasingly have employees who want to bring their own devices and connect to enterprise systems. Some call this **Bring Your Own Device (BYOD)**, and it raises some important managerial considerations. When employees connect their own devices to the corporate network, issues such as capacity, security, and compatibility arise. For example, many corporate applications are not designed to function on the small screen of a smartphone. Redesigning them for personal devices may require significant investment to accommodate the smartphone platform. And not all smartphone platforms are the same. Designing for an iPhone is different than for an Android phone. Even if a system were redesigned for these two platforms, the resources required to maintain the system increase because each platform evolves at a different rate and the applications need to appear similar on each device. In some circles, the drive to port applications to personal devices and the ensuing issues to make them work is referred to as the **consumerization of IT**.

Consumerization of IT is a growing phenomenon. Not only do employees want to use their own devices to access corporate systems but also customers increasingly expect to access company systems from their mobile devices. Making applications robust yet simple enough for customers to use from virtually any mobile device over the Web is a challenge for many information systems departments. Companies such as Good Technology have been created to provide services that allow enterprise employees to connect, communicate, and collaborate using their own devices, supplementing the IT organization's ability to meet this new demand. Websites are designed with the philosophy of "responsive design," permitting them to adapt to screens of any size.

From Strategy to Architecture to Infrastructure: An Example

This section[7] considers a simple example to illustrate the process of converting strategy to architecture to infrastructure: We introduce GiantCo.com, a fictitious competitor of Amazon and Wal-Mart, which sells a wide variety of products online.

Define the Strategic Goals

The managers at GiantCo.com recognize that they have a large amount of competition, so they have decided to try to provide outstanding customer service. In fact, their strategy is to become highly customer focused. Among their immediate strategic goals are the following:

- To increase the period of a money-back guarantee from one week to a month
- To provide cross-selling opportunities by temporarily discounting accessories or items that complement those purchased within the previous year
- To provide a return shipping label with every purchase
- To decrease out-of-stock occurrences by 20%
- To answer emails within 24 hours

Translate Strategic Goals to Business Requirements

To keep things simple, consider more closely only the first two of GiantCo.com's strategic goals: to increase the period of a money-back guarantee from one week to a month and to suggest goods that complement all those sold to a customer in the past year. How can GiantCo.com's architecture enable this goal? Its goal must be translated into business requirements. A few of the business requirements that address these two goals are to track

- At least a year's worth of sales for all customers
- All refunds provided to customers

[7] Only a few questions raised from the framework are provided; a comprehensive, detailed treatment of this situation would require more information than provided in this simple example.

- Return patterns by customer to detect excesses
- Sales of complementary goods to provide advice for future potential purchasers

Translate Business Requirements into Architecture

To support the business requirements, architectural requirements are specified that dictate the architecture to be established. One major component of the architecture deals with how to obtain, store, and use data to support the business requirements.

The database needs to store the sales data for all customers for more than an entire year. The data can be used for many purposes, including summarizing for an annual report and identifying whether customers who wish to return goods are within the 30-day period. It also provides the foundation for suggesting complementary goods when coupled with data pinpointing goods that are related. As customers use the Web site, the sales data can be very useful for their own decision making.

Translate Architecture to Infrastructure

With the architecture goals in hand, the framework presented in Figure 6.2 outlines how to build the infrastructure. The architecture outlines the functions needed by the infrastructure, enabling a functional specification to be created. Those specs are then translated into hardware, software, data protocols, interface designs, and other components that will make up the infrastructure. For GiantCo.com's database, the functional specification would include details such as how big it should be, how fast data access should be, what the format of the data will be, and more. These functional specifications then help narrow the technical specifications, which answer these questions. For example, after considering the current customer base and forecasts for growth, GiantCo.com's database might need the following:

- Sample functional specifications for a year's worth of activity
  - Space to fit transaction data for 22,500 customers who purchase 25 items a year on average with 30 facts (date, price, quantity, item number, customer number, address shipped, credit card billed, and so on) recorded for each. On average, each fact occupies 10 characters of storage.
  - Ability to insert 1,070 records per minute. One server can handle one update per second, or 60 per minute, suggesting the need for 18 servers to handle online sales. Accounting information will be placed on its own server. That totals 168,750,000,000 characters of storage for the year, indicating that 200 gigabytes will be needed for this information alone. An analysis of vendors' products and pricing indicates that one terabyte is considered more than adequate for each server given that 18 will be purchased.
  - Software to do the required tracking for suggesting complementary goods because the current system does not have that functionality.
- Hardware specifications
  - One terabyte RAID (redundant array) level 3 hard drive space.
  - Nineteen 3-gigahertz Core 2 duo servers.
- Software specifications
  - Apache operating system.
  - My SQL database.

Hardware	Software	Network	Data
19 servers: • 18 for sales • 1 for accounting LaCie 10-GB Thunderbolt RAID hard drive storage system	ERP system with modules for • Sales • Accounting • Inventory Enterprise application integration (EAI) software Apache operating system MySQL database software	• Cable modem to ISP • Dial-up lines for backup • Cicso routers, hubs, and switches • Firewalls from CheckPoint	Database • Sales • Inventory • Accounting • Complementary items

FIGURE 6.5 GiantCo.com's infrastructure components.

Additional technical specifications would be created until the entire infrastructure is designed. Then GiantCo.com's IT department is ready to pick specific hardware, software, network, data, etc., to put into its infrastructure.

Figure 6.5 lists possible infrastructure components needed by GiantCo.com.

Architectural Principles

Any good architecture is based on a set of principles, or fundamental beliefs about how the architecture should function. Architectural principles must be consistent with both the values of the enterprise as well as with the technology used in the infrastructure. The principles are designed by considering the key objectives of the organization and then translated into principles to apply to the design of the IT architecture. The number of principles vary widely, and there is no set list of what must be included in a set of architectural principles. However, a guideline for developing architectural principles is to make sure they are directly related to the operating model of the enterprise and IS organization. Principles should define the desirable behaviors of the IT systems and the role of the organization(s) that support it. A sample of architectural principles is shown in Figure 6.6.

Principle	Description of What the Architecture Should Promote
Ease of use	Ease of use in building and supporting the architecture and solutions based on the architecture
Single point of view	A consistent, integrated view of the business regardless of how it is accessed
Buy rather than build	Purchase of applications, components, and enabling frameworks unless there is a competitive reason to develop them internally
Speed and quality	Acceleration of time to market for solutions while still maintaining required quality levels
Flexibility and agility	Flexibility to support changing business needs while enabling evolution of the architecture and the solutions built on it
Innovation	Incorporation of new technologies, facilitating innovation
Data security	Data protection from unauthorized use and disclosure
Common data vocabulary	Consistent definitions of data throughout the enterprise, which are understandable and available to all users
Data quality	Accountability of each data element through a trustee responsible for data quality
Data asset	Management of data like other valuable assets

FIGURE 6.6 Sample architectural principles.
Source: Adapted from examples of IT architecture from IBM, The Open Group Architecture Framework, the U.S. Government, and the State of Wisconsin.

Enterprise Architecture

Many companies apply even more complex and comprehensive frameworks than those described earlier for developing an IT architecture and infrastructure than those described earlier. They employ an **enterprise architecture (EA)**, or the "blueprint" for all IS and their interrelationships in the firm. EA is the term used for the organizing logic for the entire organization. It often specifies how information technologies support business processes. EA differs from an IT architecture in its level of analysis, although it shares some design principles of the lower-level architectures. It identifies the core processes of the company and how they will work together, how the IT systems will support the processes, the standard technical capabilities and activities for all parts of the enterprise, and guidelines for making choices. As experts Jeanne Ross, Peter Weill, and David Robertson describe in their book, *Enterprise Architecture as Strategy*,

> Top-performing companies define how they will do business (an operating model) and design the processes and infrastructure critical to their current and future operations (enterprise architecture). . . . Then these smart companies exploit their foundation, embedding new initiatives and using it as a competitive weapon to seize new business opportunities.[8]

The components of an enterprise architecture typically include four key elements:

- *Core business processes:* The key enterprise processes that create the capabilities the company uses to execute its operating model and create market opportunities
- *Shared data:* The data that drive the core processes
- *Linking and automation technologies:* The software, hardware, and networking technologies that provide the links between applications (applications themselves are part of the IT architecture, but the way applications link together is part of the bigger picture of the enterprise architecture)
- *Customer groups:* Key customers to be served by the architecture[9]

One example of an enterprise architecture framework is the **TOGAF** (The Open Group Architecture Framework).[10] TOGAF includes a methodology and set of resources for developing an enterprise architecture. It is based on the idea of an open architecture, one whose specifications are public (as compared to a proprietary architecture whose specifications are not made public). It is based on the U.S. Department of Defense frameworks and has been developing and continuously evolving since the mid-1990s. It provides a practical, standardized methodology (called *Architecture Development Methodology*) to successfully implement an enterprise architecture for an organization. Although there is no well-accepted standard for enterprise architecture, architects who understand and use TOGAF speak a common language and use the same basic framework and processes to build their company's IS architecture. TOGAF is designed to translate strategy into architecture and then into a detailed infrastructure; however, it supports a much higher level of architecture that includes more components of the enterprise.[11]

Another example of enterprise architecture frameworks is the **Zachman framework**, which determines architectural requirements by providing a broad view that helps guide the analysis of the detailed view. This framework's perspectives range from the company's scope, to its critical models and, finally, to very detailed representations of the data, programs, networks, security, and so on. The models it uses are the conceptual business model, the logical system model, and the physical technical model.[12]

Enterprise architectures mature as firms invest resources in technologies that support their strategy. Jeanne Ross[13] theorized that enterprise architecture moves from compartmentalized "silos" to standardized technologies to enterprisewide software to business modularity. A recent study[14] shows a dramatic increase in perceived IT effectiveness as the architecture matures through those four stages.

---

[8] Jeanne W. Ross, Peter Weill, and David C. Robertson, *Enterprise Architecture as Strategy* (Boston, MA: Harvard Business School Press, 2006), viii–ix.
[9] Ibid., 50–52.
[10] The Open Group, http://www.opengroup.org.
[11] For more information on the TOGAF framework, visit the Open Group's Web site at www.opengroup.org/togaf/.
[12] For more information on the Zachman framework, visit Zachman International's Web site at www.zachman.com.
[13] J. W. Ross, "Creating a Strategic IT Architecture Competency: Learning in Stages," *MIS Quarterly Executive* 2, no. 1 (2003), 31–43.
[14] Randy V.Bradley, Renée M. E. Pratt, Terry Anthony Byrd, and Lakisha L. Simmons, "The Role of Enterprise Architecture in the Quest for IT Value," *MIS Quarterly Executive* 10, no. 2 (2011), 19–27.

Because enterprise architecture is more about how the company operates than how the technology is designed, building an EA is a joint exercise to be done with business leaders and IT leaders. IT leaders cannot and should not do this alone. Because virtually all business processes today involve some component of IT, the idea of trying to align IT with business processes would merely automate or update processes already in place. Instead, business processes are designed concurrently with IT systems. The Mohawk case at the beginning of this chapter illustrates this very well; if Mohawk had simply continued its existing business processes or had made them faster with newer technology, its profitability would have merely continued to decline. They company was able to reverse this trend only by redesigning or redirecting its business processes, an effort that was enabled by IT.

As Mohawk found, building an enterprise architecture is more than just linking the business processes to IT. It starts with organizational clarity of vision and strategy and places a high value on consistency in approach as a means of optimal effectiveness. The consistency manifests itself as some level of standardization—standardization of processes, deliverables, roles, and/or data. Every EA has elements of all these types of standardization; however, the degree and proportion of each vary with organizational needs, making it dynamic. A good enterprise architect understands this and looks for the right blend for each activity the business undertakes. That means that because organizational groups and individuals are resources for business processes, the organizational design decisions should be part of the enterprise architecture. However, this is a sophisticated approach, and new enterprise architects often seek to put more rigid standards in place and do not attempt to tackle the more complex organizational design issues.

Barclay's Bank,[15] which services more than 48 million customers worldwide, had an IT architecture that included more than 2,000 applications and spent in excess of £1 billion annually on IT. The resulting complexity was managed with an EA that specified frameworks, tools, and processes that created a common language and format. The EA governance model dictated that both business and technology executives sign off on projects to ensure accountability and ownership. Roadmaps helped clarify the enterprise architecture design and direction, which informed planning and portfolio management and created a common vision and a repeatable mechanism for future investments. The EA ensured appropriate linkages between IT investment and business needs.

Virtualization and Cloud Computing

Physical corporate data centers are rapidly being replaced by virtual infrastructure called **virtualization**. *Virtual infrastructure* originally meant one in which software replaced hardware in a way that a "virtual machine" or a "virtual desktop system" was accessible to provide computing power. Typically, computing capabilities, storage, and networking are provided by a third party or group of vendors, usually over the Internet or through a private network. In most virtual architectures, the five core components available virtually are servers, storage, backup, network, and disaster recovery. Virtualizing the desktop is a common virtualization application. In a virtualized desktop, the user's device locally accesses desktop software on a remote server, essentially separating the operating system from the applications. Virtualization is a useful way to design architecture because it enables resources to be shared and allocated as needed by the user and makes maintenance easier because resources are centralized.

Cloud computing is another term used to describe an architecture based on services provided over the Internet. It is based on the concept of a virtual infrastructure. Entire computing infrastructures are available "in the cloud." Using the cloud to provide infrastructure means that the cloud is essentially a large cluster of virtual servers or storage devices. This is called *infrastructure as a service* (IaaS).

In addition to IaaS, software as a service (Saas) and platform as a service (PaaS) are typical services found in cloud computing. These are described more fully in Chapter 10. Using the cloud for a platform means that the manager will use an environment with the basic software available, such as Web software, applications, database, and collaboration tools. Using the cloud for an entire application generally means that the software is custom designed or custom configured for the business but resides in the cloud.

[15] Adapted from Phil LeClare and Eric Knorr, "The 2010 Enterprise Architecture Awards" (September 10, 2010), http://www.infoworld.com/d/architecture/the-2010-enterprise-architecture-awards-823 (accessed August 27, 2015).

Consumers of cloud computing purchase capacity on demand and are not generally concerned with the underlying technologies. It's the next step in **utility computing**, or purchasing any part of the consumers' storage or processing infrastructure they need when they need it. Much like the distribution of electricity, the vision of utility computing is that computing infrastructure would be available when needed in as much quantity as needed. When the lights and appliances are turned off in a home, the electricity is not consumed. Ultimately, the customer is billed only for what is used. In utility computing, a company uses a third-party infrastructure to do their processing or transactions and pay only for what they use. And as in the case of the electrical utility, the economies of scale enjoyed by the computing utility enable very attractive financial models for their customers. As the cost of connectivity falls, models of cloud computing emerge.

Salesforce.com, Facebook, Gmail, Windows Azure, Apple iTunes, and LinkedIn are examples of applications in the cloud. Users access LinkedIn through the Web and build networks of business professionals on the site. But LinkedIn provides additional services, such as linking a user's blog to her or his profile, sharing and storing documents among group's members, and accessing applications such as GoodReads to see what network peers are reading and Tripit to learn about their travel plans.

Benefits of virtualization and cloud computing are many. Businesses that embrace a virtual infrastructure can consolidate physical servers and possibly eliminate many of them, greatly reducing the physical costs of the data center. Fees can be based on transaction volumes rather than large up-front investments. There is no separate cost for upgrade, maintenance, and electricity. Nor is there a need to devote physical space or to guess how many storage servers are required. Typically, the network is much simpler, too, because the virtual infrastructure mainly requires Internet connections for all applications and devices.

But the biggest benefit of virtualization and cloud computing is the speed at which additional capacity, or provisioning, can be done. In a traditional data center, additional capacity is often a matter of purchasing additional hardware, waiting for its delivery, physically installing it, and ensuring its compatibility with the existing systems. It can take weeks. In a virtual infrastructure, the nature of the architecture is dynamic by design, making adding capacity relatively easy and quick.

For example, *The New York Times* decided to make all public domain articles from 1851 to 1922 available on the Internet. To do that, the company decided to create PDF files of all the articles from the original papers in its archives. This required scanning each column of the story, creating a series of graphic pictures of the scanned image, and then cobbling them together to create the single PDF for each story. This was a lot of work and required significant computing power. Once this batch of articles was converted and added to the company's existing library, the 11 million *New York Times* stories from 1851 to 1989 were accessible on the Internet.

The manager of this project had an idea to use the cloud. He selected a service offered by Amazon.com, Amazon EC2, wrote some code to do the project he envisioned, and tested it on the Amazon servers. He used his credit card to charge the $240 it cost him to do this conversion. He calculated it would have taken him at least a month to do the conversion if he used only the few servers available to him in *The New York Times* network. However, using the Amazon cloud services, he was able to use a virtual server cluster of 100 servers, and it took just under 24 hours to process the entire 11 million articles.[16]

But managers considering virtualization and cloud computing must also understand the risks. First is the dependence on the third-party supplier. Building applications that work in the cloud may mean retooling existing applications for the cloud's infrastructure. The dominant vendor, as of the writing of this text, is VMware, a company that offers software for workstations, virtual desktop infrastructures, and servers. However, because there are no standards for virtual infrastructure, applications running on one vendor's infrastructure may not port easily to another vendor's environment.

Architectures are increasingly providing cloud computing and virtualization as alternatives to in-house infrastructures. As coordination costs drop and new platforms in the cloud are introduced, cloud computing utilization will increase.

---

[16] Galen Gruman, "Early Experiments in Cloud Computing," *InfoWorld* (April 7, 2008), http://www.infoworld.com/article/2649759/operating-systems/early-experiments-in-cloud-computing.html (accessed July 28, 2015); Derek Gottfrid, "Self-Service, Prorated Supercomputing Fun!" (November 1, 2007), http://open.blogs.nytimes.com/2007/11/01/self-service-prorated-super-computing-fun/ (accessed July 28, 2015).

Other Managerial Considerations

The infrastructure and architecture framework shown in Figure 6.3 guides the manager toward the design and implementation of an appropriate infrastructure. Defining an IT architecture that fulfills an organization's needs today is relatively simple; the problem is that by the time it is installed, those needs can change. The primary reason to base an architecture on an organization's strategic goals is to allow for inevitable future changes—changes in the business environment, organization, IT requirements, and technology itself. Considering future impacts should include analyzing the existing architecture, the strategic time frame, technological advances, and financial constraints.

Understanding Existing Architecture

At the beginning of any project, the first step is to assess the current situation. Understanding existing IT architecture allows the manager to evaluate the IT requirements of an evolving business strategy against current IT capacity. The architecture, rather than the infrastructure, is the basis for this evaluation because the specific technologies used to build the infrastructure are chosen based on the overall plan, or architecture. As previously discussed, these architectural plans support the business strategy. Assuming that some overlap is found, the manager can then evaluate the associated infrastructure and the degree to which it can be utilized going forward.

Relevant questions for managers to ask include the following:

- What IT architecture is already in place?
- Is the company developing the IT architecture from scratch?
- Is the company replacing an existing architecture?
- Does the company need to work within the confines of an existing architecture?
- Is the company expanding an existing architecture?

Starting from scratch allows the most flexibility in determining how architecture can enable a new business strategy, and a clean architectural slate generally translates into a clean infrastructure slate. However, planning effectively even when starting from scratch can be a challenge. For example, in a resource-starved start-up environment, it is far too easy to let effective IT planning fall by the wayside. Sometimes the problem is less a shortcoming in IT management and more one of poorly devised business strategy. A strong business strategy is a prerequisite for IT architecture design, which is in turn a prerequisite for infrastructure design.

Of course, managers seldom enjoy the relative luxury of starting with a clean IT slate. More often, they must deal in some way with an existing architecture, infrastructure, and legacy systems already in place. In this case, they encounter both opportunity—to leverage the existing architecture and infrastructure and their attendant human resource experience pool—and the challenge of overcoming or working within the old system's shortcomings. By implementing the following steps, managers can derive the most value and suffer the least pain when working with legacy architectures and infrastructures.

1. *Objectively analyze the existing architecture and infrastructure:* Remember that architecture and infrastructure are separate entities; managers must assess the capability, capacity, reliability, and expandability of each.
2. *Objectively analyze the strategy served by the existing architecture:* What were the strategic goals it was designed to attain? To what extent do those goals align with current strategic goals?
3. *Objectively analyze the ability of the existing architecture and infrastructure to further the current strategic goals:* In what areas is alignment present? What parts of the existing architecture or infrastructure must be modified? Replaced?

Whether managers are facing a fresh start or an existing architecture, they must ensure that the architecture will satisfy their strategic requirements and that the associated infrastructure is modern and efficient. The following sections describe evaluation criteria including strategic time frame, technical issues (adaptability, scalability, standardization, maintainability), and financial issues.

Assessing Strategic Timeframe

Understanding the life span of an IT infrastructure and architecture is critical. How far into the future does the strategy extend? How long can the architecture and its associated infrastructure fulfill strategic goals? What issues could arise and change these assumptions?

Answers to these questions vary widely from industry to industry. Strategic time frames depend on industry-wide factors such as level of commitment to fixed resources, maturity of the industry, cyclicality, and barriers to entry. The competitive environment has increased the pace of change to the point that requires any strategic decision be viewed as temporary.

Architectural longevity depends not only on the strategic planning horizon, but also on the nature of a manager's reliance on IT and on the specific rate of advances affecting the information technologies on which he or she depends. Today's architectures must be designed with maximum flexibility and scalability to ensure they can handle imminent business changes. Imagine the planning horizon for a dot-com company in an industry in which Internet technologies and applications are changing daily, if not more often. You might remember the importance of flexibility and agility to Mohawk's new business strategy and that the firm's IT architecture was created to support it.

Assessing Technical Issues: Adaptability

With the rapid pace of business, it is no longer possible to build a static information system to support businesses. Instead, adaptability is a core design principle of every IT architecture and one reason why cloud computing and virtualization are increasingly popular. A manager may think of technological advances as primarily affecting IT infrastructure, but the architecture must be able to support any such advance. Can the architecture adapt to emerging technologies? Can a manager delay the implementation of certain components until he or she can evaluate the potential of new technologies?

At a minimum, the architecture should be able to handle expected technological advances, such as innovations in storage capacity and computing power. An exceptional architecture also has the capacity to absorb unexpected technological leaps. Both hardware and software should be considered when promoting adaptability. For example, new Web-based applications that may benefit the corporation emerge daily. The architecture must be able to integrate these new technologies without violating the architecture principles or significantly disrupting business operations.

The following are guidelines for planning adaptable IT architecture and infrastructure. At this point, these two terms are used together because in most IT planning, they are discussed together. These guidelines are derived from work by Meta Group.[17]

- *Plan for applications and systems that are independent and loosely coupled rather than monolithic:* This approach allows managers to modify or replace only those applications affected by a change in the state of technology.
- *Set clear boundaries between infrastructure components:* If one component changes, others are minimally affected, or if effects are unavoidable, the impact is easily identifiable and quantifiable.
- *When designing a network architecture, provide access to all users when it makes sense to do so (i.e., when security concerns allow it):* A robust and consistent network architecture simplifies training and knowledge

---

[17] Larry R. DeBoever and Richard D. Buchanan, "Three Architectural Sins," *CIO* (May 1, 1997), 124, 126.

sharing and provides some resource redundancy. An example is an architecture that allows employees to use a different server or printer if their local one goes down.

Note that requirements concerning reliability may conflict with the need for technological adaptability under certain circumstances. If the architecture requires high reliability, a manager seldom is tempted by bleeding-edge technologies. The competitive advantage offered by bleeding-edge technologies is often eroded by downtime and problems resulting from pioneering efforts with the technology.

Assessing Technical Issues: Scalability

A large number of other technical issues should also be considered when selecting an architecture or infrastructure. A frequently used criterion is scalability. To be **scalable** refers to how well an infrastructure component can adapt to increased, or in some cases decreased, demands. A scalable network system, for instance, could start with just a few nodes but could easily be expanded to include thousands of nodes. Scalability is an important technical feature because it means that an investment can be made in an infrastructure or architecture with confidence that the firm will not outgrow it.

What is the company's projected growth? What must the architecture do to support it? How will it respond if the company greatly exceeds its growth goals? What if the projected growth never materializes? These questions help define scalability needs.

Consider a case in which capacity requirements were poorly anticipated. In early 2007, an ice storm on the East Coast of the United States forced JetBlue Airlines to scramble to take care of stranded customers, grounded planes, checked luggage, and canceled flights. In the aftermath, executives told investors that the computers didn't fail. Indeed, they did not fail, but the system failed to scale as needed. The system was set up to accommodate 650 agents and was able to be increased to 950 but no more.[18] It is unlikely that JetBlue or its software provider would have had to do any serious systems redesign to respond to the increase in demand; it simply needed to increase its infrastructure capacity. Ultimately, recovery from this planning failure cost JetBlue millions and even more in defending its image, which suffered severe negative word of mouth from the poor service that resulted. The company subsequently contracted with Verizon to manage its infrastructure as a way of responding to the scalability issue. JetBlue's plight underscores the importance of analyzing the impact of strategic business decisions on IT architecture and infrastructure and at least ensuring that a contingency plan exists for potential unexpected effects of a strategy change.

Assessing Technical Issues: Standardization

Another important feature deals with commonly used **standards**. Hardware and software that use a common standard as opposed to a proprietary approach are easier to plug into an existing or future infrastructure or architecture because interfaces often accompany the standard. For example, many companies use Microsoft Office software, making it an almost de facto standard. Therefore, a number of additional packages come with translators to the systems in the Office suite to make it easy to move data between systems.

Assessing Technical Issues: Maintainability

How easy is the infrastructure to maintain? Are replacement parts available? Is service available? Maintainability is a key technical consideration because the complexity of these systems increases the number of things that can go wrong, need fixing, or simply need replacing. In addition to availability of parts and service people, maintenance considerations include issues such as the length of time the system might be out of commission for maintenance,

[18] Mel Duvall, "What Really Happened to JetBlue," http://www.cioinsight.com/c/a/Past-News/What-Really-Happened-At-JetBlue www.cioinsight.com (April 5, 2007) (accessed August 27, 2015).

how expensive and how local the parts are, and obsolescence. Should a technology become obsolete, costs for parts and expertise skyrocket. Architectures have different inherent security profiles.

Assessing Technical Issues: Security

Securing assets in a highly centralized, mainframe architecture means building protection around the centralized core. Because data and software are stored and executed on the mainframe computer, methods of protecting these assets revolve around protecting the mainframe itself. Decentralized, server-based architecture is more difficult to secure due to the dispersion of servers. Security is a matter of protecting every server instead of one centralized system. A Web-based SOA architecture that utilizes SaaS and capacity on demand raises a whole new set of security issues. The data and applications not only reside on servers in the various vendor systems around the Web, but also the linking mechanism, the network that ties the Web together, introduces another level of security concerns. Security is discussed in more detail in Chapter 7.

Assessing Financial and Managerial Issues

Like any business investment, IT infrastructure components should be evaluated based on their expected financial value. Unfortunately, payback from IT investments is often difficult to quantify; it can come in the form of increased productivity, increased interoperability with business partners, improved service for customers, or yet more abstract improvements. This suggests focusing on how IT investments enable business objectives rather than on their quantitative returns.

Still, some effort can and should be made to quantify the return on infrastructure investments. This effort can be simplified if a manager works through the following steps with the IT staff.

1. *Quantify costs:* The easy part is costing out the proposed infrastructure components and estimating the total investment necessary. Work with the IT staff to identify cost trends in the equipment the company proposes to acquire. Don't forget to include installation and training costs in the total.
2. *Determine the anticipated life cycles of system components:* Experienced IT staff or consultants can help establish life cycle trends for both a company and an industry to estimate the useful life of various systems.
3. *Quantify benefits:* The hard part is getting input from all affected user groups as well as the IT group, which presumably knows most about the equipment's capabilities. If possible, form a team with representatives from each of these groups and work together to identify all potential areas in which the new IT system may bring value.
4. *Quantify risks:* Assess any risk that might be attributable to delaying acquisition as opposed to paying more to get the latest technology now.
5. *Consider ongoing dollar costs and benefits:* Examine how the new equipment affects maintenance and upgrade costs associated with the current infrastructure.

Once this analysis is complete, the manager can calculate the company's preferred discounted cash flow (i.e., net present value or internal rate of return computation) and the payback period. Approaches to evaluating IT investments are discussed in greater detail in Chapter 8.

Applying these considerations to the fictitious GiantCo.com company, the last task is to weigh the managerial considerations against the architectural goals that were used to determine infrastructure requirements. Figure 6.7 shows how these considerations could apply to GiantCo.com's situation.

Again, note that the criteria evaluated in Figure 6.7 do not address every possible issue for GiantCo.com, but this example shows a broad sample of the issues that will arise.

Criteria	Architecture	Infrastructure
Strategic time frame	Indefinite: GiantCo.com's strategic goal is to be able to respond to customer needs.	NA
Technology advances	Database technology is fairly stable, but transaction capacity needs to be assessed and links with smaller suppliers and customers verified.	NA
Financial Issues		
NPV of investment	NA	GiantCo.com will analyze NPV of various hardware and software solutions and ongoing costs before investing.
Payback analysis	GiantCo.com expects the new architecture to pay for itself within three years.	Specific options will be evaluated using conservative sales growth projections to see how they match the three-year goal.
Incidental investments	The new architecture represents a moderate shift in the way GiantCo.com does business and will require some training and workforce adjustment.	Training costs for each option will be analyzed. Redeployment costs for employees displaced by any outsourcing must also be considered.
Growth requirements/ scalability	Outsourcing could provide more scalability than GiantCo.com's current model, which is constrained by IT capacity. New innovations will be identified to provide scalability of volume.	The scalability required of various new hardware and software components is not significant, but options will be evaluated based on their ability to meet scalability requirements.
Standardization	NA	GiantCo.com will adopt the MySQL standard and make it a requirement of all developers for consistency.
Maintainability	The new architecture raises some maintenance issues, and new product introductions will mandate constant updates to the rules of complementary goods.	Various options will be evaluated for their maintenance and repair costs.
Staff experience	The new model will require new skills and expertise.	Current staff is not familiar with MySQL. Training and workforce adjustment will be needed. Some new staff will be hired.
Security	GiantCo.com will lock down resources for traveling personnel.	GiantCo.com will adopt a Pulse Secure VPN for securely connecting traveling personnel with network resources.

FIGURE 6.7 GiantCo.com's managerial considerations.

Social Business Lens: Building Social Mobile Applications

As companies adopt social IT, they are finding that it is closely intertwined with mobile platforms. Employees want, and in some cases expect, to be able to access their social IT from their smartphones, tablets, and more. As companies look globally, in some countries the mobile screen is the only screen used.

In 2011, more than one-third of the U.S. population used the mobile Internet. In 2014, that number grew to such an extent that 52% of device owners consider smartphones and tablets the most important devices for Internet access, while only 46% consider desktops and laptops the most important devices. Tablets have surpassed all other devices in importance.

Social business requires that companies extend their architecture to include mobile functions, called *social mobile*. Social mobile functions began to take off with the widespread adoption of smartphones. The first devices combined features of a personal digital assistant with a mobile phone, giving developers the opportunity to link applications to the Web instantly. RIM's BlackBerry was one of the first to give users mobile access to communication tools such as their e-mail. More recent devices, such as Apple's iOS, Google's Android, Microsoft's Windows Phone, Nokia's Symbian, and RIM's BlackBerry OS, use a mobile operating system.

Initial social mobile apps were social networks either ported to the mobile platform, like LinkedIn and Facebook, or designed just for the mobile platform, like Foursquare and Gowalla, social network sites linking community members who "check in" at physical locations and sometimes earn virtual rewards for doing so. Social mobile applications have extended to many other types of applications as software designers realize the large market available to them if their applications run on mobile platforms and as device users demand increasing functionality for their mobile devices.

Source: Amy Gahran, "Survey: U.S. Mobile Web Access Growing Fast" (July 8, 2010), http://articles.cnn.com/2010-07-08/tech/mobile.internet.access.pew_1_cell-phone-users-feature-phones-mobile-internet (accessed August 27, 2015); Danyl Bosomworth, "Mobile Marketing Statistics 2015," *Smart Insights* (July 22, 2015), http://www.smartinsights.com/mobile-marketing/mobile-marketing-analytics/mobile-marketing-statistics/ (accessed August 27, 2015).

SUMMARY

- Strategy drives architecture, which drives infrastructure. Strategic business goals dictate IT architecture requirements. These requirements provide an extensible blueprint suggesting which infrastructure components will best facilitate the realization of the strategic goals.
- Enterprise architecture is the broad design that includes both the information systems architecture and the interrelationships in the enterprise. Often this plan specifies the logic for the entire organization. It identifies core processes, how they work together, how IT systems will support them, and the capabilities necessary to create, execute, and manage them.
- Four configurations for IT architecture are centralized, decentralized, SOA (or Web-based), and software-defined architectures. Applications are increasingly being offered as services, reducing the cost and maintenance requirements for clients. Virtualization and cloud computing provide architectures for Web-based delivery of services.
- The manager's role is to understand how to plan IT to realize business goals. With this knowledge, he or she can facilitate the process of translating business goals to IT architecture and then modify the selection of infrastructure components as necessary.
- Frameworks guide the translation from business strategy to IS design. This translation can be simplified by categorizing components into broad classes (hardware, software, network, data), which make up both IT architecture and infrastructure.
- Enterprise leaders increasingly have requests for new devices that employees want to connect to the corporate network. The consumerization of IT describes the trend to redesign corporate systems for smartphones, tablets, and other consumer-oriented devices.
- While translating strategy into architecture and then infrastructure, it is important to know the state of any existing architecture and infrastructure, to weigh current against future architectural requirements and strategic time frame, and to analyze the financial consequences of the various systems options under consideration. Systems performance should be monitored on an ongoing basis.

KEY TERMS

applications (p. 129)
architecture (p. 125)
bring-your-own-device (BYOD) (p. 133)
capacity-on-demand (p. 132)
centralized architecture (p. 130)
cloud architecture (p. 132)
cloud computing (p. 137)
consumerization of IT (p. 133)
data center (p. 130)
decentralized architecture (p. 130)
enterprise architecture (p. 136)
infrastructure (p. 125)
mainframe (p. 130)
peer-to-peer (p. 132)
platform (p. 129)
reuse (p. 130)
scalable (p. 141)
server-based architecture (p. 130)
service-oriented architecture (SOA) (p. 130)
software-as-a-service (p. 130)
software-defined architecture (p. 130)
standards (p. 141)
system software (p. 129)
TOGAF (p. 136)
utility computing (p. 138)
virtualization (p. 137)
Web-based architectures (p. 132)
Web services (p. 130)
wireless (mobile) infrastructures (p. 132)
infrastructures (p. 125)
Zachman framework (p. 136)

DISCUSSION QUESTIONS

1. Think about a company you know well. What would be an example of IT architecture at that company? An example of the IT infrastructure?
2. What, in your opinion, is the difference between a decentralized architecture and a centralized architecture? What is an example of a business decision that would be affected by the choice of the architecture?
3. From your personal experience, what is an example of software as a service? Of BYOD?
4. Each of the following companies would benefit from either software-defined architecture or conventional, owned hardware and software. State which you would advise each of the following fictitious firms (plus the IRS) to adopt and explain why.
   a. StableCo is a firm that sells industrial paper shredders. Its business has remained steady for two decades and it has a strong and diverse customer base.
   b. DynamicCo is a fast-growing six-year old firm that has relied on three to five key wholesale customers for its entire existence. However, the list of key customers changes every year, and during two of the years, sales declined sharply.
   c. Plastics3000 is an old, stable plastics manufacturing firm that has kept its sales steady in the face of competitors as the result of an active research and development team that uses advanced software to analyze large amounts of data to develop new compounds. Once or twice a week, office personnel complain of the network becoming very slow.
   d. A downtown Las Vegas casino monitors each slot machine continuously for early detection of malfunctions such as winnings or losses trending beyond their threshold limits.
   e. CallPerfect provides call center services to pharmacies. Phone calls are routed to the company after hours and messages are delivered to the pharmacy manager the next morning.
   f. At the IRS, tax forms are available online for citizens to complete and file with the IRS electronically by April 15. A call center routes calls to agents who answer taxpayers' questions.
   g. At LittlePeople, Inc., a day care center, parents are called using software on the administrator's computer when there is a weather emergency. The school has averaged 120 families for many years.

CASE STUDY 6-1 Enterprise Architecture at American Express

Enterprise architecture (EA) at American Express was the framework the organization used to align IT and the business. EA provided a common language for leaders to use to collaborate and transform the business. At American Express, enterprise architects were the change agents who streamlined processes and designed ways to more effectively do business using IT resources. In 2011, American Express was named an InfoWorld/Forrester Enterprise Architecture Award recipient for its EA practices. As American Express leaders considered new payment methods using mobile devices, the EA guided their progress.

Mobile payments were forcing the payments industry to review their practices and significantly transform the way business was done. The new business environment introduced additional complexity with the addition of new delivery channels and the need for shorter time-to-market of payment products and services. American Express's business strategy for its payments products focused on delivering a "consistent, global, integrated customer experience based on services running on a common application platform."

To achieve this goal, the EA team created reference architectures and road maps for standardized applications across the firm. This team then worked with multiple business solution delivery teams to create and manage the common application architecture and create strategies that facilitated each business's objectives. Each strategy included a road map of initiatives that included a set of actions, the metrics to evaluate the success of these actions, and the commitments IT and the businesses made to make it happen. The road map was American Express's way to standardize language, tools, life cycle management of the applications, and architecture and governance processes. The elements of the road map included technology, reference architecture, and capabilities for the business.

The next steps for American Express were to extend the road maps to cover the maturing of SOA and to develop new reference architectures and a new taxonomy to increasingly align IT with the needs of the business. As new technologies emerged and new ways of doing business over social tools created opportunities for new payment products and services, American Express expected to continually evolve its EA.

Discussion Questions

1. What are the key components of the architecture American Express has created?
2. Why was it important to standardize so much of the architecture? What are the advantages and disadvantages of a standard EA for American Express?

3. Describe how the new architecture supports the goals and strategy of American Express.
4. What types of future payment products and services should be anticipated and prepared for by the EA group? What is your vision of how payments might work? If you were advising the CIO of American Express, what would you suggest his group prepare for?

Source: Adapted from Phil LeClare and Eric Knorr, "The 2011 Enterprise Architecture Awards" (September 19, 2011), http://www.infoworld.com/d/enterprise-architecture/the-2011-enterprise-architecture-awards-173372 (accessed August 27, 2015).

CASE STUDY 6-2 The Case of Extreme Scientists

Scientists doing research often need serious computing capability to run simulations and crunch data. Often that meant working for a large company that could provide the significant investment in information systems infrastructure. But cloud computing changed all that. Consider the case of biologist Dr. Eric Schadt, a researcher who claims that approaches to studying the complexity of living systems have failed. Studying one gene at a time doesn't explain what causes diseases, making it impossible to find the cures sought by the scientific and pharmacology communities. Dr. Schadt's vision is to manage this area of research, and the large amount of data generated, which appears to be too much for any one individual or company to manage, by creating a human social network. He believes that this organization reflects the complexity of the living systems he studies and therefore it's necessary to understand it.

Dr. Schadt cofounded a nonprofit organization dedicated to biological research using an open-source sharing of data, Sage Bionetworks. He deeply believes that sharing is the key to finding cures and creating drugs that will combat diseases. And his company has millions of dollars worth of data from some of the major pharmaceutical companies to use to begin the research. But by day, he's the Chief Scientific Officer of a start-up, Pacific Biosciences (PacBio), whose technology helps biologists look at individual molecules of DNA in real time. His job is to work on how to use this technology for PacBio and to collaborate with others who want to use it for their research. So he travels a lot. But to do his research, he needs access to the capacity of a supercomputer because the amount of data he needs to use for his research is very large.

With the use of the Web, Dr. Schadt is able to do his work anyplace. Planes are especially favored because he has significant uninterrupted time. According to one article about him,

> He has the same access to supercomputers that every other American with an Internet connection and a credit card has. He waits till the plane climbs to a cruising altitude, then when allowed to use electronic devices, he uses the plane's WiFi to get on Amazon.

Dr. Schadt is able to initiate a complex analysis of his data using Amazon's services, which crunch the data while he flies across the country. When he lands, the analysis is done and he has the results. This would be equivalent to the computing power of a scientist working on his company's multimillion-dollar supercomputer, but in this case, the cost is just a few hundred dollars.

Companies like Amazon.com have become vendors of extreme computing power. Some have compared the amount of computing power Dr. Schadt uses while flying on an airplane to the amount of computing power available to a scientist at major pharmaceutical companies that have multimillion-dollar supercomputers. With services like the computing power available in the cloud, Dr. Schadt may even have more power available to him than that scientist.

Discussion Questions

1. How would you describe the architecture Dr. Schadt uses to do his research?
2. What are the risks Dr. Schadt faces by using Amazon for his supercomputing? What are the benefits?
3. If you were advising a company trying to make a decision about using cloud computing for key business applications, what would you advise and why?

Source: Adapted from Tom Junod, "Adventures in Extreme Science" (March 22, 2011), http://www.esquire.com/features/eric-schadt-profile-0411-4 (accessed August 27, 2015).

Security

chapter

7

Information technology (IT) security is one of the top issues of concern to businesses—hacked systems or stolen data can put a company out of business. General managers must understand the basics to ensure continuance of operations. This chapter explores managing security in five areas: strategy, infrastructure, policies, training, and investments. Lessons from some of the largest and most well-known breaches are covered as well as how they occurred according to security experts. The chapter also discusses common tools that aim to secure access, data storage, and data transmission to prevent these breaches and their advantages and disadvantages. Policies general managers can implement to decrease risk of security issues and economic damage are presented followed by a discussion of education, training, and awareness issues.

During lunchtime on June 6, 2015, a white van pulled in front of the U.S. Office of Personnel Management in Washington, D.C. A team of three expert hackers entered the front door, displaying the credentials of three janitors who were bound and gagged back at their office. As the hackers stood at a supply room door next to a highly secure server room, the target of their attack, one feigned having to crouch to tie his shoe, the other two stood in the way of the security cameras, and the crouching bandit used a lock-picking tool to gain access to the supply room. They figured they had only a few minutes to clip a monitoring device to the network wires that led to the servers containing security clearance information for millions of employees and past employees. The device monitored electrical activity right through the insulation and transmitted it to the van.

The hackers closed and relocked the supply room door, exited the building, and re-entered the van just as the clock struck 1 P.M. The tallest of the three declared "right on schedule!" and set a timer for 10 minutes. He tuned his laptop into the monitoring device and the other two did the same. They watched communications to and from the server, waiting for an employee, any employee, returning from lunch to log-in. Monitoring was risky due to random sweeps for rogue wireless connections, so after 10 minutes they would abort the mission.

The three typed frantically at their keyboards but nothing seemed to work for several agonizing minutes. Ten seconds before their time was up, one of the perpetrators hastily wrote some computer code and then smiled. He was just in time to reveal a log-in conversation complete with password. The hackers set the timer for another 10 minutes, which they had budgeted for the next phase.

The hackers searched frantically for large files that might contain the security clearance information they were hired to obtain. One of them found a large file called "SecurClearRecs," and the three cursed when they saw that the file was larger than anticipated. They immediately typed commands to upload the file through the Internet to a server in Shanghai, China. They kept one eye on the building and the other eye on the red "progress bar" that indicated "5% complete" for 20 full seconds before it changed to "10% complete." The time required for each 5% seemed to vary widely; moving from 15% to 20% took almost an entire minute. They realized it would take the entire 10 minutes they had allocated or more. They could almost hear their own pulses pounding as they anticipated the million dollar reward that awaited them if they were successful but also dreaded the fact that their overall budgeted 20 minutes might not be quite enough. Maybe they could chance it and go just a little longer.

A few terror-filled minutes past the budgeted 20 minutes, at 90% complete, they saw a guard step outside of the building and point at the van. Another officer joined him, and the pair started walking cautiously toward the van, trying to talk into his radio. The hackers had wisely jammed police channel communications and flattened the patrol cars' tires, but they wanted to avoid physical contact as much as possible. Trouble was certain to loom ahead; one of the officers turned to run back to the building. The tallest hacker jumped into the driver's seat and started the van. The hackers looked down at the progress bar, which said "99% complete," just as an alarm sounded. The remaining guard began running to the van. Four flat tires would mean a 10-minute delay waiting for another officer from the security firm's headquarters. The hackers waited 5 more seconds for "100% complete" and then screeched away to a secluded clearing a one-half mile away in the woods where a blue turbocharged Hyundai Sonata awaited them. They pushed a red "self-destruct" button in the van to start a timer, jumped in the Hyundai, and sped down back roads as distant sirens blared and the van exploded. Two weeks later, on June 20, 2015, an article in *Computerworld* stated that "The U.S. government still isn't saying how much data it fears was stolen."[1]

This story is notable for two reasons: (1) It is exactly the type of story that we would all imagine when hearing about data breaches, largely thanks to big-budget Hollywood movies. However, (2) the story is almost completely false; the only true parts are that a large number of private security clearance files were indeed stolen from the Office of Personnel Management, and the June 20 article in *Computerworld* did display the preceding quote. If managers expect only such "urgent and frantic" physical attacks, they will focus their attention on the wrong threats. It is important to learn the true story of this very real breach.

Governmental officials learned in May 2015 that at least 4 million records likely had been stolen several months earlier. Subsequent estimates placed the number at 14 million records.[2] The records contained much more than names, addresses, and social security numbers of current and former employees, possibly as far back as the 1980s. The 127-page dossier for each person also included information on alcohol and drug use, financial, psychological, employment, and criminal history as well as sensitive personal information about contacts and relatives. There were even comments from acquaintances, which could include neighbors, enemies, and potential enemies of each person.[3] In short, according to the *International Business Times,* the stolen information was "invasive enough to ruin potentially millions of American lives."[4] As a consequence, the Chairman of the U.S. House Oversight Committee asked for the resignation of the person in charge, the Director of the Office of Personnel Management.[5]

In reality, the following important issues are true for this case as well as many others:

1. *The hackers were far away* and did not need any physical contact or any escape plan.
2. *They were able to spend an extended period of time*—possibly over a year—to carry out their attack.[6]
3. *It took the victim organization months to discover the breach,* which enabled the hackers to cover their tracks. In fact, a 2015 report from consulting firm Mandiant revealed that the median time that it took in 2014 for firms to detect a threat group's presence was 205 days, and the maximum was a whopping 2,982 days (11 years).[7]
4. *The hackers exploited a stolen password,* likely obtained by various means described later in this chapter.

[1] O'Connor, Fred, "Hackers Had Access to Security Clearance Data for a Year," *Computerworld* (June 20, 2015), http://www.computerworld.com/article/2938654/cybercrime-hacking/hackers-had-access-to-security-clearance-data-for-a-year.html (last accessed June 22, 2015).

[2] Kim Zetter and Andy Greenberg, "Why the OPM Breach Is Such a Security and Privacy Debacle," *Wired* (June 11, 2015), http://www.wired.com/2015/06/opm-breach-security-privacy-debacle/ (accessed June 22, 2015).

[3] Ibid.

[4] Jeff Stone "Hacked US Security Clearances Are Giving Beijing Insanely Personal Information about American Citizens" (June 12, 2015), http://www.ibtimes.com/hacked-us-security-clearances-are-giving-beijing-insanely-personal-information-about-1964882 (last accessed August 25, 2015).

[5] Erin Kelly, "House Oversight to OPM Chief: 'Time for You to Go,'" *In Brief* (June 26, 2015), 2A.

[6] "Blackmail Looms after Government Cyber Breaches," WND.com (June 13, 2015). http://www.wnd.com/2015/06/blackmail-looms-after-government-cyber-breaches/ (accessed June 22, 2015).

[7] "M-Trends: A View from the Front Lines," Fireeye.com, https://www2.fireeye.com/rs/fireye/images/rpt-m-trends-2015.pdf (last accessed June 24, 2015).

Many other firms have been victimized, and hundreds of millions of records filled with personal information have been stolen just over the last two years. Security consulting firm FireEye estimates that 97% of all firms have been breached.[8] Managers must understand how large breaches occur to clarify the picture of what is going on out in the wild frontier and to protect their own company from similar fates. Only when threats are more fully understood can management begin to formulate and implement effective security plans.

IT Security Decision Framework

The first step on the road to an effective security plan is for management to adopt a broad view of security. This can be done by establishing an information security strategy and then putting the infrastructure (tools) and policies (tactics) in place that can help the organization realize its strategy. To round out the picture, users need to become familiar with security, and investments need to be made. The whole security picture can be reflected in five key information security decisions. Understanding these decisions and who is responsible for them (that is, who has the decision rights for them) is presented in Figure 7.1. We introduced decision rights in Chapter 3, and we use the concept to illustrate appropriate roles of business and IT managers in making a company's security decisions.

Information Security Decision	Who Is Responsible	Rationale	Major Symptoms of Improper Decision Rights Allocation
Security Strategy	Business leaders	Business leaders have the knowledge of the company's strategies on which security strategy should be based. No detailed technical knowledge is required.	Security is an afterthought and patched on to processes and products.
Infrastructure	IT leaders (CISO)	In-depth technical knowledge and expertise are needed.	There is a misspecification of security and network typologies or a misconfiguration of infrastructure. Technical security control is ineffective.
Security Policy	Shared: IT and business leaders	Technical and security implications of behaviors and processes need to be analyzed, and trade-offs between security and productivity need to be made. The particulars of a company's IT infrastructure need to be known.	Security policies are written based on theory and generic templates. They are unenforceable due to a misfit with the company's specific IT and users.
Security Education, Training, and Awareness	Shared: IT and business leaders	Business buy in and understanding are needed to design programs. Technical expertise and knowledge of critical security issues are needed to build them.	Users are insufficiently trained, bypass security measures, or do not know how to react properly when security breaches occur.
Investments	Shared: IT and business leaders	They require financial (quantitative) and qualitative evaluation of business impacts of security investments. A business case has to be presented for rivaling projects. Infrastructure impacts of funding decisions need to be evaluated.	Under- or overinvestment in information security occurs. The human or technical security resources are insufficient or wasted.

FIGURE 7.1 Key information security decisions.

Sources: Adapted from Yu Wu, "What Color is Your Archetype? Governance Patterns for Information Security," (Ph.D. Dissertation, University of Central Florida, 2007); Yu Wu and Carol Saunders, "Governing Information Security: Governance Domains and Decision Rights Allocation Patterns," *Information Resources Management Journal* 24, no. 1 (January–March 2011), 28–45.

[8] Bill Whitaker, "What Happens When You Swipe Your Card?" *60 Minutes* (November 30, 2014), transcript, http://www.cbsnews.com/news/swiping-your-credit-card-and-hacking-and-cybercrime/ (accessed June 24, 2015).

1. *Information security strategy:* A company's information security strategy is based on such IT principles as protecting the confidentiality of customer information, strict compliance with regulations, and maintaining a security baseline that is above the industry benchmark. Security strategy is not a technical decision. Rather, it should reflect the company's mission, overall strategy, business model, and business environment. Deciding on the security strategy requires decision makers who are knowledgeable about the company's strategy and management systems. An organization's information systems (IS) likely need to provide the required technical input for supporting the decision.

2. *Information security infrastructure:* Information security infrastructure decisions involve selecting and configuring the right tools. Common objectives are to achieve consistency in protection, economies of scale, and synergy among the components. Top business executives typically lack the experience or expertise to make these decisions. For these reasons, corporate IT typically is responsible for managing the dedicated security mechanisms and general IT infrastructure, such as enterprise network devices. Thus, corporate IT should take the lead and make sure that the technology tools in the infrastructure are correctly specified and configured.

3. *Information security policy:* Security policies encourage standardization and integration. Following best practices, they broadly define the scope of and overall expectations for the company's information security program. From these security policies, lower-level tactics are developed to control specific security areas (e.g., Internet use, access control) and/or individual applications (e.g., payroll systems, telecom systems). Policies must reflect the delicate balance between the enhanced information security gained from following them versus productivity losses and user inconvenience. As security attacks become more sophisticated, obeying security measures to deflect those attacks places cognitive demands on users. For example, they may need a different password for every account, and these passwords must often be long and hard to remember because they must have special characters. Productivity of users is often sacrificed when they have to come up with new passwords every month or when they have to spend time judging the legitimacy of dozens of e-mails each day. Not surprisingly, both IT and business perspectives are important in setting policies. Business users must be able to say what they want from the information security program and how they expect the security function to support their business activities. On the other hand, IT leaders should be consulted for two reasons: (1) their judgment prevents unrealistic goals for standardization and integration and (2) policy decisions require the ability to analyze the technical and security implications of user behaviors and business processes. If either users or IT leaders are not consulted, unenforceable policies will probably result.

4. *Information security education, training, and awareness (SETA):* It is very important to make business users aware of security policies and practices and to provide information **security education, training, and awareness (SETA)**. Training and awareness programs build a security-conscious culture. To promote effectiveness and post-training retention, training and awareness programs must be linked to the unique requirements of individual business processes. Business user participation in planning and implementing training and awareness programs helps gain acceptance of security initiatives. However, IT security personnel are in the best position to know critical issues. Thus, both IT security managers and business users must be actively involved in planning SETA activities.

5. *Information security investments:* The fear, uncertainty, and doubt ("FUD") factor once was all that was needed to get top management to invest in information security. As information security becomes a routine concern in daily operations, security managers increasingly must justify their budget requests financially. But it is difficult to show how important security is until there has been a breach—and even then it is hard to put a dollar amount on the value of security. As when determining business needs, different units within the company may have rival or conflicting "wish lists" for information security-related purchases that benefit their unique needs. The IS organization also should have a significant say in these decisions because it is in the best position to assess whether and how the investments may fit with the company's current IT infrastructure and application portfolio. Thus, both IT and business leaders should participate in investment and prioritization decisions. One way to ensure this joint participation is to use executive committees/councils

composed of business and IT executives, such as the IT steering committee and budget committee, with the CIO having overlapping memberships in both. These committees are where IT and business leaders make business cases for their proposed investments and debate the merit and priorities of the investments. These decisions about the appropriate level of investment are made with the company's best interests in mind.

Breaches and How They Occurred

In 2013 and 2014, before the Office of Personnel Management's attack, the most famous breaches infiltrated the systems at EBay (twice), Target, Home Depot, and Anthem Blue Cross. See Figure 7.2 for the magnitude and cause of each breach.

Password Breaches

It is important to emphasize the damage that can be done by password breaches. As the following descriptions indicate, trusting and trustworthy users might have no idea they are opening a security hole by clicking on an attachment, using public WiFi, or following a link to an authentic-looking site. Executives should not believe that employees who use their personal laptops away from the office are harmless to the firm. When employees whose systems are infected log onto work e-mail systems or intranets, a hacker can gain access to the firm.

60 Minutes reported in 2015 that 80% of breaches are conducted by stealing a password.[9] There are many ways to steal a person's password. One common method is to conduct a successful **phishing attack**,[10] which sends a person a counterfeit e-mail that purports to be from a known entity. The e-mail includes either a virus-laden

Date Detected	Company	What Was Stolen	How
November 2013	Target	40 million debit and credit card account numbers[a]	Contractor's opening of an e-mail attachment containing a virus, revealing a password[b]
May 2014	EBay #1	145 million user names, e-mails, physical addresses, phone numbers, birth dates, encrypted passwords[c]	Obtaining an employee's password[d]
September 2014	EBay #2	Small but unknown	Cross-site scripting
September 2014	Home Depot	56 million credit card numbers 53 million e-mail addresses	Obtaining a vendor's password and exploiting an operating system's vulnerability[e]
January 2015	Anthem Blue Cross	80 million names, birthdays, e-mails, social security numbers, addresses, and employment data (including income)[f]	Obtaining passwords of at least five high-level employees[g]

[a] Brian Krebs, "Target Hackers Broke in Via HVAC Company," Krebs on Security (February 14, 2014), http://krebsonsecurity.com/2014/02/target-hackers-broke-in-via-hvac-company/ (accessed June 22, 2015).
[b] Brian Krebs, "Home Depot: Hackers Stole 53M Email Addresses," Krebs on Security (November 14, 2014), http://krebsonsecurity.com/2014/11/home-depot-hackers-stole-53m-email-addreses/ (accessed June 28, 2015).
[c] Andy Greenberg, "EBay Demonstrates How Not to Respond to a Huge Data Breach, Wired (May 23, 2014), http://www.wired.com/2014/05/ebay-demonstrates-how-not-to-respond-to-a-huge-data-breach/(accessed June 22, 2015).
[d] Bill Whitaker, "What Happens When You Swipe Your Card?" 60 Minutes (November 30, 2014), transcript, http://www.cbsnews.com/news/swiping-your-credit-card-and-hacking-and-cybercrime/ (accessed June 24, 2015).
[e] Ashley Carman, "Windows Vulnerability Identified as Root Cause in Home Depot breach," SC Magazine (November 10, 2014), http://www.scmagazine.com/home-depot-breach-caused-by-windows-vulnerability/article/382450/ (accessed June 28, 2015).
[f] Michael Hiltzik, "Anthem Is Warning Consumers about Its Huge Data Breach. Here's a Translation," LA Times (March 6, 2015), http://www.latimes.com/business/hiltzik/la-fi-mh-anthem-is-warning-consumers-20150306-column.html#page=1 (accessed June 28, 2015).
[g] Ibid.

FIGURE 7.2 Well-known breaches, what was stolen, and how.

---

[9] Ibid.

[10] Brian Honan, "Reactions to the EBay Breach," http://www.net-security.org/secworld.php?id=16905 (accessed June 22, 2015).

attachment or a link that invites the user to click and visit a page to either solve a problem or accomplish a task (as described in detail at the end of this chapter).

The only limit is the phisher's imagination to create a scenario that would motivate a user to click on a link. The attachment or link in a phishing message often initiates a **key logger**, or software that traps keystrokes and stores them for hackers to inspect later. A key logger can even be hidden on a thumb drive plugged into a public computer in a hotel's business center. A key logger might also be triggered by visiting an unfamiliar Web site. Just by clicking on a search result, a user might inadvertently download and install the key logging software. Asking the user to log-in will reveal his or her user name and password, opening a world of opportunity for the hacker.

Another way to obtain a password is simply to guess it. Experts warn that large breaches can be caused by using a **weak password**, such as "123456," which, incredibly, won again as the most common password of all in 2014.[11] Passwords can be troublesome. Creating a strong password that cannot be guessed results in a hard-to-remember string of nonsense characters. The name of a hometown, a team, an employer, or a family member would be among the first guesses of a hacker. Also, even if it is difficult to guess, many people use the same password for multiple purposes, and if one account is breached, all of their other accounts are then wide open. It is challenging to keep track of difficult passwords that are different for every account. Tools such as LastPass, Dashlane, and Sticky Password allow access with one password to a set of highly complex and impossible-to-remember passwords synchronized across Windows and Mac computers as well as Android and iOS smartphones.[12]

Yet another way to open a firm to a large breach is for employees to use an unsecured network at a coffee shop, hotel, or airport.[13] Many users do not realize that, even if the network's name matches the coffee shop's name, someone in the shop might have set up a so-called **evil twin connection** WiFi connection and that all incoming and outgoing Internet traffic becomes routed through the perpetrator's system. Without the proper tools or training, most users can't validate a public WiFi connection. Once connected, the unwitting users' keystrokes, including their user names and passwords, are captured as they shop online, do Internet banking, or log into their company's intranet site.[14] The only solution might be for companies to establish policies forbidding their employees to use public WiFi and use their smartphones as their PC's sole Internet connection even when tempted by free WiFi in public places.

Other Attack Approaches

Cross-Site Scripting

As shown in Figure 7.2, a second EBay breach is another important attack for management to understand. It was discovered in September 2014 by an astute user who nagged EBay to fix the problem for over a year.[15] He even created a surprising YouTube video to show how it worked.[16] The damage is unclear, affecting only the users who clicked on one particular search result that was eventually removed. However, the cause is clear in this case:[17] **cross-site scripting (XSS)**, which involves booby traps that appear to lead users to their goal, but in reality, they lead to a fraudulent site that requires a log-in. EBay permits users to install some computer code in their listings to make their items in EBay search results grab shoppers' attention. It is intended to allow animation in listings, but malicious code was inserted instead, designed for a nefarious purpose: to alter the listing's address to point to a bogus log-in screen. Users assumed they needed to log-in once again for security purposes, but in reality everyone who "logged-in" that second time provided the crooks with user names and passwords.

---

[11] Jamie Condliff, "The 25 Most Popular Passwords of 2014: We're All Doomed," *Gizmodo* (January 20, 2015), http://gizmodo.com/the-25-most-popular-passwords-of-2014-were-all-doomed-1680596951 (accessed June 22, 2015).

[12] Neil J. Rubenking, "The Best Password Managers for 2015," *PC Magazine* (June 2, 2015), http://www.pcmag.com/article2/0,2817,2407168,00.asp (accessed June 25, 2015).

[13] Sergio Galindo, "Reactions to the EBay breach," http://www.net-security.org/secworld.php?id=16905 (accessed June 22, 2015).

[14] Andrew Smith, "Strange Wi-Fi Spots May Harbor Hackers: ID Thieves May Lurk Behind a Hot Spot with a Friendly Name," *Dallas Morning News* (May 9, 2007), http://cloud-computing.tmcnet.com/news/2007/05/09/2597106.htm (accessed August 25, 2015).

[15] Chris Brook, "A Year Later, XSS Vulnerability Still Exists in EBay," *Threatpost* (April 29, 2015), https://threatpost.com/a-year-later-xss-vulnerability-still-exists-in-ebay/112493 (accessed August 27, 2015).

[16] Paul Kerr, "Ebay Hacked Proof!" (September 16, 2014), https://www.youtube.com/watch?v=WT5TG_LvZz4&feature=youtu.be (accessed June 22, 2015).

[17] Phil Muncaster, "EBay Under Fire After Cross-Site Scripting Attack," *Infosecurity* (undated), http://www.infosecurity-magazine.com/news/ebay-under-fire-after-cross-site/ (accessed June 22, 2015).

Third Parties

Several breaches have involved third parties. The Target attackers broke into the network using credentials stolen from a heating, ventilation, and air conditioning (HVAC) contractor and installed malware on the retail sales system. The malware captured and copied the magnetic stripe card data right from the computer's memory before the system could encrypt and store it. Why would an HVAC contractor have access? Security expert and blogger Brian Krebs reports that it is common for large retailers to install on their systems temperature and energy-monitoring software provided by contractors. HVAC companies need to update and maintain their software, and are given access to their main systems so they don't have to endure delays in those updates. Access to the retailing system enabled the malware to spread to a majority of Target's cash registers, collecting information from debit and credit cards and sending it to various drop points in Miami and Brazil to be picked up later by hackers in Eastern Europe and Russia.[18]

Home Depot's story echoed that of Target from a year earlier. Logon credentials were stolen from a vendor that had access to Home Depot's system, and the same malware was unleashed to cash registers. Target's story motivated Home Depot to update its system but the attack occurred before the company could complete all of the improvements.[19]

The attack at Anthem Blue Cross demonstrates that stealing high-level user names and passwords can provide quick access to large and important files. Target and Home Depot hackers had to wait until transactions were recorded to gain valuable information, which takes several days. But at Anthem, being able to download important employment and identity information from 80 million people at one pass was easy with the high-level passwords. Log-in credentials of lower-level employees would involve transaction-by-transaction data collection. Therefore, log-in accounts of executives need special attention, and their activities should be monitored regularly.

System Logs and Alerts

Early news reports of Target's hack outraged customers when it was revealed that the newly installed, state-of-the-art $1.6 million security system detected what was going on. It sent several warnings to the IT department, even before the first files were transferred, but those alerts were unheeded.[20] However, some security experts explain that there are perhaps hundreds of generic alerts each day, and it is difficult to follow up on every one. One expert was quoted aptly: "it is completely understandable how this happened."[21]

The Cost of Breaches

A Ponemon study places the cost of a data breach in 2015 to be at an all-time high, between $145 and $154 per each lost or stolen record containing sensitive information.[22] If a breach exposes 100 million records, the costs could escalate to about $15 billion. Many firms facing such costs would be put in serious jeopardy. The Target breach cost $61 million in just two months,[23] $162 million a year later,[24] and potentially billions of dollars in damage control over the long run.[25] The CIO resigned, fourth quarter profit fell 46%, and revenue declined 5.3%.[26] The Home Depot

[18] Brian Krebs, "Target Hackers Broke in Via HVAC Company," Krebs on Security (February 14, 2014), http://krebsonsecurity.com/2014/02/target-hackers-broke-in-via-hvac-company/ (accessed June 22, 2015).

[19] Shelly Banjo, "Home Depot Hackers Exposed 53 Million Email Addresses," *The Wall Street Journal* (November 6, 2014), http://www.wsj.com/articles/home-depot-hackers-used-password-stolen-from-vendor-1415309282 (accessed June 22, 2015).

[20] Michael Riley, Ben Elgin, Dune Lawrence, and Carol Matlack, "Missed Alarms and 40 Million Stolen Credit Card Numbers: How Target Blew It," *Bloomberg Business* (March 13, 2014), http://www.bloomberg.com/bw/articles/2014-03-13/target-missed-alarms-in-epic-hack-of-credit-card-data (accessed August 25, 2015).

[21] Joel Christie, "Target Ignored High-Tech Security Sirens Warning Them of a Data Hack Operation BEFORE Cyber-Criminals in Russia Made Off with 40 Million Stolen Credit Cards," http://www.dailymail.co.uk/news/article-2581314/Target-ignored-high-tech-security-sirens-warning-data-hack-operation-BEFORE-cyber-criminals-Russia-40-million-stolen-credit-cards.html (last accessed June 24, 2015).

[22] Ponemon Institute, "2015 Cost of Data Breach Study," IBM, http://www-03.ibm.com/security/data-breach/ (accessed June 23, 2015).

[23] Riley, Elgin, Lawrence, and Matlack, "Missed Alarms and 40 Million Stolen Credit Card Numbers."

[24] PYMNTS@pymnts, "How Much Did the Target, Home Depot Breaches Really Cost?" PYMNTS.com (February 26, 2015), http://www.pymnts.com/news/2015/target-home-depot-reveal-full-breach-costs/#.VYr_6EZZV34 (accessed June 24, 2015).

[25] Christie, "Target Ignored High-Tech Security Sirens."

[26] Associated Press. "Target's Tech Boss Resigns as Retailer Overhauls Security in Wake of Massive Payment Card Breach," *Financial Post* (March 5, 2014), http://business.financialpost.com/fp-tech-desk/cio/target-cio-resigns?__lsa=011c-8001 (accessed August 27, 2015).

breach cost $33 million (after insurance proceeds of $30 million reduced the initial outlays of $63 million),[27] and the company's stock price fell 2.1% the day after the breach was announced.[28] Sales were not affected, however, which might indicate that customers have become numb to these announcements.[29]

The Impossibility of 100% Security

To obtain 100% security for an organization, a first step would be to list all of the potential threats, and the second step would be to obtain tools that would guard against them. However, as in our personal lives, the challenge would be overwhelming and the solution untenable. To keep ourselves completely safe and injury free, we would need thick steel walls and air bags around us not only when we drive but also when we run, walk, and even just sit at home. We would avoid germs by spraying disinfectants on all surfaces, including our own skin before touching anything. But paradoxes exist that make it impossible to be completely safe: We would want to be high on a hill to avoid floods but low in a valley to avoid lightning strikes—an impossible paradox. We learn quickly that it is perhaps impossible to be 100% safe, 24/7.

Likewise, data stored in a firm would be easier to protect if they would just "stay still" as well and not be connected to the Internet. Although some paradoxes exist in locating the data, the security closest to 100% would be to place them in a remote area, removed from Internet access, and under several locks without any keys at all. In short, the closest we can get to perfect safety is to make data inaccessible. But this is not feasible.

Just as we accept some degree of risk to our safety even when we move from the living room to the kitchen, management must accept some level of risk as well when it makes any part of its treasure trove of data accessible to even a single person inside or outside an organization. Wider data accessibility entails great risk.

Back in 1995, the late L. Dain Gary, former manager of the U.S. Computer Emergency Response Team (CERT) in Pittsburgh appeared on an episode of *60 Minutes* and let the public in on a unpleasant fact with a sobering statement: "You cannot make a computer secure. You can reduce the risk, but you can't guarantee security."[30] Because of the futility of seeking 100% security, many companies take out insurance policies to mitigate the financial impacts of a breach. It is important to also consider the so-called "Poulsen's law" that states that information is secure when it costs more to get it than it's worth.[31] This is a good rule to remember, and the role of management is to work with the IT function to make it harder to break in than it is worth.

And stolen information is worth a lot. A security expert reported that in 2014, stolen credit cards sold for between $1 and $50 each, depending on the type of card (e.g., platinum, silver, suggesting its credit limit) and expiration date. Of the 40 million Target credit card numbers stolen, about 2 million (5%) were sold at an average price of $20, yielding $4 million to the hackers. A member of a street gang who bought one of those credit cards for $20 was likely to yield $400 in purchases of gift cards and electronics.[32]

Further, a complete identity-theft "kit" containing not only a card but social security number and medical information is worth far more—between $100 and $1,000 each on the black market.[33] The value is high because identity-theft information can be used to open new credit cards again and again, generating quite a bit of revenue.

The hackers do not keep stolen credit cards or identity theft information for their own use, given the staggering volume they acquire. They quickly sell them online to others all over the world who use them before they are

---

[27] PYMNTS@pymnts, "How Much Did the Target, Home Depot Breaches Really Cost?"

[28] Hiroko Tabuchi, "Home Depot Posts a Strong 3rd Quarter Despite a Data Breach Disclosure," *The New York Times* (November 18, 2014), http://www.nytimes.com/2014/11/19/business/home-depot-reports-strong-third-quarter-growth-despite-data-breach-disclosure.html (accessed June 23, 2015).

[29] Anne D'Innocenzio, "4 Reasons Shoppers Will Shrug Off Home Depot Hack," *USA Today* (September 11, 2014), http://www.usatoday.com/story/money/business/2014/09/11/4-reasons-shoppers-will-shrug-off-home-depot-hack/15460461/ (accessed June 23, 2015).

[30] *60 Minutes*, "E-Systems" (February 26, 1995).

[31] "Anything Made by a Man Can Be Hacked," *DSL Reports* (March 6, 2006), http://www.dslreports.com/forum/remark,15623829 (accessed September 15, 2015).

[32] Whitaker, "What Happens When You Swipe Your Card?"

[33] Tim Greene, "Anthem Hack: Personal Data Stolen Sells for 10x Price of Stolen Credit Card Numbers," *Networkworld* (February 6, 2015), http://www.networkworld.com/article/2880366/security0/anthem-hack-personal-data-stolen-sells-for-10x-price-of-stolen-credit-card-numbers.html (accessed June 24, 2015).

reported as stolen. Those cards even come with a return policy in case they are declined, because the black market shops need to maintain their reputations. However, the guarantees come with a warning that they run out after only a few hours.[34]

One final discouraging word is important. A study by the Software Engineering Institute in 2002 revealed that over time, the knowledge needed by an intruder for an attack reached an all-time low whereas the potential impact of the intruders' attack reached an all-time high.[35] The intruders' tools have not only become more sophisticated but also have actually become user friendly. Automated tools can be purchased on the **Deep Web**, which is a part of the Internet that is reputed to be 400 times larger than the public Web. The Deep Web includes unindexed Web sites that are accessible only by a browser named "Tor," which guarantees anonymity and provides access to sites offering both legal and illegal items. Examples of illegal items offered are passports, citizenship, and even murders for hire.[36] Also for sale are tools that can scan for vulnerable systems, exploit the weaknesses found, and even generate viruses. Payment could reach hundreds of thousands of dollars, usually made through *Bitcoin,* an electronic currency that is difficult to track.

The outlook is certainly grim, but some of the clues in the stories told here can provide some prescriptions for management.

What Should Management Do?

Five critical elements to build security described earlier include security strategy, infrastructure, policies, training, and investments. Security strategy needs to come first, and top management must determine the general strategy as well as investments that are needed. Infrastructure, policy, and training decisions have to be made in more detail, and these three areas will now be discussed. Fortunately, general managers can easily understand key issues for each of these elements and participate fully in design and implementation of the resulting security plans.

Infrastructure

Hackers have significant tools to breach security barriers as previously described. In this rapidly escalating cyber war, management must use its own set of technologies and specialists to reduce risk and increase security. Many firms employ a chief information security officer (CISO), described in Chapter 8, to keep abreast of new threats that emerge and manage the policies and education necessary to reduce risk. In other firms, this responsibility falls to the CIO or simply the facilities security staff. Even with specialists, managers need to have a broad understanding of these tools to communicate effectively with them.

Tools can be divided into two categories: those that provide protection from access by undesired intruders and those that provide protection for storage and transmission. See Figure 7.3 for a list of common system tools to prevent access and their advantages and disadvantages and Figure 7.4 for a list of common storage and transmission tools and their advantages and disadvantages.

Passwords are by far the most popular security tool even though they have proven to be the cause of most breaches. Some security specialists claim that passwords are obsolete and should be discontinued.[37] Also, all access protection tools have the disadvantage of requiring an additional access method if it fails. For instance, because users often forget a password, firms need to make additional investments to create an automated resetting mechanism through an alternate method, such as an e-mail to a known address or a text message to a mobile phone.

[34] Aaron Sankin, "Inside the Black Markets for Your Stolen Credit Cards," *The Kernel* (September 28, 2014), http://kernelmag.dailydot.com/issue-sections/features-issue-sections/10362/inside-the-black-markets-for-your-stolen-credit-cards/ (accessed August 27, 2015).

[35] Howard F. Lipson, "Tracking and Tracing Cyber-Attacks: Technical Challenges and Global Policy Issues," Special Report CMU/SEI-2002-SR-009, http://www.sei.cmu.edu/reports/02sr009.pdf (accessed August 27, 2015).

[36] Nyshka Chandran, "From Drugs to Killers: Exploring the Deep Web," CNBC Technology (June, 2015), http://www.cnbc.com/id/102782903 (accessed June 25, 2015).

[37] Justin Balthrop, "Passwords Are Obsolete," Medium.com (April 12, 2014), https://medium.com/@ninjudd/passwords-are-obsolete-9ed56d483eb (accessed June 24, 2015).

Access Tool	Concept	Ubiquity	Notable Advantages	Notable Disadvantages
Physical locks	Physically protect computing resources	Very high	• They are excellent as long as the lock is highly secure and guarded • Few criminals can access physical devices	• Many popular locks can be picked with tools sold online • Most information resources do not require physical access • Users often lose keys or combinations
Passwords	Invent a set of characters known only by the user	Very high	• They have very high acceptance and familiarity • They are easy to use unless forgotten • Mature best practices replace forgotten passwords (no longer a need to call the help line to reset)	• They prove to be poor by themselves • They are sometimes forgotten • They are sometimes derived from key loggers or social engineering • They can be guessed by "brute force" software
Biometrics	Scan a body characteristic, such as fingerprint, voice, iris, head, or hand geometry	Medium overall; popularized by iPhone	• It is somewhat better than passwords • It can be very reliable (e.g., iris scanning) • It cannot be forgotten • It cannot be derived from key loggers or social engineering • It can be quite inexpensive (e.g., voice, fingerprint)	• It can present false positives and false negatives (e.g., voice; facial recognition) • It can be relatively expensive and intrusive techniques (e.g., iris scanning) • It is possible to change characteristics over time, such as voice • It can result in lost limbs • It can create "loopholes" such as using a photo of a face or fingerprint on paper
Challenge questions	Prompt with a follow-up question such as "model of first car?"	Medium overall; very high in banking	• The answers are usually not forgotten • Shuffling through several different questions can enhance security	• Some answers can be derived from social network sites • Some answers can be derived by those who know the user • Spelling inconsistencies can be a nuisance
Token	Use small electronic device that generates a new supplementary passkey at frequent intervals	Low overall; very high in highly secure environments	• Even if passkey is stolen, the system is still secure when the passkey changes	• Access requires physical possession of token device • If the device is lost, access is lost until a new one is obtained • Alternative access control (e.g., password) is essential if token device is stolen
Text message	Send a text message with a passkey	Medium	• Even if a password is stolen, the system is still secure • Mobile phone saturation is very high; no additional equipment is needed • It is very useful when password is forgotten	• It requires mobile phone from all users • Home phone option requires text to speech hardware/ software • Alternative access control (e.g., password) is essential if mobile device is stolen

FIGURE 7.3 Common system access security tools and their advantages and disadvantages.

Access Tool	Concept	Ubiquity	Notable Advantages	Notable Disadvantages
Multifactor authentication	Couple two or more access techniques, for instance • Passwords and tokens • Biometrics and follow-up questions • Passwords and text messaging	Medium overall; very high in banking and other high-security environments	• It enhances security greatly • Even if a password is stolen, the system is still secure	• It requires an additional access authentication technique if one or more of the techniques fails • Users might be tempted to use an easy password, which removes the advantage of a second factor

FIGURE 7.3 (Continued)

Storage and/or Transmission Tool	Concept	Ubiquity	Notable Advantages	Notable Disadvantages
Antivirus/ antispyware	Software scans incoming data and evaluates the periodic state of the whole system to detect threats of secret software that can either destroy data or inform a server of your activity	Very high	• Products block known threats very effectively • Products have a large database and can detect hundreds of thousands of patterns that reveal a virus • Some products reveal a limited set of zero-day threats (brand-new outbreaks) by tracking suspicious behavior	• Products sometimes slow down the device • Products are not as effective for a clever zero-day threat (brand-new outbreak)
Firewall	Software and sometimes hardware-based filter prevent or allow outside traffic from accessing the network	High	• Is flexible and can prevent traffic from a particular user, device, method, or geography	• It can filter only known threats • It can have well-known "holes"
System logs	They keep track of system activity, such as successful or failed login attempts, file alterations, file copying, file deletion, or software installation	Very high	• If an irregularity occurs, the IP address of the attacker could be discovered • The extent of the irregularity can be estimated	• Some anonymizing software can hide the true IP address of the attacker • Some attackers erase or disable the logs • Logs can be huge and difficult to wade through • Some firms fail to inspect logs regularly
System alerts	System detects unusual activity, such as scores of unsuccessful log-in attempts, log-ins from countries without any branches, alterations of files, or copying of files	High	• They can aid in combing through logs more quickly • Administrators can be alerted to an irregularity while it is occurring • Many breaches can be detected this way[a] (high *sensitivity*)	• Many firms receive hundreds of alerts each day • It is difficult to discern real attacks from false alarms (low *selectivity*)

FIGURE 7.4 Common storage and transmission security tools.

Storage and/or Transmission Tool	Concept	Ubiquity	Notable Advantages	Notable Disadvantages
Encryption	System follows a complex formula, using a unique **key** (set of characters) to convert plain text into what looks like unreadable nonsense and then to decode back to plain text when presented with the decoding key	Very high	• It is very difficult to use or read a stolen computer file without the key • Long and complex keys would take years of computer time to break	• The key can be unnecessary if access password is known • If the key is not strong, hackers can uncover it by trial and error
WEP/WPA (wired equivalent privacy and wireless protected access)	Encryption is used in a wireless network	Very high	• *It is same as encryption* • Nearly all modern user devices have capabilities • It provides a secure connection between the user's device and the WiFi router	• *It is same as encryption* • Some older devices might not be able to be connected • WEP is not secure yet is still provided for compatibility
Virtual private network	Software provides a trusted, encrypted connection between your site and a particular server	Medium	• Trusted connection works as if you are connected at your office; it is useful for mobile workers • Eavesdroppers cannot easily decrypt VPN communications	• If the device is stolen while connected, the hacker has access to all resources • It sometimes slows the connection or complicates use

[a] Vinod Khosia, "Behavioral Analysis Could Have Prevented the Anthem Breach," Forbes.com (February 24, 2015), http://www.forbes.com/sites/frontline/2015/02/24/behavioral-analysis-could-have-prevented-the-anthem-breach/ (accessed June 28, 2015).

FIGURE 7.4 (Continued)

A study in the United Kingdom found that 39% of IT professionals admit that passwords are the only IT security measure in their firms, and one-third believes that biometrics are likely to be used in five years.[38] There is a general trend toward **multifactor authentication**, or the use of two or more authorization methods to gain access. Examples are use of a password followed by a passkey sent to a mobile phone as a text message or a password followed by a **challenge question**. Between 2013 and 2014, the organizations around the world using multifactor authentication increased from 30% to 37%, and this number continues to increase rapidly.[39]

Fears of making passwords intrusive or lowering convenience are likely to factor into IT's reluctance to adopt multifactor authentication. For instance, in Apple's "I'm a Mac" campaign in 2008, Apple poked fun at Microsoft Vista's "Cancel or Allow" messages,[40] emphasizing the diminished convenience caused by security warnings. Security and convenience are indeed generally at odds with each other,[41] but our current state of convenience is untenable over the long run, and the days of single-factor authentication using a password are undoubtedly going to become a distant memory.

Not only access controls are important, but also the way that information is stored and transmitted requires security tools. Figure 7.4 provides a representative list of those tools. Although these tools are likely to help limit security problems, managers also need to provide a strong security policy as described in the next section.

[38] SecureAuth, "The Password's Pulse Beats On. Hackers Still One Step away from Your Information," SecureAuth.com (March 18, 2015), https://www.secureauth.com/Company/News/March-2015/The-Password%E2%80%99s-Pulse-Beats-On-Hackers-Still-One-St.aspx (accessed June 24, 2015).

[39] SafeNet, "More Enterprises Plan to Strengthen Access Security with Multi-Factor Authentication," SafeNet Survey Report (May 21, 2014), http://www.safenet-inc.com/news/2014/authentication-survey-2014-reveals-more-enterprises-adopting-multi-factor-authentication/ (accessed June 24, 2015).

[40] Renee Quinn, "Comparative Advertising: Mac vs. PC," IP Watchdog (November 16, 2008), http://www.ipwatchdog.com/2008/11/16/comparative-advertising-mac-vs-pc/id=268/ (accessed June 24, 2015).

[41] David Jeffers, "Why Convenience Is the Enemy of Security," PC World (June 18, 2012), http://www.pcworld.com/article/257793/why_convenience_is_the_enemy_of_security.html (accessed June 25, 2015).

Security Policy

Management needs to approach security in a way that expresses its importance and instructs users on what they need to do to achieve safety. Without sound management policy, access and storage technologies will be useless. If employees write their passwords on sticky notes and put them near their workstations, passwords will be ineffective from the start. Figure 7.5 provides a list of management policy tactics to prevent security weaknesses.

Several of these policy areas are quite interesting. For instance, some managed security services provider (MSSP) firms offer the services of **white hat hackers** who break into a firm's systems to help it uncover weaknesses. White hat hackers lie in sharp contrast to **black hat hackers**, who break in for their own gain or to wreak havoc on a firm. **Grey hat hackers** test organizational systems without any authorization and notify a company when they find a weakness. Although they can be helpful, what they do is nevertheless illegal.

Another interesting area is that of social media. We are still in the early stages of understanding the impacts of being on social media for employees and firms themselves. Companies continue to set up policies about acceptable behavior on social media including the appropriateness of sharing company secrets, security procedures, and

Policy	Concept	Notable Advantages	Notable Disadvantages
Perform security updates promptly	Make sure all security updates are applied as soon as possible	• Most operating systems have automatic updates	• Sometimes the added security causes some older applications to "break" • There is an option to prevent automatic updates
Separate unrelated networks	Disconnect distinct and unrelated parts of the network. For instance, Target's HVAC system should have been disconnected from the financial system	• Protect one part of the system when the other part is attacked	• Sometimes there are connections that are unknown or unexpected • Each requires different log-in credentials, complicating its usage
Keep passwords secret	Forbid users from sharing passwords	• If everyone complies, any activities on the site will be traceable to one user's access	• It will be harder if the user is on the road and needs an assistant to help with something
Perform mobile device management	Provide a BYOD (bring your own device) policy on permitted products and required connection methods	• It will prevent, or at least allow IT to trace, potential security problems	• It will restrict users to apps they might not wish to use • It might restrict users to certain devices they might not desire to use
Data policies	Require disposal of e-mails and other documents of a certain age	• Data that are not owned cannot be stolen • Legal liability is dramatically reduced by destroying memos and e-mails that can be taken out of context	• Workers might be unable to refer back to the details of a previous successful assignment for guidance
Social media management	Provide rules about what can be disclosed on social media, who can Tweet, and how employees can identify themselves	• It will prevent misrepresentation and confusion • It will limit liability by avoiding errors	• It might appear restrictive to workers • It might appear to be meddling in workers' personal use of social media
Managed security services providers (MSSP)	Consultants who bring their expertise and checklists, most often to medium and large enterprises	• It can help build a comprehensive security plan	• It can be too expensive for a very small company • It can provide a bewildering set of options

FIGURE 7.5 Commonly used management security policies.

personal information that could be linked back to a company. Given the large size of some firms, it is difficult to control personal behavior. But lacking policy, devastating impacts of uncontrolled behavior can be high.

Education, Training, and Awareness

Users' behavior cannot be expected to change unless they are aware of security policy and tools, understand them, and know what to do. Merely dictating rules to employees and providing the required tools will not guarantee compliance. Security education, training, and awareness (SETA) can provide well-rounded preparation to users. Because 50%–75% of security incidents originate from within an organization, researchers have found that SETA was effective in reducing IS misuse and that severity of punishment was more potent than certainty of punishment if users were caught. As one might expect, the researchers also found that monitoring behavior was quite important.[42] Each component of SETA is discussed next.

Awareness

Although awareness comes at the end of the SETA acronym, it is an important first step merely to let users know that security is a complex but important issue and that there are consequences when policies are not followed. Users must see the importance of the security policies and the need to use the appropriate tools. Awareness includes an explanation of what might occur if users are relaxed about security, such as in the cases discussed in this chapter.

Awareness creates attitudes, and researchers note that attitudes are important in predicting compliance. Importantly, users' feelings of efficacy (ability to comply) and normative beliefs (social pressure to comply) are both important for forming favorable attitudes toward compliance,[43] suggesting that the awareness stage is crucial for security success. Managers should be cautious not to overwhelm users all at once; this is where education programs can help.

Education and Training

Education provides frameworks, reveals concepts, and builds understanding. Training usually provides procedures to follow and practice in following them. For example, 69% of company breaches have been discovered by outsiders, not insiders.[44] In some cases, customers complain of irregularities in their accounts, such as unauthorized charges. However, it takes time for that information to reach the breached firm, if ever, as the unsettling recent 60 Minutes interview revealed; after hacking, Visa and MasterCard do not reveal which retailer was involved. Further, in the case of Home Depot, it took Brian Krebs to notify the firm after seeing credit cards for sale on Deep Web sites. He says he did some "detective work" and tracked the stolen cards to Home Depot.[45]

Apparently, insiders do not always notice signals that might indicate a problem. Some of that can be alleviated through education. Users need to be educated about the potential for different types of suspicious activities, such as strange cars parked with the motor running, which might indicate tapping into a company's WiFi, or strangers standing near active equipment, which might indicate surveillance or potential invasive action. Employees must be trained to make sure active equipment is watched and suspicious activity reported. Training also instructs on powering down equipment, logging users out of systems, closing browser windows, and frequently updating passwords.

In a recent alarming situation, a security researcher claimed on Twitter to have tapped into the avionics system through the entertainment system on an airplane, causing the plane to go into a brief, unscheduled climb. While on the plane, the person bent over and wiggled and squeezed the under-seat electronic box's cover to pry it off.[46] The person then attached a modified Ethernet cable to an open port in the entertainment equipment below two passenger seats. Although pilots were able to quickly take over in this situation, the FBI took his Tweet seriously.

---

[42] John D'Arcy, Anat Hovav, and Dennis Galletta, "Awareness of Security Countermeasures and Its Impact on Information Systems Misuse: A Deterrence Approach," *Information Systems Research* 20, no. 1 (March 2009), 79–98.

[43] Burcu Bulgurcu, Hasan Cavusoglu, and Izak Benbasat, "Information Security Policy Compliance: An Empirical Study of Rationality-Based Beliefs and Information Security Awareness," *MIS Quarterly* 34, no. 3 (2010), 523–48.

[44] Mandiant, "M-Trends 2015: A View from the Front Lines," https://www2.fireeye.com/rs/fireye/images/rpt-m-trends-2015.pdf (accessed June 24, 2015).

[45] Whitaker, "What Happens When You Swipe Your Card?"

[46] Kim Zetter, "Is It Possible for Passengers to Hack Commercial Aircraft?" Wired (May 26, 2015), http://www.wired.com/2015/05/possible-passengers-hack-commercial-aircraft/ (accessed June 25, 2015).

Subject	Sample Educational Activities	Sample Training Activities
Access tools	Advantages and limitations of passwords Why passwords should be complex and long How often passwords should be changed Strengths of multifactor authentication	How to choose a password How to change your password How to use multifactor authentication How to use a password manager
Bringing your own devices (BYOD)	Why there are rules What the rules are	How to follow the rules What to do if something goes wrong
Social media	Why there are rules Examples of issues that have occurred in the past How those issues could have been avoided	What to do in particular situations on social media What to do if you need help or clarification on an issue
Vigilance	What signals you might see under certain situations (warning messages; phishing e-mails; customer complaints) What physical intrusions look like What the signals mean Which pieces of equipment have ports (USB, ethernet)	Where and how to look for warning signs What to do when you see the various signals (for instance, a number to call or way to shut down) How to protect your laptop when traveling

FIGURE 7.6 Major areas for education and training, with examples.

Agents seized the plane's equipment to investigate his claims and found evidence that boxes under his seat and under the seat in front of him on one of his flights had indeed been tampered with.[47] Had flight attendants been educated that this was the possible action of a hacker and been trained to notice passengers preoccupied with something below the seat, the hack might have been stopped earlier. See Figure 7.6 for a list of areas for education and training along with possible activities for each.

New employee onboarding processes include education in security policies including vulnerabilities and the tools and practices used to avoid problems. Types and levels of passwords or other access tools should be described to employees. "Dos" and "Don'ts" of social media should be presented in a well-organized manner so they are understood. And these policies must be reinforced at regular intervals to ensure compliance.

The goal of education is to avoid the consequences of phishing by helping individuals identify ways to recognize these scams. There are certain "classic" signs of a phishing message:

- An e-mail or bank account is closed, and the user needs to click to log-in and reactivate it.
- An e-mail inbox is too full, and the user is asked to click to increase storage.
- The user just won a contest or lottery and is asked to click to claim the prize.
- A user just inherited a fortune or will receive a commission to administer an inheritance after clicking to claim it.
- A product delivery failed, and the user needs to click to retry.
- An odd or unexpected Web address shows up when hovering a mouse pointer over a link in an e-mail.
- A familiar name in the "from" box is followed by an odd e-mail address.
- Poor grammar and spelling are in a note that purports to be from a large company.
- Goods or services are offered at an impossibly low price.
- An attachment is executable, often with an extension such of ZIP, EXE, or BAT.

[47] Even Perez, "FBI: Hacker Claimed to Have Taken Over Flight's Engine Controls," CNN.com (May 18, 2015), http://www.cnn.com/2015/05/17/us/fbi-hacker-flight-computer-systems/ (accessed June 25, 2015).

Paypal customer View online

We Need Your Help

Dear Customer,

We need your help resolving an issue with your account. To give us time to work together on this, we've temporarily limited what you can do with your account until the issue is resolved.

We understand it may be frustrating not to have full access to your PayPal account. We want to work with you to get your account back to normal as quickly as possible.

Why my PayPal™ account is limited?

We recently noticed a pattern of account activity that, in our experience, is usually high risk. For more information, see Restricted Activities identified in our User Agreement.

What can I do to resolve the problem?

It's usually pretty easy to take care of things like this. Most of the time, we just need you to verify your account. Click the link below

Please mark this email as "Not Spam" to enable link, if this email appears in your spam or junk mail .

Verify your Account

FIGURE 7.7 Actual phishing message received February 21, 2015.

Even if the signals are not present, security experts recommend not to click on any link or open any attachment in an e-mail unless it was requested and expected from a known source. Unexpected e-mail, even from a known source could breed viruses because of any one of the following: (1) The e-mail might not really be from the known source, and someone is **spoofing** (counterfeiting) the address, (2) the e-mail might be from a known source's computer but the e-mail had a virus, which will infect the recipient's computer, or (3) the e-mail might have been sent from a familiar person who doesn't know that a virus is attached. Opening the attachment or clicking the link would likely infect the recipient's computer and continue the spread of the virus to her or his contacts.

An actual phishing message received by one of the authors of this text on November 21, 2014, had the subject header of "PAYMENT OF A CONTRACT/INHERITANCE FUNDS" (all caps in the original), and the first sentence was "We have expected *receiving you in the office*, but no one has ever *head* from you" (italics added to highlight errors). Another recent phishing message (Figure 7.7) was more believable, but had some minor grammatical issues. Some messages are nearly flawless, looking identical to genuine ones from the named company, and making it critical to suspect every link or attachment in any e-mail.

Education programs describe phishing and spoofing and how to guard against clicking on dangerous links. Users must understand that opening a virus-laden Web page or file leads to "catching" the virus. Education programs might also include the different types of threats and include training on how to avoid scams, the loading of key-logging software on unsuspecting users' systems, and the breach of security measures already put in place. Training would demonstrate how to examine a link, what cues to evaluate, and what to do if a site is suspicious.

SUMMARY

- Five key IT security decisions focus on security strategy, infrastructure, policies, training, and investments.
- Perpetrators (hackers) most often work from a great distance, over long periods of time, and not by accessing data center buildings in person.
- Of breaches, 80% are enabled by stolen passwords. Those passwords are obtained from phishing messages, cross-site scripting, weak passwords, key loggers, and evil-twin connections.
- The statistics are staggering: It takes 205 days for the average breach to be detected, and the longest breach recorded took 11 years to detect. The message is that hackers have plenty of time to figure out how to steal files. Also, 97% of all firms have been hacked, and the average cost of a data breach is estimated to range from \$145–\$154 per stolen record containing sensitive information. Many breaches involve tens of millions of records.

- Perfect security of data and digital assets is not possible. However, there are best practices for reducing risks by using tools, implementing tactics (policies) and providing training (and education).
- Infrastructure technologies can limit access to authorized people and protect data storage and transmission.
- Policies need to be created to cover the need to install updates, separate unrelated networks, keep passwords secret, manage mobile devices, destroy data at the proper time, manage social media, and properly use managed security services providers.
- SETA refers to security education, training, and awareness, each of which has a specialized purpose.

KEY TERMS

antivirus/antispyware (p. 157)
biometrics (p. 156)
black hat hacker (p. 159)
challenge question (p. 158)
cross-site scripting (XSS) (p. 152)
deep Web (p. 155)
encryption (p. 158)
evil twin connection (p. 152)
firewall (p. 157)
grey hat hacker (p. 159)
key logger (p. 152)
mobile device management (p. 159)
multifactor authentication (p. 158)
phishing attack (p. 151)
security education training and awareness (SETA) (p. 150)
social media management (p. 159)
spoofing (p. 162)
token (p. 156)
weak password (p. 152)
white hat hacker (p. 159)
zero-day threat (p. 157)

DISCUSSION QUESTIONS

1. Did you change your shopping habits after hearing of the widespread breaches at Target, Home Depot, and dozens of other stores during 2013–2015? Why or why not?
2. Evaluate your password habits and describe a plan for new ones. Explain why you chose the new habits and how they reduce the risk of compromising your system's security.
3. Across all access tools listed in Figure 7.3 which have the most compelling advantages? What are the most concerning weaknesses? Provide support for your choices.
4. What is the likely future of access tools? Will they continue to be useful security measures? In your discussion, predict what you believe is the future of passwords.
5. What is an evil twin WiFi connection? What should you do to increase your security in a coffee shop the next time you want to connect?
6. Name three commonly used management security policy areas and describe an example policy for each area.
7. Create an outline for a training session to help your team avoid phishing. What would you include in that training session? What are some typical signs that an e-mail might be fraudulent?

CASE STUDY 7-1 The Aircraft Communications Addressing and Reporting System (ACARS)

On June 22, 2015, LOT, the state-owned Polish airline had to ground at least 10 national and international flights because hackers breached the network at Warsaw's Chopin airport and intercepted the flight plans that pilots need before taking off. The grounding affected about 1,400 passengers and lasted over five hours before the problem was solved. A month earlier, United Airlines was reported to have experienced the same problem in the United States, and pilots reported bogus flight plans repeatedly popping up on the system.

A consultant explained that the radio network that carried flight plans did not need authentication and was designed to trust the communications. A committee was then set up to develop a proposed standard for flight plan security.

Fortunately, the flight plan did not control the plane, and a pilot had to accept and enter the plan. A strange result, such as heading to a distant city in the wrong direction, would not be entered or accepted. Even if the bogus plan were entered and accepted by the pilot, there was no danger of collision or crash because of the fraudulent plans.

Any changes received to the plan while in flight had to be confirmed with air traffic controllers, who analyzed the new plan for safety. Alarms would also indicate a possible collision.

Discussion Questions

1. Which of the two aircraft breaches is more serious: the breach described here or the breach created by the hacker (described earlier in the chapter) who took control of a plane's throttle briefly through the entertainment system and then tweeted about it? Why?
2. Which of the access controls and storage/transmission controls would be most helpful for the ACARS problem? The entertainment system problem? Why?
3. If password control is used to solve the ACARS weakness, what might hackers do next?

Sources: Kim Zetter, "All Airlines Have The Security Hole That Grounded Polish Planes," *Wired* (June 22, 2015), http://www.wired.com/2015/06/airlines-security-hole-grounded-polish-planes/ (accessed August 25, 2015); and "Hackers Ground 1,400 Passengers at Warsaw in Attack on Airline's Computers," *The Guardian* (June 21, 2015), http://www.theguardian.com/business/2015/jun/21/hackers-1400-passengers-warsaw-lot (accessed June 26, 2015).

CASE STUDY 7-2 Sony Pictures: The Criminals Won

The Tech section in *Forbes* magazine reported that the "criminals won" in the Sony pictures breach. An anonymous threat posted on an obscure site warned that people who watch the to-be-released movie *The Interview* would be "doomed" to a "bitter fate" and recalled the tragic events of September 11. The threat said that the movie inappropriately made light of North Korean officials.

As a result of the threat, five large theater chains in the United States and Canada canceled plans to include the film on their screens. Ultimately, Sony had no choice but to cancel the theater release of the film for reasons that are both economic and legal. The former was due to a lack of revenue given the small number of remaining theaters that might go ahead and run the film. The latter was driven by what would happen if an attack was carried out. A Steve Carell project that featured North Korea was also canceled.

The Guardian reported that a group named the Guardians of Peace retaliated against Sony. They hacked into Sony's systems and stole over 100 terabytes of files, including unreleased movies, social security numbers for thousands of Sony employees, and internal e-mails, some of which show embarrassing conversations between Sony employees. The hackers began distributing the files in various locations online, making them free for the taking.

The officials of that government denied any involvement in the hack but said that it might have been a "righteous deed" of those who support the government.

North Korean officials demanded some changes to the movie, including taming down a death scene of its leader. Sony initially refused but then decided to go ahead and edit the scene. The movie eventually opened without incident on a limited basis in some cinemas on Christmas Day and then was made available via online rental.

According to the *Mirror* in the United Kingdom, neither the Department of Homeland Security nor the FBI could find evidence that the violence was a credible threat, but the FBI believed North Korea was behind the hacking. In turn, North Korea claimed that the U.S. government was responsible for creation of the movie.

Discussion Questions

1. Setting aside the political issues between North Korea and the United States, is there a reasonable way to respond to an anonymous threat found on the Internet somewhere? What elements would you require before canceling the film if you were CEO of Sony? If you were CEO of a chain of theaters?
2. What access and data protection controls would you recommend Sony use to provide better security for unreleased digital films and e-mails?
3. If you were a hacker, what approach would you have used to break into Sony's system? What do you think the most important SETA elements would be to prevent future hacker attacks against Sony or other media firms?

Sources: Dave Lewis, "Sony Pictures: The Data Breach and How the Criminals Won," *Forbes Tech* (December 17, 2014), http://www.forbes.com/sites/davelewis/2014/12/17/sony-pictures-how-the-criminal-hackers-won/ (accessed June 25, 2015); Oliver Laughland, "The Interview: Film at Center of Shocking Data Breach Scandal Opens in LA," *The Guardian* (December 12, 2014) http://www.theguardian.com/film/2014/dec/12/the-interview-sony-data-hack (accessed June 25, 2015); and Anthony Bond, "Sony Hack: The Interview WILL Be Released Despite Huge Cyber Attack Against Film Maker," *Mirror* (December 23, 2014), http://www.mirror.co.uk/news/world-news/sony-hack-interview-released-despite-4868965 (accessed June 25, 2015).

chapter

8

The Business of Information Technology

This chapter explores the business of information technology (IT) and the customers it serves. Beginning with the introduction of a maturity model to understand the balancing act between the supply and business demand for information systems (IS), the chapter describes key IT organization activities and relates them to one of three maturity levels. The chapter continues with a discussion about the work done by the IT organization and how the leadership within the IT organization ensures that activities are conducted efficiently and effectively, both domestically and globally. We then examine business processes within the IT department, including building a business case, managing the IT portfolio, and valuing and monitoring IT investments. The remainder of the chapter focuses on funding models and total cost of ownership.

After several months in the job of chief information officer (CIO) of Alcoa's Industrial Chemicals Business, Kevin Horner received a wake-up call from the president of the business:[1]

> We chose you because you were the best of the IT group, and you are doing a great job completing IT projects and managing the IT organization. But I am afraid that you don't know the business of your business. You haven't thoroughly answered my repeated questions about how much IT costs the business! Furthermore, you can't communicate with the people running the business in words they understand!

As a high-achieving math major in college with minors in computer science and business, Horner was quite savvy about his craft and did not expect to hear these remarks. When he protested that the structure of the financial information in European and Asian subsidiaries made it really difficult to find the answer, his boss's response surprised him: "If it wasn't a hard problem, I wouldn't need you here!"

Interpreting this unpleasant meeting as his being "under review" for possible ouster, Horner saw this as a wake-up call to the true meaning of being a C-level executive. He had found some answers about cost issues, but many of the financial numbers were "buried"—inextricably intertwined in general categories of financial statements in Europe and Asia. He had some early results, but managing the IT group took most of his time and effort.

Further, his early presentations were heavy with technical details and were often met with glazed eyes and yawns. Horner reported that he began to realize that this audience did not want to hear about the technology. "They certainly wanted me to handle technology issues, but they wanted me to communicate with them in words they understood . . . people, time, money and the possibilities technology created for them in their businesses. Most importantly they wanted me to help them to use IT to grow the business at either the top line (sales) or bottom line (net income)."

[1] This story and all the quotes are based on a personal interview with Kevin Horner and one of our authors, March 23, 2015.

Horner embarked on a re-energized mission to answer all of the president's concerns in a more complete way, and that mission ultimately paid handsome dividends both to him and Alcoa. If success can be measured by promotions, he went far beyond redeeming himself. After five years as CIO of Alcoa Chemical, he had many promotions until he ultimately became CIO of Alcoa Global. In 2011, he took an opportunity to become chief executive officer (CEO) of Mastech, a $100 million publicly traded IT staffing firm where he remains.

How did he achieve such resounding success? The first thing he did was to partner with the CFO to understand the financials of the business. The CFO was able to determine how to peel back the layers of accounting numbers and truly wrestle the IT costs from the general accounting categorizations where they comfortably hid. Within 60 days, the president and his management team had their answers.

But Horner did not stop at a good, solid set of internal cost numbers, a remarkable achievement in and of itself. Rather than only gaze inside the firm, he found it most helpful to use the Hackett Group, an external benchmarking consulting firm, to compare his costs against those of similar firms. This analysis was most helpful for the leadership of the business because after finding that the company was high on some key IT costs, the leaders all saw the writing on the wall for the next mission: Find ways to reduce costs but continue to provide improved services.

Two key examples of how Horner addressed those needs will help explain his early success. He accompanied salespeople on actual sales calls to see exactly how the overall supply chain process worked. Then with that information as a base, he was able to have the business provide reliable product information to customers, accelerating delivery of the products customers needed without creating excessive inventory buffers.

Horner also worked with procurement officials to renegotiate contracts for the highest-cost elements within the company's IT spending. For example, two very costly areas included telecommunications costs (including cell phones) and PCs. He found two important cost-savings opportunities: eliminate unnecessary services and negotiate many small separate contracts as a larger unit, raising the business's bargaining power. As contracts would come up for renewal, a joint team from IT and procurement spearheaded an intense process to streamline costs, focusing on the highest cost elements first. These contract negotiations led to another benefit: standardization, which enabled further savings by simplifying items such as interconnectivity between segments of the business, and PC and mobile phone support.

The lessons learned in Horner's initial CIO role in the chemicals business transferred naturally into his next role as CIO of Alcoa Europe, which was a collection of historical Alcoa businesses and locations along with several newly acquired companies representing what Horner called "kind of a $3B 'start-up' company." He knew immediately that he had to get a clear picture of the IT business in Europe from several perspectives—technology, applications, people, vendors, cost, and "quick wins," which solved problems for his business leadership colleagues. This time Horner didn't need the questions from the business president to guide him: He had to quickly assess talent in his team, determine total IT cost in the business, assist the management team to move to Europe from a structure focusing on legal entity driven reporting and reporting finances in a new structure that aligned with corporate Alcoa and unified pan-European business units. As a result of his business-focused thrusts, within 24 months, the entire unified structure was created and implemented; legal entity fiscal reporting was maintained; a shared service function for finance, accounting, HR, and procurement plus the technology to operate it was implemented; Y2K remediation was completed; and European IT costs were reduced by 25%.

What does this experience demonstrate? It shows that there are common denominators that every business leader understands: people, time, and money. When a business leader wants to invest capital to produce more product or a new product, that investment is scrutinized for cost and benefit. Horner says that a CIO should make sure IT is not the exception to that rule. "Don't talk about ERP or mobile apps, talk about what is going to happen to the business . . . [and] to people, time, and money when you have the ERP or the mobile app," he says. "Getting the cost side of the IT organization in order represents table stakes for the CIO," implying that you would wear out your welcome by focusing inward. Rather than focusing only on managing the technologies and IT people and describing new investments and initiatives by using "techy" jargon, a CIO should take a business viewpoint. If you follow that advice, you will not only be welcome at the table but also will thrive. This demonstrates the Business of Information Technology, the title of this chapter.

In this chapter, issues related to the business side of IT are explored. We begin by looking at key activities managers can expect of their IT organization and, probably just as importantly, what the IT organization does not provide. The chapter continues with a discussion of key business processes within the IT organization, such as building a business case, managing an IT portfolio, and valuing and monitoring IT investments. This is followed by a discussion of ways of funding the IT department and an exploration of several ways to calculate the cost of IT investments, including total cost of ownership and activity-based costing. These topics are critical for the IT manager to understand, but a general manager must also understand how the business of IT works to successfully propose, plan, manage, and use information systems.

Organizing to Respond to Business: A Maturity Model

The Alcoa situation just discussed reveals that IT leaders must make sure they have the right resources and organization to respond to business needs. It is not enough to focus inward on managing personnel, software, and equipment, which can seem like a full-time responsibility. IT managers must go beyond internal matters and partner with their business colleagues. Responding to business demands adds substantially to IT managers' responsibilities because it requires them not only to manage the complexity within the IT function, but also to go well beyond what seem to be the boundaries of IT and understand intricacies of their business partners.

Merlyn's **business-IT maturity model** in Figure 8.1 provides characteristics of how engaged the IT function can be with the rest of the organization at three unique levels of maturity. At Level 1, representing an immature IT organization, IT managers maintain an inward focus. They merely react to specific needs that are brought to their attention, often in an environment that emphasizes cost reduction. As the IT organization matures to Level 2, the focus shifts to business processes, and IT personnel search for solutions to business problems. Level 3 represents IT managers as business partners who search for ideas that provide value to the organization and value relationships both inside and outside not only the IT organization but also the firm. They seek ideas that provide not only new revenue but also help identify new opportunities that redefine the business.

This model illustrates that for IT to provide the most value to the business, IT managers and business managers must recognize their mutual dependency and ensure that business capability has the technology support needed for success. This model does not comment on the type of technology used but on the way the business organization approaches its use of IT. For example, in Level 3, business leaders see IT's role as a business partner that they can include in high-level meetings that explore new lines of business. Compare this approach with lower levels of maturity. At Level 2, the focus would instead be on creating an effective business process, which has a much more limited scope and impact. At Level 1, where the business demand for IT is primarily all about cost

Maturity Level	Nature of the Level	Engagement Characteristics
Level 3	IT as business partner	• Proactive • Outside-in • Relationship centric • Focused on business growth • Framed on a context of business value
Level 2	IT as solutions provider	• Active • Process centric • Focused on solutions • Framed in a context of projects
Level 1	IT as order taker	• Reactive • Inside-out • Technology centric • Framed in a context of cost

FIGURE 8.1 Business-IT maturity model.
Source: Adapted from Vaughan Merlyn, http://vaughanmerlyn.com/2014/04/01/the-disciplines-of-business-it-engagement/ (accessed April 22, 2015).

savings and foundation systems, the IT function might be seen more as a necessary evil that needs to be pushed into a corner rather than expanded to flex organizational muscles. When the maturity of the IT organization rises to Level 3, it is able not only to keep up with business demands but also to enhance the business in ways that were not envisioned before.

This chapter describes the complex, multifaceted tasks for which an IT organization takes responsibility and how IT is organized. The chapter describes both the internal and external issues that must be handled by IT leaders and the personnel responsible for them. The description is presented in a context of how the IT organization must make it a priority to partner with business leaders. Because running the business of IT requires funding, we also explore how to fund IT projects to support business and how to cover the operational costs.

Understanding the IT Organization

Consider the analogy of a ship to help explain the purpose of an IT organization and how it functions. A ship transports people and cargo to a particular destination in much the same way that an IT organization directs itself toward the strategic goals set by the larger enterprise. All ships navigate waters, but different ships have different structures, giving them unique capabilities such as transporting people versus cargo. Even among similar categories, ships have different features, such as those configured to transport a cargo of finished products versus one configured to transport a cargo of oil. All IT organizations provide services to their businesses, but based on the skills and capabilities of their people, the organizational focus of their management, and their state of maturity, they, too, differ in what they can do and how they work with the businesses. Sometimes the IT organization must navigate perilous waters or storms to reach port. For both the IT organization and the ship, the key is to perform more capably than any competitors. It means doing the right things at the right time and in the right way to propel the enterprise through the rough waters of business.

Different firms need to do different things when it comes to IT. Because firms have different goals, they need to act in different ways and as a result, there are differences in the IT activities that are provided. But even if two firms have similar goals, the firms' size, organization structure, and level of maturity might affect what the IT organization in each firm is expected to do.

What a Manager Can Expect from the IT Organization

We look at the IT organization from the perspective of the customer of the IT organization, the general manager, or "user," of the systems. What can a manager expect from the IT organization? Just as IT leaders benefit from understanding their business partners, a general manager benefits from understanding what the IT organization does.

Managers must learn what to expect from the IT organization so they can plan and implement business strategy accordingly. Although the nature of the activities may vary in each IT organization depending upon its overall goal, a manager typically can expect some level of support in 14 core activities: (1) developing and maintaining information systems, (2) managing supplier relationships, (3) managing data, information, and knowledge, (4) managing Internet and network services, (5) managing human resources, (6) operating the data center, (7) providing general support, (8) planning for business discontinuities, (9) innovating current processes, (10) establishing architecture platforms and standards, (11) promoting enterprise security, (12) anticipating new technologies, (13) participating in setting and implementing strategic goals, and (14) integrating social IT.[2] These activities are briefly described in Figure 8.2.

Although the activities could be found at any maturity level, we indicate in Figure 8.2 the level where they are especially important. Recall that Level 1 focuses on cost savings and efficiency of business operations; Level 2 takes a process view, provides services of an integrated nature across the organization, and supports decision making to maximize business effectiveness; and Level 3 focuses on innovation and support of business strategy. This progression implies that the scope of activities in the IT organization expands with increased IT maturity.

[2] Eight activities are described by John F. Rockart, Michael J. Earl, and Jeanne W. Ross, "Eight Imperatives for the New IT Organization," *Sloan Management Review* (Fall 1996), 52–53. Six activities have been added to their eight imperatives.

Activity	Description	Maturity Level
Developing and maintaining systems	• Together with business users, analyze needs, design, write, and test the software • Identify, acquire, and install outside software packages to fill business needs • Correct system errors or enhance the system to respond to changing business and legal environments	1
Managing supplier relationships	• Maximize the benefit of supplier relationships to the enterprise and pre-empt problems that might occur	1
Managing data, information, and knowledge	• Collect and store data created and captured by the enterprise (Level 1) • Manage enterprise information and knowledge (Level 2)	1, 2
Managing Internet and network systems	• Develop and maintain Internet access and capabilities • Manage private networks, telephone systems, and wireless technologies • Design, build, and maintain the network architecture and infrastructure	1, 2 (depending on nature of network)
Managing human resources	• Hire, train, and maintain good staff performers; fire poor performers • Work with enterprise HR personnel to learn up-to-date regulations and practices	1
Operating the data center	• Operate and maintain large mainframe computers, rows of servers, or other hardware on which the company's systems are built • Provide connections between the firm's systems and cloud services	1
Providing general support	• Manage diverse help desk activities • Collect and record support information • Assign appropriate personnel to support cases • Follow up with vendors as needed • Follow up with business contacts with updates or solutions	1
Planning for business discontinuities	• Develop and implement business continuity plan • Make preparations to counter physical or electronic attacks, hacking attempts, weather disasters, and other events that could cripple the enterprise	1
Innovating current processes	• Work with managers to innovate processes that can benefit from technological solutions • Explore modifications that can reduce costs, improve service, or connect with customers • Design systems that facilitate new ways of doing business	2
Establishing architecture platforms and standards	• Develop, maintain, and communicate standards • Maintain consistency and integrity of the firm's data	2
Promoting enterprise security	• Maintain the integrity of the enterprise infrastructure • Develop and implement enterprise information security policies, strategy, and controls • Identify, prioritize, and guard against threats to the enterprise's information assets • Work with business units to enhance security of operational practices • Train employees to raise awareness, importance, and understanding of security risks • Participate in discussions about security investments	2
Anticipating new technologies	• Scout new technology trends and help the business integrate them into planning and operations • Assess the costs and benefits of new technologies for the enterprise • With business partners, prioritize the most promising opportunities on strategic and operational grounds, and schedule their implementation • Limit investments in technologies that are incompatible with current or planned systems or that quickly become obsolete	3

FIGURE 8.2 IT organization activities and related level of maturity.

Activity	Description	Maturity Level
Participating in setting and implementing strategic goals	• Enable business managers to achieve strategic goals by acting as educators or consultants • Advise managers on best practices within IT • Work with managers to develop IT-enhanced solutions to business problems • Serve as partners in moving the enterprise forward	3
Integrating the use of social IT	• Leverage the use of social IT to transform the business • Adapt social IT from personal to business use • Encourage engagement, collaboration, and innovation in customer-, supplier-, and employee-directed applications • Manage the data resulting from social IT to provide business insights	3

FIGURE 8.2 (Continued)

The IT organization can be expected to be responsible for most, if not all, of the activities listed in Figure 8.2. However, instead of actually performing the activities, the IT organization increasingly identifies and then works with vendors who provide them. More traditional activities such as data center operations, network management, and system development and maintenance (including application design, development, and maintenance) have been outsourced to vendors for decades. More recently, enterprises are outsourcing providers to perform more newly acquired IT activities such as process management (alternatively called *business process outsourcing*). In our increasingly flat world, many companies are successfully drawing from labor supplies in other parts of the world to meet the business demand that they can't handle internally in their own IT organization. Managing the sourcing relationships and global labor supply is so important that a whole chapter (i.e., Chapter 10) is devoted to discussing these sourcing issues in greater depth.

What the IT Organization Does Not Do

This chapter presents core activities for which the IT organization is typically responsible. It is enlightening to examine tasks that should *not* be performed by the organization. Clear examples include core business functions, such as selling, manufacturing, and accounting, and few functional managers would attempt to delegate these tasks to IT professionals. However, some functional managers inadvertently delegate key operational decisions to the IT organization. For example, when general managers ask the IT professional to build an information system for their organization and do not become active partners in the design of that system, they are in effect turning over control of their business operations. Likewise, asking an IT professional to implement a software package or app without partnering with that professional to ensure that the package meets both current and future needs is ceding control.

Partnerships between the general managers and IT professionals are also important for a number of other decisions. For instance, IT professionals should not have the sole responsibility for deciding which business projects receive IT dollars. Giving carte blanche to the IT professional would mean that the IT organization decides what is important to the business units. If IT professionals try to respond to every request from their business counterparts, they would likely face a backlog of delayed initiatives and become overwhelmed. Business partners participate in prioritizing IT projects to ensure that resources are applied appropriately. Similarly, IT professionals should not solely decide the acceptable level of IT services or security. Because senior managers run the business, they are the ones who must decide on the level of service and security that should be delivered by the IT organization.[3] These are examples of decisions that should be made jointly with business counterparts. Perfection comes at a price that many business leaders may be unwilling to pay. Not every system needs to have gold-plated functionality, and not every system needs to be fortified from every conceivable danger.

[3] J. W. Ross and P. Weill, "Six IT Decisions Your IT People Shouldn't Make," *Harvard Business Review* 80, no. 11 (November 2002), 84–95. (2002), 1–8.

As discussed in Chapter 2, the senior management team, including the CIO, sets business strategy. However, in many organizations, the general manager delegates critical technology decisions to the IT professional alone, and this can lead to technology decisions that might hinder business opportunities. The strategy formulation process is a joint process including business and IT professionals. The role for the IT professional in the discussion of strategy includes such things as suggesting technologies and applications that enable it, identifying limits to the technologies and applications under consideration, reporting on best practices and new technologies that might enhance opportunities of the firm, and consulting all those involved with setting the strategic direction to make sure they properly consider the role and impact of IT on the decisions they make. The IT organization does not set business strategy. It does, however, participate in the discussions and partner with the business to ensure that IT can provide the infrastructure, applications, and support necessary for the successful implementation of the business strategy. The IT organization can also provide ideas of new business capabilities afforded by new technologies. In that sense, IT leaders must be part of key business strategy discussions.

Chief Information Officer

If an IT organization is like a ship, the chief information officer is like the captain. The **chief information officer (CIO)** is the most senior executive in the enterprise responsible for technology vision and leadership for designing, developing, implementing, and managing IT initiatives for the enterprise to operate effectively in a constantly changing and intensely competitive marketplace. The CIO is an executive who manages IT resources to implement enterprise strategy and who works with the executive team in strategy formulation processes.

CIOs are a unique breed. They have a strong understanding of the business and of the technology. In many organizations, they take on roles that span both of these areas. One recently coined term is **business technology strategist,** the strategic business leader who uses technology as the core tool in creating competitive advantage and aligning business and IT strategies.[4] The CIO, as the most senior IT professional in the corporate hierarchy, must champion the IT organization by promoting IT as a strategic tool for growth and innovation. The title *CIO* signals to both the organization and to outside observers that this executive is a strategic IT thinker and is responsible for linking IS strategy with the business strategy. In other words, CIOs must know the business vision and understand how the IT function contributes to making this vision happen. This means that CIOs must work effectively not only in the technical arena but also in the overall business management arena. They need the technical ability to plan, conceive, build, and implement multiple IT projects on time and within budget. However, their technical skills must be balanced against business skills such as the ability to realize the benefits and manage the costs and risks associated with IT, to articulate and advocate for a management vision of IT, and to mesh well with the existing management structure.

Just as the chief financial officer (CFO) is somewhat involved in operational management of the financial activities of the organization, the CIO is involved with operational issues related to IT. More often than not, CIOs are asked to perform strategic tasks at some part of their day and operational tasks at other times. Some of their operational activities include identifying and managing the introduction of new technologies into the firm, negotiating partnership relationships with key suppliers, setting purchasing and supplier policies, and managing the overall IT budget. Actual day-to-day management of the data center, IT infrastructure, application development projects, vendor portfolio, and other operational issues are typically not handled directly by the CIO but by one of the managers in the IT organization. Ultimately, whether they directly function as operational managers or as leaders with oversight of other operational managers, the CIO must assume responsibility for all the activities described in Figure 8.2 that the IT organization is charged to perform.

Where the CIO fits within an enterprise is often a source of controversy. In the early days of the CIO position, when it was predominantly responsible for controlling costs (Level 1), the position reported to the CFO. Because the CIO was rarely involved in enterprise governance or in discussions of business strategy, this reporting structure worked. However, as IT became a source for competitive advantage in the marketplace, reporting to the CFO proved too limiting. Conflicts arose because the CFO misunderstood the vision for IT or saw only the costs of technology. They also arose because management still saw the CIO's primary responsibility as providing services

[4] M. Carter, V. Grover, and J. B. Thatcher, "The Emerging CIO Role of Business Technology Strategist," *MIS Quarterly Executive* 10, no. 1 (2011), 19–29.

whose costs had to be controlled. More recently, CIOs often report directly to the CEO, president, or other executive manager. This elevated reporting relationship not only signals that the role of IT is critical to the enterprise and indicates Level 3 maturity but also makes it easier to implement strategic IT initiatives.

Some organizations choose not to have a CIO. These organizations do not believe that a CIO is necessary, in part because technology is highly integrated into virtually every aspect of the business and no single officer need provide oversight. These firms typically hire an individual to be responsible for running the computer systems and possibly to manage many of the activities described later in this chapter. But they signal that this person is not a strategist by giving him or her the title of data processing manager, director of information systems, or some other name that clearly differentiates this person from other top officers in the company. Using the words *chief* and *officer* usually implies a strategic focus, and some organizations that do not see the value of having an IT person on their executive team choose not to use these words.

Although the CIO's role is to guide the enterprise toward the future, this responsibility is frequently too great to accomplish alone. Many organizations recognize that certain strategic areas of the IT organization require more focused guidance. This recognition led to the creation of new positions, such as the chief knowledge officer (CKO), chief technology officer (CTO), chief telecommunications officer (also CTO), chief network officer (CNO), chief information security officer (CISO), chief privacy officer (CPO), chief resource officer (CRO), chief mobility officer (CMO), and chief social media officer (CSMO). See Figure 8.3 for a list of the different responsibilities for each position that, with the occasional exception of the CTO, typically is subordinate to the CIO. Together, these officers form a management team that leads the IT organization.

Many large corporations take the concept of CIO one step further and identify the CIO of a business unit. This is someone who has responsibilities similar to those of a corporate CIO, but the scope is the business unit and there is not as much concern about defining corporate standards and policies to ensure consistency across the business units. The business unit CIO is responsible for aligning the IT investment portfolio with the business unit's strategy. Typically, the business unit CIO has dual reporting responsibility to both the corporate CIO and the president of the business unit. At IBM, the CIO is a manager from a business unit who serves a two- to three-year term.[5]

Title	Responsibility
Chief technology officer (CTO)	Track emerging technologies; advise on technology adoption; design and manage IT architecture
Chief knowledge officer (CKO)	Create knowledge management infrastructure; build a knowledge culture; make corporate knowledge payoff
Chief data officer (CDO)	Create and maintain the definition, storage, and retirement of data in the firm; streamline access to the data; reduce data redundancy
Chief analytics officer (CAO)	Take advantage of data analysis opportunities, often used for understanding customers, transactions, markets, or trends
Chief telecommunications officer (CTO)	Manage phones, networks, and other communications technology across the entire enterprise
Chief network officer (CNO)	Build and maintain internal and external networks
Chief resource officer (CRO)	Manage outsourcing relationships
Chief information security officer (CISO)	Ensure that information management practices are consistent with security requirements
Chief privacy officer (CPO)	Establish and enforce processes and practices to meet privacy concerns of customers, employees, and vendors
Chief mobility officer (CMO)	Oversee and ensure the viable use of mobile platforms and apps
Chief social media officer (CSMO)	Maintain a social IT perspective that results in effectively implementing social media

FIGURE 8.3 The CIO's lieutenants.

[5] Ann Majchrzak, Luba Cherbakov, and Blake Ives, "Harnessing the Power of the Crowds with Corporate Social Networking Tools: How IBM Does It," *MIS Quarterly Executive* 8, no. 2 (2009), 103–8.

Building a Business Case

In order to meet demand, the IT organization is often charged with providing solutions. Businesses managers often turn to IT for good solutions, but IT projects end up competing with those of other managers in tight economic times when there clearly aren't enough budget resources to cover them all. After all, there is often no shortage of other business investments such as new production machinery for higher product quality and lower costs or funding for product research and development on product innovations. Thus, managers need to show that the solution they want would be not only a good IT investment but also a good business investment.

To gain support and a "go-ahead" decision, every manager must often create a business case. Similar to a legal case, a **business case** is a structured document that lays out all the relevant information needed to make a go/no-go decision. The business case for an IT project is also a way to establish priorities for investing in different projects, an opportunity to identify how IT and the business can deliver new benefits, gain commitment from business managers, and create a basis for monitoring the investment.[6]

The components of a business case vary from corporation to corporation, depending on the priorities and decision-making environment. However, there are several primary elements of any business case (see Figure 8.4). Critical to the business case is the identification of both costs and benefits, both in financial and nonfinancial terms.

In building, it is particularly important for the business case to describe the benefits to be gained with the acceptance of the project the case is selling. Ward, Daniel, and Peppard[7] suggested a framework for identifying and describing both financial and nonfinancial benefits (Figure 8.5). The first step in this framework is to identify each benefit as innovation (allowing the organization to do new things), improvement (allowing the organization to do

Section or Component	Description
Executive summary	One- or two-page description of the overall business case document summarizing key points
Overview and introduction	Brief business background, the current business situation, a clear statement of the business problem or opportunity, and a recommended solution at a high level
Assumptions and rationale	Issues driving the proposal (e.g., operational, human resources, environmental, competitive, industry or market trends, or financial)
Project summary	High-level and detailed descriptions of the project: scope, objectives, contacts, resource plan, key metrics, implementation plan, and key success factors
Financial discussion and analysis	Overall summary followed by projected costs/revenues/benefits, financial metrics, financial model, cash flow statement, underlying assumptions, and total cost of ownership (TCO) analysis
Benefits and business impacts	Summary of business impacts followed by details on nonfinancial matters such as new business, transformation, innovations, competitive responses, organizational, supply chain, and human resource impacts
Schedule and milestones	Entire schedule for the project with milestones and expected metrics at each stage; if appropriate, can include a marketing plan and schedule
Risk and contingency analysis	Analysis of risks and ways to manage those risks, sensitivity analysis of scenarios, and interdependencies and the impact they will have on potential outcomes
Conclusion and recommendation	Primary recommendation and conclusions
Appendices	Backup materials not directly provided in the body of the document, such as detailed financial investment analysis, marketing materials, and competitors' literature.

FIGURE 8.4 Components of a business case.

[6] John Ward, Elizabeth Daniel, and Joe Peppard, "Building Better Business Cases for IT Investments," *MIS Quarterly Executive* 7, no. 1 (March 2008), 1–15.

[7] Ibid.

		Type of Business Change		
		Innovation (do new things)	Improvement (do things better)	Cessation (stop doing things)
High ↑	Financial benefits	Financial value can be calculated by applying a cost/price or other valid financial formula to a quantifiable benefit.		
	Quantifiable benefits	There is sufficient evidence to forecast how much improvement/benefit should result from the changes.		
Degree of Explicitness	Measurable benefits	Although this aspect of performance is currently measured or an approximate measure could be implemented, it is not possible to estimate how much performance will improve when changes are implemented.		
↓ Low	Observable benefits	By using agreed criteria, specific individuals or groups will use their experience or judgment to decide the extent the benefit will be realized.		

FIGURE 8.5 Classification framework for benefits in a business case.
Source: Adapted from John Ward, Elizabeth Daniel, and Joe Peppard, "Building Better Business Cases for IT Investments," *MIS Quarterly Executive* 7, no. 1 (March 2008), 1–15.

things better), or cessation (stopping things). Then the benefits can be classified by degree of explicitness or the ability to assign a value to the benefit. As shown in Figure 8.6, benefits fall into one of these categories:

- *Financial:* There is a way to express the benefit in financial terms. These are the metrics that are most easily used to judge the go/no-go decision because financial terms are universal across all business decisions. An example is improvement in profit.
- *Quantifiable:* There is a way to measure the size or magnitude of the benefit, but financial benefits are not directly determinable. For example, a firm might expect a 20% increase in customer retention, but to determine the financial benefit of resulting increased sales, it would require an analysis of what items they would buy. Most business cases revolve around quantifiable benefits, so it is important to ensure the collection of a comprehensive list of quantifiable benefits and any associated costs.
- *Measurable:* There is a way to measure the benefit, but it is not necessarily connectable to any organizational outcome. Management must ensure alignment with the business strategy. For example, many organizations collect satisfaction or web engagement data and are able to detect improvements.
- *Observable:* They can be detected only by opinion or judgment. These are the subjective, intangible, soft, or qualitative benefits. Things seem better but no measures are available. For example, customers might be expected to be happier or less argumentative.

Benefits	**Innovation: Chat Function and Customer Support Forum**	**Improvement: Remodeled Facebook Page**	**Cessation: Reduce Phone Support by 90%**
Financial	Fewer returns; higher sales	Sales from redemption of special coupons by new customers	Overall costs reduced
Quantifiable	Shorter customer wait time	Number of new customers	Wait time for phone lines
Measurable	Higher customer satisfaction scores	Number of "shares" by new customers	Overall customer service satisfaction scores
Observable	Fewer complaints	Supportive comments on the page	Decrease in verbal complaints by phone-in customers

FIGURE 8.6 Benefit examples for a business case.

Consider the example of a small manufacturing firm that hopes to differentiate itself with excellent customer service but that has customers who are confused from time to time, an expanding customer support department, long customer wait time, and growing dissatisfaction. The firm identified a potential three-pronged social network project that included a remodeled Facebook page, a new chat function, and a new customer support forum. The project would be funded from reducing the phone support department by 90%. See Figure 8.6 for examples from a potential benefit analysis for the social network project.

Of course, the benefit analysis is only part of the story because costs and risks need to be considered as well. Projected costs would include purchase of hardware and software, consulting help, internal costs, training costs, and other new expenditures. There would also be technical risks, financial risks, and organizational risks. Technical risks could include complexity in usage of the new chat and customer support forum and incomplete statistics from the Facebook page. Examples of financial risks would be a lack of accuracy in estimating costs, overestimates of usage, and overly optimistic call center reduction. Organizational risks would include inadequate monitoring of the new functionality or inability to recruit knowledgeable monitors for the chat function, support forum, and Facebook page.

IT Portfolio Management

Managing the set of systems and programs in an IT organization is similar to managing resources in a financial organization. There are different types of IT investments or projects, and together they form the business's IT portfolio. **IT portfolio management** refers to "evaluating new and existing applications collectively on an ongoing basis to determine which applications provide value to the business in order to support decisions to replace, retire, or further invest in applications across the enterprise."[8] This process requires thinking about IT systems as a cohesive set of core assets, not as a discontinuous stream of one-off (one-time only), targeted investments as often has been the case in the past. IT portfolio management involves continually deciding on the right mix of investments from funding, management, and staffing perspectives. The overall goal of IT portfolio management is for the company to fund and invest in the most valuable initiatives that, taken together as a whole, generate maximum benefits for it.

Professor Peter Weill and colleagues at MIT's Center for Information Systems Research (CISR) describe four asset classes of IT investments that typically make up the company's IT portfolio:[9]

- *Transactional systems:* Streamline or cut costs on the way business is done (equivalent to Level 1 in the Business Maturity Model)
- *Infrastructure systems:* Provide the base foundation of shared IT services used for multiple applications such as servers, networks, tablets, or smartphones (equivalent to Level 2 in the Business Maturity Model)
- *Informational systems:* Provide information used to control, manage, communicate, analyze, or collaborate (equivalent to Level 2 in the Business Maturity Model)
- *Strategic systems:* Gain competitive advantage in the marketplace (equivalent to Level 3 in the Business Maturity Model)

In analyzing the composition of any single company's IT portfolio, one can find a profile of the relative investment made in each IT asset class. Weill's study found that the average firm allocates 46% of its total IT investment each year to infrastructure and only 25% of its total IT investment in transactional systems. Weill also found that firms in diverse industries allocate their IT resources differently.[10]

[8] James D. McKeen and Heather A. Smith, "Developments in Practice XXXIV: Application Portfolio Management," *Communications of the Association for Information Systems* 26, no. 9 (2010), http://aisel.aisnet.org/cais/vol26/iss1/9 (accessed September 4, 2015).

[9] Peter Weill and Marianne Broadbent, *Leveraging the New Infrastructure: How Market Leaders Capitalize on Information Technology* (Cambridge, MA: Harvard Business School Press, June 1998). © MIT Sloan Center for Information Systems Research 2005–12. Used with permission. For more information, see http://cisr.mit.edu.

[10] Ibid.

Weill's work also suggests that a different balance between IT investments is needed for a cost-focused strategy compared to an agility-focused strategy. A company with a cost-focused strategy would seek an IT portfolio that helps lower costs as the primary business objective. In that case, Weill's work suggests that on average, 27% of the IT investments are made in transactional investments, suggesting higher use of applications that automate processes and typically lower operational costs.[11] On the other hand, a company with an agility focus would be more likely to invest a higher percent of its IT portfolio in infrastructure (e.g., 51% on average) and less in transactional systems (e.g., 24% on average). The infrastructure investment would create a platform that would likely be used to more quickly and nimbly create solutions needed by the business whereas the transactional systems might lock in the current processes and take more effort and time to change.

From the portfolio management perspective, potential new systems are evaluated on their own merits and compared against other systems in the prospective portfolio. Often applications can't stand alone and require integration with other applications, some of which would need to be acquired or developed. A complete picture is required for a fair comparison of portfolio alternatives. Portfolio management helps prioritize IT investments across multiple decision criteria, including value to the business, urgency, and financial return. Just like an individual or company's investment portfolio is aligned with its objectives, the IT portfolio must be aligned with the business strategy.

Valuing IT Investments

New IT investments are often justified by the business managers proposing them in terms of monetary costs and benefits. The monetary costs and benefits are important but are not the only considerations in making IT investments. Soft benefits, such as the ability to make future decisions, are often part of the business case for IT investments, making the measurement of the investment's payback (length of time to recoup the cost) difficult.

Several unique factors of the IT organization make it very challenging to determine the value from IT investments. First, the systems are complex, and calculating the costs is an art, not a science. Second, because many IT investments are for infrastructure, calculating a **payback period** may be more complex than other types of capital investments. Third, many times the payback cannot be calculated because the investment is a necessity rather than a choice without any tangible payback. For example, upgrading to a newer version of software may be required because the older version simply is no longer supported. Many managers do not want to have to upgrade just because the vendor insists that an upgrade is necessary. Instead, managers may resist IT spending on the grounds that the investment adds no incremental value. These factors and more fuel a long-running debate about the value of IT investments. IT managers need to learn to express benefits in a businesslike manner such as **return on investment (ROI)** or increased customer satisfaction.

IT managers, like the business managers who propose IT projects, are expected to understand and even try to calculate the true return on these projects. Measuring this return is difficult, however. To illustrate, consider the relative ease with which a manager might analyze whether the enterprise should build a new plant. The first step would be to estimate the costs of construction. The plant capacity dictates project production levels. Demand varies, and construction costs frequently overrun, but the manager can find sufficient information to make a decision about whether to build. Most of the time, the benefits of investing in IT are less tangible than those of building a plant because the IT cannot be felt and touched like a physical building can be. Such benefits might include tighter systems integration, faster response time, more accurate data, and more leverage to adopt future technologies, among others. How can a manager quantify these intangibles? He or she should also consider many indirect, or downstream, benefits and costs, such as changes in how people behave, where staff report, and how tasks are assigned. In fact, it may be impossible to pinpoint who will benefit from an IT investment when making the decision.[12]

Despite the difficulty, the task of evaluating IT investments is necessary. Knowing which approaches to use and when to use them are important first steps. A number of financial valuation approaches are summarized in Figure 8.7. Managers should choose based on the attributes of the project. For example, ROI or payback analysis

---

[11] Ibid.

[12] John C. Ford, "Evaluating Investment in IT," *Australian Accountant* (December 1994), 3.

Valuation Method	Description
Return on investment (ROI)	Excess of return over the investment is calculated as ROI = (Revenue – Investment)/ Investment.
Net present value (NPV)	Accounting for the time value of money, the NPV discounts cash flows from future periods as being worth less than immediate cash flows. Discounting is performed by using a present value factor, which is 1/(1 + Discount rate)^{years}
Economic value added (EVA)	The amount of benefit of an investment that exceeds the costs of the capital used for investments. It is sometimes implemented **firmwide** as net operating profit after taxes (Capital × Cost of capital).
Payback period	This is a simple and popular method that, assuming there are regular or irregular financial benefits of an investment, computes how long a firm estimates it must wait until it breaks even on the investment (all costs are finally recouped).
Internal rate of return (IRR)	Like an interest rate, IRR represents the rate that is earned on an investment. The rate is compared to a target that is determined by corporate policy.
Weighted scoring methods	Costs and revenues are weighted based on their strategic importance, level of accuracy or confidence, and comparable investment opportunities.

FIGURE 8.7 Financial valuation methods.

can be used when detailed analysis is not required, as when a project is short lived and its costs and benefits are clear. When the project lasts long enough that the time value of money becomes a factor, **net present value (NPV)** and **economic value added (EVA)** are better approaches. EVA is particularly appropriate for capital-intensive projects.

Both IT and business managers may encounter a number of pitfalls when analyzing return on investment. First, some situations are heavy in soft benefits and light in projected financial benefits. That is, increased customer satisfaction might not result in actual financial inflows.

Second, it is difficult to reconcile projects of diverse size, benefits, and timing in light of a fixed budget available for new projects. The budget might contain enough funding for only one large project with moderate but quick return, and then there is no room for other smaller projects with higher but slower return.

Third, circumstances may alter the way managers make estimates. For instance, in a software implementation, if experience shows that it usually takes 20% longer than budgeted to build a system, managers might begin to routinely add 20% to future estimates when preparing schedules and budgets to account for the uncertainty.

Fourth, managers can fall into "analysis paralysis." Reaching a precise valuation may take longer than is reasonable to make an investment decision. Because a single right valuation may not exist, "close enough" usually suffices. Experience and an eye to the risks of an incorrect valuation help decide when to stop analyzing.

Finally, even when the numbers say a project is not worthwhile, the investment may be necessary to remain competitive. For example, UPS faced little choice but to invest heavily in IT. At the time, FedEx had made IT a competitive advantage and was winning the overnight delivery war. More recently, companies are finding that they must re-invest in their applications in order to make them work on mobile devices.

Monitoring IT Investments

An old adage says: "If you can't measure it, you can't manage it." Management's role is to ensure that the money spent on IT results in value for the organization. Therefore, a common, accepted set of metrics must be created, and those metrics must be monitored and communicated to senior management and customers of the IT department. These metrics are often financial in nature (i.e., ROI, NPV). But financial measurement is only one category of measures used to manage IT investments. Other IT metrics include logs of errors encountered by users, end-user surveys, user turnaround time, logs of computer and communication up-/downtime, system response time, and percentage of projects completed on time and/or within budget. An example of a business-focused method is the extent to which the technology innovation improves the number of contacts with external customers, increases sales revenue, and generates new business leads.

The Balanced Scorecard

Deciding on appropriate measures is half of the equation for effective IT organizations. The other half of the equation is ensuring that those measures are accurately communicated to the business. Two methods for communicating these metrics are scorecards and dashboards.

Financial measures may be the language of stockholders, but managers understand that such measures can be misleading if used as the sole means of making management decisions. One methodology used to solve this problem, created by Robert Kaplan and David Norton and first described in the *Harvard Business Review* in 1992, is the **balanced scorecard**, which focuses attention on the organization's value drivers (which include, but are not limited to, financial performance).[13] Companies use this scorecard to assess the full impact of their corporate strategies on their customers and work force as well as their financial performance.

The balanced scorecard methodology allows managers to look at the business from four perspectives: customer, internal business, innovation/learning, and financial. For each perspective, the goals and measures are designed to answer these basic questions:

- How do customers see us? (customer perspective)
- At what must we excel? (internal business perspective)
- Can we continue to improve and create value? (innovation and learning perspective)
- How do we look to shareholders? (financial perspective)

Figure 8.8 graphically shows the relationship of these perspectives.

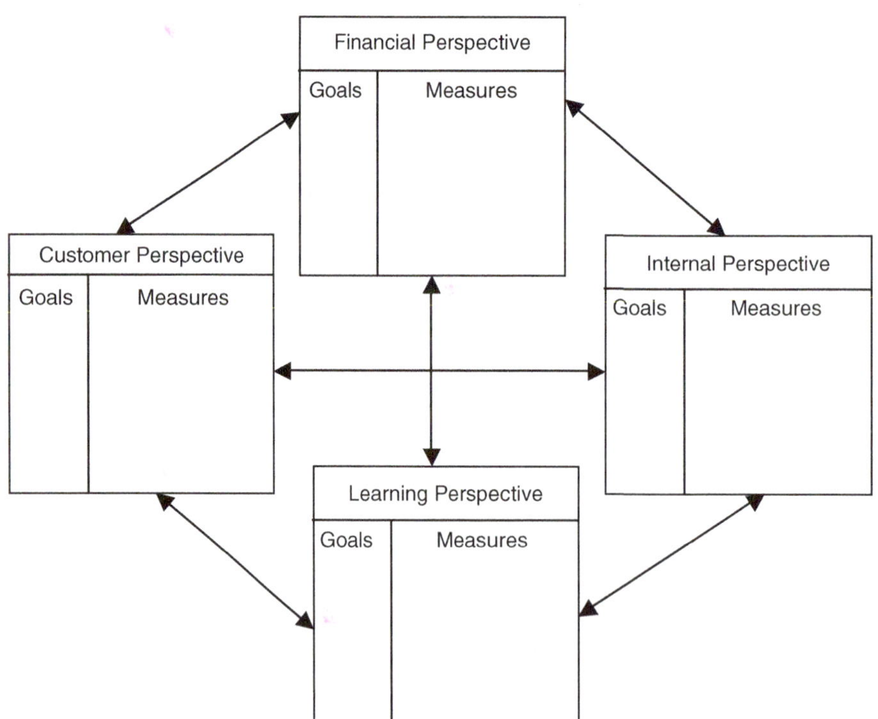

FIGURE 8.8 The balanced scorecard perspectives.
Source: Based on R. Kaplan and D. Norton, "The Balanced Scorecard—Measures That Drive Performance," *Harvard Business Review* (January–February 1992), 72.

[13] For more detail, see R. Kaplan and D. Norton, "The Balanced Scorecard—Measures That Drive Performance," *Harvard Business Review* 70, no. 1, (January–February 1992), 71–79.

Since the introduction of the balanced scorecard, many people have modified it or adapted it to apply to their particular organization. Managers of information technology find the concept of a scorecard useful in managing and communicating the value of the IT department.

Applying the categories of the balanced scorecard to IT might mean interpreting them more broadly than originally conceived by Kaplan and Norton. For example, the original scorecard speaks of the customer perspective, but for the IT scorecard, the customer might be a user within the company, not an external customer of the company. The questions asked when using this methodology within the IT department are summarized in Figure 8.9.

David Norton comments, "[D]on't start with an emphasis on metrics—start with your strategy and use metrics to make it understandable and measurable (that is, to communicate it to those expected to make it happen and to manage it)."[14] He finds the balanced scorecard to be the most effective management framework for achieving organizational alignment and strategic success.

FirstEnergy, a multibillion-dollar utility company, is a good example of how the IS scorecard can be used. One of its strategic, albeit nonfinancial, goals was to create "raving fans" among its customers. The MIS group interpreted "raving fans" to mean satisfied internal customers. It used three metrics to measure the performance toward this goal:[15]

- Percentage of projects completed on time and on budget
- Percentage of projects released to the customer by agreed-on delivery date
- End-of-project customer satisfaction survey results

A scorecard used within the IT organization helps senior IT managers understand their organization's performance and measure it in a way that supports its business strategy. The IT scorecard is linked to the corporate scorecard and ensures that the measures used by IT are those that support the corporate goals. At DuPont Engineering, the balanced scorecard methodology forces every action to be linked to a corporate goal, which helps promote alignment and eliminate projects with little potential impact. The conversations between IT and the business focus on strategic goals, the merits of the project at hand, and the actual impact rather than on technology and capabilities.[16]

Dimension	Description	Example of IT Measures
Customer perspective	*How do customers see us?* Measures that reflect factors that really matter to customers	Impact of IT projects on users, impact of IT's reputation among users, and user-defined operational metrics
Internal business perspective	*What must we excel at?* Measures of what the company must do internally to meet customer expectations	IT process metrics, project completion rates, and system operational performance metrics
Learning perspective	*Can we continue to improve and create value?* Measures of the company's ability to innovative, improve, and learn	IT R&D, new technology introduction success rate, training metrics
Financial perspective	*How do we look to shareholders?* Measures to indicate contribution of activities to the bottom line	IT project ROI, NPV, IRR, cost/benefit, TCO, ABC

FIGURE 8.9 Balanced scorecard applied to IT departments.
Source: Adapted from R. Kaplan and D. Norton, "The Balanced Scorecard—Measures That Drive Performance," *Harvard Business Review* (January–February 1992), 72.

[14] "Ask the Source: Interview with David Norton," cio.com (July 25, 2002) (accessed February 22, 2003).
[15] Adapted from Eric Berkman, "How to Use the Balanced Scorecard," *CIO Magazine* 15, no. 15 (May 15, 2002), 1–4.
[16] Ibid; also Hall of Fame Organizations: Dupont, http://www.thepalladiumgroup.com/about/hof/Pages/HofViewer.aspx?MID=27 (accessed February 19, 2012).

IT Dashboards

Scorecards provide summary information gathered over a period of time. Another common IT management monitoring tool is the IT **dashboard**, which provides a snapshot of metrics at any given point in time. Much like the dashboard of an automobile or airplane, the IT dashboard summarizes key metrics for senior managers in a manner that provides quick identification of the status of the organization. Like scorecards, dashboards are useful outside the IT department and are often found in executive offices as a tool for keeping current on critical measures of the organization. This section focuses on the use of these tools within the IT department. The contents of a dashboard depend on what is important to management, but in most cases graphical representations provide quick, at-a-glance results. Dashboards are often quite colorful, but as Figure 8.10 illustrates, they can be very useful even without using color.

IT dashboards are also used in an IT department, which provide frequently updated information on areas of interest such as the status of projects of various sizes or operational systems of various types. For example, a dashboard used by General Motors (GM) North America's IT leadership team monitors project status.[17] Because senior managers question the overall health of a project rather than the details, the dashboard they designed provides red, yellow, or green highlights for rapid comprehension. A green highlight means that the project is progressing as planned and performance is within acceptable limits. A yellow highlight means at least one key target has been missed. A red highlight means the project is significantly behind and needs some attention or resources to get back on track.

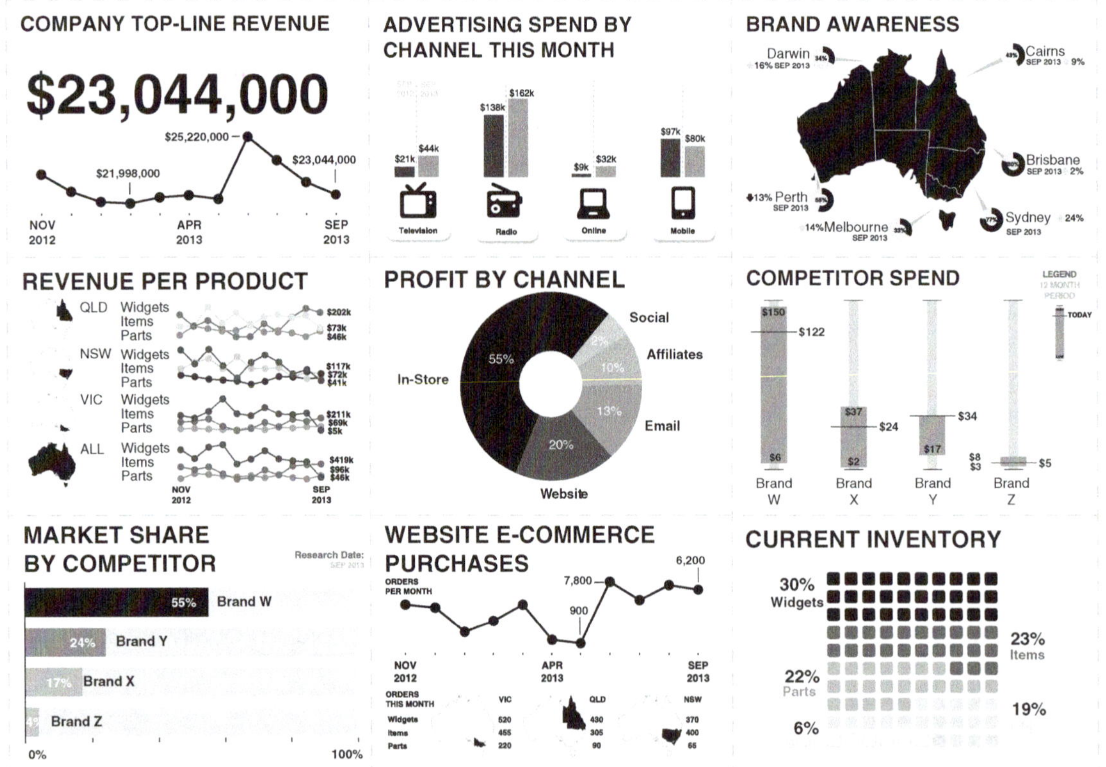

FIGURE 8.10 Example of an executive dashboard.
Source: http://www.datalabs.com.au/business-intelligence-dashboards/.

[17] Adapted from Tracy Mayor, "Red Light, Green Light," *CIO Magazine* 15, no. 1 (October 1, 2001), 108.

At GM, each project is tracked and rated monthly. GM uses four dashboard criteria: (1) performance to budget, (2) performance to schedule, (3) delivery of business results, and (4) risk. At the beginning of a project, these metrics are defined and acceptable levels set. The project manager assigns a color status monthly based on the defined criteria, and the results are reported in a spreadsheet. When managers look at the dashboard, they can immediately tell whether projects are on schedule based on the amount of green, yellow, or red highlights on the dashboard. They can then drill down into yellow or red metrics to get the projects back on track. The dashboard provides an easy way to identify where their attention should be focused. The director of IT operations explains, "Red means I need more money, people or better business buy-in. . . . The dashboard provides an early warning system that allows IT managers to identify and correct problems before they become big enough to derail a project."[18]

There are really four types of IT dashboards.[19] *Portfolio dashboards* like GM's help senior IT leaders manage IT projects. These dashboards show senior IT leaders the status, problems, milestones, progress, expenses, and other metrics related to specific projects. *Business-IT dashboards* show relevant business metrics and link them to the IT systems that support them. The metrics on the balanced scorecard provide a sample of the type of metrics followed by this dashboard. A *service dashboard* is geared toward the internal IS department, showing important metrics about the IS such as up time, throughput, service tickets, progress on bug fixes, help desk satisfaction, and so on. The fourth type is an *improvement dashboard*, which monitors the three to five key improvement goals for the IT group. Like the portfolio dashboard, the metrics to be monitored are based on the projects undertaken, but unlike the other dashboards, this one is geared toward monitoring progress toward important goals of the IT organization itself.

In order to increase its transparency, the U.S. government created an IT dashboard Web site[20] in 2009. This Web site, which was built in six weeks, displays the status of each IT project (termed an "investment") currently under development within the U.S. government. This dashboard provides status information by project and agency and offers the ability to drill down for details. For each project, it provides color-coded (i.e., green, yellow, and red) performance metrics for cost, schedule, and CIO evaluation along with a project history. For each agency, it provides an agency rating and count of projects in each color grouping. For example, in September 2015, one could click the "Portfolio" button for a list of departments and their overall ratings.[21] Across all projects, pie charts revealed green, yellow, and red counts of 575, 129, and 34, respectively. The Department of Homeland Security (DHS) had average project rating of 3.9 out of 5 over 89 projects.

Clicking on the DHS name allowed drilling down for detail about its projects, and clicking on each project provided 2015 spending along with ratings and commentary.[22] For instance, the $163.5 million "FEMA—Infrastructure" project had a very low rating of 2.0 out of 5. A narrative and graphical rating history[23] allows the user to understand the problems and when they occurred. The FEMA—Infrastructure evaluation score fell in April 2013, largely because the project was over budget and behind schedule. It is apparent that the increased transparency provides increased accountability for managing the investments.[24]

Dashboards are built on the information contained in the other applications, databases, and analytical systems of the organization (see Chapter 12 for a more complete discussion of business intelligence and business analytics). Refer to Figure 8.11 for the architecture of a sample dashboard for Western Digital, a $3-billion global designer and manufacturer of high-performance hard drives for PCs, networks, storage devices, and entertainment systems.[25]

---

[18] Ibid.

[19] Adapted from Chris Curran, "The 4 Types of CIO Dashboards," *CIO.com* (June 15, 2009), http://www.ciodashboard.com/metrics-and-measurement/the-4-types-of-cio-dashboards/ (accessed April 9, 2012).

[20] See https://itdashboard.gov/ (accessed September 4, 2015).

[21] http://www.itdashboard.gov/portfolios (accessed September 4, 2015).

[22] https://itdashboard.gov/portfolios/agency=024 (accessed September 4, 2015).

[23] https://itdashboard.gov/investment?buscid=163 (accessed September 4, 2015).

[24] U.S. government IT Dashboards, http://www.itdashboard.gov/portfolios (accessed on accessed April 23, 2015).

[25] Robert Houghton, O. A. El Sawy, P. Gray, C. Donegan, and A. Joshi, "Vigilant Information Systems for Managing Enterprises in Dynamic Supply Chains: Real-Time Dashboards at Western Digital," *MISQE* 3, no. 1 (March 2004), 19–35.

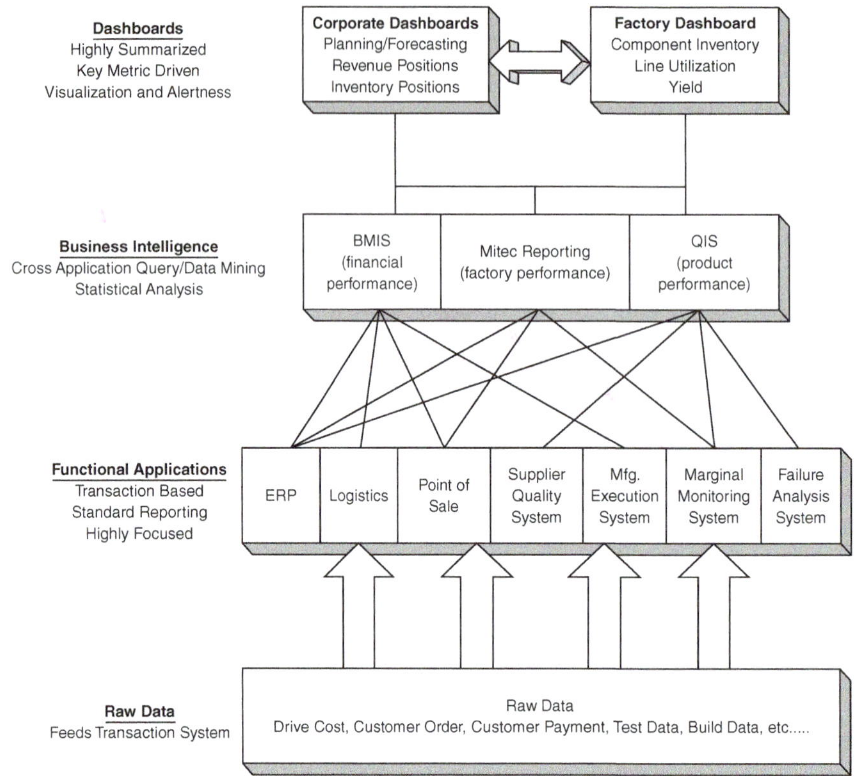

FIGURE 8.11 Example architecture of a dashboard.
Source: Robert Houghton, O. A. El Sawy, P. Gray, C. Donegan, and A. Joshi, "Vigilant Information Systems for Managing Enterprises in Dynamic Supply Chains: Real-Time Dashboards at Western Digital," *MIS Quarterly Executive* 3, no. 1 (March 2004).

Funding IT Resources

Who pays for IT? The users? The IT organization? Headquarters? Certain costs are associated with designing, developing, delivering, and maintaining the IT systems. How are these costs recovered? The three main funding methods are chargeback, allocation, and corporate budget. Both chargeback and allocation methods distribute the costs back to the businesses, departments, or individuals within the company. This distribution of costs is used so that managers can understand the costs associated with running their organization or for tax reasons when the costs associated with each business must be paid for by the appropriate business unit. Corporate budgeting, on the other hand, is a completely different funding method in which IT costs are not linked directly with any specific user or business unit; costs are recovered using corporate coffers.

Chargeback

With a **chargeback funding method**, IT costs are recovered by charging individuals, departments, or business units based on actual usage and cost. The IT organization collects usage data on each system it runs. Rates for usage are calculated based on the actual cost to the IT group to run the system and billed out on a regular basis. For example, a PC might be billed at $100/month, which includes the cost of maintaining the system, any software license fees for the standard configuration, e-mail, network access, a usage fee for the help desk, and other related services. Each department receives a monthly bill showing the number of units it has, such as PCs, printers, or servers, multiplied by the charge for each unit. Services such as mainframe processing time and special project consulting help can also be included. When the IT organization wants to recover administrative and overhead costs using a chargeback system, these costs are built into rates charged for each service.

Chargeback systems are popular because they are viewed as the most equitable way to recover IT costs. Costs are distributed based on usage or consumption of resources, ensuring that the largest portion of the costs is paid for by the group or individual who consumes the most. Chargeback systems can also provide managers a "menu" of options for managing and controlling their IT costs. For example, a manager may decide to select tablets rather than laptops because the unit charge is less expensive. The chargeback system gives managers the details they need to understand both what IT resources they use and how to account for IT consumption in the cost of their products and services. Because the departments get a regular bill, they know exactly what their costs are.

Creating and managing a chargeback system, however, is a costly endeavor itself. IT organizations must build systems to collect details that might not be needed for anything other than the bills they generate. For example, if PCs are the basis for charging for network time, the network connect time per PC must be collected, stored, and analyzed each billing cycle. The data collection quickly becomes large and complex, which often results in complicated, difficult-to-understand bills. In addition, picking the charging criteria is challenging. For example, it is relatively easy to count the number of PCs located in a particular business unit, but is that number a good measure of the network resources used? It might be more accurate to charge based on units of network time used, but how would that be captured and calculated? Chargeback methods are most appropriate when there is a wide variation in usage among users or when actual costs need to be accounted for by the business units.

Allocation

To simplify the cost recovery process, an allocation system can be used. An **allocation funding method** recovers costs based on something other than usage, such as revenues, log-in accounts, or head count (number of employees) in each business unit or department. For example, suppose the total spending for IT for a year is $1 million for a company with 10,000 employees. A business unit with 1,000 employees might be responsible for 10%, or $100,000, of the total IT costs. Of course, with this type of allocation system, it does not matter whether these employees even use the IT; the department is still charged the same amount.

The allocation mechanism is simpler than the chargeback method to implement and apply each month. Actual usage does not need to be captured. The rate charged is often fixed at the beginning of the year. Allocation offers two main advantages. First, the level of detail required to calculate the allocations is much less, which reduces record keeping expenses. Second, the charges from the IT organization are predictable. Unlike the chargeback mechanism, where each bill opens up an opportunity for discussion about the charges incurred, the allocation mechanism seems to generate far less frequent arguments from the business units. Often, quite a bit of discussion takes place at the beginning of the year when rates and allocation bases are set, but less discussion occurs each month because the managers understand and expect the bill.

Two major complaints are made about allocation systems. First is the free-rider problem: A large user of IT services pays the same amount as a small user when the charges are not based on usage. Second, deciding the basis for allocating the costs is an issue. Choosing the number of employees over the number of desktops or other basis is a management decision, and whichever basis is chosen, someone will likely pay more than his or her actual usage would imply. Allocation mechanisms work well when a corporate directive requires the use of this method and when the units agree on the basis for dividing the costs.

Often when an allocation process is used, a follow-up process is needed at the end of the fiscal year to compare the total IT expenses against the total IT funds recovered from the business units, and any extra funds are given back to the business. Sometimes this process is called a "true-up" process because true expenses are balanced against payments made. In some cases, additional funds are needed; however, IT managers try to avoid asking for funds to make up for shortfalls in their budget. The true-up process is needed because the actual cost of the information system is difficult to predict at the beginning of the year. Cost changes over the year because hardware, software, or support costs fluctuate in the marketplace and because IT managers, like all managers, work constantly on improving efficiency and productivity, resulting in lower costs. In an allocation process that charges a fixed rate for each service for the year, a true-up process allows IT managers to pass along any additional savings to their business counterparts. Business managers often prefer the predictability of their monthly IT bills along with a true-up process over the relative unpredictability of being charged actual costs each month.

Funding Method	Description	Why Do It?	Why Not Do It?
Chargeback	Charges are calculated based on actual usage.	It is the fairest method for recovering costs based on actual usage. IT users can see exactly what their usage costs are.	IT department must collect details on usage, which can be expensive and difficult. IT must be prepared to defend the charges, which takes time and resources.
Allocation	Total expected IT expenditures are divided by agreed upon basis such as number of login IDs, number of employees, or number of workstations.	It requires less bookkeeping for IT because rate is set once per fiscal year, and basis is well understood. Monthly costs for the business units are predictable.	IT department must defend allocation rates; it may charge a low-usage department more than its usage would indicate is fair.
Corporate Budget	Corporate allocates funds to IT at annual budget session.	There is no billing to the business units. IT exercises more control over what projects are done. It is good for encouraging the use of new technologies.	It competes with all other budgeted items for funds; users might draw on excessive resources, lacking any incentive to economize.

FIGURE 8.12 Comparison of IT funding methods.

Corporate Budget

An entirely different way to pay for IT costs is to simply consider them all to be corporate overhead and pay for them directly out of the corporate budget. With the **corporate budget funding method**, the costs fall to the corporate bottom line, rather than levying charges on specific users or business units.

Corporate budgeting is a relatively simple method for funding IT costs. It requires no calculation of prices of the IT systems. And because bills are not generated on a regular cycle to the businesses, concerns are raised less often by the business managers. IT managers control the entire budget, giving them control of the use of those funds and, ultimately, more input into what systems are created, how they are managed, and when they are retired. This funding method also encourages the use of new technologies because learners are not charged for exploration and inefficient system use.

As with the other methods, certain drawbacks come with using the corporate budget. First, all IT expenditures are subjected to the same process as all other corporate expenditures, namely, the budgeting process. In many companies, this process is one of the most stressful events of the year: Everyone has projects to be done, and everyone is competing for scarce funds. If the business units are not billed in some way for their usage, many companies find that the units do not control their usage. Getting a bill for services motivates the individual business manager to reconsider his or her usage of those services. Finally, if the business units are not footing the bill, the IT group may feel less accountable to them, which may result in an IT organization that is less end-user or customer oriented.

Figure 8.12 summarizes the advantages and disadvantages of these methods.

How Much Does IT Cost?

The three major IT funding approaches in the preceding discussion are designed to recover the costs of building and maintaining the information systems in an enterprise. The goal is to simply cover the costs, not to generate a profit (although some IT organizations are actually profit centers for their corporation). The most basic method for calculating the costs of a system is to add the costs of all the components, including hardware, software, network, and the people involved. IT organizations calculate the initial costs and ongoing maintenance costs in just this way.

Activity-Based Costing

Another method for calculating costs is known as *activity-based costing (ABC)*. Traditional accounting methods account for direct and indirect costs. Direct costs are those that can be clearly linked to a particular process or product, such as the components used to manufacture the product and the assembler's wages for time spent building the product. Indirect costs are the overhead costs, which include everything from the electric bill, the salary of administrative managers, and the expenses of the administrative function to the wages of the supervisor overseeing the assembler, the cost of running the factory, and the maintenance of machinery used for multiple products. Further, depending on the funding method used by the enterprise, indirect costs are allocated or absorbed elsewhere in the pricing model. The allocation process can be cumbersome and complex and often is a source of trouble for many organizations. The alternative to the traditional approach is ABC.

Activity-based costing calculates costs by counting the actual activities that go into making a specific product or delivering a specific service. *Activities* are processes, functions, or tasks that occur over time and produce recognized results. They consume assigned resources to produce products and services. Activities are useful in costing because they are the common denominator between business process improvement and information improvement across departments.

Rather than allocate the total indirect cost of a system across a range of services according to an allocation formula, ABC calculates the amount of time that system supported a particular activity and allocates only that cost to that activity. For example, an accountant would look at the enterprise resource planning (ERP) system and divide its cost over the activities it supports by calculating how much of the system is used by each activity. Product A might take up one-twelfth of an ERP system's capacity to control the manufacturing activities needed to make it, so it would be allocated one-twelfth of the system's costs. The help desk might take up a whole server, so the entire server's cost would be allocated to that activity. In the end, the costs are put in buckets that reflect the products and services of the business rather than the organization structure or the processes of any given department. In effect, ABC is the process of charging all costs to "profit centers" instead of to "cost centers."

Jonathan Bush, CEO of management services company Athenahealth, did activity-based costing for Children's Hospital in Boston. When he found that it cost the hospital about $120 to admit a patient, he recommended a solution of using the information received from the primary care doctor. He argues, "Your primary-care doctor has already created 90% of that information to see you for your regular visit. Why wouldn't the hospital give the doctor $100 if it was costing them $120 to do it themselves?"[26] The ABC approach allowed the hospital to realize the cost of running the hospital systems to perform the activity and to compare it with the cost of an alternative source that turned out to be cheaper. But until the thorny issues of electronic medical records are sorted out, the doctors and the hospitals will likely continue to create their own records.

Total Cost of Ownership

When a system is proposed and a business case is created to justify the investment, summing up the initial outlay and the maintenance cost does not provide an entirely accurate total system cost. In fact, if only the initial and maintenance costs are considered, the decision is often made on incomplete information. Other costs are involved, and a time value of money affects the total cost. One technique used to calculate a more accurate cost that includes all associated costs is **total cost of ownership (TCO)**. It has become the industry standard. Gartner Group introduced TCO in the late 1980s when PC-based IT infrastructures began gaining popularity.[27] Other IT experts have since modified the concept, and this section synthesizes the latest and best thinking about TCO.

TCO looks beyond initial capital investments to include costs associated with technical support, administration, training, and system retirement. Often, the initial cost is an inadequate predictor of the additional costs necessary to successfully implement the system. TCO techniques estimate annual costs per user for each potential infrastructure choice; these costs are then totaled. Careful estimates of TCO provide the best investment numbers to compare with financial return numbers when analyzing the net returns on various IT options. The alternative, an analysis without TCO, can result in an "apples and oranges" comparison. Consider a decision about printers. The initial cost of a laser printer may be much less than an inkjet printer, but when considering the cost of toner and ink over the expected lifetime of the printers, the total cost of ownership of the laser printer is much lower. A similar analysis of a larger IT system clarifies similar alternatives and comparisons.

[26] David Lidsky, "#43 Athenahealth," fastcompany.com (February 17, 2010), http://www.fastcompany.com/mic/2010/profile/athenahealth (accessed January 30, 2012).

[27] M. Gartenberg, "Beyond the Numbers: Common TCO Myths Revealed," Gartner Group Research Note: Technology (March 2, 1998).

A major IT investment is for infrastructure. The hardware, software, network, and data framework can be used to organize the TCO components the manager needs to evaluate each infrastructure option. Hardware, software, and networking units can include the obvious equipment and packages but also "invisible" significant items such as technical support, administration, training, and disposal costs can easily be overlooked. "Soft" data costs can include removable media such as thumb drives or portable hard drives, as well as on-site and off-site storage.

Even if managers can't get a completely accurate figure of costs, they can be more aware of areas where costs can be cut. More or less detail can be used in each area as needed by the business environment. The manager can adapt this framework for use with varying IT infrastructures.

TCO Component Breakdown

TCO is sometimes difficult for managers to fully comprehend. To clarify how the TCO framework is used, this section examines the hardware category in more detail. For shared components, such as servers and printers, TCO estimates should be computed per component and then divided among all users who access them.

For more complex situations, such as when only certain groups of users possess certain components, it is wise to segment the hardware analysis by platform. For example, in an organization in which every employee possesses a desktop computer that accesses a server and half the employees also possess stand-alone laptops that do not access a server, one TCO table could be built for desktop and server hardware and another for laptop hardware. Each table would include software, network, and data costs associated only with its specific platforms.

Soft costs, such as technical support, administration, and training, are easier to estimate than they may first appear. For example, as Figure 8.13 depicts, technical support costs include areas such as phone support, troubleshooting, hot swaps, and repairs. These and all other costs are summed and divided by the number of devices to derive an amount per unit, which is when added to the initial cost of a device, and reflects a truer sense of cost of ownership, or TCO.

The final soft cost, informal support, may be harder to determine, but it is important nonetheless. Informal support comprises the sometimes highly complex networks that develop among co-workers through which many problems are fixed and much training takes place without the involvement of any official support staff. In many circumstances, these activities can prove more efficient and effective than working through official channels. Still, managers want to analyze the costs of informal support for two reasons:

1. The costs—both in salary and in opportunity—of a nonsupport employee providing informal support may prove significantly higher than analogous costs for a formal support employee. For example, it costs much more in both dollars per hour and forgone management activity for a midlevel manager to help a line employee troubleshoot an e-mail problem than it would for a formal support employee to provide the same service.

2. The quantity of informal support activity in an organization provides an indirect measure of the efficiency of its IT support organization. The formal support organization should respond with sufficient promptness and thoroughness to discourage all but the briefest informal support transactions.

Various IT infrastructure options affect informal support activities differently. For example, a more user-friendly systems interface may alleviate the need for much informal support, justifying a slightly higher software expenditure. Similarly, an investment in support management software may be justified if it reduces the need for informal support. Web-based applications change the equation even further. Those companies that use a vendor-supplied Web-based application may find that support activities are provided by the vendor or the applications are written in such a way as to minimize or eliminate support entirely.

TCO as a Management Tool

This discussion focused on TCO as a tool for evaluating which infrastructure components to choose, but TCO also can help managers understand how infrastructure costs break down. Research has consistently shown that the labor costs associated with an IT infrastructure far outweigh the actual capital investment costs. TCO provides the

Soft Cost Areas	Example Components of Cost	Source
Technical support	Hardware phone support	Call center
	In-person hardware troubleshooting	IT operations
	Hardware hot swaps	IT operations
	Physical hardware repair	IT operations
	Total cost of technical support	
Administration	Hardware setup	System administrator
	Hardware upgrades/modifications	System administrator
	New hardware evaluation	IT operations
	Total cost of administration	
Training	New employee training	IT operations
	Ongoing administrator training	Hardware vendor
	Total cost of training	
	Total soft costs for hardware	

FIGURE 8.13 Soft cost considerations.

fullest picture of where managers spend their IT dollars. Like other benchmarks, TCO results can be evaluated over time against industry standards (much TCO target data for various IT infrastructure choices are available from industry research firms). Even without comparison data, the numbers that emerge from TCO studies assist in making decisions about budgeting, resource allocation, and organizational structure.

However, like the ABC approach, the cost of implementing TCO can be a detriment to the program's overall success. Both ABC and TCO are complex approaches that may require significant effort to determine the costs to use in the calculations. Managers must weigh the benefits of using these approaches with the costs of obtaining reliable data necessary to make their use successful.

SUMMARY

- IT organizations can be expected to anticipate new technologies, participate in setting and implementing strategic goals, innovate current processes, develop and maintain information systems, manage supplier relationships, establish architecture platforms and standards, promote enterprise security, plan for business discontinuities, manage data/information/knowledge, manage Internet and network services, manage human resources, operate the data center, provide general support, and integrate social IT.
- IT activities can reveal the group's level of maturity. The most mature IT organizations are proactive and partner with business executives.
- The chief information officer (CIO) is a high-level IS officer who oversees many important organizational activities. The CIO must display both technical and business skills. The role requires both strategic and operational skills.
- A business case is a tool used to support a decision or a proposal of a new investment. It is a document containing a project description, financial analysis, marketing analysis, and all other relevant documentation to assist managers in making a go/no-go decision.
- Benefits articulated in a business case can be categorized as observable, measurable, quantifiable, and financial. These benefits are often for innovations, improvements, or cessation.
- The portfolio of IT investments must be carefully evaluated and managed.
- The investments may be valued using such methods as return on investment (ROI), net present value (NPV), economic value added (EVA), payback period, internal rate of return (IRR), and weighted scoring.
- Benefits derived from IT investments are sometimes difficult to quantify and to observe or are long range in scope.

- Monitoring and communicating the status and benefits of IT is often done through the use of balanced scorecards and IT dashboards.
- IT is funded using one of three methods: chargeback, allocation, or corporate budget.
- Chargeback systems are viewed as the most equitable method of IT cost recovery because costs are distributed based on usage. Creating an accounting system to record the information necessary to do a chargeback system can be expensive and time consuming and usually has no other useful application.
- Allocation systems provide a simpler method to recover costs because they do not involve recording system usage to allocate costs. However, allocation systems can sometimes penalize groups with low usage.
- The corporate budget method does not allocate costs at all. Instead, the CIO seeks and receives a budget from the corporate overhead account. This method of funding IT does not require any usage record keeping but is also most likely to be abused if the users perceive it to be "free."
- Activity-based costing (ABC) is another technique to group costs into a meaningful bucket. Costs are accounted for based on the activity, product, or service they support. ABC is useful for allocating large overhead expenses.
- Total cost of ownership (TCO) is a technique used to understand all the costs beyond the initial investment costs associated with owning and operating an information system. It is most useful as a tool to help evaluate which infrastructure components to choose and to help understand how infrastructure costs occur.

KEY TERMS

activity-based costing (ABC) (p. 185)
allocation funding method (p. 183)
balanced scorecard (p. 178)
business case (p. 173)
business-IT maturity model (p. 167)
business technology strategist (p. 171)
chargeback funding method (p. 182)
chief information officer (CIO) (p. 171)
corporate budget funding method (p. 184)
dashboard (p. 180)
economic value added (EVA) (p. 177)
IT portfolio management (p. 175)
net present value (NPV) (p. 177)
payback period (p. 176)
return on investment (ROI) (p. 176)
total cost of ownership (TCO) (p. 185)

DISCUSSION QUESTIONS

1. Using an organization with which you are familiar, describe the role of the most senior IS professional. Is that person a strategist or an operational manager?
2. What advantages does a CIO bring to a business? What might be the disadvantages of having a CIO?
3. Under what conditions would you recommend using each of these funding methods to pay for information systems expenses: allocation, chargeback, and corporate budget?
4. In the following table are comparative typical IT portfolio profiles for different business strategies from Weill and Broadbent's study.[28] Explain why infrastructure investments are higher and transactional and informational investments are lower for a firm with an agility focus than a firm with a cost focus. Also, how would you explain the similar values for strategic investments among the three profiles?

	Transactional Investments	Infrastructure Investments	Informational Investments	Strategic Investments
Average firm	25%	46%	18%	11%
Cost focus	27%	44%	18%	11%
Agility focus	24%	51%	15%	10%

5. Describe the conditions under which ROI, payback period, NPV, and EVA are most appropriately applied to information systems investments.

[28] Weill and Broadbent, *Leveraging The New Infrastructure*.

6. A new inventory management system for ABC Company could be developed at a cost of $260,000. The estimated net operating costs and estimated net benefits over six years of operation would be:

Year	Estimated Net Operating Costs	Estimated Net Benefits
0	$260,000	$0
1	7,000	42,000
2	9,400	78,000
3	11,000	82,000
4	14,000	115,000
5	15,000	120,000
6	25,000	140,000

   a. What would the payback period be for this investment? Would it be a good or bad investment? Why?
   b. What is the ROI for this investment?
   c. Assuming a 15% discount rate, what is this investment's NPV?

7. Compare and contrast the IT scorecard and dashboard approaches. Which, if either, would be most useful to you as a general manager? Please explain.

8. TCO is one way to account for costs associated with a specific infrastructure. This method does not include additional costs such as disposal costs—the costs to dispose of the system when it is no longer of use. What other additional costs might be of importance in making total cost calculations?

9. Check out the U.S. government IT dashboard site at http://www.itdashboard.gov/portfolios. Based upon the site:
   a. Describe the portfolio for the Department of Justice.
   b. Which investments, if any, appear to be in trouble in the Department of Justice? Based on the information that is provided, can you estimate the status of those projects? Is there any additional information that you think a manager would like to see about the status of the project?

CASE STUDY 8-1 KLM Airlines

KLM Airlines, headquartered in the Netherlands, is one of the world's leading international airlines. Following its merger with Air France in 2004, KLM employs 33,000 people worldwide (1,000 of whom work in the IT function) and operates about 200 planes.[29]

Following the 9/11 terrorist attack in 2001, the challenging business environment for airlines caused KLM's CEO to appoint a new CIO from the operations area, clearly outside of the IT area, to make a structural break from the past. Three priorities included examining outsourcing IT, creating a board of business and IT representatives, and fashioning a process for governance of IT that is shared between the IT function and business units.

The result of the ensuing efforts over several years was to create four levels of committee governance: An executive committee kept an eye on matching the business strategy with IT strategies; A business/IT board, which was composed of the CEO, CIO, and all business unit executive vice presidents, was formed to manage the portfolio and budget; an IT management team worked on tactical planning for the business/IT board; and finally, the CIO/information services management team planned and managed IT operations. KLM also established a set of key principles and practices and developed a standard business case template that had to be used whenever requesting an investment greater than 150,000 euros.

KLM experienced five benefits attributed to the governance structure: reduced IT costs per kilometer flown, increased capacity for IT innovation, better alignment of investments to business goals, increased trust between functional units and the IT organization, and a mind-set of the value of IT.

[29] Adapted from Steven De Haes, Dirk Gemke, John Thorp, and Wim Van Grembergen, "KLM's Enterprise Governance of IT Journey: From Managing IT Costs to Managing Business Value," *MIS Quarterly Executive* 10, no. 3 (2011), 109–20.

Discussion Questions

1. What is likely to have led to increased trust for the IT organization?
2. What might explain an item that is seemingly quite unrelated to IT (costs per kilometer flown) decreased as a result of the new CIO structure?
3. What maturity level did KLM appear to exhibit (a) in 2000 and (b) in 2011? Why?
4. Why do you think that KLM requires its employees to use a standard business case template when they want to make an investment?

Sources: Adapted from Steven De Haes, Dirk Gemke, John Thorp, and Wim Van Grembergen, "KLM's Enterprise Governance of IT Journey: From Managing IT Costs to Managing Business Value," *MIS Quarterly Executive* 10, no. 3 (2011), 109–20, and "Analyzing IT Value Management at KLM Through the Lens of Val IT," http://www.isaca.org/JOURNAL/ARCHIVES/2011/VOLUME-5/Pages/Analyzing-IT-Value-Management-at-KLM-Through-the-Lens-of-Val-IT.aspx (accessed May 30, 2015).

CASE STUDY 8-2 Balanced Scorecards at BIOCO

BIOCO is a profitable and growing medium-sized biopharmaceutical company located in the southeast United States. It develops, produces, and markets vaccines and antibody-based pharmaceutical products. As part of the company's strategic transformation, BIOCO's CEO introduced a top-down, strategy-driven management process called the "BIOCO Way." The CEO has a strong conviction that the success of a company starts with a clear vision of what the company wants to be and a corporate strategy that reflects that vision. In the BIOCO Way, the corporate vision and strategy are translated into a long-term corporate strategic plan, which in turn is used to generate the corporate strategy map. To measure progress against the strategy map, a cascade of balanced scorecards (corporate, division/department) are developed and used. As a result of the full integration of the levels of balanced scorecards into the planning process, the BIOCO Way emphasizes how the strategies and related tactics should be carried out and measured at all levels. The CEO is a strong champion of balanced scorecards and is considered an in-house guru for the method.

Each year, BIOCO managers at the corporate and department levels review performance and assess the appropriateness of their respective balanced scorecards for the prior year. Based on the results of the performance reviews and a short-term execution plan for the upcoming year, strategic initiatives are added, modified, or removed, and the metrics in the scorecards are adjusted accordingly. The CIO thinks that the balanced scorecards help the departments look beyond their own operations, and the vice president thinks they mobilize everyone in the company by setting up tangible goals that are clearly linked to the overall goals of the company. The CIO thinks the scorecard enhances communications because it "provides a focal point and common language around the key value drivers of the organization," and it helps IT understand other business areas. To overcome cultural differences among the departments, he added culture as a fifth perspective in the scorecards.

Discussion Questions

1. What benefits has BIOCO realized from its use of balanced scorecards?
2. Do you think the BIOCO Way was useful in helping the IT department align its goals with that of the company? Why or why not?
3. Do you think that the BIOCO approach could be implemented successfully in large companies? Why or why not? If so, what, if any, adjustments need to be made?
4. BIOCO recently was sold and now has a new CEO. Do you think the BIOCO Way will be as successful under the new CEO? Why or why not?

Sources: Q. Hu and C. D. Huang, "Using the Balanced Scorecard to Achieve Sustained IT-Business Alignment: A Case Study," *Communications of the Association for Information Systems* 17, no. 1 (2006); Organized Change Consultancy, "Examples of Companies Using the Balanced Scorecard" (2010), https://www.organizedchange.com/examplesofcompaniesusingthebalancedscorecard.htm (accessed May 30, 2015).

Governance of the Information Systems Organization

chapter

9

Governance structures define the way decisions are made in an organization. This chapter explores four models of governance based on the location of decision making in organization structure (centralized, decentralized, and federal), decision rights, digital ecosystems, and control, considering frameworks from the Committee of Sponsoring Organizations of the Treadway Commission (COSO), Control Objectives for Information and related Technology (COBIT), and Information Technology Infrastructure Library (ITIL). Examples and strategies for implementation are discussed.

Intel's information technology (IT) performance reports for 2013[1] and 2015[2] boast about how the company increased its storage capacity from 25 petabytes in 2010 to 106 petabytes in 2014, and over the same interval raised the number of handheld devices from 19,400 to 53,700. Intel also exploited other highly visible opportunities of using predictive data analytics. It reduced the amount of time required to detect data threats from two weeks in 2013 to 20 minutes in 2014. Finally, Intel enjoyed a revenue increase of $351 million from advanced analytics in the areas of sales leads, supply, demand, and pricing.

An outsider might assume that Intel stepped up spending and IT investments to accomplish these goals. However, it actually *reduced* the number of data centers from 91 in 2010 to 61 in 2014 and reduced IT spending from 2.64% to 2.30% of revenue during that same five-year interval.

How did Intel accomplish these and other laudable goals? Its approach was the result of 23 years of evolution of its strategy that began by creating a centralized IT organization in 1992 with control resting in IT. Intel has come a long way from its original governance structure, which was centered on mainframes and wide-area networks. Later, in 2003, Intel initiated its "Protect Era" in response to two events: the then-new Sarbanes–Oxley legislation and a virus that had infected Intel's internal networks through an employee's home-based network connection. The company's "Protect Era" was led by IT and locked down resources to such an extent that employees had to devise risky policy workarounds to be able to complete some of their tasks. Data could be used only within a particular functional area, not shared among areas.

Intel's current "Protect to Enable Era" in information governance began in 2009 after managers found that its overly restrictive policies on bring your own device (BYOD) had frustrated its employees who saw those policies as both expensive and detrimental to innovation over the long run. This led Intel to discover that **consumerization** is a powerful force. That six-syllable mouthful describes the increasingly powerful tools available in the consumer space that can impact the corporate space. Mobility has been the major breakthrough in consumerization, and the increasing use of

[1] http://www.intel.com/content/dam/www/public/us/en/documents/reports/2012-2013-intel-it-performance-report.pdf (accessed September 1, 2015).

[2] http://www.intel.com/content/www/us/en/it-management/intel-it-best-practices/intel-it-annual-performance-report-2014-15-paper.html (accessed September 1, 2015).

smartphones, tablets, and smaller/more powerful laptops coupled with Web-based applications that offer everything from free business productivity tools, such as Google Docs to sharing applications like YouTube and SlideShare and to social tools such as Twitter and LinkedIn, have created a new IT environment.

Intel found that cloud services, desktop applications, social networking, mobile devices, and the management policies surrounding them had changed the business of IT. BYOD forced IT leaders at Intel and many other firms to re-evaluate how IT services are offered. Intel's traditional command and control mentality—with IT leaders making all technology decisions—no longer could work. The consumerization of technology changed Intel's management approach[3] from "How do we stop it?" to "How do we work with this?"

Intel's governance structure also resulted in a lost opportunity to exploit data and analytics (described in Chapter 13). Because information was restricted to the particular department in which it was generated, Intel could not explore connections between manufacturing decisions and consumer reactions or between social media trends and product design decisions. A new approach to governance was clearly needed, and Protect to Enable has addressed those needs.

More recently, Intel has extended the governance framework's reach by its new six-pronged focus on social networking, mobile devices, analytics, cloud technologies, Internet of Things, and security. Intel reports that it has now moved to the top of a three-tiered pyramid of IT leadership of (1) developing programs and delivering services, (2) contributing business value, and (3) transforming the company.

How does a governance framework provide these benefits? Intel now uses information governance boards that include representatives from a variety of its functions, including marketing, manufacturing, product design, human resources (HR), legal, business development, internal audit, and IT. Sharing the governance with business units is one of five key success factors, according to an analysis of the Intel case.[4] Intel reports that they have moved beyond categorizing challenges as IT problems or business problems. They assert that only integrated solutions work to "disrupt instead of being disrupted."[5]

Although each information systems (IS) organization is unique in many ways, all have elements in common. The focus of this chapter is to introduce managers to issues related to the way decisions about IT are made in the organization. These issues should reflect the typical activities of an IS organization that were discussed in Chapter 8. The current chapter examines governance of the IS organization as it relates to decisions about IT issues.

IT Governance

Expectations (or more specifically, what managers should and should not expect from the IS organization) are at the heart of IT governance. **Governance** in the context of business enterprises is all about making decisions that define expectations, grant authority, or ensure performance. In other words, governance is about aligning behavior with business goals through empowerment and monitoring. Empowerment comes from granting the right to make decisions, and monitoring comes from evaluating performance. As noted in Chapter 3, a decision right is an important organizational design variable because it indicates who in the organization has the responsibility to initiate, supply information for, approve, implement, and control various types of decisions.

Four perspectives of IT governance are described here. The first, a traditional perspective of IT governance, focuses on how decision rights can be distributed to facilitate centralized, decentralized, or hybrid modes of decision making. In this view of governance, the organization structure plays a major role. The second focuses on the interaction between accountability and allocation of decision rights to executives, business unit leaders, or IT leaders. The third focuses on an "ecosystem" that reflects the significant impacts of the large variety of resources available from individuals, organizational units, and outside service providers. The final perspective, control structures developed in response to important legislation, also provides governance guidelines to firms.

---

[3] Paul P. Tallon, James E. Short, and Malcolm Harkins, "The Evolution of Information Governance at Intel," *MIS Quarterly Executive* 12, no. 4 (2013), 189–98.

[4] Ibid.

[5] http://www.intel.com/content/www/us/en/it-management/intel-it-best-practices/intel-it-annual-performance-report-2014-15-paper.html, 20 (accessed September 3, 2015).

Centralized versus Decentralized Organizational Structures

Companies' organizational strategies exist along a continuum from centralization to decentralization. At one end of the continuum, **centralized IS organizations** bring together all staff, hardware, software, data, and processing into a single location. **Decentralized IS organizations** scatter these components across different locations to address local business needs. These two approaches do not refer to IT architectures but to decision-making frameworks. A combination, or hybrid, of the two is called *federalism,* found in the middle (see Figure 9.1). Enterprises of all shapes and sizes can be found at any point along the continuum. Over time, however, each enterprise may gravitate toward one end of the continuum or the other, and often reorganization is in reality a change toward one end to the other.

Centralization and decentralization trends have evolved through the five eras of information usage (see Chapter 2, Figure 2.1). In the 1960s, mainframes dictated a centralized approach to IS because the mainframe resided in one physical location. Centralized decision making, purchasing, maintenance, and staff kept these early computing behemoths running. The 1970s remained centralized due in part to the constraints of mainframe computing, although minicomputers planted early seeds for decentralizing. In the 1980s the advent of the personal computer (PC), which allowed computing power to spread beyond the raised-floor, super-cooled rooms of mainframes, provided further fuel for decentralization. Users especially liked the shift to decentralization because it put them more in control and increased their agility. However, the pressures for secure networks and massive corporate databases in the 1990s shifted some organizations back to a more centralized approach. Yet, the increasingly global nature of many businesses makes complete centralization impossible. The most recent global survey found that 70.6% of the participating organizations were centralized in terms of IT, 13.5% were decentralized, and 12.7% were federated.[6] Although the high percentage of centralized companies in the sample may seem surprising, the study suggested that with the increasing appreciation for governance found in companies with high levels of governance maturity comes the need for control that is made possible in the centralized structure.

The survey also found that two-thirds of responding enterprises had governance activities for enterprise IT (GEIT). These companies indicated that the main driver for GEIT activities is to ensure that IT functionality aligns with business needs, and, like Intel's findings, the most commonly experienced outcomes were improvements in management of IT-related risk and communication and relationships between business and IT. Good governance therefore can increase the transparency of IT supply and demand and help in assigning priorities for IT projects and services.

What are the most important considerations in deciding how much to centralize or decentralize? Figure 9.2 shows some advantages and disadvantages of each approach.

Consider two competing parcel delivery companies, UPS and FedEx, in the year that they both reported spending about $1 billion on IT. UPS's IT strategy focused on delivering efficiencies to meet the business demands of consistency and reliability. UPS's centralized, standardized IT environment supported dependable customer service at a relatively low price. In contrast, FedEx chose a decentralized IT strategy that allowed it to focus on flexibility in meeting business demands generated from targeting various customer segments. The higher costs of the decentralized approach to IT management were offset by the benefits of localized innovation and customer responsiveness.[7]

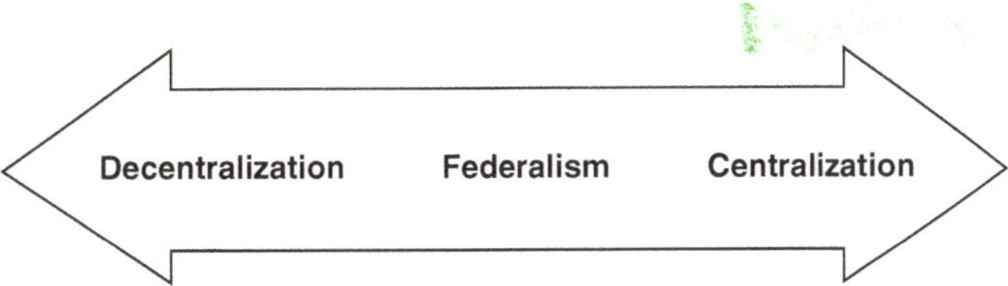

FIGURE 9.1 Organizational continuum.

[6] IT Governance Institute, "Global Status Report on the Governance of Enterprise IT (GEIT)" (2011), 49, http://www.isaca.org/Knowledge-Center/Research/Documents/Global-Status-Report-GEIT-10Jan2011-Research.pdf (accessed February 27, 2011).

[7] J. W. Ross and P. Weill, "Six IT Decisions Your IT People Shouldn't Make," *Harvard Business Review* (November 2002), 1–8.

Approach	Advantages	Disadvantages	Companies Adopting
Centralized	• Global standards; common data • "One voice" for negotiating supplier contracts • Greater leverage in deploying strategic IT initiatives • Economies of scale and a shared cost structure • Access to large capacity • Improved recruitment and training of IT professionals • Improved control of security and databases • Consistent with centralized enterprise structure	• Technology may not meet local needs • Slow support for strategic initiatives • Schism between business and IT organization • "Us versus them" mentality when technology problems occur • Lack of business unit control over overhead costs	Zara, UPS[a]
Decentralized	• Technology customized to local business needs • Close partnership between IT and business units • Greater flexibility • Reduced telecommunication costs • Consistency with decentralized enterprise structure • Business unit control of overhead costs	• Difficulty in maintaining global standards and consistent data • Higher infrastructure costs • Difficulty in negotiating preferential supplier agreements • Loss of control • Duplication of staff and data	VeriFone, FedEx[b]

[a] J. W. Ross and P. Weill, "Six IT Decisions Your IT People Shouldn't Make," *Harvard Business Review* (November 2002), 1–8.
[b] Ibid.

FIGURE 9.2 Advantages and disadvantages of organizational approaches.

Zara, the global retail and apparel manufacturer introduced in Chapter 2, also used a centralized approach, which differs from other clothing chains. The head of IS, who was not a CIO, reported directly to the deputy general manager, who was two levels below the CEO.[8] This way of structuring the IS department was consistent with the organization's predominantly centralized structure. It was also well suited to organizational processing about which most administrative decisions were made in the headquarters at Lacoruña, Spain. The users did not require a lot of hand-holding with regard to the point-of-sale (POS) systems in the stores. For these reasons, a centralized approach was a good fit for Zara. The store managers, however, did retain some decision rights about which products to order. Thus, Zara was not totally at the centralization end of the continuum. In contrast, Verifone, which we discuss in Chapter 4, needs a decentralized structure for its globally distributed employees.

Companies adopt a strategy based on lessons learned from earlier years of centralization and decentralization. Most companies want to achieve the advantages derived from both organizational paradigms. This desire leads to **federalism**,[9] a structuring approach that distributes power, hardware, software, data, and personnel between a central IS group and IS in business units. Many companies adopt a form of federal IT yet still count themselves as either decentralized or centralized, depending on their position on the continuum. Organizations such as Home Depot and the U.S. Department of Veteran Affairs recognize the advantages of a more hybrid approach and actively seek to benefit from adopting a federal structure. See Figure 9.3 for the interrelationship of these approaches.

Archetypes of Accountability and Decision Rights

Sometimes the centralized/decentralized/federal approaches to governance are not fine-tuned enough to help managers deal with the many contingencies facing today's organizations. This issue is addressed by a framework

[8] Andrew McAfee, Vincent Dessain, and Anders Sjman, "Zara: IT for Fast Fashion," Harvard Business School Case 9-604-081 (September 6, 2007).
[9] John F. Rockart, Michael J. Earl, and Jeanne W. Ross, "Eight Imperatives for the New IT Organization," *Sloan Management Review* (Fall 1996), 52–53.

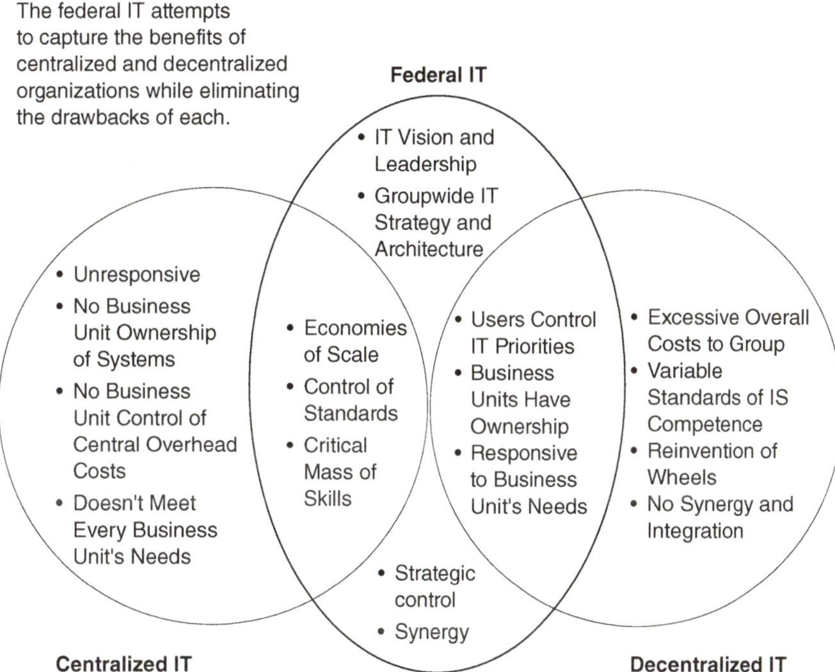

FIGURE 9.3 Federal IT.
Source: Michael J. Earl, "Information Management: The Organizational Dimension," *The Role of the Corporate IT Function in the Federal IT Organization*, ed. S. L. Hodgkinson (New York: Oxford University Press, 1996), Figure 12.1. By permission of Oxford University Press, Inc.

developed by Peter Weill and Jeanne Ross. They define **IT governance** as "specifying the decision rights and accountability framework to encourage desirable behavior in using IT."[10] IT governance is not about what decisions are actually made but rather about who is making them (i.e., who holds the decision rights) and how the decision makers are held accountable for them.

It is important to match the manager's decision rights with his or her accountability for a decision. Figure 9.4 indicates what happens when there is a mismatch. Where the CIO has a high level of decision rights and accountability, the firm is likely to be at maturity Level 3 (which was introduced in Chapter 8). Where both the decision rights and accountability are low, the company is likely to be at Level 1. Mismatches result in either an oversupply of IT resources or the inability of IT to meet business demand.

Good IT governance provides a structure to make good decisions. It can also limit the negative impact of organizational politics in IT-related decisions. IT governance has two major components: (1) assignment of decision-making authority and responsibility and (2) decision-making mechanisms (e.g., steering committees, review boards, policies). When it comes specifically to IT governance, Weill and his colleagues proposed five generally applicable categories of IT decisions: IT principles, IT architecture, IT infrastructure strategies, business application needs, and IT investment and prioritization.[11] A description of these decision categories with an example of major IS activities affected by them is provided in Figure 9.5.

Weill and Ross's study of 256 enterprises shows that a defining trait of high-performing companies is the use of proper decision right allocation patterns for each of the five major categories of IT decisions. They use six political archetypes with highly descriptive names (business monarchy, IT monarchy, feudal, federal, IT duopoly, and anarchy) to label the combinations of people who either input information or have decision rights for the key

[10] Peter Weill and Jeanne W. Ross, *IT Governance: How Top Performers Manage IT Decision Rights for Superior Results* (Cambridge, MA: Harvard Business School Press, 2004); Peter Weill, "Don't Just Lead, Govern: How Top-Performing Firms Govern IT," *MIS Quarterly Executive* 3, no. 1 (2004), 1–17. The quote is on page 3.

[11] P. Weill, "Don't Just Lead, Govern: How Top-Performing Firms Govern IT," *MIS Quarterly Executive* 3, no. 1 (2004).

		Accountability	
		Low	High
Decision Rights	High	**Technocentric gap** • There is danger of overspending on IT, creating an oversupply • IT assets may not be utilized to meet business demand • Business group might become frustrated with IT group	**Strategic norm (Level 3 balance)** • IT is viewed as competent • IT is viewed as strategic to business
	Low	**Support norm (Level 1 balance)** • It works for organizations where IT is viewed as a support function • Its focus is on business efficiency	**Business gap** • Cost considerations dominate IT decision • IT assets may not utilize internal competencies to meet business demand • IT group might cause frustration for business group

FIGURE 9.4 IS Decision rights accountability gap.
Source: Adapted from V. Grover, R. M. Henry, and J. B. Thatcher, "Fix IT-Business Relationships through Better Decision Rights," *Communications of the ACM* 50, no. 12 (December 2007), 82, Figure 1.

Category	Description	Examples of Affected IS Activities
IT principles	How to determine IT assets that are needed	Participating in setting strategic direction
IT architecture	How to structure IT assets	Establishing architecture and standards
IT infrastructure strategies	How to build IT assets	Managing Internet and network services, data, human resources, mobile computing
Business application needs	How to acquire, implement, and maintain IT (insource or outsource)	Developing and maintaining information systems
IT investment and prioritization	How much to invest and where to invest in IT assets	Anticipating new technologies

FIGURE 9.5 Five major categories of IT decisions.
Source: Adapted from P. Weill, "Don't Just Lead, Govern: How Top-Performing Firms Govern IT," *MIS Quarterly Executive* 3, no. 1 (2004), 4, Figure 2.

IT decisions.[12] An **archetype** is a pattern resulting from allocation of decision rights. Decisions can be made at several levels in the organization: top executives, IT executives, or business unit executives. Figure 9.6 summarizes the level and function for the allocation of decision rights in each archetype.

For each decision category, the organization adopts an archetype as the means to obtain inputs for decisions and to assign accountability for them. Although there is little variation in the selection of archetypes regarding who provides information for decision making, there is significant variation across organizations in terms of archetypes selected for decision right allocation. For instance, the duopoly is used by the largest portion (36%) of organizations for IT principles decisions whereas the IT monarchy is the most popular for IT architecture and infrastructure decisions (i.e., 73% and 59%, respectively).[13]

There is no one best arrangement for the allocation of decision rights. Rather, the most appropriate arrangement depends on a number of factors, including the type of performance indicator. Some common performance indicators are asset utilization, profit, or growth.

[12] Peter Weill and Jeanne W. Ross, *IT Governance: How Top Performers Manage IT Decision Rights for Superior Results* (Cambridge, MA: Harvard Business School Press, 2004).
[13] Weill and Ross, *IT Governance.*

Decision rights or inputs rights for a particular IT decision are held by:		CxO Level Execs	Corp. IT and/or Business Unit IT	Business Unit Leaders or Process Owners
Business Monarchy	A group of, or individual, business executives (i.e., CxOs). Includes committees comprised of senior business executives (may include CIO). Excludes IT executives acting independently.	✓		
IT monarchy	Individuals or groups of IT executives.		✓	
Feudal	Business unit leaders, key process owners or their delegates.			✓
Federal	C level executives and at least one other business group (e.g., CxO and BU leaders)—IT executives may be an additional participant. Equivalent to a country and its states working together.	✓	✓	✓
		✓		✓
IT duopoly	IT executives and one other group (e.g., CxO or BU leaders).	✓	✓	
			✓	✓
Anarchy	Each individual user.			

FIGURE 9.6 IT governance archetypes.
Source: P. Weill, "Don't Just Lead, Govern: How Top-Performing Firms Govern IT," *MIS Quarterly Executive* 3, no. 1 (2004), 5, Figure 3.

Emergent Governance—The Digital Ecosystem

New consumer technologies challenge a "top-down" governance approach for making all decisions in a planned and methodical manner. The best-laid plans are often derailed. Intel's decree to lock down data and strictly control devices used by employees grew so difficult that it impeded the company's ability to not only compete but also to fulfill everyday tasks. Sometimes the best plans aren't even prescribed far in advance; in some situations, they simply emerge. For instance, social networking was ignored by many firms in its early days because they failed to recognize its impact. Most firms now realize that social networking needs not only recognition but also strategic investments.

There are many freely available and widely used apps, Web sites, social networks, smartphones, and other IT assets; it would be foolish to try to invent something identical in house, so firms often exploit them. Using a variety of such assets implies that governance might need to be more flexible and follow patterns of adaptation much like biological ecosystems, forming an interrelated set of interacting species.[14] Just as a species cannot ignore predators, prey, and complementary species, an information systems department cannot ignore new technologies and information assets that emerge suddenly and unexpectedly. One interesting definition of **digital ecosystem** regards those systems as self-interested, self-organizing, and autonomous digital entities.[15]

A simple example can be useful. Before YouTube, firms had to find their own way to provide digital video content to customers on the Web. Some used animations that were available in special image formats whereas others had to choose between requiring a download of a video file that they hoped would be playable on a user's computer or streaming a file to users who had to also install a particular streaming player that was compatible with the streaming video. Providing that content widely was not generally considered to be feasible or even desirable. With YouTube, firms can now simply use a link or even embed the video into their own Web site. Coupling this

[14] Maja Hadzic and Elizabeth Chang, "Application of Digital Ecosystem Design Methodology within the Health Domain," *IEEE Transactions on Systems, Man and Cybernetics, Part A: Systems and Humans* 40, no. 4 (2010): 779–88.
[15] Rahnuma Kazi and Ralph Deters, "Mobile Event-Oriented Digital Ecosystem," *Digital Ecosystems Technologies (DEST), 2012 6th IEEE International Conference* (2012).

new simplicity with an ability to display a map from Google Maps forms new and very useful interdependencies between these digital assets.

In recent years, mobile computing, GPS, and social media have indeed presented new, unexpected challenges and opportunities as described earlier. However, other technological developments have also provided digital ecosystem opportunities, such as cloud computing, the Internet of Things (IoT), radio frequency ID (RFID), and smart cards. Interconnecting firms with each other allows connectivity in new, unpredictable, and very helpful ways.

A good example in the health care arena is an electronic medical record (EMR).[16] An EMR is filled with a variety of information about a patient (for instance, patient demographics, appointments, medications, medical history, billing records). Not only can a doctor's computer pick out the relevant information about a patient to use but also a pharmacy can identify potential drug interactions and a laboratory can be informed of certain medical conditions when processing a specimen. In addition, both the pharmacy process and the insurance company can bill for the medication and the appointment.

Some or all of these functions could have been in the original plans for EMRs, but others might occur to enterprising designers along the way. For instance, a bank that is administering the patient's flexible spending account can be provided medical billing information for properly disbursing funds. Also, a tax authority might be provided billing information from the EMR to verify deductible expenses. Each party would be privy only to the relevant information for it, and the rest would be kept confidential.

A smartphone provides another example of how a digital ecosystem can form between applications, firms, and digital entities. Even just the junction of identity, date, location, preference, and relationship information can provide real-time driving directions, invitations to nearby events, alerts about nearby friends, personalized advertising, and chatter on social network alerts. Many of these uses were not even imagined 15 years ago, and it is hard to imagine the possible new connections and uses that will occur in another 15 years. For instance, new ecosystem connections will be made possible when the IoT places more technology into automobiles. A self-driving car could actually react independently to an urgent situation with a family member and safely make a split-second decision to change course before all of the information is fully comprehended by the occupant (formerly called the "driver"). Individual devices and applications that are difficult to imagine today might be combined in new ways on the road, in the home, and at the office.

Strong governance implications emerge from ecosystems. The symbiotic multifirm and adaptive situations cannot be completely planned or orchestrated by a single entity. Much of the decision making exists outside the firm, and, therefore, complete plans no longer can be made in a single boardroom. Along with the good news of synergies between with and among various "apps" and devices, there is the potential danger of changes to the information passed between them or even the complete failure of an outside entity. Imagine what hotels would need to do if Google Maps would disappear altogether. Further, what would need to be done with location-based ads if predictions come true that one or more of the GPS satellites would fail[17] and are also vulnerable to attack?[18]

Fortunately, most ecosystems have adopted stringent standards for data exchange, and the most useful ones are quite successful. The likelihood of a permanent failure of Google Maps is quite remote for the foreseeable future. Even if Google were to divest the app, a new firm would likely be able to maintain the tightly specified connections. IT governance is perhaps most vulnerable to an inability to imagine strategic potential from new devices, applications, and connections. A firm should explore whether plans can be changed in mid-year. Can competitors become allies? Can business processes be changed quickly? Can new capabilities that might be contrary to previous activities or directions be enabled? Firms in the future will probably need to answer all of these questions in the affirmative for their ultimate survival.

To summarize the three governance frameworks, see Figure 9.7 for the main concept and potential best practice of each framework.

[16] Hadzic and Chang, "Application of Digital Ecosystem Design Methodology within the Health Domain."

[17] "GPS System Close to Breakdown," http://www.theguardian.com/technology/2009/may/19/gps-close-to-breakdown (accessed September 4, 2015).

[18] "Global Positioning System Is a Single Point of Failure," http://www.afcea.org/content/?q=global-positioning-system%E2%80%A8-single-point-failure (accessed September 4, 2015).

Governance Framework	Main Concept	Possible Best Practice
Centralization-Decentralization	Decisions can be made by a central authority or by autonomous individuals or groups in an organization.	Use a hybrid, federal approach.
Decision archetypes	Patterns based upon allocating decision rights and accountability are specified.	Tailor the archetype to the situation.
Digital ecosystems	Members of the ecosystem contribute their strengths, giving the whole ecosystem a complete set of capabilities that can impact decision making and operations.	Build flexibility and adaptability into governance.

FIGURE 9.7 Three governance frameworks.

Decision-Making Mechanisms

Many different types of mechanisms can be created to ensure good IT governance. Policies are useful for defining the process of making a decision under certain situations. However, when the environment is complex, policies are often too rigid. In a recent worldwide study of IT governance, almost 60% of the respondents relied on policies and standards for governance, making it the most popular mechanism for governance.[19] A second method, a **review board**, or committee that is formally designated to approve, monitor, and review specific topics, can be an effective governance mechanism. For example, Twila Day, CIO of Sysco, established an architecture review board to look at new technologies and processes.[20]

A third mechanism that is used very frequently for IT decisions is the **IT steering committee**, also called an IT *governance council*. Such a committee is composed of key stakeholders or experts who provide guidance on important IT issues. Steering committees work especially well with the federal archetype, which calls for joint participation of IT and business leaders in the decision-making process. Steering committees can be geared toward different levels of decision making. The highest level of steering committees report to the board of directors or the CEO and are often composed of top-level executives and the CIO. At this level, the steering committee provides strategic direction and funding authority for major IT projects and ensures that adequate resources be allocated to the IS organization for achieving strategic goals.

Committees with lower-level players typically are involved with allocating scarce resources effectively and efficiently. Lower-level steering committees provide a forum for business leaders to present their IT needs and to offer input and direction about the support they receive from IT operations.

Either level may have working groups to help increase the steering committee's effectiveness and to measure the performance of the IS organization. The assessment of performance differs for each group. For example, the lower-level committee likely would include more details and would focus on the progress of the various projects and adherence to the budget. The higher-level committee would focus on the performance of the CIO and the ability of the IS organization to contribute to the company's achievement of its strategic goals.

Although an organization may have both levels of steering committees, it is more likely to have one or the other. If the IS organization is viewed as being critical for the organization to achieve its strategic goals, the firm's C-level executives are likely to be on the committee. Otherwise, the steering committee tends to be larger so that it can have widespread representation from the various business units. In this case, the steering committee is an excellent mechanism for helping the business units realize the competing benefits of proposed IT projects and develop an approach for allocating among the project requests.

[19] IT Governance Institute, "Global Status Report on the Governance of Enterprise IT (GEIT)" (2011), 49, http://www.isaca.org/Knowledge-Center/Research/Documents/Global-Status-Report-GEIT-10Jan2011-Research.pdf (accessed February 27, 2011).

[20] Martha Heller, "*How to Make Time for Strategy*," CIO.com (April 22, 2010), http://www.cio.com/article/591719/How_to_Make_Time_for_Strategy (accessed January 16, 2012).

For example, when Hilton Worldwide's CIO started working on a project to create a new loyalty program, he and the business sponsor of the project convened a lower-level steering committee made up of people from IT, marketing, HR, finance, and other departments. They discussed change management and business issues that arose as they designed the system to be used in 85 countries in over ten brands in the Hilton portfolio. The project went very smoothly. But earlier, another project to outsource the hotel help desk had not gone as well. The CIO learned from both experiences that there is no such thing as too much communication and created weekly steering committee meetings for each project. The CIO is quoted as saying, "E-mail is great for scheduling meetings, but it's the steering committees where we are working through really difficult issues together, and making promises and keeping promises, where the foundations of trust are established."[21]

Governance Frameworks for Control Decisions

The framework described previously focuses on which department is responsible for decisions. More recently, governance frameworks have been employed specifically to define responsibility for control decisions. They are being implemented to help ward off future accounting fiascos. These frameworks focus on processes and risks associated with them.

Sarbanes–Oxley Act of 2002

In response to rogue accounting activity by major global corporations such as Enron and WorldCom and their accounting firms, such as Arthur Andersen, the **Sarbanes–Oxley Act (SoX)** was enacted in the United States in 2002 to increase regulatory visibility and accountability of public companies and their financial health. The U.S. government wanted to assure the investing public that they could rely on financial markets to deliver valid performance data and accurate stock valuation. All corporations that fall under the jurisdiction of the U.S. Securities and Exchange Commission are subject to SoX requirements. This includes not only U.S. and foreign companies that are traded on U.S. exchanges but also those entities that make up a significant part of a U.S. company's financial reporting. Within five years of SoX's passage, 15,000 U.S. companies, 1,200 non-U.S.-based companies. and over 1,400 accounting firms in 76 countries have been affected by SoX.[22]

According to SoX, CFOs and CEOs must personally certify and be accountable for their firms' financial records and accounting (Section 302), auditors must certify the underlying controls and processes that are used to compile the financial results of a company (Section 404), and companies must provide real-time disclosures of any events that may affect their stock price or financial performance within a 48-hour period (Section 409). Penalties for failing to comply range from monetary fines to a 20-year jail term.

A comprehensive Public Company Accounting Oversight Board (PCAOB) review of 2,800 engagements of the largest audit firms found hundreds of cases involving audit failures, suggesting that improvements could be made in audit firm performance as well as the PCAOB's process for assessing and reporting on engagements. However, the review reported that SoX has been successful in increasing corporate focus on a strong ethical culture in publicly owned companies.[23]

Although SoX was not originally aimed at IT departments, it soon became clear that IT played a major role in raising the accuracy of financial data. Consequently, in 2004 and 2005, there was a flurry of activity as IT managers

---

[21] Adapted from "Candid Talk Trumps the Blame Game," CIO.com (November 2011), http://www.cio.com/article/693018/Candid_Talk_Trumps_the_Blame_Game (accessed September 4, 2015); "How CIOs Build Bridges with Other C-Level Execs," CIO.com (November 2011), http://www.cio.com/article/2402725/relationship-building-networking/how-cios-build-bridges-with-other-c-level-execs.html (accessed September 4, 2015).

[22] These figures were derived from the Public Company Accounting Oversight Board (PCAOB) as reported in Ashley Braganza and Arnoud Franken, "SoX, Compliance, and Power Relationships," *Communications of the ACM* 50, no. 9 (September 2007), 97–102.

[23] Curtis Vershoor, "Has SoX Been Successful," September 5, 2012, http://www.accountingweb.com/article/has-sox-been-successful/219796 (accessed March 27, 2015).

identified controls, determined design effectiveness, and validated operational controls through testing. Five IT control weaknesses repeatedly were uncovered by auditors:[24]

1. Failure to segregate duties within applications, set up new accounts, and terminate old ones in a timely manner.
2. Lack of proper oversight for making application changes, including appointing a person to make a change and another to perform quality assurance on it.
3. Inadequate review of audit logs to ensure that systems are running smoothly and that there is an audit of the audit log.
4. Failure to identify abnormal transactions in a timely manner.
5. Lack of understanding of key system configurations.

Although SoX's focus is on financial controls, many auditors encouraged (forced) IT managers to extend their focus to organizational controls and risks in business processes. This means that IT managers must assess the level of controls needed to mitigate potential risks in organizational business processes. As companies move beyond SoX certification into maintaining compliance, IT managers must be involved in ongoing and consistent risk identification, actively recognize and monitor changes to the IS organization and environment that may affect SoX compliance, and continuously improve IS process maturity. It is likely that managers will turn to software to automate many of the needed controls.

Frameworks for Implementing SoX

COSO

The Enron and WorldCom major financial scandals were not the first. In the wake of financial scandals in the mid-1980s, the Treadway Commission (or National Commission on Fraudulent Financial Reporting) was created. Its head, James Treadway, had previously served as commissioner of the SEC. The members of the Treadway Commission came from five highly esteemed accounting organizations: Financial Executives International (FEI), American Accounting Association (AAA), American Institute of Certified Public Accountants (AICPA), Institute of Internal Auditors (IIA), and Institute of Management Accountants (IMA). These organizations became known as the *Committee of Sponsoring Organizations of the Treadway Commission (COSO)*. The commission created three control objectives for management and auditors that focused on addressing risks to internal control. These control objectives deal with:

- *Operations:* To help the company maintain and improve its operating effectiveness and protect the assets of shareholders
- *Compliance:* To ensure that the company is in compliance with relevant laws and regulations
- *Financial reporting:* To ensure that the company's financial statements are produced in accordance with generally accepted accounting principles (GAAP). *SoX is focused on this control objective.*

To make sure a company meets its control objectives, COSO established five essential control components for managers and auditors: (1) create a control environment that addresses the overall culture of the company; (2) assess the most critical risks to internal controls; (3) create control structures that outline important processes and guidelines; (4) provide clear information about employees' responsibilities and procedures to be followed; and (5) monitor internal controls. The Sarbanes–Oxley Act requires public companies to define their control framework and specifically recommends COSO as that business framework for general accounting controls. It is not IT specific.

[24] Ben Worthen, "The Top Five IT Control Weaknesses" (July 1, 2005), http://www.cio.com/article/2448687/project-management/the-top-five-it-control-weaknesses.html (accessed September 4, 2015).

COBIT

Control Objectives for Information and Related Technology (COBIT) COBIT (Control Objectives for Information and Related Technology) is an IT governance framework that is consistent with COSO controls, and also a governance tool to ensure that IT provides the systematic rigor needed for the strong internal controls and Sarbanes–Oxley compliance. It provides a framework for linking IT processes, IT resources, and IT information to a company's strategies and objectives. As a governance framework, it provides guidelines about who in the organization should make decisions about IT processes, resources, and information.

Information Systems Audit & Control Association (ISACA) issued COBIT in 1996. COBIT consists of several overlapping sets of guidance with multiple components, which almost form a cascade of process goals, metrics, and practices. At the highest level, key areas of risks are defined in four major domains: planning and organization, acquisition and implementation, delivery and support, and monitoring and evaluating. When implementing a COBIT framework, a company determines the processes that are the most susceptible to the risks that it judiciously chooses to manage. There are far too many risks for a company to try to manage all of them.

Once the company identifies processes that it is going to manage, it sets up a control objective and then more specific key goal indicators. As with any control system, metrics called *key performance indicators (KPIs)* need to be established to enable measurement of progress in meeting the goals. Then activities to achieve the KPIs are selected. These activities, or *critical success factors,* are the steps that need to be followed to successfully provide controls for a selected process. When a company wants to compare itself with other organizations, it uses a well-defined maturity model. The components of COBIT and examples of each component are provided in Figure 9.8.

One advantage of COBIT is that it is well suited to organizations focused on risk management and mitigation. Another advantage is that it is very detailed. However, this high level of detail unfortunately can serve as a disadvantage in the sense that it makes COBIT very costly and time consuming to implement. Yet, despite the costs, companies are starting to realize benefits from its implementation. As a governance framework, it designates clear ownership and responsibility for key organizational processes in such a way that is understood by all organizational

Component	Description	Example
Domain	One of four major areas of risk: plan and organize (PO), acquire and implement (AI), deliver and support (DS), and monitor and evaluate (ME); each domain consists of multiple processes	Deliver and support (or DS)
Control objective	Focus on control of a process associated with risk; can be 34 processes	DS (deliver and support) objective #11—Manage data: ensures delivery of complete, accurate, and valid data to the business
Key goal indicator	Specific measures of the extent to which the goals of the system have been met in regard to a control objective	A measured reduction in the data preparation process and tasks
Key performance indicator	Actual, highly specific measures for measuring accomplishment of a goal	Percent of data input errors (Note: percentage should decrease over specified periods of time)
Critical success factor	Description of the steps that a company must take to accomplish a control objective; can be 318 critical success factors	Data entry requirements clearly stated, enforced, and supported by automated techniques at all levels, including database and file interfaces
Maturity model	A uniquely defined six-point ranking of a company's readiness for each control objective made in comparison with other companies in the industry	Level 0: Data not recognized as corporate resources and assets; no assigned data ownership or individual accountability for data integrity and reliability; data quality and security poor or nonexistent

FIGURE 9.8 Components of COBIT and their examples.
Source: Adapted from Hugh Taylor, *The Joy of SoX* (Indianapolis, IN: Wiley, 2006).

stakeholders. Consistent with the Information Systems Strategy Triangle discussed in Chapter 1, COBIT provides a formal framework for aligning IS strategy with the business strategy. It does so by using a governance framework and focusing on risks of internal control and associated processes to recognize who is responsible for important control decisions. Finally, COBIT makes possible the fulfillment of the COSO requirements for the IT control environment that is encouraged by the Sarbanes–Oxley Act.

Other Control Frameworks

Although COBIT is the most common set of IT control guidelines for SoX, it is by no means the only control framework. Others include those provided by the International Standards Organization (ISO), as well as the **Information Technology Infrastructure Library (ITIL).** A set of concepts and techniques for managing information technology infrastructure, development, and operations, ITIL was developed in the United Kingdom. It is a widely recognized framework for IT service management and operations management that has been adopted around the globe. ITIL 2011 has five distinct volumes: service strategy; service design; service transition; service operation; and continual service improvement.

IS and the Implementation of Sarbanes–Oxley Act Compliance

Because of the level of detail, the involvement of the IS department and the CIO in implementing SoX—most notably Section 404, which deals with management's assessment of internal controls—is considerable. Although the IS department typically plays a major role in SoX compliance, it often lacks formal authority. Thus, the CIO needs to tread carefully when working with auditors, the CFO, the CEO, and business leaders. Braganza and Franken provide six tactics that CIOs can use in working effectively in these relationships. These strategies include knowledge building, knowledge deployment, innovation directive, mobilization, standardization, and subsidy. Figure 9.9 provides a definition for each of these tactics, along with examples of activities to enact them.

Tactic	Definition	Examples of Activities
Knowledge building	Establish a knowledge base to implement SoX	Acquire technical knowledge about SoX and Section 404
Knowledge deployment	Disseminate knowledge about SoX and develop an understanding of this knowledge by management and other organizational members	Move IT staff with knowledge of 404 to parts of the organization that are less knowledgeable; create a central repository of 404 knowledge; absorb 404 requirements from external bodies; conduct training programs to spread an understanding of SoX
Innovation directive	Organize for implementing SoX and announce the approach	Issue instructions that encourage the adoption of 404 compliance practices; publish reports of each unit's progress toward implementation; deploy drivers for implementation; direct implementation from top down and/or bottom up
Mobilization	Persuade decentralized players and subsidiaries to participate in SoX implementation	Create a positive impression of SoX (and 404) implementation; conduct promotional and awareness campaigns
Standardization	Negotiate agreements between organizational members to facilitate the SoX implementation	Use mandatory controls, often embedded within the technology; indicate formal levels of compliance required; establish *firmwide* standards of control; create an overarching corporate compliance architecture
Subsidy	Fund the implementers' costs during the SoX implementation and the users' costs during its deployment and use	Centralize template development; develop Web-based resources; train IT staff for implementing 404; fund short-term skill gaps; track implementation; target funds during implementation for specific IT-related 404 goals

FIGURE 9.9 CIO tactics for implementing SoX compliance.
Source: Adapted from Ashley Braganza and Arnoud Franken, "SoX, Compliance, and Power Relationships," *Communications of the ACM* 50, no. 9 (September 2007), 97–102.

Social Business Lens: Governing the Content

Since the beginning of social applications like Facebook, Twitter, and Instagram, there has been a debate about who gets to decide on what's allowed to be posted. Should the users decide? Should the application company decide? This debate still rages today.

One perspective is that the users own and manage their content. Aside from the legal issues, which are discussed in Chapter 13 of this text, users have control over what they post and what they block from their pages on most social media. Most social networks have controls that allow users to block others from posting on their page, but it's not the default in most cases. For example, when a user tags another Facebook user in a post or photo, the content then also shows up on the tagged person's timeline. Even though a control can be set to minimize this, some have found it troublesome that items can be placed in their timeline in this manner. Most users feel that they should have control of their content on their social media page.

Now ratchet this up to the group level. Should the "crowd" decide what is appropriate to put on a social media site or should the company decide? The crowd has a say in some manner; members of the community can vote or "like" a post and in some cases, content with the most votes rises to the top for others to see.

But the social media company also has a say in what content is appropriate. Again, aside from content that crosses legal boundaries, which of course vary country by country, some companies have taken a stronger stance. For example, Instagram removed a number of users from its Web site for not following instructions. Its Web site plainly stated two new policies:

> We want Instagram to continue to be an authentic and safe place for inspiration and expression. Help us foster this community. Post only your own photos and videos and always follow the law. Respect everyone on Instagram, don't spam people or post nudity.*

> We want . . . to maintain the best possible experience on Instagram, so spam, fake accounts and other people and posts that don't follow our Community Guidelines may be removed from Instagram.†

*From Instagram's Community Guidelines, https://help.instagram.com/477434105621119/ (accessed May 22, 2015).
† From Instagram's Help Center, https://help.instagram.com/309501049246773 (accessed May 22, 2015).

Sources: "Chaos Ensues As Instagram Deletes Millions of Accounts," http://www.businessinsider.com/chaos-ensues-as-instagram-deletes-millions-of-accounts-2014-12#ixzz3MJXUmhlm (accessed September 4, 2015); and Instagram company website, www.instagram.com; "Instagram Users Report Mass Deletion of Profiles for 'violating' Terms of Service," http://tech.firstpost.com/news-analysis/instagram-users-report-mass-deletion-of-profiles-for-violating-terms-of-service-86660.html (accessed September 4, 2015); "Instagram Deletes Millions of Accounts in Spam Purge," http://www.bbc.com/news/technology-30548463 (accessed September 4, 2015).

The extent to which a CIO could use these various tactics depends on the power that he or she holds relating to the SoX implementation. Those few CIOs who are given carte blanche by their CEOs to implement SoX compliance can employ compelling activities, such as subsidy, standardization, and innovation directives. Those CIOs can establish standards and enforce their compliance, creating an overarching corporate compliance architecture. They can direct the SoX implementation from top down and put Section 404 implementation drivers in place. If, on the other hand, the CEO does not vest the CIO with the considerable power to employ such tactics, the CIO may need to take more of a persuasive stance and focus on training programs and building an electronic knowledge database of SoX documents. In this case, it is especially important to sell the CIO and CFO on the importance of complying with prescribed procedures and methods. In either situation, the CIO needs to acquire and manage the considerable IT resources to make SoX compliance a reality.

These new guidelines sound reasonable enough, but they are much more stringent than the previous set of guidelines they replaced. Instagram deleted not only thousands of accounts, which mostly involved spam and fake identities, but also others that the company deemed inappropriate. According to some sources, the crowd was not happy. A mass campaign to stop following Instagram's own official Instagram account followed, and that account lost 30% of its followers. Does the crowd govern the content or the company?

SUMMARY

- Alternative approaches to governance of information systems organization are possible. One approach is based on where IS decisions are made in the organization's structure. Centralized IS organizations place IT staff, hardware, software, and data in one location to promote control and efficiency. At the other end of the continuum, decentralized IS organizations with distributed resources can best meet the needs of local users. Federalism in IS organizations is in the middle of the centralization/decentralization continuum.
- A second governance approach involves decision rights. In this approach, IT governance specifies how to allocate decision rights in such a way as to encourage desirable behavior in the use of IT. The allocation of decision rights can be broken down into six archetypes (business monarchy, IT monarchy, feudal, federal, IT duopoly, and anarchy). High-performing companies use the proper decision rights allocation patterns for each of the five major categories of IT decisions.
- A third governance approach recognizes the power of combining complementary technologies in ways that were not predicted or controlled by an organization. This so-called digital ecosystem represents formal recognition of a firm's healthy adaptation and synergistic adoption to new hardware, applications, and connections with customers, employees, and other firms. Much of this has been driven by consumerization of technology.
- A fourth governance approach is based on controls. The Sarbanes–Oxley Act (2002) was enacted to improve organizations' internal controls. COBIT is an IT governance framework based on control that can be used to promote IT-related internal controls and Sarbanes–Oxley compliance.

KEY TERMS

archetype (p. 196)
centralized IS organizations (p. 193)
COBIT (Control Objectives for Information and Related Technology) (p. 202)
Consumerization (p. 191)
decentralized IS organizations (p. 193)
digital ecosystem (p. 197)
federalism (p. 194)
governance (p. 192)
Information Technology Infrastructure Library (ITIL) (p. 203)
IT governance (p. 195)
review board (p. 199)
Sarbanes–Oxley Act (SoX) (p. 200)
steering committee (p. 199)

DISCUSSION QUESTIONS

1. The debate about centralization and decentralization is heating up again with the advent of BYOD and the increasing use of the Web. Why does the Internet make this debate topical?
2. Why is the discussion of decision rights among managers in a firm important?
3. Why can an IT governance archetype be good for one type of IS decision but not for another?

CASE STUDY 9-1 IT Governance at University of the Southeast

University of the Southeast[25] was (and still is) one of the largest universities in the United States. It had been growing rapidly; that growth was spurred, in part, by information technology. The university embraced lecture capture technologies that allowed lectures to be streamed to students in a classroom, in dorm rooms, on the grass near the main campus central fountain, and at a variety of other places of the students' choosing whenever they chose to watch. This made it possible to have sections of classes with over 1,000 students without having to build physical classrooms with enough seats to accommodate each person enrolled. It also made it possible to offer classes that were streamed to students at remote campuses. Each student was charged a technology fee (i.e., $5.16 for undergraduates and $13.85 for graduates per credit hour each semester), which was administered by the Information Technologies and Resources (IT&R) Office to help fund the costs of providing IT to students and faculty.

[25] The name University of the Southeast is made up but the school and situation were real.

IT&R was responsible for providing computer services, technologies, and telecommunications across the campus (Computer Services and Technology), helping faculty with their instructional delivery and multimedia support (Office of Instructional Resources), helping faculty develop and deliver Web-based and lecture capture courses (Center for Distributed Learning), and the library. The IT&R Office developed IT-related policies with very little input from the faculty and was responsible for deciding and implementing decisions concerning IT architecture and infrastructure. IT&R worked with the university president and other top administrators in making IT investment decisions. IT&R staff also worked with the various colleges, administrative offices, and an advisory board in making decisions about applications that needed to be developed. However, faculty were not consulted at all when the lecture capture system was selected.

As was often the case at large universities, many decision rights on a wide range of issues had been allocated to the colleges. The College of Business Administration had its own server and Technology Support Department (TSD). A recent survey of faculty and staff in the college indicated a high level of satisfaction with the TSD but far less satisfaction with the services provided by the university-level IT&R. Some college respondents indicated their displeasure about IT&R's support of the technology for the lecture capture courses, help desk, and classroom technologies.

The problems with the technology support for lecture capture software were particularly troublesome. The software would not authenticate students who had paid to enroll in some lecture capture courses, making it impossible for them to download the lectures even though they were registered in the course. Further, some university-affiliated housing did not have adequate network bandwidth to allow students to download the lectures. When problems occurred—which they did on a daily basis—the IT&R help desk often referred the students to instructors who could not resolve their problems. One faculty member who was teaching a lecture class with 1,400 students exclaimed, "It is utter chaos for me when something goes wrong with the system and hundreds of my students are trying to call, see or email me in panic to get me to fix something that I can't fix."

To fix some of these issues, the CIO argued that all e-mail accounts should be placed on one central server. This would allow the IT&R greater control and make maintenance easier and more efficient. It also would considerably improve security. But it was not ideal for the faculty. A faculty meeting about e-mail revealed some concerns with this move. First, faculty wanted e-mails sent to the central university server to be forwarded to their accounts on their other university-based servers (i.e., the college, department, or institute servers) but found that this was impossible to do so. Second, faculty wanted to retain their control over archiving e-mails. Third, faculty wanted to have control over their preferred e-mail address. In some cases, the faculty e-mail addresses that they had used for a decade had been changed in the printed university directory to the e-mail address on the central university server without their knowledge. This meant that faculty did not receive (or even know about) messages sent to them via the address on the university server. They could not change the printed e-mail address in the university directory to the address on the college server that they had been using or forward the mail sent to the central server to a different account.

The IT&R spokesman said that having a centralized server for e-mail accounts was more secure, reliable and efficient. He said that faculty shouldn't have control over their preferred e-mail address, even if it were on a campus server, because of the identity management problems that it would create. A frustrated faculty member at the meeting asked the IT&R spokesman to describe one time when issues about ease of use and functionality of the system by the user were weighted more than security in decisions about e-mail. The IT&R spokesman could not think of an example.

Discussion Questions

1. Describe the IT governance system that was in place at the University of the Southeast using both decision rights and structure as the bases of governance.
2. The CIO wanted to implement a centralized IT governance system. As demonstrated in this case, what are the advantages of a centralized IT governance system? What are the disadvantages?
3. In your opinion, what assignment of decision rights would be best for University of the Southeast? Please explain.

CASE STUDY 9-2 The "MyJohnDeere" Platform

"The customer is in control of the data and can share with dealers, crop consultants, and anyone in their network of trusted advisers; securely, from any internet enabled device," says Chris Batdorf, a marketing manager at John Deere.[26] The MyJohnDeere project was designed with the realization that there was synergy in linking together disparate sources of information into this "platform."[27]

Who would be interested in using this application? You might expect that John Deere customers and employees would be the only parties. But according to Accenture, a multinational management consulting, technology services, and outsourcing company, John Deere realized that there was value in opening access to its system to farmers, ranchers, landowners, banks, and government workers. The platform is useful for all those people because it integrates information about equipment, production data, and farm operations and helps users improve their profitability.[28]

A farmer described how the John Deere Operations Center allowed him to upload a treasure trove of data about planting, spraying, fertilizing, and harvesting. He said that he accessed that information later not only to diagnose problems about the equipment but also to make decisions about the use of land and personnel. He said that he can send that information to consultants for real-time recommendations on what to change even while he was harvesting.[29]

A platform such as MyJohnDeere could introduce new capabilities that can provide strategic value to customers, other firms, and, of course, its host. According to Accenture, the platform integrated the Internet of Things with social, mobile, analytics, and cloud technology. The combination encouraged the development of new applications over time and represented a recent pivotal technology trend. Such a platform provided reusable components that can evolve over time.[30]

Discussion Questions

1. What governance approach did John Deere appear to have adopted? Did it fit the profile of an "old" heavy industry player?
2. What difficulties do you think an "old" heavy industry player such as John Deere encountered internally when proposing to develop the MyJohnDeere platform?
3. What difficulties do you believe John Deere faced externally among the proposed users?
4. How do you think John Deere might have overcome those internal and external difficulties?
5. What other parties might have been interested in obtaining the information in John Deere's cloud? What might they have done with it?

Sources: Adapted from John Deere press release, "The MyJohnDeere Operations Center—New Tools to Manage Data" (August 21, 2014), https://www.deere.com/en_US/corporate/our_company/news_and_media/press_releases/2014/agriculture/2014aug21_mjd_operations_center.page (accessed September 4, 2015); Cindy Zimmerman, "MyJohnDeere Operations Center Connectivity" (March 2, 2015); http://precision.agwired.com/2015/03/02/myjohndeere-operations-center-connectivity/ (accessed September 4, 2015); and William Lesieur, "Proliferating Digital Ecosystems through 'The Platform (R)evolution'—Accenture Technology Vision 2015," http://www.accenture.com/us-en/blogs/technology-blog/archive/2015/01/26/proliferating-digital-ecosystems-through-the-platform-%28R%29evolution-acn-technology-vision-2015.aspx (accessed September 4, 2015).

[26] https://www.deere.com/en_US/corporate/our_company/news_and_media/press_releases/2014/agriculture/2014aug21_mjd_operations_center.page (accessed September 4, 2015).

[27] http://www.accenture.com/us-en/blogs/technology-blog/archive/2015/01/26/proliferating-digital-ecosystems-through-the-platform-%28R%29evolution-acn-technology-vision-2015.aspx (accessed September 4, 2015).

[28] Ibid.

[29] http://precision.agwired.com/2015/03/02/myjohndeere-operations-center-connectivity/ (accessed September 4, 2015).

[30] http://www.accenture.com (accessed September 4, 2015).

chapter

10 Information Systems Sourcing

This chapter is organized around decisions in the Sourcing Decision Cycle. The first question regarding information systems (IS) in the cycle relates to the decision to *make* (insource) or *buy* (outsource) them. This chapter's focus is on issues related to outsourcing whereas issues related to insourcing are discussed in other chapters of this book. Discussed are the critical decisions in the Sourcing Decision Cycle: *how* and *where* (cloud computing, onshoring, offshoring). When the choice is offshoring, the next decision is *where abroad* (farshoring, nearshoring, or captive centers). Explored next in this chapter is the final decision in the cycle, *keep as is or change* in which case the current arrangements are assessed and modifications are made to the outsourcing arrangement, a new outsourcing provider is selected, or the operations and services are backsourced, or brought back in house. Risks and strategies to mitigate risks are discussed at each stage of the cycle.

After 13 years, Kellwood, an American apparel maker, ended its soups-to-nuts IS outsourcing arrangement with EDS. The primary focus of the original outsourcing contract was to integrate 12 individually acquired units with different systems into one system. Kellwood had been satisfied enough with EDS's performance to renegotiate the contract in 2002 and 2008, even though at each renegotiation point, Kellwood had considered bringing the IS operations back in house, or backsourcing. The 2008 contract iteration resulted in a more flexible $105 million contract that EDS estimated would save Kellwood $2 million in the first year and $9 million over the remaining contract years. But the situation at Kellwood had changed drastically. In 2008, Kellwood had been purchased by Sun Capital Partners and taken private. The chief operating officer (COO), who was facing a mountain of debt and possibly bankruptcy, wanted to consolidate and bring the operations back in house to give some order to the current situation and reduce costs. Kellwood was suffering from a lack of IS standardization as a result of its many acquisitions. The chief information officer (CIO) recognized the importance of IS standardization and costs, but she was concerned that the transition from outsourcing to insourcing would cause serious disruption to IS service levels and project deadlines if it went poorly. Kellwood hired a third-party consultant to help it explore the issues and decided that backsourcing would save money and respond to changes caused by both the market and internal forces. Kellwood decided to backsource and started the process in late 2009. It carefully planned for the transition, and the implementation went smoothly. By performing streamlined operations in house, it was able to report an impressive $3.6 million savings, or about 17% of annual IS expenses after the first year.[1]

The Kellwood case demonstrates a series of decisions made in relation to sourcing. Both the decision to outsource IS operations and then to bring them back in house were based on a series of

[1] For more information see Stephanie Overby, "Company Saves Millions by Ending Outsourcing Deal," CIO.com, http://www.cio.com/article/549463/Company_Saves_Millions_By_Ending_IT_Outsourcing_Deal?page=1&taxonomyId=3195 (accessed January 31, 2012); B. Bacheldor, "Kellwood Stayed on Top of Its Outsourcing All the Way to the End," CIO.com, http://blogs.cio.com/beth_bacheldor/kellwood_stayed_ on_top_of_its_outsourcing_all_the_way_to_the_end?page=0 (accessed February 10, 2012).

factors. These factors, similar to those used by many companies in their sourcing decisions, are discussed later in this chapter. The global outsourcing market has been growing steadily. Companies of all sizes pursue outsourcing arrangements, and many multimillion-dollar deals have been widely publicized. As more companies adopt outsourcing as a means of controlling IS costs and acquiring "best-of-breed" capabilities, managing these supplier relationships has become increasingly important. IS departments must maximize the benefit of these relationships to the enterprise and pre-empt problems that might occur. Failure in this regard could result in deteriorating quality of service, loss of competitive advantage, costly contract disputes, low morale, and loss of key personnel.

How IS services are provided to a firm has become an important strategic and tactical discussion. As briefly mentioned in Chapter 6, there are numerous alternatives to sourcing computing power, applications, and infrastructure. This chapter examines the sourcing cycle to consider the full range of decisions related to who should perform the IS work of an organization. The cycle begins with a decision to make or buy information services and products. Once the decision to make or buy has been finalized, a series of questions must be answered about where and how these services should be delivered or products developed. The discussion in this chapter is built around the Sourcing Decision Cycle framework discussed in the next section. Considering the answers to sourcing questions can help explain a number of terms associated with sourcing: *insourcing, outsourcing, cloud computing, full outsourcing, selective outsourcing, multisourcing, onshoring, offshoring, nearshoring, farshoring,* and *backsourcing*. For each type of sourcing decision, the risks, or likelihood of something negative occurring as a result of the decision, are discussed, and some steps that can be taken to manage the risks are proposed.

Sourcing Decision Cycle Framework

Sourcing does not really just involve only one decision. It involves many decisions. The rest of this chapter is built around the critical sourcing decisions shown in Figure 10.1. Many of the chapter headings are tied to key decisions in Figure 10.1. Although the Sourcing Decision Cycle starts anywhere, we choose to start with the original make-or-buy decision. If an organization decides to "make," that means that it plans to create and run its own applications. "Buy," on the other hand, means the organization plans to obtain its applications from an outside

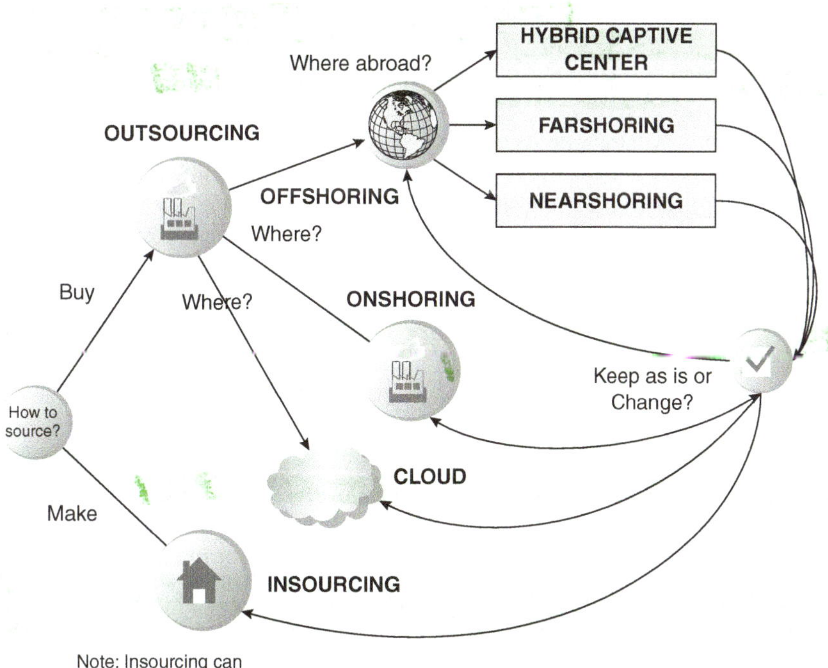

FIGURE 10.1 Sourcing Decision Cycle framework.

vendor or vendors. When the "buy" option is selected, the organization becomes a client company that must then decide on "how" and "where" to outsource. The answers to the "how" question include the scope of the outsourcing and the steps that should be taken to ensure its success. The answers to the "where" question focus on whether the client company should work with an outsourcing provider (i.e., vendor) in its own country, offshore, or in a cloud. If the client company decides to go offshore because labor is cheaper or needed skills are more readily available, it must make another decision: It must decide whether it wants the work done in a country that is relatively nearby or in a country that is quite distant. Finally, the client company chooses an outsourcing provider (or decides to do its own IS work). After a while, the client company faces another decision. It periodically must evaluate the sourcing arrangement and see whether a change is in order. If the in house work is unsatisfactory or other opportunities that are preferable to the current arrangement have become available, then the client company may turn to outsourcing. If, on the other hand, the outsourcing arrangement is unsatisfactory, the client company has several options to consider: to correct any existing problems and continue outsourcing with its current provider, to outsource with another provider, or to backsource. If the company decides to make a change in its sourcing arrangements at this point, the Sourcing Decision Cycle starts over again.

Starting the Cycle: The Make-or-Buy Sourcing Decision

Managers decide whether to make or buy information services and products. The products can include an application or a system, and services can range from help desk support, telecommunications, running data centers, and even implementing and operating business processes as in business process outsourcing (BPO). A simple "make" decision often involves insourcing some or all of the business's IS infrastructure, and a simple "buy" decision often involves outsourcing, although it could also include purchasing packaged software. In its simplest form, the make-or-buy decision hinges on whether to insource ("make") or outsource ("buy").

Insourcing

The most traditional approach to sourcing is **insourcing**, or providing IS services or developing them in the company's own in house IS organization and/or in its local cloud. Several "yes" answers to the questions posed in Figure 10.2 favor the decision to insource. Probably the most common reason is to keep core competencies in house. Managers are concerned that if they outsource a core competency, they risk losing control over it or losing contact with suppliers who can help them remain innovative in relation to that competency. Failing to control the competency or stay innovative is a sure way to forfeit a company's competitive advantage. On the other hand, by outsourcing commodity work, a firm can concentrate on its core competencies. Other factors that weigh in favor of insourcing are having an IS service or product that requires considerable security, confidentiality, or adequate resources in house (e.g., time to complete the project with current staffing or IS professionals with the needed skills and training).

In some companies, the IS function is underappreciated by top management. As long as everything is running smoothly, top managers may not notice the work done by or appreciate the services and products of the IS organization. Often an IS department that insources has found it necessary to compete for resources differently than if it outsources. It is necessary for the department to have enough respect and support from top management to acquire resources and get the department's job done. A major risk of insourcing is that the complexities of running IS in house requires management attention and resources that might better serve the company if focused on other value-added activities.

Captive centers are a new variation of insourcing. A **captive center** is an overseas subsidiary that is created to serve its main "client," the parent company, but it may serve other clients as well. Firms have set up such subsidiaries to operate like an outsourcing provider, but the firms actually own the subsidiaries. They are launched in less expensive locations, usually away from the company's headquarters or major operating units. The three most common types of captive centers are basic, shared, and hybrid.[2] The *basic captive center* provides services only to the parent firm. The *shared captive center* performs work for both a parent company and external customers.

[2] I. Oshri, J. Kotalarsky and C.-M. Liew, "What to Do with Your Captive Center: Four Strategic Options," *The Wall Street Journal* (May 12, 2008), http://www.wsj.com/articles/SB121018777870174513 (accessed September 2, 2015).

Make or Buy Questions	Suggests Insourcing	Suggests Outsourcing	Examples of Associated Risk in Worse-Case Scenarios
Does it involve a core competency?	Yes	No	*If outsourced:* Loss of control over strategic initiatives; loss of strategic focus
Does it involve confidential or sensitive IS services or software development?	Yes	No	*If outsourced:* Competitive secrets may be leaked
Is there enough time available to complete software development projects in house?	Yes	No	*If insourced:* Project not completed on time
Do the in-house IS professionals have adequate training, experience, or skills to provide the service or develop the software?	Yes	No	*If outsourced:* Technological innovations limited to what provider offers; overreliance on provider's skills
Are there reliable outsourcing providers who are likely to stay in business for the duration of the contract?	No	Yes	*If outsourced:* Project not completed or, if completed, is over budget and late when another provider takes it over
Is there an outsourcing provider that has a culture and practices that are compatible with the client?	No	Yes	*If outsourced:* Conflict between client and provider personnel
Does the provider have economies of scale that make it cheaper to provide the service or develop the software than in house?	Most likely No	Most likely Yes	*If outsourced:* Excessive costs of project or operations because of the way the contract is written
Does it offer a better ability to handle peaks?	Most likely No	Most likely Yes	*If insourced:* Loss of business
Does it involve consolidating data centers?	Most likely No	Most likely Yes	*If insourced:* Inefficient operations

FIGURE 10.2 Make or buy? Questions and risks.

The *hybrid captive center* typically performs the more expensive, higher profile or mission-critical work for the parent company and outsources the more commoditized work that is more cheaply provided by an offshore provider.

Outsourcing

Outsourcing means purchasing a good or service that was previously provided internally or that could be provided internally but is now provided by outside vendors. In the early days of outsourcing, outside providers often took over entire IS departments, including people, equipment, and management responsibility. Reducing costs was the primary motivation for outsourcing. This classic approach prevailed through most of the 1970s and 1980s but then experienced a decline in popularity. In 1989, Eastman Kodak Company's multivendor approach to meeting its IS needs created the "Kodak effect." Kodak outsourced its data center operations to IBM, its network to Digital Equipment Company, and its desktop supply and support operations to Businessland.[3] Kodak managed these relationships through strategic alliances.[4] It retained a skeleton IS staff to act for its business personnel with outsourcing providers. Its approach to supplier management became a model emulated by Continental Bank, General Dynamics, Continental Airlines, National Car Rental, and many more.[5]

Kodak's watershed outsourcing arrangement ushered in new outsourcing practices that put all IS activities up for grabs, including those providing competitive advantage. As relationships with outsourcing providers become

[3] L. Applegate and R. Montealegre, "Eastman Kodak Co.: Managing Information Systems Through Strategic Alliances," Harvard Business School case 192030 (September 1995).

[4] Anthony DiRomualdo and Vijay Gurbaxani, "Strategic Intent for IT Outsourcing," *Sloan Management Review* (June 22, 1998).

[5] Mary C. Lacity, Leslie P. Willcocks, and David F. Feeny, "The Value of Selective IT Sourcing," *Sloan Management Review* (March 22, 1996).

more sophisticated, companies realize that even such essential functions as customer service are sometimes better managed by experts on the outside. Over the years, motives for outsourcing broadened beyond cost control. The next section examines factors and risks to be considered in making the outsourcing decision. The sourcing strategy suggested by the answers to the key how to source question and associated risks are listed in Figure 10.2.

Factors in the Outsourcing Decision

Under what conditions would an organization decide to outsource? There are three primary factors that are likely to favor the decision to seek to buy the services or products of an outsourcing provider: lower costs due to economies of scale, ability to handle processing peaks, and the client company's need to consolidate data centers. These and other factors are listed in Figure 10.2.

One of the most common reasons given for outsourcing is the desire to reduce costs. Outsourcing providers derive savings from economies of scale that client companies often cannot realize. Outsourcing providers achieve these economies through centralized (often "greener") data centers, preferential contracts with suppliers, and large pools of technical expertise. Most often, enterprises lack such resources on a sufficient scale within their own IS departments. For example, a single company may need only 5,000 PCs, but an outsourcing provider might negotiate a contract for 50,000 to spread over many clients and at a much lower cost per computer. Second, the outsourcing provider's larger pool of resources than the client company's allows the provider leeway in assigning available capacity to its clients on demand. For instance, at year-end, an outsourcing provider potentially can allocate additional mainframe capacity to ensure timely completion of nightly processing in a manner that would be impossible for an enterprise running its own bare-bones data center. Third, an outsourcing provider may help a client company to consolidate data centers following a merger or acquisition or when the internal group cannot overcome the inertia of its top management. Outsourcing may also offer an infusion of cash as a company sells its equipment to the outsourcing vendor.

If the service or product involves a core competency, then the organization should strongly consider insourcing to protect the benefits the organization enjoys from its own competency. However, if the product or service is considered to be a commodity instead of a core competency, then there are some distinct advantages to outsourcing. By bringing in outside expertise, client company management often can pay more attention to its core activities rather than to IS operations. Further, if an organization does not have employees with the training, experience, or skills in house to successfully implement new technologies, it should consider outsourcing. This is because outsourcing providers generally have larger pools of talent with more current knowledge of advancing technologies and best practices. For example, many outsourcing providers gain vast experience solving business intelligence problems whereas IS staff within a single company would have only limited experience, if any. That is why client companies turn to outsourcing providers to help them implement such technologies as Enterprise 2.0, Web 2.0 tools, cloud computing, and enterprise resource planning (ERP) systems. However, it is important to remember that client company managers are ultimately still responsible for IS services and products provided to their firm.

Outsourcing providers also have an added advantage because they can specialize in IS services. Outsourcing providers' extensive experience in dealing with IS professionals helps them to understand how to hire, manage, and retain IS staff effectively. Often they can offer IS personnel a professional environment in which to work that a typical company cannot afford to build. For example, a Web designer would have responsibility for one Web site within a company but for multiple sites when working for an outsourcing provider. It becomes the outsourcing provider's responsibility to find, train, and retain highly marketable IS talent. Outsourcing relieves a client of costly investments in continuous training to keep its IS staff current with the newest technologies and the headaches of hiring and retaining highly skilled staff that easily can change jobs.

Outsourcing Risks

Opponents of outsourcing cite a considerable number of risks with it (see Figure 10.2). A manager should consider each of these before making a decision about outsourcing. Each risk can be mitigated with effective planning and ongoing management.

First, outsourcing requires that a client company surrender a degree of control over critical aspects of the enterprise. The potential loss of control could extend to several areas: project control, scope creep, technologies employed, costs, financial controls, accuracy and clarity of financial reports, and even the company's IS direction. By turning over data center operations, for example, a company puts itself at the mercy of an outsourcing provider's ability to manage this function effectively. A manager must choose an outsourcing provider carefully and negotiate terms that encourage an effective working relationship.

Second, outsourcing client companies may not adequately anticipate new technological capabilities when negotiating outsourcing contracts. Outsourcing providers may not recommend so-called bleeding-edge technologies for fear of losing money in the process of implementation and support, even if their implementation would best serve the client company. Thus, poorly planned outsourcing can result in a loss in IS flexibility. For example, some outsourcing providers were slow to adopt social technologies for their clients because they feared the benefits would not be as tangible as the costs of entering the market. This reluctance impinged on clients' ability to realize social business strategies. To avoid this problem, an outsourcing client should have a chief technology officer (CTO) or technology group that is charged with learning about and assessing emerging technologies that can be used to support its company's business strategy.

Third, by surrendering IS functions, a client company gives up any real potential to develop them for competitive advantage—unless, of course, the outsourcing agreement is sophisticated enough to comprehend developing such an advantage in tandem with the outsourcing company. However, the competitive advantage may be compromised if it is made available to the outsourcing provider's other clients. Under many circumstances, the outsourcing provider becomes the primary owner of any technological solutions that it develops for the client. This allows the outsourcing provider to leverage the knowledge to benefit other clients, possibly even competitors of the initial client company.

Fourth, contract terms may leave client companies highly dependent on their outsourcing provider with little recourse in terms of terminating troublesome provider relationships. That is, the clients may be locked into an arrangement that they no longer want. It may be too expensive to switch to another outsourcing provider should the contract sour. Despite doing due diligence and background checks, the outsourcing provider may be unreliable or go out of business before the end of the contract. The risk of over-reliance for any number of reasons typically increases as the size of the outsourcing contract increases. DHL Worldwide Express entrusted 90% of its IT development and maintenance projects to a large Indian-based company, Infosys. "There's a lot of money wrapped up in a contract this size, so it's not something you take lightly or hurry with," said Ron Kifer, DHL's Vice President of Program Solutions and Management.[6] Clearly, DHL faced considerable risk in offshoring with Infosys because of its reliance on the provider.

Fifth, it might be harder to keep its competitive secrets when a company employs an outsourcing provider. Although outsourcing providers are sensitive to keeping client information separated in their systems, an outsourcer's staff will usually work with multiple customers. Some managers are concerned that their company databases are no longer kept in house, and the outsourcing provider's other customers may have easier access to sensitive information. Although all outsourcing agreements contain clauses to keep customer data and systems secure, managers still voice concern about data security and process skills when they are managed by a third party. Thinking through the security issues carefully and implementing controls where possible mitigate this risk. Often, the outsourcing provider has more secure processes and practices in place simply because its business depends on it—it's a competitive necessity and often a core competency of the outsourcing provider.

Sixth, the outsourcing provider's culture or operations may be incompatible with that of the client company, making the delivery of the contracted service or system difficult. Conflicts between the client's staff and the staff of the outsourcing provider may delay progress or harm the quality of the service or product delivered by the outsourcing provider.

Finally, although many companies turn to outsourcing because of perceived cost savings, these savings may never be realized. Typically, the cost savings are premised on the old way that the company performed the processes.

[6] Stephanie Overby, "The Hidden Costs of Offshore Outsourcing" (September 1, 2003), http://www.cio.com/article/29654/The_Hidden_Costs_of_Offshore_Outsourcing (accessed June 4, 2012).

Social Business Lens: Crowdsourcing

Crowdsourcing is a form of outsourcing that is provided by a very large number of individuals. Two forms of crowdsourcing are available: collaboration and tournament. *Collaboration crowdsourcing* occurs when individuals use social media to collectively create a common document or solution. Examples are Wikipedia or crowdsourcing for innovation as was discussed in Chapter 5. *Tournament crowdsourcing* also uses social media to solicit and collect independent solutions from a potentially large number of individuals but selects one or a few of the contributions in exchange for financial or nonfinancial compensation.

Some sites offer marketplaces to promote particular types of tournament crowdsourcing. Consider 99designs (99designs.com), which is the largest online graphic design marketplace where people or firms can go to get affordable designs for such things as logos, labels, business cards, and Web sites. It is anticipated that by 2016, the site will have over a million members offering graphic services. Businesses can source graphic design work by launching design contests to the 99design community, working individually with designers who are members of the community, or purchasing design templates from 99designs' ready-made logo store. Recently, 99designs opened a new site, Swiftly, for customers who want to get small design tasks done quickly for a flat fee.

Sources: I. Blohm, J. M. Leimeister, and H. Krcmar, "Crowdsourcing: How to Benefit from (Too) Many Great Ideas" *MIS Quarterly Executive 12*, no. 4 (2013), 199–211; About 99designs, http://99designs.com/about (downloaded May 22, 2015).

However, new technologies may usher in new processes, and the anticipated savings on the old processes become moot. Further, the outsourcing client is, to some extent, at the mercy of the outsourcing provider. Increased volumes due to unspecified growth, software upgrades, or new technologies not anticipated in the contract may end up costing a firm considerably more than it anticipated when it signed the contract. Also, some savings, although real, may be hard to measure.

Decisions about How to Outsource Successfully

Clearly, the decision about whether to outsource must be made with adequate care and deliberation. It must be followed with numerous other decisions about how to mitigate outsourcing risks and make the outsourcing arrangement work. Once these decisions have been made, they should be openly communicated to all relevant stakeholders. Three major decision areas are selection, contracting, and scope.

Selection

Selection-related decisions focus on finding compatible outsourcing providers whose capabilities, managers, internal operations, technologies, and culture complement those of the client company. This means that compatibility and cultural fit might trump price, especially when long-term partnerships are envisioned. Selection factors are discussed more fully in the "where" and "where abroad" decisions.

Contracting

Many "how" decisions center around the outsourcing contract. In particular, client companies must ensure that contract terms allow them the flexibility they require to manage and, if necessary, sever supplier relationships. The 10-year contracts that were so popular in the early 1990s are being replaced with contracts of shorter duration lasting 3 to 5 years and full life cycle service contracts that are broken up into stages. Deal size also has declined this millennium. Although the numbers of megadeals and midrange contracts awarded each year have remained relatively stable since 2002, smaller contracts valued at $100 million or less had more than tripled a decade later.[7]

[7] Stephanie Overby, "IT Outsourcing Deal Size Data Shows Decade-Long Decline," http://www.cio.com/article/2399755/it-organization/it-outsourcing-deal-size-data-shows-decade-long-decline.html (accessed March 9, 2015).

Often client companies and outsourcing providers have formal outsourcing arrangements, called **service level agreements (SLAs)** that define the level of service to be provided. SLAs often describe the contracted delivery time and expected performance of the service. Contracts are tightened by adding clauses describing actions to be taken in the event of a deterioration in quality of service or noncompliance with the SLA. Service levels, baseline period measurements, growth rates, and service volume fluctuations are specified in the contracts to reduce opportunistic behavior on the part of the outsourcing provider. Research demonstrates that tighter contracts tend to lead to more successful outsourcing arrangements.[8] To write tighter contracts, it is a good idea for the client company to develop contract management skills and to hire both outsourcing and legal experts. Unfortunately, a tight contract does not provide much solace to a client company when an outsourcing provider goes out of business. It also does not replace having a good relationship with the outsourcing provider that allows the client to work out problems when something unanticipated occurs.

Scope

Most enterprises outsource at least some IS functions. This is where scope questions come into play. Defining the scope of outsourcing means that the client must decide whether to pursue outsourcing fully or selectively with one (single sourcing) or more providers (multisourcing). If a client decides to go the selective outsourcing route, it may insource most of its IS duties but selectively outsource the remaining functions.

Full outsourcing implies that an enterprise outsources all its IS functions from desktop services to software development. An enterprise typically outsources everything only if it does not view IT as a strategic advantage. Full outsourcing can free resources to be employed in areas that add greater value. This choice can also reduce overall cost per transaction due to size and economies of scale.[9] Many companies outsource IS simply to allow their managers to focus attention on other business issues. Others outsource to accommodate growth and respond to their business environment. Kellwood, the case discussed at the beginning of the chapter, appeared to have used full outsourcing to improve operations.

With **selective outsourcing**, an enterprise chooses which IT capabilities to retain in house and which to give to one or more outsiders. A "best-of-breed" approach is taken to choose suppliers for their expertise in specific technology areas. Possible areas for selective sourcing include Web site hosting, Web 2.0 applications, cloud services, business process application development, help desk support, networking and communication, social IT services, and data center operations. Although an enterprise can acquire top-level skills and experience through such relationships, the effort required to manage them grows tremendously with each new provider. Still, selective outsourcing, sometimes called *strategic sourcing,* reduces the client company's reliance on outsourcing with only one provider. It also provides greater flexibility and often better service due to the competitive market.[10] To illustrate, an enterprise might retain a specialist firm to develop social business applications and at the same time select a large outsourcing provider, such as IBM, to assume mainframe maintenance.

Consider JetBlue, an airline that turned to Verizon to manage its IT infrastructure—its network, data center, and help desk. The six-year contract with Verizon allows the data centers to scale as JetBlue grows and helps JetBlue "reduce the cycle time for delivery of those capabilities and allow the rest of IT to focus on other capabilities," said JetBlue CIO, Joe Eng. Eng asserted that JetBlue can still have control over IT: "We own the decision paths, the service-level agreements and what direction we want to take, but Verizon will be key in the implementation."[11] Verizon was chosen over other providers for a number of reason, especially because the operation of networks is its core business.

A client company that decides to use multiple providers when fully or selectively outsourcing is multisourcing. **IT multisourcing** is defined as delegating "IT projects and services in a managed way to multiple vendors

[8] See, for example, C. Saunders, M. Gebelt, and Q. Hu, "Achieving Success in Information Systems Outsourcing," *California Management Review* 39, no. 2 (1997), 63–79; M. Lacity and R. Hirschheim, *Information Systems Outsourcing: Myths, Metaphors and Realities* (Hoboken, NJ: John Wiley, 1995).
[9] Tom Field, "An Outsourcing Buyer's Guide: Caveat Emptor" (April 1, 1997).
[10] Ibid.
[11] M. Hamblen, "Verizon to Manage JetBlue's Network, Data Centers and Help Desk," CIO.com (October 6, 2009), http://www.computerworld.com/s/article/9138965/Verizon_to_manage_JetBlue_s_network_data_centers_and_help_desk (accessed January 31, 2012).

who must (at least partly) work cooperatively to achieve the client's business objectives."[12] Over the last 15 years, numerous benefits of IT multisourcing have made this approach take off markedly in terms of number of companies using it and contract sizes. In particular, it helps companies limit the risks associated with working with just one provider. It can also help client firms lower their IT service costs due to competition among providers, improve the quality through best-of-breed services, enhance their flexibility in adapting to changing market conditions, and provide easier access to specialized IT expertise and capabilities.[13] However, multisourcing comes with its downsides. Having more providers requires more coordination than with working with a single outsourcing provider. Further, when a major problem occurs, there may be a tendency to "finger-point." That is, each outsourcing provider may claim that the problem is caused by or can be corrected only by another provider. And as outsourcing providers expand their service offerings, unexpected competition among providers can hurt the client if not managed well.

Adidas, a multinational footwear and sports apparel company, recently adopted a multisourcing strategy, which carefully pitted three IT providers against each other at the same time that they were working cooperatively together.[14] Adidas split virtually all of its huge IT budget allocated for outsourcing among three providers: a large Indian outsourcing company with which it had worked for a decade and two "hungry" smaller firms. Adidas selected the three firms in such a way that at least two vendors, and sometimes all three, could perform particular services that it needed. The large Indian outsourcing provider had become complacent, and the competition provided better IT services at a lower price. In addition, all three vendors were charged to be more innovative. Through careful management, Adidas orchestrated the delicate balance between provider cooperation and competition among the providers.

Deciding Where—In the Cloud, Onshoring, or Offshoring?

Until recently, outsourcing options were either to use services onshore (work performed in the same country as the client) or offshore (work performed in another country). More recently, a new sourcing option has become more available and more accepted by managers: cloud computing. We next describe the three sourcing options. We also describe some answers to the "how" question: how to make the arrangement successful. Many best practices were discussed in the previous subsection because they are common to all three outsourcing options. A few more unique practices are discussed in the next sections.

Cloud Computing

As discussed in Chapter 6, **cloud computing** is the dynamic provisioning of third-party-provided IT services over the Internet using the concept of shared services. Companies offering cloud computing make an entire data center's worth of servers, networking devices, systems management, security, storage, and other infrastructure available to their clients. In that way, their clients can buy the exact amount of storage, computing power, security, or other IT functions that they need, when they need it, and pay only for what they use. Thus, the client company can realize cost savings by sharing the provider's resources with other clients. The providers also provide 24/7 access using multiple mobile devices, high availability for large backup data storage, and ease of use.

Cloud computing's many advantages make it quite popular with executives. The total global cloud computing market is estimated to spurt from $61 billion in 2012 to $241 billion in 2020.[15] This growth was originally fueled by small- to medium-size businesses that lacked large IT functions or internal capabilities. More recently, larger companies have been signing up for cloud services to take advantage of the cloud's many benefits.

---

[12] Martin Wiener and Carol Saunders, "Forced Coopetition in IT Multi-Sourcing," *The Journal of Strategic Information System* 23, no. 3 (2014), 210–25.

[13] Ibid.

[14] Ibid.

[15] Till Winkler, Alexander Benlian, Marc Piper, and Henry Hirsch, "Bayer HealthCare Delivers a Dose of Reality for Cloud Payoff Mantras in Multinationals," *MIS Quarterly Executive* 13, no. 4 (2014), 193–207.

Advantages and Risks/Challenges of Cloud Computing Cloud computing offers a number of advantages. Because resources can be shared, costs for IT infrastructure and services can be slashed. There are no up-front investment costs, and ongoing costs are variable according to the firm's needs, especially for those with multinational units in large countries.[16] The Commonwealth Bank of Australia claimed that its IT costs dropped by approximately 40% when it moved to a cloud for IT infrastructure, software, and development.[17] Further, with companies such as Amazon, Google, IBM, and Microsoft vying for customers, pricing is still rather competitive. Flexibility is enhanced because infrastructure needs that vary over time can be met dynamically. For many companies, cloud computing means "pay-as-you-go." They can get the exact level of IT support that they need when they need it. Further, cloud computing is scalable, which means that more providers can be added if requirements increase, or they theoretically can be taken out of play if the needs decrease. This allows business units to focus on their core competencies as long as they do not need to deal with local idiosyncrasies and customizations.[18]

Netflix realized the advantages of cloud computing to support its strategic initiative to stream movies to its customers instead of mailing them DVDs. To do so, it needed so much more infrastructure that the cloud appeared to be its only option. "Netflix.com is nearly 100% in the cloud. . . . We really couldn't build data centers fast enough," says Jason Chan, Netflix's cloud security architect. The introduction of a Netflix application for iPhones will place even greater spikes in demand, at least temporarily. But Chan isn't concerned: "That's what cloud is really intended for."[19]

As with any sourcing decision, organizations considering cloud computing must weigh its benefits against its risks and challenges. Executives worry over many of the same types of risks that are found with other types of outsourcing. In particular, they fear technical lock in, long-term business commitments, and lost IT capabilities, which ultimately could lead to overdependence on the outsourcing provider.[20] IT executives are particularly concerned that they might lose control over the IT environment for which they bear responsibility. One big concern with cloud computing has been security, specifically with external threats from remote hackers and security breaches as the data travel to and from the cloud. Tied to the concerns about security are concerns about data privacy. The standards, monitoring, and maintenance tools for cloud computing are still not mature. This makes security, interoperability, and data mobility difficult. However, knowing that their business is on the line, many cloud providers have strengthened their security and are willing to deal with the security issues of individual customers. For example, when Bayer HealthCare ran into security risks related to its pharmaceutical customer data in its cloud customer relationship management (CRM), a middleware solution was implemented to protect internal systems against intrusions from outside the firewall.

Another challenge that causes some managers to shy away from cloud computing is the fact that the ability to tailor service-level requirements, such as uptime, response time, availability, performance, and network latency, to the specific needs of a client is far less than with insourcing or many other outsourcing options. To manage this risk, an SLA needs to spell out these requirements. For multinationals, a related challenge is data sovereignty, which means that data are subject to the laws of the country in which they are located.[21] The Commonwealth Bank of Australia has excluded some application providers because the core data need to remain in Australia.[22] Bayer Healthcare took a different, far more time-consuming approach. It adopted a global solution that took into account the different regulatory requirements and processes across its business units in different countries. It also used a two-platform approach: The business units in small and medium countries used an in-house system as their "common platform," while business units in larger countries with more complex systems relied on cloud providers that offered an "advanced" cloud-based platform.[23]

---

[16] Ibid.

[17] Daniel Schlagwein, Alan Thorogood, and Leslie Willcocks, "How Commonwealth Bank of Australia Gained Benefits Using a Standards-Based, Multiprovider Cloud Model," *MIS Quarterly Executive* 13, no. 4 (2014), 209–22.

[18] Winkler et al., "Bayer HealthCare Delivers a Dose of Reality," 193–207.

[19] Tim Greene, "Netflix Deals with Cloud Security Concerns," CIO.com (September 21, 2011), http://www.cio.com/article/print/690236 (accessed September 22, 2011).

[20] Schlagwein, Thorogood, and Willcocks, "How Commonwealth Bank of Australia Gained Benefits," 209–22.

[21] Winkler et al., "Bayer HealthCare Delivers a Dose of Reality," 193–207; Schlagwein, Thorogood, and Willcocks, "How Commonwealth Bank of Australia Gained Benefits," 209–22.

[22] Schlagwein, Thorogood, and Willcocks, "How Commonwealth Bank of Australia Gained Benefits."

[23] Winkler et al., "Bayer HealthCare Delivers a Dose of Reality," 193–207.

Cloud Computing Options Cloud computing comes in many different forms. Options include on-premise or private clouds, community clouds, hybrid clouds and public clouds. In **private clouds**, data are managed by the organization and remain within its existing infrastructure, or it is managed offsite by a third party for the organization (client company). In a **community cloud**, the cloud infrastructure is shared by several organizations and supports the shared concerns of a specific community. An example of a community cloud is Norway's BankID community. BankID relies on a cloud infrastructure to provide a system that enables electronic identification, authentication, and signing. Members of the BankID community include Norwegian banks, the Norwegian government, the Norwegian Banking Federation, and merchants.[24]

A **hybrid cloud** is a combination of two or more other clouds. Mohawk, a U.S. manufacturer of premium paper products discussed in Chapter 6, has a hybrid cloud. It is part of a computing environment with on-premises ERP and manufacturing systems, a secure suite of private cloud services to send and receive data files among on-premises databases and to integrate with its business partners, and a suite of cloud services to integrate public cloud applications with internal applications and business processes.[25]

In a **public cloud**, data are stored outside of the corporate data centers in the cloud provider's environment. As discussed in Chapter 6, public clouds include:

- *Infrastructure as a service (IaaS):* Provides infrastructure through grids or clusters or virtualized servers, networks, storage, and systems software designed to augment or replace the functions of an entire data center. The customer may have full control of the actual server configuration allowing more risk management control over the data and environment. The earlier Netflix example illustrates the IaaS cloud option.

- *Software as a service (SaaS):* Provides software application functionality through a Web browser. Mohawk uses the Web for a variety of SaaS applications (e.g., e-marketing, CRM, and human resources [HR]).[26] Both the platform and the infrastructure are fully managed by the cloud provider, which means that if the operating system or underlying service is not configured correctly, the data at the higher application layer may be at risk. This is the most widely known and used form of cloud computing. A provider of SaaS is sometimes called *application service provider (ASP)*.[27]

- *Platform as a service (PaaS):* Provides services using virtualized servers on which clients can run existing applications or develop new ones without having to worry about maintaining the operating systems, server hardware, load balancing, or computing capacity; the cloud provider manages the hardware and underlying operating system, which limits its enterprise risk management capabilities. Bayer Healthcare's cloud platform-based component development (PaaS) is used to customize cloud solutions when the existing SaaS solutions are unable to satisfy the complex, idiosyncratic needs of its large business units.[28]

Onshoring

Outsourcing does not necessarily mean that IT services and software development are shipped abroad. **Onshoring**, also called *inshoring*, means performing outsourcing work domestically (i.e., in the same country). Onshoring may be considered the "opposite" of offshoring. In scope, it involves either selective or full outsourcing.

A growing trend in onshoring in the United States is rural sourcing, which is hiring outsourcing providers with operations in rural parts of the country. Rural sourcing firms can be competitive because they take advantage of lower salaries and living costs when compared to firms in metropolitan areas. Dealing with a rural company can have advantages in terms of different time zones, similar culture, and fewer hassles compared with dealing with foreign outsourcing providers. However, the rural sourcing firms are usually too small to handle large-scale projects

---

[24] Ben Eaton, Hanne Kristine Hallingby, Per-Jonny Nesse, Ole Hanset, "Achieving Payoffs from an Industry Cloud Ecosystem at BankID," *MIS Quarterly Executive* 13, no. 4 (December 2014), 51–60.

[25] Paul J. Stamas, Michelle L. Daarst-Brown, and Schoot A. Bernard, "The Business Transformation Payoffs of Cloud Services at Mohawk," *MIS Quarterly Executive* 13, no. 4 (December 2014), 177–92.

[26] Ibid.

[27] Diana Kelley, "How Data-Centric Protection Increases Security in Cloud Computing and Virtualization" (2011), http://www.securitycurve.com (accessed September 22, 2011).

[28] Ibid.; Winkler et al., "Bayer HealthCare Delivers a Dose of Reality," 193–207.

and may not have the most technologically advanced employees. Rural sourcing is often viewed as more politically correct than offshoring.[29]

Offshoring

Offshoring (which is short for *offshore sourcing*) occurs when the IS organization uses contractor services, or even its own hybrid captive center in a distant land. The functions sent offshore range from routine IT transactions to increasingly higher-end, knowledge-based business processes.

Programmer salaries can be a fraction of those in the home country in part because the cost of living and the standard of living in the distant country are much lower, maybe as much as 70% lower when only considering direct labor costs. However, these savings come at a price because other costs increase. Additional technology, telecommunications, travel, process changes, and management overhead are required to relocate and supervises overseas operations. For example, during the transition period, which can be rather lengthy, offshore workers must often be brought to the home country headquarters for extended periods to become familiar with the company's operations and technology. Because of the long transition period, it can often take several years for offshoring's labor savings to be fully realized. And even if they are realized, they may never reflect the true cost to a company. Many, especially those who have lost their jobs to offshore workers, argue that offshoring cuts into the very fiber of the society in the country of origin whose companies are laying off workers. Yet, it helps the economies of the countries where offshoring is performed. For example, India's IT services industry, the largest private sector employer, was a $108 billion industry in fiscal year 2013 with $76 billion derived from exports of services and products.[30]

Even though the labor savings are often very attractive, companies sometimes turn to offshoring for other reasons. The employees in many offshore companies are typically well educated (often holding master's degrees) and proud to work for an international company. The offshore service providers are often "profit centers" that have established Six Sigma, ISO 9001, Capability Maturity Model (CMM), or another certification program. These offshore providers usually are more willing to "throw more brainpower at a problem" to meet their performance goals than many companies in the United States or Western Europe. In offshore economies, technology know-how is a relatively cheap commodity in ample supply.[31]

Offshoring raises the fundamental question of what to send offshore and what to keep within the enterprise IS organization when implementing the selective outsourcing model. Because communications are made difficult by differences in culture, time zones, and possibly language, outsourced tasks are usually those that can be well specified. They typically, but not always, are basic noncore transactional systems that require the users or customers to have little in-depth knowledge. In contrast, early stage prototypes and pilot development are often kept in house because this work is very dynamic and requires familiarity with business processes. Keeping the work at home allows CIOs to offer learning opportunities to in house staff. In summary, the cost savings that lure many companies to turn to offshoring need to be assessed in relation to the increased risks and communication problems in working with offshore workers and relying on them to handle major projects.

Deciding Where Abroad—Nearshoring or Farshoring?

Offshoring can be either relatively proximate (nearshoring) or in a distant land (farshoring). Each of these offshore options is described in more detail here. They are also shown in Figure 10.3 with other domestic and nondomestic sourcing options in Figure 10.3. In some cases, the distinction is hard to make because some cloud computing can be considered as insourcing if it is a local private cloud or local community cloud or some hybrid. However, in most cases, cloud computing tends to be a form of outsourcing either domestically or nondomestically in the ether. Further, although most captive centers could be considered a form of insourcing, hybrid captive centers sometimes outsource a client's simple, more commoditized work.

[29] Bob Violino, "Rural Outsourcing on the Rise in the U.S." (March 7, 2011), http://www.computerworld.com/s/article/353556/Lure_of_the_Countryside?taxonomyId=14&pageNumber=1 (accessed September 22, 2011).

[30] India Brand Equity Foundation, http://www.ibef.org/industry/information-technology-india.aspx (accessed March 9, 2015).

[31] Aditya Bhasin, Vinay Couto, Chris Disher, and Gil Irwin, "Business Process Offshoring: Making the Right Decision" (January 29, 2004), http://www2.cio.com/consultant/report2161.html (accessed August 14, 2005).

	Insourcing	Outsourcing
Domestic (local)	Situation in which a firm provides IS services or develops IS in its own in house organization and/or in its local private cloud or, possibly, local community cloud	Purchase of a good or services that was previously provided internally or that could be provided internally but is now provided by an outside domestic outsourcing provider (i.e., onshoring), or outsourced to a rural or local cloud provider
Nondomestic	Situation in which a firm uses an offshore captive center	Situation when the IS organization uses contractor services in a distant land or in the ether; may include nearshoring, farshoring, cloud computing, or a hybrid captive center

FIGURE 10.3 Different forms of sourcing.
Source: Adapted from http://www.dbresearch.com/PROD/DBR_INTERNET_EN-PROD/PROD0000000000179790/Offshoring%3A+Globalisation+wave+reaches+services+se.PDF (downloaded May 22, 2015).

Geographic Lens: Corporate Social Responsibility

Many outsourcing clients are increasing their corporate social responsibility (CSR) expectations for themselves and for their global IS outsourcing providers. Pessimists of global IS outsourcing are concerned that it maximizes profit for the rich but offers little or no benefits for other groups, especially the poor in developing countries. The pessimists are concerned that global IS outsourcing will deepen income inequalities and have disruptive effects on society around the globe. Optimists of global IS outsourcing see it as a way of sharing wealth on a global basis. It is ethically justified because it can improve efficiency, help developing countries where unemployment is very high by providing jobs, lead to transfers of knowledge and information technology, and encourage better educational systems in less developed countries so that people can do the outsourcing work. Ironically, global IS outsourcing may benefit both the more developed origin country (frequently the United States, Western Europe, and Australia) as well as the destination country through free trade and reduced prices for computers and communications equipment. It also may fuel the creation of high-level jobs for workers in more developed countries.

To promote corporate social responsibility, both clients and outsourcing providers should implement the following guidelines: understand relevant CSR regulatory requirements to ensure compliance, establish measures and report CSR performance and compliance to stakeholders, respond to inquiries about CSR compliance, embed CSR in ongoing operations, and develop a CSR culture through hiring and education.

Sources: R. Babin and B. Nicholson, "Corporate Social and Environmental Responsibility and Global IT Outsourcing," *MIS Quarterly Executive* 8, no. 4 (2009), 203–12; Laura D'Andrea Tyson, "Outsourcing: Who's Safe Anymore?" (February 23, 2004).

Farshoring

Farshoring is a form of offshoring that involves sourcing service work to a foreign, lower-wage country that is relatively far away in distance or time zone (or both). For countries such as the United States and United Kingdom that outsource large amounts of work, India and China are the most popular farshoring destinations. Ironically, companies in India and China are now themselves farshoring to countries with lower labor costs.

Nearshoring

Nearshoring, on the other hand, uses providers in foreign, lower-wage countries that are relatively close in distance or time zones to the client company. With nearshoring, the client company hopes to benefit from one or more dimensions of being close: geographic, temporal, cultural, linguistic, economical, political, or historic linkages. Nearshoring basically challenges the assumption on which farshoring is premised: Distance doesn't matter. The advocates of nearshoring argue that distance does matter, and when closer on one or more of these dimensions, the client company faces fewer challenges in terms of communication, control, supervision, coordination, or social bonding.

Three major global clusters of countries are focused on building a reputation as a home for nearshoring: a cluster of 20 nations around the United States and Canada, a cluster of 27 countries around Western Europe, and a smaller cluster of three countries in East Asia: China, Malaysia, and Korea.[32]

The dimensions of being close clearly extend beyond distance and time zone. For example, language makes a difference in nearshoring. That is why Latin American nearshoring destinations are appealing to Texas and Florida where there is a large Spanish-speaking population and why French-speaking North African nations are appealing to France. These dimensions likely play a key role when companies are trying to decide between a nearshore or farshore destination (particularly India). Ironically, India, which exports roughly five times the software of the strictly nearshoring nations in the three major nearshoring clusters, is responding to the competitive threat that these nations pose by offering its clients nearshoring options. For example, India-based Tata Consulting Services (TCS) offers its British clients services that are nearshore (Budapest, Hungary), farshore (India), or onshore (London, United Kingdom). It is likely that the differentiation based on "distance" will continue to be important in the outsourcing arena.

Selecting an Offshore Destination: Answering the "Where Abroad?" Question

A difficult decision that many companies face is selecting an offshoring destination. To answer the *where abroad* question, client companies must consider attractiveness, level of development, and cultural differences.

Attractiveness Approximately 100 countries are now exporting software services and products. For various reasons, some countries are more attractive than others as hosts of offshoring business because of the firm's geographic orientation. With English as the predominant language of outsourcing countries (i.e., United States and United Kingdom), countries with a high English proficiency are more attractive than those where different languages are spoken. Geopolitical risk is another factor that affects the use of offshore firms in a country. Countries on the verge of war, with high rates of crime, and with hostile relationships with the client company's home country are typically not suitable candidates for this business. Other factors including regulatory restrictions, trade issues, data security, and intellectual property also affect the attractiveness of a country for an offshoring arrangement. Hiring legal experts who know the laws of the outsourcing provider's company can mitigate legal risks. Nonetheless, some countries are more attractive than others because of their legal systems. The level of technical infrastructure available in some countries also can add to or detract from the attractiveness of a country. Although a company may decide that a certain country is attractive overall for offshoring, it still must assess city differences when selecting an offshore outsourcing provider. For example, Chennai is a better location in India for finance and accounting, but Delhi has better call center capabilities.[33]

Some countries have created an entire industry of providing IT services through offshoring. India, for example, took an early mover advantage in the industry. With a large, low-cost English-speaking labor pool, many entrepreneurs set up programming factories that produce high-quality software to meet even the toughest standards. One measure of the level of proficiency of the development process within an IS organization is the Software Engineering Institute's Capability Maturity Model (CMM).[34] Its Level 1 means that the software development processes are immature, bordering on chaotic. Few processes are formally defined, and output is highly inconsistent. At the other end of the model is Level 5 in which processes are predictable, repeatable, and highly refined. Level 5 companies are consistently innovating, growing, and incorporating feedback. The software factories in many Indian enterprises are well known for their CMM Level 5 software development processes, making them extremely reliable, and, thus, desirable as vendors. However, if the client company is not at the same CMM level as the provider, it may want to specify which CMM processes it will pay for to avoid wasting money. Further, it may seek to elevate its own CMM certification to close the process gap between what it can do and what the outsourcing provider can do.

---

[32] Erran Carmel and Pamela Abbott, "Why 'Nearshore' Means that Distance Matters," *Communications of the ACM* 50, no. 10 (October 2007), 40–46.

[33] Ben Worthen and Stephanie Overby, "USAA IT Chief Exits" (June 15, 2004), http://www.cio.com/archive/061504/tl_management.html (accessed August 14, 2005).

[34] CMM is now referred to as Capability Maturity Model Integration (CMMI).

Development Tiers A very important factor in selecting an offshore destination is the level of development of the country, which often subsumes a variety of other factors. For example in the highest tier, the countries have an advanced technological foundation and a broad base of institutions of higher learning. Carmel and Tjia suggest that there are three tiers of software exporting nations:[35]

- *Tier 1—Mature software-exporting nations:* These include such highly industrialized nations as the United Kingdom, the United States, Japan, Germany, France, Canada, the Netherlands, Sweden, and Finland. It also includes the three "I's" (i.e., India, Ireland, and Israel) that became very prominent software exporters in the 1990s as well as China and Russia, which entered the tier in the 2000s.
- *Tier 2—Emerging software-exporting nations:* These nations are the up-and-comers. They tend to have small population bases or unfavorable conditions such as political instability or an immature state of economic development. Countries in this tier include Brazil, Costa Rica, South Korea, and many Eastern European countries.
- *Tier 3—Infant stage software-exporting nations:* These nations have not significantly affected the global software market, and their software industries are mostly "cottage industries" with small, isolated firms. Some of the 15 to 25 Tier 3 countries are Cuba, Vietnam, and Jordan.

The tiers were determined on the basis of industrial maturity, the extent of clustering of some critical mass of software enterprises, and export revenues. The higher-tiered countries tend to offer higher levels of skills but also charge higher prices.

Cultural Differences Often misunderstandings arise because of differences in culture and, sometimes, language. For example, GE Real Estate's CIO quickly learned that U.S. programmers have a greater tendency to speak up and offer suggestions whereas Indian programmers might think something does not make sense, but they go ahead and do what they were asked, assuming that this is what the client wants.[36] Thus, a project, such as creating an automation system for consumer credit cards that is common sense for a U.S. worker, may be harder to understand and take longer when undertaken by an offshore worker. The end result may be a more expensive system that responds poorly to situations unanticipated by its offshore developers. It is important to be aware of and to manage the risks due to cultural differences.

Sometimes cultural and other differences are so great that companies take back in house operations that were previously outsourced offshore. Carmel and Tjia outlined some examples of communication failures with Indian developers due to differences in language, culture, and perceptions about time:[37]

- What is funny in one culture is not necessarily funny in another culture.
- Indians are less likely than Westerners, especially the British, to engage in small talk.
- Indians, like Malaysians and other cultures, are hesitant about saying "no." Answers to questions to which one option for response is "no" are extremely difficult to interpret.
- Indians often are not concerned with deadlines. When they are, they are likely to be overly optimistic about their ability to meet the deadlines of a project. One cultural trainer was heard to say, "When an Indian programmer says the work will be finished tomorrow, it only means it will not be ready today."[38]

Re-evaluation—Keep as Is or Change Decision

The final decision in the Sourcing Decision Cycle requires an assessment as to whether the sourcing arrangement is working as it should be. If everything is basically satisfactory, then the arrangement can continue as is. Otherwise, the arrangement may need to be adjusted. If the arrangement is very unsatisfactory, another outsourcing provider

---

[35] Erran Carmel and Paul Tjia, *Offshoring Information Technology* (Cambridge, UK: Cambridge University Press, 2005).
[36] Overby, "The Hidden Costs of Offshore Outsourcing."
[37] Carmel and Tjia, *Offshoring Information Technology.*
[38] Ibid., 181.

may be selected or backsourcing may occur. **Backsourcing** is a business practice in which a company takes back in house assets, activities, and skills that are part of its information systems operations and were previously outsourced to one or more outside IS providers.[39] Kellwood, the company described at the beginning of this chapter, frequently re-evaluated its outsourcing arrangements and eventually backsourced.

Backsourcing may be partial or complete reversal of an outsourcing contract. A growing number of companies around the globe have brought their outsourced IS functions back in house after terminating, renegotiating, or letting their contracts expire. Some companies, such as Continental Airlines, Cable and Wireless, Halifax Bank of Scotland, Sears, Bank One, and Xerox, have backsourced contracts worth a billion dollars or more.

The most expensive contract that was backsourced to date was the one that JP Morgan Chase signed with IBM for a whopping $5 billion dollars. JP Morgan Chase terminated its contract and brought information systems (IS) operations back in house only 21 months into a seven-year mega-contract. The CIO of JP Morgan Chase, Austin Adams, stated at that time, "We believe managing our own technology infrastructure is best for the long-term growth and success of our company, as well as our shareholders. Our new capabilities will give us competitive advantages, accelerate innovation, and enable us to become more streamlined and efficient."[40] A number of factors appear to have played a role in the decision to bring the IS operations back in house. Outsourcing appeared to stagnate IT at JP Morgan Chase under the outsourcing arrangement. Another factor is that the company had undergone a major change with its July 2004 merger with Bank One, which had gained a reputation for consolidating data centers and eliminating thousands of computer applications. And the man who had played a big role in the consolidation was Bank One's CIO, Austin Adams. In his new role at JP Morgan Chase, Adams managed the switch from IBM to self-sufficiency by taking advantage of the cost-cutting know-how he had gained at Bank One. Thus, the underperforming JP Morgan Chase learned much from the efficient Bank One.[41]

It is not only large companies that are backsourcing. Small- to medium-size firms also report having negative outsourcing experiences, and many of these have backsourced or are considering backsourcing. Given the size and number of the current outsourcing contracts and the difficulties of delivering high-quality information services and products, backsourcing is likely to remain an important option to be considered by many client companies.

Ironically, the reasons given for backsourcing often mirror the reasons for outsourcing in the first place. That is, companies often claim that they backsource to reduce costs and become more efficient. Based on reports in the popular press, the most common reasons given for backsourcing are a change in the way the IS is perceived by the organization, the need to regain control over critical activities that had been outsourced, a change in the executive team (where the new executives favored backsourcing), higher than expected costs, and poor service. The studies found that backsourcing was not always due to problems. Sometime companies saw opportunities, such as mergers, acquisitions, or new roles for IS, that required backsourcing to be realized.[42]

Outsourcing decisions can be difficult and expensive to reverse because outsourcing requires the enterprise to acquire the necessary infrastructure and staff. Unless experienced IT staff from elsewhere in the firm can contribute, outsourcing major IT functions means losing staff to either the outsourcing provider or other companies. When IT staff gets news that their company is considering outsourcing, they often seek work elsewhere. Even when staff are hired by the outsourcing provider to handle the account, they may be transferred to other accounts, taking with them critical knowledge. Although backsourcing represents the final decision in one Sourcing Decision Cycle, it is invariably followed by another cycle of decisions as the company seeks to respond to its dynamic environment.

---

[39] Rudy Hirschheim, "Backsourcing: An Emerging Trend" (1998); Mary C. Lacity and Leslie P. Willcocks, "Relationships in IT Outsourcing: A Stakeholder's Perspective," *Framing the Domains of IT Management. Projecting the Future . . . Through the Past*, ed. Robert W. Zmud (Cincinnati, OH: Pinnaflex Education Resources, 2000), 355–84.

[40] Stephanie Overby, "Outsourcing—and Backsourcing—at JP Morgan Chase" (2005), http://www.cio.com/article/print/10524 (accessed July 23, 2008).

[41] Paul Strassmann, "Why JP Morgan Chase Really Dropped IBM" (January 13, 2005), http://www.baselinemag.com/c/a/Projects-Management/Why-JP-Morgan-Chase-Really-Dropped-IBM/.

[42] N. Veltri, C. Saunders, and C. B. Kavan, "Information Systems Backsourcing: Correcting Problems and Responding to Opportunities" (2008). These economic and relationship issues are similar to those found in the three empirical studies that have performed backsourcing research to date: Bandula Jayatilaka, "IS Sourcing a Dynamic Phenomena: Forming an Institutional Theory Perspective," *Information Systems Outsourcing: Enduring Themes, New Perspectives and Global Challenges*, ed. Rudy Hirschheim, Armin Heinzl, and Jens Dibbern (Berlin: Springer-Verlag, 2006), 103–34; R. Hirschheim and M. C. Lacity, "Four Stories of Information Systems Sourcing," *Information Systems Outsourcing: Enduring Themes, New Perspectives and Global Challenges*, ed. R. Hirschheim, Armin Heinzl, and J. Dibbern (Berlin: Springer-Verlag, 2006), 303–46; Dwayne Whitten and Dorothy Leidner, "Bringing IT Back: An Analysis of the Decision to Backsource or Switch Vendors," *Decision Sciences* 37, no. 4 (2006), 605–21.

Outsourcing in the Broader Context

Most of our discussion about outsourcing has focused on the dyadic relationship between a client and its outsourcing provider(s). However, as business becomes more complex and organizations become more intertwined with one another, it becomes increasingly important to consider outsourcing in a broader context that includes strategic networks and business ecosystems.

Strategic Networks

Typically, outsourcing relationships are couched in terms of an outsourcing provider and a client—just as we have done in this chapter. A different approach to viewing outsourcing arrangements is the **strategic network**, a long-term, purposeful "arrangement by which companies set up a web of close relationships that form a veritable system geared to providing product or services in a coordinated way."[43] The client company becomes a hub and its suppliers, including its outsourcing providers, are part of its network. The advantage of the strategic network is that it lowers the costs of working with others in its network. In doing so, the client company can become more efficient than its competitors as well as flexible enough to respond to its rapidly changing environment. Perhaps the strategic network is the best way to think about outsourcing arrangements in today's world.

An example of a strategic network is a Japanese *keiretsu* that has a hub company, a policy that encourages specialization within the network, and investments (financial and otherwise) in long-term relationships.[44] Japanese companies manage their outsourcing activities based on inputs from different types of suppliers.[45] The strategic suppliers (*kankei kaisa*) fall into the keiretsu category whereas independent suppliers (*dokuritsu kaisha*) do not. Japanese companies work very closely with other companies in the keiretsu.

Another type of strategic network that increasingly affects outsourcing arrangements is a network with a parent or multinational organization and a number of its subsidiaries. Often one subsidiary performs outsourcing services for another subsidiary in the network. Given the increasingly complex structure of today's multinationals, the role of strategic networks in outsourcing arrangements is likely to grow.

Business Ecosystems

Digital ecosystems are discussed in Chapter 9. Another type of ecosystem is the **business ecosystem**, which is defined as "an economic community supported by a foundation of interacting organizations and individuals—the organisms of the business world."[46] This economic community is comprised of customers, suppliers, lead producers, competitors, outsourcing providers, and other stakeholders. Over time, the community members' investments, capabilities, and roles become aligned as they all move toward a shared vision.

In Norway, a business ecosystem was created by Norwegian banks using the BankID cloud community discussed earlier in the chapter.[47] The community with its cloud infrastructure was established in 2000 by two major Norwegian banks. Eventually, other Norwegian banks, the Federation of Norwegian Banking, and the government joined in as core members to subsidize and nurture the ecosystem. Merchants were brought into the ecosystem to grow the community and its offerings. Students and landlords were brought in when BankID was expanded to allow students to pay for their housing online. The BankID ecosystem also includes the main cloud infrastructure suppliers as core members and equipment vendors and the outsourcing companies as peripheral members. Systems such as BankID are becoming more and more common.

---

[43] Ibid., 7.

[44] Ibid., 122.

[45] Masaaki Kotabe and Janet Y. Murray, "Global Sourcing Strategy and Sustainable Competitive Advantage," *Industrial Marketing Management* 33 (2004), 7–14.

[46] James F. Moore, "Predators and Prey: A New Ecology of Competition," *Harvard Business Review* 71, no. 3 (May/June 1993), 75–83.

[47] Eaton et al., "Achieving Payoffs from an Industry Cloud Ecosystem at BankID," 51–60.

SUMMARY

- Firms typically face a range of sourcing decisions. The Sourcing Decision Cycle Framework highlights decisions about where the work will be performed. Decisions include insourcing versus outsourcing; onshoring versus cloud computing versus offshoring; and selecting among offshoring options (nearshoring versus farshoring). The cycle involves an assessment of the adequacy of the IS service/product delivery. The assessment can trigger a new cycle.
- Cost savings or filling the gaps in the client company's IT skills are powerful reasons for outsourcing. Other reasons include the ability of the company to adopt a more strategic focus, manage IS staff better, better handle peaks, or consolidate data centers. The numerous risks involved in outsourcing arrangements must be carefully assessed by IS and general managers alike.
- Full or selective outsourcing offers client companies an alternative to keeping top-performing IS services in house. These firms can meet their outsourcing needs by using single-vendor or multiple-vendor models (multisourcing).
- Cloud computing allows client firms to buy the exact amount of storage, computing power, security, or other IT functions that they need, when they need it. It includes infrastructure as a service (IaaS), platforms as a service (PaaS), and software as a service (SaaS).
- Offshoring may be performed in a country that is proximate along one or a number of dimensions (nearshoring) or that is distant (farshoring). Offshoring must be managed carefully and take into consideration functional differences.
- As business becomes more complex, outsourcing should be considered in the broader context of strategic networks and business ecosystems.

KEY TERMS

backsourcing (p. 223)
business ecosystem (p. 224)
captive center (p. 210)
cloud computing (p. 216)
community cloud (p. 218)
crowdsourcing (p. 214)
farshoring (p. 220)
full outsourcing (p. 215)
hybrid cloud (p. 218)
insourcing (p. 210)
IT multisourcing (p. 215)
nearshoring (p. 220)
offshoring (p. 219)
onshoring (p. 218)
outsourcing (p. 211)
private clouds (p. 218)
public cloud (p. 218)
selective outsourcing (p. 215)
service level agreements (SLA) (p. 215)
strategic network (p. 224)

DISCUSSION QUESTIONS

1. The make-versus-buy decision is important every time a new application is requested of the IS group. What, in your opinion, are the key reasons an IS organization should make its own systems? What are the key reasons it should buy an application?
2. Is offshoring a problem to your country? To the global economy? Please explain.
3. When does cloud computing make sense for a large corporation that already has an IS organization? Give an example of cloud computing that might make sense for a start-up company.
4. Does a captive center resolve the concerns managers have about outsourcing to a third party vendor? Why or why not?

■ CASE STUDY 10-1 Crowdsourcing at AOL

Where would you go if you needed to find hundreds of people each willing to take on a tiny portion of a large task for minimal pay? Projects like these include filling out surveys, verifying or entering data, writing articles, and transcribing audio files. They are increasingly common in the digital age, so you might turn to an online marketplace such as Crowdsourcing.com, CrowdFlower, or Amazon's Mechanical Turk where people around the globe go to find work.

Daniel Maloney, an AOL executive, recently turned to crowdsourcing for help inventorying AOL's vast video library. (*Note: This definition of crowdsourcing differs from the one used in Chapter* 5 *as a way to spur innovation.*) He broke the large job into microtasks and described the tasks that he needed to be done on Mechanical Turk. In particular, each worker was asked to find Web pages containing a video and identify the video's source and location on those pages. The over one-half million workers that were registered at Mechanical Turk could read about the tasks and decide if they wanted to perform them.

Using the crowdsourcing service, the AOL project took less than a week to get up and running and only a couple of months to reach completion. The total cost was about as much as it would have been to hire two temp workers for the same period.

Maloney was pleased with the cost savings and added, "We had a very high number of pages we needed to process. Being able to tap into a scaled work force was massively helpful."[48] However, he really did not know very much about the workers who did the work for AOL, and he likely had to make sure that their work was done correctly.

Critics of crowdsourcing feel it can lead to "digital sweatshops," where workers, many of whom may be underage, put in long hours to generate very little pay and no benefits. Some also believe that crowdsourcing will eliminate full-time jobs. The crowdsourcing marketplace services counter that they are trying to register stay-at-home parents or college students with spare time.

Discussion Questions

1. Is crowdsourcing as used by AOL a form of outsourcing? Why or why not?
2. What steps do you think Maloney might have taken to ensure that the crowdsourcing would be a success for the inventory project?
3. What factors should be considered when deciding whether to crowdsource a particular part of a business?
4. Describe the advantages and disadvantages of crowdsourcing.

Sources: http://aws.amazon.com/mturk (accessed April 17, 2012); Haydn Shaughnessy, "How to Cut Consulting Costs by 90% and Keep Your Talent Happy!" www.forbes.com (accessed April 16, 2012); Scott Kirsner, "My Life as a Micro-Laborer," www.boston.com (accessed April 1, 2012); R. E. Silverman, "Big Firms Try Crowdsourcing," http://online.wsj.com/article/SB10001424052970204409004577157493201863200.html?mod=djem_jiewr_IT_domainid (accessed November 2, 2011) (accessed January 17, 2012).

CASE STUDY 10-2 Altia Business Park

The road to Altia Business Park in San Pedro Sula, Honduras, is quite memorable. On one side of the road are gated communities with small but neatly maintained stucco houses. On the other side of the road is a small river with clear running water. One bank of the river is covered with tightly cramped shanties. Further down the road towers a 13-story monolith in black glass. This is the home of Altia Business Park, a technological park developed by Grupo Karims, a multinational corporation with core businesses in textiles and real estate and operations in Asia, North America, Central America, and the Caribbean. The building is antiseismic and Leed Certified, which means that it follows green building practices. It is energy self-sufficient and connected to North and South America through three fiber optic submarine cables. The building is the first of two that will comprise the Business Park.

On a recent visit, Corporate Marketing Director Barbara Rivera guided an American student group through the marbled halls of the building. She introduced Marcus, who was a manager in the call center in the building. Marcus explained that call center business, especially to North America, was picking up. He was born and raised in the United States and graduated from the University of Maryland. Because he could not find work in the United States upon graduation, he moved to Honduras where he has family. Rivera also introduced Lena, a 20-something professional, who spoke to the visiting group in perfect English, complete with current idioms. Lena had recently graduated from a university in Honduras with a master's degree in graphical design. She said this degree was very helpful in managing the room full of graphic designers working for the company that maintains the Web site for Sandal Resorts. Rivera told the visitors that the average salary of the workers in

[48] R. E. Silverman, "Big Firms Try Crowdsourcing" (January 17, 2012), http://online.wsj.com/article/SB10001424052970204409004577157493201863200.html?mod=djem_jiewr_IT_domainid (accessed November 2, 2011).

the companies in the Business Park was $4,800 a year[49] and people were eager to get the jobs because of the excellent pay in a country where 65% of the population lives below the poverty line. The country has a literacy rate of 84.3%, and 47% of the employable work force is between the ages of 20 and 34, so the competition for good jobs can be fierce. Honduras actually has more English speakers as a proportion of population than the average Central American economy.

Discussion Questions

1. Discuss offshoring from the perspective of potential workers in your country. Discuss offshoring from the perspective of potential workers in Honduras.
2. Barbara Rivera is marketing Altia Business Park as a nearshoring site to companies in North America. What characteristics make it a desirable nearshoring site to them?
3. Is this a good idea to market Altia Business Park as a nearshoring site to people in North America? Why or why not?

[49] The GDP was $4,300 at the time of the case according to CIA—World Fact Book—Honduras, https://www.cia.gov/library/publications/the-world-factbook/geos/ho.html (accessed February 13, 2012); GDP is now $4,800, https://www.cia.gov/library/publications/the-world-factbook/geos/ho.html (accessed March 9, 2015); and 65% of the population still live below the poverty line; see also http://hondurasoutsourcing.nearshoreamericas.com/.

chapter

11

Managing IT Projects

A major function of the information systems (IS) organization always has been to build and implement systems. This chapter begins with a discussion about defining a project and identifying key players and then follows up with a description of how information technology (IT) projects are managed. Various system development methodologies and approaches are introduced and compared. The chapter concludes with a discussion of two critical management areas for project success: risk management and change management.

The Rural Payments Agency (RPA), an agency responsible for administering agricultural subsidies to farmers in the United Kingdom (U.K.) blamed poor planning and lack of testing of its IT system for delays in paying out £1.5 billion of European Union (EU) subsidies.[1] The U.K. government developed a complex system for administering the Single Payment Scheme, which maps farmers' land to a database that was used to calculate subsidy payments. By the end of 2006, only 15% of the subsidies had been paid to farmers and, as a result, a large number of farmers faced bankruptcy after not receiving subsidies due. Problems still plagued the system in early 2012 when the RPA's CEO stated that the agency had deep-rooted problems that included inaccurate data sources of past, present, and future scheme claims, a lack of standard processes and controls, aging systems, unsuitable technology, and an organizational structure and associated corporate services that did not offer a good fit with the RPA's purpose. The agency's new three-year framework document included a vision of openness, efficiency, simplification, availability of authoritative data, and a promise of correcting the problems in early 2014.[2]

In 2014, the Single Payment Scheme was indeed rolled out two months ahead of the adjusted deadline, but the story does not end there. In response to new agreements in the EU, the RPA announced a new system, the Basic Payment Scheme, which repaired some inequities and allowed richer data to be collected. That system was intended to be 100% online and required farmers to verify their identity and accurately measure and map their properties, including certain surface features of the property such as terrain and vegetation.[3]

In January 2015, the identity verification process proved to be a barrier for many farmers because it was difficult to use. A telephone service for assistance was consequently overloaded and difficult or impossible to reach.[4] Also, even with only a few farmers online, the servers operated at 100% of capacity, and the system became intolerably slow.[5] In March, the CEO announced that "all farmers

[1] At that time, that amount represented about U.S.$2.77 billion when the exchange rate was £1.7 to U.S.$1.00. By spring, 2015, the exchange rate had dropped to £1.52 to U.S.$1.00.

[2] Warmwell postings (February 26, 2012), http://www.warmwell.com/rpa.html (accessed April 10, 2012).

[3] Warmwell postings (June 2014), http://www.warmwell.com/rpa.html (accessed September 1, 2015).

[4] Warmwell postings (January 2015), http://www.warmwell.com/rpa.html (accessed September 1, 2015).

[5] Bryan Glick, "What Went Wrong with Defra's Rural Payment Scheme?" *Computer Weekly* (March 20, 2015), http://www.computerweekly.com/news/2240242763/What-went-wrong-with-Defras-rural-payments-system (accessed September 1, 2015).

are now being offered the opportunity to complete applications on paper," using forms that were "tried and tested" in the past.[6]

An independent watchdog group investigated the situation and learned that the implementation of the system began before final specifications and regulations were agreed on by the European Commission (the executive body of the European Union). The RPA then had to make many substantial changes to the system after implementation. Further, the investigation found that testing did not take into account the real environment, leading to unanticipated work to populate the database with what has now been realized to be largely inaccurate data. Four separate governmental reviews have all been deeply critical of the system and its implementers. The RPA's July 2010 report commented, "the review process was made unnecessarily difficult by the RPA leadership resisting its commencement."[7]

Despite receiving three "red" warnings from the Office of Government Commerce during reviews, the implementation continued. Time was not built into the schedule for testing the whole system as well as the individual components. The components were not compatible with the business processes they were supposed to support.[8] The Single Payment Scheme system itself has cost £350 million, which is considerably more than the original estimated cost of £75.5m. An additional £304 million has been spent on staff costs to respond to the early payment fiascos. As of March 2015, the Single Payment Scheme has been abandoned and the Basic Payment Scheme cost an additional £154 million but does not work properly.[9] All told, since the project began, £600 million in EU fines had accumulated.[10]

This example highlights the possible financial and social consequences of a failed IS project. Such failures occur at an astonishing rate. The Standish Group, a technology research firm, found that 67% of all software projects are challenged—that is, are delivered late, are over budget, or simply fail to meet their performance criteria.[11] Business projects increasingly rely on IS to attain their objectives, especially with the increased focus of business over the Internet. Thus, managing a business project means managing, often to a large degree, an IS project. To succeed, a general manager must be both a project manager and a risk manager.

In the current business environment, the quality that differentiates firms in the marketplace—and destines them for success or failure—is often the ability to adapt existing business processes and systems to produce innovative ideas faster than the competition. The process of continual adaptation to the changing marketplace drives the need for business change and thus for successful project management. Typical adaptation projects include the following:

- Rightsizing the organization
- Re-engineering business processes
- Adopting more comprehensive, integrative processes
- Incorporating new information technologies

Projects are made up of a set of one-time activities that transforms a set of resources into a new information system. Firms seek to compete through new products and processes, but the work of initially building or radically changing them falls outside the scope of normal business operations. That is where projects come in. When work can be accomplished only through methods that fundamentally differ from those employed to run daily operations, the skilled project manager must play a crucial role.

Successful business strategy requires executive management to decide which objectives can be met through normal daily operations and which require a specialized project. Rapidly changing business situations make it difficult to keep the IT projects aligned with dynamic business strategy. Furthermore, the complexity of IT-intensive

---

[6] Warmwell postings (March 20, 2015), http://www.warmwell.com/rpa.html (accessed September 1, 2015).

[7] Warmwell postings (July 20, 2010), http://www.warmwell.com/rpa.html (accessed April 10, 2012).

[8] Adapted from http://www.silicon.com/publicsector/0, 3800010403, 39168359, 00.htm (accessed July 28, 2008); "Review Calls for Rationalisation of Rural Payments Agency IT Systems," Computing.co. United Kingdom (July 21, 2010), http://www.computing.co.uk/ctg/news/1842966/review-calls-rationalisation-rural-payments-agency-it-systems (accessed January 22, 2012).

[9] Glick, "What Went Wrong with Defra's Rural Payment Scheme?"

[10] Parliamentary business report (March 24, 2015), http://www.publications.parliament.uk/pa/cm201415/cmselect/cmenvfru/942/94203.htm (accessed September 1, 2015).

[11] The information from the Standish Group CHAOS Report for 2006 was quoted in C. Sauer, A. Gemino, and B. H. Reich, "The Impact of Size and Volatility on IT Project Performance," *Communications of the ACM* 50, no. 11 (November 2007), 79–84.

projects has increased over the years, magnifying the risk that the finished product or process will no longer satisfy the needs of the business originally targeted to benefit from the project in the first place. Thus, learning to manage projects successfully, especially their IT component, is a crucial competency for every manager. Executives acknowledge skilled IT project management as fundamental to business success.

This chapter provides an overview of what a project is and how to manage one. It begins with a general discussion of project management and then continues with aspects of IT-intensive projects that make them uniquely challenging. It identifies the issues that shape the role of the general manager in such projects and help them to manage risk. Finally, the chapter considers what it means to successfully complete IT projects.

What Defines a Project?

In varying degrees, organizations combine two types of work—projects and operations— to transform resources into profits. Both types are performed by people and require a flow of limited resources. Both are planned, executed, and controlled. The flight of an airplane from its point of departure to its destination is an operation that requires a pilot and crew, the use of an airplane, and fuel. The operation is repetitive: After the plane is refueled and maintained, it takes new passengers to another destination. The continuous operation the plane creates is a transportation service. However, developing the design for such a plane is a project that may require years of work by many people. When the design is completed, the work ends. Figure 11.1 compares characteristics of both project and operational work. The last two characteristics are distinctive and form the basis for the following formal definition:

> [A] **project** is a temporary endeavor undertaken to create a unique product, service or result. Temporary means that every project has a definite beginning and a definite end[12] [emphasis added].

All projects have stakeholders. **Project stakeholders** are the individuals and organizations that either are involved in the project or whose interests may be affected as a result of the project.[13] The most obvious project stakeholders are the project manager and project team. But other stakeholders include the project sponsor who typically is a general manager who provides the resources for the project and who often expects to use the project deliverables. Customers, also stakeholders, are individuals or organizations who use the project product. Multiple layers of customers may be involved. For example, the customers for a new pharmaceutical product may include the doctors who prescribe the medications, the patients who take them, and the insurers who pay for them. Finally, employees in the organization undertaking the project are stakeholders with varying degrees of involvement.

To organize the work of a project team, the project manager may break a project into subprojects. He or she then organizes these subprojects around distinct activities, such as quality control testing. This organization method allows the project manager to contract certain kinds of work externally to limit costs or other drains on crucial project resources. At the macro level, a general manager may choose to organize various projects as elements of a larger *program* if doing so creates efficiencies. A **program** is a collection of related projects that is often related to

Characteristics	Operations	Projects
Purpose	To sustain the enterprise	To reach a specific goal or accomplish a task
Trigger to change	Operation no longer allows an enterprise to meet its objectives	Project goal is reached or task is completed
Quality control	Formal	Informal
Product or service	Repetitive	Unique
Duration	Ongoing	Temporary

FIGURE 11.1 Characteristics of operational and project work.

[12] Project Management Institute, *A Guide to the Project Management Body of Knowledge*, 3rd ed. (Newtown Square, PA: Project Management Institute, 2004), 5.
[13] Ibid., 24.

a strategic organizational objective.[14] There is often some uncertainty about how that objective will be achieved. For example, total quality management (TQM) and workplace safety are *programs,*[15] and each might involve several IT (and non-IT) *projects*. TQM might require projects to develop defect databases, deploy on-line training programs, and implement measurement systems to track improvements. Other programs include the space program or the development of Boeing's Dreamliner. Such programs provide a framework from which to manage competing resource requirements and assign priorities among a set of projects.

What Is Project Management?

Project management is the "application of knowledge, skills, tools, and techniques to project activities in order to meet project requirements."[16] Project management always involves continual trade-offs, and it is the manager's job to manage them. Even the tragic sinking of the *Titanic* has been attributed, in part, to project trade-offs. The company that built the *Titanic*, Harland and Wolff of Belfast, Northern Ireland, had difficulty finding the millions of rivets it needed for the three ships it was building at the same time. Under time and cost pressures to build these ships, the company managers decided to sacrifice quality by purchasing low-grade rivets that were used on some parts of the *Titanic*. When making the trade-offs, it was unlikely that the company's management knew that they were purchasing something so substandard that their ship would sink if it hit an iceberg. Nonetheless, the trade-off proved disastrous.[17]

The three well-known trade-offs are depicted in the project triangle (see Figure 11.2), which highlights the importance of balancing scope, time, and cost. *Scope* may be subdivided into that of the product (the detailed description of the system's quality, features, and functions) and of the project itself (the work required to deliver a product or service with the intended product scope). *Time* refers to the time required to complete the project, whereas *cost* encompasses all the resources required to carry out the project. In the tragic case of the *Titanic*, the managers were willing to trade off *quality* for lower-*cost* rivets that allowed them to build all three ships (*scope*) in a more timely fashion *(time)*. In contrast, a successful balance of scope, time, and cost yields a high-quality project—one in which the needs and expectations of the users are met.

The tricky part of project management is successfully juggling these three elements. Changes in any one of the sides of the triangle affect one or both of the other sides. For example, if the project scope increases, more time and/or more resources (cost) are needed to do the additional work. This increase in scope after a project has begun is aptly called *scope creep*.

In most projects, only two of these elements can be optimized, and the third must be adjusted to maintain balance. A project can be finished in a specific amount of time for a specific budget, but then the scope must be adjusted accordingly. Or if the project is needed quickly and with a specific scope, then the cost must be adjusted

FIGURE 11.2 Project triangle.

[14] Savvy Project Manager (April 9, 2008), https://thesavvypm.wordpress.com/2008/04/09/definition-of-program-vs-project/ (accessed September 1, 2015).

[15] Dan Friedmann, "Program vs. Project Management," http://www.proj-mgt.com/PMC_Program_vs_Project.htm (accessed September 1, 2015).

[16] Ibid., 8.

[17] This research was described in J. H. McCarty and T. Foecke, *What Really Sank the Titanic* (New York: Citadel Press, 2008) and is based on J. H. McCarty, PhD Thesis, The Johns Hopkins University (2003).

accordingly. It is usually not possible to complete a project cheaply, quickly, and with a large scope. To do so usually means introducing errors and completion at a quality level that is too low for acceptance testing. The reasoning is that many cutting-edge technologies can be acquired, but they are often proprietary and unique, requiring steep fees or specialized "rock star" developers to adapt or install them. The final choice is to attempt to build an excellent system cheaply; however, it will take a long time if the firm waits for competing vendors to offer less expensive alternatives. Sometimes a firm might hire college interns with up-to-date, excellent skills at a very low rate, but their availability is often limited because of classes, homework, or exams. If a firm waits several years, it might find technologies available at no cost from an open source provider.

It is important that the project stakeholders decide on the overriding "key success factor" (i.e., time, cost, or scope) although the project manager has the important responsibility of demonstrating to the stakeholders the impact on the project of selecting any of these. In the RPA case at the beginning of this chapter, scope was a key success factor that was managed inappropriately, ultimately resulting in a much longer time and much higher cost.

But the key success factor is only one metric to use when managing a project. Stakeholders are concerned about all facets of the project. Measuring and tracking progress is often done by tracking time (How are we doing compared to the schedule?), cost (How are we doing compared to the budget?), scope (Are we on track to provide the intended functionality?), resources (How much of our resources have we consumed so far?), quality (Is the quality of the output/deliverables at the level required for success?), and risks (How are we doing managing the risk associated with this project?).

A successful business project often begins with a well-written business case that spells out the components of the project. The business case clearly articulates the details of the project and argues for resources for it. For example, UPS prioritizes projects on the strength of their business cases and financial metrics. They also make nonfinancial considerations such as weighing international projects more heavily to spur the company's growth.[18] The components of a business case and common financial metrics are discussed in Chapter 8.

The process used to develop the business case sets the foundation for the project itself. Therefore, detailed planning and contingency planning are important parts of project management. It is often in the planning phase that implementation issues, areas of concern, and gaps are first identified. Further, a strong business plan developed from the business case gives all members of the project team a reference document to help guide decisions and activities.

Project management software is often used to manage projects and keep track of key metrics. A recent well-known survey by Capterra[19] revealed that the top five project management systems are Microsoft Project, Atlassian Jira, Podio, Smartsheet, and Basecamp but that 13 others are used by at least 200,000 users. Those packages can keep track of team members, deliverables, schedules, budgets, priorities, tasks, and other resources. Many of these systems provide a dashboard of key metrics to help project managers quickly identify areas of concern or potentially critical issues that need attention. Some packages have "moved to the cloud" and enable employees to access status reports and plans anywhere.[20]

Organizing for Project Management

Although managing projects is not a new set of activities for management, it is a struggle for many to bring a project in on time, on budget, and within scope. Some organizations create a **project management office (PMO)**, which is a department responsible for boosting efficiency, gathering expertise, and improving project delivery. A PMO operates at the project level and often is tasked with accomplishing goals defined in various organizational programs. A PMO is created to bring discipline to the project management activities within the enterprise. The Sarbanes–Oxley Act is also a driver because it forces companies to pay close attention to project expenses and progress.

[18] UPS, "IT Governance: The Key to Aligning Technology Initiatives with Business Direction," http://www.pressroom.ups.com (accessed July 22, 2008).
[19] Jordan Barrish, "The 20 Most Popular Project Management Software Products" (November 13, 2013), http://blog.capterra.com/20-popular-project-management-software-products-infographic/ (accessed September 2, 2015).
[20] Don Reisinger, "10 Cloud-Based Project Management Tools to Serve Every Company's Needs" (July 5, 2013), http://www.eweek.com/cloud/slideshows/10-cloud-based-project-management-tools-to-serve-every-companys-needs (accessed September 2, 2015).

Although companies may not immediately realize cost savings, the increased efficiencies and project discipline from a PMO may eventually lead to cost savings.

PMOs can be expected to function in the following seven areas, according to *CIO Magazine*:

- Project support
- Project management process and methodology
- Training
- Project manager home base
- Internal consulting and mentoring
- Project management software tools and support
- Portfolio management (managing multiple projects)

The responsibilities of a PMO range widely based on the preferences of the chief information officer (CIO) under which the PMO typically falls. Sometimes the PMO is simply a clearinghouse for best practices in project management, and other times it is the organization that more formally manages all major projects. At risk management company Assurant Group, for example, a number of project managers work in the PMO under the direction of the chief operating officer (COO). Using well-defined software development and project management methodologies, these PMO managers work with business managers to refine their project management efforts—from requirements definition to postimplementation audits. Within four years of the installation of its PMO, 97% of Assurant's projects were delivered on schedule and within budget.[21]

Project Elements

Project work requires in-depth situational analyses and the organization of complex activities into often coincident sequences of discrete tasks. The outcomes of each activity must be tested and integrated into the larger process to produce the desired result. The number of variables affecting the performance of such work is potentially enormous.

Four elements essential for any project include (1) project management, (2) a project team, (3) a project cycle plan, and (4) a common project vocabulary. Project management includes the project sponsor who initiates the project and a **project manager** who makes sure that the entire project is executed appropriately and coordinated properly. A good project manager defines the project scope realistically, and then manages the project so that it can be completed on time and within budget.

The project team has members who work together to ensure that all parts of the project come together correctly and efficiently. The plan represents the methodology and schedule to be used by the team to execute the project. Finally, a common project vocabulary allows all those involved with the project to understand the project and communicate effectively.

It is essential to understand the interrelationships among these elements and with the project itself. Both a commitment to working together as a team and a common project vocabulary must permeate the management of a project throughout its life. The project plan consists of the sequential steps of organizing and tracking the work of the team. Finally, the project manager ensures the completion of work by team members at each step of the project cycle plan (see later discussion) and as situational elements evolve throughout the project cycle.

Project Management

Two key players in project management are the sponsor and the manager. The project sponsor liaises between the project team and the other stakeholders. The sponsor is the project champion and works with the project manager in providing the leadership to accomplish project objectives. Often the sponsor is a very senior-level executive in

[21] M. Santosus, "Why You Need a Project Management Office (PMO)," http://www.cio.com/article/29887/Why_You_Need_a_Project_Management_Office_PMO_/1 (accessed July 15, 2008).

the firm, someone who has influence with the key stakeholders and C-level team. The project sponsor secures the financial resources for the project.

The project manager is central to the project. The project manager role is not an easy one because it requires a range of management skills to make the project successful. The challenge facing a project manager is to learn and apply these skills properly in the situations that require them. The skills include (1) identifying requirements of the systems to be delivered, (2) providing organizational integration by defining the team's structure, (3) assigning team members to work on the project, (4) managing risks and leveraging opportunities, (5) measuring the project's status, outcomes, and exceptions to provide project control, (6) making the project visible to general management and other stakeholders, (7) measuring project status against plan, often using project management software, (8) taking corrective action when necessary to get the project back on track, and (9) providing project leadership. The first three of these skills are formulative; they require considerable planning and designing ability. The remaining skills are all about taking action and reacting. When a project deviates from its desired path, corrective action is needed to get it back on track.[22]

Another way to understand this list of skills is that the last one, providing project leadership, guides the first eight skills. Lack of leadership can result in unmotivated or confused people doing the wrong things and ultimately derailing the project. Strong project leaders skillfully manage team composition, reward systems, and other techniques to focus, align, and motivate team members. Figure 11.3 reflects the inverse relationship between the magnitude of the project leader's role and the experience and commitment of the team. In organizations with strong processes for project management and professionals trained for this activity, the need for aggressive project leadership is reduced.

A number of factors influence project managers and, ultimately, their team's performance. These include organizational culture and socioeconomic influences. *Organizational culture* affects the leadership style of the project manager and the communication between team members. For example, a culture that rewards individual achievement over team participation may hinder a project team. Members might hoard information instead of sharing it. A leader who sets a good example for the team and who encourages teamwork has the opportunity to eliminate these barriers. *Socioeconomic influences* on projects include government and industry standards, globalization, and cultural issues.

Project Team

The project team consists of those people who work together to complete the project. Business teams often fail because members don't understand the nature of the work required to make their team effective. Teamwork begins by clearly defining the team's objectives and each member's role in achieving these objectives. Teams

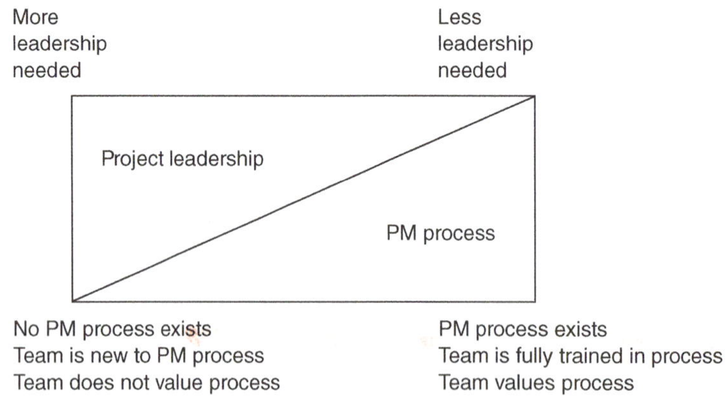

FIGURE 11.3 Project leadership versus project management (PM) process.

[22] Adapted from K. Forsberg, H. Mooz, and H. Cotterman, *Visualizing Project Management* (Hoboken, NJ: John Wiley, 1996).

need to have norms about conduct, shared rewards, a shared understanding of roles, and team spirit. Project managers should leverage team member skills, knowledge, experiences, and capabilities when assigning the team members to complete specific activities on an as-needed basis. In addition to completing their team activities, team members also represent their departments and transmit information about their department to other team members. Such information sharing constitutes the first step toward building consensus on critical project issues that affect the entire organization. Thus, effective project managers use teamwork both to organize and apply human resources, to motivate an acceptance of change, and to collect and share information throughout the organization.

Project Cycle Plan

The project cycle plan organizes discrete project activities and sequences them in steps along a timeline so that the project fulfills the requirements of customers and stakeholders. It identifies critical beginning and end dates and breaks the work spanning these dates into phases. Using the plan, the time and resources needed to complete the work based on the project's scope are identified, and tasks are assigned to team members. The general manager tracks the phases to coordinate the eventual transition from project to operational status, a process that culminates in the "go-live" date. The project manager uses the phases to control the progress of work. He or she may establish "control gates" at various points along the way to verify that project work to date has met key requirements regarding cost, quality, and features. If it has not met these requirements, he or she can make changes, which could also delay the project plan's "go-live" date.

The project cycle plan can be developed using various approaches and software tools. The three most common approaches are the project evaluation and review technique (PERT), critical path method (CPM), and Gantt chart. PERT identifies the tasks within the project, orders them in a time sequence, identifies their interdependencies, and estimates the time required to complete the task. The *critical path* is a set of important tasks that must be performed sequentially without skipping any of them. Together, these critical tasks account for the total elapsed time of the project. Noncritical tasks are those that can be performed in parallel and for which some slack time can be built into the schedules without affecting the duration of the entire project. A PERT chart is shown in Figure 11.4. Note that talking with a selected group of customers must be done before holding the first approval meeting. Likewise, that meeting must be held before the needs assessment can be completed.

CPM is a project planning and scheduling tool that is similar to PERT. Unlike PERT, CPM incorporates a capability for identifying relationships between costs and the completion date of a project and the amount and value of resources that must be applied in alternative situations. The two approaches differ in terms of time estimates. PERT builds on broad estimates of the time needed to complete project tasks. It takes into account the optimistic, most probable, and pessimistic time estimates for each task. In contrast, CPM assumes that all time requirements for completion of individual tasks are relatively predictable. Because of these differences, CPM tends to be used on projects for which direct relationships can be established between time and resources (costs).

Gantt charts are commonly used as visual tools for displaying time relationships of project tasks and for monitoring the progress toward project completion. Gantt charts list project tasks. For each task, a bar indicates the relative amount of time expected to complete the task. Milestones (i.e., due dates) are noted with diamonds. At the start of the project, Gantt charts are especially useful for planning and monitoring purposes. As the project progresses, the chart is modified to reflect the extent to which each task is completed at the time the project is monitored. A Gantt chart is displayed in Figure 11.5.

Figure 11.6 presents a comparison of a generic project cycle plan, the Project Management Institute's project life cycle, and a typical high-tech commercial business cycle. Notice that although each of these life cycles has unique phases, all can loosely be described by three major periods (shown at the top of the diagram): study, implementation, and operations.

Projects are all about change. They bring new products, services, or systems into organizations or make them available for the organization's customers. These project deliverables need to be integrated into the organization's (or its customers') operations. Not surprisingly, the three major periods in the project life cycle in Figure 11.6

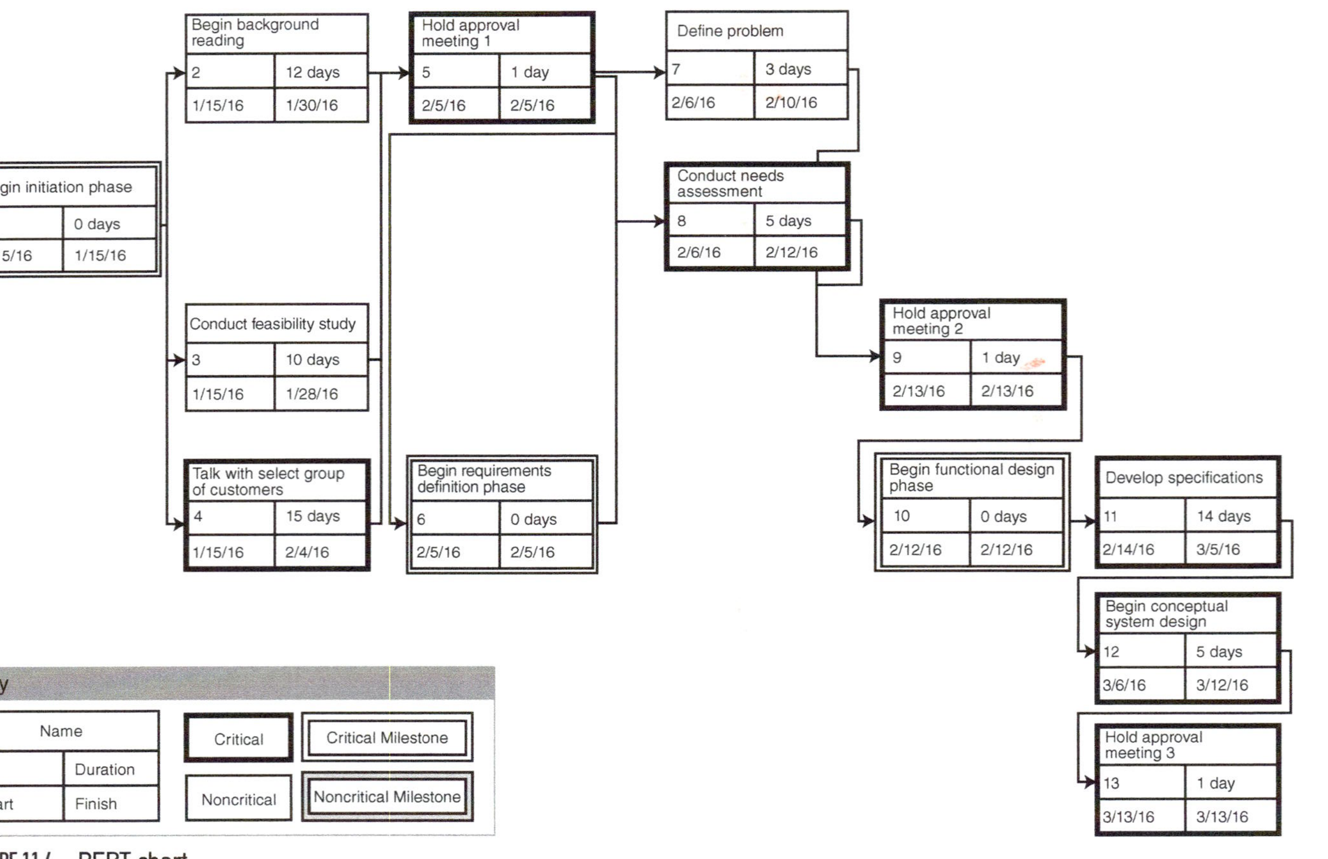

FIGURE 11.4 PERT chart.

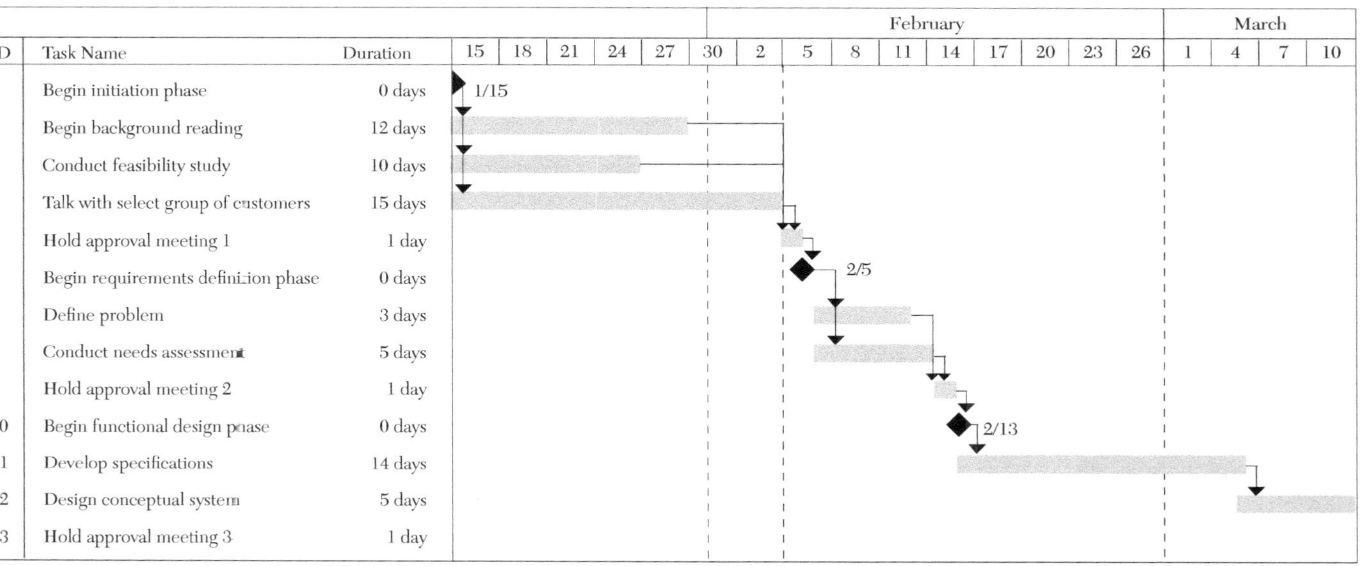

FIGURE 11.5 Gantt chart.

<table>
<tr><td colspan="3">Study Period</td><td colspan="6">Implementation Period</td><td colspan="2">Operation Period</td></tr>
<tr><td colspan="11">Typical High-Tech Commercial Business</td></tr>
<tr><td>Product requirements</td><td>Product definition</td><td>Product proposal</td><td>Product development</td><td colspan="2">Engineer model</td><td colspan="2">Internal test</td><td>External test</td><td>Production</td><td>Manufacturing sales and support</td></tr>
<tr><td colspan="11">Generic Systems Development Life Cycle Template (See also Figure 11.7 for more detail)</td></tr>
<tr><td>Initiation and feasibility</td><td>Requirements definition</td><td>Functional design</td><td colspan="2">Technical design and construction</td><td colspan="2">Verification</td><td colspan="2">Implementation</td><td colspan="2">Maintenance and review</td></tr>
<tr><td colspan="11">Project Management Institute Process Groups in a Project Life Cycle</td></tr>
<tr><td colspan="2">Initiating</td><td>Planning</td><td colspan="6">Executing</td><td>Monitoring and controlling</td><td>Closing</td></tr>
</table>

FIGURE 11.6 Project cycle template.
Source: Adapted from K. Forsberg, H. Mooz, and H. Cotterman, *Visualizing Project Management*, 3rd ed. (Hoboken, NJ: John Wiley, 2005). Used with permission.

(study, implementation, and operations) correspond respectively to Lewin's classic change model introduced in Chapter 4: unfreezing, changing, and refreezing.[23] First, according to Lewin, people need to be given a motivation for change in the unfreezing stage. People don't want to change unless they see some reason for doing so. This is what happens in the study period when it is determined what needs to be changed and why. The project sponsor is often a key mover in providing answers to these questions. Then in the changing stage, when the system is built (or purchased) and installed, people in the organization are made aware of what the change is and receive training about how to take advantage of it. It is not possible for people to fully understand the change until the implementation period, after the service, product, or system has been designed or built, and they are then trained to use it. Those on the project team can better understand what the project deliverable is and why it was designed the way it was. Finally, the refreezing stage occurs when the organization helps the employees integrate the change into their normal way of working. This occurs in the operations period.

Common Project Vocabulary

Typical project teams include a variety of members from different backgrounds and parts of the organization. Often the team is made up of consultants who are new to the organization, a growing number of technical specialists, and business members. Each area of expertise represented by team members uses a different technical vocabulary. For example, an accountant in a manufacturing firm might consider the "end of year" to be June 30, the end of the company's fiscal year, but a sales representative might consider the "end of year" as December 31 when the frantic sales activity ends for a while. Also, an executive might refer to the sale of a subsidiary as a "sale" whereas an accountant would call it a "divestment." When used together in the team context, these different vocabularies make it difficult to carry on conversations, meetings, and correspondence.

To avoid misunderstandings, project team members need to commit to a consistent meaning for terms used on their project. After agreeing on definitions and common meanings, the project team should record and explain the terms in its own common project vocabulary. The common project vocabulary includes many terms and meanings that are unfamiliar to the general manager and the team's other business members. To improve their communications with general managers, users, and other nontechnical people, technical people should limit their use of acronyms and cryptic words and should strive to place only the most critical ones in the common project vocabulary. Good management of the common project vocabulary, the project management, the project team, and the project life cycle are all essential to project success.

IT Projects

An IT project is a specific type of business project. One industry saying is that there is no such thing as an IT project; all projects are really business projects involving varying degrees of IT. Sometimes managing the IT component of a project is referred to separately as an IT project not only for simplicity but also because the business world perceives that managing an IT project is somehow different from managing any other type of project. However, projects done by the IT department typically include an associated business case and other components of business projects; even though the project owner may be an IT person, mounting evidence indicates that IT projects are just business projects involving significant amounts of technology. However, the more complex the IT aspect of the project is, the higher is the risk of failure of the project, which makes these types of projects worthy of special consideration.

IT projects are difficult to estimate despite the increasing amount of attention given to mastering this task. Like the case of the RPA's Single Payment Scheme, most software projects fail to meet their schedules and budgets. Managers attribute that failure to poor estimating techniques, poorly monitored progress protocols, and the misinformed idea that schedule slippage can be solved by simply adding additional people to the team.[24] This fallaciously

[23] Kurt Lewin, "Frontiers In Group Dynamics II. Channels of Group Life; Social Planning and Action Research," *Human Relations* 1, no. 2 (1947): 143–53.

[24] Frederick Brooks, *The Mythical Man-Month: Essays on Software Engineering* (Reading, MA: Addison-Wesley, 1982).

assumes not only that people and months are interchangeable but also that if the project is off schedule, it may be that it was incorrectly designed in the first place, and putting additional people on the project just hastens the process to an inappropriate end.

Many projects are measured in terms of **function points**, or the functional requirements of the software product, which can be estimated earlier than total lines of code. Others are measured in "man-months," the most common unit for discussing the size of a project. For example, a project that takes 100 man-months means that it will take one person 100 months to do the work, or 10 people can do it in 10 months.

A recent study found that managing projects using the man-months metric was linked to more underperforming projects than those using any other metric of size (i.e., budget, duration, team size).[25] Man-months may be a poor metric for project management because some projects cannot be sped up with additional people. An analogy is that of pregnancy. It takes one woman nine months to carry a baby, and putting nine people on the job for one month cannot speed that process. Software systems often involve highly interconnected, interdependent, and complex sets of tasks that rely on each other to make a completed system. Further, adding people means that more communication is needed to coordinate all the team members' activities. In sum, additional people can speed the process in some cases, but most projects cannot be made more efficient simply by adding talent. Often, adding people to a late project only makes the project later.[26]

IT Project Development Methodologies and Approaches

The choice of development methodologies and managerial influences also distinguishes IT projects from other projects. The general manager needs to understand the issues specific to the IT aspects of projects to select the right management tools for the particular challenges presented in such projects. The **systems development life cycle (SDLC)** is a traditional tool for developing IS or for implementing software developed by an outsourcing provider or software developer. Many steps in the SDLC are used by other methodologies, although not to the same extent. For example, most other methodologies try to determine user needs and test the new system, even though these other methodologies don't perform all of the other steps in the SDLC. Thus, this chapter provides greater detail on SDLC than on the other methodologies. The SDLC discussion is followed by a short description of two key iterative approaches—agile programming and prototyping.

Systems Development Life Cycle

Systems development refers to the set of activities used to create an IS, a process in which the phases of the project are well documented, milestones are clearly identified, and all individuals involved in the project fully understand what exactly the project consists of and when deliverables are to be made. The SDLC typically refers to the process of designing and delivering the entire system. Although the system includes hardware, software, networking, and data (as discussed in Chapter 6), the SDLC generally is used in one of two distinct ways. On the one hand, it is the general project plan of all the activities that must take place for the entire system to be put into operation, including the analysis and feasibility study, development or acquisition of components, implementation activities, maintenance activities, and retirement activities. In the context of an information system, however, the term *SDLC* can refer to a highly structured, disciplined, and formal process for design and development of system software. In either view, the SDLC is grounded on the systems approach and allows the developer to focus on system goals and trade-offs.

The SDLC approach is much more structured than other development approaches, such as agile programming or prototyping. However, despite being a highly structured approach, no single well-accepted SDLC process exists. For any specific organization, and for a specific project, the actual tasks under each phase may vary. In addition, the checkpoints, metrics, and documentation may vary somewhat. The SDLC typically consists of seven phases (see Figure 11.7).

---

[25] Sauer, Gemino, and Reich, "The Impact of Size and Volatility on IT Project Performance."

[26] Brooks, *The Mythical Man-Month.*

Phase	Description	Sample Activities
Initiation and feasibility	Project is begun with a formal initiation and overall project is understood by IS and user/customers.	• Document project objectives, scope, benefits, assumptions, constraints, estimated costs and schedule, and user commitment mechanisms • Plan for human resources, communication, risk management, and quality
Requirements definition	The system specifications are identified and documented.	• Define business functionality; review existing systems • Identify current problems and issues, potential solutions • Identify and prioritize user requirements • Develop user acceptance plan, user documentation needs, and user training strategy
Functional design	The system is designed.	• Complete a detailed analysis of new system including entity-relationship diagrams, data flow diagrams, and functional design diagrams • Define security needs; revise system architecture • Identify standards; define systems acceptance criteria • Define test scenarios • Revise implementation strategy • Freeze design
Technical design and construction	The system is built or a purchased system is customized and implemented.	• Finalize architecture, technical issues, standards, and data needs • Complete technical definition of data access, programming flows, interfaces, special needs, inter-system processing, conversion strategy, and test plans • Construct system • Monitor and control the development process • Revise schedule, plan, and costs, as necessary
Verification	The system is reviewed to make sure it meets specifications and requirements.	• Finalize verification testing, user testing, security testing, error-handling procedures, acceptance testing, end-user training, documentation, and support
Implementation	The system is brought up for use.	• Put system into production environment • Establish security procedures • Deliver user documentation • Execute training and complete monitoring of system
Maintenance and review	The system is maintained and repaired as needed throughout its lifetime.	• Run system • Conduct user review and evaluation • Conduct internal review and evaluation • Check metrics to ensure usability, reliability, utility, cost, satisfaction, business value, etc. • Fix errors and add new features • Ensure contract closure

FIGURE 11.7 Systems development life cycle (SDLC) phases.

Note that system construction or acquisition cannot begin until the requirements are specified and the functional and technical designs are completed. After the new system is built or bought, it is tested, and users must approve it before the implementation phase can begin. The implementation phase is the "cutover" where the new system is put in operation and all links are established. Cutover may be performed in several ways: The old system may run alongside the new system (**parallel conversion**), the old system may stop running as soon as the new system is installed (**direct cutover**), or the new system may be installed in stages across locations, or in phases. The safest way to convert from an old system to a new system is parallel conversion because if the new system fails, users easily can revert to the old system. The riskiest approach is direct cutover because there is no backup system to turn to in the event of problems with the new system. Usually direct cutover is reserved for small, less-critical systems or for systems that weren't previously available. An instance when direct cutover was a good idea was Dagen H (*Högertrafik*) Day, September 3, 1967, when Swedish drivers were to change from driving on the left-hand to the right-hand side of the road. On Dagen H Day, all non-essential vehicles needed to be off the roads between 1:00 and 6:00 P.M. Those that remained pulled over at 4:50 P.M, moved carefully to the right-hand side of the road, and remain stopped for the next ten minutes. Then at 5:00 P.M, they were permitted to proceed.[27]

Also, note that implementation is not the final stage. Periodic evaluation is conducted in the maintenance and review stage to ensure that the project continues to meet the needs for which it was designed. The system development project is evaluated using postproject feedback (sometimes called *postimplementation audit*) from all involved in the project. Postproject feedback brings closure to the project by identifying what went right and what could be done better next time. Maintenance is conducted on the system and enhancements made until it is decided that a new system should be developed and the SDLC begins anew. The maintenance and review phase is typically the longest phase of the life cycle.

Agile Development

Several problems arise with using traditional SDLC methodology for newer IT projects. First, many systems projects fail to meet objectives even with the structure of the SDLC. The primary reason is often because the skills needed to estimate costs and schedules are difficult to obtain, and each project is often unique so that previous experience may not provide the skills needed for the current one. Second, even though objectives that were specified for the system were met, those objectives may reflect a scope that is too broad or too narrow or has changed since the project was initiated. Thus, the problem that the system was designed to solve may or may not still exist, or the opportunity that it was to capitalize on may not be appropriately leveraged. Third, organizations need to respond quickly because of the dynamic nature of the business environment. Not enough time is available to adequately complete each step of the SDLC for each IT project. Newer methodologies designed to address these concerns use an iterative approach (Figure 11.8).

One of the dangers developers face is expecting a predictable development process when in reality it's not predictable at all. In response to this challenge, **agile development** methodologies are being championed. These include extreme programming (XP), crystal, scrum, feature-driven development, and dynamic system development method (DSDM). To deal with unpredictability, agile methodologies tend to be people- rather than process-oriented. They adapt to changing requirements by iteratively developing systems in small stages and then testing the new code extensively. The mantra for agile programming is "Code a little; test a little." Some agile methodologies build on existing methodologies. For example, DSDM is an extension of rapid applications development (RAD) used in the United Kingdom that draws on the underlying principles of active user interaction, frequent deliveries, and empowered teams. It incorporates a project planning technique that divides the schedule into a number of separate time periods (timeboxes) with each part having its own deliverables, deadline, and budget. DSDM is based on four types of iterations: study (business and feasibility), functional model, design and build, and implementation. These iterations occur (and recur) in cycles of between two and six weeks. In contrast is XP, a more prescriptive agile methodology that revolves around 12 practices, including pair programming, test-driven development, simple design, and small releases.[28]

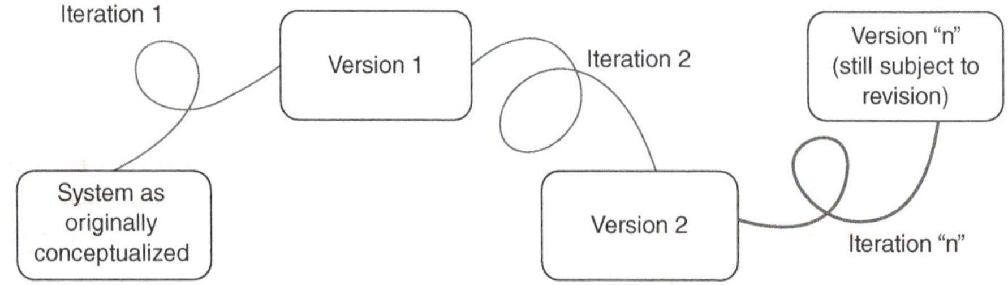

FIGURE 11.8 Iterative approach to systems development.

[27] H. Dagen, Wikipedia, http://en.wikipedia.org/wiki/Dagen_H (accessed September 2, 2015).

[28] Kent Beck, *Extreme Programming Explained: Embrace Change* (Reading, MA: Addison-Wesley Longman, 1999).

Although it allows speedy development and creates happy customers, there are some downsides to agile development. For large projects, it is difficult to estimate the effort that will be required. Further, in the rush to get the project completed, designing and documentation might be underemphasized. Also, an agile development project can easily get off track if the customer representatives are not clear about what final outcome they want.

Prototyping

Another iterative approach is **prototyping**, a type of evolutionary development that uses the method of building systems in which developers get a general idea of what is needed by the users and then build a fast, high-level version of the system at the beginning of the project. The idea of prototyping is to quickly get a version of the software in the hands of the users and to jointly let the system evolve through a series of iterative cycles of design. In this way, the system is done either when the users are happy with the design or when the system is proven impossible, too costly, or too complex. Some IS groups use prototyping as a methodology by itself because users are involved in the development much more closely than is possible with the traditional SDLC process. Users see the day-to-day growth of the system and contribute frequently to the development process. In other cases, prototyping is used as a phase in the SDLC to capture project requirements. Through this iterative process, the system requirements usually are made clear.

There are several drawbacks to prototyping. First, documentation may be more difficult to write as the system evolves, because of frequent changes over time. Second, users often do not understand that a final prototype may not be scalable to an operational version of the system without additional costs and organizational commitments. Once users see a working model, they typically assume that the work is also almost done, which is not usually the case. An operational version of the system needs to be developed using enterprise-level tools rather than desktop tools. In many cases, a system built with desktop tools can serve only one or a small number of users at a time. An enterprise-ready system can often serve hundreds or thousands of users simultaneously. A seemingly operational version may be difficult to complete because the user is unwilling to give up a system that is up and running, and she or he often has unrealistic expectations about the amount of work involved in creating an enterprise-ready version. This reluctance leads to the fourth drawback. Because it may be nearly impossible to definitively say when the prototype is complete, the prototyping development process may be difficult to manage.

A fifth problem with prototyping is caused by the difficulty of integration across a broad range of requirements; this approach is best suited for "quick-and-dirty" types of systems. Developers should rely on a more structured approach such as the SDLC for extremely large and complex systems. Finally, because of the speed of development and reliance on a small number of people for quick (perhaps hasty) feedback, there may be flaws in the system's design. The advantages and disadvantages of the SDLC, agile development, and prototyping approaches are summarized in Figure 11.9.

Other Development Methodologies and Approaches

A variety of other methodologies and approaches exist. These include RAD; joint applications development; user-centered design; object-oriented analysis, design, and development; and open sourcing.

Rapid Applications Development and Joint Applications Development

Rapid applications development (RAD) is similar to prototyping in that it is an interactive process, in which tools are used to drastically speed the development process. RAD systems typically have tools for developing the user interface—called the *graphical user interface (GUI)*—reusable code, code generation, and programming language testing and debugging. These tools make it easy for the developer to build a library of standard sets of code (sometimes called *objects*) that can easily be used (and reused) in multiple applications. Similarly, RAD systems typically have the ability to allow the developer to simply "drag and drop" many objects such as buttons, tables, menus, and drop-down lists into the design, and the RAD system automatically writes some or all of the code necessary to include the desired functionality. Even platforms like Facebook and Web hosting sites such as WordPress allow the user to create feature-rich sites without writing a single line of computer code.

Methodology	Advantages	Disadvantages
SDLC	• Has a structured approach with milestones and approvals for each phase • Uses system approach • Focuses on goals and trade-offs • Emphasizes documentation • Requires user sign-offs	• Has systems that often fail to meet objectives • Needs skills that are often difficult to obtain • Has scope that may be defined too broadly or too narrowly • Is very time consuming
Agile development	• Is good for adapting to changing requirements • Is good for understanding and responding to changing user requirements • Allows face-to-face communication and continuous inputs from users • Speeds up development process • Is liked by users	• Is hard to estimate system deliverables at start of project • Underemphasizes designing and documentation • Is easy to get project off track if user not clear about what the final outcome should be
Prototyping	• Improves user communications • Is liked by users • Speeds up development process • Is good for eliciting system requirements • Provides a tangible model to serve as basis for production version	• Is often underdocumented • Is not designed to be an operational version • Often creates unrealistic expectations • Has a difficult-to-manage development process • End result is often difficult to integrate • Is more likely to experience design flaws than in SDLC • Is often hard to maintain

FIGURE 11.9 Comparison of IT development methodologies.

Finally, RAD includes a set of tools to create, test, and debug the programs written in the pure programming language. However, one must remember that "a fool with a tool is still a fool." RAD is more than just using advanced systems development tools. Rather, it is about making systems developers work more effectively.

RAD is commonly used for developing user interfaces and rewriting legacy applications. It may incorporate prototyping to involve users early and actively in the design process. Although RAD is an approach that works well in the increasingly dynamic environment of systems developers, it does have some drawbacks. Sometimes basic principles of software development (e.g., programming standards, documentation, data-naming standards, backup, and recovery) are overlooked in the race to finish the project. Also, the process may be so speedy that requirements are frozen too early.[29] As a result, systems developed by using RAD may lack quality.

Joint applications development (JAD) is a version of RAD or prototyping in which users are more integrally involved, as a group, with the entire development process up to and, in some cases, including coding. JAD uses a group approach to elicit requirements in a comprehensive manner. Interviewing groups of users saves interviewing and data collection time, but it can be expensive in terms of the travel and living expenses needed to get the participants together.

User-Centered Design

User-centered design uses tools for RAD, JAD, agile development, and prototyping to provide assurance that users' needs will be met. Early in the process, users are involved on the project team and are asked to evaluate impacts on system utility, usability, organizational/social/cultural impact, and the holistic human experience. The goals of user-centered design are to improve efficiency and reduce effort; reduce or prevent errors; strive for a fit between the user's task, the information provided, and the format of the information provided; enable an enjoyable, engaging, and satisfying interaction experience; promote trust; and keep the design simple.[30]

[29] Joey F. George, "The Origins of Software: Acquiring Systems at the End of the Century," *Framing the Domains of IT Management*, ed. R. Zmud (Cincinnati, OH: Pinnaflex Education Resources, 2000).

[30] Dov Te'eni, Jane Carey, and Ping Zhang, *HCI: Developing Effective Organizational Information System* (New York: John Wiley, 2006).

The U.S. government maintains the Web site Usability.gov, which provides over 200 design guidelines, such as "do not require users to remember information from place to place on a Web site" and "make upper and lower case search terms equivalent." Each guideline provides an assessment of importance and the strength of evidence that supports it.[31] Although it might be difficult to remember and follow hundreds of recommendations, heeding them will likely reduce frustration and confusion and perhaps save millions of dollars by reducing the amount of maintenance that could be needed.

However, the guidelines do not cover all possible ways in which to simplify design and engage users. Some of the most popular technologies, such as those from Apple, Microsoft, and Google, offer particular usability advantages and disadvantages. Apple's famous designs have led to long lines in front of retail outlets when new products are introduced. Most have been wildly successful with notably few exceptions. In 2000, Microsoft offered a touch-screen-capable PC operating system when it introduced Windows XP, one of its most popular operating systems ever. Interestingly, when the interface was adapted in 2012 to include larger icons, making for easier finger targets using a special "tiled" display in Windows 8, users balked at the change. Windows 10 moved back to a more "classic" look and feel. Apple's OSX exhibits a future touchscreen path with a large icon screen "app" view. Google quietly adapted its Android and Chromebook software to conform to its material design approach in which system elements look and behave like tactile reality, image choices are bold and intentional, and motion is used to convey meaningful feedback and guidance on what to do next.[32]

Often technologies fail but form the basis of very successful products as time goes on. For example, Apple's Newton boasted ground-breaking mobile device features but relied on hardware of its time—the early 1990s—and users found it slow with a dim screen and short-lived batteries. Twenty years later, better screens, processors, and batteries became available, and Apple tried again with an unprecedented successor to the Newton that also served as a phone, music player, and camera: the iPhone. It is obvious that the iPhone has revolutionized not only the product category and the entire company but also the entire electronics industry.

These examples demonstrate that in software projects, usability has great commercial value in the marketplace. Research on usability and the user experience (UX) has been conducted for decades, but many systems even today are not very usable. For instance, smartphones and tablets famously lack an "undo" function, often requiring users to start from scratch if they press the wrong key.[33]Web sites sometimes use language in their links that is unfamiliar to users, and it is difficult to understand precisely where to click next. Search functions sometimes fail to unearth the desired results. Users just simply dislike some designs, such as the unusual "tile" design of Windows 8 that was discarded in Windows 10 in the summer of 2015.

Why do these failures occur? First, product delivery deadlines sometimes push usability to the back burner because feature lists tend to be the main force in selling software.[34] Also, usability involves a large number of disciplines, such as psychology, graphic art, Internet technologies, and business needs. It is difficult to master a large set of tools from so many disciplines.[35] Finally, systems are quite complex and are difficult to test thoroughly from a usability standpoint.[36] Testing requires designing a comprehensive list of tasks to perform, assembling groups of users who try to perform them, and acting on feedback received by observing errors, confusion, and misinterpretations. One encouraging factor is that over time, most poor systems suffer a Darwinian fate: They must evolve or die. The fit survivors will eventually either outnumber the endangered ones or perhaps serve as good examples to those that started out poorly.

---

31 Usability.Gov. Research Based Web Design and Usability Guidelines, Department of Health and Human Services and General Services Administration, http://www.usability.gov/sites/default/files/documents/guidelines_book.pdf (accessed September 2, 2015).

32 Google, http://www.google.com/design/spec/material-design/introduction.html#introduction-principles (accessed September 2, 2015).

33 D. Norman and J. Nielsen, "Gestural Interfaces: A Step Backward In Usability," *Interactions* (2010).

34 Chris Ward, "Feature-zilla! Will Featureful Kill Usable on the Web?" January 23, 2014, http://www.sitepoint.com/featureful-vs-usable/ (accessed September 2, 2015).

35 K. Instone, "User Experience: An Umbrella Topic,"*CHI'05 Extended Abstracts on Human Factors in Computing Systems* (Association for Computing Machinery, 2005), 1087–88.

36 Jim Ross, "17 Usability Testing Myths and Misconceptions" (January 5, 2015), http://www.uxmatters.com/mt/archives/2015/01/17-usability-testing-myths-and-misconceptions.php (accessed September 2, 2015).

Object-Oriented Development

Object-oriented development is becoming increasingly popular as a way to avoid the pitfalls of procedural methodologies. Object-oriented development, unlike more traditional development using the SDLC, builds on the concept of objects. An **object** encapsulates both the data stored about an entity and the operations that manipulate that data. A program developed using an object orientation is basically a collection of objects. The object orientation makes it easier for developers to think in terms of reusable components. Using existing components can save programming time. Such component-based development, however, assumes that the components have been saved in a repository and can be retrieved when needed and assumes that the components in the programs in newly developed information systems can communicate with one another.

Open Sourcing Approach

Linux, the brainchild of Linus Torvalds, is a world-class operating system created from part-time hacking by several thousand developers scattered all over the planet and connected only by the Internet. This system was built using a development approach called **open sourcing**, or building and improving "free" software by an Internet community. The brilliance of Linux was that Torvalds took a very powerful but proprietary operating system, Unix, and rewrote it to make it available as an open source. In fact, the kernel of Linux contains the statement, "Linux is a Unix clone written from scratch by Linus Torvalds with assistance from a loosely-knit team of hackers across the Net."[37] Torvalds managed the development process by releasing early and often, delegating as much as possible, being open to new ideas, and archiving and managing the various versions of the software.

Eric Raymond, the author of *The Cathedral and the Bazaar*, suggests that the Linux community resembles a great bazaar of differing agendas and approaches (with submissions from *anyone*) out of which a coherent and stable system emerged. This development approach is in contrast to cathedrals in which software is carefully crafted by company employees working in isolation. The most frequently cited example of a cathedral is Microsoft, a company known, if not ridiculed, for espousing a proprietary approach to software development.[38] However, Microsoft has endorsed a movement toward open source code in many of its projects.[39] One example is the adoption of open XML file formats to replace the proprietary and secret formats in previous versions of Word, PowerPoint, and Excel files.[40]

Software is **open source software (OSS)** if it is released under a license approved by the Open Source Initiative (OSI). The most widely used OSI license is the GNU general public license (GPL), which is premised on the concept of free software. *Free software* offers the following freedoms for the software users:

- To run the program for any reason you want
- To study how the program works and to adapt it to your needs, assuming you have access to the source code
- To distribute copies so that you can help your neighbor
- To improve and release your improvements to the public so that the whole community benefits, assuming you have access to the source code[41]

A user who modifies the software must observe the rule of *copyleft*, which stipulates that the user cannot add restrictions to deny other people their central freedoms regarding the free software.

Open sourcing is a movement that offers a speedy way to develop software. Further, because it is made available to a whole community, testing is widespread. Finally, its price is always right—it is free. However, a number of managerial issues are associated with its use in a business organization.

---

[37] See the "read-me" file at https://www.kernel.org/pub/linux/kernel/README (accessed September 2, 2015).
[38] Eric S. Raymond, "The Cathedral and the Bazaar," http://www.catb.org/~esr/writings/cathedral-bazaar/cathedral-bazaar/ (accessed June 4, 2012).
[39] Microsoft. "Openness," http://openness.microsoft.com/blog/ (accessed September 2, 2015).
[40] Microsoft. "Overview of the XML file formats in Office 2010," https://technet.microsoft.com/en-us/library/cc179190.aspx (accessed September 2, 2015).
[41] GNU Project—Free Software Foundation, "The Free Software Definition," http://www.gnu.org/philosophy/free-sw.html (accessed February 27, 2002).

Social Business Lens: Mashups

Social IT applications are often designed with an open architecture to make them easy to adapt. One way organizations take advantage of this feature and create new applications is by using **mashups**. These are Web apps that combine other apps to create a new app, data, functionality, and even interface. The goal of a mashup is to be able to create new applications quickly using existing applications, data, and infrastructure. Some mashups are used internally within a firm, but others are set up on the Web and become a new app.

An example of a mashup is Zillow.com, the real estate Web site. It has a relationship with numerous data providers across the country and accesses public records, which are used in its service. But in addition, Zillow uses Google's street views and displays the Google logo. It also uses home data from walkscore.com and gives credit to that site for that data. In 2012, Zillow launched a social home shopping site, called Neighborhood Advice, which links users' search for a home with information about their community of friends on Facebook. Zillow then displays circles on a map to indicate where the user's friends live or have checked in, enabling the user to locate areas where they have many, or few, friends.

- *Preservation of intellectual property:* The software is open to the whole community. It cannot be sold, and its use cannot be restricted. Thus, the community is the "owner" of the code. But how are the contributions of individuals recognized?
- *Updating and maintaining open source code:* A strength of the open source movement is that it is open to the manipulation of members of an entire community. That very strength makes it difficult to channel the updating and maintenance of code.
- *Competitive advantage:* Because the code is available to all, a company would not want to open-source a system that it hopes can give it a competitive advantage.
- *Tech support:* The code may be free, but technical support usually isn't. Users of an open-source system must still be trained and supported.
- *Standards:* Standards are open. Yet, in a technical world that is filled with incompatible standards, open sourcing may take a very long time to provide a viable strategy for its many organizations.

Applications written following the open source standards were initially rejected by corporate IT organizations. Executives wondered how code that was free, open, and available to all could be counted on to support critical business applications. However, executives began to see the benefits of open source code after OSI created a series of examples and case studies that highlighted the benefits. In addition to Linux, Android (Google's smartphone operating system), Mozilla (a popular Web browser core), Apache (Web server), PERL (Web scripting language), OpenOffice (a Sun Microsystems-originated set of office applications that support the Microsoft Office suite formats), and PNG (graphics file format) are examples of very popular software that is based on open source efforts. Advances in the applications available on the Internet, particularly many of the Web 2.0 applications that are making their way slowly into the corporate infrastructure, are open sourced. Corporations are learning to manage the open-source process by more clearly stating their requirements and interfacing with developers on what typically begin as their noncore or least critical systems (those that, if copied, do not endanger the firm).

Many good references are available for systems development, but further detail is beyond the scope of this text. The interested general manager is referred to a more detailed systems development text for a deeper understanding of this critical IS process.

Managing IT Project Risk

IT projects are often distinguished from many non-IT projects on the basis of their high levels of risk. Although every manager has an innate understanding of what risk is, there is little consensus as to its definition. Risk is perceived as the possibility of additional cost or loss due to the choice of an alternative. Some alternatives have a lower associated risk than others. Risk can be quantified by assigning a probability of occurrence and a financial consequence to each alternative. We consider project risk to be a function of complexity, clarity, and size.[42]

Complexity

The first determinant of risk on an IT project is its complexity level, or the extent of difficulty and number of interdependent components. Several factors contribute to increased complexity in IT projects. The first is the sheer pace of technological change. The increasing numbers of products and technologies affecting the marketplace cause rapidly changing views of any firm's future business situation. For example, introducing a new development approach such as open sourcing creates significantly different ideas in people's minds about the future direction of IT development in the firm. Such uncertainty makes it difficult for project team members to identify and agree on common goals. This fast rate of change also creates new vocabularies to learn as technologies are implemented, which can undermine effective communication.

The development of more complex technologies accelerates the trend toward increased specialization among project team members and multiplies the number of interdependencies that must be tracked in project management. Team members must be trained to work on the new technologies. More subprojects must be managed, which, in turn, means developing a corresponding number of interfaces to integrate the pieces (i.e., subprojects) back into a whole.

High complexity played a part in the 2008 failure at Heathrow Airport's terminal 5.[43] The project involved 180 IT suppliers and over 160 IT systems. There are more than 9,000 devices connected to the system along with another 2,100 PCs. The system includes 175 lifts (elevators), 131 escalators, and 18 kilometers of conveyor belts for baggage handling. According to the British Airports Authority (BAA), "It has taken 400,000 man-hours of software engineering just to develop the complex system, and coding work is set to continue even after the initial installation begins."[44] The British Airways CIO was quoted as saying that "the construction of T5 involved creating a small town with a full telecommunications network for the construction workers, merely to enable the terminal to be built."[45] But the failure in 2008 resulted in canceled flights, lost baggage, substantial delays, and frustrated customers and employees. According to blogger Michael Krigsman, "The systems incorporated in T5 severely taxed BA's planning, testing and deployment capabilities."[46]

Complexity can be determined once the context of a project has been established. Consider the hypothetical case of a manager given six months and $500, 000 to build a corporate Web site to sell products directly to customers. Questions that might be used to build context for this case include the following:

- How many products will this Web site sell?
- Will this site support global, national, regional, or local sales?
- How will this sales process interface with the existing customer fulfillment process?
- Does the company possess the technical expertise in house to build the site?
- What other corporate systems and processes will this project affect?
- How and when will these other systems be coordinated?

[42] The ideas were derived from this source, but we used different names and expanded the application. L. Applegate, F. W. McFarlan, and J. L. McKenney, *Corporate Information Systems Management: Text and Cases*, 5th ed. (Homewood, IL: Irwin/McGraw-Hill, 1999).
[43] Michael Krigsman, "IT Failure at Heathrow T5: What Really Happened" (April 7, 2008), blogs.zdnet.com/projectfailures/?p=681 (accessed September 2, 2015).
[44] Ibid.
[45] CIO UK, www.cio.co.uk/concern/change/news/index.cfm?articleid=2487&pn=2 (accessed April 11, 2012).
[46] Michael Krigsman, "IT Failure at Heathrow T5: What Really Happened."

Clarity

A project is risky if it is hard to define. Clarity is concerned with the ability to define the requirements of a system. A project has low clarity if the users cannot easily state their needs or define what they want from the system. A project also has low clarity if user demands for the system or regulations that guide its structure change considerably over the life of the project. A project with high clarity is one in which the systems requirements do not change and can be easily documented. A payroll package that calculates gross pay and deductions and then automatically deposits net pay into predetermined bank accounts is an example of a high-clarity project for most firms; each firm could likely use exactly the same package with minimal tailoring. In contrast, one of the authors interviewed a developer on a low-clarity project that was to monitor competitor advertising. The system measured magazine ads by the square inch and radio and TV ads by the minute. There was no established single way in which this monitoring had to take place, and various other options were viable, such as measuring the use of particular words, humor, or particular types of images. The field was, and still is, quite undefined as to what it means to monitor competitors' ads.

Size

Size also plays a big role in project risk. All other things being equal, big projects are riskier than small ones. A project can be considered big if it has the following characteristics:

- Large budget relative to other budgets in the organization
- Large number of team members (and, hence, a large number of man-months)
- Large number of organizational units involved in the project
- Large number of programs/components
- Large number of function points
- Large number of source lines of code (i.e., the number of lines of code in the software product's source file)

It is important to consider the relative size. At a small company with an average project budget of $30,000, $90,000 would be a large project. However, to a major corporation that just spent $2 million implementing an ERP, a $90,000 budget would be peanuts.

Managing Project Risk Level

Risk management is usually a two-stage process: first the risk is assessed and then actions are taken to control it.[47] The project's complexity, clarity, and size determine the level of risk. Varying levels of these three determinants differentially affect the amount of project risk. At one extreme, large, highly complex projects that are low in clarity are extremely risky. In contrast, small projects that are low in complexity and high in clarity have low risk. Everything else is somewhere in between.

The level of risk determines how formal the project management system and detailed the planning should be. When it is difficult to estimate how long or how much a project will cost because it is so complex or what should be done because its clarity is so low, using formal management practices or planning is inappropriate. A high level of planning makes it almost impossible in these circumstances because of the uncertainty surrounding the project and makes it difficult to adapt to external changes that are bound to occur. On the other hand, formal planning tools

[47] R. Schmidt, K. Lyytinen, M. Keil, and P. Cule, "Identifying Software Project Risks: An International Delphi Study," *Journal of Management Information Systems* 17, no. 4 (Spring 2001), 5–36.

may be useful in low-risk projects because they can help structure the sequence of tasks and provide realistic cost and time targets.[48]

Managing the Complexity Aspects of Project Risk

The more complex the project, the greater is the risk. The increasing dependence on IT in all aspects of business means that managing the risk level of such a project is critical to a general manager's job. Organizations increasingly embed IT more deeply into their business processes, not only raising efficiency but also increasing risk. Many companies now rely entirely on IT for their revenue-generating processes whether the processes use the Internet or not. For example, airlines depend on IT for generating reservations and ultimately sales. If the reservation system goes down, that is, if it fails, agents simply cannot sell tickets. In addition, even though the airplanes technically can fly if the reservation system fails, the airline cannot manage seat assignments, baggage, or passenger loads without the reservation system. In short, the airline would have to stop doing business should its reservation system fail. That type of dependence on IT raises the risk levels associated with adding or changing the system. A manager may adopt several strategies in dealing with complexity, including leveraging the technical skills of the team, relying on consultants to help deal with project complexity, and a host of internal integration strategies.

Leveraging the Technical Skills of the Team When a project is complex, it is helpful to have a project manager with experience in similar situations or who can translate experiences in many different situations to a new complex one. For projects high in complexity, it also helps to have team members with significant work experience, especially if it is related.

Relying on Consultants and Vendors Few organizations develop or maintain the in-house capabilities they need to complete complex IT projects. Risk-averse managers want people who possess crucial IT knowledge and skills. Often that skill set can be attained only from previous experience on similar IT projects. Such people are easier to find at consulting firms because consultants' work is primarily project based. Consulting firms rely on processes that develop the knowledge and experience of their professionals. Thus, managers often choose to "lease" effective IT team skills rather than try to build them with their own people. However, the project manager must balance the benefits achieved from bringing in outsiders at the cost of not developing in house the skill set that the outsiders have. When the project is over and the consultants leave, will the organization be able to manage without them? Having too many outsiders on a team also increases the difficulty of alignment. Outsiders may have different objectives, such as selling more business or learning new skills, which might conflict with the project manager's goal for the project.

Integrating Within the Organization Highly complex projects require good communication among the team members, which helps them to operate as an integrated unit. Ways of increasing internal integration include holding frequent team meetings, documenting critical project decisions, and conducting regular technical status reviews.[49] These approaches ensure that all team members are "on the same page" and are aware of project requirements and milestones.

Managing Clarity Aspects of Project Risk

When a project has low clarity, project managers need to rely more heavily on the users to define system requirements. It means managing project stakeholders and sustaining commitment to projects.

Managing Project Stakeholders A project's low clarity may be the result of its multiple stakeholders' conflicting needs and expectations for the system. The project manager must balance the goals of the various project stakeholders to achieve desired project outcomes. The project manager may also need to specifically manage stakeholders. It is

[48] H. Barki, S. Rivard, and J. Talbot, "An Integrative Contingency Model of Software Project Risk Management," *Journal of Management Information Systems* 17, no. 4 (Spring 2001), 37–69.
[49] Ibid. and Applegate, McFarlan, and McKenney, *Corporate Information Systems Management*.

not always a simple task to identify project stakeholders. They may be employees, managers, users, other departments, or even customers. However, failure to manage these stakeholders can lead to costly mistakes later in the project if a particular group does not support the project.

Managing stakeholders' expectations and needs often involves both the project manager and the general manager. Project sponsors are especially critical of IT projects with organizational change components. Sponsors use their power and influence to remove project barriers by gathering support from various social and political groups both inside and outside the organization. They also prove to be valuable when participating in communication efforts to build the visibility of the project.

Sustaining Commitment to Projects An important way to increase the likelihood of project success is to gain commitment from stakeholders and to sustain that commitment throughout the life of the project. Research indicates five primary determinants of project commitment: project, psychological, social, organizational, and cultural.[50] (See Figure 11.10.) Project teams often focus on only the project factors, ignoring the other four because of their complexity.

By identifying how these factors are manifest in an organizational project, managers can use tactics to ensure a sustained commitment. For example, to maintain commitment, a project team might continually remind stakeholders of the benefits to be gained from completion of this project. Likewise, assigning the right project champion the task of selling the project to all levels of the organization can maintain commitment. Other strategies encourage stakeholder, especially user, buy-in so that they can help clarify project requirements. Examples include making a user or the project sponsor the project team leader; encouraging the project sponsor to provide public support for the project; placing key stakeholders on the project team; placing key stakeholders in charge of the change process, training, or system installation; and formally involving stakeholders in the specification approval process. Being involved in the project makes stakeholders more aware of the trade-offs that inevitably occur during a system implementation and perhaps more willing to accept the consequences of the trade-offs. In addition, being involved in the project allows stakeholders who are users to better understand how the system works and thus may make it easier for them to use it.

Determinant	Description	Example
Project	Objective attributes of the project such as cost, benefits, expected difficulty, and duration	Projects more likely to have higher commitment if they involve a large potential payoff
Psychological	Factors managers use to convince themselves things are not so bad, such as previous experience, personal responsibility for outcome, and biases	Projects more likely to have higher commitment when there is a previous history of success
Social	Elements of the various groups involved in the process, such as rivalry, norms for consistency, and need for external validation	Projects more likely to have higher commitment when external stakeholders have been publicly led to believe the project will be successful
Organizational	Structural attributes of the organization, such as political support, and alignment with values and goals	Projects more likely to have higher commitment when there is strong political support from executive levels
Cultural	Cultural attributes such as appreciation for teamwork or a focus on technical issues	Projects more likely to have higher commitment when there is a culture of teamwork

FIGURE 11.10 Determinants of commitment for IT projects.
Sources: Adapted from Mark Keil, "Pulling the Plug: Software Project Management and the Problem of Project Escalation," *MIS Quarterly* 19, no. 4 (December 1995), 421–47; Michael Newman and Rajiv Sabherwal, "Determinants of Commitment to Information Systems Development: A Longitudinal Investigation," *MIS Quarterly*, 20, no. 1 (March 1996), 23–54.

[50] See, for example, Mark Keil, "Pulling the Plug: Software Project Management and the Problem of Project Escalation," *MIS Quarterly* 19, no. 4 (December 1995), 421–47; Michael Newman and Rajiv Sabherwal, "Determinants of Commitment to Information Systems Development: A Longitudinal Investigation," *MIS Quarterly* 20, no. 1 (March 1996), 23–54.

Pulling the Plug

The risk management strategies described here are designed to turn potentially troubled projects into successful ones. Often projects in trouble persist long after they should be abandoned. Interestingly, this would be a case of sustaining too much commitment to a project. Research shows that the amount of money already spent on a project biases managers toward continuing to fund the project even if its prospects for success are questionable.[51]

Other factors can also enter in the decision to keep projects too long. For example, when the penalties for failure within an organization are high, project teams are often willing to go to great lengths to ensure that their project persists even if that means extending resources. Also, a propensity for taking risks or an emotional attachment to the project by powerful individuals within the organization can contribute to the continuation of a troubled project well beyond reasonable time limits. A recent global survey found that ultimately the plug is pulled on approximately one project of every five.[52]

Gauging Success

How does a manager know when a project has been a success? At its start, the general manager who built the business case would have considered several aspects based on achieving the business goals. It is important that the goals be measurable so that they can be used throughout the project to provide the project manager real-time feedback. The general manager probably also wants to know whether the system meets the specifications and project requirements set in the project scope, but measuring this is complex. Metrics may be derived specifically from the requirements and business needs that generated the project to determine whether the system meets expectations. Such metrics need to be based on the specific system, such as automating the order entry process or building a knowledge management system for product design.

Four dimensions that are useful in determining whether a project is successful are shown in Figure 11.11. The dimensions are defined as follows:

- *Resource constraints:* Does the project meet the established time and budget criteria? Was there *schedule slip* (i.e., the current scheduled time divided by the original scheduled time)? Most projects set some measure of short-term success along this dimension that is easy to measure.
- *Impact on customers:* How much benefit does the customer receive from this project? Although some IT projects are transparent to the organization's end customer, every project can be measured on the benefit to the immediate customer of the IS. This dimension includes performance and technical specification measurements.
- *Business success:* How high are the profits and how long do they last? Did the project meet its return on investment goals? This dimension must be aligned with the organization's business strategy.
- *Prepare the future:* Has the project altered the organization's infrastructure so that its future business success and positive customer impact are likely? Today, many companies are building Internet infrastructures in anticipation of future business and customer benefits. Overall success of this strategy is measurable only in the future, although projects underway now can be evaluated on how well they prepare the business for future opportunities.

What other considerations should be made when defining success of an IS? Is it enough just to complete a project? Is it necessary to finish on time and on budget? If other dimensions are important, what are they? The type of project can greatly influence how critical each of these dimensions is in determining overall success. It is the responsibility of the general manager to coordinate the company's comprehensive business strategy with the project

[51] Hal Arkes and Catherine Blumer, "The Psychology of Sunk Cost," *Organizational Behavior and Human Decision Processes* 35 (1985), 124–40; Daniel Kahneman and Amos Tversky. "Prospect Theory: An Analysis of Decision under Risk," *Econometrica: Journal of the Econometric Society* 47, no. 2 (1979), 263–91.

[52] Governance Institute, Global Status Report on the Governance of Enterprise IT (GEIT) (2011), 11, http://www.isaca.org/Knowledge-Center/Research/ResearchDeliverables/Pages/Global-Status-Report-on-the-Governance-of-Enterprise-IT-GEIT-2011.aspx (accessed September 8, 2015).

Success Dimension	Low Tech	Medium Tech	High Tech
	Existing technologies with new features	*Most technologies new but available before the project*	*New, untested technologies*
Resource constraint	Important to meet	Overruns acceptable	Overruns most likely
Impact on customers	Added value	Significantly improved capabilities	Quantum leap in effectiveness
Business success	Profit; return on investment	High profits; market share	High profits and market share but may come much later; market leader
Prepare the future	Gain of additional capabilities	New market; new service	Leadership core and future technologies

FIGURE 11.11 Success dimensions for various project types.
Source: Adapted from Aaron Shenhar, Dov Dvir, and Ofer Levy, and Alan C. Maltz "Project Success: A Multidimensional Strategic Concept," *Long Range Planning* 34, no. 6 (2001), 699–725.

type and the project success measurements. In this way, the necessary organizational changes can be coordinated to support the new information system. After the project is completed, postproject feedback should be elicited to ensure that the system meets its requirements and its development process is a good one.

SUMMARY

- A general manager fulfills an important role in project management. As a project sponsor, the general manager may be called on to select the project manager, provide resources to the project manager, and to give direction to and support for the project.
- The business case provides the foundation for a well-managed project by specifying its objectives, required resources, critical elements, and stakeholders.
- Project management involves continual trade-offs. The project triangle highlights the need to delicately balance cost, time, and scope to achieve quality in a project.
- Four important project elements are project management, project team, project cycle plan, and common project vocabulary.
- Understanding the complexity of the project, the environment in which it is developed, and the dimensions used to measure its success allows the general manager to balance the trade-offs necessary for using resources effectively and to keep the project's direction aligned with the company's business strategy.
- Three popular information technology project development methodologies are SDLC, agile programming, and prototyping. Each of these methodologies offers both advantages and drawbacks. Other methodologies and approaches are emerging.
- The project management office (PMO) brings focus and efficiency to project management activities. Often the PMO is a formal organization under the chief information officer (CIO).
- In increasingly dynamic environments, it is important to manage project risk, which is a function of project size, clarity, and level of complexity. For low-clarity projects, interfacing with users and gaining their commitment in the project are important. Projects that are highly complex require leveraging the technical skills of the team members, bringing in consultants when necessary and using other strategies to promote internal integration.
- Projects are here to stay, and every general manager must be a project manager at some point in his or her career. In that capacity, the general manager is expected to lead the daily activities of the project. This chapter offers insight into the necessary skills, processes, and roles that project management requires.
- Mashups are new applications derived from combining existing applications on the Web.

KEY TERMS

agile development (p. 242)
direct cutover (p. 241)
function points (p. 240)
joint applications development (JAD) (p. 244)
mashups (p. 247)
object (p. 246)
open source software (OSS) (p. 246)
open sourcing (p. 246)
parallel conversion (p. 241)
program (p. 230)
project (p. 230)
project management (p. 231)
project management office (PMO) (p. 232)
project manager (p. 233)
project stakeholders (p. 230)
prototyping (p. 243)
rapid applications development (RAD) (p. 243)
systems development life cycle (SDLC) (p. 240)
user-centered design (p. 244)

DISCUSSION QUESTIONS

1. What are the trade-offs between cost, quality, and time designing a project plan? What criteria should managers use to manage this trade-off?
2. Why does it often take a long time before troubled projects are abandoned or brought under control?
3. What are the critical success factors for a project manager? What skills should managers look for when hiring someone who would be successful in this job?
4. What determines the level of technical risk associated with a project? What determines the level of organizational risk? How can a general manager assist in minimizing these risk components?
5. Lego's Mindstorms Robotics Invention System was designed for 12-year-olds. But after more than a decade of development at the MIT Media Lab using the latest advances in artificial intelligence, the toy created an enormous buzz among grown-up hackers. Despite its stiff $199 price tag, Mindstorms sold so quickly that store shelves were emptied two weeks before its first Christmas in 1998. In its first year, a staggering 100,000 kits were sold, far beyond the 12,000 units the company had projected. Of Mindstorms' early customers, 70% were old enough to vote. These customers bought the software with the intention of hacking it. They wanted to make the software more flexible and powerful. They deciphered Mindstorms' proprietary code, posted it on the Internet, began writing new advanced software, and even wrote a new operating system for their robots. To date, Lego has done nothing to stop this open source movement even though thousands of Lego's customers now operate their robots with software the company didn't produce or endorse and can't support. In fact, Lego actively supports the open source movement by providing source code on its site.[53] There is said to be some danger: software that others develop may end up damaging the robot's expensive infrared sensors and motors.[54]
   a. What are the advantages of Lego's approach to open sourcing?
   b. What are the disadvantages of Lego's approach to open sourcing?
   c. How should Lego manage the open source movement?

■ CASE STUDY 11-1 Implementing Enterprise Change Management at Southern Company

Atlanta-based Southern Company, a leading utility provider in the southeast United States, is valued by its 4.4 million electricity customers for its excellent service, and it ranks as *Fortune* magazine's "most admired" company in its industry. That means quality is important in everything the company does. When David Traynor, the company's business excellence manage, was charged with implementing a new enterprise change management (ECM) suite, [55] he knew its key users, employees in the IT department, would scrutinize the new system and be very critical if anything didn't work exactly as it should.

---

[53] John Baichtal, "Lego Mindstorms EV3 Source Code Available," Makezine Blog (August 2, 2013), http://makezine.com/2013/08/02/lego-mindstorms-ev3-source-code-available/ (accessed September 2, 2015); Lego, http://www.lego.com/en-us/mindstorms/downloads (accessed September 2, 2015).
[54] Paul Keegan, "Intellectual Property Is Not a Toy," *Business 2.0* 2, no. 8 (October 2001), 90.
[55] An enterprise change management suite is a series of programs that increase the readiness of people in an organization to be able to accept and thrive under organizational change. Such readiness comes with developing skills as well as handling resistance to change.

The projected investment for the ECM was in the seven figures range, but the business case was straightforward. The justification was based on the savings in time and costs from reduced meetings and the ability to devote more attention to risky projects. The IT department was handling over 7,000 change requests a year, each of which required a time-consuming approval process no matter how small or routine it was. Each change request needed to be approved at one of the three hour-long review committee meetings that were held each week. Some frustrated employees were even starting to circumvent the approval process. Clearly, something had to be done. But even though the ECM suite had clear benefits, the IT department was not eager to work on a system that didn't promise to be very exciting. Further, installing the ECM suite promised to markedly change the way the IT folks performed their work. "They had to log all their changes, gain approval, take all these steps that they weren't being tasked with before," said Traynor.

The department selected BMC's Remedy software suite after spending 6 months designing the new process. Next came 10 months of customizing the systems and 7 months to build them. The first ECM phase was rolled out in August 2010. Surprisingly, the new system produced even more change requests than before—almost 3,000 additional ones each year. Traynor reasoned that before the ECM was switched on, a lot of changes must have been processed without any review. That was problematic given that about 8 of 10 requested projects have at least some level of risk, and 100% require resources to complete. Now the change advisory board meets monthly (rather than three times weekly) and deals only with emergency changes and high-risk changes that could affect critical sites or many users. Routine change requests are preapproved using standard formats.

Traynor hadn't spent much time getting buy in from the IT department during the first phase of the ECM project. He now believes he should have started the ECM communication and training effort much sooner in the first phase. The second phase of the implementation, the incident and problem management system, was done differently. Traynor appointed "ambassadors" from each IT unit as before, but this time they participated from the very first day of the second phase. Traynor encouraged them to talk with the IT employees in their unit so the employees were not playing catch-up as they had been in the first phase. Rather, the ambassadors were actively involved in designing system changes: "They've put their fingerprints on it. . . . We get a lot of mileage from [the ambassadors]." Traynor wants them to learn the ECM and play a major role in training and testing the system. He adds, "The hope is that [they] . . . become the go-to person after we go live."

Discussion Questions

1. What type of development methodology appears to have been employed at Southern Company for the ECM project? Was this a good approach? Provide a rationale for your response.
2. Describe how Traynor could have applied Lewin's three-stage model of change in implementing the ECM. What would have been the advantages of applying Lewin's three-stage model?
3. Assess Southern's ECM system on the four dimensions of project success. How successful do you think this project is?

Sources: Southern Company Web site, www.southerncompany.com (accessed April 18, 2012); S. Overby, "How Southern Company Revamped IT Change Management," Cio.com (October 18, 2010), http://www.cio.com/article/2414206/it-organization/how-southern-company-revamped-it-change-management.html (accessed September 2, 2015).

CASE STUDY 11-2 Dealing with Traffic Jams in London

As London entered the 21st century, it confronted a major issue that plagues many cities throughout the world—excessive automobile traffic. Many Londoners—particularly the business community—rated traffic congestion as the city's most serious problem. At peak periods, the average speed was less than 10 miles per hour, a slower speed than the horse-drawn carriages of previous centuries. Drivers spent about half their time waiting in traffic. This congestion nightmare was not only a major source of driver frustration but also a contributor to both environmental and economic problems. By one estimate, traffic-related problems cost London businesses roughly £2 million—more than $3 million—every week. Clearly, the city needed an aggressive policy to address this issue. The solution, proposed by the government study *Road Charging Options for London* (ROCOL) authorized by the 1999 Greater London Authority Act and endorsed by incoming mayor Ken Livingstone, was *congestion charging*. As the name suggests, the city would assess a fee, or charge, on every automobile that entered high-traffic sections of London during peak hours.

Rather than attempt a broad citywide implementation, the government focused specifically on the highly congested section of central London where roughly 1 million people entered every day, about 150,000 of them by private automobile. Beginning in February 2003, drivers who entered this area between 7 A.M. and 6:30 P.M. had to pay a fee of £5 (roughly $8) by midnight. The fee has steadily increased over the years, and by 2014 it had increased to £11.50 (roughly $18).[56] Certain types of vehicles, such as ambulances, buses, and taxis, are exempt. Drivers have the option to pay the charge by mail (prepay), text messaging, telephone, or in person at various pay points. Failure to pay the fee results in a fine of £130 (roughly $200).[57] Significantly, this solution makes extensive use of current technologies. From the start, the city installed almost 700 cameras at more than 200 sites in the designated high-traffic area to photograph the license plates of every vehicle that entered the area. The city transmitted these photos to a data center that translated the photographic images into license plate numbers utilizing automatic number plate recognition technology. Drivers who failed to pay the fee received a notice of the fine in the mail.

To create and implement the congestion charge plan, the government had a number of project risks:

- *Tight schedule:* The project needed to be completed under tight deadlines in order to meet multiple statutory requirements and minimize disruptions to commuters.
- *Technology:* The cameras had to be strategically placed in order to accurately photograph tens of thousands of license plates every day.
- *Lack of pre-existing models:* There were no pre-existing models in the world to follow.
- *Limited experience and expertise:* Livingstone had been recently elected mayor, and the supervising governmental agency—Transport for London—had only recently been created. Thus, neither was experienced in building such a system.
- *Political fallout:* The political risk of a system failure to Livingstone was so huge that it would be extremely damaging to his career.

Transport for London adopted a series of management strategies to navigate these waters and limit the risks resulting from its limited experience, IT ability, and management time. Perhaps the most significant decision was to outsource the basic management activities to firms that specialized in these areas. For example, PricewaterhouseCoopers first and then Deloitte & Touche were contracted to manage the competitive bidding process.

Early in the project, project managers identified the critical technical elements and divided the project into five "packages" that could, if required, be bought and managed separately. These included (1) the camera component, (2) the so-called image store (storage) component that collected images, converted them into license numbers, and condensed the images (duplicates would occur when one vehicle was photographed by several cameras), (3) the telecommunications links between the cameras and the image store component, (4) the customer services infrastructure, including the ability to pay by phone, Web, and mail, and (5) an extensive network of retail outlet kiosks and gas stations where people could pay the toll.

The retail (driver's) side of the system was seen as such a big risk that it was bought and managed separately. To further reduce the risks, it was decided to select the best available technologies for each of the five packages. Another risk-aversive move was to utilize only established technologies for the actual process of identifying the vehicles in the designated zone. For example, Transport for London rejected proposals to employ electronic tags because this technology had not been proved effective in scenarios such as this one. Finally, the city added roughly 200 buses to its fleet to accommodate increased ridership.

Transport for London requested bids on the project early in 2001. The estimated $116.2 million project was large enough to require listing in the European Union's public sector register. Companies throughout Europe were allowed to bid on it. Separate bids could be tendered for the camera and communications packages whereas the remaining three packages could receive bids on a combined basis or individually. Deloitte & Touche reviewed more than 40 bids before deciding on a single contractor to manage the entire program. Its choice was The Capita Group, England's largest business process outsourcing firm. Significantly, before accepting Capita's bid, Deloitte & Touche required both that firm and the other final candidate to submit technical design studies. In addition, Capita's contract included penalties if the company failed to meet the established deadlines.

[56] Transport for London, https://tfl.gov.uk/modes/driving/congestion-charge (accessed September 2, 2015); BBC News, "London's Congestion Charge Rises to £11.50" (June 16, 2014), http://www.bbc.com/news/uk-england-london-27865252 (accessed September 2, 2015).
[57] BBC News, "London's Congestion Charge Rises."

After awarding the contract to Capita, Deloitte & Touche closely monitored every step of the process, and it kept additions to the original plan to a minimum. As a result, scope creep—the process whereby a project increases in both size and costs as new features are added—was never a serious issue. One of the few changes added to the requirements was an option for motorists to pay fees through the popular SMS text-messaging format.

Throughout the implementation of the new system, the city continually sought feedback from key stakeholders. In addition, it regularly updated the public concerning the project's status. Consequently, few drivers were caught unaware when the new policy went into effect on February 17, 2003. The mayor also wisely decided to begin operations during a school holiday period when traffic volumes would be significantly lower. Thus, by the time traffic returned to normal, drivers generally had adapted to the new procedures.

What were the results of these concerted efforts? Unlike so many systems projects, London's congestion charging plan was completed on time and within budget. Significantly, however, the demanding schedule did not compromise the quality of the work. Instead, five months after it was begun, the new program appeared to have achieved its basic goals when a follow-up study[58] indicated that traffic in central London had diminished by as much as 20%, and average driving speeds had improved. A 10-year study found sustained reductions in central London, averaging 23% over the longer period.[59] The fines and fees resulted in a project payback period of about one and one-half years. It was estimated that total revenues would amount to $2.2 billion over a 10-year period. Moreover, vehicular emissions of toxic substances such as nitrogen dioxide were also reduced. However, a study found it difficult to determine the precise causes of London's decreased emissions between 2003 and 2011.[60] Because half of the European Union's automobiles have diesel engines, nitrogen dioxide levels might have fallen further if Volkswagens had proper emission controls.[61]

One potential problem that did *not* emerge was "rat runs" in which traffic jams would appear in areas outside the zone as drivers altered their routes to avoid the charges. After reviewing the outcomes of the London program, many observers predicted that congestion charging would become a standard practice in cities throughout the world.

Discussion Questions

1. Assess the risks of this project. Given your assessment of the project complexity, clarity, and size, what management strategies would you recommend for it? What, if any, of these strategies were adopted in this project?
2. Describe the development methodology that was applied to this project. Was this the most appropriate approach? Provide a rationale for your response.
3. When a project is outsourced, who should manage the project—the internal group or the outsourcer? Why?

Sources: Ken Livingstone, "The Challenge of Driving through Change: Introducing Congestion Charging in Central London," *Planning Theory and Practice* 5, no. 4 (December 2004), 490–98; Bradford Wernie, Wim Oude Weernink, and Sylviane de Saint-Seine, "The World Watches As London Tries to End Congestion," *Automotive News Europe* 8, no. 2 (January 27, 2003) 3–4; Malcolm Wheatley, "How IT Fixed London's Traffic Woes," *CIO*16, no. 19 (July 15, 2003), http://www.cio.com/article/2439968/it-organization/how-technology-fixed-london-s-traffic-woes.html (accessed September 3, 2015); "Transport for London Study: Public and Stakeholder Consultation on a Variation Order to Modify the Congestion Charging Scheme: Impact Assessment" (January 2014), https://consultations.tfl.gov.uk/roads/cc-changes-march-2014/user_uploads/cc-impact-assessment.pdf (accessed September 3, 2015).

[58] Malcolm Wheatley, "How IT Fixed London's Traffic Woes," CIO16, no. 19 (July 15, 2003), http://www.cio.com/article/2439968/it-organization/how-technology-fixed-london-s-traffic-woes.html (accessed September 3, 2015).

[59] "Transport for London Study: Public and Stakeholder Consultation on a Variation Order to Modify the Congestion Charging Scheme: Impact Assessment" (January 2014), https://consultations.tfl.gov.uk/roads/cc-changes-march-2014/user_uploads/cc-impact-assessment.pdf (accessed September 3, 2015).

[60] Green Car Congress, "HEI Study Finds London Congestion Charging Scheme shows Little Evidence of Improving Air Quality" (April 27, 2011), http://www.greencarcongress.com/2011/04/hei-study-finds-london-congestion-charging-scheme-shows-little-evidence-of-improving-air-quality.html#tp (accessed September 3, 2015).

[61] Karl Mathieson and Arthur Neslen, "VW scandal caused nearly 1m tonnes of extra pollution, analysis shows," *The Guardian* (September 23, 2015), http://www.theguardian.com/business/2015/sep/22/vw-scandal-caused-nearly-1m-tonnes-of-extra-pollution-analysis-shows (accessed September 26, 2015).

chapter 12

Business Intelligence, Knowledge Management, and Analytics

Business intelligence and analytics have become a source of strategic advantage for those firms who understand and develop skills to manage big data. This chapter provides an overview of the ways businesses make decisions. Making better decisions begins by understanding how to build capabilities in knowledge management, business intelligence, and analytics and how to protect an organization's intellectual property. Data, information, and knowledge (both tacit and explicit) are then defined and discussed because they compose the foundation of making better decisions. Knowledge is managed through four main processes, which are outlined next. A discussion of competing with analytics, and the capabilities that enable it, follows. The chapter then takes a more technical turn, addressing the components of business analytics and big data amassed in data warehouses. The chapter concludes with a discussion of the Internet of Things, social media analytics, and caveats that managers must anticipate.

Netflix knew *House of Cards* would be a blockbuster before it aired the first episode.[1] Using data from its 33 million customers worldwide, Netflix data scientists had their own internal data source of viewing customer preferences, and analysis indicated that using director David Fincher, starring Kevin Spacey, and basing the show on the British series *House of Cards* would be a success. The scientists identified patterns in the data that gave them support for a decision to create this new series. For example, they found that Netflix had a very large audience who watched the British version of *House of Cards* and watched films starring Kevin Spacey and directed by David Fincher. By "running the numbers," execs knew this new show would appeal to a very large group of people and that it would be a hit before the filming even started.

Netflix has a competitive advantage because of its big data and analytics investment—the company knows not only what is watched on its site by all of its customers but also much more information. For example, the company knows when someone pauses, rewinds, or fast forwards; what is being searched for and what is chosen from the search results; what device is used to watch the program; and when the viewer leaves the content and whether he or she ever comes back. Analytics data can be valuable from these data. Analysis shows that the analytics results differ significantly from the results obtained by convening focus groups, and it turns out the analytics algorithms give better direction for a more successful outcome. Netflix's data-driven culture extends not only to decisions about original content but many other major decisions such as what films to license, what shows to recommend to customers, and what colors and images to use on their site.

[1] Adapted from "Giving Viewers What They Want," *The New York Times* (February 24, 2013), http://www.nytimes.com/2013/02/25/business/media/for-house-of-cards-using-big-data-to-guarantee-its-popularity.html (accessed September 5, 2015); "Big Data Lessons from Netflix" (March 11, 2014), http://www.wired.com/2014/03/big-data-lessons-netflix/ (accessed September 5, 2015); "What Netflix's 'House of Cards' Means for the Future of TV" (March 4, 2013), http://www.forbes.com/sites/gregsatell/2013/03/04/what-netflixs-house-of-cards-means-for-the-future-of-tv/ (accessed September 5, 2015).

Enterprises have long sought a way to harness the value locked inside the extensive data they collect and store about customers, markets, competitors, products, people, and processes. In today's business environment, external data sources and real-time data flows add opportunities for insight that might otherwise be missed. Algorithms and analytics programs are the way this value is unlocked and used to describe, predict, and prescribe future activity. Managers use these insights to make better decisions in virtually every corner of their business from marketing and customer management to supply chains, risk management, hiring practices, and research and development activities. Moving forward, the amount of data available to analyze will continue to explode, especially with the growth of the Internet of Things, fueled by rapid growth of smart devices connected to the Web. This chapter describes how organizations compete with analytics, then addresses basic concepts of knowledge management, and reviews the current thinking about business intelligence, business analytics, big data, and intellectual property.

Competing with Business Analytics

In recent years, many companies have found success competing through better use of analytics. Companies such as Netflix as described at the beginning of this chapter have used analytics to improve on their otherwise lackluster business to become industry leaders. Caesars Entertainment, the largest gaming company in the world by some measures, found a way to more than double revenues by collecting and analyzing customer data. Capital One has also emerged from a crowded field of financial services firms to become one of the industry's leaders through the use of extensive business analytics. Those analytics enable Capital One to continuously create new products and services that appeal to new customers and to reinvigorate relationships with existing customers. The bank was founded on the idea that by mining data about individual customers it could create financial products that addressed what the big players would consider "niche markets." Although these markets were unattractive to the large players because of the smaller number of potential customers, the niche markets were profitable. Using the customer database of a small bank and running numerous analytical tests, Capital One identified characteristics that would create a profitable service. It learned, for example, that the most profitable customers were ones who charged a large amount but paid their credit cards off slowly. At the time, most credit cards companies did not differentiate between these and other customers. Capital One's innovative idea was to create a product that catered to these customers. Today, Capital One runs hundreds of experiments to identify new products that target individual customers. Using analytics to simulate and test is a very low-cost way to design and develop these products.[2]

Sports teams have propelled themselves to league success through business analytics. The systematic use of factual data in proprietary models is credited with helping the Oakland As and the Boston Red Sox. As seen in the movie, *Moneyball*, Billy Beane was one of the first general managers in Major League Baseball to build his organization, the Oakland As, around analytics. Although this industry collected data extensively, it was mostly used to manage the game in process. The Oakland As used data on things that it could measure such as the on-base percentage (the number of times a player gets on base) instead of softer criteria such as estimating the effort the player is willing to put in. The Oakland As used analytics in its recruiting efforts to predict which young players had the best chances of becoming major league players and hired players that other teams overlooked at salaries that were much more affordable. This strategy paid off, consistently carrying the Oakland As to the playoffs despite a budget for player's salaries that was a fraction of what some of its competitors had.

One reason for the rise in companies competing on analytics is that numerous companies in many industries offer similar products and use comparable technologies. Therefore, business processes are among the last remaining points of differentiation, and analytic competitors are wringing every last drop of value from those processes.[3] Business analytics fuel fact-based decision making. For example, a company may use simple inventory reports to figure out what products are selling quickly and which are moving slowly, but a company that uses analytics also knows who buys them, what price each customer pays, how many items the customer will likely purchase in a lifetime, what motivates each customer to purchase, and which incentives to offer to increase the revenue from each sale.

---

[2] Thomas Davenport and Jeanne Harris, *Competing on Analytics* (Boston, MA: Harvard Business School Press, 2007), 41–42.

[3] Ibid.

According to a study by consulting firm McKinsey and Company, there are five ways big data and analytics can help an organization:[4]

1. Making information more transparent and usable at a frequency that outpaces the competition
2. Exposing variability and boosting performance by collecting and analyzing more transactional and performance data
3. More precisely tailoring products and services using better-designed segmentation and large data samples
4. Improving decision making through experiments, forecasting and feedback, and just-in-time analysis
5. Developing the next generation of products and services more quickly using sensor data to collect after-sales information on product usage, performance, and so on.

Knowledge Management, Business Intelligence, and Business Analytics

It's all about making better decisions. Before the terms "big data" and "analytics" were all the rage, managers talked about knowledge management. Managing knowledge is not a new concept,[5] but it has been invigorated by new technologies for collaborative systems, the emergence of the Internet and intranets—which in themselves act as a large, geographically distributed knowledge repository—and the well-publicized successes of companies like Netflix that use business analytics. The discipline draws from many established sources, including anthropology, cognitive psychology, management, sociology, artificial intelligence, information technology (IT), and library science. Knowledge management remains, however, an emerging discipline with few generally accepted standards or definitions of key concepts.

Knowledge management includes the processes necessary to generate, capture, codify, integrate, and transfer knowledge across the organization to achieve competitive advantage. Individuals are the ultimate source of organizational knowledge. The organization gains only limited benefit from knowledge isolated within individuals or among workgroups; to obtain the full value of knowledge, it must be captured and transferred across the organization.

Business intelligence can be considered a component of knowledge management. **Business intelligence** (BI) is the term used to describe the set of technologies and processes that use data to understand and analyze business performance.[6] It is the management strategy used to create a more structured approach to decision making based on facts that are discovered by analyzing information collected in company databases. While knowledge management includes the processes necessary to capture, codify, integrate, and make sense of all types of knowledge as described earlier, business intelligence is more specifically about extracting knowledge from data. Davenport and Harris suggest that **business analytics** is the term used to refer to the use of quantitative and predictive models, algorithms, and evidence-based management to drive decisions.[7] By this definition, business analytics is a subset of BI. Some, however, use the terms BI and analytics interchangeably.

The most profound aspect of knowledge management and business intelligence is that an organization's sustainable competitive advantage ultimately lies in what its employees know and how they apply that knowledge to business problems. Exaggerated promises and heightened expectations couched in the hyperbole of technology vendors and consultants may create unrealistic expectations. Knowledge management is not a silver bullet, however, because it cannot solve all business problems. Knowledge must serve the broader goals of the organization, and

---

[4] James Manyika, Michael Chui, Brad Brown, Jacques Bughin, Richard Dobbs, Charles Roxburgh, and Angela Hung Byers, "Big Data: The Next Frontier for innovation, competition, and productivity," May 2011, http://www.mckinsey.com/insights/business_technology/big_data_the_next_frontier_for_innovation (accessed September 5, 2015).

[5] The cuneiform texts found at the ancient city Ebla (Tall Mardikh) in Syria are, at more than 4,000 years old, some of the earliest known attempts to record and organize information.

[6] Davenport and Harris, *Competing on Analytics*, 7.

[7] Ibid.

analytics alone do not create competitive advantage. How the information is used and how the knowledge is linked back to business processes are important components of knowledge management.

Data, Information, and Knowledge

The terms *data, information*, and *knowledge* are often used interchangeably but have significant and discrete meanings within the knowledge management domain. As was first presented in the Introduction of this textbook, there are differences (see Figure 12.1). **Data** are specific, objective facts or observations, such as "distributor ABC bought 600 of our sweaters." Standing alone, such facts have limited intrinsic meaning. But key features of data are that it can be easily captured, transmitted, and stored electronically.

Information is defined by Peter Drucker as "data endowed with relevance and purpose."[8] People turn data into information in different ways. One way is by organizing them into some unit of analysis (e.g., dollars, dates, or customers), which helps interpret the data by giving it context. Another way is by combining related data to create relevance. For example, a customer's data such as name or address become information when combined with the average order size as well as orders from that customer over time because at that point, the combined facts give a different meaning than the individual facts alone. Extending the ABC example, knowing that an average distributor buys 800 sweaters annually provides more than just the data about ABC's purchase of 600 this year. Also, knowing that ABC bought 400 sweaters last year, and 200 sweaters the year before starts to indicate much more than just the current data alone.

Knowledge is a mix of contextual information, experiences, rules, and values. It is richer and deeper than information and more valuable because someone has thought deeply about that information and added his or her own unique experience, judgment, and wisdom. Continuing with the sweater example, the sales manager might know more about distributor ABC and therefore have some additional information or experiences that add to the information. The manager knows that this is a new distributor, one with a strategy to add additional retail outlets each year. Then the information put in a richer context indicates something very different than just the sales numbers alone. The sales manager knows that his or her company has an opportunity to grow as the distributor grows.

Values and beliefs are also a component of knowledge; they determine the interpretation and the organization of knowledge. Tom Davenport and Larry Prusak, experts who have written about this relationship, say, "The power of knowledge to organize, select, learn, and judge comes from values and beliefs as much as, and probably more than, from information and logic."[9] Knowledge also involves the synthesis of multiple sources of information over time.[10]

	Data	Information	Knowledge
Definition	Simple observations of the state of the world	Data endowed with relevance and purpose	Information from the human mind (includes reflection, synthesis, context)
Characteristics	• Easily structured • Easily captured on machines • Often quantified • Easily transferred • Mere facts presented	• Unit of analysis required • Data that have been processed • Human mediation necessary	• Hard to structure • Difficult to capture on machines • Often tacit • Hard to transfer
Example	Daily inventory report of all inventory items sent to the CEO of a large manufacturing company	Daily inventory report of items that are below economic order quantity levels sent to inventory manager	Inventory manager knowing which items need to be reordered in light of daily inventory report, anticipated labor strikes, and a flood in Brazil that affects the supply of a major component.

FIGURE 12.1 The relationships between data, information, and knowledge.
Source: Adapted from Thomas Davenport, *Information Ecology* (New York: Oxford University Press, 1997).

[8] Peter F. Drucker, "The Coming of the New Organization" (January–February 1988), 45–53.
[9] Thomas H. Davenport and Laurence Prusak, *Working Knowledge* (Boston, MA: Harvard Business School Press, 1998), 12.
[10] Thomas H. Davenport, *Information Ecology* (New York: Oxford University Press, 1997), 9–10.

Value	Sources of Value
Sharing of best practices	• Avoid reinventing the wheel • Build on valuable work and expertise
Sustainable competitive advantage	• Shorten the life cycle of innovation • Promote view of an "infinite resource" that isn't used up • Impact bottom-line returns
Managing overload	• Filter data to assimilate relevant knowledge into the company • Provide organization and storage for easier data retrieval
Rapid change	• Build on previous work to make company more agile • Streamline processes/build dynamic processes • Sense and respond to changes more quickly • Customize preexisting solutions for unique customer needs
Embedded knowledge from products	• Use smart products to gather product information automatically to refine products, provide maintenance, add upgrades and identify customer usage. • Blur distinction between manufacturing and service firms when information systems are embedded in products • Add value through intangibles such as fixing systems before customers know they're broken
Globalization	• Decrease cycle times for global processes because information moves faster than physical process components • Manage global competitive pressures • Provide global access to knowledge • Adapt to local conditions
Insurance for downsizing	• Protect against loss of knowledge when workers leave • Provide portability for workers who move between roles • Reduce time for knowledge acquisition

FIGURE 12.2 The value of managing knowledge.

The amount of human contribution increases along the continuum from data to information to knowledge. Computers work well for managing data but are less efficient at managing information. The more complex and ill-defined elements of knowledge (for example, "tacit" knowledge described in the next section) are difficult if not impossible to capture electronically.

Although knowledge has always been important to the success of an organization, it was presumed that the natural, informal flow of knowledge was sufficient to meet organizational needs. But managing knowledge has become far more complex, the amount of knowledge to manage far greater than ever, and the tools to manage knowledge far more powerful. Managing knowledge provides value to organizations in several ways as summarized in Figure 12.2.

Tacit versus Explicit Knowledge

Knowledge can be further classified into two types: tacit and explicit. **Tacit knowledge** was first described by philosopher Michael Polanyi in his book, *The Tacit Dimension* with the classic assertion that "We can know more than we can tell."[11] For example, try writing, or explaining verbally, how to swim or ride a bicycle. Describe the color aqua to someone who cannot see or the sound made by a piano to someone who has never heard one. Tacit knowledge is personal, context specific, and hard to formalize and communicate. It consists of experiences, beliefs, and skills. Tacit knowledge is entirely subjective and is often acquired through physically practicing a skill or activity.

[11] Michael Polanyi, *The Tacit Dimension* (Chicago, IL: University of Chicago Press, 1966), 4.

Tacit Knowledge	Explicit Knowledge
• Knowing how to identify the key issues necessary to solve a problem • Applying similar experiences from past situations • Estimating work required based on intuition and experience • Deciding on an appropriate course of action	• Procedures listed in a manual • Books and articles • News reports and financial statements • Information left over from past projects

FIGURE 12.3 Examples of explicit and tacit knowledge.

In 2011, quarterback Drew Brees broke the NFL single-season record for the most passing yards with 5,476 yards. It would be nearly impossible to verbally describe all the factors that Brees had to consider when making those passes, yet he knew to whom to throw the ball, where to put the ball, and why to make that throw—all in a matter of seconds. Brees' ability to pass the football incorporates so much of his own personal experience and kinesthetic memory that it is impossible to separate that knowledge from the player himself. His bone structure, muscular development, and the nerves between his arm and his brain all contribute to his ability to throw the types of passes he does.

IT has traditionally focused on **explicit knowledge**, that is, knowledge that can be easily collected, organized, and transferred through digital means, such as a memorandum or financial report. Individuals, however, possess both tacit and explicit knowledge. Explicit knowledge, such as the knowledge gained from reading this textbook, is objective, theoretical, and codified for transmission in a formal, systematic method using grammar, syntax, and the printed word. Figure 12.3 summarizes these differences.

Knowledge conversion strategies are often of interest in the business environment. Companies often want to take an expert's tacit knowledge and make it explicit or to take explicit, book-learning to their new hires and make it tacit. In their book *The Knowledge Creating Company*, Ikujiro Nonaka and Hirotaka Takeuchi describe four different modes of *knowledge conversion* (see Figure 12.4). The modes are (1) from tacit knowledge to tacit knowledge, called *socialization,* (2) from tacit knowledge to explicit knowledge, called **externalization**, (3) from explicit knowledge to explicit knowledge, called **combination**, and (4) from explicit knowledge to tacit knowledge, called **internalization**.[12] **Socialization** is the process of sharing experiences; it occurs through observation, imitation, and practice. Common examples of socialization are sharing war stories, apprenticeships, conferences, and casual, unstructured discussions in the office or "at the water cooler."

FROM \ TO	Tacit Knowledge	Explicit Knowledge
Tacit Knowledge	SOCIALIZATION Transferring tacit knowledge through shared experiences, apprenticeships, mentoring relationships, on-the-job training, "talking at the water cooler"	EXTERNALIZATION Articulating and thereby capturing tacit knowledge through use of metaphors, analogies, and models
Explicit Knowledge	INTERNALIZATION Converting explicit knowledge into tacit knowledge; learning by doing; studying previously captured explicit knowledge (manuals, documentation) to gain technical know-how	COMBINATION Combining existing explicit knowledge through exchange and synthesis into new explicit knowledge

FIGURE 12.4 The four modes of knowledge conversion.
Source: Ikujiro Nonaka and Hirotaka Takeuchi, *The Knowledge-Creating Company: How Japanese Companies Create the Dynamics of Innovation* (New York: Oxford University Press, 1995), 62. By permission of Oxford University Press, Inc.

[12] Ikujiro Nonaka and Hirotaka Takeuchi, *The Knowledge-Creating Company* (New York: Oxford University Press, 1995), 62–70.

Knowledge Management Processes

Knowledge management involves four main processes: the generation, capture, codification, and transfer of knowledge. **Knowledge generation** includes all activities that discover "new" knowledge, whether such knowledge is new to an individual, a firm, or an entire discipline. **Knowledge capture** involves continuous processes of scanning, organizing, and packaging knowledge after it has been generated. **Knowledge codification** is the representation of knowledge in a manner that can be easily accessed and transferred. **Knowledge transfer** involves transmitting knowledge from one person or group to another, and the absorption of that knowledge. Without absorption, a transfer of knowledge does not occur. Generation, codification, and transfer generally take place constantly without management intervention. Knowledge management systems seek to enhance the efficiency and effectiveness of these activities and leverage their value for the firm as well as the individual. But with the increasing introduction of new and more robust systems for managing and using knowledge, knowledge management processes are dynamic and continuously evolving.

Knowledge management processes are different in the age of widespread Internet use, including robust search tools such as Google's. Whereas traditional knowledge management systems had well-defined processes for generation, capture, codification, and transfer, technologies such as large data warehouses, ubiquitous Web sites, search tools, and tagging made it possible to capture and find information without those formal processes. **Tagging**, where users themselves list key words that codify the information or document at hand, creates an ad hoc codification system, sometimes referred to as a **folksonomy**. Search engines have changed the way information is accessed, making it possible to quickly find virtually anything on any system connected to the Internet. These technologies have replaced traditional knowledge management systems and have given individuals the ability to find information that traditionally was locked within structures that had to be designed, managed, and then taught to users.

Business Intelligence

In the past, traditional BI was associated with providing real-time, easy-to-use dashboards and reports to assist managers in monitoring key performance metrics. Common elements of BI systems include reporting, querying, dashboards, and scorecards. Dashboards tend to be simple, online displays of key metrics, often graphically displayed in pie charts, bar charts, red-yellow-green coded data, and other images that easily convey both the value of the metric and, with the color coding, whether the metric is within acceptable parameters. In one example, a map of the United States was used to indicate sales performance by geography, and each state was color coded to indicate whether targets were being met. Managers could click on each state to drill down into the next level of detail, which provided information by region. Further drilling down indicated sales by city and ultimately by sales person. At each level, the data were presented and color coded to give a visual, and therefore quick, indication of who was making targets and who was missing them. Traditional BI is useful for strategic, tactical, and operational decisions.

BI today incorporates a number of additional characteristics and capabilities. Some function as a service in the cloud. Others are event driven, offer instant access to real-time information, and provide dynamically created reports that "mash up" or combine streaming data, internal data sources, and external data sources. It is also common to find systems that enable mobile/ubiquitous access. These and other newer technologies have enabled BI to move to a new level with robust user interfaces and powerful visualization and analytics tools. Algorithms are much more sophisticated than ever before, giving managers more accurate and better insights. Crowdsourcing allows the data structures and report designs to be created by the community rather than by a single designer. Data and reports are infused with narratives from the users to provide richer context. Dynamic capabilities in the BI system provide exceptions, alerts, and notifications that change based on what the system learns from the data alone. A manager who sees something in the data that requires an intervention will be able not only to perform it but also to tag it and link it with the data so that the collective knowledge grows over time.

Components of Business Analytics

To successfully build business analytics capabilities in the enterprise, companies make a significant investment in their technologies, their people, and their strategic decision-making processes. Four components are needed (see Figure 12.5).

Data Sources

Data used in the analytical processes come from various sources and are stored in corporate databases, usually as tables of data in a very structured format. One might think about a customer database that has for each customer a number of pieces of data such as name, account number, and address. These pieces contain a wide variety of data used to create a coherent picture of business conditions at a single point in time. Much of the data used by the organization is generated internally and captures operational and financial information. Other data can be gathered from external sources, such as competitor's public activities, weather patterns, and economic trends. Because the information in these data sources is clear and easily categorized into databases, it is called **structured data**.

Other data, such as conversations, Twitter streams, and videos are considered **unstructured data**. These data sources have information embedded in them but work needs to be done to extract the useful information. Other examples of unstructured data are the data in blogs, e-mails, documents, photos, audio files, presentations, Web pages, and other similar files. A single unstructured data file might contain multiple items of interest. When data are taken out of the context of the original file, they lose some of their meaning. The common characteristic of these data sources is that the data are not easily put into a tabular or other structured format and therefore do not fit neatly into a database.

Data warehouses, or collections of data designed to support management decision making, sometimes serve as repositories of all of an organization's databases. The warehouses are centralized so all the organization's departments can access the data and store new data in formats that are easily used by others. Data warehouses traditionally have held structured data, but today, there are multiple examples of data warehouses that manage large collections of unstructured data.

Real-time data sources are another type of data stream that companies use in their analytics program. Many people have seen stock prices flow across a screen for financial traders. This is a type of real-time data. The information changes constantly (or at least often). Modern analytics programs have found ways to use real-time streams of data in their algorithms.

Component	Definition	Example
Data sources	Data streams and repositories	Data warehouses; weather data
Software tools	Applications and processes for statistical analysis, forecasting, predictive modeling, and optimization	Data-mining process; forecasting software package
Data-Driven environment	Organizational environment that creates and sustains the use of analytics tools	Reward system that encourages the use of the analytics tools; willingness to test or experiment
Skilled workforce	Workforce that has the training, experience, and capability to use the analytics tools	Data scientists, chief data officers, chief analytics officers, analysts, etc. Netflix, Caesars, and Capital One are examples of companies with these types of roles

FIGURE 12.5 Components of successful business analytics programs.

2. Software Tools

At the core of business analytics are the tools. An approach used to extract information from data sources is **data mining**, which is the process of analyzing data warehouses and other sources for "gems" that can be used in management decision making. The term typically refers to the process of combing through massive amounts of customer data to understand buying habits and to identify new products, features, and enhancements. It also identifies previously unknown relationships among data. The analysis may help a business better understand its customers by answering such questions as these; Which customers prefer to contact us via the Web instead through a call center? How are customers in Location X likely to react to the new product that we will introduce next month? How would a proposed change in our sales commission policy likely affect the sales of Product Y? Using data mining to answer such questions helps a business reinforce its successful practices and anticipate future customer preferences. For example, *The New York Times* reported that by using data mining, Walmart uncovered the surprising fact that its Florida customers stocked up on beer and strawberry pop tarts when a hurricane was predicted. It now initiates quick shipments to its stores when hurricanes are on the horizon so that there are plenty of these two items when a hurricane becomes a more tangible threat.[13]

There are four categories of tools that are typically included under the business analytics umbrella. They include[14]

- *Statistical analysis:* Answers questions such as "Why is this happening?"
- *Forecasting/Extrapolation:* Answers questions such as "What if these trends continue?"
- *Predictive modeling:* Answers questions such as "What will happen next?"
- *Optimization:* Answers questions such as "What is the best that can happen?"

These tools are used with the data in the data warehouse to gain insights and support decision making.

3. Data-Driven Environment

A **data-driven culture**, an environment that supports and requires analytics, is a critical factor for success. It requires aligning information systems (IS) strategy and organizational strategy with the business strategy. Executives in the organization demand that staff provide not only a decision or recommendation but also the data to support it. Gone are the days of just evaluating results at the end of a financial period. In a data-driven culture, staff use data streams to continually evaluate and make corrections in midcourse. To achieve a data-driven organization, there must be alignment of the corporate culture, the incentive systems, the metrics used to measure success of initiatives, and the processes for using analytics with the objective of building a competitive advantage through analytics. As an example of aligning organizational strategy with a business strategy promoting the use of analytics to gain competitive advantage, one financial services firm encouraged the use of analytics by changing its appraisal system. Demonstration of skills associated with applying analytics was made a significant factor in compensation decisions.

Although many companies have some sort of analytical tools in place, most are not used for mainstream decision making, and they certainly do not drive the strategy formulation discussions of the company. Those who gain competitive advantage from analytics use these capabilities as an integral component of their business. Companies such as GE, Proctor and Gamble, Walmart, Chevron, and HP routinely expect data-driven decision making and have built strong analytics capabilities into their teams to expand the use of data in decision making.

Leadership plays a big role in creating a strong analytics environment. Leaders must move the company's culture toward an **evidence-based management** approach in which evidence and facts are analyzed as the first step in decision making. Those in this type of culture are encouraged to challenge others by asking for data support, and when no data are available, to experiment and learn to generate facts. Use of evidence-based management encourages decisions based on data and analysis rather than on experience and intuition.

---

[13] Constance Hays, "What Walmart Knows about Customers' Habits" (November 14, 2004), http://www.nytimes.com/2004/11/14/business/yourmoney/14wal.html (accessed September 6, 2015).
[14] Ibid.

4. Skilled Workforce

It's clear that to be successful with analytics, data and technology must be used. But experts point out that even with the best data and the most sophisticated analytics, people must be involved. Managers must be able to leverage their knowledge of analytics to improve decision making. Leaders must set examples for the organization by using analytics and requiring that decisions made by others use that process. Perhaps the most important role is sponsorship. Davenport and Harris point out that it was the CEO-level sponsorship and the corresponding passion for analytics that enabled firms such as Caesars Entertainment and Capital One to achieve the success they did.[15]

Although leadership is important and general management and staff must be data driven, the staff must also have analytics experts. A key role for a successful analytics program is the **data scientist**, a professional who has the skills to use the right analytics with the right data at the right time for the right business problem. Some describe this role as part science and part art because there are multiple ways to use data and analytics to answer business questions. The data scientist has the skills to look at the data in different ways to extract the appropriate information for the business.

Leading the analytics program is often a **chief analytics officer (CAO)** or **chief data officer**. As the name implies, the CAO is the individual at the helm of the analytics activities of an organization. Organizations typically create a center of excellence for analytics capabilities that operates as a shared service of expertise. The CAO would be the leader of this center. Likewise, a chief data officer has the responsibility for the data warehouse, organizational databases, relationships with vendors who supply external data sources, and sometimes the algorithms that use these data sources.

Levels of Analytical Capabilities

All businesses have data, but some do a better job than others at using it, creating a potent source of competitive advantage. Companies tend to fall into one of five levels of analytical capabilities, with each level adding to the lower levels. Understanding the different levels can help organizations envision how to improve their capabilities to gain additional advantages. Figure 12.6 summarizes these levels.

Level	Description	Source of Business Value
Level 1: Reporting	Answers "**What** happened?" by creating batch and ad hoc reports that summarize historical data; data across functions possibly not consistent or well integrated	Reduction in costs of report generation and printing
Level 2: Analyzing	Answers "**Why** did it happen?" by using ad hoc, real-time reports, and business intelligence tools to understand root causes	Understanding root causes
Level 3: Descriptive	Answers "**What** is happening now?" by linking business intelligence tools with operational systems to provide instantaneous views and updated status; data integrated, clean, and reliable	Real-time understanding of action/reaction and course correction instantly to improve operations
Level 4: Predictive	Answers "**What** will happen?" by using predictive models that extrapolate from data to enable possible scenarios for the future; may be used to see potential for strategic advantage to business	Ability to take action on predictions to help the business
Level 5: Prescriptive	Answers "**How** should we respond?" by automatically linking analytics with other systems, creating continuous updates from business intelligence tools that automatically are understood by operational tools and trigger events as needed	Automated reactions based on real-time data stream; value from dynamic process that "learns and corrects" automatically

FIGURE 12.6 Analytical capabilities levels.
Sources: Adapted from conversations with Farzad Shirzad, leader of Teradata's Center for Excellence in Analytics in 2011; Jeff Bertolucci, "Big Data Analytics: Descriptive vs. Predictive vs. Prescriptive," *Information Week* (December 31, 2013).

[15] Davenport and Harris, *Competing on Analytics*.

Big Data

One impact of our information-based economy is the very large amount of data amassing in databases inside both companies and the environment. Consider, for a moment the vast amount of data Google must process every time it is queried. Google tells the inquirer how many results are found and how fast the search process found them. A recent query of "big data" produced "about 774,000,000 results in 0.42 seconds." A second query of "lady gaga" produced 240,000,000 results in 0.33 seconds. Google indexes billions of Web sites as part of its search algorithm.

Big data is the term used to describe techniques and technologies that make it economical to deal with very large data sets at the extreme end of the scale. Data sets are usually evaluated according to their size in bytes, which are characters such as letters, numbers, and symbols. According to Wikipedia, big data sets are on the order of exabytes (10^{18} bytes, abbreviated as EB) and zettabytes (10^{21} bytes, abbreviated as ZB). A megabyte (MB) is 10^{6} bytes. Extreme data sets get so big because volumes of information are continuously created, usually quickly, and stored for analysis. These extreme data sets create difficulties in storing, searching, sharing, and analyzing; the size just cannot be handled by traditional data management tools or techniques. Having large data sets is desirable because of the potential trends and analytics that can be extracted, but when the sets are so large that the information system cannot manage them, they are considered a "big data problem." In those cases, specialized computers and tools are needed to help managers mine the data.

One reason for the explosion of data is that traditionally, managers looked at only transaction data, but now it is possible to also look at information around a transaction. Consider Netflix, described in the opening of this chapter. It tracks not only what movie or show is watched but dozens of pieces of information around that transaction, including what was in the user's search results but not chosen, when the user stopped watching and at what point in the program this occurred, and other events that occur before, during, and after the actual transaction.

Social media channels are a source of big data. Conversations contain words that get their meaning from the other words in the sentence, and companies want to know that meaning. They want to analyze the conversation, not just keywords or tags associated with it. For example, marketers want to evaluate sentiment, and that often depends on the context in which words are used. A conversation might include a phrase "wicked problems." A *wicked problem* is a problem that is difficult or impossible to solve because there is incomplete, contradicting, or too much information. However, taken alone, *wicked* means bad or evil, and *problem* might mean a situation or inquiry that needs to be solved. Without the context, the marketer might conclude that there is a particularly bad or evil problem to solve, when in actuality, that was not the sentiment at all. For that reason, social media data often is captured in its entirety so analysis can be done as needed later. However, conversations are large, unstructured clusters of words, and the resulting database is considered big data.

An important practical application of big data can illustrate how analytics of social media data can be useful. Researchers at the University of Arizona found that they can predict the number of asthma-related emergency room visits with 70% accuracy by tracking in real time pollution data and the incidence of words such as *wheezing, sneezing,* and *inhaler* found in tweets and Google searches. Although only about 1% of tweets report those words out of 464.8 million Tweets in a two and a half month period, that proportion represents about 15,000 tweets per day globally. The researchers plot the trends on a map and can alert hospitals in areas with asthma terms and conditions that indicate a likely outbreak.[16]

Big data are increasingly common in part because of the rich, unstructured data streams that are created by conversations. With the growth of social IT, managers are increasingly finding that gathering all the information about their company and their customers from all the social sites available creates a data set that has the potential to supply unique customer intelligence. Finding ways to collect, manage, and use the data, however, is significantly more difficult than managing more structured data sets.

[16] Sudha Ram, Wenli Zhang, Max Williams, and Yolande Pengetnze, "Predicting Asthma-Related Emergency Department Visits Using Big Data," *IEEE Journal of Biomedical and Health Informatics* 19, no. 4 (July 2015), 1216–23.

Internet of Things

The **Internet of Things** also creates massive amounts of data. Technology embedded in devices stream sensor data from those devices to create rich databases of operational data. Devices such as elevators, vehicles, refrigerators, industrial equipment, wristwatches, pacemakers, and more are all equipped with sensors that capture relevant operational information such as floors of buildings visited; miles driven; food stored; forklifts in use; time of day; heart health including blood flow; and sensor-maintenance information such as the health of the device, time between failures, and battery level. Advanced sensors also interact with other sensors, sending and receiving signals that guide the operations of the device. As these technologies proliferate, the information generated grows exponentially.

Kevin Ashton was a brand manager for Oil of Olay in the mid-1990s when he wondered why some products flew off the shelf and others seemed to stay forever. He came up with the idea of tagging products with sensors so they could be tracked and stores could know what was on their shelves. Fast forward to today; sensors embedded in devices generate so much data that estimates of the amount of data generated are out of date before they are published. Internet protocol (IP) version 6, the latest version, allows 3.4×10^{38} addresses on the Internet, and each address could be generating data continuously.

Sensors connected to the Internet have many uses. Imagine a sprinkler system that senses moisture in the ground, follows the weather forecast, and optimizes water consumption, or a trucking company that places sensors on each of its trucks to track where it is and to optimize its route in terms of saving gas and time and increasing responsiveness to customers. The abundance of sensors sets the stage for new business models that incorporate a "sense and respond" capability. But managers cannot successfully invest in the Internet of Things without a robust analytics capability to manage the data this type of investment will generate.

Database warehouse vendors, such as Teradata, IBM, and Oracle, have tailored tools for customers with big data problems. In order to integrate with business applications and provide appropriate accessibility, backup and security, data warehouses must be *scalable* to allow capture and storage of all the data; *agile* to accommodate changing requirements, mixed types of work, and quick turnaround of queries and reports; and *compatible* with the enterprise infrastructure.

There is a "dark side" to big data. The intense number crunching is likely to yield a number of "false discoveries." Any results should be questioned before they are applied. Extensive analysis might yield a correlation and lead to a statistical inference that is unfair or discriminatory. Big data might offer a high-tech twist to the old practice of "I know what the facts are—now let's find the ones we want." Here again, care must be applied when using powerful tools.[17] But the biggest concern is what some consumers consider an invasion of privacy. Companies now can use analytics to paint a far more accurate picture of a customer than he or she might like.

Social Media Analytics

Managers have seen a rise in interest in using social IT that can be attributed to the increase in the number and ease of ways to measure the value gained from the invested time and resources. A class of tools called **social media analytics** addresses this opportunity. The goal of social media analytics is to measure the impact of social IT investments on a business. At issue, however, is how to analyze conversations, tweets, blogs, and other social IT data to create meaningful, actionable facts from statements of preferences and emotions. For example, it might be relatively easy to measure the number of *hits* on a Web site or the number of *click-throughs* from a link. But what does that information really tell a manager? What action would the manager consider taking based on these types of data? *Hits* and *click-throughs* are meaningful only in context and with other data that indicate whether business value was achieved. That is, they become information only when they are processed to become relevant and purposeful.

[17] Davenport and Harris, *Competing on Analytics.*

Sentiment analysis uses algorithms to analyze text to extract subjective information such as emotional statements, preferences, likes/dislikes, and so on. Managers seeking to understand what is being said in social media use sentiment analysis. This type of process helps answer questions such as these:

- What do our customers think about our position on this issue?
- How well received is our latest marketing campaign?
- What is our customer's experience with this problem?

Sentiment analysis can be used to scrutinize conversations, reports, e-mails, blogs, Tweets, Facebook posts, and other unstructured files. The goal is to identify issues and spot trends before they grow into big business problems. Most sentiment analysis software extracts sentiments, identifies changes in sentiment over time, and evaluates content for positive, negative, and neutral text entries. The more useful software does this in real time to allow dynamic changes in the way business is done. Some customizing is also necessary; the asthma researchers in Arizona needed to create their own algorithms to analyze the context of each tweet to make sure it was indeed of concern. For example, a tweet describing how a person's breath was taken away after watching a video needed to be differentiated from a tweet describing how a person had trouble catching her or his breath after a run.[18]

Vendors such as Google Analytics and Salesforce.com offer platforms with social media analytics tools. A platform includes tools that enable:

- *Listening to the community:* Identifying and monitoring all conversations in the social Web on a particular topic or brand.
- *Learning who is in the community:* Identifying customer demographics such as age, gender, location, and other trends to foster closer relationships with the community.
- *Engaging people in the community:* Communicating directly with customers on social platforms such as Facebook, YouTube, LinkedIn, and Twitter using a single app.
- *Tracking what is being said:* Measuring and tracking demographics, conversations, sentiment, status, and customer voice using a dashboard and other reporting tools.
- *Building an audience:* Using algorithms to analyze data from internal and external sources to understand customer attributes, behaviors, and profiles and to then find new similar customers.

UPS, Pizza Hut, Pepsi, AMD, and Dell Computers are examples of companies with well-known case studies about their use of social analytics and monitoring tools for engaging and encouraging collaboration among their customers. For example, in a presentation to the Blogwell community, a UPS manager described how the company turned around its customer service efforts using social IT and social analytics.[19] UPS studied its customer service process and monitored the social Web for comments. Managers noticed that some customers loved it, but others had a bad experience and wrote about it on sites such as Twitter and Facebook. By using a social media analytics platform, the managers identified dissatisfied customers and addressed their problems on the social platform used by the customer. This resulted in more than 1 million positive tweets about UPS and lots of public recognition for turning around its customer service process.

Google Analytics, on the other hand, is a set of analytics tools that enable organizations to analyze traffic coming, going, and on their Web site. The Google Analytics suite thoroughly analyzes many aspects of the key words used by visitors to reach a Web site and provides statistics to help managers understand the searches potential customers use. Some of its features are:

- *Web site testing and optimizing:* Understanding traffic to Web sites and optimizing a site's content and design for increasing traffic.

---

[18] Ram et al., "Predicting Asthma-Related Emergency Department Visits Using Big Data."
[19] socialmedia.org/blogwell (November 8, 2011).

Social Business Lens: Personalization and Real-Time Data Streams

Has this happened to you? You do a search on the Internet for cuff links, read about them, but decide not to purchase them. Then for the next few days, every time you are on the Web, you see advertisements for the same cuff links. Then some ads appear for shirts with cuffs. That might be followed by ads for formal wear. Somehow the system knows that you were shopping for cuff links and makes some leaps about other items you might like. It seems like the system knows you; in fact, it does.

Storing data streams to later analyze user preferences simply to provide trends and historic data is a thing of the past. Analytics groups are able to use algorithms to analyze data in real time as they stream through the Internet. The processing power available today coupled with new means of analyzing real-time data streams makes it possible to provide services that personalize the system to individuals as they are using it.

Personalization can be done in a number of ways. In the cuff link example, it's likely that a cookie, a small data element, has been deposited in your cookies file of your laptop by a third party ad provider through an agreement with owners of many of the most popular sites today. That cookie is accessed by the third party ad provider when you navigate to other sites and provides ads that correspond to pages you have viewed in an attempt to match your latest interests and stimulate future purchases. The user can delete the cookie anytime, and most cookies are not considered useful after a month or two. But while it resides on the system, it provides Web sites a way to personalize information delivered to you. Cookies are described in more detail in Chapter 13.

Another way to personalize the information seen by a user is to draw inferences from the Internet protocol (IP) address of the user. When you access the Internet, your connection has a unique IP address. Systems can connect the IP address with your location (in the United States, that is done through Zip Codes because IP addresses are associated with specific geographic locations). Coupling the Zip Code with other demographic information provides enough clues about the user to predict her or his likes and dislikes and ultimately personalize the message delivered by the Web site.

Conversations are another source of personalization. Real-time data streams are fertile ground for clues about users. Systems "monitor" the public data streams, and analytics find patterns and trends. Managers place great value on the inferences they can draw from real-time data streams, and executives can make more impactful decisions. For example, suppose a sports event half-time show is not well received by the public. Twitter and other social media sites will begin to buzz with comments. Systems designed to monitor and notice these remarks will alert managers of a possible situation that may need action, damage control, or other decision.

As algorithms, analytics, and other data management hardware and software increase in sophistication, we can expect to see increasingly more accurate predictions and more personalized interaction.

- *Search optimization:* Understanding how Google sees an organization's Web site, how other sites link to the organization's site, and how specific search queries drive traffic to the organization's site.
- *Search term interest and insights:* Understanding interests in particular search terms globally and regionally, top searches for similar terms, and popularity over time.
- *Advertising support and management:* Identifying the best ways to spend advertising resources for online media.

RE/MAX is an example of a company using social media analytics. With franchises in 62 countries, RE/MAX is a leading provider of residential, commercial, referral, relocation, and asset management. As part of its online strategy, RE/MAX created a site that listed all properties available whether listed by its own agents or those from other companies and made it available to anyone accessing the site. The company then used Google Analytics to understand consumer behavior on the site and to drive leads to agents in their franchises. Prior to this strategy, RE/MAX had used focus groups to understand consumer behavior, but these were expensive, limited in scope, and lacked real data. Its site gets more than 2 million hits a month, mostly from visitors who searched for "remax" in queries. Google Analytics helped managers redesign the Web site so the most used tools were on the home page, further providing value to potential customers. Ultimately, Google Analytics helped RE/MAX drive an increased number of leads to agents, reducing the cost agents had been paying for leads.[20]

Intellectual Capital and Intellectual Property

Two other terms frequently encountered in discussions of knowledge and information are *intellectual capital* and *intellectual property*. **Intellectual capital** is defined as knowledge that has been identified, captured, and leveraged to produce higher-value goods or services or some other competitive advantage for a firm. *Knowledge management* and *intellectual capital* are often used imprecisely and interchangeably to describe similar concepts. To be more precise, the former describes the process for managing knowledge and the latter indicates the desired product of the process. That is, by adopting knowledge management technologies, a firm can create a treasure trove of intellectual

Geographic Lens: When Two National Views of Intellectual Property Collide

U.S. and Chinese government officials have been at odds over the issue of intellectual property for decades. For years, Chinese officials have promised to improve their protection of intellectual property. In December 2010 at a Joint Commission on Commerce and Trade meeting in Washington, China's top economic policy maker promised better protection for foreign software, better tracking of the management of software in state-owned enterprises, no discrimination against foreign intellectual property in government procurement, and improvements in the Chinese patent process.

These promises will be hard to keep because stringent protection of foreigners' intellectual property is at odds with China's development strategy and even its history and traditions. The concept of intellectual property protection did not exist in China until Westerners introduced it in the early 20th century. The emperors who ruled China prior to the 20th century were concerned about unauthorized publication because they wanted to control what was disseminated, not because they wanted to encourage private, individual expression. Unfortunately, when Western ideas of intellectual property were introduced to China, it was done in a threatening manner to protect Western economic interests. As a result, many Chinese viewed the concept of intellectual property as a foreign imposition. Furthermore, the impact of Marxist theories of collective ownership that marked China's communist period meant that it was not until the 1980s that modern notions of intellectual property were brought to China—notions that remain novel and alien to many Chinese.

In addition, many foreign companies operating in China complain that Beijing views the appropriation of foreign innovations as a viable approach for developing domestic technology. These companies claim that the Chinese government tacitly supports forcing foreigners to disclose their technology and transfer patents to gain contracts. In fact, China's new antimonopoly laws allow compulsory licensing of foreign technologies in some cases and require foreign companies that wanted to merge with or buy a Chinese company to transfer technology to China. Such policies can ratchet Chinese firms up the tech ladder more rapidly, but they are considered by many to reflect the misappropriation of intellectual property. Although the United States has made some progress at the World Trade Organization against the theft of intellectual property in China, and China has enacted some intellectual property laws, the battle over intellectual property is still raging.

Sources: Editorial, China and Intellectual Property (December 23, 2010), http://www.nytimes.com/2010/12/24/opinion/24fri1.html (accessed February 22, 2015); William Alford, "Understanding Chinese Attitudes Toward Intellectual Property (IP) Rights" (September 15, 2006), http://www.cio.com/article/2444480/it-organization/understanding-chinese-attitudes-towards-intellectual-property—ip—rights.html (accessed February 22, 2015).

[20] www.google.com/analytics/case_study_remax.html (accessed on February 20, 2012).

capital. However, there are no guarantees; IT provides an infrastructure for capturing and transferring knowledge but does not create knowledge and cannot force people to share or use the knowledge.

Individuals can own their information-based ideas in the same way they own their physical property. **Intellectual property (IP)** is the term used to describe these creative and innovative information-based outputs. However, because intellectual property is information based, it differs from physical property in two important ways. First, information-based property is nonexclusive to the extent that when one person uses it, another person can use it without degradation or loss of quality. Consider an MP3 file of music that can be easily copied and shared with another without loss of the original property. Second, unlike the cost structure of physical property, the marginal cost of producing additional copies of information-based property is negligible compared with the cost of original production. These factors create differences in the ethical treatment of physical and information-based intellectual property. The economics of information versus the economics of physical property is further explored in the Introduction of this text.

The protections available for IP make it possible for owners to be rewarded for the use of their ideas and it allows them to have a say in how their ideas are used. To protect their ideas, owners typically apply for and are granted intellectual property rights. In some cases, as soon as a record is made of what has been created, the owner can expect some protection automatically. An owner only needs to declare ownership and mark the ideas appropriately.

The four main types of intellectual property protections are patents for inventions, trademarks for brand identity, designs for product appearance, and copyrights for literary and artistic material, music, films, sound recordings, broadcasts, and software.[21] In 2002, the music-sharing Web site Napster raised controversial issues long surrounding the practice of copyright. The Audio Home Recording Act (1992), passed in the United States to prevent serial copying, didn't seem to apply to Napster, which only facilitated the sharing. In 1998, the more stringent Digital Millennium Copyright Act (DMCA) was passed by a unanimous vote in the U.S. Congress with the active support of the entertainment industry.[22] The DMCA makes it a crime to circumvent copy protection even if that copy protection impairs rights established by the Audio Home Recording Act. A senior-level position, Coordinator for International Intellectual Property Enforcement in the U.S. Department of Commerce, was created in 2009 to lead the battle against global piracy of intellectual property.

The U.S. Congress continues to propose and discuss ways to protect intellectual property, particularly from piracy of online materials by sites and companies outside of U.S. jurisdiction. But the U.S. government has additional organizations to monitor and manage these issues. The Executive Office of the President of the United States oversees the Office of the U.S. Trade Representative, which annually reviews the state of IP rights protection and enforcement with global trading partners. It publishes the "Special 301" report annually to share the status of IP management around the world.[23]

But management of IP is a concern not only to the U.S. government. In 2014, the United Kingdom passed the Intellectual Property Act of 2014,[24] introducing criminal liability and penalties for infringing on registered designs and specifying processes for determining ownership in some situations. The Australian Parliament passed a similar bill, the Intellectual Property Laws Amendment Bill 2014, which also clarified earlier IP and patent protection laws.[25] The World Intellectual Property Organization (WIPO), an agency of the United Nations, has 188 member states and works with governments to "lead the development of a balanced and effective international intellectual property system that enables innovation and creativity for the benefit of all."[26]

[21] "What Is Intellectual Property or IP?" http://www.intellectual-property.gov.uk/std/faq/question1.htm (accessed June 25, 2002).

[22] On March 10, 2004, the European Union passed the EU Copyright Directive, which is similar in many ways to DCMA.

[23] For more information on intellectual property and the Special 301 report, see Office of the U. S. Trade Representative, https://ustr.gov/issue-areas/intellectual-property (accessed September 6, 2015).

[24] http://www.legislation.gov.uk/ukpga/2014/18/contents/enacted (accessed September 6, 2015).

[25] http://www.aph.gov.au/Parliamentary_Business/Bills_Legislation/Bills_Search_Results/Result?bId=r5192 (accessed September 6, 2015); http://www.ipaustralia.gov.au/about-us/public-consultations/Consulting_on_proposals_to_streamline_IP_processes_and_support_small_business/ (accessed September 6, 2015).

[26] http://www.wipo.int/wipolex/en/news/ (accessed September 6, 2015).

Caveats for Managing Knowledge and Business Intelligence

Following such a broad review of the topics provided in this chapter, it seems appropriate to conclude with a few caveats. First, recall that BI, analytics, big data, and even knowledge management continue to be emerging disciplines. Viewing BI as a process rather than an end in and of itself requires managers to remain flexible and open minded.

Second, the objective of knowledge management is not always to make knowledge more visible or available. Like other assets, it is sometimes in the best interests of a firm to keep knowledge tacit, hidden, and nontransferable. Competitive advantage increasingly depends on knowledge assets that are difficult to reproduce. Retaining knowledge is as much a strategic issue as sharing knowledge. Business intelligence, on the other hand, is designed to make knowledge visible, at least inside the enterprise, so it can be analyzed and acted upon to meet business objectives.

Third, knowledge can create a shared context for thinking about the future. If the purpose of knowledge management and business intelligence is to help make better decisions, then it must provide value for future events, not just views of the past history. The goal is to use data to identify trends and environmental changes and then create predictions that help inform business strategy and long-term goal setting.

Finally, people lie at the heart of knowledge management and business intelligence. Establishing and nurturing a culture that values learning and sharing of knowledge enables effective and efficient knowledge management. Knowledge sharing—subject, of course, to the second caveat—must be valued and practiced by all employees for knowledge management to work. The success of knowledge management ultimately depends on a personal and organizational willingness to learn.

SUMMARY

- Competing with analytics is done by building analytics capabilities that give insights to a new way to operate a business by making faster decisions and using different business models or better information.
- Knowledge management includes the processes necessary to generate, capture, codify, and transfer knowledge across organizations. *Business intelligence* (BI) is the set of technologies and practices used to analyze and understand data and to use it in making decisions about future actions. Business analytics is the set of quantitative and predictive models used to drive decisions.
- Data, information, and knowledge should not be viewed as interchangeable. Knowledge is more valuable than information, which is more valuable than data because of the human contributions involved.
- The two kinds of knowledge are tacit and explicit. *Tacit knowledge* is personal, context specific, and hard to formalize and communicate. *Explicit knowledge* is easily collected, organized, and transferred through digital means.
- *Knowledge management* is a dynamic and continuously evolving process that involves knowledge generation, capture, codification, and transfer. Technologies have enabled user-generated codification with tagging.
- In the past, traditional business intelligence provided periodically updated dashboards to monitor key performance metrics. The current generation of BI is event driven, offers instant access, and can dynamically update dashboards in real time from streaming data, ubiquitous access, and user configurability.
- The five levels of analytics capabilities are reporting, analyzing, describing, predicting, and prescribing.
- The term *big data* refers to very large data repositories often found in environments where volumes of information are generated at a high velocity. Much big data are unstructured, requiring different algorithms to mine for insights than those used with structured data.
- The *Internet of Things* is the term used for the connection of physical devices to the Internet using sensors and creating large, real-time data streams.
- Social media analytics provide companies the tools to monitor and engage their communities and to evaluate the success of their investment in social IT. Sentiment analysis is used to extract insights from conversations and social media data streams.
- The four main types of intellectual property are patents, trademarks, designs, and copyrights.

KEY TERMS

big data (p. 268)
business analytics (p. 260)
business intelligence (p. 260)
chief analytics officer (CAO) (p. 267)
chief data officer (p. 267)
combination (p. 263)
data (p. 261)
data-driven culture (p. 266)
data mining (p. 266)
data scientist (p. 267)
data warehouses (p. 265)
evidence-based management (p. 266)
explicit knowledge (p. 263)
externalization (p. 263)
folksonomy (p. 264)
information (p. 261)
intellectual capital (p. 272)
intellectual property (IP) (p. 273)
internalization (p. 263)
Internet of Things (p. 269)
knowledge (p. 261)
knowledge capture (p. 264)
knowledge codification (p. 264)
knowledge generation (p. 264)
knowledge management (p. 260)
knowledge transfer (p. 264)
real-time data sources (p. 265)
sentiment analysis (p. 270)
socialization (p. 263)
social media analytics (p. 269)
structured and unstructured data (p. 265)
tacit knowledge (p. 262)
tagging (p. 264)

DISCUSSION QUESTIONS

1. What does it take to be a successful competitor using business analytics? What is the role of information technology (IT) in helping build this competence for the enterprise?
2. The terms *data*, *information*, and *knowledge* are often used interchangeably. But as this chapter discussed, they can be seen as three points on a continuum. What, if anything, in your opinion, is next on this continuum?
3. What is the difference between tacit and explicit knowledge? From your own experience, describe an example of each. How might an organization manage tacit knowledge?
4. How will the Internet of Things change the way managers make decisions? Give an example of a data stream from sensor data that you would like to monitor. Please explain why this would be beneficial to you.
5. How do social media analytics aid an organization? Give an example of a social media data stream and the type of insight that might be drawn from it.
6. Why is it so difficult to protect intellectual property? Do you think that the Digital Millennium Copyright Act is the type of legislation that should be enacted to protect intellectual property? Why or why not?
7. PricewaterhouseCoopers has an elegant, powerful intranet knowledge management system called *Knowledge Curve*. It makes available to its consultants and auditors a compendium of best practices, consulting methodologies, new tax and audit insights, links to external Web sites and news services, online training courses, directories of in-house experts, and other forms of explicit knowledge. Yet, according to one of the firm's managing partners, "There's a feeling it's underutilized. Everybody goes there sometimes, but when they're looking for expertise, most people go down the hall."[27] Why do you think that Knowledge Curve is underutilized?

CASE STUDY 12-1 Stop & Shop's Scan It! App

The grocery store and supermarket shopping industries have combined annual revenues in the hundreds of billions of dollars. Just food and beverage sales in the United States (U.S.) brought in $600 billion in revenue in 2014. Grocery shopping was a highly commoditized industry with over 85,000 stores in the U.S. at that time. With little variation in available item selection and less money being spent on groceries in the down economy, competition for customer loyalty continued to grow. By using business analytics to help process buying habits of its customers, Stop & Shop, a Quincy, Massachusetts-based grocer, tried to get a better grasp on the hard-to-understand concept of customer loyalty in grocery shopping.

[27] Thomas Stewart, "The Case Against Knowledge Management," *Business 2.0* (February 2002), 81, http://providersedge.com/docs/km_articles/The_Case_Against_KM.pdf (accessed September 7, 2015).

In 2009, Stop & Shop introduced Scan It!, a portable electronic device for customers shopping in its stores. The device allowed customers to "scan and bag" products, expediting checkout times at the end of their shopping trip. Additionally, the device offered deals based on the location of the scanner (and therefore the customer) in the store. Location-specific discounts in real time became increasingly popular among customers as use of Scan It! grew by 10% in both the first and second quarters of 2009. The most beneficial aspect of the Scan It!, however, came with the powerful analytics software built into the device by Modiv Media in which Stop & Shop owns a minority interest. The software kept track of each customer's purchasing habits both past and present in order to individualize coupons in real time for the customer.

The scanner resulted in three positive trends for Shop & Stop. Customer loyalty grew, allowing the company to secure an increased customer base than area demographics would predict. Additionally, each shopper's basket size increased as the individually tailored coupons enticed customers to buy more. Lastly, Shop & Stop's customer base grew as word of mouth marketing brought in more customers to try the state-of-the-art device.

However, after a couple of years, Stop & Shop saw customer adoption plateau. In October 2011, the grocer created the Scan It! app for the iPhone and Android. By eliminating the need to sign in and retrieve a scanner at the store, customer adoption of the device continued its upward climb. Additionally, as customers became increasingly concerned about saving money while shopping, Stop & Shop built in budgeting software to allow customers to track their spending more effectively. Ads for the new app proclaimed, "New Mobile App Allows Customers to Shop, Bag, and Tally Their Grocery Order with Their Personal iPhone® and Android™ Devices." Scan It! was heralded as "a first of its kind grocery app that allows customers to use their personal mobile device to scan, tally, and bag their groceries while they shop."[28]

Stop & Shop had bundled an app that not only rewarded customers who shopped at its stores by helping them save money but also tracked information on sales, which the company loaded into its data warehouse and used to understand its customers. Analytics then helped Stop & Shop put the right items on its shelves to maximize sales and create customer loyalty.

Discussion Questions

1. What is the benefit of the Scan It! data to Stop & Shop? What are some of the questions the company could answer about its customers?
2. How would you assess the level of capabilities of Stop & Shop's use of analytics? What might the company do differently with the data to gain more value?
3. What is the benefit of Scan It! for the customers? What concerns might shoppers have about their privacy? How would you advise Stop & Shop management to respond to these concerns?

Sources: Adapted from http://www.internetretailer.com/2011/10/26/stop-shop-expands-availability-scan-it-mobile-app (accessed September 6, 2015); http://stopandshop.com/shopping/shopping-tools/scanit/ (accessed September 6, 2015); http://southeastfarmpress.com/vegetables/supermarket-guru-seeking-next-big-trend (accessed September 6, 2015).

CASE STUDY 12-2 Business Intelligence at CKE Restaurants

At a time when most fast-food restaurants were touting nutrition, Hardee's proudly introduced the Monster Thickburger. It boasts a phenomenal 1,420 calories and 107 grams of fat. It consists of 2 one-third-pound charbroiled 100% Angus beef patties, three slices of American cheese, a dollop of mayonnaise, and four crispy strips of bacon on a toasted buttery sesame seed bun. What on earth was CKE Restaurants, the owners of the Hardee's chain, thinking?

Because of its business intelligence system (BIS), CKE was confident about introducing the Monster Thickburger across the United States. A BIS uses data mining, analytical processing, querying, and reporting to process a business's data and derive insights from them. CKE's BIS, known ironically inside the company as the CKE performance reporting (CPR), monitored the performance of its Monster Thickburger in test markets to ensure that the burger contributed to increases in sales and profits at restaurants without cannibalizing sales of other more modest burgers. To do so, CKE's BIS studied

[28] Adapted from http://www.internetretailer.com/2011/10/26/stop-shop-expands-availability-scan-it-mobile-app; http://www.stopandshop.com/our_stores/tools/scan_it_mobile.htm; http://southeastfarmpress.com/vegetables/supermarket-guru-seeking-next-big-trend.

a variety of factors—such as menu mixes, Monster Thickburger production costs, average unit volumes for the Monster Thickburger compared with other burgers, gross profits and total sales for each of the test stores, and the contribution that each menu item (including the Monster Thickburger) made to total sales. Because the sales of Monster Thickburger exceeded expectations in the test markets, CKE developed a $7 million dollar advertising campaign to launch its nationwide introduction. Monster Thickburger sales exceeded expectations, and Hardee's sales revenues increased immediately, eventually growing by 8%. "The Monster Thickburger was directly responsible for a good deal of that increase," says Brad Haley, Hardee's executive vice president of marketing.

Partially because of its reliance on CPR, CKE was rescued from the brink of bankruptcy. It increased sales at restaurants open more than a year, narrowed its overall losses, and finally turned a profit after three years. CPR, its proprietary system, consists of a Microsoft SQL server database and uses Microsoft development tools to parse and display analytical information. It uses econometric models to provide context and to explain performance. The company reviews and refines these models each month. The econometric models take into consideration 44 factors, including the weather, holidays, coupon activity, discounting, free giveaways, and new products. With the click of a button, for example, a sales downturn can be explained on a screen showing, for example, that 5% of the 8% decrease was due to torrential rain in the Northeast and 2% was due to free giveaways.

In the competitive restaurant chain industry, companies have to be agile and responsive to the dynamic environment that they face. They must match their BIS initiatives to their business strategies in order to improve operations and their bottom lines. BISs assist companies in making strategic decisions about menu items and closures of underperforming stores as well as tactical matters such as renegotiating contracts with food suppliers, monitoring food costs, and identifying opportunities to improve inefficient processes. To derive value from their BISs, many restaurant chains have successfully reduced the three biggest barriers to BIS success: voluminous amounts of irrelevant data, poor data quality, and user resistance.

CKE's CIO and Executive Vice President of Strategic Planning Jeff Chasney states: "If you're just presenting information that's neat and nice but doesn't evoke a decision or impart important knowledge, then it's noise. You have to focus on what are the really important things going on in your business."

Chasney stresses that a BIS should be different from the plain-vanilla standard corporate reporting tools of old. Rather, a BIS should provide managers insights rather than just data. He believes that the context from which the data were collected significantly impacts how those data should be interpreted. Systems that just report changes without enough background or information on what caused those changes are not very useful. Managers don't know what data to trust. Chasney explains, "If your business intelligence system is not going to improve your decision making and find problem areas to correct and new directions to take, nobody's going to bother to look at it."

The first step to developing a BIS is to understand the company's decision-making processes. Before information is collected, analyzed, and used in the BIS, someone has to identify what information is needed to confidently make decisions. For instance, the CEOs of CKE's restaurant chains wanted to understand what made sales fluctuate while the COOs wanted to know how to recognize good business opportunities as well as underperforming properties. Then the BIS designer must determine the appropriate presentation format, be it a report, a chart, or a Web site.

BIS must add value to the executive's decision-making processes. To do that, attention must be paid to the critical performance indicators. For CKE, as Chasney learned, those are sales, cost of sales, exceptions (such as high-performing or underperforming areas), and business trends.

Discussion Questions

1. How does the business intelligence system (BIS) at CKE add value to the business?
2. What are some tips for developing and using the BIS described in this case?
3. Was the introduction of the Monster Thickburger a good idea or an example of information leading to a wrong decision?

Sources: Christine Lagorio, "Man vs. Monster Thickburger" (February 11, 2009), http://www.cbsnews.com/news/man-vs-monster-thickburger/ (accessed September 6, 2015); Meredith Levinson, "The Brain Behind the Big, Bad Burger and Other Tales of Business Intelligence," *CIO* (May 15, 2007); http://www.cio.com/article/109454/The_Brain_Behind_the_Big_Bad_Burger_and_Other_Tales_of_Business_Intelligence (accessed September 6, 2015).

chapter

13 Privacy and Ethical Considerations in Information Management

Information technology (IT) has created a unique set of ethical issues related to the use and control of information. This chapter addresses those issues from various perspectives using three normative theories (stockholder, stakeholder, and social contract) to understand the responsible use and control of information by business organizations. Social contract theory is extended to the evolving issue of responsiveness to foreign governments when ethical tensions emerge. At the individual and corporate levels, Mason's privacy, accuracy, property, accessibility (PAPA) framework is applied to information control. Subsequently, the chapter covers the ethical role of managers in today's dynamic world of social business and security controls to keep information safe and accurate. The chapter concludes with a discussion of green computing.

When TJX Co., Target, and Home Depot fell victim to three of the largest data security breaches in the history of retailing, each faced a serious ethical dilemma that unfortunately seems to have plagued a growing number of companies in recent years. The credit card accounts of an estimated 186 million customers worldwide were stolen by these three breaches alone; 90 million for TJX, 40 million for Target, and 56 million for Home Depot.[1] Current laws from multiple state, federal, and foreign jurisdictions dictate how and when a firm must inform affected customers and what corrective steps it must take in such a case; most jurisdictions allow 45 days for a firm to act following the determination of a breach. Any delay beyond 45 days would incur heavy fines. However, ethically, it becomes an even more pressing issue. Should highly visible firms such as these inform affected customers immediately or wait until a breach has been secured and all remedial steps have been undertaken, which may take weeks?

If a firm informs customers immediately, the customers could start taking preventive steps to protect themselves from identity theft and minimize resulting financial and psychological losses. However, this means the breach would become public knowledge before the remedial steps were taken. More hackers would learn about the breach and possibly exploit the weakness in the company's IT infrastructure. Additionally, the financial markets would lose confidence in the breached company and severely punish shareholders. Such loss of image would also affect the company's ability to attract and retain high-quality employees in the long run. On the other hand, if it waited for 45 days, the financial stability of many customers would be compromised through misuse of their credit cards and other private records. This could result in major class-action litigation, which might permanently affect the company.

Information collected in the course of operations is important for conducting business and even creating valuable competitive advantage. But managers must ask ethical questions concerning just

[1] D. Paddon, "Home Depot: 56 Million Credit Cards Affected by Security Breach, Malware Eliminated," *Huffington Post Canada* (September 18, 2014; updated November 18, 2014), http://www.huffingtonpost.ca/2014/09/18/home-depot-credit-cards-eliminates_n_5845534.html (accessed September 7, 2015).

how that information will be used and by whom whether it is recorded or created inside or outside the organization. Failing to protect customer information can carry serious consequences, such as damaged shareholder relationships. Target's stock price fell 9% in the days after the breach was announced, and profit fell a whopping 46% in the quarter following the breach.[2] Likewise, TJX's stock lost 8% in value the day after the breach was announced.[3]

Acting responsibly is likely to gain legitimacy in the eyes of key stakeholders. Further, failure to adequately control information can cause a spillover effect with repercussions for an entire industry. For example, following the TJX breach, Massachusetts passed legislation with stringent requirements for any organization maintaining information about its citizens.[4] As computer networks and their products come to touch every aspect of people's lives and as the power, speed, and capabilities of computers expand, managers are increasingly challenged to govern those computer networks and to protect information residing on them in an ethical manner.

Following the Target and Home Depot breaches, Congress passed a Cybersecurity Enhancement Bill into law on December 18, 2014[5] that supports research and development to establish best practices, increase the public's awareness of the importance of cybersecurity, supports educational initiatives, and fosters a better-prepared workforce. Federal agencies are required to develop and continually update a cybersecurity strategic plan to "(1) guarantee individual privacy, verify third-party software and hardware, and address insider threats; (2) determine the origin of messages transmitted over the internet; and (3) protect information stored using cloud computing or transmitted through wireless services."[6] Additional legislation is expected to be signed into law over the coming years, and it is likely that legislation will struggle to keep up with the race between protection and breach of large pools of information for the foreseeable future. Even without any possible new legislation, managers must make decisions that don't compromise or put at risk the privacy and security of an individual's information.

Without guaranteed solutions, managers could easily become perplexed with their charge to manage both technically and ethically. They must manage the information generated and contained within their systems for the benefit not only of the corporation but also of society as a whole. The predominant issue, which arises due to the omnipresence of corporate IS, concerns the just and ethical use of the information that companies collect in the course of everyday operations. Without official guidelines and codes of conduct, who decides how to use this information? More and more, this challenge falls on corporate managers. They must understand societal needs and expectations to determine what they ethically can and cannot do in their quest to learn about their customers, suppliers, and employees and to provide greater service.

In a society whose legal standards are continually challenged, managers must serve as guardians of the public and private interest, although many may have no formal legal training and, thus, no firm basis for judgment. This chapter addresses many such concerns. It begins by expanding on the definition of ethical behavior and introduces several heuristics that managers can employ to help them make better decisions. Then the chapter elaborates on the most important issues behind the ethical treatment of information and some newly emerging controversies that will surely test society's resolve concerning the increasing presence of IS in every aspect of life.

This chapter takes a high-level view of ethical issues facing managers in today's environment. It focuses primarily on providing a set of frameworks the manager can apply to a wide variety of ethical issues. Outside the scope of this chapter are several important issues such as the digital divide (the impact of computer technology on the poor or "have-nots," racial minorities, and third world nations), cyberwar (politically motivated hacking to conduct sabotage and espionage), cyberbullying, or social concerns that arise from artificial intelligence, neural networks, and expert systems. Such problems have no easy answers, and researchers are just beginning to define and understand them, a necessary step in finding future solutions. Although these are interesting and important areas for concern, the objective in this chapter is to provide managers a way to think about the issues of information ethics and corporate responsibility.

---

[2] M. McGrath, "Target Profit Falls 46% on Credit Card Breach and the Hits Could Keep Coming," *Forbes* (February 26, 2014), http://www.forbes.com/sites/maggiemcgrath/2014/02/26/target-profit-falls-46-on-credit-card-breach-and-says-the-hits-could-keep-on-coming/ (accessed September 7, 2015).

[3] R. Kerber, "Cost of Data Breach at TJX Soars to $256m," Boston Globe Connection (August 15, 2007), http://www.boston.com/business/articles/2007/08/15/cost_of_data_breach_at_tjx_soars_to_256m/?page=full (accessed September 7, 2015).

[4] M. Culnan and C. Williams, "How Ethics Can Enhance Organizational Privacy: Lessons from the ChoicePoint and TJX Data Breaches," *MIS Quarterly* 33, no. 4 (2009), 673–87.

[5] https://www.congress.gov/bill/113th-congress/senate-bill/1353 (accessed September 7, 2015).

[6] Ibid.

Responsible Computing

The technological landscape is changing daily. Increasingly, however, technological advances come about in a business domain lacking ethical clarity. Because of its newness, this area of IT often lacks accepted norms of behavior or universally accepted decision-making criteria. Companies daily encounter ethical dilemmas as they try to use their IS to create and exploit competitive advantages. These ethical dilemmas arise when a decision or an action reflects competing moral values that may impair or enhance the well-being of an individual or a group of people. These dilemmas arise when there is no one clear way to deal with the ethical issue.

Managers must assess current information initiatives with particular attention to possible ethical issues. Collecting customer information in an uncontrolled manner can lead to unintended consequences, such as the increasing number of breaches that are occurring and invasion of privacy. There are indeed benefits for both buyers and sellers in storing and using detailed information, making purchases more convenient and presenting products that are truly interesting to customers. Using high volumes of data that are stored about customers can raise the efficiency of the browsing and shopping experience. However, managers need to also consider **information ethics**, or the "ethical issues associated with the development and application of information technologies."[7] Stated more directly, just because we can do something does not mean we should.

It is useful to consider three theories of ethical behavior in the corporate environment that managers can develop and apply to the particular challenges they face. These normative theories of business ethics—stockholder theory, stakeholder theory, and social contract theory—are widely applied in traditional business situations. They are "normative" in that they prescribe behavior, specifying what people should do. Smith and Hasnas also refer to them as "intermediate-level" principles that can be understood by ordinary businesspeople and that can be applied to the "concrete moral quandaries of the business domain."[8] Following is a description of each theory accompanied by an illustration of its application using the TJX example, the first of the three widespread retail data breaches outlined at the beginning of this chapter.

Stockholder Theory

According to **stockholder theory**, stockholders provide funding for a firm, and expect its managers to act as agents in furthering the stockholders' goals.[9] The nature of this contract binds managers to act in the interest of the shareholders (i.e., to maximize shareholder value). As Milton Friedman wrote, "There is one and only one social responsibility of business: to use its resources and engage in activities designed to increase its profits so long as it stays within the rules of the game, which is to say, engages in open and free competition, without deception or fraud."[10]

Stockholder theory qualifies the manager's duty in two salient ways. First, managers are bound to employ legal, nonfraudulent means. Second, managers must take the long-term view of shareholder interest (i.e., they are obliged to forgo short-term gains if doing so will maximize value over the long-term).

The stipulation under stockholder theory that the pursuit of profits must be legal and nonfraudulent would not have prevented TJX from waiting to announce the security breach until it had taken corrective action. The delay allowed by law might also have a positive impact on TJX's stock price. Delaying would satisfy the test of maximizing shareholder value because it would help keep the price of its stock from dropping. Further, a recent survey indicated that customers are reluctant to shop in stores once data breaches have been announced,[11] so delaying may be important for maintaining a steady stream of revenues for as long as possible. On the other hand, disgruntled customers would definitely stop shopping at its stores if TJX waited too long.[12] Any lost revenues would weigh

[7] M. G. Martinsons and D. Ma, "Sub-Cultural Differences in Information Ethics Across China: Focus on Chinese Management Generation Gaps," *Journal of AIS* 10 (Special Issue) (2009).

[8] H. Jeff Smith and John Hasnas, "Ethics and Information Systems: The Corporate Domain," *MIS Quarterly* (March 1999), 112.

[9] Ibid.

[10] M. Friedman, *Capitalism and Freedom* (Chicago, *IL: University of Chicago Press*, 1962), 133.

[11] Brett Conradt, "Think Shoppers Forget Retail Data Breaches? Nope," CNBC.com (June 22, 2015), http://www.cnbc.com/2015/06/22/ (accessed September 12, 2015).

[12] There is an interesting presentation of a similar breach with commentaries from the CIOs of ChoicePoint, Motorola, Visa International, and Theft Resource Center in Eric McNulty, "Boss I Think Someone Stole Our Customer Data," *Harvard Business Review* (September 2007), 37–50.

against managers' success in meeting the ethical obligation to work toward maximizing value. It appears that TJX took only the actions necessary to bring its practices in line with those expected in industry.[13]

Stakeholder Theory

Stakeholder theory holds that managers, although bound by their relation to stockholders, are entrusted also with a responsibility, fiduciary or otherwise, to all those who hold a stake in or a claim on the firm.[14] The word *stakeholder* is currently taken to mean any group that vitally affects the survival and success of the corporation or whose interests the corporation vitally affects. Such groups normally include stockholders, customers, employees, suppliers, the local community, and, possibly, many other groups who may hold a stake in the firm. At its most basic level, stakeholder theory states that management must balance the rights of all stakeholders without impinging on the rights of any one particular stakeholder.

Stakeholder theory diverges most consequentially from stockholder theory in affirming that the interests of parties other than the stockholders also play a legitimate role in a firm's governance and management. As a practical matter, it is often difficult, if not impossible, to figure out what is in the best interest of each stakeholder group and then balance any conflicting interests.

When stakeholders feel that their interests haven't been considered adequately by the managers making the decisions, their only recourse may be to stop participating in the corporation: Customers can stop buying the company's products, stockholders can sell their stock, and so forth. But some stakeholders are not in a position to stop participating in the corporation. In particular, employees may need to continue working for the corporation even though they dislike practices of their employers or experience considerable stress due to their jobs.

Viewed in light of stakeholder theory, the ethical issue facing TJX presented a more complex dilemma. John Philip Coghlan, CEO of Visa USA noted, "A data breach can put an executive in an exceedingly complex situation, where he must negotiate the often divergent interests of multiple stakeholders."[15] TJX's shareholders stand to gain in the short term by delaying an announcement, but what would be the effects on other stakeholders? One stakeholder group, the customers, definitely could benefit from knowing about the breach and its severity as soon as possible because they could take steps to protect themselves through a special Web page, toll-free information hotlines, or Webcasts. TJX could also offer them a free credit-monitoring service and compensate those who are injured. Research has shown that customers who receive adequate compensation after making a complaint are actually more loyal than those without complaints.[16] On the other hand, if the breach were not announced, fewer hackers might be attracted to the situation or inspired to be a "copy cat" and break into systems. Nonetheless, it probably could be shown that the costs to customers outweighed the benefits within the larger stakeholder group.

Social Contract Theory

Social contract theory places responsibility on corporate managers to consider the needs of the society (societies) in which the corporation is embedded. Social contract theorists assert that a corporation is permitted legally to form to create more value to society than it consumes. Thus, society gives legal recognition to the organization and charges it with enhancing society's welfare by satisfying particular interests of consumers and workers in exploiting the advantages of the corporate form.[17] The social contract comprises two distinct components: social welfare and justice. *Social welfare* addresses the issue of providing benefits exceeding their associated costs, and the need for *justice* addresses the need for corporations to pursue profits legally without fraud or deception and avoid activities that injure society. The social contract obliges managers to pursue profits in ways that are compatible with the well-being of society as a whole.

---

[13] Culnan and Williams, "How Ethics Can Enhance Organizational Privacy," 673–87.
[14] Smith and Hasnas, "Ethics and Information Systems," 115.
[15] McNulty, "Boss I Think Someone Stole Our Customer Data."
[16] Ibid.
[17] Smith and Hasnas, "Ethics and Information Systems," 116.

Social contract theory is sometimes criticized because no mechanism exists to actuate it. In the absence of a real contract whose terms subordinate profit maximization to social welfare, most critics find it hard to imagine that corporations are willing to lose profitability in the name of altruism. Yet, the strength of the theory lies in its broad assessment of the moral foundations of business activity.

Applied to the TJX case, social contract theory would demand that the manager ask whether the delay in notifying customers about the security breach could compromise fundamental tenets of fairness or social justice. If customers were not apprised of the delay as soon as possible, TJX's actions could be seen as unethical because it would not seem fair to delay notifying the customers. If, on the other hand, the time prior to notification were used to take corrective action with the consequence of limiting not only hackers from stealing confidential customer information but also of forestalling future attacks that would impact society as a whole, the delay conceivably could be considered ethical.

Although these three normative theories of business ethics possess distinct characteristics, they are not completely incompatible. All offer useful metrics for defining ethical behavior in profit-seeking enterprises under free market conditions. The theories provide managers an independent standard by which to judge the ethical nature of superiors' orders as well as their firms' policies and codes of conduct. Upon inspection, the three theories appear to represent concentric circles with stockholder theory at the center and social contract theory at the outer ring. Stockholder theory is narrowest in scope, stakeholder theory encompasses and expands on it, and social contract theory covers the broadest area. Figure 13.1 summarizes these three theories.

What, ultimately, did TJX do? It disclosed the breach in January 2007 but did not release a comprehensive executive summary of the attack until March 2007 when it made a regulatory filing. The preceding December TJX had actually noticed suspicious software, at which point it hired IBM and General Dynamics to investigate. Three days later, these investigators determined that TJX's systems had been compromised due to its failure to implement adequate information security procedures and detect and limit unauthorized access.[18] Further, the attacker still had access. Unfortunately, it took TJX 17 months to find out that its computer systems had been breached on numerous occasions on a colossal scale.[19] It was over a year later, on February 29, 2008, when President and CEO Carol Meyrowitz wrote a letter to "valued customers" about the breach that had been announced in January 2007. The TJX retail chain agreed to pay $24 million and $41 million in restitution to MasterCard- and Visa-issuing lenders, respectively, who were affected by the breach. TJX also offered free credit monitoring for cardholders and a $30 store voucher.[20] Not until June 2009 did TJX finally reach a settlement of US$9.75 million with 41 states to compensate them for their investigations of the breach.[21] Based on media coverage at that time, one could surmise that TJX's overriding approach was more consistent with the stockholder theory than social contract theory. At least one set of stakeholders, the customers, were not well served.

Theory	Definition	Metrics
Stockholder	Maximize stockholder wealth, in a legal and non-fraudulent manner	Will this action maximize long-term stockholder value? Can goals be accomplished without compromising company standards and without breaking laws?
Stakeholder	Maximize benefits to all stakeholders while weighing costs to competing interests	Does the proposed action maximize collective benefits to the company? Does this action treat one or more of the corporate stakeholders unfairly?
Social contract	Create value for society in a manner that is just and non-discriminatory	Does this action create a "net" benefit for society? Does the proposed action discriminate against any group in particular, and is its implementation socially just?

FIGURE 13.1 Three normative theories of business ethics.

[18] Culnan and Williams, "How Ethics Can Enhance Organizational Privacy," 673–87.

[19] Kevin Murphy, "TJX Hack Is Biggest Ever" (March 29, 2007), *Computer Business Review*, http://www.cbronline.com/news/tjx_hack_is_biggest_ever (accessed September 7, 2015).

[20] Martin Bosworth, "TJX to Pay MasterCard $24 Million for Data Breach," ConsumerAffaris.com (April 6, 2008), http://www.consumeraffairs.com/news04/2008/04/tjx_mc.html (accessed July 29, 2008).

[21] J. Vijayan, "TJX Reaches $9.75 Million Breach Settlement with 41 States" (June 24, 2009), http://www.computerworld.com/s/article/9134765/TJX_reaches_9.75_million_breach_settlement_with_41_ states (accessed January 28, 2012).

Corporate Social Responsibility

Application of social contract theory helps companies adopt a broad perspective. In this section, we address a "big picture" by exploring three areas in which corporate social responsibility is particularly visible: responsible use of information, ethical tensions with governments, and green computing.

Responsible Use of Information

Beyond the concerns of data breaches, organizations today are sitting on more data than ever before thought imaginable. Those data enable a company to profile us, estimate our incomes, predict our needs, and tempt us to make purchases. Sometimes this activity strikes customers as being a "Big Brother" situation, but the name for this has become "big data."

As described in Chapter 12, modern statistical packages provide advanced methods to detect patterns in enormous sets of data. Large data sets are difficult for people to envision, but the larger the data set, the clearer the picture becomes for detecting and understanding those patterns. The data indicate that many behaviors tend to cluster together; for example, camera purchases tend to be accompanied by photography accessories. Zip Codes in affluent neighborhoods tend to predict purchases of more expensive equipment and more accessories. Those who qualify and who also frequently purchase hiking and sporting goods might be ripe for a new GoPro™ complete with accessories. A merchant who passes up the opportunity to advertise similar waterproof personal travel cameras to carefully targeted individuals will not be in a good position to compete in today's world. However, there is a downside to these practices.

Target inadvertently revealed a teen's concealed pregnancy to her parents by mailing to her home address ads for maternity clothes and diapers.[22] The mailing was triggered by analysis of purchases of unscented soaps, vitamins, and cotton balls, which matched purchasing patterns of tens of thousands of other pregnant women. Although Target now sprinkles in other ads to be less blatant, the fact that it is aware of such personal facts is a stark illustration of the potential for large retailers to learn an alarming amount of private information by keeping track of purchasers and combining it with other identifying information they receive along the way or from other organizations.

That story becomes more surprising when consumers consider that even data with concealed but uniquely coded account numbers can reveal personal information, as a recent study reported in *Science* reported.[23] The researchers found that knowing three other facts, such as time and date, location, and approximate amount spent while visiting a merchant, 90% of individuals can be identified even with a data set that includes 1.1 million records spread over three months. Knowing when a person visited a particular restaurant or coffee shop can be discerned quickly with the use of social media entries and pictures that can establish what a person is eating. Identification of the person's identity can, of course, identify all of his or her credit card transactions throughout the entire data set. The message is quite clear: Be cautious about identifying exactly where you are and exactly when you are there on social media such as Facebook, Foursquare, and Instagram.

The *Science* study might imply feelings of futility are in order; that just when a manager tightens security practices to thwart yesterday's criminals, new threats render those practices inadequate. After all, few would have expected even disguised data to be a threat to customers. Further, many security professionals warn that it is not possible to provide 100% assurance of security in any system.[24]

However, that does not mean that managers should give up. As Chapter 7 discusses, failures often occur when firms don't take even basic precautions. TJX used basic WiFi encryption that could be broken into in about a half an hour in 2005. Hackers sat outside of a Marshall's store using a laptop and antenna to access data. More surprisingly,

---

[22] K. Hill, "How Target Figured Out a Teen Girl Was Pregnant Before Her Father Did," *Forbes* (February 16, 2012), http://www.forbes.com/sites/kashmirhill/2012/02/16/how-target-figured-out-a-teen-girl-was-pregnant-before-her-father-did/ (accessed September 7, 2015).

[23] Y. A de Montjoye, L. Radaelli, V. K. Singh, and A. S. Pentland, "Unique in the Shopping Mall: On the Re-identifiability of Credit Card Metadata," *Science* 347, no. 6221 (January 30, 2015), 536–39.

[24] M. Pringle, "Security Expert: All Systems Vulnerable to Cyberattacks" (December 23, 2014), http://www.wbaltv.com/money/security-expert-all-systems-vulnerable-to-cyberattacks/30350212 (accessed September 7, 2015).

a security professional reported in 2007 that most major retailers had similar weaknesses.[25] The Target hack was perpetrated by data thieves posing as heating/air conditioning repair professionals; they were able to tap into the system using their assigned terminals. The Home Depot breach involved installation of malware at self-service checkout counters.[26]

These stories will undoubtedly and unfortunately be augmented by others in the future, but they illustrate that security personnel should be armed with knowledge of best practices, common sense in handling people who request access to computer systems, and vigilance at points of vulnerability. Chapter 7 provides specific strategies to try to carry out a firm's responsibility for protecting data.

Ethical Tensions with Governments

Organizations are also facing a dilemma reconciling their corporate policies with regulations in countries where they want to operate. "Managers may need to adopt much different approaches across nationalities to counter the effects of what they perceive as unethical behaviors."[27] For example, the United Arab Emirates threatened to shut off BlackBerry messaging, e-mail, and Web browsing services if the device's maker, Research in Motion (RIM) did not provide certain information necessary for national security. RIM managers did not want to disclose confidential information. But they also didn't want to endanger UAE's national security. Even though a compromise was reached shortly before the shutdown was to go into effect, the case reflects the challenges of dealing with foreign governments.[28]

Censorship posed an ethical dilemma for companies such as Sony and Google. Just before planning to release the film *The Interview*, Sony Pictures suffered terroristic threats and eventually widespread hacks of their computers that President Barak Obama and the NSA blamed on North Korea.[29] Sony reacted swiftly to the threats and postponed plans to release the film. Eventually, the film was released, at first online and then in a small number of theaters. A firm suffering threats from governmental agencies faces unexpected options requiring quick action.

Enticed by the lure of a gigantic market, Google tried to set up business in China. The Chinese government, quite accustomed to developing and enforcing regulations, wanted to limit the overseas Web sites that Google's search engine could retrieve when operating in China. The Chinese government also interfered with Google's e-mail services, making it difficult for users to gain access to Gmail. Google continues to face the dilemma of how to deliver the level of services it deems appropriate in the face of stiff government regulation. This dilemma is likely to become very common with increased globalization. In this case, the balancing act is at an international level.

PAPA: Privacy, Accuracy, Property, and Accessibility

In an economy that is rapidly becoming dominated by knowledge workers, the value of information is paramount. Those who possess the "best" information and know how to use it will win. The recent trends in cloud computing and big data permit high levels of computational power and storage to be purchased for relatively small amounts of money. Although this trend means that computer-generated or stored information now falls within the reach of a larger percentage of the populace, it also means that collecting and storing information is becoming easier and more cost effective. Although this circumstance can affect businesses and individuals for the better, it also can affect them substantially for the worse.

---

[25] G. Ou, "TJX's Failure to Secure Wi-Fi Could Cost $1B" (May 7, 2007), http://www.zdnet.com/article/tjxs-failure-to-secure-wi-fi-could-cost-1b/ (accessed September 7, 2015).

[26] B. Krebs, "Home Depot: 56M Cards Impacted, Malware Contained," Krebs On Security (September 18, 2014), http://krebsonsecurity.com/2014/09/home-depot-56m-cards-impacted-malware-contained/ (accessed September 7, 2015).

[27] D. Leidner and T. Kayworth, "A Review of Culture in Information Systems Research: Toward a Theory of Information Technology Culture Conflict," *MIS Quarterly* 30, no. 2 (2006), 357–99.

[28] "For Data, Tug Grows Over Privacy vs. Security" (August 3, 2010), http://query.nytimes.com/gst/fullpage.html?res=9504E4D6113CF930A3575BC0A9669D8B63 (accessed January 28, 2012).

[29] J. Diamond, "NSA Hacking Since 2010 Led U.S. to Blame North Korea for Sony Attack," CNN (January 20, 2015), http://www.cnn.com/2015/01/19/politics/nsa-north-korea-hacking-2010/ (accessed September 12, 2015).

Area	Critical Questions
Privacy	What information must people reveal about themselves to others? Are there some things that people do not have to reveal about themselves? Can the information that people provide be used to identify their personal preferences or history when they don't want those preferences or history to be known? Can the information that people provide be used for purposes other than those for which the people were told that it would be used?
Accuracy	Who is responsible for the reliability, authenticity, and accuracy of information? Who is accountable for errors in the information?
Property	Who owns the information? Who owns the channels of distribution, and how should they be regulated? What is the fair price of information that is exchanged?
Accessibility	What information does a person or organization have a right to obtain, with what protection, and under what conditions? Who can access personal information in the files? Does the person accessing personal information "need to know" the information that is being accessed?

FIGURE 13.2 Mason's areas of managerial control.
Source: Adapted from Richard O Mason, "Four Ethical Issues of the Information Age," *MIS Quarterly* 10, no. 1 (March 1986), 5.

Consider several areas of information ethics in which the control of information is crucial. Richard O. Mason[30] identified four such areas, which can be summarized by the acronym PAPA: privacy, accuracy, property, and accessibility (see Figure 13.2). Mason's framework has limitations in terms of accommodating the range and complexity of ethical issues encountered in today's information-intensive world. However, this framework helps to understand information ethics because it is both popular and simple.

Privacy

Many people consider privacy to be the most important area in which their interests need to be safeguarded. **Privacy** has long been considered "the right to be left alone."[31] Although it has been argued that so many different definitions exist that it is hard to satisfactorily define the term,[32] it is "fundamentally about protections from intrusion and information gathering by others."[33] Typically, it has been defined in terms of individuals' ability to personally control information about themselves. But requiring individuals to control their own information would severely limit what is private. In today's information-oriented world, individuals really have little control.

In July 2015, the issue of privacy became a frequent subject of discussion due to the discovery of a breach at marital affair facilitation firm Ashley Madison, revealing account and credit card information for 37 million users.[34] Users had assumed that their covert affairs would remain a secret, but blackmailers demanded money to keep the information from being published widely.[35] Reportedly, the hackers subsequently released information from 32 million of the users.[36] Two suicides have been linked to the breach, underscoring the seriousness of online privacy.[37]

[30] Richard O. Mason, "Four Ethical Issues of the Information Age," *MIS Quarterly* 10, no. 1 (March 1986).

[31] Samuel D. Warren and Louis D. Brandeis, "The Right to Privacy," *Harvard Law Review* 4, no. 5 (December 1890), 193–200.

[32] Paul Pavlou, "State of the Inform Privacy Literature: Where Are We Now and Where Should We Go?" *MIS Quarterly* 35, no. 4 (2011), 977–85.

[33] E. F. Stone, D. G. Gardner, H. G. Gueutal, and S. McClure, "A Field Experiment Comparing Information-Privacy Values, Beliefs, and Attitudes Across Several Types of Organizations," *Journal of Applied Psychology* 68, no. 3 (August 1983), 459–68.

[34] Daniel Victor, "The Ashley Madison Data Dump, Explained," *The New York Times* (August 19, 2015), http://www.nytimes.com/2015/08/20/technology/the-ashley-madison-data-dump-explained.html (accessed September 7, 2015).

[35] Jonah Bromwich, "Ashley Madison Users Face Threats of Blackmail and Identity Theft," *The New York Times* (August 27, 2015), http://www.nytimes.com/2015/08/28/technology/ashley-madison-users-face-threats-of-blackmail-and-identity-theft.html (accessed September 7, 2015).

[36] Rishi Iyengar, "Hackers Release Data from Cheating Website Ashley Madison Online," *Time* (August 18, 2015), http://time.com/4002647/ashley-madison-hackers-data-released-impact-team/ (accessed September 7, 2015).

[37] Hilary Shenfield, "Suicides Possibly Linked to Release of Ashley Madison Client Names: Toronto Police," *People* (August 25, 2015), http://www.people.com/article/suicides-possibly-linked-to-ashley-madison-hack-toronto-police-say (accessed September 7, 2015).

Privacy Paradox

Managers must consider the *privacy paradox*, which trades off convenience, irritation, and even entertainment for privacy. For instance, a company might store credit card numbers of its customers so that they do not have to enter that information every time they visit the firm's Web site. However, by doing so, there is additional risk of theft of that information. There is also convenience in tailoring advertisements according to a person's unique interests. Rather than suffer with relentless advertisements that have little relevance, ad networks that share information across sites potentially provide less irritation to consumers. Finally, teenagers and adults alike post private information about location, friends, and activities, largely for entertainment purposes in spite of abundant warnings.

A study of 15,000 consumers in 15 countries reported that 51% said they would not trade off privacy for convenience but 27% said they would. Results differed by country with India reporting 40% in the "no" camp and 48% in the "yes" camp. In contrast, Germans were most negative with 71% saying "no" and 12% saying "yes."[38]

Interestingly, regardless of the survey results, recent studies reveal that many consumers *behave* as if they are unconcerned. Teenagers in a study posted sensitive information widely although many regretted their disclosures later.[39] Many people are finding out that talking about their latest bashes in detail on Facebook does not go over very well with potential employers who access their pages. An interesting study reported that 70% of U.S. recruiters and human resource professionals have rejected candidates based on data found online.[40] Fewer than 20% of Facebook's members had adjusted the default privacy settings prior to Facebook's change in policy (when it came under fire) to enhance customer privacy.[41] The concern about privacy on Facebook (and other Internet sites) varies across the globe; for example, it is greater in Europe than in the United States.

Even more telling is the fact that privacy notices are widely ignored, perhaps due to their length, legal language, and uninteresting nature. Facebook's Terms of Service (TOS) agreement outlines its privacy policy in over 9,000 words, and Pen Pal's TOS 36,000 tops the number of words in Shakespeare's *Hamlet*. [42] A recent prank confirmed a previous University of California–Berkeley survey that found that fewer than 2% of users read license agreements. Thousands actually agreed to give up their souls by agreeing to an "immortal soul clause" buried in an agreement notice at a Web site in the United Kingdom.[43]

The Federal Trade Commission (FTC) is currently seeking more understandable privacy notices for consumers that will result in more transparency about data provided to firms "in the fine print." In a recent speech, FTC Director Jessica Rich warned of corporate practices that compromise privacy, especially in the ways in which big data can work against consumers.[44] Managers must avoid ethical blunders while they seek to provide customers convenient and useful opportunities.

Taking Control

Although total control is difficult in today's digital world, individuals can exert control by making efforts to manage their privacy through *choice*, *consent*, and *correction*. In particular, individuals can *choose* situations that offer the desired level of access to their information ranging from "total privacy to unabashed publicity."[45]

---

[38] S. Lohr, "The Privacy Paradox, a Challenge for Business," *The New York Times* (June 12, 2014), http://bits.blogs.nytimes.com/2014/06/12/the-privacy-paradox-a-challenge-for-business/ (accessed September 7, 2015).

[39] Y. Wang, S. Komanduri, P. G. Leon, G. Norcie, A. Acquisti, and L. F. Cranor, "I Regretted the Minute I Pressed Share: A Qualitative Study of Regrets on Facebook," Symposium on Usable Privacy and Security (2011), https://cups.cs.cmu.edu/soups/2011/proceedings/a10_Wang.pdf (accessed September 7, 2015).

[40] Andrew LaVallee, "Facebook Outlines Privacy Changes" (December 9, 2009), http://blogs.wsj.com/digits/2009/12/09/facebook-outlines-privacy-changes/ (accessed May 11, 2011).

[41] Lori Andrews, "Facebook Is Using You," *The New York Times* (February 4, 2012), http://www.nytimes.com/2012/02/05/opinion/sunday/facebook-is-using-you.html (accessed September 7, 2015).

[42] Marc Goodman, *Future Crimes* (Toronto, Ontario: Random House, 2015).

[43] J. Temple, "Why Privacy Policies Don't Work—and What Might," *SFGate* (January 29, 2012), http://www.sfgate.com/business/article/Why-privacy-policies-don-t-work-and-what-might-2786252.php (accessed September 7, 2015).

[44] J. Rich, "The FTC's Consumer Protection Program: Current Priorities in Advertising and Privacy," speech at the FTC Privacy and Advertising Law Summit, June 12, 2014, https://www.ftc.gov/system/files/documents/public_statements/411821/140612kdwspeech.pdf (accessed September 7, 2015).

[45] H. T. Tavani and James Moore, "Privacy Protection, Control of Information, and Privacy-Enhancing Technologies," *Computers and Society* (March 2001), 6–11.

Individuals may also exert control when they manage their privacy through *consent*. When they give their consent, they are granting access to otherwise restricted information and they are specifying the purposes for which it may be used. In granting access, people should recognize that extensive amounts of data that can personally identify them are being collected and stored in databases and that these data can be used in ways that the individuals had not intended. When giving their consent, individuals should try to anticipate how their information might be reused as a result of data mining or aggregation. They should also try to anticipate unauthorized access through security breaches or internal browsing in companies whose security is lax. Finally, individuals should have control in managing their privacy by being able to access their personal information and correct it if it is wrong. To protect the integrity of information collected about individuals, federal regulators have recommended allowing consumers limited access to corporate information databases. Consumers thus could update their information and correct errors.

A new **online reputation management** industry has sprung up in recent years, targeting both individuals (such as CEOs)[46] and firms.[47] For a fee, firms such as Reputation.com and Elixir continuously search for negative formal or informal reviews about companies or individuals on Web sites and report results periodically. Experts advise managers to take an active role in protecting their brand by improving the presentation of search results, creating and controlling brand pages on popular social networks, participating actively in blogs, and providing press releases.[48]

For organizations, the tension between the proper use of personal information and information privacy is considered to be one of the most serious ethical debates of the Information Age.[49] One of the main organizational challenges to privacy is surveillance of employees.[50] For example, to ensure that employees are productive, employers can monitor their employees' e-mail and computer utilization while they are at work even though companies have not historically monitored employees' telephone calls.

Individuals are also facing privacy challenges from organizations providing them with services. Their actions are being traced not only with **cookies** but perhaps also with "beacons," "flash cookies," and even "supercookies" that can follow individuals' surfing behaviors without them knowing it. Every time someone uses one of the main search engines or merely visits a site directly, a "cookie," or small coded text message, is placed on or retrieved and updated from the at person's hard drive. The cookie file is sent back to the host company each time the browser requests a page from the server, [51] enabling these companies to track their surfing habits. Cookies have been ruled to be legal by U.S. courts.

Although the cookie is accessible only to the server that created it, third-party services can contribute an advertisement on Web site pages on servers owned by hundreds of different firms, obtaining information about browsing practices across a wide variety of sites. The cookie can store information about which page a person viewed. For instance, product pages that he or she views can be identified. The firms obtaining that information then can use it to determine which advertisements to provide or even to sell their databases to other firms. A revealing examination of the 50 most popular U. S. Web sites determined that more than two-thirds of the 3,000 plus tracking files installed by a total of 131 companies after people visited these Web sites were used to create rich databases of consumer profiles that could be sold.[52]

Although cookies are often criticized for their use in actions that violate privacy, they also serve useful purposes. Without cookies, it would not be possible to have a "shopping cart" when visiting an online store; without cookies, every click would be considered to be from an arbitrary source and the Web site would not know who it is when

[46] C. Connor, "5 New Reasons CEOs Should Maintain Stellar Online Reputation Management," *Forbes* (January 18, 2014), http://www.forbes.com/sites/cherylsnappconner/2014/01/18/5-new-reasons-ceos-should-maintain-a-stellar-reputation-online/ (accessed September 7, 2015).

[47] C. Connor, "Top Online Reputation Management Tips for Brand Marketers," *Forbes* (March 4, 2014), http://www.forbes.com/sites/cherylsnappconner/2014/03/04/top-online-reputation-management-tips-for-brand-marketers/ (accessed September 7, 2015).

[48] Ibid.

[49] Pavlou, "State of the Inform Privacy Literature," 977–85.

[50] B. C. Stahl, "The Impact of UK Human Rights Act 1998 on Privacy Protection in the Workplace," *Computer Security, Privacy, and Politics: Current Issues, Challenges, and Solutions* (Hershey, PA: Idea Group, 2008), 55–68.

[51] Webopedia, http://www.webopedia.com/TERM/c/cookie.html (accessed June 28, 2002).

[52] Julia Angwin, "The Web's New Gold Mine: Your Secrets" (July 30, 2010), http://online.wsj.com/article/SB10001424052748703940904575395073512989404.html (accessed January 28, 2010).

the user goes from one page to the next. It is also important to note that the user's actual identity is not sold to other parties but that the cookie reveals a person's browsing practices to determine what ads should be provided as she or he continues surfing the Web. Another benefit is thus that ads, in theory, should be more interesting and appropriate for users. Someone who spends all of his or her spare time browsing digital camera accessories, for example, would likely find it more useful to see ads for new lenses than ads for clothing. Selling this information can create a revenue source for a company and provide the user useful leads for potentially valued products.

Apple and Google recently came under fire for collecting and storing unencrypted location information from both personal computers and mobile devices. The information was obtained after the computer or mobile device searched for available wireless networks that were nearby. Typically the users gave permission to the companies to determine the computer's approximate location, but many people did not know that the information was being stored. Going against previous policy about keeping information about Internet searches sacrosanct, Google now combines user information from its sister sites, Gmail, Google +, and YouTube, to direct user searches and sell the information to advertisers.[53]

Do customers have a right to privacy while searching the Internet? Courts have decided that the answer is no, but as society moves ahead, the right to monitor customer habits in terms of their phone usage, location, e-mailing behaviors, and a myriad of other behaviors will be affected by how managers decide to use the information that they have collected.

Why would people be willing to give up this privacy? First, by supplying the information to vendors, they can receive personalized services in return. For example, the location device on their mobile might alert them that the restaurant that they are just walking by has a special offer on one of their favorite foods—sushi. Second, they might be paid for the information at a price that exceeds what they are giving up. Third, they might see providing information, such as that contained on many Facebook pages, as something that everybody is doing. Some individuals, especially younger ones, share information that would otherwise be considered private simply because they view it as a way to have their friends know them and to get to know their friends. "Digital natives" who have grown up in the Internet age do not know a society without the Web. They are comfortable building relationships, and, consequently, sharing information on the Web that others might consider private. Unfortunately, what's posted on the Web is there forever, and it may be fun to share it now, but its presence may have unintended consequences in the future.

Governments around the world are grappling with privacy legislation. Not surprisingly, they are using different approaches for ensuring the privacy of their citizens. The National Security Agency (NSA) computer system administrator Edward Snowden engaged in "whistle-blowing" but revealed many government secrets, violating several laws and perhaps endangering enforcement agents. In the coming years, if he returns to the United States and engages in extensive dialog, history will draw more definitive and perhaps more holistic conclusions than those that are available today.

The United States' so-called "sectorial" approach relies on a mix of legislation, regulation, and self-regulation. It is based upon a legal tradition with a strong emphasis on free trade. In the United States, privacy laws are enacted in response to specific problems for specific groups of people or specific industries. Examples of the relatively limited privacy legislation in the United States include the 1974 Privacy Act that regulates the U.S. government's collection and use of personal information and the 1998 Children's Online Privacy Protection Act that regulates the online collection and use of children's personal information.

The Gramm–Leach–Bliley Act of 1999 applies to financial institutions. It followed in the wake of banks selling sensitive information, including account information, Social Security numbers, credit card purchase histories, and so forth to telemarketing companies. This U.S. law somewhat mitigates the sharing of sensitive financial and personal information by allowing customers of financial institutions the limited right to "opt out" of the information sharing by these institutions with nonaffiliated third parties. This means that the financial institution may use the information unless the customer specifically tells the institution that his or her personal information cannot be used or distributed.

[53] Julia Angwin, "Google Widens Its Tracks" (July 30, 2010), http://online.wsj.com/article/SB10001424052970203806504577181371465957162.html?mod=djem_jiewr_IT_domainid (accessed January 28, 2012). Also see Goodman, *Future Crimes*.

The Health Insurance Portability and Accountability Act (HIPAA) of 1996 is designed to safeguard the electronic exchange privacy and security of information in the health care industry. Its Privacy Rule ensures that patients' health information is properly protected while allowing its necessary flow for providing and promoting health care. HIPAA's Security Rule specifies national standards for protecting electronic health information from unauthorized access, alteration, deletion, and transmission.

The Fair Credit Reporting act limits the use of credit reports provided by consumer reporting agencies to "permissible purposes" and grants individuals the right to access their reports and correct errors in them.

In contrast to the sectorial approach of the United States and with strong encouragement of self-regulation by industry, the European Union relies on omnibus legislation that requires creation of government data protection agencies, registration of databases with those agencies, and, in some cases, prior approval before processing personal data. The legislation is linked with the continental European legal tradition where privacy is a well-established right.[54] Because of pronounced differences in governmental approaches, many U.S. companies were concerned that they would be unable to meet the European "adequacy" standard for privacy protection specified in the European Commission's Directive 95/46/EC on Data Protection that went into effect in 1998. This directive sets standards for the collection, storage, and processing of personal information. It prohibits the transfer of personal

Social Business Lens: Personal Data

Social IT, especially Facebook, is redefining how people think about themselves and define themselves to others. Sherry Turkle, the author of *Alone Together* and a professor at Massachusetts Institute of Technology, says about Facebook and the new marketplace for personal data: "I can't think of another piece of passive software that has gotten so embedded in the cultural conversation. . . . It crystallized a set of issues that we will be defining for the next decade—self, privacy, how we connect and the price we are willing to pay for it."

What many people who supply these data about themselves may not realize is that that data may exist indefinitely in the ether. Furthermore, the data about personal lives and wants may be mined indefinitely by technology companies. Lori Andrews, in her book *I Know Who You Are and I Saw What You Did: Social Networks and the Death of Privacy*, is concerned that the Internet companies are in business for the money and hence they really would prefer to keep their customers in the dark about how their personal data are being used to generate profits.

And what is Andrews' solution? She proposes a social network constitution that can be used to judge the activities of social networks. Her constitution has 10 articles and begins with: "We the people of Facebook nation." Articles such as "No person shall be discriminated against based on his or her social network activities or profile" or "Each individual shall have control over his or her image from a social network, including over the image created by data aggregation" point to the need for people who supply data to social networks to demand respect for the data. Her focus is on rights, but not individuals' responsibilities in keeping private information private.

It could be argued that individuals need to recognize that surrendering their privacy in exchange for coupons, free music, and videos or customized products and services may lead to the loss of something of value—And that the data may remain accessible far longer than they want it to be.

Sources: Lori Andrews, *I Know Who You Are and I Saw What You Did: Social Networks and the Death of Privacy* (Simon and Schuster, 2012); J. Wortham, "It's Not About You, Facebook. It's About Us," *The New York Times* (February 12, 2012), http://www.nytimes.com/2012/02/12/business/facebook-and-its-users-so-mutually-dependent.html (accessed September 7, 2015); E. Morozov, "Sharing It All," *The New York Times* (January 29, 2012), http://www.socialnetworkconstitution.com/uploads/8/6/6/0/8660362/morozov_sharing_it_all_nytimes_book_review_01.29.12.pdf (accessed September 7, 2015); T. McNichol, "Fixing the Reputation of Reputation Managers" (February 2, 2012), http://www.businessweek.com/magazine/fixing-the-reputations-of-reputation-managers-02022012.html (accessed April 5, 2012).

[54] Stahl, "The Impact of UK Human Rights Act 1998 on Privacy Protection in the Workplace," 55–68.

data to non-European Union nations that do not meet the European privacy standards. Many U.S. companies believed that this directive would significantly hamper their ability to engage in many trans-Atlantic transactions. However, the U.S. Department of Commerce (DOC), in consultation with the European Commission, developed a "safe harbor" framework in 2000 that outlines practices that would protect a firm from prosecution. This framework allows U.S. companies to be placed on a list maintained by the DOC. They must demonstrate through a self-certification process that they are enforcing privacy at a level practiced in the European Union.[55]

Accuracy

The **accuracy**, or the correctness, of information assumes real importance for society as computers come to dominate in corporate record-keeping activities. When records are entered incorrectly, who is to blame? In December 2010, a couple was told by Bank of America, their mortgage holder, that they would have to vacate their house by Christmas Eve unless they put their house up for forced sale. The couple was flabbergasted because they had never missed making a house payment. They had, however, refinanced their home less than a year earlier. Although they used a conventional mortgage, they had checked out loan rates on the Make Home Affordable Program. Unbeknown to them, the mere initiation of this type of loan application triggers to the credit world that the applicant is in bad financial straits. A series of unfortunate errors ensued in which the limit on their credit card was reduced, their good accounts were canceled, and their credit score was ruined. Earlier that same year, another unit of Bank of America admitted to erroneously reporting to credit agencies that the couple was seeking a loan modification, ruining their credit rating and, as a result, putting their mortgage into default. This unit sent a letter of apology and turned the case over to a special unit at Bank of America that is charged with dealing with severe customer issues. The special unit was supposed to notify the credit reporting agencies that the couple was a good credit risk. Unfortunately, it didn't do so, costing the couple much anxiety and financial loss.[56] Although this incident may highlight the need for better controls over the bank's internal processes, it also demonstrates the risks that can be attributed to inaccurate information retained in corporate systems. In this case, the bank was responsible for the error, but it paid little—compared to the family—for its mistake. Although they cannot expect to eliminate all mistakes from the online environment, managers must establish controls to ensure that situations such as this one do not happen with any frequency.

Over time, it becomes increasingly difficult to maintain the accuracy of some types of information. Although a person's birth date does not typically change (my grandmother's change of her birth year notwithstanding), addresses and phone numbers often change as people relocate, and even their names may change with marriage, divorce, and adoption. The European Union Directive on Data Protection requires accurate and up-to-date data and tries to make sure that data are kept no longer than necessary to fulfill their stated purpose. This is a challenge many companies don't even attempt to meet.

Property

The increase in monitoring leads to the question of **property**, or who owns the data. Now that organizations have the ability to collect vast amounts of data on their clients, do they have a right to share the data with others to create a more accurate profile of an individual? Consider what happens when a consumer provides information for one use, say a car loan. This information is collected and stored in a data warehouse and then "mined" to create a profile for something completely different. And if some other company creates such consolidated profiles, who owns that information, which in many cases was not divulged willingly for that purpose?

Also consider what happens when you "like" a product. Your face is displayed on your friend's page when she or he sees an advertisement for that product, which might surprise you. This raises the question of who owns images that are posted in cyberspace. The images are *by* a photographer, *of* you, and *on* Facebook's servers. All can argue

---

[55] U.S. Department of Commerce, "Safe Harbor Overview," http://export.gov/safeharbor/eu/eg_main_018476.asp (accessed January 28, 2012).

[56] G. Gombossy, "Bank of America's Christmas Present: Foreclose Even Though Not a Payment Missed" (December 24, 2010), http://ctwatchdog.com/finance/bank-of-americas-christmas-present-foreclose-even-though-not-a-payment-missed (accessed February 27, 2012).

ownership to some extent. Further, with ever more sophisticated methods of computer animation, another question can arise: Can companies use newly "created" images or characters building on models in other media without paying royalties? Mason suggests that information, which is costly to produce in the first place, can be easily reproduced and sold without the individual who produced it even knowing what is happening—and certainly not being reimbursed for its use. In talking about this information that is produced, Mason notes:

> . . . information has the illusive quality of being easy to reproduce and to share with others. Moreover, this replication can take place without destroying the original. This makes information hard to safeguard since, unlike tangible property, it becomes communicable and hard to keep it to one's self.[57]

Accessibility

In the age of the information worker, **accessibility**, or the ability to obtain the data, becomes increasingly important. Would-be users of information must first gain the physical ability to access online information resources, which broadly means they must access computational systems. Second and more important, they then must gain access to the information itself. In this sense, the issue of access is closely linked to that of property. Looking forward, the major issue facing managers is how to create and maintain access to information for society at large without harming individuals who have provided much, if not all, of the information.

Today's managers must ensure that information about their employees and customers is accessible only to those who have a right to see and use it. Managers should take active measures to see that adequate security and control measures are in place in their companies. It is becoming increasingly clear that they also must ensure that adequate safeguards are working in the companies of their key trading partners. The managers at TRICARE, a military health provider, were no doubt embarrassed when they reported to 4.9 million active and retired military personnel and their families that their personal and medical records had been compromised. Back-up tapes containing records back to 1992 had been left in the care of an employee of TRICARE's data contractor, Science Applications International Corp. The tapes were stolen from the employee's car in San Antonio, Texas, while they were being transferred from one federal facility to another.[58] Accessibility clearly is an issue that extended beyond TRICARE's internal systems.

Accessibility is becoming increasingly important with the surge in **identity theft**, or "the taking of the victim's identity to obtain credit, credit cards from banks and retailers, steal money from the victim's existing accounts, apply for loans, establish accounts with utility companies, rent an apartment, file bankruptcy or obtain a job using the victim's name."[59] Identity theft is covered in Chapter 7, and you can see an obvious link between accessibility of information and security.

Managers' Role in Ethical Information Control

Managers must work to implement controls over information highlighted by the PAPA principles. Managers should not only deter identity theft by limiting inappropriate access to customer information but also respect their customers' privacy. Three best practices can be adopted to help improve an organization's information control by incorporating moral responsibility.[60]

- *Create a culture of responsibility:* CEOs and top-level executives should lead in promoting responsibility for protecting both personal information and the organization's information systems. Internet companies should post their policies about how they will use private information in understandable language and make a good case as to why they need the personal data that they gather from customers and clients. Author Mary Culnan

[57] Mason, "Four Ethical Issues of the Information Age," 5.
[58] Jim Forsyth, "Records of 4.9 mln Stolen from Car in Texas Data Breach" (September 29, 2011), http://www.reuters.com/article/2011/09/29/us-data-breach-texas-idUSTRE78S5JG20110929 (accessed February 28, 2012).
[59] Identity Theft Organization, Frequently Asked Questions, http://www.identitytheft.org (accessed April 5, 2012).
[60] Culnan and Williams, "How Ethics Can Enhance Organizational Privacy," 673–87.

Geographic Lens: Should Subcultures Be Taken into Account When Trying to Understand National Attitudes Toward Information Ethics?

Ethics can naturally be expected to vary across countries. An interesting study of 1,100 Chinese managers showed that it can also vary over time in the same country, depending upon subcultures resulting from major events within a country. Maris Martinsons and David Ma studied the responses to PAPA-based ethical situations made by three different Chinese generations: *republican*—people born before the People's Republic of China was established in 1949; *revolution*—people born between 1950 and 1970 under Communist rule during Mao Zedong's Cultural Revolution in 1966 and the Great Leap Forward (1958–1961); and *reform*—people born after 1970 when Deng Xiaoping's government introduced the Open Door and the One Child policies as part of economic and social reforms.

Survey results indicate significant differences in information ethics across generations. The revolution generation experienced a profound event that appears to have increased its ethical acceptance of both inaccurate information and intellectual property violations. Chinese managers from the reform generation are much less accepting of privacy violations than are those from the older generations. They are more conscious of the right to privacy and less inclined to compromise the privacy of others.

Source: M. G. Martinsons and D. Ma, "Subcultural Differences in Information Ethics across China: Focus on Chinese Management Generation Gaps," *Journal of AIS* 10 (Special Issue) (2009), 816–33.

noted in *CIO* magazine about customers providing information: "If there are no benefits or if they aren't told why the information is being collected or how it's being used, a lot of people say 'Forget it.'"[61] The costs of meaningfully securing the information may outweigh the obvious benefits—unless there is a breach. Thus, it is unlikely that an organization can create a culture of integrity and responsibility unless there is a moral commitment from the CEO.

- *Implement governance processes for information control:* In Chapter 9, we discuss the importance of mechanisms to identify the important decisions that need to be made and who would make them. Further, control governance structures, such as Control Objectives for Information and Related Technology (COBIT) and Information Technology Infrastructure Library (ITIL), can help identify risks to the information and behaviors to promote information control. Organizations need governance to make sure that their information control behaviors comply with the law and reflect their risk environment.
- *Avoid decoupling:* Often organizations use complex processes to treat personal privacy issues. Should an apparent conflict appear, managers can decouple the impact of institutional processes and mechanisms on individuals. In that way, managers can shift the responsibility away from themselves and onto the company. It would be much better if the managers were to act as if the customer's information were actually their own. This would mean that in delicate situations involving privacy or other issues of information control, managers would ask themselves "How would I feel if my information were handled in this way?"[62]

Green Computing

Green computing is concerned with using computing resources efficiently. The need for green computing is becoming more obvious considering the amount of power needed to drive the world's PCs, servers, routers, switches, and data centers. It was recently estimated that the digital economy uses up 10% of the world's electricity to run

[61] "Saving Private Data," *CIO Magazine* (October 1, 1998).
[62] Culnan and Williams, "How Ethics Can Enhance Organizational Privacy," 685.

data centers, charge smartphone and tablet batteries, and transmit data globally.[63] Usage patterns in 2007 when the 2.4 gigawatts of computing power consumed by the five largest search companies exceeded even the Hoover Dam's 2 gigawatt capacity seemed to be a "wake-up call." The situation was also exacerbated by the cooling systems that companies added to combat the heat generated by their highest-performing systems. Since 2007, many firms have developed sustainability plans that extend from manufacturing to executive travel to information systems use. The increased focus on sustainability and the use of more energy-saving technologies have contributed to reduced energy use, although energy use is still substantial.[64]

Sustainability measures taken by firms include replacing older systems with more energy-efficient ones, moving workloads based on energy efficiency, using the most power-inefficient servers only at times of peak usage, improving air flows in data centers, and turning to cloud computing as well as using virtualization. As introduced in Chapter 6, virtualization lets a computer run multiple operating systems or several versions of the same operating system at the same time. SAP used virtualization to eliminate 1,400 servers and increased the number of virtual servers from 37% in 2009 to 49% in 2010.[65] SAP noted that green IT "presents some of the greatest opportunities to increase our efficiency, improve our operations and reach our sustainability goals. It is one of the best examples of how creating positive impact also benefits our business. By reducing our total energy consumption, we can be both sustainable and profitable."[66]

Google's high energy needs to power servers has resulted in many ambitious plans to save power.[67] Google has reportedly been very secretive about current plans[68] although it did transform a paper mill in Hamina, Finland, into a data center with massive computing facilities. Part of the appeal of the mill was its underground tunnel system that pulls water from the Gulf of Finland. Originally, that frigid Baltic water cooled a steam generation plant at the mill, but Google saw it as a way to cool its servers.[69]

Green programs can have a triple bottom line (TBL, or 3BL): economic, environmental, and social. That is, green programs create economic value while being socially responsible and sustaining the environment, or "people, planet, profit."

Green computing can be considered from the social contract theory perspective by considering the first two of these: "people" and "planet." Managers benefit society by conserving global resources when they make green, energy-related decisions about their computer operations. In addition, stockholder theory explains the "profit" side of a firm's actions because energy-efficient computers reduce not only the direct costs of running the computing-related infrastructure, but also the costs of complementary utilities, such as cooling systems for the infrastructure components.

SUMMARY

- Because of the asymmetry of power relationships, managers tend to frame ethical concerns in terms of refraining from doing harm, mitigating injury, and paying attention to dependent and vulnerable parties. As a practical matter, ethics is about maintaining one's own personal perspective about the propriety of business practices. Managers must make systematic, reasoned judgments about right and wrong and take responsibility for them. Ethics is about taking decisive

[63] B. Walsh, "The Surprisingly Large Energy Footprint of the Digital Economy [UPDATE]," *Time* (August 14, 2013). http://science.time.com/2013/08/14/power-drain-the-digital-cloud-is-using-more-energy-than-you-think/ (accessed September 7, 2015).

[64] Two articles contrast energy use in 2007 and 2011: G. Lawton, "Powering Down the Computing Infrastructure" *Computer* (February 2007), 16–19, https://www.computer.org/csdl/mags/co/2007/02/r2016.pdf (accessed September 7, 2015); J. Markoff, "Data Centers' Power Use Less Than Was Expected, *The New York Times* (July 31, 2011), http://www.nytimes.com/2011/08/01/technology/data-centers-using-less-power-than-forecast-report-says.html?_r=2 (accessed February 28, 2012).

[65] "Data Center Energy Report," SAP Sustainability Report, http://www.sapsustainabilityreport.com/data-center-energy (accessed January 30, 2012).

[66] "Total Energy Consumed," SAP Sustainability Report, http://www.sapsustainabilityreport.com/total-energy-consumed (accessed January 30, 2012).

[67] J. Mick, "Google Looks at Floating Data Centers for Energy" (September 16, 2008), http://www.dailytech.com/Google+Looks+to+Floating+Data+Centers+for+Energy/article12966.htm (accessed October 1, 2008).

[68] D. Terdiman, "San Francisco's Bay Barge Mystery: Floating Data Center or Google Glass Store?" Cnet (October 27, 2013), http://www.cnet.com/news/san-franciscos-bay-barge-mystery-floating-data-center-or-google-glass-store/ (accessed September 7, 2015).

[69] Cade Metz, "Google Reincarnates Dead Paper Mill as Data Center of Future" (January 26, 2012), http://www.wired.com/wiredenterprise/2012/01/google-finland/ (accessed January 28, 2012).

action rooted in principles that express what is right and important and about taking action that is publicly defensible and personally supportable.

- Three important normative theories describing business ethics are (1) stockholder theory (maximizing stockholder wealth), (2) stakeholder theory (maximizing the benefits to all stakeholders while weighing costs to competing interests), and (3) social contract theory (creating value for society that is just and nondiscriminatory).
- Social contract theory offers the broad perspective to display corporate responsibility in areas such as green computing and dealing with ethical issues in tensions with foreign governments about IT and its use.
- PAPA is an acronym for the four areas in which control of information is crucial: privacy, accuracy, property, and accessibility.
- To enhance ethical control of information systems, companies should create a culture of responsibility, implement governance processes, and avoid decoupling.

KEY TERMS

accessibility (p. 291)
accuracy (p. 290)
cookies (p. 287)
green computing (p. 292)
identity theft (p. 291)
information ethics (p. 280)
online reputation management (p. 287)
privacy (p. 285)
property (p. 290)
social contract theory (p. 281)
stakeholder theory (p. 281)
stockholder theory (p. 280)

DISCUSSION QUESTIONS

1. Private corporate data are often encrypted using a key, which is needed to decrypt the information. Who within the corporation should be responsible for maintaining the "keys" to private information collected about consumers? Is that the same person who should have the keys to employee data?
2. Check out how Google has profiled you. Using your own computer, go to Ad Preferences: www.google.com/ads/preferences. How accurate is the picture Google paints about you in your profile?
3. Consider arrest records, which are mostly computerized and stored locally by law enforcement agencies. They have an accuracy rate of about 50%—about half of them are inaccurate, incomplete, or ambiguous. People other than law enforcement officials use these records often. Approximately 90% of all criminal histories in the United States are available to public and private employers. Use the three normative theories of business ethics to analyze the ethical issues surrounding this situation. How might hiring decisions be influenced inappropriately by this information?
4. The European Community's Directive on Data Protection strictly limits how database information is used and who has access to it. Some restrictions include registering all databases containing personal information with the countries in which they are operating, collecting data only with the consent of the subjects, and telling subjects of databases the intended and actual use of the databases. What effect might these restrictions have on global companies? In your opinion, should these types of restrictions be made into law? Why or why not? Should the United States bring its laws into agreement with the EU directive?
5. If you were a consultant to ICANN.org and were asked to create a global Internet privacy policy, what would you include in it? Create a summary of your recommendations.
6. Do you believe sending targeted advertising information to a computer using cookies is objectionable? Why or why not?

CASE STUDY 13-1 Ethical Decision Making

Situation 1

Google Glass makes it possible to record video all day in a format that is much less obtrusive than holding a camera in front of your face. In fact, it might not be detected.

Discussion Questions

1. Argue whether it is reasonable for you to be recording video in the following scenarios, and state why or why not using the PAPA paradigm.
   a. In a bank
   b. As you drive your car
   c. In a casino
   d. In class
   e. In a bar

Situation 2

The help desk is part of the group assigned to Doug Smith, the manager of office automation. The help desk has produced very low-quality work for the past several months. Smith has access to the passwords for each of the help desk members' computer accounts. He instructs the help desk supervisor to go into each hard drive after hours and obtain a sample document to check for quality control for each pool member.

Discussion Questions

1. If you were the supervisor, what would you do?
2. What, if any, ethical principles have been violated by this situation?
3. If poor quality was found, could the information be used for disciplinary purposes? For training purposes?
4. Apply PAPA to this situation.

Situation 3

Kate Essex is the supervisor of the customer service representative group for Enovelty.com, a manufacturer of novelty items. This group spends its workday answering calls from and sometimes placing calls to customers to assist in solving a variety of issues about orders previously placed with the company. The company has a rule that personal phone calls are allowed only during breaks. Essex is assigned to monitor each representative on the phone for 15 minutes a day as part of her regular job tasks. The representatives are aware that Essex will be monitoring them, and customers are immediately informed of this when they begin their calls. Essex begins to monitor James Olsen and finds that he is on a personal call regarding his sick child. Olsen is not on break.

Discussion Questions

1. What should Essex do?
2. What, if any, ethical principles help guide decision making in this situation?
3. What management practices should be in place to ensure proper behavior without violating individual "rights"?
4. Apply the normative theories of business ethics to this situation.

Situation 4

Jane Mark is the newest hire in the IS group at We_Sell_More.com, a business on the Internet. The company takes in $30 million in revenue quarterly from Web business. Jane reports to Sam Brady, the vice president of IS. Jane is assigned to a project to build a new capability into the company Web page that facilitates linking products ordered with future offerings of the company. After weeks of analysis, Jane concluded that the best way to incorporate that capability is to buy a software package from a small start-up company in Silicon Valley, California. She convinces Brady to accept her decision and is authorized to lease the software. The vendor e-mails Jane the software in a ZIP file and instructs her on how to install it. At the initial installation, Jane is asked to acknowledge and electronically sign the license agreement. The installed system does not ask Jane if she wants to make a backup copy of the software, so as a precaution, Jane takes it on herself to copy the ZIP files that were sent to her onto a thumb drive. She stores the thumb drive in her desk drawer.

A year later, the vendor is bought by another company, and the software is removed from the market to prevent further sale. The new owner believes this software will provide it a competitive advantage that it wants to reserve for itself. The new vendor terminates all lease agreements and revokes all licenses on their expiration. But Jane still has the thumb drive she made as backup.

Discussion Questions

1. Is Jane obligated to stop using her backup copy? Why or why not?
2. If We_Sell_More.com wants to continue to use the system, can it? Why or why not?
3. Would your opinion change if the software is a critical system for We_Sell_More.com? If it is a noncritical system? Explain.

Situation 5

Some of the Internet's biggest companies (i.e., Google, Microsoft, Yahoo, IBM, and Verisign) implemented a "single sign-on" system, called OpenID, that is available at thousands of Web sites. It allows the widespread practice that users who are logged into Facebook to click a Facebook button for an instant login. The benefits are obvious; the system makes it easier for users to sign on to a number of sites without having to remember multiple user IDs, passwords and registration information. Under OpenID, the companies share the sign-on information, personal information such as credit card data, billing addresses, and personal preferences for any Web user who agrees to participate.

Discussion Questions

1. Discuss any potential and real threats to privacy in this situation. Search for news articles about Facebook to find problematic incidents, if any.
2. Who would own the data? Explain.
3. Who do you think should have access to the data? How should that access be controlled?

Situation 6

SpectorSoft markets eBlaster as a way to keep track of what your spouse or children are doing online. Operating in stealth mode, eBlaster tracks every single keystroke from instant messages to passwords entered into a computer. It also records every e-mail sent and received and every Web site visited by the unsuspecting computer user. The data are sent anonymously to an IP address of the person who installed eBlaster. It could also be installed on the computers of a business.

Discussion Questions

1. Do you think it would be ethical for a business to install eBlaster to ensure that its employees are engaged only in work-related activities? If so, under what conditions would using it be appropriate? If not, why not?
2. Apply the normative theories of business ethics to this situation.

Situation 7

Google, Inc. had a unique advantage beginning in March 2012. By combining information about user activity from its many popular applications (such as Gmail, Google+, and YouTube), Google algorithms were able to alert users to things that might be of interest. This vast amount of information, analyzed properly, gave Google a way to compete. By combining data with information from Internet searches, Google could better compete against applications such as Facebook.

But this was a departure from its earlier privacy policy. In June 2011, the executive chairman of Google had declared, "Google will remain a place where you can do anonymous searches [without logging in]. We're very committed to having you have control over the information we have about you."

This may be possible for users who don't login to a Google account, but for those with Gmail or other personal accounts or an Android mobile phone, it's more difficult to remain anonymous. Offering a counter viewpoint, Chirstopher Soghoian, an independent privacy and security researcher said, "Google now watches consumers practically everywhere they go on the Web [and anytime they use an Android phone]. No single entity should be trusted with this much sensitive data."

Discussion Questions

1. Do you see any ethical issues involved in Google's recent approach to combining information from a particular user? Why or why not?
2. How might users change their behaviors if they were aware of this new approach?
3. Apply the normative theories of business ethics to Google's new policy about combining user information?

Situation 8

Spokeo is a company that gathers online data for employers, the public, or anybody who is willing to pay for its services. Clients include recruiters and women who want to find out whether their boyfriends are cheating on them. Spokeo recruits via ads that urge "HR-Recruiters—Click Here Now."

Discussion Questions

1. Do you think it would be ethical for a business to hire Spokeo to find out about potential employees? If so, under what conditions would it be appropriate? If not, why not?
2. Do you think it is ethical for women to hire Spokeo to see if their boyfriends are cheating on them? Why or why not?

Sources: Situations 2 to 5 are adapted from short cases suggested by Professor Kay Nelson, Southern Illinois University—Carbondale. The names of people, places, and companies have been made up for these stories. Any similarity to real people, places, or companies is purely coincidental. Situation 7 is from Julia Angwin, "Google Widens Its Tracks," *The Wall Street Journal* (July 30, 2010), http://online.wsj.com/article/SB10001424052970203806504577181371465957162.html?mod=djem_jiewr_IT_domainid (accessed on January 28, 2010). Situation 8 is from Lori Andrews, "Facebook Is Using You" (February 5, 2012), SR7, http://www.nytimes.com/2012/02/05/opinion/sunday/facebook-is-using-you.html (accessed September 7, 2015).

CASE STUDY 13-2 Midwest Family Mutual Goes Green

Midwest Family Mutual Insurance Co., an insurance company with $120 million worth of written premiums in 2014, considers itself to be "environmentally green." Through a variety of initiatives, it has reduced its annual energy, natural gas, and paper consumption by 63%, 76%, and 65%, respectively. Ron Boyd, the carrier's CEO, attributes most of the improvements in energy usage to creating a virtual work-from-home environment as a result of implementing a series of electronic processes and applications. These include imaging and workflow technology, networking technology, and a Voice over IP (VoIP) network. In 2006, the year these savings were reported, all but two of Midwest Family Mutual's 65 employees worked from home. In addition to the energy savings that the company has directly experienced, Boyd estimated that in 2008, the company's telecommuting policy resulted in fuel savings of at least 25,000 gallons.

Although green computing was a commendable goal in itself, Midwest Family Mutual's bottom line also has benefited from the company's socially responsible approach. Over a five-year period, Midwest Family Mutual's was able to shave its expense ratio to 25.9% from 33.5%. Its Web site states, "Being green environmentally and operationally CAN [emphasis in original] equate to being green financially."

Green computing grew out of Midwest Family Mutual's IT successes, according to Boyd. As the company started realizing savings from the electronic processes it implemented, management started thinking about telecommuting arrangements that allowed its employees to work from home. Boyd adds, "It became obvious that many of our jobs could be done wherever a high-speed connection existed. . . . VoIP completed the technology requirements for all [employees] to work from home."

Boyd summarizes that the company "became green as a side benefit of saving resources and cost." The company continued its green policy with its decision to sell its 24,000-square-foot office building in Minnetonka, Minnesota. However, to provide more centralized regional service to agents in the new states in which it was recently licensed (i.e., Arizona, Nevada, Utah, Colorado, Idaho, Washington, and Oregon), the company built a new home domicile in Chariton, Iowa, in 2012.

Discussion Questions

1. Do you think that the economic benefits that Midwest Family Mutual realized as a result of green computing are unusual? Do you think that most companies could see similar types of economic gains? Explain.
2. What are some possible disadvantages that the employees of Midwest Family Mutual might be experiencing as a result of its virtual work-from-home office environment?
3. Apply the normative theories of business ethics to this situation.

Sources: Adapted from Anthony O'Donnell, "Plymouth, Minnesota-Based Midwest Family Mutual's Move to a Paperless, Work-at-Home Operational Paradigm Has Yielded Both Environmental and Bottom-Line Benefits," *Insurance & Technology* (February 24, 2008), http://www.insurancetech.com/resources/fss/showArticle.jhtml;jsessionid=AYMVWDKZBGIFIQSNDLOSKHSCJUNN2JVN?articleID=206801556 (accessed April 23, 2008); Midwest Family Mutual News Archive, "MFM Announces 2011 Results and Plans for 2012," https://midwestfamily.com/news.php?detail=589 (accessed on April 14, 2012); "Midwest Family Goes Green," https://midwestfamily.com/page.php?detail=6 (accessed March 11, 2015).

Glossary

Accessibility: An area of information control involved with the ability to obtain data.

Accuracy: An area of information control dealing with the correctness of information or lack of errors in information.

Activity-based costing (ABC): The costing method that calculates costs by counting the actual activities that go into making a specific product or delivering a specific service.

Agile (business) processes: Processes designed with the intention of simplifying redesign and reconfiguration by making it possible to make incremental changes in order to easily adapt to the business environment.

Agile development: The term that refers to system development methodologies used to deal with unpredictability. They adapt to changing requirements by iteratively developing systems in small stages and then testing the new code extensively. They include extreme programming (XP), crystal, scrum, feature-driven development, and dynamic system development method (DSDM).

Allocation funding method: The method for funding IT costs by recovering costs based on something other than usage, such as revenues, log-in accounts, or number of employees.

Antivirus/Antispyware: A software that scans incoming data and evaluates the periodic state of the whole system to detect threats of secret software that can either destroy data or inform a server of destructive software activity.

Application: A software program designed to facilitate a specific practical task as opposed to control resources. Examples of applications include Microsoft Word, a word processing application; Lotus 1-2-3, a spreadsheet application; and SAP R/3, an enterprise resource planning application. Contrast with *operating system*.

Application service provider (ASP): An Internet-based company that offers a software application used through its Web site. For example, a company might offer small business applications that a small business owner could use on the Web rather than buying software to load on the company's own computers.

Archetype: A pattern resulting from decision rights allocation.

Architecture: The plan that provides a blueprint for translating business strategy into a plan for IS.

ASP: See *Application service provider*.

Assumption: The deepest layer of culture or the fundamental part of every culture that helps discern what is real and important to a group; it is unobservable because it reflects organizational values that have become so taken for granted that they guide organizational behavior without any of the groups thinking about them.

Balanced scorecard: The method that focuses attention on the organization's value drivers (which include, but are not limited to, financial performance). Companies use it to assess the full impact of their corporate strategies on their customers and workforce as well as their financial performance.

Behavior control: A type of formal control in which specific actions, procedures, and rules for employees are explicitly prescribed and their implementation is monitored.

Beliefs: The perceptions that people hold about how things are done in their community.

Backsourcing: A business practice in which a company takes back in house assets, activities, and skills that are part of its information systems operations and were previously outsourced to one or more outside IS providers.

Big data: The term used to describe techniques and technologies that make it economical to deal with very large data sets at the extreme end of the scale.

Biometrics: An access tool that scans a body characteristic, such as fingerprint, voice, iris, or head or hand geometry.

Black hat hackers: The hackers who break into an organization's Web sites or systems for their own gain or to wreak havoc on a firm.

Blue ocean strategy: A business strategy in which firms try to find new market spaces where they have the "water" to themselves. That is, they enter a market space(s) when the goal is not to beat the competition but to make it irrelevant.

Bring your own device (BYOD): The term used to refer to the scenario when employees bring their own devices—commonly smart phones, tablets, and laptops—to work and connect to enterprise systems.

Business analytics: The use of data, analysis, and modeling to arrive at business decisions. Some organizations use business analytics to create new innovations or to support the modification of existing products or services.

Business case: A structured document that lays out all the relevant information needed to make a go/no-go decision. It contains an executive summary, overview, assumptions, program summary, financial discussion and analysis, discussion of benefits and business impacts, schedule and milestones, risk and contingency analysis, conclusion, and recommendations.

Business ecosystem: A type of ecosystem that is an economic community where organizations and individuals interact.

Business intelligence: The term for the broad practice of using technology, applications, and processes to collect and analyze data to support business decisions.

Business-IT maturity model: A framework that displays the demands on the business side and the IT offerings on the supply side to help understand differences in capabilities and suggests the degree to which the IT function should be engaged with the rest of the organization.

Business process management (BPM): A well-defined and optimized set of IT processes, tools, and skills used to manage business processes.

Business process reengineering (BPR): A radical change approach in the organization that occurs over a short amount of time.

Business strategy: A plan articulating where a business seeks to go and how it expects to get there.

Business technology strategist: The strategic business leader who uses technology as the core tool in creating competitive advantage and aligning business and IT strategies.

BYOD: See *Bring your own device.*

Capacity-on-demand: The availability of additional processing capability for a fee.

Captive center: An overseas subsidiary that is set up to serve the parent company. Companies set up captive centers as an alternative to offshoring.

Centralized architecture: A way of organizing computer hardware and systems in which everything is purchased, supported, and managed centrally, usually in a data center.

Centralized IS organization: The organization structure that brings together all power, staff, hardware, software, data, and processing into a single location/position.

Challenge question: The access tool to a computer account that prompts a user with a follow-up question such as "Model of first car?"

Chargeback funding method: The method for funding IT costs in which costs are recovered by charging individuals, departments, or business units based on actual usage and cost.

Chief analytics officer (CAO): The individual at the helm of an organization's analytics activities.

Chief data officer: An individual who has the responsibility for the data warehouse, organizational databases, relationships with vendors who supply external data sources, and sometimes the algorithms that use these data sources.

Chief information officer (CIO): The most senior officer responsible for the information systems activities within the organization. The CIO is a strategic thinker, not an operational manager, is typically a member of the senior management team, and is involved in all major business decisions that come before that team, bringing an information systems perspective to the team.

Client: A software program that requests and receives data and sometimes instructions from another software program, usually running on a separate computer.

Cloud computing: The style of infrastructure for which capacity, applications, and services (such as development, maintenance, or security) are provided dynamically by a third-party provider over the Internet, often on a "fee-for-use" basis. Customers go to the Web for the services they need.

COBIT: See *Control objectives for information and related technologies.*

Collaboration: The use of social IT to extend the reach of stakeholders, both employees and those outside the enterprise walls. Social IT such as social networks enable individuals to find and connect with each other to share ideas, information, and expertise.

Combination: The mode of knowledge conversion from explicit knowledge to explicit knowledge.

Community cloud: Cloud infrastructure that is shared by several organizations and supports the common concerns of a specific community.

Complementor: One of the players in a co-opetitive environment. It is a company whose product or service is used in conjunction with a particular product or service to make a more useful set for the customer. (See *Value net.*)

Consumerization of IT: The drive to port applications to personal devices and the ensuing issues involved in making them work in business organizations.

Control Objectives for Information and Related Technology (COBIT): The IT governance framework for decision controls that is consistent with the Committee of Sponsoring Organizations of the Treadway Commission (COSO) and that provides systematic rigor needed for the strong internal controls and Sarbanes–Oxley compliance.

Cookie: A small coded text message placed on or retrieved and updated from a person's hard drive to allow companies to track the person's movements through a site or sites.

Co-opetition: A business strategy by which companies cooperate and compete at the same time.

Corporate budget funding method: The method for funding IT costs in which they fall to the corporate bottom line rather than being levied to specific users or business units.

Cost leadership strategy: A business strategy by which the organization aims to be the lowest-cost producer in the marketplace. (See *Differentiation strategy; Focus strategy.*)

CRM: See *Customer relationship management.*

Cross-site-scripting (XSS): The security breach involving booby traps that appear to lead users to their goal, but in reality lead to a fraudulent site that requires a log-in.

Crowdsourcing: The act of taking a task traditionally performed by an employee or a contractor and outsourcing it through the form of an open call to an undefined, generally large group of people.

Culture: A set of shared values and beliefs that a group holds and that determines how the group perceives, thinks about, and appropriately reacts to its various environments; a collective programming of the mind that distinguishes not only societies (or nations) but also industries, professions, and organizations.

Customer relationship management (CRM): The management activities performed to obtain, enhance, and retain customers. CRM is a coordinated set of activities revolving around the customer.

Cycle plan: A project management plan that organizes project activities in relation to time. It identifies critical beginning and end dates and breaks the work spanning these dates into phases. The general manager tracks the phases to coordinate the eventual transition from project to operational status, a process that culminates on the "go-live" date.

Dashboard: A common management monitoring tool that provides a snapshot of metrics at any given point in time.

Data: A set of specific, objective facts or observations that standing alone have no intrinsic meaning.

Database: A collection of data formatted and organized to facilitate ease of access, searching, updating, addition, and deletion. It is typically so large that it must be stored on disk, but sections may be kept in RAM for quicker access. The software program used to manipulate the data in a database is also often referred to as a "database."

Database administrator (DBA): The person within the information systems department who manages the data and the database. Typically, this person makes sure that all the data that go into the database are accurate and appropriate, and that all applications and individuals who need access have it.

Data center: The place where a firm's computers, servers, and peripherals are housed together, typically to store, process, and distribute large amounts of data.

Data-driven culture: The organizational environment that supports and encourages the use of analytics to support decision making.

Data mining: The process of analyzing databases for "gems" that will be useful in management decision making. Typically, data mining is used to refer to the process of combing through massive amounts of customer data to understand buying habits and to identify new products, features, and enhancements.

Data scientist: A professional who has the skills to use the right analytics with the right data at the right time for the right business problem.

Data warehouse: A centralized collection of data designed to support management decision making. It sometimes includes all the organization's databases.

Debugging: The process of examining and testing software and hardware to make sure they operate properly under every condition possible. The term is based on calling any problem a "bug"; therefore, eliminating the problem is called "debugging."

Decentralized architecture: The arrangement of hardware, software, networking, and data in a way that distributes the processing and functionality between multiple small computers, servers, and devices that rely heavily on a network to connect them.

Decentralized IS organization: The IS organization structure that scatters power, hardware, software, networks, and data components in different locations/positions to address local business needs.

Decision model: The IS-based model used by managers for scenario planning and evaluation. The information system collects and analyzes the information from automated processes and presents them to the manager to aid in decision making.

Decision right: The position(s) in the organization that have been allocated the responsibility to initiate, supply information for, approve, implement, and control a type of decision.

Deep Web: A large part of the Web that includes unindexed Web sites that are accessible only by a browser named "Tor," which guarantees anonymity and provides access to sites offering both legal and illegal items and services.

Differentiation strategy: A business strategy by which the organization qualifies its product or service in a way that allows it to appear unique in the marketplace. (See *Cost leadership strategy; Focus strategy*.)

Digital native: An individual who has grown up completely fluent in the use of personal technologies and the Web.

Digital signature: A digital code applied to an electronically transmitted message used to prove that the sender of a message (e.g., a file or e-mail message) is truly who he or she claims to be.

Direct cutover: The conversion stage in a system development life cycle in which the old system is disconnected and a new system takes its place rather than operating both simultaneously for a period of time.

Dynamic business process: The process that reconfigures itself as it learns while iterating through a constant renewal cycle of design, deliver, evaluate, redesign, and so on.

Economic value added (EVA): The valuation method that accounts for opportunity costs of capital to measure true economic profit and revalues historical costs to give an accurate picture of the true market value of assets.

Ecosystem: A collection of interacting participants, including vendors, customers, and other related parties acting in concert to do business.

E-mail (electronic mail): A way of transmitting messages over communication networks.

Enacted values: The values and norms that are actually exhibited or displayed in employee behavior.

Encryption: The translation of data into a code or a form that can be read only by the intended receiver. Data are encrypted using a key or alphanumeric code and can be decrypted only by using the same key or code.

Engagement: The use of social IT to involve stakeholders in the traditional business of the enterprise social IT such as communities and blogs to provide a platform for individuals to join in conversations, create new conversations, offer support to each other, and engage in other activities that create a deeper feeling of connection to the company, brand, or enterprise.

Enterprise 2.0: A term used to describe a company using the technologies and practices resulting from Web 2.0 architectures, applications, and services. Enterprise 2.0 typically refers to a flat organization with unimpeded information flows between all levels and individuals in the organization. Companies adopting these practices seek to be agile, flexible, user driven, on demand, and transparent.

Enterprise architecture (EA): The term used for a "blueprint" for the corporation that includes the business strategy, the IT architecture, the business processes, and the organization structure and how all these components relate to each other. Often this term is IT-centric, specifying the IT architecture and all the interrelationships with the structure and processes.

Enterprise information systems (EIS): Another term for enterprise systems.

Enterprise resource planning (ERP) software: A large, highly complex software program that integrates many business functions under a single application. ERP software can include modules for inventory management, supply chain management, accounting, customer support, order tracking, and human resource management. ERP software is typically integrated with a database.

Enterprise system: A set of IS tools that many organizations use to enable information to flow within and between processes across the organization.

Espoused values: The explicitly stated, preferred organization values.

Evidence-based management: An approach in which evidence (data) and facts are analyzed as the first step in decision making.

Evil twin connection: A bogus WiFi connection that appears to be genuine but is actually a counterfeit connection that is set up to deceive people into providing information unwittingly.

Explicit knowledge: Objective, theoretical, and codified knowledge for transmission in a formal, systematic method using grammar, syntax, and the printed word. (In contrast, see *Tacit knowledge*.)

Externalization: The mode of knowledge conversion from tacit knowledge to explicit knowledge.

Extranet: A network based on the Internet standard that connects a business with individuals, customers, suppliers, and other stakeholders outside the organization's boundaries. An extranet typically is similar to the Internet; however, it has limited access to those specifically authorized to be part of it.

Farshoring: A form of offshoring that involves sourcing service work to a foreign, low-wage country that is relatively far in distance or time zone (or both) from the client company.

Federalism: The organization structuring approach that distributes power, hardware, software, data, and personnel between a central IS group and IS in business units.

File transfer: The means of transferring a copy of a file from one computer to another over the Internet.

Firewall: A security measure that blocks undesirable requests for entrance into a Web site and keeps those on the "inside" from reaching outside.

Flat organization structure (horizontal organization structure): The organization structure with a less well-defined chain of command and with ill-defined, fluid jobs.

Focus strategy: The business strategy by which the organization limits its scope to a narrower segment of the market and tailors its offerings to that group of customers. This strategy has two variants: *cost focus*, in which the organization seeks a cost advantage within its segment, and *differentiation focus*, in which the organization seeks to distinguish its products or services within the segment. This strategy allows the organization to achieve a local competitive advantage even if it does not achieve competitive advantage in the marketplace overall. (See *Cost strategy; Differentiation strategy*.)

Folksonomy: The collaborative creation and management of a structure for any type of collection, such as ideas, data, or documents. The term is the merger of *folk* and *taxonomy,* meaning that it is a user-generated taxonomy.

Full outsourcing: The situation in which an enterprise outsources all its IS functions from desktop services to software development.

Function points: The functional requirements of a software product that can be estimated earlier than total lines of code.

Governance (in the context of business enterprises): The established process of making decisions, defining expectations, granting power, or verifying performance.

Graphical user interface (GUI): The term used to refer to the use of icons, windows, colors, and text as the means of representing information and links on a computer screen. GUIs give the user the ability to control actions by clicking on objects rather than by typing commands to the operating system.

Green computing: An upcoming technology strategy in which companies become more socially responsible by using computing resources efficiently.

Grey hat hackers: The hackers who test organizational systems without any authorization and notify the IT staff when they find a weakness.

Groupware: The software that enables a group to work together on a project whether in the same room or from remote locations by allowing the group simultaneous access to the same files. Calendars, written documents, e-mail messages, discussion tools, and databases can be shared.

Hierarchical organization structure: An organization form or structure based on the concepts of division of labor, specialization, spans of control, and unity of command.

Hybrid cloud: A cloud infrastructure that is a combination of private and public clouds.

Hypercompetition: A theory about industries and marketplaces that suggests that the speed and aggressiveness of moves and countermoves in any given market create an environment in which advantages are quickly gained and lost. A hypercompetitive environment is one in which conditions change rapidly.

Identity theft: The taking of a victim's identity to obtain credit and/or credit cards from banks and retailers, steal money from the victim's existing accounts, apply for loans, establish accounts with utility companies, rent an apartment, file for bankruptcy, or obtain a job using the victim's name.

Information: Data endowed with relevance and purpose.

Information ethics: The ethical issues associated with the development and application of information technologies.

Information integration: The coordination involved in determining the information to share, the format of that information, the technological standards used to share it, and the security used to ensure that only authorized partners access it.

Information model: A framework for understanding what information will be crucial to the decision, how to get it, and how to use it.

Information resource: The available data, technology, people, and processes within an organization to be used by the manager to perform business processes and tasks.

Information system (IS): The *combination* of technology (the "what"), people (the "who"), and process (the "how") that an organization uses to produce and manage information.

Information systems (IS) strategy: The plan an organization uses in providing information services.

Information Systems Strategy Triangle: The framework connecting business strategy, information system strategy, and organizational systems strategy.

Information technology: All forms of technology used to create, store, exchange, and use information, usually including hardware, software, data, and networks.

Information technology (IT) asset: Anything, tangible or intangible, that can be used by a firm in its processes for creating, producing, and/or offering its products (goods or services).

Information technology (IT) capability: Something that is learned or developed over time for the firm to create, produce, or offer its products.

Information technology (IT) governance: The established decision rights and accountability framework to encourage desirable behavior in using IT.

Information Technology Infrastructure Library (ITIL): The control framework that offers a set of concepts and techniques for managing information technology infrastructure, development, and operations that was developed in United Kingdom.

Information technology (IT) portfolio management: The evaluation of new and existing applications collectively on an ongoing basis to determine which applications provide value to the business in order to support decisions to replace, retire, or further invest in applications across the enterprise.

Infrastructure: Everything that supports the flow and processing of information in an organization including hardware, software, data, and network components. It consists of components chosen and assembled in a manner that best suits the organization's plan and enables the overarching business strategy.

Innovation: The use of social IT to identify, describe, prioritize, and create new ideas for the enterprise. Social IT offers the community members a forum in which to suggest new ideas, comment on other ideas, and vote for their favorite idea, giving managers a new way to generate and make decisions on products and services.

Insourcing: The manner in which a firm provides IS services or develops IS from its own in house IS organization.

Instant messaging (IM): An Internet protocol (IP)-based application that provides real-time text-based communication between people using a variety of different device types, including computer-to-computer and mobile devices.

Integrated supply chain: An enterprise system that crosses company boundaries and connects vendors and suppliers with organizations to synchronize and streamline planning and deliver products to all members of the supply chain.

Intellectual capital: The knowledge that has been identified, captured, and leveraged to produce high-value goods or services or some other competitive advantage for the firm.

Intellectual property (IP): The term used to describe a creative information-based output. It is information based and, unlike physical property, it is nonexclusive and has a negligible marginal cost to produce additional copies.

Internalization: The mode of knowledge conversion from explicit knowledge to tacit knowledge.

Internet: The system of computers and networks that together connect individuals and businesses worldwide. The Internet is a global, *inter*connected *net*work of millions of individual host computers.

Internet of Things: The technology embedded in devices that streams sensor data from those devices to the Internet to create rich databases of operational data.

Intranet: A network used within a business for individuals and departments to communicate. An intranet is an application on the Internet but is limited to internal business use. It is a password-protected set of interconnected nodes under the company's administrative control. (See *Extranet*.)

IS: See *Information system.*

IT: See *Information technology.*

IT asset: See *Information technology asset.*

IT capability: See *Information technology capability.*

IT governance: See *Information technology governance.*

IT portfolio management: See *Information technology portfolio management.*

ITIL: See *Information Technology Infrastructure Library.*

Joint applications development (JAD): A version of RAD or prototyping in which users as a group are more integrally involved with the entire development process up to and, in some cases, including coding.

Key logger: A type of surveillance device that hackers use to track keystrokes either through hardware (an unseen thumb drive on a public computer) or software (i.e., a compromised Web site).

Knowledge: The information synthesized and contextualized to provide value.

Knowledge capture: The continuous processes of scanning, organizing, and packaging knowledge after it has been generated.

Knowledge codification: The representation of knowledge in a manner that can be easily accessed and transferred.

Knowledge generation: All activities that discover "new" knowledge, whether such knowledge is new to the individual, the firm, or the entire discipline.

Knowledge management: The processes necessary to capture, codify, and transfer knowledge across the organization to achieve competitive advantage.

Knowledge repository: A physical or virtual place that stores documents with knowledge embedded, such as memos, reports, or news articles so they can be retrieved easily.

Knowledge transfer: The transmission of knowledge from one person or group to another and the absorption of that knowledge.

Legacy system: A mature information system that has worked for a long time (often 20 to 30 years old).

List server: A type of e-mail mailing list to which users subscribe; when any user sends a message to the server, a copy of the message is sent to everyone on the list. This allows for restricted-access discussion groups: Only subscribed members can participate in or view the discussions because they are transmitted via e-mail.

Local Area Network (LAN): A network of interconnected (often via Ethernet) workstations that reside within a limited geographic area (typically a single building or campus). LANs are typically employed so that the machines on them such as printers or servers can share resources and/or can exchange e-mail or other forms of messages (e.g., to control industrial machinery).

Mainframe: A large, central computer that handles all the functionality of a system.

Managerial levers: The organizational, control, and cultural variables that are used by decision makers to effect changes in their organizations.

Mashup: A term used in the Web 2.0 community to mean the combination of data from multiple sources into one Web page, for example, the combination of Google Maps with real estate data to produce a diagram showing home price ranges for certain neighborhoods.

Matrix organization structure: An organizational form or structure in which workers are assigned two or more supervisors, each supervising a different aspect of the employees' work in an effort to make sure multiple dimensions of the business are integrated.

Middleware: The software used to connect processes running in one or more computers across a network.

Mission: A clear and compelling statement that unifies an organization's effort and describes what the firm is all about (i.e., its purpose).

Mobile device management: A type of security policy that focuses on bring your own device (BYOD) and is related to permitted products and required connection methods.

Mobile workers: Individuals who work from wherever they are.

Multifactor authentication: The use of two or more authorization methods to gain access to a computer system.

Multisourcing: A type of sourcing in which IT projects and services are allocated to multiple vendors who work together to achieve the client's business objectives.

Nearshoring: A form of offshoring service work to a foreign, low-wage country that is relatively close in distance or time zone (or both) to the client company.

Net present value (NPV): The valuation method that takes into account the time value of money in which cash inflows and outflows are discounted.

Network effect: The increased value of a network node to a person or organization in the network when another joins the network.

Networked organization structure: The organization form or structure in which rigid hierarchies are replaced by formal and informal communication networks that connect all parts of the company; known for its flexibility and adaptiveness.

Object: An item that encapsulates both the data stored about an entity and the operations that manipulate that data.

Observable artifact: The most visible layer of culture that includes physical manifestations such as traditional dress, symbols in art, acronyms, awards, myths and stories about the group, rituals, and ceremonies.

Offshoring (outsourcing offshore): The situation in which an IS organization uses contractor services or even builds its own data center in a distant land.

Online reputation management: The service provided to a person or company for a fee to find negative formal or informal reviews on Web sites and report results to the client periodically.

Onshoring (inshoring): The situation in which outsourcing work is performed domestically.

Open source software (OSS): The software released under a license approved by the Open Source Initiative (OSI).

Open sourcing: A development approach in which an Internet community builds and improves "free" software.

Operating system (OS): A program that manages all other programs running on, as well as all the resources connected to, a computer. Examples include Microsoft Windows, DOS, and UNIX.

Oracle: A provider of widely used enterprise resources planning and database systems.

Organizational strategy: A plan that answers the question: "How will the company organize to achieve its goals and implement its business strategy?" It includes the organization's design as well as the choices it makes to define, set up, coordinate, and control its work processes.

Organizational systems: The fundamental elements of a business including people, work processes, structure, and the plan that enables them to work efficiently to achieve business goals.

Outcome control: The type of formal control in which the controller/manager explicitly defines intermediate and final goals for an employee.

Outsourcing: The business arrangement in which third-party providers and vendors manage the activities of the information systems. In a typical outsourced arrangement, the company finds vendors to perform operational, support, and systems development activities, saving strategic decisions for the internal information systems personnel.

Parallel conversion: The conversion in which both the old system and new system are run at the same time.

Payback period: The length of time needed to recoup the cost of an investment.

Peer to peer: The description of infrastructure that allows networked computers to share resources without a central server playing a dominant role.

Personnel control: The type of control that represents a proper fit between a person and a job, often involving picking the right person for the task.

Phishing attack: A type of security breach in which a person receives a convincing e-mail calling for a response to a phony urgent situation or opportunity, with a link pretending to be a step towards performing the response. Often the sender is an imposter and the response actually can lead to theft of identity information, account passwords, or monetary funds.

Platform: The hardware and software on which applications are run. For example, the iPhone is considered a platform for many applications and services that can be run on it.

Portal: Easy-to-use Web sites that provide quick access to search engines, critical information, research, applications, and processes that individuals want.

Privacy: The area of information control involved with the right to be left alone; an individual's ability to personally control information about himself or herself; it is involved with the protections from intrusion and information gathering by others.

Private cloud: A cloud infrastructure in which data are managed by the organization itself.

Process: An interrelated, sequential set of activities and tasks that turn inputs into outputs and has a distinct beginning, a clear deliverable at the end, and a set of metrics that are useful to measure performance.

Process perspective: The "big picture" view of a business from the perspective of the business processes performed. Typically, the view is made up of cross-functional processes that traverse disciplines, departments, functions, and even organizations. (In contrast, see *Silo perspective*.)

Program: A collection of related projects that is often related to a strategic organizational objective. It also refers to a set of instructions to execute one or more tasks on the computer.

Project: A temporary endeavor undertaken to create a unique product, service, or result. *Temporary* means that a project has a definite beginning and a definite end.

Project manager: A person who makes sure that an entire project is executed appropriately and coordinated properly and defines project scope realistically and manages the project so that it can be completed on time and within budget.

Project management office (PMO): The organizational unit within which the expertise for managing projects resides.

Project stakeholder: An individual or organization that is actively involved in a project or whose interests may be affected as a result of project execution or project completion.

Property: An area of information control focused on who owns the data.

Protocol: A special, typically standardized, set of rules used by computers to enable communication between them.

Prototyping: An evolutionary development method for building an information system. Developers get the general idea of what is needed by the users and then build a fast, high-level version of the system at the beginning of the project. The idea of prototyping is to quickly get a version of the software in the hands of the users and to jointly evolve the system through a series of cycles of design and build and then to use and evaluate.

Public cloud: A cloud infrastructure in which data are stored outside of the corporate data centers in the cloud provider's environment.

Rapid application development (RAD): The process similar to prototyping in that it is an interactive process in which tools are used to speed development. RAD systems typically have tools for developing the user, reusable code, code generation, and programming language testing and debugging. These tools make it easy for the developer to build a library of common, standard sets of code that can easily be used in multiple applications.

Really simple syndication (RSS); also *Web feeds*: The structured file format for porting data from one platform or information system to another.

Real-time data source: A type of data stream that companies use in analytics programs that capture data as they occur.

Reengineering: A management process of redesigning business processes in a relatively radical manner. Reengineering traditionally meant taking a "blank piece of paper" and designing (then building) a business process from the beginning. This was intended to help the designers eliminate any blocks or barriers that a current process or environment might have. This process is sometimes called *business process redesign (BPR), reengineering,* or *business reengineering.*

Resource-based view (RBV): A view that attaining and sustaining competitive advantage comes from creating value using information and other resources of the firm.

Return on investment (ROI): The amount of financial benefit (either revenue or reduced expense) over and above an investment in a particular IS, divided by the investment amount itself. The result is a percentage.

Review board: A committee that is formally designated to approve, monitor, and review specific topics related to the IS department and systems.

Reuse: A relatively small chunk of functionality available for many applications.

SAP: The company that produces the leading ERP software, technically named "SAP R/3" but often simply referred to as SAP.

Sarbanes–Oxley (SoX) Act of 2002: The U.S. act to increase regulatory visibility and accountability of public companies and their financial health.

Scalable: A criterion used to determine how well an infrastructure component can adapt to increased or, in some cases, decreased demands.

SDLC: See *Systems development life cycle.*

Security education/training/awareness (SETA): The training to make business users aware of security policies and practices and to build a security-conscious culture.

Selective outsourcing: The action taken when an enterprise chooses which IT capabilities to retain in house and which to give to an outsider.

Sentiment analysis: The type of analytics that uses algorithms to analyze text to extract subjective information such as emotional statements, preferences, likes/dislikes, and so on.

Server-based architecture: A decentralized plan or format that uses numerous servers often located in different physical locations. A *server* is a software program or computer intended to provide data and/or instructions to another software program or computer. The hardware that a server program runs is often also referred to as "the server."

Service-level agreement (SLA): Portion of the formal service contract between clients and outsourcing providers that describes the level of service including delivery time and expected service performance.

Service-oriented architecture (SOA): The type of architecture in which business processes are built using services delivered over a network (typically the Internet). Services are software programs that are distinct units of business functionality residing on different parts of a network and can be combined and reused to create business applications.

Silo perspective; also ***Functional view or perspective*:** The view of an organization based on the functional departments, typically including manufacturing, engineering, logistics, sales, marketing, finance, accounting, and human resources. (In contrast, see *Process Perspective.*)

Six sigma: An incremental data-driven approach to quality management for eliminating defects from a process. The term comes from the idea that if the quality of all output from a process were to be mapped on a bell-shaped curve, the tail of the curve, six sigma from the mean, would be where there were less than 3.4 defects per million.

Social business: An enterprise whose basic business model engages communities as a core competency and builds processes based on capabilities available only through the use of social IT.

Social business strategy: A plan of how a firm will use social IT to engage, collaborate, and innovate. It is aligned with organizational strategy and IS strategy and includes a vision of how the business would operate if it seamlessly and thoroughly incorporated social and collaborative capabilities throughout the business model.

Social contract theory: The theory used in business ethics that places responsibility on corporate managers to consider the needs of the society (societies) in which a corporation is embedded. Social contract theorists ask what conditions would have to be met for the members of such a society to agree to allow a corporation to be formed. Thus, society bestows legal recognition on a corporation to allow it to employ social resources toward given ends.

Social IT: The term that refers to technologies used for collaboration, engagement, and innovation over the Web. Typically, these tools enable communities of people to chat, network, and share information. Common examples are social networks such as Facebook and Linked In, crowdsourcing services such as Kickstarter, blogs or microblogs such as Twitter, and location-based applications such as Foursquare.

Social media: The marketing and sales applications of social IT.

Social media analytics: A class of tools to measure the impact of social IT investments (i.e., tweets, blogs, Facebook) on the business.

Social media management: A type of security policy that provides rules about what can be disclosed on social media, such as who can Tweet and how employees can identify themselves.

Social network: An IT-enabled network that links individuals together in ways that enable them to find experts, get to know colleagues, and see who has relevant experience for projects across traditional organization lines.

Social networking site: A Web site available from a Web-based service that allows its members to create a public profile within a bounded system, list other users with whom they share a connection, and view and interact with their list of connections and those made by others within the system. Examples are MySpace, Facebook, and LinkedIn.

Socialization: The mode of knowledge conversion from tacit knowledge to tacit knowledge using the process of sharing experiences; it occurs through observation, imitation, and practice.

Software-as-a-service (SaaS): The term used to describe a model of software deployment that uses the Web to deliver applications on an "as-needed" basis. Often when software is delivered as a service, it runs on a computer on the Internet rather than on the customer's computer and is accessed through a Web browser.

Spoofing: A security breach in which a hacker counterfeits an Internet address.

Stakeholder theory: A theory used in business ethics that suggests that managers, although bound by their relation to stockholders, are also entrusted with a fiduciary responsibility to all those who hold a stake in or a claim on the firm, including employees, customers, vendors, neighbors, and so forth.

Standard: The technical specifications to be followed throughout the infrastructure. Often standards are agreed on for development processes, technology, methods, practices, and software.

Steering committee: An IT governance mechanism that calls for joint participation of IT and business leaders in making decisions about IT as a group.

Stockholder theory: A theory used in business ethics suggesting that stockholders advance capital to corporate managers who act as agents in advancing the stockholders' ends. The nature of this contract binds managers to act in the interest of the shareholders (i.e., to maximize shareholder value).

Strategic alliance: An interorganizational relationship that affords one or more companies in the relationship a strategic advantage.

Strategy: A coordinated set of actions to fulfill objectives, purposes, and goals.

Structured data: The facts gathered from external sources that are clear and easily categorized when stored in databases or used.

Supply chain management (SCM) system: The system that manages the integrated supply chain; its processes are linked across companies with a companion process used by a customer or supplier.

Synchronized planning: The agreement by partners on a joint design of planning, forecasting, and replenishing activities and what to do with the information.

Systems development life cycle (SDLC): The process of designing and delivering an entire system using these seven phases: initiation of the project, requirements definition phase, functional design phase, technical design and construction phase, verification phase, implementation phase, and maintenance and review phase.

System software: Software such as Microsoft Windows, Apple OSX, and Linux that provides instructions to the hardware.

Tacit knowledge: The personal, context-specific knowledge that is hard to formalize and communicate. It consists of experiences, beliefs, and skills and is entirely subjective and often acquired through physically practicing a skill or activity. (In contrast, see *Explicit knowledge*.)

Tagging: The process in which users list key words that codify information or a document at hand and that create an ad hoc codification system, sometimes referred to as a *folksonomy*.

Telecommuting: The combination of *telecommunications* with *commuting*. This term usually refers to the practice of individuals who regularly work from home instead of commuting to an office. However, it is often used to mean anyone who works regularly from a location outside her or his company's office.

The Open Group Architecture Framework (TOGAF): The framework that includes a methodology and set of resources for developing an enterprise architecture based on the idea of an open architecture whose specifications are public (as compared to a proprietary architecture whose specifications are not made public).

Token: A small electronic device that generates a new supplementary passkey at frequent intervals.

Total cost of ownership (TCO): A costing method that looks beyond initial capital investments to include costs associated with technical support, administration, training, and system retirement.

Total quality management (TQM): A management philosophy in which quality metrics drive the performance evaluation of people, processes, and decisions. The objective of TQM is to continually, and often incrementally, improve the activities of the business to reach the goal of eliminating defects (or achieving zero defects) and producing the highest-quality outputs possible.

Unified communications (UC): An evolving communications technology architecture that automates and unifies all forms of human and device communications in context and with a common experience.

Unstructured data: The facts that are embedded (i.e., in blogs, tweets, conversations) that have to be extracted before they can become useful information. They are not straightforward.

User-centered design: The development approach that uses tools for RAD, JAD, agile development, and prototyping to provide assurance that users' needs are being met efficiently and responsively.

Utility computing: The purchasing of an entire computing capability on an as-needed basis.

Value net: The set of players in a co-opetitive environment including a company and its competitors and complementors as well as its customers and suppliers and the interactions among all of them. (See *Complementor*.)

Value: A principle or quality that reflects a community's aspirations about the way things should be done.

Video teleconference (videoconference): A set of interactive telecommunication technologies that allow two or more locations to interact simultaneously via two-way video and audio transmissions.

Virtual corporation: A temporary network of companies (or individuals) linked by information technology to exploit fast-changing opportunities.

Virtual private network (VPN): A private network that uses a public network such as the Internet to connect remote sites or users. It maintains privacy through the use of a tunneling protocol and security procedures.

Virtual team: A team of two or more people who (1) work together interdependently with mutual accountability for achieving common goals, (2) do not work in either the same place and/or at the same time, and (3) must use electronic technology to communicate, coordinate their activities, and complete their team's tasks.

Virtual world: A computer-based simulated environment intended for its users to inhabit and interact via avatars.

Virtualization: The process that allows a computer to run multiple operating systems or several versions of the same operating system at the same time; is a virtual infrastructure in which software replaced hardware in a way that a "virtual machine" or a "virtual desktop system" was accessible to provide computing power.

Voice over Internet protocol (VoIP): A method for taking analog audio signals, such as the kind heard when someone talks on the phone, and turning them into digital data that can be transmitted over the Internet.

Wide Area Network (WAN): A computer network that spans multiple offices, often over a wide geographic area. A WAN typically consists of transmission lines leased from telephone companies.

Weak password: A password such as "123456" that is easy to guess.

Web 2.0: The term given to the Internet and its applications that support collaboration, social networking, social media, RSS, mashups, and a number of other information-sharing tools. The term is used to distinguish it from Web 1.0, which was mostly used for transactions and information dissemination. Web 2.0 is not about different technical specifications but about using the Internet in different ways than was done with Web 1.0.

Web-based architecture: The format or plan in which significant hardware, software, and possibly data elements reside on the Internet.

Web logs (Blogs): The online journals that link together into a very large network of information sharing.

Web services: The software systems that are offered over the Internet and executed on a third party's hardware. Often the term refers to more fundamental software that uses XML messages and follows simple object access protocol (SOAP) standards.

White hat hackers: The hackers who break into a firm's systems to uncover weaknesses.

Wiki: The software that allows users to work collaboratively to create, edit, and link Web pages easily.

Wireless (mobile) infrastructure: The infrastructure that allows communication from remote locations using a variety of wireless technologies (e.g., fixed microwave links; wireless LANs; cellular networks; wireless WANs; satellite links; digital dispatch networks; one-way and two-way paging networks; diffused infrared, laser-based technology; keyless car entry; and global positioning systems).

Wisdom: The knowledge fused with intuition and judgment that facilitates the ability to make decisions.

Workflow: The term that describes activities that take place in a business process.

Workflow diagram: A picture or map of the sequence and detail of each step in a process.

Zachman framework: The enterprise architecture that determines requirements by providing a broad view that helps guide the analysis of the detailed view.

Zero-day threat: The brand-new outbreaks of a security problem.

Zero time organization: An organization designed around responding instantly to the demands of customers, employees, suppliers, and other stakeholders.

Index

D